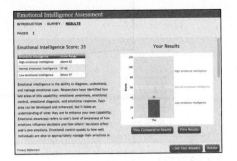

Personal Inventory Assessments is a collection of online exercises designed to promote **self-reflection** and engagement in students, enhancing their ability to connect with management concepts.

"I most liked the Personal Inventory Assessments because they gave me a deeper understanding of the chapters. I would read about personalities and then find out which category I fit into using the assessment."

— Student, Kean University

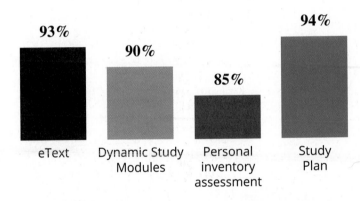

% of students who found learning aid helpful

Dynamic Study Modules use the latest developments in cognitive science and help students study chapter topics by adapting to their performance in real time.

Pearson eText enhances student learning with engaging and interactive lecture and example videos that bring learning to life.

The **Gradebook** offers an easy way for you and your students to see their performance in your course.

86% of students would tell their instructor to keep using MyLab Management

For additional details visit: www.pearson.com/mylab/management

DEVELOPING MANAGEMENT SKILLS

TENTH EDITION

David A. Whetten
BRIGHAM YOUNG UNIVERSITY

Kim S. Cameron
UNIVERSITY OF MICHIGAN

Vice President, Business, Economics, and UK
   Courseware: Donna Battista
Director of Portfolio Management: Stephanie Wall
Specialist Portfolio Manager: Kris Ellis-Levy
Editorial Assistant: Amanda McHugh
Vice President, Product Marketing: Roxanne McCarley
Senior Product Marketer: Carlie Marvel
Product Marketing Assistant: Marianela Silvestri
Manager of Field Marketing, Business Publishing:
   Adam Goldstein
Field Marketing Manager: Nicole Price
Vice President, Production and Digital Studio, Arts
   and Business: Etain O'Dea
Director, Production and Digital Studio, Business
   and Economics: Ashley Santora

Managing Producer, Business: Melissa Feimer
Senior Content Producer: Claudia Fernandes
Operations Specialist: Carol Melville
Design Lead: Kathryn Foot
Manager, Learning Tools: Brian Surette
Learning Tools Strategist: Michael Trinchetto
Managing Producer, Digital Studio and GLP:
   James Bateman
Managing Producer, Digital Studio: Diane Lombardo
Digital Studio Producer: Monique Lawrence
Digital Studio Producer: Alana Coles
Full Service Project Management, Interior Design,
   Cover Design: Integra Software Services Pvt Ltd.
Printer/Binder: LSC Communications, Inc.
Cover Printer: LSC Communications, Inc.

Library of Congress Cataloging-in-Publication Data is available on file at the Library of Congress.

1   19

ISBN 10:   0-13-517546-1
ISBN 13: 978-0-13-517546-0

BRIEF TABLE OF CONTENTS

CONTENTS

7   NEGOTIATING AND RESOLVING CONFLICT   307

PART III   GROUP SKILLS   369

8   EMPOWERING AND ENGAGING OTHERS   371

9   BUILDING EFFECTIVE TEAMS AND TEAMWORK   405

Why Focus on Management Skill Development?

Given that a "skill development" course requires more time and effort than a course using the traditional lecture/discussion format, we are sometimes asked this question by students, especially those who have relatively little work experience.

Reason #1: It focuses attention on what effective managers *actually* do.

In an influential article, Henry Mintzberg (1975) argued that management education had almost nothing to say about what managers actually *do* from day to day. He further faulted management textbooks for introducing students to the leading theories about management while ignoring what is known about effective management practice. Sympathetic to Mintzberg's critique, we set out to identify the defining competencies of effective managers.

Although no two management positions are exactly the same, the research summarized in the Introduction highlights ten personal, interpersonal, and group skills that form the core of effective management practice. Each chapter addresses one of these skills:

Personal Skills

1. Developing Self-Awareness
2. Managing Stress and Well-Being
3. Solving Problems Analytically and Creatively

Interpersonal Skills

4. Building Relationships by Communicating Supportively
5. Gaining Power and Influence
6. Motivating Performance
7. Negotiating and Resolving Conflict

Group Skills

8. Empowering and Engaging Others
9. Building Effective Teams and Teamwork
10. Leading Positive Change

Consistent with our focus on promoting effective management practice, the material in these chapters provides guidance for a variety of contemporary management challenges, including: "How can I help others accept new goals, new ideas, new approaches?" "How can I invigorate those who feel outdated and left behind?" "How do I help the 'survivors' of a downsizing pick up the pieces and move on?" "How do I help people with very different agendas and philosophies work together, especially during periods of high stress and uncertainty?"

Anyone tempted to dismissively argue that the answers to these questions are "common sense" would do well to recall Will Rogers' pithy observation: "Common sense ain't necessarily common practice." In addition, the research reported in the Introduction suggests that, in many cases, managers' "common sense" isn't necessarily "good sense."

The premise of this book and associated course is that the key to effective management practice is practicing what effective managers—those with "good sense"—do consistently.

Reason #2: It is consistent with proven principles of effective teaching and learning.

A seasoned university professor advised a young colleague, "If your students aren't learning, you're not teaching—you're just talking!" Here's what some authorities on higher education have to say about how effective teachers foster learning:

> "All genuine learning is active, not passive. It is a process of discovery in which the student is the main agent, not the teacher." (Adler, 1982)

> "Learning is not a spectator sport. Students do not learn much just by sitting in a class listening to teachers, memorizing pre-packaged assignments, and spilling out answers. They must talk about what they are learning, write about it, relate it to past experiences, apply it to their daily lives. They must make what they learn part of themselves." (Chickering & Gamson, 1987)

In their classic book, Bonwell and Elson (1991) list seven defining characteristics of active learning:

1. Students are involved in more than passive listening.
2. Students are engaged in activities (e.g., reading, discussing, writing).
3. There is less emphasis placed on information transmission and greater emphasis placed on developing student skills.
4. There is greater emphasis placed on the exploration of attitudes and values.
5. Student motivation is increased, especially in adult learners.
6. Students receive immediate feedback from their instructor and peers.
7. Students are involved in higher order thinking (analysis, synthesis, evaluation).

Our goals in writing this book were to bridge the academic realm of theory and research and the organizational realm of effective practice and to help students consistently translate proven principles from both realms into personal practice. To accomplish these goals, we formulated a five-step "active" learning model, described in the Introduction. Based on the positive feedback we've received from teachers and students as well as multiple empirical research studies, we can state with confidence that the form of active learning pioneered in this book is a proven pedagogy for management skill mastery.

MYLAB MANAGEMENT SUGGESTED ACTIVITIES

For the 10th edition we the authors are excited that Pearson's MyLab Management has been integrated fully into the text. These new features are outlined below. Making assessment activities available on line for students to complete before coming to class will allow you the professor more discussion time during the class to review areas that students are having difficulty in comprehending.

Watch It

MyLab recommends video clips that can be assigned to students for outside classroom viewing or that can be watched in the classroom. The videos correspond to the chapter material and is accompanied by multiple choice questions that re-enforce student's comprehension of the chapter content.

Personal Inventory Assessments (PIA)

Students learn better when they can connect what they are learning to their personal experience. PIA (Personal Inventory Assessments) is a collection of online exercises designed to promote self-reflection and engagement in students, enhancing their ability to connect with concepts taught in principles of management, organizational behavior, and human resource management classes. Assessments are assignable by instructors who can then track students' completions. Student results include a written explanation along with a graphic display that shows how their results compare to the class as a whole. Instructors will also have access to this graphic representation of results to promote classroom discussion.

DETAILED CHAPTER BY CHAPTER CHANGES

Based on suggestions from reviewers, instructors, and students, we have made a number of changes in the tenth edition of Developing Management Skills.

Introduction

- Updated references
- Clarified writing, especially sensitive to international perspectives and gender

Chapter 1 – Developing Self-Awareness

- Updated pre-assessment instruments, paying special attention to gender and nationality
- Updated references throughout the chapter
- Created new cases in the Skill Analysis section
- Updated scenarios in the Skill Practice section

Chapter 2 – Managing Stress and Well-Being

- Updated references throughout the chapter
- Added cases on stress and stress management among Millennials in the Skill Analysis section
- Added an up-to-date Skill Practice exercise

Chapter 3 – Solving Problems Analytically and Creatively

- Updated references and examples throughout the chapter
- Replaced cases in the Skill Analysis section
- Updated the Creative Problem-Solving Practice scenarios

Chapter 4 – Building Relationships by Communicating Supportively

- Updated references throughout the chapter
- Updated cases in the Skill Analysis section
- Updated exercises in the Skill Practice section

Chapter 5 – Gaining Power and Influence

- Updated references throughout the chapter
- Enhanced material on social capital
- Added a section on Sexual Harassment
- Updated the cases in Skill Analysis section

Chapter 6 – Motivating Performance

- Adopted new chapter title, emphasizing the use of motivation to enhance performance
- Updated references and examples throughout the chapter
- Expanded section on intrinsic reinforcement
- Added section on diagnosing and correcting unacceptable performance
- Added new Skill Practice exercise

Chapter 7 – Negotiating and Resolving Conflict

- Adopted new chapter title, reflecting expanded focus
- Updated references and examples throughout the chapter
- Added a section on negotiations
- Added new negotiations exercises in the Skill Practice section
- Updated the cases and exercises

Chapter 8 – Empowering and Engaging Others

- Updated references throughout the chapter
- Added a new case to the Skill Analysis section
- Updated exercises in the Skill Practice section

Chapter 9 – Building Effective Teams and Teamwork

- Updated references and examples throughout the chapter
- Created a new case in the Skill Analysis section
- Updated Skill Practice exercises

Chapter 10 – Leading Positive Change

- Updated references throughout the chapter
- Updated Corporate Vision Statements in the Skill Analysis section
- Added an exercise to the Skill Practice section

Tips for Getting the Most Out of This Course

Whether you are an undergraduate or MBA student, or an experienced manager, based on our years of teaching management skills, here are some suggestions for making this course a personally meaningful learning experience:

- Read the Introduction carefully. Although this is not a typical management text-book, it is important that you understand its distinctive learner-focused features, especially the five-step learning model: Skill Assessment, Skill Learning, Skill Analysis, Skill Practice, and Skill Application. You'll also find informative research on how much managers' actions impact individual and organizational performance and the characteristics of effective managers.

- Thoughtfully complete the Skill Assessment surveys for each chapter. These diagnostic tools are designed to help you identify which specific aspects of each skill topic most warrant your personal attention.

- Carefully study the Behavioral Guidelines and the summary model at the conclusion of the Skill Learning section of each chapter before reading that section. These written and graphical summaries are designed to bridge the research-informed description of each topic with the skill development activities that follow. To help you internalize research-informed "good sense," be sure to use the Behavioral Guidelines as your frame of reference when reading and discussing Skill Analysis cases and participating in Skill Practice and Skill Application exercises.

- Be sure to complete the Skill Application exercises in each chapter. Management skill mastery requires out-of-class skill practice. How to do this is pretty straight-forward if you are currently working in an organization, regardless of whether you are an experienced manager or a new, part-time employee. Whether or not you are currently employed, we encourage you to seek out skill practice opportunities in all aspects of your life, including working in assigned teams in this and other courses, planning social events for a campus or community organization, counseling a troubled sibling or friend, managing end-of-semester deadlines, or handling a difficult issue with a boy/girlfriend or spouse. The sooner you begin—and the more you persist in—practicing what you learn in this course, the more you'll be able to count on these skills as "automatic responses" when you need them as a manager.

INSTRUCTOR RESOURCE CENTER

At Pearson's Higher Ed catalog, https://www.pearsonhighered.com/sign-in.html, instructors can easily register to gain access to a variety of instructor resources available with this text in downloadable format. If assistance is needed, our dedicated technical support team is ready to help with the media supplements that accompany this text. Visit https://support.pearson.com/getsupport for answers to frequently asked questions and toll-free user support phone numbers.

The following supplements are available with this text:

- Instructor's Resource Manual
- Test Bank
- TestGen® Computerized Test Bank
- PowerPoint Presentation

This title is available as an eBook and can be purchased at most eBook retailers.

Acknowledgments

In addition to the informal feedback we have received from colleagues around the world, we would especially like to thank the following people who have formally reviewed material and provided valuable feedback, vital to the revision of this and previous editions:

Richard Allan, University of Tennessee–Chattanooga
Joseph S Anderson, Northern Arizona University
Forrest F. Aven, University of Houston
Lloyd Baird, Boston University
Bud Baker, Wright State University
John D. Bigelow, Boise State University
Ralph R. Braithwaite, University of Hartford
Julia Britt, California State University
Tim Bothell, Brigham Young University
David Cherrington, Brigham Young University
John Collins, Syracuse University
Kerri Crowne, Temple University
Joseph V. DePalma, Farleigh Dickerson University
Todd Dewett, Wright State University
Andrew J. Dubrin, Rochester Institute of Technology
Steven Edelson, Temple University
Crissie M. Frye, Eastern Michigan University
Norma Givens, Fort Valley State University
Barbara A. Gorski, St. Thomas University
Sara Grant, New York University
David Hampton, San Diego State University
Jason Harris-Boundy. San Francisco State University

Stanley Harris, Auburn University
Richard E. Hunt, Rockhurst College
Daniel F. Jennings, Baylor University
Avis L. Johnson, University of Akron
Jay T. Knippen, University of South Florida
Roland Kushner, Lafayette College
Roy J. Lewicki, Ohio State University
Michael Lombardo, Center for Creative Leadership
Charles C. Manz, University of Massachusetts–Amherst
Ralph F. Mullin, Central Missouri State University
Thomas J. Naughton, Wayne State University
J. Randolph New, University of Richmond
Jon L. Pierce, University of Minnesota–Duluth
Lyman Porter, University of California–Irvine
Lyle F. Schoenfeldt, Appalachian State University
Jacop P. Siegel, University of Toronto
Charles Smith, Hofstra University
Noel M. Tichy, University of Michigan
Wanda V. Trenner, Ferris State University
Ulya Tsolmon, Brigham Young University
Kenneth M. York, Oakland University

We especially thank our collaborators who adapted the book for the European and Australian markets as well as those who translated *Developing Management Skills* into Spanish, Russian, Chinese, and Dutch.

We are grateful for the assistance of many dedicated associates who have helped us continually upgrade and enhance *Developing Management Skills*. We wish to acknowledge our colleague, Jeffrey Thompson, Director of the Romney Institute of Public Management, Brigham Young University. Jeff has been a valuable collaborator on our recent revisions and has become a major part of the authoring team.

Finally, and most importantly, we express appreciation to our families for their ongoing patience and support, which is reflected in their willingness to share their time with this competing "labor of love"—and to forgive our own gaps between common sense and common practice.

David A. Whetten
Kim S. Cameron

MANAGEMENT CONCEPTS

- The Critical Role of Management Skills
- The Importance of Competent Managers
- The Skills of Effective Managers
- Employability
- What Are Management Skills?
- Improving Management Skills
- An Approach to Skill Development
- Leadership and Management
- Contents of the Book
- Organization of the Book
- Diversity and Individual Differences
- Summary

SUPPLEMENTARY MATERIAL

- Personal Assessment of Management Skills (PAMS)
- What Does It Take to Be an Effective Manager?
- SSS Software In-Basket Exercise

SCORING KEY AND COMPARISON DATA

INTRODUCTION

The Critical Role of Management Skills

LEARNING OBJECTIVES

1. Introduce the importance of management skills

2. Identify essential management skills

3. Explain a learning model for developing management skills

4. Review the contents of the book

Introduction

The Critical Role of Management Skills

No one doubts that the twenty-first century will continue to be characterized by chaotic, transformational, rapid-fire change. In fact, almost no sane person is willing to predict what the world will be like 50, 20, or even 10 years from now. Change is just too rapid and ubiquitous. Three-quarters of the content on the Web was not available three years ago. The development of "nanobombs" has caused some people to predict that personal computers and desktop monitors will land on the scrap heap of obsolescence within 20 years. The new computers will be a product of etchings on molecules leading to personalized data processors injected into the bloodstream, implanted in eyeglasses, or included in wrist bands.

Warren Bennis, a colleague of ours, half-jokingly predicted that the factory of the future would have only two employees, a person and a dog. The person would be there to feed the dog. The dog would be there to keep the person from touching the equipment! Almost no one would argue with the claim that "permanent white water" best characterizes our current environment. Almost everything is in flux, from our technology and methods of transacting business to the nature of education and the definition of the family.

Despite all this change in our environment, there is something that has remained relatively constant. With minor variations and stylistic differences, what have not changed in several thousand years are the basic skills that lie at the heart of effective, satisfying, growth-producing human relationships. Freedom, dignity, trust, love, and respect in relationships have always been among the goals of human beings, and the same principles that brought about those outcomes in the second or seventeenth centuries still bring them about in the twenty-first century. Despite our circumstances, in other words, and despite the technological resources we have available to us, the same basic human skills still lie at the heart of effective human interaction.

This book is built on the presumption that developing management skills—that is, the skills needed to manage one's own life as well as relationships with others—is a ceaseless endeavor. These skills were largely the same a century ago as they are today. The basic behavioral principles that lie at the foundation of these skills are timeless. This is one reason why the shelves of bookstores, blogs, and online newsletters are filled with descriptions of how one more executive or one more company struck it rich or beat out the competition. Thousands of books trumpet prescriptions for how to be successful in business, or in life. Many of these books have made it to the best-seller lists, where they have enjoyed lengthy stays.

Our intention in this book is not to try to duplicate the popular appeal of the best-selling books or to utilize the common formula of recounting anecdotal incidents of successful organizations or well-known managers. We have produced a book that is based on, and remains true to, social science and business research. We want to share with you what is known and what is not known about how to develop management skills and how to foster productive, healthy, satisfying, and growth-producing relationships with others in your work setting. *Developing Management Skills* is designed to help you actually improve your personal management competencies—to change your behavior.

In a recent survey of 985 college instructors sponsored by Pearson, the publisher of this book, 82 percent rated the development of *employability skills* to be important or very important for their students. Employability skills in the survey referred to the very same competencies that are covered in this text—that is, problem-solving, communication, teamwork, self-management, creative thinking, and leadership. More than 90 percent of instructors indicated that these skills should be developed in the classroom. Seldom, however, are materials available or courses designed to produce those outcomes, so these instructors expressed the need for a book to assist them in that endeavor.

This book, therefore, serves as a practicum or a guide to effective managerial skills, and it will assist in the development of the skills you need to be more employable. Not only will the skills covered in this book assist you in becoming employable in your first job, but after your first promotion, you will most likely be in a managerial role, and these management skills will be even more important in contributing to your success. Whereas the skills in this book focus on "management skills," their relevance is not limited just to an organization or work setting. This book could be retitled "life skills," "leadership skills," or even "employability skills." We focus mainly on work settings here because our primary goal is to help you prepare for and improve your own competency in a managerial role. You will discover, however, that these skills are applicable in most areas of your life—with families, friends, volunteer organizations, and your community.

In the next section, we review some of the scientific evidence that demonstrates how management skills are associated with personal and organizational success, and we review several studies of the key management skills that seem to be the most important in our modern-day environment. It is on those key skills that this book is targeted. We then describe a model and a methodology for helping you develop management skills.

A large number of fads abound proclaiming a new way to be a leader, get rich, or both, but our intent is to rely on a proven methodology that has grounding in the scientific literature. We present what has been shown to be a superior process for improving management skills, and we base our claims on scholarly evidence. This Introduction concludes with a brief description of the organization of the rest of the book and the importance of keeping in mind individual differences among people.

The Importance of Competent Managers

In the last couple of decades, an abundance of evidence has been produced demonstrating that skillful management is the single most powerful determinant of organizational success. Surveys by a variety of consulting firms in the past five years (e.g., Deloitte, Gallup, McKinsey, Mercer) have reconfirmed that leadership and management account for the most variance in organizational performance and employee well-being. These studies have been conducted across numerous industry sectors, international settings, and organization types. The research findings now make it almost unquestionable that if organizations want to succeed, they must have competent, skillful managers.

As an example, a study of 968 firms—the organizations whose managers were rated as effective in managing their people; that is, they implemented effective people management strategies and demonstrated personal competency in management skills—had, on average, more than a 7 percent decrease in turnover, increased profits of $3,814 per employee, $27,044 more in sales per employee, and $18,641 more in stock market value per employee, compared to firms that had less-effective people management (Huselid, 1995; Pfeffer & Veiga, 1999). In a follow-up study of 702 firms, shareholder wealth was an amazing $41,000 per employee higher in companies demonstrating strong people management skills than in firms that had a lower emphasis on people management (Huselid & Becker, 1997).

A study of German firms in 10 industrial sectors produced similar results: "Companies that place workers at the core of their strategies produce higher long-term returns...than their industry peers" (Blimes, Wetzker, & Xhonneux, 1997). A study of five-year survivability in 136 nonfinancial companies that issued IPOs in the late 1980s found that the effective management of people was the most significant factor in predicting longevity, even when accounting for industry type, size, and profits. Firms that did a good job of managing people tended to survive; others did not (Welbourne & Andrews, 1996).

A study at the University of Michigan investigated the factors that best accounted for financial success over a five-year span in 40 major manufacturing firms. The five most powerful predictors included market share (assuming that the higher the market share of a firm, the higher its profitability); firm capital intensity (assuming that the more a firm is automated and up to date in technology and equipment, the more profitable it is); size of the firm in assets (assuming that economies of scale and efficiency can be used in large firms to increase profitability); industry average return on sales (assuming that firms would reflect the performance of a highly profitable industry); and the ability of managers to effectively manage their people (assuming that an emphasis on good people management helps produce profitability in firms). The results revealed that one factor—the ability to manage people effectively—was three times more powerful than all other factors combined in accounting for firm financial success over a five-year period! We repeat: Good management was more important than all other factors taken together in predicting profitability.

This is just a small sampling of studies that indicate overwhelmingly that good management fosters financial success, whereas less-effective management fosters financial distress. Successful organizations have managers with well-developed management skills. Moreover, the data are clear that management skills are more important in accounting for success than industry, environment, competition, and economic factors combined.

The Skills of Effective Managers

What, then, differentiates effective managers from less-effective managers? If developing management skills is so crucial for organizational success, what skills ought to be the focus of our attention? In writing this book, we wanted to identify the skills and competencies that separate extraordinarily effective performers from the rest of us. So, in addition to reviewing the managerial and leadership literature, we also identified 402 individuals who were rated by their peers as highly effective managers in their own organizations in the fields of business, health care, education, and state government. We then interviewed those people to determine what attributes are associated with managerial effectiveness. We asked questions such as:

❑ How have you become so successful in this organization?
❑ Who fails and who succeeds in this organization, and why?

❏ If you had to train someone to take your place, what knowledge and what skills would you make certain that person possessed in order to perform successfully as your successor?

❏ If you could design an ideal curriculum or training program to teach you to be a better manager, what would it contain?

❏ Think of other effective managers you know. What skills do they demonstrate that explain their success?

Our analysis of the interviews produced about 60 characteristics of effective managers. The 10 identified most often are listed in Table 1. Not surprisingly, these 10 characteristics are all behavioral skills. They are not personality attributes or styles, nor are they generalizations such as "luck," "charisma," or "timing." They also are common across industries, levels, and job responsibilities. The characteristics of effective managers are not a secret, and they are similar to the lists developed in other studies.

For example, the Miles Group and Stanford University conducted a study of the skills in which most CEOs and corporate directors needed coaching and development (Executive Coaching, 2013). The study identified the following skills, listed in the order of emphasis.

❏ Conflict management
❏ Listening
❏ Delegation
❏ Planning
❏ Mentoring and empowering
❏ Communication
❏ Team-building
❏ Compassion
❏ Persuasion and influence
❏ Interpersonal relationships
❏ Motivation

Note that these skills are almost exactly the same as those listed in Table 1, so each is addressed in this book. That is, this book provides you with the opportunity to develop and improve the most important skills that account for managerial success.

Table 1	Skills of Effective Managers—One Study
1. Verbal communication (including listening)	
2. Managing time and stress	
3. Rational and creative problem-solving	
4. Recognizing, defining, and solving problems	
5. Motivating and influencing others	
6. Delegating and engaging others	
7. Setting goals, articulating a vision, and leading change	
8. Self-awareness	
9. Team building	
10. Managing conflict	

What Are Management Skills?

There are several defining characteristics of management skills that differentiate them from other kinds of characteristics and practices. First, management skills are *behavioral*. They are not personality attributes or stylistic tendencies. Management skills consist of actions that lead to positive outcomes. Skills can be observed by others, unlike attributes that are purely attitudinal, stylistic, or embedded in personality.

Second, management skills are *controllable*. The performance of these behaviors is under your own control. Skills may involve other people and require cognitive work, but they are behaviors that you can govern yourself.

Third, management skills are *developable*. Performance can improve. Unlike IQ or certain personality or temperament attributes that remain relatively constant throughout life, you can improve your competency in skill performance through practice and feedback. You can progress from less competence to more competence in management skills, and that outcome is the primary objective of this book.

Fourth, management skills are *interrelated* and *overlapping*. It is difficult to demonstrate just one skill in isolation from others. Skills are not simplistic, repetitive behaviors; rather, they are integrated sets of complex responses. Improving one management skill will help you improve others.

Fifth, management skills are sometimes *contradictory* or *paradoxical*. For example, the core management skills are neither all soft and humanistic nor all hard-driving and directive. They are not exclusively oriented toward teamwork and interpersonal relations, nor are they exclusively oriented toward individualism and solitary decision-making. A variety of skills are typical of the most effective managers, and some of them may appear incompatible.

To illustrate, Cameron and Tschirhart (1988) assessed the skill performance of more than 500 midlevel and upper-middle managers in about 150 organizations. The 25 most frequently mentioned management skills, taken from about a dozen studies in the academic literature (such as those in Table 2), were measured. Statistical analyses revealed that the skills fell into four main groups, or clusters. One group of skills focused on participative and human relations skills (for example, supportive communication and team building), while another group focused on just the opposite; that is, competitiveness and control (for example, assertiveness, power, and influence skills). A third group focused on innovativeness and individual entrepreneurship (for example, creative problem-solving),

Table 2	A Model for Developing Management Skills	
Components	**Contents**	**Objectives**
1. Skill assessment	Survey instruments Role-plays	Assess current level of skill competence and knowledge; create readiness to change.
2. Skill learning	Written text Behavioral guidelines	Teach validated principles and present a rationale for behavioral guidelines.
3. Skill analysis	Cases	Provide examples of appropriate and inappropriate skill performance. Analyze behavioral principles and reasons they work.
4. Skill practice	Exercises Simulations Role-plays	Practice behavioral guidelines. Adapt principles to personal style. Receive feedback and assistance.
5. Skill application	Assignments (behavioral and written)	Transfer classroom learning to real-life situations. Foster ongoing personal development.

while a fourth group emphasized the opposite type of skills; namely, maintaining order and rationality (for example, managing time and rational decision-making). One conclusion from this study is that effective managers are required to demonstrate paradoxical skills. That is, the most effective managers are both participative and hard-driving, both nurturing and competitive. They were able to be flexible and creative while also being controlled, stable, and rational (also see Cameron, et al., 2014). Our objective in this book is to help you develop that kind of behavioral competency and complexity.

Improving Management Skills

It is a bit unnerving that while average IQ scores have jumped approximately 25 points in the last century, emotional intelligence scores (EQ) have fallen. In a survey of 110 Fortune 500 CEOs, 87 percent were satisfied with the level of competence and analytic skills of business school graduates, 68 percent were satisfied with conceptual skills of graduates, but only 43 percent of the CEOs were satisfied with graduates' management skills, and only 28 percent were satisfied with their interpersonal skills and emotional intelligence!

The good news is that improvement in management skills has been found in both students and managers who have been exposed to the learning model presented in *Developing Management Skills*. For example, MBA students showed improvement of 50 to 300 percent on social skills over two years after taking courses based on the approach to developing management skills presented here. A greater amount of improvement occurred among students who applied these skills to aspects of their lives outside the classroom. In addition, a cohort of 45- to 55-year-old executives produced the same results as the MBA students. They also improved dramatically in their management skills even though most were already experienced in senior managerial positions (Boyatzis, 1996, 2000, 2005; Boyatzis, Cowen, & Kolb, 1995; Boyatzis, et al., 1996; Leonard, 1996; Rhee, 1997; Wheeler, 1999).

An Approach to Skill Development

The method that has been found to be most successful in helping individuals develop management skills is based on an adaptation of social learning theory (Bandura, 1977; Boyatzis, et al., 1995; Davis & Luthans, 1980). This learning theory relies on several principles.

1. In order to improve, individuals must be aware of their current level of skill competency so that they can be motivated to improve. For comparison, think about a weight-loss plan: You will have a difficult time losing weight if you don't know how much you weigh to begin with. Most of us receive very little feedback about our level of skill competency, so it is difficult to know how to get better. Therefore, to help you understand what skills to improve and why, an assessment activity is part of the learning model. The assessment activities take the form of self-evaluation instruments, case studies, or problems that help highlight personal strengths and weaknesses in a particular skill area.

2. Management skills and behavioral guidelines must be grounded in empirical evidence and social science theory. Because leaders and managers have such an important impact on their organizations' performance and on employee well-being, when we provide advice about how to be an effective manager, the advice and guidance needs to be grounded in evidence. A great number of self-help books have trumpeted advice for leaders and managers, but empirical evidence showing that this advice actually works is very rare. Scientifically based knowledge about the effects of the management principles being presented is a prerequisite for an effective

learning model, so the Skill Learning section of each chapter is based on empirically verified principles.

3. Case examples of best practices, applications in different circumstances, and the nuances associated with management skills are often helpful in developing competency. Therefore, a skill analysis section is included in each chapter so that you can analyze when various aspects of the skills are best utilized and in what ways they can be applied.

4. Simply learning guidelines or principles, or analyzing how others demonstrate the skills, will not help people become better managers. You can read several books about bicycle riding, for example, but you won't get any better as a rider until you actually get on a bicycle and practice. The same is true of management skills. Each chapter in the book provides exercises, assignments, and activities that will help you practice management skills in a classroom setting where feedback is immediate. This provides a relatively safe environment in which you can try out new behaviors and make mistakes. The goal is to help you improve your behavioral competence.

5. An application component is also an important part of the learning model. If learning only takes place in a classroom setting, transferring learning to an actual job setting is often difficult. Therefore, application exercises in each chapter take the form of outside-of-class interventions, consulting assignments, self-analysis through journal writing, problem-centered interventions, or teaching assignments that you can practice in a real-world setting.

In summary, empirical evidence suggests that a five-step learning model is most effective for helping you develop management skills. Table 2 outlines such a model. Step 1 involves the *assessment* of current levels of skill competency and knowledge of the behavioral principles. Step 2 consists of the presentation of validated, scientifically based *principles and guidelines* for effective skill performance. Step 3 is an *analysis* step in which models or cases are presented in order to analyze behavioral principles in real organizational settings. This step also helps demonstrate how the behavioral guidelines can be adapted to different personal styles and circumstances. Step 4 consists of *practice* exercises in which experimentation can occur and immediate feedback can be received in a relatively safe environment. Step 5 is the *application* of the skill to a real-life setting outside the classroom with follow-up analysis of the relative success of that application.

Research on the effectiveness of training programs using this general learning model has shown that it produces results superior to those based on more traditional lecture, discussion, or case method approaches (Boyatzis, et al., 1995; Burnaska, 1976; Kolb, 1984; Latham & Saari, 1979; Moses & Ritchie, 1976; Porras & Anderson, 1981; Smith, 1976; Vance, 1993).

To assist you in improving your own management skills, this book emphasizes practicing management skills rather than just reading about them. We have organized the book with this specific approach in mind.

Leadership and Management

Before outlining the organization of this book, we want to briefly discuss the place of leadership in this volume. Some writers have differentiated between the concepts of "leadership" and "management" (Bass, 1990; Katzenbach, 1995; Nair, 1994; Quinn, 2000; Tichy, 1999). Some have wondered why we concentrate on "management" skills instead of "leadership" skills in this book. We have also been asked by professors, business executives, and students why we have not changed the title of the book to *Developing Leadership Skills* or at least included one chapter on leadership in this volume. These queries and suggestions are important and have motivated us to clarify at the outset of the book what we mean by management, and why our approach also lies at the heart of leadership as typically defined.

One of the most popular models of leadership is based on the "Competing Values Framework," an organizing framework for leadership and managerial skills. It was developed by examining the criteria used to evaluate organizational performance (Cameron, et al., 2014; Quinn & Rohrbaugh, 1983). Extensive research has been conducted on this framework for more than three decades, and a brief explanation will help clarify the relationship between management and leadership skills. This research has shown that leadership and management skills fall into four clusters, or categories, as illustrated in Figure 1.

In order to be an effective leader and manager, the research suggests that you must be competent in: (1) people skills, collaboration, teamwork, and interpersonal communication. These are referred to in the academic literature as *clan skills* or *collaborate skills*; (2) creativity, innovativeness, entrepreneurship, and fashioning a vision for the future. These are referred to in the academic literature as *adhocracy skills* or *create skills*; (3) producing results, making fast decisions, competing aggressively, and being comfortable taking charge. These are referred to in the academic literature as *market skills* or *compete skills*; and (4) maintaining stability and predictability, increasing quality, being efficient, and maintaining control. These are referred to in the academic literature as *hierarchy skills* or *control skills*.

Clan or collaborate skills include those required to build effective interpersonal relationships and develop others (e.g., building teamwork, communicating supportively). Adhocracy or create skills include those required to manage the future, innovate, and promote change (e.g., solving problems creatively, articulating an energizing vision). Market or compete skills include those required to compete effectively and manage external relationships (e.g., motivating others, using power and influence). Hierarchy or control skills include those required to maintain control and stability (e.g., managing personal stress and time, solving problems rationally). (See Cameron & Quinn, 2006.)

Figure 1	Leadership and Management Skills Organized by the Competing Values Framework

Flexibility Change

CLAN SKILLS—COLLABORATE

Communicating Supportively
Building Teams and Teamwork
Empowering

ADHOCRACY SKILLS—CREATE

Solving Problems Creatively
Leading Positive Change
Fostering Innovation

Internal Maintenance - **External Positioning**

HIERARCHY SKILLS—CONTROL

Managing Personal Stress
Managing Time
Maintaining Self-Awareness
Analytical Problem Solving

MARKET SKILLS—COMPLETE

Motivating Others
Gaining Power and Influence
Managing Conflict

Stability Control

In Figure 1, the two top quadrants in the Competing Values Framework—clan and adhocracy—are usually associated with leadership: i.e., "doing the right things," such as setting direction, articulating a vision, transforming organizations, building teams, and creating something new. The two bottom quadrants—market and hierarchy—are usually associated with management: "doing things right," such as maintaining control, monitoring, refining performance, solving problems, competing aggressively. Traditionally, leadership is often associated with what individuals do under conditions of change. When organizations are dynamic and undergoing transformation, people at the top are expected to exhibit leadership (i.e., pay attention to clan and adhocracy issues). "Management," on the other hand, has traditionally been used to describe what executives do under conditions of stability; thus, management has been linked with the status quo (i.e., pay attention to market and hierarchy issues). In summary, leadership has been equated with dynamism, vibrancy, and charisma; management with hierarchy, equilibrium, and control.

However, the recent research is clear that such distinctions between leadership and management are neither accurate nor useful (Cameron, et al., 2014; Quinn, 2000). Managers cannot be successful without being good leaders, and leaders cannot be successful without being good managers. No longer do organizations and individuals have the luxury of holding onto the status quo; worrying about doing things right but failing to do the right things; keeping the system stable instead of leading change and improvement; monitoring current performance instead of formulating a vision for the future; concentrating on equilibrium and control instead of vibrancy and charisma. Effective management and leadership are inseparable. The skills required to do one are also required for the other.

No organization in a postindustrial, hyperturbulent, twenty-first-century environment will survive without executives capable of demonstrating both management and leadership skills. Leading change and managing stability, establishing vision and accomplishing objectives, breaking the rules and monitoring conformance, although paradoxical, all are required for success.

All of us, in other words, need to develop competencies that will enhance our ability to be both leaders and managers. The specific skills in this book represent all four quadrants in the Competing Values Framework of leadership. They serve as the foundation for effective management and for effective leadership. *The skills discussed in this book cover both management skills and leadership skills.* We have chosen to use the label "management skills" to incorporate the skills associated with leadership as well as with management. When you are promoted, you will be given a managerial role, and your success in that role will depend on the extent to which you have mastered specific skills. You can act as a leader in any context or role, so this book is designed to prepare you to be an effective manager as well as an effective leader.

Contents of the Book

To repeat, this book focuses on the skills that research has identified as critically important for successful management and leadership. Each chapter discusses a cluster of related behaviors, and these clusters of interrelated behaviors comprise the overall management skill indicated in the chapter's title. Figure 2 also points out that each skill cluster is related to and overlaps with other personal management skills, so each relies at least partially on others to be performed successfully.

Part I contains three chapters on *personal skills*: Developing Self-Awareness, Managing Stress and Well-Being, and Solving Problems Analytically and Creatively. These skills focus on issues that may not involve other people but instead relate to the management of the self—hence they are called personal skills.

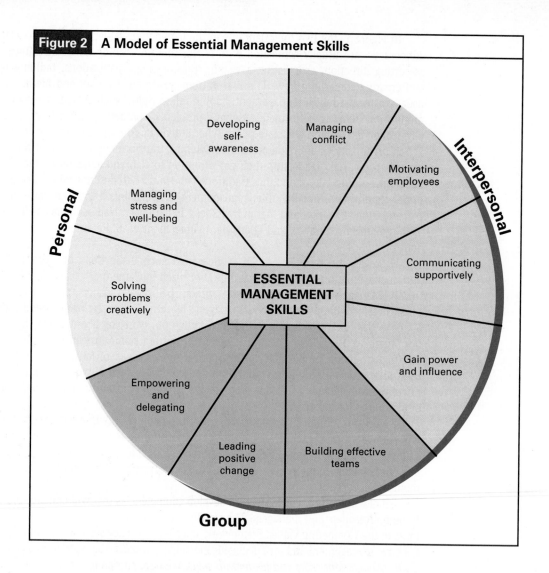

Figure 2 **A Model of Essential Management Skills**

Developing self-awareness

Managing conflict

Interpersonal

Motivating employees

Managing stress and well-being

Personal

Communicating supportively

ESSENTIAL MANAGEMENT SKILLS

Solving problems creatively

Gain power and influence

Empowering and delegating

Leading positive change

Building effective teams

Group

Part II focuses on *interpersonal skills*: Building Relationships by Communicating Supportively, Gaining Power and Influence, Motivating Others, and Managing Conflict. These skills focus primarily on issues that arise in your interactions with other people. Part III includes three chapters on *group skills*: Empowering and Engaging Others, Building Effective Teams and Teamwork, and Leading Positive Change. These skills focus on key issues that arise when you are involved with other people either as a leader or as a member of the group. As you progress from personal to interpersonal to group skills, the core competencies developed in the previous skill area help support successful performance in the new skill area.

At the outset of this introductory chapter, we mentioned that Pearson Publishers conducted a survey of a large sample of college instructors. These instructors rated *employability skills* as being important or very important for their students to learn. A large majority of these faculty members also expressed a desire to have access to textbooks that would address these specific skills. Table 3 highlights the sections of this book that directly address employability skills. Sections of the book that help foster behavior change and improved competence in employability skills are highlighted, and the specific chapters whose content directly addresses these employability skills are noted.

Appendix I contains a glossary of key terms in the text, and Appendix II lists references for excerpted material in the book.

Table 3 — Employability Skills and Developing Management Skills Content

Employability Skill	Content that assists in development
Critical Thinking	Skill Analysis section of each chapter Skill Practice section of each chapter Skill Application section of each chapter Especially content in Chapters 1, 3, 6, 7, and 10
Communication	Skill Analysis section of each chapter Skill Practice section of each chapter Skill Application section of each chapter Especially content in Chapters 4, 5, 6, 7, and 10
Collaboration	Skill Analysis section of each chapter Skill Practice section of each chapter Skill Application section of each chapter Especially content in Chapters 2, 3, 4, 6, 7, 8, and 9
Knowledge Application and Analysis	Skill Analysis section of each chapter Skill Practice section of each chapter Skill Application section of each chapter Especially content in Chapters 1, 3, and 10
Ethics and Social Responsibility	Skill Analysis section of each chapter Skill Practice section of each chapter Skill Application section of each chapter Especially content in Chapters 1, 3, 8, and 10

Organization of the Book

Each chapter is organized on the basis of the learning model summarized in Table 4. Specifically, each chapter begins with *Skill Assessment* instruments, followed by the largest section of the chapter, an explanation of the key behavioral guidelines along with evidence that confirms their validity. This is the *Skill Learning* section. The third section, *Skill Analysis*, provides brief case histories that illustrate both effective and ineffective applications of the behavioral principles. The *Skill Practice* section provides exercises, problems, and role-play assignments in order for you to practice the behavioral guidelines in a safe, simulated managerial situation and to receive feedback from peers and instructors. The last section of

Table 4 — The Organization of Each Chapter

Section	Contents
Skill Assessment	Instruments designed to identify your current level of skill competency, your styles, and/or key dimensions of the skill. These instruments can be used to identify individual differences, issues surrounding diversity, and areas for personal improvement plans.
Skill Learning	Behavioral guidelines and key principles associated with the skill are explained. Scientific research is used as the basis for prescribed skill performance. Clarifying how to successfully develop and perform the skill is the purpose of this section.
Skill Analysis	Cases and examples provide examples of successful and unsuccessful skill performance. Analytic problem-solving is facilitated as recommendations are made for what the key issues are, how performance might be modified, and why success was achieved.
Skill Practice	Exercises and role-plays make it possible for individuals to actually practice the skill. Feedback from peers and the instructor will facilitate improvement of the skill in a setting where failure is not costly.
Skill Application	Suggested assignments are provided so that the skill can be applied in a real-life setting. A feedback mechanism is also suggested so that individuals analyze their own success in applying the skill outside the classroom. Improvement plans should always be associated with the application exercises.

each chapter is *Skill Application*. It contains a form to help you generate your own improvement agenda, as well as assignments and ideas for applying the skill in real-world situation.

Diversity and Individual Differences

One reason it is difficult to develop management skills is because all of us possess our own unique styles, personalities, and inclinations. We all know that everyone doesn't react in the same way to similar circumstances. It is impossible, therefore, to manage each relationship in exactly the same way, or even to behave the same way from one encounter to the next. Sensitivity to individual differences is an important part of an effective manager's repertoire.

A great deal of research has been conducted on cultural differences, gender differences, ethnic differences, and age differences in organizations (e.g., Abramson & Moran, 2017; Cameron, 2017). While we do not summarize that extensive research, we do want to highlight the importance of being sensitive to individuality. Two kinds of sensitivities are necessary: one to the uniqueness displayed by each person, and the other to distinctive but general patterns of behavior that characterize groups of people. For example, it is essential that you not only become aware of the differences that characterize people with whom you associate, but also that you value and capitalize on these differences. People's general tendency is to fear or oppose those who are different from us. Therefore, we provide a framework to help us all better understand and appreciate differences. We don't emphasize *managing diversity* as much as *diagnosing individual differences* so they can be valued, understood, and appreciated.

In Chapter 1, Developing Self-Awareness, we explain a model developed by Frans Trompenaars that relies on seven dimensions found to differ across national and cultural boundaries. These dimensions have been found to be very helpful in helping people understand key differences in others. They are: *universalism versus particularism, individualism versus communitarianism, specificity versus diffuseness, neutral versus affective, achievement versus ascription oriented, internal versus external,* and *past versus present versus future time emphasis*. These dimensions will help you adjust your behaviors when you interact with others from a different culture or nationality. Although the behavioral principles upon which the management skills are based are applicable across cultures, genders, ethnic groups, and age cohorts, important nuances may be required of you as you practice among people characterized by these differences. Women may not behave the same way as men. Japanese colleagues may not respond in the same way as German colleagues. Individuals in their sixties may not see the world in the same way as someone in their twenties. So being sensitive to and valuing individual differences is key.

Summary

In sum, *Developing Management Skills* is not intended just for individuals who plan to enter managerial positions or who currently manage organizations. It is meant to help you better manage many aspects of your life and relationships. It is intended to help you actually improve your behavior, to elevate your competence, and to become more effective in your relationships with different kinds of people. It is intended to improve your social and emotional intelligence. John Holt (1964, p. 165) succinctly summarized our intention by equating management skill to intelligence:

> *When we talk about intelligence, we do not mean the ability to get a good score on a certain kind of test or even the ability to do well in school; these are at best only indicators of something larger, deeper, and far more important. By intelligence we mean a style of life, a way of behaving in various situations. The true test of intelligence is not how much we know how to do, but how we behave when we don't know what to do.*

Fostering the development of such intelligence is the goal of *Developing Management Skills*.

SUPPLEMENTARY MATERIAL

Diagnostic Survey and Exercises

Personal Assessment of Management Skills (PAMS)

Step 1: To get an overall profile of your level of skill competence, respond to the following statements using the rating scale below. Please rate your behavior as it is, not as you would like it to be. If you have not engaged in a specific activity, answer according to how you think you would behave based on your experience in similar activities. Be realistic; this instrument is designed to help you tailor your learning to your specific needs. After you have completed the survey, the scoring key at the end of the chapter will help you generate an overall profile of your management skill strengths and weaknesses.

Step 2: Get copies of the associates' version of this instrument from your instructor. An alternate version has been provided in the Instructor's Manual that uses "he" or "she" instead of "I" in the questions. Give copies to at least three other people who know you well or who have observed you in a situation in which you have had to lead or manage others. Those people should complete the instrument by rating your behavior. Bring the completed surveys back to class and compare: (1) your own ratings to your associates' ratings, (2) your associates' ratings to the ratings received by others in the class, and (3) the ratings you received to those of a national norm group.

Subsections of this instrument appear in each chapter throughout the book.

Rating Scale

1 Strongly disagree
2 Disagree
3 Slightly disagree
4 Slightly agree
5 Agree
6 Strongly agree

In regard to my level of self-knowledge:

_____ 1. I seek information about my strengths and weaknesses from others as a basis for self-improvement.

_____ 2. In order to improve, I am willing to be self-disclosing to others (that is, to share my beliefs and feelings).

_____ 3. I am very much aware of my preferred style in gathering information and making decisions.

_____ 4. I have a good sense of how I cope with situations that are ambiguous and uncertain.

_____ 5. I have a well-developed set of personal standards and principles that guide my behavior.

When faced with stressful or time-pressured situations:

_____ 6. I use effective time-management methods such as keeping track of my time, making to-do lists, and prioritizing tasks.

_____ 7. I frequently affirm my priorities so that less important things don't drive out more important things.

_____ 8. I maintain a program of regular exercise for fitness.

_____ 9. I maintain an open, trusting relationship with someone with whom I can share my frustrations.

_____ 10. I know and practice several temporary relaxation techniques, such as deep breathing and muscle relaxation.

_____ 11. I maintain balance in my life by pursuing a variety of interests outside of work.

When I approach a typical, routine problem:

_____ 12. I state clearly and explicitly what the problem is. I avoid trying to solve it until I have defined it.

_____ 13. I always generate more than one alternative solution to the problem, instead of identifying only one obvious solution.

_____ 14. I keep steps in the problem-solving process distinct; that is, I define the problem before proposing alternative solutions, and I generate alternatives before selecting a single solution.

When faced with a complex or difficult problem that does not have an easy solution:

_____ 15. I try out several definitions of the problem. I don't limit myself to just one way to define it.

_____ 16. I try to unfreeze my thinking by asking lots of questions about the nature of the problem before considering ways to solve it.

_____ 17. I try to think about the problem from both the left (logical) side of my brain and the right (intuitive) side of my brain.

_____ 18. I do not evaluate the merits of an alternative solution to the problem before I have generated a list of alternatives. That is, I avoid deciding on a solution until I have developed many possible solutions.

_____ 19. I have some specific techniques that I use to help develop creative and innovative solutions to problems.

When trying to foster more creativity and innovation among those with whom I work:

_____ 20. I make sure there are divergent points of view represented or expressed in every complex problem-solving situation.

_____ 21. I try to acquire information from individuals outside the problem-solving group who will be affected by the decision, mainly to determine their preferences and expectations.

_____ 22. I try to provide recognition not only to those who come up with creative ideas (the idea champions) but also to those who support others' ideas (supporters) and who provide resources to implement them (orchestrators).

_____ 23. I encourage informed rule-breaking in pursuit of creative solutions.

In situations where I have to provide negative feedback or offer corrective advice:

_____ 24. I am able to help others recognize and define their own problems when I counsel them.

_____ 25. I am clear about when I should coach someone and when I should provide counseling instead.

_____ 26. When I give feedback to others, I avoid referring to personal characteristics and focus on problems or solutions instead.

_____ 27. When I try to correct someone's behavior, our relationship is almost always strengthened.

_____ 28. I am descriptive in giving negative feedback to others. That is, I objectively describe events, their consequences, and my feelings about them.

_____ 29. I take responsibility for my statements and point of view by using, for example, "I have decided" instead of "They have decided."

_____ 30. I strive to identify some area of agreement in a discussion with someone who has a different point of view.

_____ 31. I don't talk down to those who have less power or less information than I.

_____ 32. When discussing someone's problem, I usually respond with a reply that indicates understanding rather than advice.

In a situation where it is important to obtain more power:

_____ 33. I always put forth more effort and take more initiative than expected in my work.

_____ 34. I am continually upgrading my skills and knowledge.

_____ 35. I strongly support organizational ceremonial events and activities.

_____ 36. I form a broad network of relationships with people throughout the organization at all levels.

_____ 37. In my work I consistently strive to generate new ideas, initiate new activities, and minimize routine tasks.

_____ 38. I consistently send personal notes to others when they accomplish something significant or when I pass along important information to them.

_____ 39. I refuse to bargain with individuals who use high-pressure negotiation tactics.

_____ 40. I always avoid using threats or demands to impose my will on others.

When another person needs to be motivated:

_____ 41. I always determine if the person has the necessary resources and support to succeed in a task.

_____ 42. I use a variety of rewards to reinforce exceptional performances.

_____ 43. I design task assignments to make them interesting and challenging.

_____ 44. I make sure the person gets timely feedback from those affected by task performance.

_____ 45. I always help the person establish performance goals that are challenging, specific, and timebound.

_____ 46. Only as a last resort do I attempt to reassign or release a poorly performing individual.

_____ 47. I consistently discipline when effort is below expectations and capabilities.

_____ 48. I make sure that people feel fairly and equitably treated.

_____ 49. I provide immediate compliments and other forms of recognition for meaningful accomplishments.

When I see someone doing something that needs correcting:

_____ 50. I avoid making personal accusations and attributing self-serving motives to the other person.

_____ 51. I encourage two-way interaction by inviting the respondent to express his or her perspective and to ask questions.

_____ 52. I make a specific request, detailing a more acceptable option.

When someone complains about something I've done:

_____ 53. I show genuine concern and interest, even when I disagree.

_____ 54. I seek additional information by asking questions that provide specific and descriptive information.

_____ 55. I ask the other person to suggest more acceptable behaviors.

When two people are in conflict and I am the mediator:

_____ 56. I do not take sides but remain neutral.

_____ 57. I help the parties generate multiple alternatives.

_____ 58. I help the parties find areas on which they agree.

In situations where I have an opportunity to engage people in accomplishing work:

_____ 59. I help people feel competent in their work by recognizing and celebrating their small successes.

_____ 60. I provide regular feedback and needed support.

_____ 61. I try to provide all the information that people need to accomplish their tasks.

_____ 62. I highlight the important impact that a person's work will have.

When engaging others in work:

_____ 63. I specify clearly the results I desire.

_____ 64. I specify clearly the level of initiative I want others to take (for example, wait for directions, do part of the task and then report, do the whole task and then report, and so forth).

_____ 65. I allow participation by those accepting assignments regarding when and how work will be done.

_____ 66. I avoid upward delegation by asking people to recommend solutions, rather than merely asking for advice or answers, when a problem is encountered.

_____ 67. I follow up and maintain accountability for delegated tasks on a regular basis.

When I am in the role of leader in a team:

_____ 68. I know how to establish credibility and influence among team members.

_____ 69. I am clear and consistent about what I want to achieve.

_____ 70. I build a common base of agreement in the team before moving forward with task accomplishment.

_____ 71. I articulate a clear, motivating vision of what the team can achieve, along with specific short-term goals.

When I am in the role of team member:

_____ 72. I know a variety of ways to facilitate task accomplishment in the team.

_____ 73. I know a variety of ways to help build strong relationships and cohesion among team members.

When I desire to make my team perform well, regardless of whether I am a leader or member:

_____ 74. I am knowledgeable about the different stages of team development experienced by most teams.

_____ 75. I help the team avoid groupthink by making sure that sufficient diversity of opinions is expressed in the team.

_____ 76. I can diagnose and capitalize on my team's core competencies, or unique strengths.

_____ 77. I encourage the team to achieve dramatic breakthrough innovations as well as small continuous improvements.

When I am in a position to lead change:

_____ 78. I create positive energy in others when I interact with them.

_____ 79. I emphasize a higher purpose or meaning associated with the change I am leading.

_____ 80. I express gratitude frequently and conspicuously, even for small acts.

_____ 81. I emphasize building on strengths, not just overcoming weaknesses.

_____ 82. I use a lot more positive comments than negative comments.

_____ 83. When I communicate a vision, I capture people's hearts as well as their heads.

_____ 84. I know how to get people to commit to my vision of positive change.

What Does It Take to Be an Effective Manager?

The purpose of this exercise is to help you get a firsthand picture of the role of a manager and the skills required to perform that job successfully.

Your assignment is to interview at least three managers who are employed full-time. You should use the questions below in your interviews, plus use others that you think might help you identify effective management skills. The purpose of these interviews is to give you a chance to learn about critical managerial skills from those who have to use them.

Please treat the interviews as confidential. The names of the individuals do not matter—only their opinions, perceptions, and behaviors. Assure the managers that no one will be able to identify them from their responses. Keep written notes of your interviews. These notes should be as detailed as possible so you can reconstruct the interviews later. Be sure to keep a record of each person's job title and a brief description of his or her organization.

1. Please describe a typical day at work. What do you do all day?

2. What are the most critical problems you face as a manager?

3. What are the most critical skills needed to be a successful manager in your line of work?

4. What are the major reasons managers fail in positions like yours?

5. What are the outstanding skills or abilities of other effective managers you have known?

6. If you had to train someone to replace you in your current job, what key abilities would you focus on?

7. On a scale of 1 (very rarely) to 5 (constantly), please rate the extent to which you use the following skills or behaviors during your workday:

_____ Managing personal time and stress

_____ Facilitating group decision-making

_____ Creative problem-solving

_____ Articulating an energizing vision

_____ Managing conflict

_____ Gaining and using power

_____ Delegating

_____ Active listening

_____ Conducting interviews

_____ Building teams and teamwork

_____ Conducting meetings

_____ Fostering continuous improvement and quality

_____ Making analytical decisions

_____ Using interpersonal communication skills

_____ Motivating others

_____ Capitalizing on your self-awareness

_____ Facilitating organizational change

_____ Setting specific goals and targets

_____ Empowering others

_____ Giving speeches or presentations

_____ Defining and/or solving complex problems

_____ Negotiating

SSS Software In-Basket Exercise

One way to assess your own strengths and weaknesses in management skills is to engage in an actual managerial work experience. The following exercise gives you a realistic glimpse of the tasks faced regularly by practicing managers. Complete the exercise, and then compare your own decisions and actions with those of classmates.

SSS Software designs and develops customized software for businesses. It also integrates this software with the customer's existing systems and provides system maintenance. SSS Software has customers in the following industries: airlines, automotive, consumer products, electronics, finance/banking, government, and health/hospital. The company has also begun to generate important international clients. These include the European Airbus consortium and a consortium of banks and financial firms based in Kenya.

SSS Software has grown rapidly since its inception eight years ago. Its revenue, net income, and earnings per share have all been above the industry average for the past several years. However, competition in this technologically sophisticated field has grown very rapidly. Recently, it has become more difficult to compete for major contracts. Moreover, although SSS Software's revenue and net income continue to grow, the rate of growth declined during the last fiscal year.

SSS Software's 250 employees are divided into several operating divisions, with employees at four levels: nonmanagement, technical/professional, managerial, and executive. Non-management employees take care of the clerical and facilities support functions. The Technical/Professional staff performs the core technical work for the firm. Most Managerial employees are group managers who supervise a team of Technical/Professional employees working on a project for a particular customer. Staff who work in specialized areas such as finance, accounting, human resources, nursing, and law are also considered Managerial employees. The Executive level includes the 12 highest-ranking employees at SSS Software. An organization chart in Figure 3 illustrates SSS Software's structure. There is also an Employee Classification Report that lists the number of employees at each level of the organization.

In this exercise, you will play the role of Chris Perillo, vice president of operations for Health and Financial Services. You learned last Wednesday, October 13, that your predecessor, Michael Grant, had resigned and gone to Universal Business Solutions Inc. You were offered his former job, and you accepted it. Previously, you were the Group Manager for a team of 15 software developers assigned to work on the Airbus consortium project in the Airline Services Division. You spent all of Thursday and Friday and most of the weekend finishing up parts of the project, briefing your successor, and preparing for an interim report you will deliver in Paris on October 21.

It is now 7:00 a.m. Monday and you are in your new office. You have arrived at work early so you can spend the next two hours reviewing material in your in-basket (including some memos and messages to Michael Grant), as well as your voicemail and email. Your daily planning book indicates that you have no appointments today or tomorrow but will have to catch a plane for Paris early Wednesday morning. You have a full schedule for the remainder of the week and all of next week.

Assignment

During the next two hours, review all the material in your in-basket, as well as your voicemail and email. Take only two hours. Using the response form below as a model, indicate how you want to respond to each item (that is, via letter/memo, email, phone/voicemail, or personal meeting). If you decide not to respond to an item, check "no

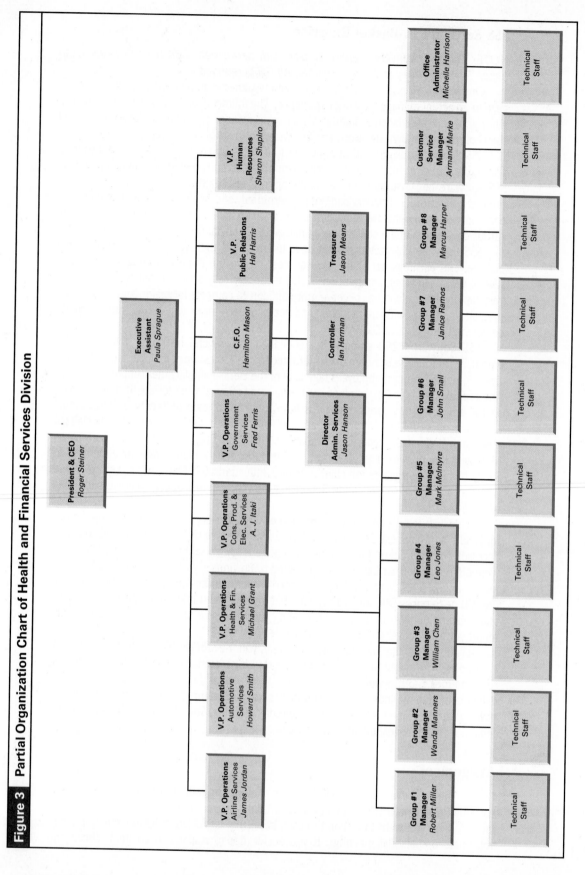

Figure 3 Partial Organization Chart of Health and Financial Services Division

response" on the response form. All your responses must be written on the response forms. Write your precise, detailed response (do not merely jot down a few notes). For example, you might draft a memo or write out a message that you will deliver via phone/voicemail. You may also decide to meet with an individual (or individuals) during the limited time available on your calendar today or tomorrow. If so, prepare an agenda for a personal meeting and list your goals for the meeting. As you read through the items, you may occasionally observe some information that you think is relevant and want to remember (or attend to in the future) but that you decide not to include in any of your responses to employees. Write down such information on a sheet of paper titled "note to self."

Sample Response Form

Relates to:

Memo # _____   Email # _____   Voicemail # _____

Response form:

_____ Letter/Memo   _____ Meet with person (when, where)

_____ Email   _____ Note to self

_____ Phone call/Voicemail   _____ No response

ITEM 1 – EMAIL

TO: All Employees
FROM: Roger Steiner, Chief Executive Officer
DATE: October 15

I am pleased to announce that Chris Perillo has been appointed as Vice President of Operations for Health and Financial Services. Chris will immediately assume responsibility for all operations previously managed by Michael Grant. Chris will have end-to-end responsibility for the design, development, integration, and maintenance of custom software for the health and finance/banking industries. This responsibility includes all technical, financial, and staffing issues. Chris will also manage our program of software support and integration for the recently announced merger of three large health maintenance organizations (HMOs). Chris will be responsible for our recently announced project with a consortium of banks and financial firms operating in Tanzania. This project represents an exciting opportunity for us, and Chris's background seems ideally suited to the task.

Chris comes to this position with an undergraduate degree in computer science from the California Institute of Technology and an MBA from the University of Virginia. Chris began as a member of our technical/professional staff six years ago and has most recently served for three years as a Group Manager supporting domestic and international projects for our airlines industry group, including our recent work for the European Airbus consortium.

I am sure you all join me in offering congratulations to Chris for this promotion.

ITEM 2 – EMAIL

TO: All Managers
FROM: Hal Harris, Vice President, Community and Public Relations
DATE: October 15

For your information, the following article appeared on the front page of the business section of Thursday's *Los Angeles Times*.

In a move that may create problems for SSS Software, Michael Grant and Janice Ramos have left SSS Software and moved to Universal Business Solutions Inc. Industry analysts see the move as another victory for Universal Business Solutions Inc. in their battle with SSS Software for share of the growing software development and integration business. Both Grant and Ramos had been with SSS Software for over seven years. Grant was most recently Vice President of Operations for all SSS Software's work in two industries: health and hospitals, and finance and banking. Ramos brings to Universal Business Solutions Inc. her special expertise in the growing area of international software development and integration.

Hillary Collins, an industry analyst with Merrill Lynch, said, "The loss of key staff to a competitor can often create serious problems for a firm such as SSS Software. Grant and Ramos have an insider's understanding of SSS Software's strategic and technical limitations. It will be interesting to see if they can exploit this knowledge to the advantage of Universal Business Solutions Inc."

ITEM 3 – EMAIL

TO: Chris Perillo
FROM: Paula Sprague, Executive Assistant to Roger Steiner
DATE: October 15

Chris, I know that in your former position as a Group Manager in the Airline Services Division, you probably have met most of the Group Managers in the Health and Financial Services Division, but I thought you might like some more personal information about them. These people will be your direct reports on the management team.

Group #1: Bob Miller, 55-year-old white male, married (Anna) with two children and three grandchildren. Active in local Republican politics. Well regarded as a "hands-off" manager heading a high-performing team. Plays golf regularly with Mark McIntyre, John Small, and a couple of V.P.s from other divisions.

Group #2: Wanda Manners, 38-year-old white female, single with one school-age child. A fitness "nut" has run in several marathons. Some experience in Germany and Japan. Considered a hard-driving manager with a constant focus on the task at hand. Will be the first person to show up every morning.

Group #3: William Chen, 31-year-old male of Chinese descent, married (Harriet), two young children from his first marriage. Enjoys tennis and is quite good at it. A rising star in the company, he is highly respected by his peers as a "man of action" and a good friend.

Group #4: Leo Jones, 36-year-old white male, married (Janet) with an infant daughter. Recently returned from paternity leave. Has traveled extensively on projects, since he speaks three languages. Has liked hockey ever since the time he spent in Montreal. Considered a strong manager who gets the most out of his people.

Group #5: Mark McIntyre, 45-year-old white male, married (Mary Theresa) to an executive in the banking industry. No children. A lot of experience in Germany and Eastern Europe. Has been writing a mystery novel. Has always been a good "team player," but several members of his technical staff are not well respected and he hasn't addressed the problem.

Group #6: John Small, 38-year-old white male, recently divorced. Three children living with his wife. A gregarious individual who likes sports. Spent a lot of time in Mexico and Central America before he came to SSS Software. Recently has been doing mostly contract work with the federal government. An average manager; has had some trouble keeping his people on schedule.

Group #7: This position vacant since Janice Ramos left. Roger thinks we ought to fill this position quickly. Get in touch with me if you want information on any in-house candidates for any position.

Group #8: Marcus Harper, 42-year-old African American, married (Tamara) with two teenage children. Recently won an award in a local photography contest. Considered a strong manager who gets along with peers and works long hours.

Customer Service: Armad Marke, 38-year-old male, divorced. A basketball fan. Originally from Armenia. Previously a Group Manager. Worked hard to establish the Technical Services Phone Line, but now has pretty much left it alone.

Office Administrator: Michelle Harrison, 41-year-old white female, single. Grew up on a ranch and still rides horses whenever she can. A strict administrator.

There are a number of good folks here, but they don't function well as a management team. I think Michael played favorites, especially with Janice and Leo. There are a few cliques in this group and I'm not sure how effectively Michael dealt with them. I expect you will find it a challenge to build a cohesive team.

ITEM 4 – EMAIL

TO: Chris Perillo
FROM: Wanda Manners, Group 2 Manager
DATE: October 15

Confidential and Restricted

Although I know you are new to your job, I feel it is important that I let you know about some information I just obtained concerning the development work we recently completed for First National Investment. Our project involved the development of asset management software for managing their international funds. This was a very complex project due to the volatile exchange rates and the forecasting tools we needed to develop.

As part of this project, we had to integrate the software and reports with all their existing systems and reporting mechanisms. To do this, we were given access to all of their existing software (much of which was developed by Universal Business Solutions Inc.). Of course, we signed an agreement acknowledging that the software to which we were given access was proprietary and that our access was solely for the purpose of our system integration work associated with the project.

Unfortunately, I have learned that some parts of the software we developed actually "borrow" heavily from complex application programs developed for First National Investment by Universal Business Solutions Inc. It seems obvious to me that one or more of the software developers from Group 5 (that is, Mark McIntyre's group) inappropriately "borrowed" algorithms developed by Universal Business Solutions Inc. I am sure that doing so saved us significant development time on some aspects of the project. It seems very unlikely that First National Investment or Universal Business Solutions Inc. will ever become aware of this issue.

Finally, First National Investment is successfully using the software we developed and is thrilled with the work we did. We brought the project in on time and under budget. You probably know that they have invited us to bid on several other substantial projects.

I'm sorry to bring this delicate matter to your attention, but I thought you should know about it.

ITEM 5A – EMAIL

TO: Chris Perillo
FROM: Paula Sprague, Executive Assistant to Roger Steiner
DATE: October 15
RE: Letter from C.A.R.E. Services (copies attached)

Roger asked me to work on this C.A.R.E. project and obviously wants some fast action. A lot of the staff are already booked solid for the next couple of weeks. I knew that Elise Soto and Chu Hung Woo have the expertise to do this system and when I checked with them, they were relatively free. I had them pencil in the next two weeks and wanted to let you know. Hopefully, it will take a "hot potato" out of your hands.

ITEM 5B – COPY OF FAX

C.A.R.E.
Child and Adolescent Rehabilitative and Educational Services
A United Way Member Agency
200 Main Street
Los Angeles, CA 90230

DATE: October 11
Roger Steiner, CEO
SSS Software
13 Miller Way
Los Angeles, CA 90224

Dear Roger,

This letter is a follow-up to our conversation after last night's board meeting. I appreciated your comments during the board meeting about the need for sophisticated computer systems in nonprofit organizations, and I especially appreciate your generous offer of assistance to have SSS Software provide assistance to deal with the immediate problem with our accounting system. Since the board voted to fire the computer consultant, I am very worried about getting our reports done in time to meet the state funding cycle.

Thanks again for your offer of help during this crisis.

Sincerely yours,

Janice Polocizwic

Janice Polocizwic

Executive Director

ITEM 5C – COPY OF A LETTER

SSS SOFTWARE
13 Miller Way
Los Angeles, CA 90224
DATE: October 12
Janice Polocizwic
Executive Director, C.A.R.E. Services
200 Main Street
Los Angeles, CA 90230

Dear Janice,

I received your fax of October 11. I have asked Paula Sprague, my executive assistant, to line up people to work on your accounting system as soon as possible. You can expect to hear from her shortly.

Sincerely,

Roger Steiner

Roger Steiner

cc: Paula Sprague, Executive Assistant

ITEM 6 – EMAIL

TO: Michael Grant
FROM: Harry Withers, Group 6 Technical Staff
DATE: October 12

PERSONAL AND CONFIDENTIAL

Our team is having difficulty meeting the submission deadline of November 5 for the Halstrom project. Kim, Fred, Peter, Kyoto, Susan, Mala, and I have been working on the project for several weeks, but we are experiencing some problems and may need additional time. I hesitate to write this letter, but the main problem is that our group manager, John Small, is involved in a relationship with Mala. Mala gets John's support for her ideas and brings them to the team as required components of the project. Needless to say, this has posed some problems for the group. Mala's background is especially valuable for this project, but Kim and Fred, who have both worked very hard on the project, do not want to work with her. In addition, one member of the team has been unavailable recently because of childcare needs. Commitment to the project and team morale have plummeted. However, we'll do our best to get the project finished as soon as possible. Mala will be on vacation the next two weeks, so I'm expecting that some of us can complete it in her absence.

ITEM 7 – VOICEMAIL MESSAGE

Hello, Michael. This is Jim Bishop of United Hospitals. I wanted to talk with you about the quality assurance project that you are working on for us. When Jose Martinez first started talking with us, I was impressed with his friendliness and expertise. But recently, he doesn't seem to be getting much accomplished and has seemed distant and on-edge in conversations. Today, I asked him about the schedule and he seemed very defensive and not entirely in control of his emotions. I am quite concerned about our project. Please give me a call.

ITEM 8 – VOICEMAIL MESSAGE

Hi, Michael. This is Armand. I wanted to talk with you about some issues with the technical services phone line. I've recently received some complaint letters from phone line customers whose complaints have included long delays while waiting for a technician to answer the phone, technicians who are not knowledgeable enough to solve problems, and, on occasion, rude service. Needless to say, I'm quite concerned about these complaints.

I believe that the overall quality of the phone line staff is very good, but we continue to be understaffed, even with the recent hires. The new technicians look strong, but they are working on the help line before being fully trained. Antolina, our best tech, often brings her child to work, which is adding to the craziness around here.

I think you should know that we're feeling a lot of stress here. I'll talk with you soon.

ITEM 9 – VOICEMAIL MESSAGE

Hi, Chris, it's Pat. Congratulations on your promotion. They definitely picked the right person. It's great news—for me, too. You've been a terrific mentor so far, so I'm expecting to learn a lot from you in your new position. How about lunch next week?

ITEM 10 – VOICEMAIL MESSAGE

Chris, this is Bob Miller. Just thought you'd like to know that John's joke during our planning meeting has disturbed a few of the women in my group. Frankly, I think the thing's being blown out of proportion, especially since we all know this is a good place for both men and women to work. Give me a call if you want to chat about this.

ITEM 11 – VOICEMAIL MESSAGE

Hello. This is Lorraine Adams from Westside Hospital. I read in today's *Los Angeles Times* that you will be taking over from Michael Grant. We haven't met yet, but your division has recently finished two large million-dollar projects for Westside. Michael Grant and I had some discussion about a small conversion of a piece of existing software to be compatible with the new systems. The original vendor had said that they would do the work, but they have been stalling, and I need to move quickly. Can you see if Harris Wilson, Chu Hung Woo, and Elise Soto are available to do this work as soon as possible? They were on the original project and work well with our people.

Um...(long pause) I guess I should tell you that I got a call from Michael offering to do this work. But I think I should stick with SSS Software. Give me a call.

ITEM 12 – VOICEMAIL MESSAGE

Hi, Chris, this is Roosevelt Moore calling. I'm a member of your technical/professional staff. I used to report to Janice Ramos, but since she left the firm, I thought I'd bring my concerns directly to you. I'd like to arrange some time to talk with you about my experiences since returning from six weeks of paternity leave. Some of my major responsibilities have been turned over to others. I seem to be out of the loop and wonder if my career is at risk. Also, I am afraid that I won't be supported or seriously considered for the opening created by Janice's departure. Frankly, I feel like I'm being screwed for taking my leave. I'd like to talk with you this week.

ITEM 13 – EMAIL

TO: Michael Grant
FROM: Jose Martinez, Group 1 Technical Staff
DATE: October 12

I would like to set up a meeting with you as soon as possible. I suspect that you will get a call from Jim Bishop of United Hospitals and want to be sure that you hear my side of the story first. I have been working on a customized system design for quality assurance for them using a variation of the J-3 product we developed several years ago. They had a number of special requirements and some quirks in their accounting systems, so I have had to put in especially long hours. I've worked hard to meet their demands, but they keep changing the ground rules. I keep thinking, this is just another J-3 I'm working on, but they have been interfering with an elegant design I have developed. It seems I'm not getting anywhere on this project. Earlier today, I had a difficult discussion with their Controller. He asked for another major change. I've been fighting their deadline and think I am just stretched too thin on this project. Then Jim Bishop asked me if the system was running yet. I was worn out from dealing with the Controller, and I made a sarcastic comment to Jim Bishop. He gave me a funny look and just walked out of the room.

I would like to talk with you about this situation at your earliest convenience.

ITEM 14 – EMAIL

TO: Chris Perillo
FROM: John Small, Group 6 Manager
DATE: October 15

Welcome aboard, Chris. I look forward to meeting with you. I just wanted to put a bug in your ear about finding a replacement for Janice Ramos. One of my technical staff, Mala Abendano, has the ability and drive to make an excellent group manager. I have encouraged her to apply for the position. I'd be happy to talk with you further about this, at your convenience.

ITEM 15 – EMAIL

TO: Chris Perillo
FROM: Paula Sprague, Executive Assistant to Roger Steiner
DATE: October 15

Roger asked me to let you know about the large contract we have gotten in Tanzania. It means that a team of four managers will be making a short trip to determine current needs. They will assign their technical staff the tasks of developing a system and software here over the next six months, and then the managers and possibly some team members will be spending about 10 months on-site in Tanzania to handle the implementation. Roger thought you might want to hold an initial meeting with some of your managers to check on their interest and willingness to take this sort of assignment. Roger would appreciate an email of your thoughts about the issues to be discussed at this meeting, additional considerations about sending people to Tanzania, and about how you will put together an effective team to work on this project. The October 15 memo I sent to you will provide you with some information you'll need to start making these decisions.

ITEM 16 – EMAIL

TO: Chris Perillo
FROM: Sharon Shapiro, V.P. of Human Resources
DATE: October 15
RE: Upcoming meeting

I want to update you on the ripple effect of John Small's sexual joke at last week's planning meeting. Quite a few women have been very upset and have met informally to talk about it. They have decided to call a meeting of all people concerned about this kind of behavior throughout the firm. I plan to attend, so I'll keep you posted.

ITEM 17 – EMAIL

TO: All SSS Software Managers

FROM: Sharon Shapiro, V.P. of Human Resources

DATE: October 15

RE: Promotions and External Hires

Year-to-Date (January through September) Promotions and External Hires

| | Race | | | | | Sex | | |
Level	White	African American	Asian	Hispanic	Native American	M	F	Total
Hires into Executive Level	0 (0%)	0 (0%)	0 (0%)	0 (0%)	0 (0%)	0 (0%)	0 (0%)	0
Promotions to Executive Level	0 (0%)	0 (0%)	0 (0%)	0 (0%)	0 (0%)	0 (0%)	0 (0%)	0

| | Race | | | | | Sex | | |
Level	White	African American	Asian	Hispanic	Native American	M	F	Total
Hires into Management Level	2 (67%)	1 (33%)	0 (0%)	0 (0%)	0 (0%)	2 (67%)	1 (33%)	3
Promotions to Management Level	7 (88%)	0 (0%)	1 (12%)	0 (0%)	0 (0%)	7 (88%)	1 (12%)	8
Hires into Technical/ Professional Level	10 (36%)	6 (21%)	10 (36%)	2 (7%)	0 (0%)	14 (50%)	14 (50%)	28
Promotions to Technical/ Professional Level	0 (0%)	0 (0%)	0 (0%)	0 (0%)	0 (0%)	0 (0%)	0 (0%)	0
Hires into Non-Management Level	4 (20%)	10 (50%)	2 (10%)	4 (20%)	0 (0%)	6 (30%)	14 (70%)	20
Promotions to Non-Management Level	NA	NA	NA	NA	NA	NA	NA	NA

SSS Software Employee (EEO) Classification Report as of June 30

| | Race | | | | | Sex | | |
Level	White	African American	Asian	Hispanic	Native American	M	F	Total
Executive Level	11 (92%)	0 (0%)	1 (8%)	0 (0%)	0 (0%)	11 (92%)	1 (8%)	12
Management Level	43 (90%)	2 (4%)	2 (4%)	1 (2%)	0 (0%)	38 (79%)	10 (21%)	48
Technical/ Professional Level	58 (45%)	20 (15%)	37 (28%)	14 (11%)	1 (1%)	80 (62%)	50 (38%)	130
Non-Management Level	29 (48%)	22 (37%)	4 (7%)	4 (7%)	1 (2%)	12 (20%)	48 (80%)	60
Total	141 (56%)	44 (18%)	44 (18%)	19 (8%)	2 (1%)	141 (56%)	109 (44%)	250

If your instructor is utilizing **MyLab Management**, log on to www.pearson.com/mylab/management and select the Personal Inventory Assessment (PIA) section to complete the following instrument Personal Assessment of Management Skills (PAMS).

SCORING KEY AND COMPARISON DATA

⭐ Go to www.pearson.com/mylab/management for scoring keys and comparison data for the following instrument:

Personal Assessment of Management Skills

Personal Assessment of Management Skills

Scoring Key

SKILL AREA	ITEMS	ASSESSMENT	
		PERSONAL	ASSOCIATES
Developing Self-Awareness	**1–5**		
Self-disclosure and openness	1–2		
Awareness of self	3–5		
Managing Stress	**6–11**		
Eliminating stressors	6–7		
Developing resiliency	8–9		
Short-term coping	10–11		
Solving Problems Creatively	**12–23**		
Rational problem-solving	12–14		
Creative problem-solving	15–19		
Fostering innovation and creativity	20–23		
Communicating Supportively	**24–32**		
Coaching and counseling	24–25		
Effective negative feedback	26–28		
Communicating supportively	29–32		
Gaining Power and Influence	**33–40**		
Gaining power	33–37		
Exercising influence	38–40		
Motivating Others	**41–49**		
Managing Conflict	**50–58**		
Initiating	50–52		
Responding	53–55		
Mediating	56–58		
Empowering and Engaging	**59–67**		
Empowering	59–62		
Delegating	63–67		

Skill Area	Items	Assessment	
		Personal	Associates
Building Effective Teams and Teamwork	**68–77**		
Leading teams	68–71		
Team membership	72–73		
Teamwork	74–77		
Leading Positive Change	**78–84**		
Fostering positive deviance	78–80		
Leading positive change	81–82		
Mobilizing others	83–84		

Comparison Data (N = 5,000 students)

Compare your scores with at least four referents: (1) If you asked others to rate you using the associates' version, compare how you rated yourself with how your associates rated you; (2) Compare the ratings you received to those received by other students in the class; (3) Compare the ratings you received to a norm group of approximately 5,000 business school students (see the information below); and (4) Compare your score against the maximum possible (510).

For the survey as a whole, if you scored

394.35	=	mean
422 or above	=	you are in the top quartile
395–421	=	you are in the second quartile
369–394	=	you are in the third quartile
368 or below	=	you are in the bottom quartile

What Does It Take to Be an Effective Manager?

This exercise does not have a solution or scoring data. Answers will vary among students.

SSS Software In-Basket Exercise

This exercise does not have a solution or scoring data. Answers will vary among students.

Part I

Personal Skills

CHAPTERS

SKILL ASSESSMENT

- Self-Awareness Assessment
- Emotional Intelligence Assessment
- The Defining Issues Test
- VIA Assessment
- Cognitive Style Indicator
- Locus of Control Scale
- Tolerance of Ambiguity Scale
- Core Self-Evaluation Scale (CSES)

SKILL LEARNING

- Key Dimensions of Self-Awareness
- The Enigma of Self-Awareness
- Understanding and Appreciating Individual Differences
- Important Areas of Self-Awareness
- Summary
- Behavioral Guidelines

SKILL ANALYSIS

- The Case of Heinz
- Computerized Exam
- Decision Dilemmas

SKILL PRACTICE

- Shipping the Part
- Through the Looking Glass
- Diagnosing Managerial Characteristics
- An Exercise for Identifying Aspects of Personal Culture:
  A Learning Plan and Autobiography

SKILL APPLICATION

- Suggested Assignments
- Application Plan and Evaluation

SCORING KEYS AND COMPARISON DATA

MyLab Management

Go to www.pearson.com/mylab/management to complete the exercises marked with this icon ✪.

1

Developing Self-Awareness

LEARNING OBJECTIVES

Increase personal awareness of your:

1. Sensitive line
2. Emotional intelligence
3. Personal values and moral maturity
4. Character strengths
5. Cognitive style
6. Orientation toward change
7. Core self-evaluation

SKILL ASSESSMENT ?

DIAGNOSTIC SURVEYS FOR DEVELOPING SELF-AWARENESS

MyLab Management Personal Inventory Assessments

 PERSONAL INVENTORY ASSESSMENT

The assessment instruments in this chapter are briefly described below. The assessments appear either in your text or in MyLab. The assessments marked with ✪ are available only in MyLab. If assigned, go to www.pearson.com/mylab/management to complete these assessments. The assessments without the ✪ appear only in the text.

All assessments should be completed before reading the chapter material.

After completing the first assessment, save your response to your hard drive. When you have finished reading the chapter, re-take the assessment and compare your responses to see what you have learned.

- ✪ ❑ The *Self-Awareness Assessment Instrument* measures the extent to which you are self-aware and effectively engage in self-awareness practices.
- ✪ ❑ The *Emotional Intelligence Assessment* measures your emotional style and intelligence.
- ❑ The *Defining Issues Test* assesses your moral and values maturity based on your responses to controversial social issues.
- ❑ The *VIA Instrument* (http://www.viacharacter.org/www/Character-Strengths-Survey) assesses your character strengths and, in particular, identifies your signature strengths.
- ❑ The *Cognitive Style Indicator* assesses the way you gather and evaluate information and make decisions.
- ✪ ❑ The *Locus of Control Scale* measures your opinion about the causes and influences of certain events in your life.
- ❑ The *Tolerance of Ambiguity Scale* assesses the extent to which you are comfortable in situations where ambiguity and uncertainty are present.
- ❑ The *Core Self-Evaluation Scale* measures core personality attributes that predict human behavior.

DEVELOPING SELF-AWARENESS

Assessment Section

THE DEFINING ISSUES TEST

This instrument assesses your opinions about controversial social issues. Different people make decisions about these issues in different ways. You should answer the questions for yourself without discussing them with others.

You are presented with three stories. Following each story you are asked to choose between three decisions. Next, you will rate the importance of 12 questions about the story in influencing your decision. After you have completed your ratings, select the four most important questions and rank them from 1 to 4 in the spaces provided.

Some statements will raise important issues, but you should ask yourself whether your decision should rest on that issue. Some statements sound high and lofty but are largely gibberish. If you cannot make sense of a statement, or if you don't understand its meaning, mark it 5—"Of no importance." Use the following scale for rating the importance of the statements.

Rating Scale

1	Of great importance	This statement or question makes a crucial difference in making a decision about the problem.
2	Of much importance	This statement or question is something that would be a major factor (though not always a crucial one) in making a decision.
3	Of some importance	This statement or question involves something you care about, but it is not of great importance in reaching a decision.
4	Of little importance	This statement or question is not very important to consider in this case.
5	Of no importance	This statement or question is completely unimportant in making a decision. You would waste your time thinking about it.

The Escaped Prisoner

A man had been sentenced to prison for 10 years. After one year, however, he escaped from prison, moved to a new area of the country, and took on the name of Thompson. For eight years he worked hard, and gradually he saved enough money to buy his own business. He was fair to his customers, gave his employees top wages, and gave most of his own profits to charity. Then one day, Ms. Jones, an old neighbor, recognized him as the man who had escaped from prison eight years before and for whom the police had been looking.

What should Ms. Jones do? (Check one.)

_____ Report him—send him back to prison
_____ Can't decide
_____ Not report him

Importance

1. _____ Hasn't Mr. Thompson been good enough for such a long time to prove he isn't a bad person?
2. _____ Every time someone escapes punishment for a crime, doesn't that just encourage more crime?
3. _____ Wouldn't we be better off without prisons and the oppression of our legal system?
4. _____ Has Mr. Thompson really paid his debt to society?
5. _____ Would society be unfairly treating Mr. Thompson?
6. _____ What benefit would prison be apart from society, especially for a charitable man?
7. _____ How could anyone be so cruel and heartless as to send Mr. Thompson back to prison?
8. _____ Would it be fair to prisoners who have to serve out their full sentences if Mr. Thompson is let off?
9. _____ Was Ms. Jones a good friend of Mr. Thompson?
10. _____ Wouldn't it be a citizen's duty to report an escaped criminal, regardless of the circumstances?
11. _____ How would the will of the people and the public good best be served?
12. _____ Would going to prison do any good for Mr. Thompson or protect anybody?

From the list of questions, select the four most important:

_____ Most important
_____ Second most important
_____ Third most important
_____ Fourth most important

The Doctor's Dilemma

A woman was dying of incurable cancer and had only about six months to live. She was in terrible pain, but she was so weak that a large dose of a pain killer such as morphine would probably kill her. She was delirious with pain, and in her calm periods, she would ask her doctor to give her enough morphine to kill her. She said she couldn't stand the pain and that she was going to die in a few months anyway.

What should the doctor do? (Check one.)

_____ Give the woman an overdose that will make her die
_____ Can't decide
_____ Don't give her the overdose

Importance

_____   1. Is the woman's family in favor of giving her the overdose?
_____   2. Is the doctor bound by the same laws as everybody else?
_____   3. Would people be better off without society regimenting their lives and even their deaths?
_____   4. Should the doctor make the woman's death from a drug overdose appear to be an accident?
_____   5. Does the state have the right to force continued existence on those who don't want to live?
_____   6. What is the value of death prior to society's perspective on personal values?
_____   7. Should the doctor have sympathy for the woman's suffering, or should he care more about what society might think?
_____   8. Is helping to end another's life ever a responsible act of cooperation?
_____   9. Can only God decide when a person's life should end?
_____   10. What values has the doctor set for himself in his own personal code of behavior?
_____   11. Can society afford to let anybody end his or her life whenever he or she desires?
_____   12. Can society allow suicide or mercy killing and still protect the lives of individuals who want to live?

From the list of questions above, select the four most important:

_____ Most important
_____ Second most important
_____ Third most important
_____ Fourth most important

The Newspaper

Rami, a senior in high school, wanted to publish a newspaper for students so that he could express his opinions. He wanted to speak out against military buildup and some of the school's rules, such as the rule forbidding boys to have long hair.

When Rami started his newspaper, he asked his principal for permission. The principal said it would be all right if before every publication Rami would turn in all his articles for the principal's approval. Rami agreed and turned in several articles for approval. The principal approved all of them, and Rami published two issues of the paper in the next two weeks.

However, the principal had not expected that Rami's newspaper would receive so much attention. Students were so excited by the paper that they began to organize protests against the government, hair regulation, and other school rules. Angry parents objected to Rami's opinions. They phoned the principal, telling him that the newspaper was unpatriotic and should not be published. As a result of the rising excitement, the principal wondered if he should order Rami to stop publishing on the grounds that the controversial newspaper articles were disrupting the operation of the school.

What should the principal do? (Check one.)

_____ Stop Rami's newspaper
_____ Can't decide
_____ Don't stop it

Importance

1. Is the principal more responsible to the students or to the parents?
2. Did the principal give his word that the newspaper could be published for a long time, or did he just promise to approve the newspaper one issue at a time?
3. Would the students start protesting even more if the principal stopped the newspaper?
4. When the welfare of the school is threatened, does the principal have the right to give orders to students?
5. Does the principal have the freedom of speech to say no in this case?
6. If the principal stopped the newspaper, would he be preventing full discussion of important problems?
7. Would the principal's stop order make Rami lose faith in him?
8. Is Rami really loyal to his school and patriotic to his country?
9. What effect would stopping the paper have on the students' education in critical thinking and judgment?
10. Is Rami in any way violating the rights of others in publishing his own opinions?
11. Should the principal be influenced by some angry parents when it is the principal who knows best what is going on in the school?
12. Is Rami using the newspaper to stir up hatred and discontent?

From the list of questions above, select the four most important:

_____ Most important
_____ Second most important
_____ Third most important
_____ Fourth most important

SOURCE: *Adapted from* Rest, et al., 1999.

Cognitive Style Indicator

This instrument assesses the way you gather and evaluate information and make decisions. There are no right or wrong answers, and the accuracy of your results will depend on the extent to which you honestly answer each question. Please use the following scale in responding to each item.

Rating Scale

1 Totally disagree
2 Disagree
3 Neither agree nor disagree
4 Agree
5 Totally agree

_____ 1. Developing a clear plan is very important to me.
_____ 2. I like to contribute to innovative solutions.
_____ 3. I always want to know what should be done when.
_____ 4. I prefer to look at creative solutions.
_____ 5. I want to have a full understanding of a problem.
_____ 6. I like detailed action plans.
_____ 7. I am motivated by ongoing innovation.
_____ 8. I like to analyze problems.
_____ 9. I prefer a clear structure to do my job.
_____ 10. I like a lot of variety in my life.
_____ 11. I engage in detailed analyses.
_____ 12. I prefer well-planned meetings with a clear agenda.
_____ 13. New ideas attract me more than existing solutions.
_____ 14. I study each problem until I understand the underlying logic.
_____ 15. I make definite appointments and follow up meticulously.
_____ 16. I like to extend the boundaries.
_____ 17. A good task is a well-prepared task.
_____ 18. I try to avoid routine.

SOURCE: *Cognitive Style Indicator, Cools, E. and H. Van den Broeck. (2007) "Development and Validation of the Cognitive Style Indicator."* Journal of Psychology, *14: 359–387.*

Tolerance of Ambiguity Scale

This assessment helps you better understand how comfortable you are with situations that are inherently ambiguous. Inasmuch as this is a self-diagnostic tool, candid, realistic responses are essential.

Please respond to the following statements by indicating the extent to which you agree or disagree with them. Fill in the blanks with the number from the rating scale that best represents your evaluation of the item.

Rating Scale

1 Strongly disagree
2 Moderately disagree
3 Slightly disagree
4 Neither agree nor disagree
5 Slightly agree
6 Moderately agree
7 Strongly agree

_____ 1. An expert who doesn't come up with a definite answer probably doesn't know too much.
_____ 2. I would like to live in a foreign country for a while.
_____ 3. There is really no such thing as a problem that can't be solved.
_____ 4. People who fit their lives to a schedule probably miss most of the joy of living.

_____ 5. A good job is one where what is to be done and how it is to be done are always clear.

_____ 6. It is more fun to tackle a complicated problem than to solve a simple one.

_____ 7. In the long run it is possible to get more done by tackling small, simple problems rather than large and complicated ones.

_____ 8. Often the most interesting and stimulating people are those who don't mind being different and original.

_____ 9. What we are used to is always preferable to what is unfamiliar.

_____ 10. People who insist upon a yes or no answer just don't know how complicated things really are.

_____ 11. A person who leads an even, regular life in which few surprises or unexpected happenings arise really has a lot to be grateful for.

_____ 12. Many of our most important decisions are based upon insufficient information.

_____ 13. I like parties where I know most of the people more than ones where all or most of the people are complete strangers.

_____ 14. Teachers or supervisors who hand out vague assignments give one a chance to show initiative and originality.

_____ 15. The sooner we all acquire similar values and ideals the better.

_____ 16. A good teacher is one who makes you wonder about your way of looking at things.

SOURCE: *S. Budner (1962), "Intolerance of Ambiguity as a Personality Variable," from* Journal of Personality, *30: 29–50. Reprinted with the permission of Blackwell Publishing, Ltd.*

Core Self-Evaluation Scale (CSES)

Research has identified four core elements of self-evaluations. This instrument will help you identify the component parts of your overall self-evaluation. Because this is a diagnostic tool, candid, realistic responses are essential.

Below are several statements with which you may agree or disagree. Using the response scale below, indicate your level of agreement or disagreement with each statement.

Rating Scale

1 Strongly disagree
2 Disagree
3 Neutral
4 Agree
5 Strongly agree

_____ 1. I am confident I get the success I deserve in life.

_____ 2. Sometimes I feel depressed.

_____ 3. When I try, I generally succeed.

_____ 4. Sometimes when I fail I feel worthless.

_____ 5. I complete tasks successfully.

_____ 6. Sometimes, I do not feel in control of my work.

_____ 7. Overall, I am satisfied with myself.

_____ 8. I am filled with doubts about my competence.

_____ 9. I determine what will happen in my life.

_____ 10. I do not feel in control of my success in my career.

_____ 11. I am capable of coping with most of my problems.

_____ 12. There are times when things look pretty bleak and hopeless to me.

SOURCE: *T. Judge, A. Erez, J. Bono, and C. Thoreson. The core self-evaluation scale: Development of a measure,* Personnel Psychology, *2003: 303–331.*

Key Dimensions of Self-Awareness

For more than 2,000 years, knowledge of the self has been considered at the very core of human behavior. The ancient dictum "Know thyself" has been variously attributed to Plato, Pythagoras, Thales, and Socrates. Plutarch noted that this dictum was inscribed in the temple of Delphi, that mystical sanctuary where kings and generals sought advice from the oracle at Delphi on matters of greatest importance to them. Probably the most oft-quoted passage on the self is Polonius' advice in Hamlet: "To thine own self be true, and it must follow, as the night the day, thou canst not then be false to any man." Philip Massinger reminded us: "He that would govern others must first master himself." Lao Tsu famously stated: "Knowing others is intelligence. Knowing oneself is true wisdom. Mastering others is strength; mastering yourself is true power."

Because **self-awareness** lies at the heart of the ability to master oneself and therefore to lead and manage others effectively, this chapter serves as the foundation for managing oneself and others. Of course, a host of techniques and methods for achieving self-knowledge have long been available—including mindfulness training, group methods, meditation and contemplation techniques, altered consciousness procedures, aromatherapy, assorted massages, physical exercise regimens, and biofeedback. More than one million self-help books are currently available on Amazon.com, and it is estimated that Americans spend approximately $100 billion on self-help therapies.

In this chapter, we do not summarize these various approaches to enhanced self-awareness, nor do we espouse any one technique in particular. Instead, our objective is to help you understand the importance of self-awareness as a foundation for improving your ability to be a successful manager and a successful person. We provide you with some powerful self-assessment instruments that are predictive of managerial success. By completing these instruments, you will develop an understanding of several key aspects of your own strengths, inclinations, and styles. Our emphasis in this chapter, and throughout the book, is on scientifically validated information linking self-awareness to successful management. We try to avoid generalizations and prescriptions that have not been tested in research.

The Enigma of Self-Awareness

Erich Fromm (1939) was one of the first behavioral scientists to observe the close connection between self-concept and our feelings about others: "Hatred against oneself is inseparable from hatred against others." Carl Rogers (1961) later proposed that self-awareness and self-acceptance are prerequisites for psychological health, personal growth, and the ability to know and accept others. In fact, Rogers suggested that the basic human need is for self-regard, which, in his clinical cases, he found to be more powerful than physiological needs. In addition, Brouwer (1964, p. 156) asserted that all personal change is preceded by self-awareness:

> The function of self-examination is to lay the groundwork for insight, without which no growth can occur. Insight is the "Oh, I see now" feeling which must consciously or unconsciously precede change in behavior. Insights—real, genuine glimpses of ourselves as we really are—are reached only with difficulty and sometimes with real psychic pain. But they are the building blocks of growth. Thus, self-examination is a preparation for insight, a groundbreaking for the seeds of self-understanding which gradually bloom into changed behavior.

We cannot improve ourselves or develop new capabilities unless we know what level of capability we possess. Considerable empirical evidence suggests that individuals who are self-aware are healthier, perform better in managerial and leadership roles, and are more productive at work (Alberts, Martijn, & DeVrioes, 2011; Ashley & Reiter-Palmon, 2012; Boyatzis, 2008; Higgs & Rowland, 2010; Showry & Manasa, 2014).

On the other hand, self-knowledge may inhibit personal improvement rather than facilitate it. Individuals may resist acquiring additional information in order to protect their self-esteem or self-respect. If they acquire new knowledge about themselves, it's possible that it will be negative or lead to feelings of inferiority, weakness, incompetence, or shame. So, they avoid new self-knowledge. As Maslow (1962, p. 57) notes:

We tend to be afraid of any knowledge that would cause us to despise ourselves or to make us feel inferior, weak, worthless, evil, shameful. We protect ourselves and our ideal image of ourselves by repression and similar defenses, which are essentially techniques by which we avoid becoming conscious of unpleasantness or dangerous truths.

We avoid personal growth, then, because we fear finding out that we are not all we would like to be. If there is a better way to be, then our current state must be inadequate or inferior. This resistance is the "denying of our best side, of our talents, of our finest impulses, of our highest potentialities, of our creativeness. In brief, this is the struggle against our own greatness" (Maslow, 1962, p. 58). Freud (1956) asserted that to be completely honest with oneself is the best effort an individual can make because complete honesty requires a continual search for more information about the self and a desire for self-improvement. The results of that search are often uncomfortable.

Seeking knowledge of one's self, therefore, is an enigma: It is a prerequisite for and motivator of growth and improvement, but it may also inhibit growth and improvement. It may lead to progress and advancement or to stagnation and defensiveness because of fear of knowing more. How, then, can improvement be accomplished? How can management skills be developed if the self-knowledge necessary for the development of those skills is resisted?

THE SENSITIVE LINE

One answer relies on the concept of the **sensitive line**. This concept refers to the point at which individuals become defensive or protective when encountering information about themselves that is inconsistent with their self-concept or when encountering pressure to alter their behavior.

Most people regularly experience information about themselves that doesn't quite fit or that is marginally inconsistent. For example, a friend might say, "You look tired today. Are you feeling okay?" If you are feeling fine, the information is inconsistent with your self-awareness. But because the discrepancy is relatively minor and does not confront your fundamental self-image, it would not likely offend you or evoke a strong defensive reaction. It would probably not require that you reexamine and change your self-concept.

On the other hand, the more discrepant the information or the more serious its implications for your self-concept, the closer it would approach your sensitive line—and you would feel a need to defend yourself against it. For example, having a coworker judge you as incompetent may cross your sensitive line if you think of yourself as an effective and productive employee. This would be especially true if the coworker were an influential person. Your response would probably be to defend yourself against the information in order to protect the image you hold of yourself.

This response is known as the **threat-rigidity response** (Staw, Sandelands, & Dutton, 1981; DeDreu, Carsten, & Nijstad, 2008). When individuals are threatened, when they encounter uncomfortable information, or when uncertainty is created, they tend to become rigid. They hunker down, protect themselves, and become risk averse. Consider what happens when you are startled or suddenly shocked by something unexpected. Physically, your body tends to become rigid in order to protect itself. It tightens up to safeguard stability. Similarly, individuals also become rigid—psychologically and emotionally—when they encounter information that threatens their self-concept. They tend to redouble their efforts to protect what is comfortable and familiar (Cameron, Kim, & Whetten, 1987; Weeks, 2017; Weick & Sutcliffe, 2000). They rely on first-learned or most reinforced behavior patterns and emotions. Crossing the sensitive line creates rigidity and self-preservation.

In light of this defensiveness, then, how can increased self-knowledge and personal change ever occur? There are at least two answers. One is that information that is verifiable, predictable, and controllable is less likely to cross the sensitive line than information without those characteristics. That is, if an individual can test the validity of the discrepant information (for example, if some objective standard exists for evaluating the accuracy of the information), if the information is not unexpected or "out of the blue" (for example, if it is received at regular intervals), and if there is some control over what, when, and how much information is received (for example, if it is requested), the feedback is more likely to be heard and accepted.

The information you receive about yourself from the instruments and exercises in this chapter is verifiable, controllable, and predictable. You have already completed several self-assessment instruments that have been used extensively in research. Their reliability and validity have been established, and they have been associated with managerial success. Therefore, as you

LEARNING

analyze your scores and seek honestly to understand more about your underlying attributes, you can gain important insight that will prove very useful.

A second answer to the problem of overcoming resistance to self-examination lies in the role other people can play in helping us gain self-understanding. It is almost impossible to increase self-awareness unless we interact with and disclose ourselves to others. Unless we are willing to open up to others, to discuss aspects of ourselves that seem ambiguous or unknown, little growth can ever occur. **Self-disclosure**, therefore, is a key to improvement in self-awareness. Harris (1981) points out:

> In order to know oneself, no amount of intro-spection or self-examination will suffice. You can analyze yourself for weeks, or meditate for months, and you will not get an inch further—any more than you can smell your own breath or laugh when you tickle yourself.
>
> You must first be open to the other person before you catch a glimmering of yourself. Our self-reflection in a mirror does not tell us what we are like; only our reflection in other people. We are essentially social creatures, and our self-understanding resides in associa-tion, not in isolation.

As you engage in the practice exercises in this chapter, you are encouraged to discuss your insights with someone else. These interactions should be sin-cere, honest, and motivated by the desire for self-understanding and self-improvement. Never should the information you share or receive be used to judge or wound another person. Maintaining a trusting relation-ship with someone with whom you can share is a criti-cal prerequisite to self-understanding.

Several studies have shown that low self-disclosers are less healthy and more self-alienated than high self-disclosers. College students give the highest ratings for **interpersonal competence** to high self-disclosers.

Individuals who are high self-disclosers are liked better, have closer relationships, and are perceived to be more similar to and more enjoyable than individu-als who display excessive or insufficient self-disclosure (see, for example, Goleman, 1998b; Sprecher, et al., 2013). The enigma of self-awareness can be managed, then, by exercising some control over when and what kind of information you receive about yourself and by involving others in your pursuit of self-understanding. The support and feedback individuals receive from others during the **process** of self-disclosure—besides

helping to increase feedback and self-awareness—helps information contribute to greater self-awareness without crossing the sensitive line.

Understanding and Appreciating Individual Differences

Another important reason for focusing on self-awareness is to help you develop the ability to diagnose and appre-ciate important differences among others with whom you interact. Considerable evidence shows that an in-dividual's effectiveness as a manager is closely related to his or her ability to recognize, value, and capitalize on fundamental differences among others. This topic is commonly discussed in the management literature under the subject of "managing diversity."

Although it is difficult to understand all the rami-fications of "managing diversity," it is not difficult to be sensitive to certain important differences that affect the way you manage others. This chapter, therefore, has two objectives: (1) to help you better understand your own uniqueness as an individual—to become bet-ter equipped to manage yourself—and (2) to help you diagnose, value, and utilize the differences you find in other people.

One suggestion for successfully managing, valuing, and capitalizing on individual differences is to focus on *differences*—not *distinctions*. Recognizing differences is not the same as evaluating distinctions. One is help-ful. The other is hurtful. We observe differences. We create distinctions. Recognizing differences allows us to take advantage of others' unique contributions. Cre-ating distinctions creates social barriers between peo-ple for the express purpose of reinforcing advantages and disadvantages.

To repeat, self-awareness and understanding dif-ferences cannot occur without self-disclosure, sharing, and trusting conversations. Self-knowledge requires an understanding and valuing of differences—not the cre-ation of distinctions. We encourage you, therefore, to use the information you discover about yourself and oth-ers to build, grow, and improve your managerial skills.

Important Areas of Self-Awareness

Of course, a large number of dimensions are available to explore in order to develop in-depth self-awareness. For example, numerous aspects of cognitive style have been measured; authors have identified more than a dozen "intelligences" (ranging from social and practi-cal to cognitive and creative); hundreds of personal-ity factors have been investigated in the psychological literature; the mapping of the human chromosome has raised the possibility that thousands of physiological differences may be crucial in understanding behavior; and gender, age, cultural, ethnic, and experience differences all develop individually over time. It is impossible, of course, to accurately select the best or most central aspects of self-awareness, because the options are just too numerous.

With this in mind, however, we chose five of the most critical areas of self-awareness that have been found in research to be key in producing successful management. They are: *emotional intelligence, personal values, cognitive style, orientation toward change*, and *core self-evaluation*. These areas have been found to be among the most important predictors of effective personal and managerial performance—including achieving life success, performing effectively in teams, competent decision-making, lifelong learning and development, creativity, communication competency, job satisfaction, and job performance (Alberts, Martijn, & DeVrioes, 2011; Ashley & Reiter-Palmon, 2012; Cools & Van den Broeck, 2007; Goleman, 1998b; Grant, 2013; Judge, et al., 2003).

Research on **emotional intelligence**—the ability to correctly diagnose and manage one's own emotions and relationships with others—has been identified as an important factor in accounting for success in leaders and managers (Boyatzis, Goleman, & Rhee, 2013; Goleman, 1998a; Joseph & Newman, 2010; O'Boyle, et al., 2011; Oginska-Bulik, 2005). Self-awareness has been identified as a crucial aspect of emotional intelligence, and it is more powerful than IQ in predicting success in life (Zeidner, Matthews, & Roberts, 2012).

One study, for example, tried to identify differences between star performers and average managers in 40 companies. Emotional intelligence competencies, including self-awareness, were *twice* as important in contributing to excellence as cognitive intelligence (IQ) and technical expertise (Goleman, 1998a). In a study of a multinational consulting firm, superior performing partners were compared to average performing partners. Superior performers—who had significantly higher emotional intelligence and self-awareness scores—contributed more than twice the revenues to the firm and were four times more likely to be promoted than those with low self-awareness and emotional intelligence (Boyatzis, Goleman, & Rhee, 2013).

Recent research on a second important area of self-awareness—namely, values and character strengths—has revealed that being aware of and building on your personal values and strengths significantly enhances the quality of relationships, problem-solving abilities,

job performance, and well-being in work and in life. The most effective managers are aware of and capitalize on their most closely held values and character strengths, and the happiest and most successful people are able to capitalize on these same factors.

Values are the stable, closely held attributes that you consider to be at the very heart of who you are and what you believe is good and right. Character strengths are the means by which you manifest those values (Peterson & Seligman, 2004). Being aware of and demonstrating your most important character strengths has been found to be crucial in managerial success as well as long-term personal well-being. A well-known instrument is available for you to assess your personal character strengths.

A third area of self-awareness is **cognitive style**, which refers to the manner in which you gather and process information. Researchers have found that individual differences in cognitive style influence perception, learning, problem-solving, decision-making, communication, and creativity (Cools & Van den Broeck, 2007; Hayes & Allinson, 1994; Kirton, 2003). A large number of dimensions of cognitive style have been identified, but we have selected an instrument in this chapter that captures the most frequently studied dimensions (Cools & Van den Broeck, 2007). The instrument is empirically validated and links cognitive style to successful managerial behavior.

Fourth, a discussion of **orientation toward change** focuses on methods people use to cope with change in their environment. In the twenty-first century, we are faced with increasingly fragmented, rapidly changing, tumultuous conditions; knowing your orientation toward coping with such change is an important aspect of self-awareness. Two dimensions—*locus of control* (Tillman, Smith, & Tillman, 2010) and *intolerance of ambiguity* (Furnham & Marks, 2013)—are measured by two instruments, and research connecting these two dimensions to effective management is discussed in the sections that follow.

The fifth area of self-awareness relates to **core self-evaluation**. This is a construct that captures the essential aspects of core personality (Judge, et al., 2003). More than 50,000 studies have been conducted on what has been referred to as "the Big Five" personality dimensions—neuroticism, extroversion, conscientiousness, agreeableness, and openness—but a single underlying factor has been found to account for the effects of these personality dimensions: core self-evaluation. By analyzing your scores on the assessment instrument, you not only learn about your underlying personality dimensions, but you also will learn how they are associated with outcomes such as motivation, problem-solving, creativity, life satisfaction, and work performance (Chang, et al., 2012; Johnson, Rosen, & Levy, 2008; Judge, et al., 2005).

These five areas of self-awareness—emotional intelligence, personal values, **learning style**, orientation toward change, and core self-evaluation—constitute important aspects of the self-concept. Figure 1.1 summarizes these five aspects of self-awareness, along with their functions in defining the self-concept.

Again, many other aspects of self-awareness could be considered, but what we value, how we feel about ourselves, how we behave toward others, what we want to achieve, and what we are attracted to all are strongly influenced by our emotional intelligence, values, cognitive style, orientation toward change, and core self-evaluation. These are among the most important building blocks on which other aspects of the self emerge.

EMOTIONAL INTELLIGENCE

Emotional intelligence has become a very popular topic that suffers from the problem that almost all trendy concepts encounter: Its meaning and measurement have become confusing and ambiguous. Emotional intelligence has come to encompass almost everything that is not IQ. Since the publication of Daniel Goleman's book *Emotional Intelligence* in 1995, interest in the concept of emotional intelligence has mushroomed (even though the concept was introduced in 1990 by Salovey and Mayer). Almost 20,000 books have been published on the topic, and scores of consulting companies and executive coaches now advertise themselves as experts in helping others develop emotional intelligence. The number of instruments available to assess emotional intelligence is voluminous (more than 100), although only three or four have been scientifically validated and used in any systematic investigations.

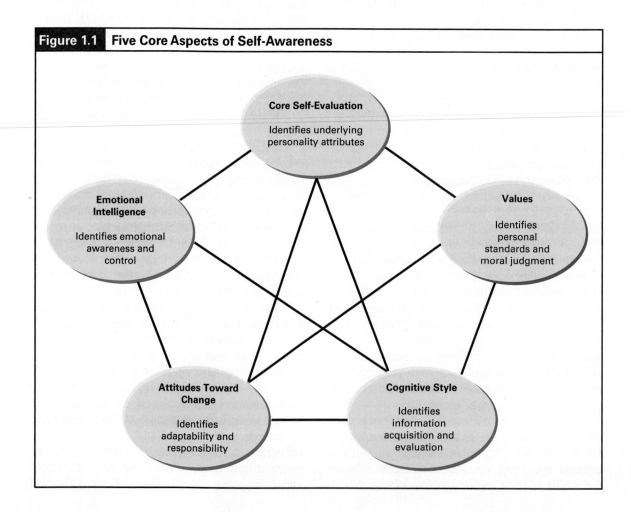

| Figure 1.1 | Five Core Aspects of Self-Awareness |

Core Self-Evaluation
Identifies underlying personality attributes

Emotional Intelligence
Identifies emotional awareness and control

Values
Identifies personal standards and moral judgment

Attitudes Toward Change
Identifies adaptability and responsibility

Cognitive Style
Identifies information acquisition and evaluation

A scan of the scientific and popular writing on emotional intelligence confirms that almost everything is defined as an aspect of emotional intelligence. Multiple definitions abound and are frequently incompatible and contradictory. One way to clarify this problem of multiple definitions is to differentiate between *emotional intelligence* and *emotional competence*. Emotional intelligence refers to the ability to diagnose, understand, and manage emotional cues. Emotional competence refers to the noncognitive capabilities and skills—including social skills—that affect human functioning.

The first definition is the one we have adopted in this chapter. This is because emotional competencies are covered by the topics discussed in the remainder of this text. Whereas emotional competencies are critical for predicting success, in this chapter we adopt a more precise and refined definition of emotional intelligence. Emotional intelligence is, in fact, a prerequisite for developing emotional competence, and we will assist you in other chapters to develop and improve on what is often referred to as emotional competence.

Emotional intelligence refers specifically to: (1) the ability to diagnose and recognize your own emotions, (2) the ability to control your own emotions, (3) the ability to recognize and diagnose emotions displayed by others, and (4) the ability to respond appropriately to those emotional cues. These abilities are not inherent but can be developed and improved. Unlike IQ, for example, which remains relatively constant over a lifetime, emotional intelligence can be enhanced with practice. With effort, you can change your level of emotional intelligence. The instrument you completed in the Skill Assessment section assesses these four dimensions, and we briefly explain them below.

Emotionally intelligent people are able to accurately recognize and label the emotions they are experiencing as well as to *regulate* and control them (Grant, 2013). They are less likely to blow up and lose control, less likely to experience debilitating depression and anxiety, and more likely to manage their own emotional states than those with less emotional intelligence.

Think, for example, of how you behave at a sporting event when the officials make a bad call; when someone gets angry at you; when you are criticized for something you did; or when you receive special accolades and recognition. Emotionally intelligent people remain in control of their emotions, whereas less emotionally intelligent people tend to lose control.

Remaining in control of one's emotions does not mean being bland or even-tempered all the time. Rather, it means that a person is aware of his or her emotions and can control them so that they are not unrestrained. Emotionally intelligent people may display a wide range of emotions and intensity.

Emotionally intelligent people are also able to accurately diagnose and empathize with the feelings of others. Empathy refers to the ability to understand and connect with others' feelings. It does not mean sympathizing or adopting others' feelings, and it is not based on a memory of having experienced the same emotions. If someone has experienced a tragedy or loss, for example, emotionally intelligent people can share in and understand those feelings even if they have never experienced something similar. They need not be depressed themselves, for example, in order to understand the depression of others.

Emotionally intelligent people also *respond* appropriately to the emotions of others. Their responses match the intensity of the emotions other people feel, and they support and encourage emotional expressions (Salovey & Grewal, 2005). That is, if others are excited and happy, emotionally intelligent people do not remain aloof and withdrawn. On the other hand, they are not merely manipulated in their feelings and responses by the emotions of others. They don't respond merely on the basis of others' feelings. Rather, they remain in personal control of their responses.

One reason emotional intelligence is so important is that it has deteriorated over time. Whereas average IQ points have increased almost 25 points over the last 100 years—people tend to be smarter now than 100 years ago—emotional intelligence scores have actually declined (Goleman, 1998a; Slaski & Cartwright, 2003). Think, for example, of the amount of litigation, conflict, disrespect, bullying, and divorce that characterizes our society. Less emphasis is placed on emotional intelligence development now than in the past.

This is a problem because emotional intelligence has strong predictive power regarding success in management and in life—much stronger, in fact, than IQ scores. For example, it is estimated that IQ accounts for only about 10 percent of the variance in job performance and in life success (Sternberg, 1996), but by adding emotional intelligence to the equation, we can account for four times more variance. Emotional intelligence is more important than IQ in accounting for success.

For example, in a study of 450 boys who grew up in a small town in Massachusetts, two-thirds lived

LEARNING

in welfare families and one-third had IQ scores below 90. They were followed over 40 years, and it was found that IQ had almost nothing to do with life success. Emotional intelligence, on the other hand, was the most predictive factor (Snarey & Vaillant, 1985).

A study of 80 PhDs in science who attended the University of California at Berkeley in the 1950s found that what accounted for life success 40 years after graduation was mainly emotional intelligence scores. Emotional intelligence was four times more important than IQ in determining who had achieved success in their careers, who were evaluated by experts as being highly successful, and who were listed in sources such as *Who's Who* and *American Men and Women of Science* (Feist & Barron, 1996).

In a study of business school undergraduate students, higher emotional intelligence scores were typical of those involved in clubs, Greek organizations, sports teams, and activities in which social interaction was frequent. Higher emotional intelligence was also associated with higher GPAs in both business classes and university classes (Rozell, Pettijohn, & Parker, 2002). Emotional intelligence has also been found to be an important predictor of managerial success. In a study of managers on three continents, for example, 74 percent of successful managers had emotional intelligence as their most salient characteristic, whereas this was the case in only 24 percent of the failures. A study at PepsiCo found that company units headed by managers with well-developed emotional intelligence skills outperformed yearly revenue targets by 15 to 20 percent. Those with underdeveloped skills underperformed their targets by about the same amount (Goleman, Boyatzis, & McKee, 2002). Emotional intelligence was found to be the major predictor of success when managers engaged in teamwork, managing conflict, and transformational leadership (Clarke, 2010), after controlling for personality and cognitive ability. And, in still another study, emotional intelligence was the primary factor in explaining who emerged as a leader, and it was more important than cognitive intelligence, gender, or personality traits (Cote, et al., 2010; Joseph & Newman, 2010; O'Boyle, et al., 2011).

A McBer study comparing outstanding managers with average managers found that 90 percent of the difference was accounted for by emotional intelligence. In a worldwide study of what companies were looking for in hiring new employees, 67 percent of the most desired attributes were emotional intelligence competencies (Goleman, et al., 2002). The point of these studies should be clear: Effective managers have developed high levels of competency in emotional intelligence.

The Emotional Intelligence Assessment instrument you completed in the Skill Assessment section provides an evaluation of your competency in the four general areas of emotional intelligence—emotional awareness, emotional control or balance, emotional diagnosis or empathy, and emotional response. A comprehensive and fully valid measure of these factors would require an instrument many times longer than the one included here, so this assessment merely provides an abbreviated but reasonably accurate summary of your emotional intelligence capability. Your scores will help you identify areas of strength as well as aspects of emotional intelligence that you can pursue to become more capable. Becoming aware of your own emotional intelligence is an important aspect of becoming a more effective manager.

VALUES AND CHARACTER STRENGTHS

Values are among the most stable and enduring characteristics of individuals. They are the foundation on which attitudes and personal preferences are formed. They help define our morality and our conceptions of what is "good." Much of what we are is a product of the basic values we have developed throughout our lives.

The trouble with values is that they are taken for granted, and people are often unaware of them. Unless a person's values are challenged, they remain largely undetected. People are especially not aware that they hold some values as being more important than others. This unawareness leads to actions or behaviors that are sometimes contrary to values. Until people encounter a contradiction or a threat to their basic values, they seldom articulate their values or seek to clarify them.

The values held by each of us are affected by a variety of factors, and a number of methods have been employed to measure and describe values. We point out several ways in this chapter—each of which has been widely used in research and in management practice.

One factor is the general value orientations that characterize large groups, such as nationalities, ethnic groups, industries, or organizations. Much research has been done, for example, on identifying the differences in values that arise across cultural groups. The point of this research is to identify ways in which nationalities differ from one another, since almost all managers now face the need to manage across national boundaries. In your own life, it is likely that you interact with individuals who do not share your birth country, and knowing something about their value orientations helps your interactions be more effective. Some values differ systematically across national cultures, and at least some of our values are affected significantly by the country and culture in which we are raised.

The Values of National Cultures

Trompenaars, (2011; Trompenaars & Hampden-Turner, 2012) identified seven value dimensions in which significant differences exist among national cultures. Certain cultures emphasize some values more than others do. Table 1.1 identifies Trompenaars' seven dimensions, and we provide examples of countries that represent each of the value dimensions. No national culture emphasizes one of these dimensions to the exclusion of another, but there are clear differences in the amount of emphasis placed on each dimension.

The first five dimensions of the model refer to how individuals relate to other people. For example, some countries (e.g., the United States, Norway, Sweden, and Switzerland) emphasize a value of **universalism**, in which other people's behavior is governed by universal standards and rules—for example, do not

lie; do not cheat; do not run a red light even if no one is coming the other way. General societal rules govern behavior. Other countries (e.g., China, Indonesia, Korea, and Singapore) hold a value of **particularism**, in which the relationship with an individual governs behavior—for example, is the other person a friend, a family member, a relative?

To illustrate the differences, consider your answer to this question: *You are riding in a car with a close friend who hits a pedestrian while going 40 miles an hour in a 25-mile-per-hour zone. There are no witnesses, and your friend's lawyer says that if you'll testify that he was only traveling 25 miles an hour, he'll get off. Will you lie for him?* Managers in universalistic cultures are more likely to refuse than people in particularistic cultures. For example, 97 percent of the Swiss and 93 percent of North Americans (Canada and the United States) would refuse to testify, whereas 32 percent of Venezuelans and 37 percent of South Koreans would refuse.

A second value dimension differentiates cultures that value **individualism**—an emphasis on the self, on independence, and on uniqueness—versus **collectivism**—an emphasis on the group, on the combined unit, and on joining with others. Individualistic values hold the contributions of individuals to be most valuable, whereas collectivism values team contributions.

Table 1.1	Cultural Values Dimensions	
Value Dimensions	**Explanation**	**Example of Countries with Dominance**
Universalism	Societal rules and norms are valued.	Norway, Sweden, Switzerland, United States
Particularism	Individual relationships are valued.	China, Indonesia, Korea, Venezuela
Individualism	Individual contributions are valued.	Austria, Denmark, Nigeria, United States
Collectivism	Team contributions are valued.	Indonesia, Japan, Mexico, Philippines
Affective	Showing emotions is valued.	France, Iran, Spain, Switzerland
Neutral	Unemotional responses are valued.	China, Ethiopia, Japan, Korea
Specific	Segregating life's roles is valued.	Denmark, Holland, Sweden, United Kingdom
Diffuse	Integrating life's role is valued.	China, Korea, Nigeria, Singapore,
Achievement	Personal accomplishment is valued.	Austria, Canada, Norway, United States
Ascription	Inherent attributes are valued.	Czech Republic, Egypt, Indonesia, Korea
Past and Present	Past is tightly connected to future.	France, Japan, United Kingdom
Future	Future is disconnected but valued.	Netherlands, United States
Internal	Individual control is valued.	Austria, Canada, United Kingdom, United States
External	Control comes from outside forces.	China, Czech Republic, Egypt, Japan

SOURCE: F. Trompenaars and C. Hampden-Turner (2012). Riding the Waves of Culture. Reprinted with the permission of the McGraw-Hill Companies.

For example, consider your answer to this question: *What kind of job is found most frequently in your organization: one where everyone works together and you do not get individual credit, or one where everyone is allowed to work individually and you receive individual recognition?* Eastern Europeans (e.g, Russia, Czech Republic, Hungary, Poland) average above 80 percent in agreeing that individual credit is received, whereas Asians (e.g., Japan, India, Nepal) average below 45 percent. (The United States score is 72 percent.)

A third value dimension refers to the display of feelings in public. It identifies an **affective** versus **neutral** orientation. Cultures with high affective values tend to show emotions openly and to deal with problems in emotional ways. Loud laughter, anger, and intense passion may all be displayed in the course of a business negotiation, for example. Cultures with neutral values are more rational and stoic in their approach to problem-solving. Instrumental, goal-directed behaviors rather than emotions dominate interactions.

For example, *if you became very upset at work or in class—say you feel slighted, offended, or angry—how likely would you be to display your feelings openly in public?* Managers in Japan, Ethiopia, and Hong Kong, for example, average 64 percent, 74 percent, and 81 percent, respectively, in refusing to show emotions publicly. On the other hand, 15 percent of Kuwaiti managers, 18 percent of Egyptian managers, and 19 percent of Spanish managers would refuse. (The United States score is 43 percent.)

A fourth dimension—**specificity** versus **diffusion**—describes the difference between cultures that segregate the different roles in life to maintain privacy and personal autonomy compared to cultures that integrate and merge their roles. Cultures with specific values separate work relationships from family relationships, for example, whereas diffuse cultures entangle work and home relationships. People with specific values may seem hard to get to know because they keep a boundary between their personal lives and their work lives. People with diffuse values may seem too forward and too superficial because they seem to share personal information freely.

To illustrate the difference, consider how you would respond to this question: *Your boss asks you to come to her home to help her paint her house. You don't want to do it because you hate painting. Would you refuse?* More than 90 percent of the Dutch and Swedes would refuse, whereas only 32 percent of the Chinese and 46 percent of Nigerians would refuse. (In the United States, 82 percent would refuse.)

A fifth value dimension differentiates cultures that emphasize an **achievement** orientation versus an **ascription** culture. In some cultures, people tend to acquire high status based on their personal accomplishments, whereas in other cultures status and prestige are based more on ascribed characteristics such as age, gender, family heritage, or ethnic background. Who you know (ascription) versus what you can do (achievement) helps identify the difference on this value dimension.

For example, the following statement helps highlight achievement versus ascription value differences: *It is important to act the way you are, to be consistent with your true self, even if you do not accomplish the task at hand.* Only 10 percent of managers from Uruguay, 12 percent from Argentina, and 13 percent from Spain disagree with the statement, whereas 77 percent of Norwegian managers and 75 percent of managers from the United States disagree.

A sixth value dimension relates to how people interpret and manage time. It distinguishes the emphasis placed on the past, present, or future in various cultures. Some cultures, for example, value past and tradition more than future; other cultures place more value on the future than the past. What you have achieved in the past matters more in some cultures than where you are headed in the future. Time differences also exist regarding short- versus long-time horizons. For example, some people are oriented toward very short time horizons in which they think in terms of minutes and hours (a short-time horizon). Other people think in terms of months or years (a long-time horizon).

Complete the following brief exercise to get a sense of your own time horizon. *Use the following scale to assign a number to each of the following statements: My past started _____ ago and ended _____ ago. My present started _____ ago and will end _____ from now. My future will start _____ from now and will end _____ from now. Use this rating scale: 7 = years, 6 = months, 5 = weeks, 4 = days, 3 = hours, 2 = minutes, 1 = seconds.*

By way of comparison, managers in the Philippines averaged 3.40 on the scale, Irish managers averaged 3.82, and Brazilians averaged 3.85. On the other hand, managers in Hong Kong averaged 5.71, Portuguese managers averaged 5.62, and Pakistani managers averaged 5.47. (Managers in the United States averaged 4.30.)

The seventh and final value dimension focuses on internal and external control. (We will discuss this value dimension in more detail later in the chapter.) It differentiates cultures that presume individuals are in control of their own destinies from those that presume nature or external forces control much of what happens. For example, some countries emphasize the value of individuals inventing or creating things (internal control), whereas other countries emphasize the value of taking what already exists or has been created elsewhere and then refining or improving it (external control).

Two statements that illustrate this difference are: (1) *What happens to me is my own doing,* and (2) *Sometimes I feel that I do not have enough control over the direction my life is taking.* More than 80 percent of managers from Uruguay, Norway, Israel, and the United States agree with the first statement, whereas less than 40 percent of Venezuelans, Chinese, and Nepalese agree.

Because almost every manager will be faced with the opportunity to interact with and manage individuals born in other cultures, being aware of value differences and being able to diagnose and manage those differences is an important prerequisite for success. Of course, stereotyping people based on their national culture, or overgeneralizing based on trends such as those reported here, can be dangerous and misleading. None of us would like to be pigeonholed based on a general country profile. These dimensions, as you will see, are most useful for increasing sensitivity and helping with diagnosis rather than placing people in categories.

Like countries, organizations, too, have value systems, referred to as an **organizational culture**. Research has found that employees who hold values congruent with their organization's values are more productive and satisfied (Cameron & Quinn, 2011; Glew, 2009; Meyer, et al., 2010; Posner, 2010). Holding values that are inconsistent with company values, on the other hand, is a major source of frustration, conflict, and nonproductivity. Being aware of your own priorities and values, the values of your organization, and the general value priorities of your country is important if you expect to achieve compatibility at work and in a long-term career (Fisher, Macrosson, & Yusuff, 1996). For an in-depth discussion on organizational culture, see Cameron and Quinn (2011).

Several authors have argued that individuals differ in their level of values development, so different sets of instrumental values are held by individuals at different stages of development (Kohlberg, 1969; Kohlberg & Ryncarz, 1990). People progress from one level of maturity to another, and as they do, their value priorities change. Individuals who have progressed to more mature levels of values development possess a qualitatively different set of values than those at less mature levels.

This theory of values maturity or moral development has received a great deal of attention from researchers, and research findings have important implications for self-awareness and managerial effectiveness. Therefore, we briefly discuss this notion of values maturity.

Values Maturity

Values maturity focuses on the kind of reasoning used to reach a decision about an issue that has value or moral connotations. The model consists of three major levels, each of which contains two stages. Table 1.2 summarizes the characteristics of each stage.

The levels are called *preconventional, conventional,* and *postconventional.*

The first level of maturity, the *preconventional* or *self-centered level*, includes the first two stages of values development. Moral reasoning and instrumental values are based on personal needs or wants and on the consequences of an act. For example, something is judged as right or good if it helps an individual obtain a reward or avoid punishment and if the consequences are not negative for someone else. Stealing $50,000 is worse than stealing $500 in the self-centered level because the consequences (that is, the losses) are more negative for someone else. Most children operate at this level of values maturity.

The second level, the *conventional* or *conformity level*, includes stages 3 and 4. Moral reasoning is based on conforming to and upholding the conventions and expectations of society. This level is sometimes referred to as the "law and order" level because the emphasis is on adherence to laws and norms. Right and wrong are judged on the basis of whether or not behaviors conform to the rules of those in authority. Respect from others based on obedience is a prized outcome. Stealing $50,000 and stealing $500 are equally wrong at this level because both violate the law. Most American adults function at this level of values maturity.

Third is the *postconventional* or *principled level*. It includes the final two stages of maturity and represents the most advanced level of moral reasoning and the most mature set of values development. Right and wrong are judged on the basis of the internalized principles of the individual. Judgments are made on the basis of a set of core values that take precedence.

In the highest stage of maturity, this set of principles is comprehensive (it covers all contingencies), consistent (it is never violated), and universal (it does not change with the situation or circumstance). Thus, stealing $50,000 and stealing $500 are still judged to

Table 1.2 Classification of Moral Judgment into Stages of Development

Level Basis of Moral Judgment	Stage of Development
A PRECONVENTIONAL LEVEL (SELF-CENTERED) Moral value resides in external factors and consequences, not persons or relationships.	**1. Punishment and Obedience** What is right is determined by avoiding punishment and not breaking an authority's rules. **2. Individual Instrumental Purpose and Exchange** What is right is meeting one's own immediate interests and what is fair or equal for others.
B CONVENTIONAL LEVEL (CONFORMITY) Moral value resides in duty, maintaining social contracts, and keeping commitments.	**3. Mutual Interpersonal Expectations, Relationships, and Conformity** What is right is determined by others' feelings and maintaining trust as a result of keeping expectations and commitments. The golden rule is relevant. **4. Social System and Conscience Maintenance** What is right is conforming to social norms and expectations and upholding the social order.
C POSTCONVENTIONAL (PRINCIPLED) Moral value resides in commitment to freely selected standards, rights, and duties.	**5. Prior Rights and Social Contract or Utility** What is right is upholding the rights, values, and contracts of others in society; moral behavior is freely chosen. **6. Universal Ethical Principles** What is right is guided by internal, universal ethical principles. When laws violate principles, the laws are ignored.

Source: *Adapted from Kohlberg, 1981.*

be wrong, but the basis for the judgment is not the violation of laws or rules; rather, it is the violation of a set of comprehensive, consistent, universal principles developed by the individual. Few individuals, according to Kohlberg, reach this highest level of maturity on a consistent basis. It may be characterized by individuals we consider to be especially wise and exemplary, such as Gandhi, Buddha, or Moses.

In short, self-centered individuals view rules and laws as outside themselves, but they obey because by doing so they may obtain rewards or avoid punishment. Conformist individuals view rules and laws as outside themselves, but they obey because they have learned and accepted those rules and laws, and they seek the respect of others. Principled individuals examine the rules and laws and develop a set of internal principles that they believe are morally right. If there is a choice to be made between obeying a law or obeying a principle, they choose the principle. Internalized principles supersede rules and laws in principled individuals.

To help you determine your own level of values maturity, an instrument developed by James Rest at the University of Minnesota's Moral Research Center is included in the Assessment section. It has been used extensively in research because it is easier to administer than a more comprehensive instrument developed by the author of values or moral maturity framework, Lawrence Kohlberg (1976). Rather than placing a person on one single level of values maturity, Rest's instrument identifies the stage that the person relies on most. By completing this instrument, therefore, you will identify your predominant level of values maturity. To determine your maturity level, refer to the self-scoring instructions in the MyLab section associated with this chapter. Exercises in the Skill Analysis and Skill Practice sections will help you develop or refine principles at the stage 5 and stage 6 levels of maturity.

Character Strengths

Character strengths emerge from your strongly held values and are the means by which your values are manifest (Peterson & Seligman, 2004). They are the attributes you hold as most important, and they represent the behavioral manifestations of these basic inclinations. They are what you desire the most and what help you be your very best. When demonstrated, character strengths constitute what you consider to be

Table 1.3	The 24 Main Character Strengths	
• Appreciation of beauty	• Hope	• Perseverance
• Bravery	• Humility	• Perspective
• Creativity	• Humor	• Prudence
• Curiosity	• Judgment	• Self-regulation
• Fairness	• Kindness	• Social intelligence
• Forgiveness	• Leadership	• Spirituality
• Gratitude	• Love	• Teamwork
• Honesty	• Love of learning	

SOURCE: *Peterson & Seligman, 2004.*

the good life for yourself and for others; what produces desirable outcomes; what are reflected in thoughts, feelings, and actions; and what are morally valued even in the absence of beneficial outcomes. Displaying character strengths does not detract from other people, and, therefore, people admire their presence rather than feeling competitive or threatened by them.

The best-known framework for identifying and assessing character strengths was developed by our colleagues, Martin Seligman and the late Chris Peterson (2004). Their framework has been successfully measured by the *Values-in-Action* (or VIA) instrument, which is the best-known and most-utilized assessment instrument available. It has been completed by millions of respondents and has been applied in thousands of research studies.

The VIA assessment instrument is found online at *http://www.viacharacter.org/www/Character-Strengths-Survey*. We encourage you to complete the VIA instrument, which is free of charge. You will receive a personalized feedback report showing your signature character strengths as well as an interpretation of what your profile means.

The character strengths assessed by the VIA instrument are listed in Table 1.3.

A large amount of research across more than 70 countries highlights the importance of character strengths in helping you be an effective manager as well as a successful person in life. In one study of 1,031 working adults, for example, utilizing *signature strengths* (i.e., the strengths you prioritize and the values you consider to be the most important in your life) was the most important predictor of job performance, citizenship behavior, productivity, and personal satisfaction (Littman-Ovadia, Lavy, & Boiman-Meshita, 2016; Lavy & Littman-Ovadia, 2016). In a study of 10,000 New Zealand workers, individuals who were aware of and demonstrated their most important character

strengths were 18 times more likely to flourish at work than those who were not aware of and did not demonstrate their strengths (Hone, et al., 2015).

In classrooms, students who were exposed to a character strengths curriculum and who became aware of their character strengths experienced more positive emotions in the classroom, developed more cohesion as a class, exhibited better interpersonal relationships, demonstrated higher levels of integrity, revealed greater perseverance, displayed greater enjoyment, and had more classroom engagement than those who did not (Quinlan, et al., 2014; Seider, Novick, & Gomez, 2013; Seligman, et al., 2009). Significantly fewer depressive symptoms and negative emotions were experienced by students exposed to a character strengths-based curriculum (Gillham, et al., 2011). Importantly, these results held across multiple cultures and age groups, indicating that the character strengths measured by the VIA are not affected by national culture, gender, or other demographic factors.

ETHICAL DECISION-MAKING

MyLab Management Watch it!
If your instructor has assigned this activity, go to www.pearson.com/mylab/management to complete the video exercise.

In addition to its benefits for self-understanding, awareness of your own level of values maturity also has important practical implications for **ethical decision-making**. By and large, the American public rates American business executives' honesty, integrity, and concern for moral values as abysmal. A large majority of the public thinks managers are dishonest, overly profit-oriented, and willing to step on other people to get what they want. Business executives are rated near the bottom in ethical decision-making, along with advertisers, Congress, used-car salespeople, and lobbyists (Bazerman & Tenbrunsel, 2011; Gallup, 2017; Harris & Sutton, 1995; Lozano, 1996). Although 9 out of 10 companies have a written code of ethics, evidence exists that these documents are not influential in ensuring high moral conduct (Elliott & Schroth, 2002; Mitchell, 2002).

Unethical actions by a company or a leading executive in business are reported in the media almost every day. Record levels of fines ranging in the billions, long-term prison sentences, and public embarrassment are common nowadays. Almost no one has confidence that our leaders—from politics to business—are playing it absolutely, totally straight.

A recent list of the most unethical companies includes Barrick Gold Corporation, Chevron, Dow Chemical, ExxonMobil, General Electric, Halliburton, Monsanto, Papa John's Pizza, Philip Morris, RCA, Siemens, and Walmart. Well-known ethical scandals involving A.H. Robins, Amazon, Bank of America, Bank of Boston, Dow Corning, EF Hutton, Enron, Facebook, Firestone, Ford, General Dynamics, General Motors, Global Crossing, Google, J.P. Morgan, Lockheed Martin, Martin Marietta, Microsoft, Rockwell Automation, Toyota, Tyco, and Wells Fargo have had their day in the press. One cartoon that seems to summarize these goings-on depicts a group of executives sitting at a conference table. The leader remarks, "Of course, honesty is one of the better policies."

Corporate behavior that exemplifies unethical decision-making is not our principal concern here. More to the point is a study by the American Management Association that included 3,000 managers in the United States. It reported that most individual managers felt they were under pressure to compromise personal standards to meet company goals (Harris & Sutton, 1995). A more recent study found that at least a quarter of Wall Street executives say they have to be unethical to succeed (Plaue, 2012).

Moreover, most individuals have encountered someone else violating ethical standards, but in a majority of cases, nothing is reported. For example, in a survey of federal employees asked whether they had observed any of the following activities in the past year, more than 50 percent answered yes to seeing: stealing funds, stealing property, accepting bribes, sexual harassment, ineligible people receiving funds, deficient goods or services, use of position for personal benefit, taking unfair advantage of a contractor, and serious violation of the law. More than two-thirds did not report what they saw. A survey of senior executives in major corporations showed similar results (Plaue, 2012).

Ethical decision-making would be relatively simple if all trade-offs were between an obvious right and an obvious wrong. The trouble is, this is seldom the case. One case in the Skills Analysis section—Shipping the Part—illustrates this trade-off between at least two desirable choices—economic benefits or social benefits. Individuals who effectively manage these kinds of ethical trade-offs are those who have a clear sense of their own values and character strengths and who have developed a principled level of moral maturity. They have articulated and clarified their own internal set of universal, comprehensive, and consistent principles on which to base their decisions. This is not a simple matter, so we offer some standards against which to test your own values and principles for making moral or ethical choices. These standards are neither comprehensive nor absolute, and they are not independent of one another. They simply serve as a reference against which to test your ethical decision-making and some principles you may include in your personal values statement.

- *Front page test:* Would I be embarrassed if my decision became a headline in the local newspaper? Would I feel comfortable describing my actions or decision to a customer or stockholder?
- *Golden rule test:* Would I be willing to be treated in the same manner?
- *Dignity and liberty test:* Are the dignity and liberty of others preserved by this decision? Is the basic humanity of the affected parties enhanced? Are their opportunities expanded or curtailed?
- *Equal treatment test:* Are the rights, welfare, and betterment of minorities and people of lower status given full consideration? Does this decision benefit those with privilege but without merit?
- *Personal gain test:* Is an opportunity for personal gain clouding my judgment? Would I make the same decision if the outcome did not benefit me in any way?
- *Congruence test:* Is this decision or action consistent with my espoused personal principles? Does it violate the spirit of any organizational policies or laws?
- *Procedural justice test:* Can the procedures used to make this decision stand up to scrutiny by those affected?
- *Cost-benefit test:* Does a benefit for some cause unacceptable harm to others? How critical is the benefit? Can the harmful effects be mitigated?

- *Good night's sleep test:* Whether or not anyone else knows about my action, will it produce a good night's sleep?
- *Virtuousness test:* Does this represent the best of the human condition or the highest aspirations to which human beings aspire?

In the Skill Application section of this chapter, you may want to consider these alternatives when constructing your own set of comprehensive, consistent, and universalistic principles. You should be aware, however, that your set of personal principles will also be influenced by your orientation for acquiring and responding to the information you receive. This orientation is called cognitive style.

COGNITIVE STYLE

Each of us is constantly exposed to an overwhelming amount of information, and only part of it can be given attention and acted on at a time. For example, right now you have information entering your brain relating to the functioning of your physical body, the attributes of the room in which you are sitting, the words on this page, the ideas and memories that spring to mind as you read about self-awareness, long-held beliefs, recollections of recent events, and so on. Of course, you are not processing all of this information consciously; if you were, your brain would become overloaded and you would become psychotic. Over time, we all develop strategies for suppressing some kinds of information and paying attention to other kinds. These strategies become habitual and ingrained, and they result in a unique cognitive style for each of us.

Cognitive style refers to the inclination each of us has to perceive, interpret, and respond to information in a certain way. Cognitive style is based on two key dimensions: (1) the manner in which you *gather information*, and (2) the way in which you *evaluate* and *act on* information. A large number of instruments are available to measure different dimensions of cognitive styles (see Cassidy, 2004; Eckstrom, French, & Harmon, 1979; Myers-Briggs Type Inventory— MBTI; Sternberg & Zhang, 2000), but here we focus on dimensions that have emerged in the most recent research on cognitive style. These dimensions are the ones that most researchers now identify as being at the heart of cognitive style.

It is important to note that cognitive styles are not the same as personality types. They are not inherent attributes. Rather, they are inclinations toward information and learning that we have developed over time. Hence, cognitive styles can be altered and changed through practice and conscious development (Vance, et al., 2007). No one is predestined to think in a particular way.

Based on an extensive literature review of models of cognitive style, we selected an instrument developed by Cools and Van den Broeck (2007) to assess your cognitive style. You completed this instrument in the Skill Assessment section. This instrument assesses three dimensions of your cognitive style—knowing style, planning style, and creating style. These dimensions are independent in the sense that any person can score high or low on any of the three sections. They are not polar opposites from one another but are just different ways that people process information. Each style emphasizes a different kind of information seeking and response, and the main attributes are summarized in Table 1.4.

Table 1.4	Attributes of Three Dimensions of Cognitive Style	
	Attributes	**Possible Liabilities**
Knowing	Emphasizes facts, details, and data Seeks clear, objective solutions Focuses on validity, credibility of data Emphasizes accuracy and precision	Slow to make decisions Not very creative Resistant to innovation Intolerant of multiple views
Planning	Emphasizes planning and preparation Seeks agendas and outlines Focuses on methods, processes, and follow-up Emphasizes clear actions and routine	Frustrated by the status quo Intolerant of ambiguity Stressed by complexity Difficulty handling illogical issues
Creating	Emphasizes creativity, risk-taking, and innovation Seeks novelty and ambiguity Focuses on spontaneity and possibilities Emphasizes interaction and getting many inputs	Resistant to structure Tends to break rules May make many mistakes Tends to ignore data and facts

Knowing Style

Individuals who score high on the knowing style tend to emphasize facts, details, and data. They seek clear and objective solutions to problems. They are careful, so decisions are usually not made quickly. They do things in the correct way and tend to be critical of unexpected or aberrant behavior. They excel at solving problems that are structured and have one correct answer. They prefer multiple-choice exams over essay exams.

Research has suggested that these individuals are inclined toward careers in technology, engineering, and law. In college, students with a knowing style tend to major in the physical sciences, engineering, law, and computer programming. In business, they tend to select careers in areas where numbers and data predominate (e.g., auditing, finance, MIS), and they prefer jobs that have a technical problem-solving emphasis (Kolb, Boyatzis, & Mainemelis, 2000; Cools & Van den Broeck, 2007).

Planning Style

Individuals who score high on the planning style are inclined toward preparation and planning. They produce agendas and well-developed outlines for handling information. Having a systematic methodology for gathering and responding to information is important to these people, so they prepare in advance and are especially sensitive to details and methods.

People with a planning style are best at processing a wide range of information and thinking through problems to reach a solution. Research has shown that people with a planning style are inclined toward information and science careers, and they prefer lectures, readings, analytical models, and thinking time as their learning activities. In college, these people tend to major in economics, accounting, operations, mathematics, engineering, and medicine. They tend to select careers in the information sciences and in research fields (e.g., educational research, information, and theology), and they prefer jobs in which information gathering predominates (e.g., research and analysis) (Kolb, Boyatzis, & Mainemelis, 2000; Cools & Van den Broeck, 2007).

Creating Style

Individuals who score high on the creating style tend to prefer experimentation and creativity. They seek uniqueness and novelty, and they are comfortable with ambiguity. They tend to search for information broadly and from many sources, so they are usually more social and extroverted (Cools & Van den Broeck, 2007; Furnham, et al., 2009) than people with other cognitive styles. These people often view rules and procedures as obstacles and constraints, so they may appear disorganized.

Research shows that these individuals tend to be imaginative and emotional and prefer working in groups in order to hear a variety of different opinions. In college, people with a creating style tend to major in the arts, history, political science, English, and psychology. They tend to select careers in social services (e.g., psychology, nursing, and public policy) and in arts and communication (e.g., theater, literature, and journalism), and they prefer jobs in which personal interactions predominate (Kolb, Boyatzis, & Mainemelis, 2000; Cools & Van den Broeck, 2007). In business schools, students in sales and marketing and in human resources tend to have higher scores in this style.

Research on these cognitive dimensions has found that no matter what type of problem people face, most use their preferred cognitive style to approach it. They prefer, and even seek, decision situations and problem types consistent with their own style.

In one study, for example, managers who had a planning style implemented more computer-based systems and rational procedures for decision-making than did creating-style managers. Managers in another study defined identical problems differently depending on their different cognitive styles (e.g., some thought the problem required more data, whereas others thought it required brainstorming new ideas). Other studies found that differences in cognitive style led to significantly different decision-making processes in managers (see Henderson & Nutt, 1980; Chenhall & Morris, 1991; Ruble & Cosier, 1990; Kirton, 2003).

It is important to point out that very little relationship has been found between cognitive style and academic performance among college students (Armstrong, 2000; Cools & Van den Broeck, 2007). Cognitive style does not indicate intelligence or capability. Smart people may score high or low on any of the cognitive styles.

Knowing your cognitive style, however, can prove advantageous in several ways, such as when selecting career options, choosing compatible business environments, identifying the best work assignments, selecting complementary teammates, and improving your decision-making. It can also help you determine which academic courses or study methods will be most suited to your cognitive style—for example, someone with a knowing style may feel more comfortable in accounting, someone with a planning style may feel more comfortable in operations, and someone with a creating style may feel more comfortable in advertising. No single course represents only one cognitive style, of course, but the way in which you process information is often more compatible with one kind of course than others.

People can modify their cognitive styles, of course, as they engage in different kinds of activities, interact with different kinds of people, or manage in different kinds of work environments. Most people tend to adapt to their circumstances. However, substantial evidence shows that people tend to select an occupation that reinforces and is consistent with their dominant cognitive style (Agor, 1985; Chan, 1966; Jones, & Wright, 2010). When they do, they tend to be more successful.

The Cognitive Style Instrument you completed in the Skill Assessment section of this chapter helps you identify the tendencies you have toward gathering, evaluating, and responding to information. Comparing your scores against three different comparison groups will help you gauge your own tendencies and inclinations toward processing information. To fully capitalize on this information, you will also want to consider your own orientation toward change in the next section.

ATTITUDES TOWARD CHANGE

In order to capitalize fully on the strengths of your own cognitive style, you also should be aware of your orientation toward change. This is important because, as the environment in which managers operate continues to become more chaotic, more temporary, more complex, and more overloaded with information, your ability to process information is at least partly constrained by your fundamental attitude about change.

Almost everyone agrees with the prediction that change will increase in the future, both in pace and scope. The challenge of students and managers in the twenty-first century is to prepare for a world that cannot be predicted by the experiences of the past.

No manager at the beginning of the twenty-first century would boast of his or her organization as being stable, preserving constancy, or maintaining the status quo. Even now, stability is interpreted more as stagnation than steadiness, and organizations not in the business of major transformation and revolution are generally viewed as recalcitrant. All this is to say that the environment of the twenty-first century is characterized by turbulence, gigantic change, rapid-fire decisions, and chaos. No one will have time to read and analyze a case study. E-business has changed the rules of the game. No one can predict the competitive environment anymore. Customers are no longer geographically constrained, and the standards for servicing them have changed completely.

In this chaotic pace of change—what some refer to as "permanent white water"—being aware of your own orientation toward change is an important prerequisite for successfully coping with it. Two dimensions of change orientation particularly relevant for managers are discussed on the following pages.

Tolerance of Ambiguity

The first important dimension is **tolerance of ambiguity**, which refers to the extent to which individuals are threatened by or have difficulty coping with situations that are ambiguous, where change occurs rapidly or unpredictably, where information is inadequate or unclear, or where complexity exists. People vary in their aptitude for operating successfully in stimulus-rich and information-overloaded environments or in the extent to which they can cope with ambiguous, incomplete, unstructured, dynamic situations. Individuals who have a high tolerance of ambiguity also tend to be more cognitively complex. They tend to pay attention to more information, interpret more cues, and possess more sense-making categories than less cognitively complex individuals.

Research has found that people who are more tolerant of ambiguity and are more cognitively complex are better transmitters of information, more sensitive to internal (nonsuperficial) characteristics of others when evaluating their performance at work, and more behaviorally adaptive and flexible under ambiguous and overloaded conditions than less tolerant and less cognitively complex individuals. Managers with higher tolerance-of-ambiguity scores are more likely to be entrepreneurial in their actions; to be open to new information; and to cope more effectively with major organizational change, downsizing, and role stress and conflict (Armstrong-Stassen, 1998; Furnham & Marks, 2013; Teoh & Foo, 1997; Timothy, et al., 1999).

The downside is that individuals who are more tolerant of ambiguity have more difficulty focusing on a single important element of information, generating one best answer, and concentrating without being distracted by interruptions. However, for the most part, in an information-rich environment, tolerance of ambiguity and cognitive complexity are more adaptive than the opposite characteristics.

In the Assessment section of this chapter, a Tolerance of Ambiguity Scale (Budner, 1962) assesses the extent to which you have a tolerance for these kinds of complex situations. In scoring the Tolerance of Ambiguity Scale, three different subscale scores are assessed. One is the *novelty* score, which indicates the extent to which you are tolerant of new, unfamiliar information or situations. The second subscale is the *complexity* score, which indicates the extent to which you are tolerant of multiple, distinctive, or unrelated information. The third subscale is the *insolubility* score, which indicates the extent to which you are tolerant of problems that are very difficult to solve because, for example, alternative solutions are not evident, information is unavailable, or the problem's components seem unrelated to each other. In general, the more tolerant people are of novelty, complexity, and insolubility, the more likely they are to succeed as managers in information-rich, ambiguous environments. They are less overwhelmed by ambiguous circumstances.

It is important to note that cognitive complexity and tolerance for ambiguity are not related to cognitive intelligence, and your score on the Tolerance of Ambiguity Scale is not an evaluation of how smart you are. Most important, individuals can learn to tolerate more complexity and more flexibility in their information-processing abilities.

The first step toward increasing tolerance is becoming aware of where you are now by completing the Assessment section. Then the Skill Analysis and Skill Practice sections of this chapter, along with discussions such as the one in the chapters on problem-solving and creativity, provide ways to improve your tolerance for ambiguity and your cognitive complexity. It is also important to note that a positive correlation exists between tolerance of ambiguity and the second dimension of orientation toward change discussed here: locus of control.

Locus of Control

The second dimension of orientation toward change is labeled **locus of control**. It is one of the most studied and written-about aspects of orientation toward change. Locus of control refers to the attitude people develop regarding the extent to which they are in control of their own destinies. When individuals receive information about the success or failure of their own actions or when something changes in the environment, they differ in how they interpret that information. People receive reinforcements, both positive and negative, as they attempt to make changes around them. If individuals interpret the reinforcement they receive to be contingent on their own actions, it is called an **internal locus of control** (that is, "I was the cause of the success or failure of the change"). If they interpret the reinforcement as being a product of outside forces, it is called an **external locus of control** (that is, "Something or someone else caused the success or failure"). Over time, people develop a "generalized expectancy" about the dominant sources of the reinforcements they receive. Thus, they become largely internally focused or largely externally focused with regard to the source of control they perceive in a changing environment.

More than 10,000 studies have been done using the locus of control scale. In general, the research suggests that managers in North America have a far greater tendency to have an internal locus of control than, say, Middle Eastern and Far East managers (April, Dharani, & Peters, 2012; Trompenaars & Hampton-Turner, 2012). Individuals who have an internal locus of control are less alienated from the work environment, more satisfied with their work, have better relationships with their managers, enjoy better health, and experience less job strain and more position mobility (promotions and job changes) than individuals with an external locus of control (Barbuto, Weltmer, & Pennisi, 2010; Bernardi, 1997, 2011; Coleman, Irving, & Cooper, 1999; Martin, et al., 2005; Ng & Feldman, 2011; Valentine, Godkin, & Doughty, 2008).

A study of leadership and group performance found that internals were more likely to be leaders and that groups led by internals were more effective than those led by externals. Internals also were found to outperform externals in stressful situations, to engage in more entrepreneurial activity, to be more active in managing their own careers, and to have higher levels of job involvement than externals (Karimi & Alipour, 2011; Roddenberry & Renk, 2010; Trompenaars & Hampton-Turner, 2012). Firms led by internals performed significantly better than firms led by externals (Bowling, Eschleman, & Wang, 2010). In summarizing the results of this massive array of research on locus of control, the conclusion is consistent. Leaders tend to be handicapped by an external locus of control. On the other hand, research also has found that an internal locus of control is not a panacea for all management problems. Internal locus of control is not always a positive attribute. For example, individuals with an external locus of control have been found to be more inclined to initiate structure as leaders (to help clarify roles). Internals are less likely to comply with leader directions and are less accurate in processing feedback about successes and failures than are externals. Internals also have more difficulty arriving at decisions with serious consequences for someone else (Coleman, et al., 1999; Trompenaars & Hampton-Turner, 2012). Moreover, some researchers have found that a balance between internal and external locus of control is more functional than an overemphasis on either one (April, Dharani, & Peters, 2012).

It is important to note that locus of control can shift over time, particularly as a function of the position held at work, and that external locus of control does not inhibit individuals from attaining positions of power and influence at the top of organizations. Therefore, no matter what your internal–external score, you can be a successful manager in the right setting, or you can alter your locus of control.

The Locus of Control Scale in the Skill Assessment section helps you generate a score showing the extent to which you have an internal or external locus of control. The scoring key identifies your *External Locus of Control* score. Comparing your own score to the mean scores of several other groups can help you determine the extent to which you are internal (below the mean scores) or external (above the mean scores) in your orientation toward change.

In summary, two key attitudes toward change—tolerance of ambiguity and locus of control—have been found to be associated with success in management roles. Knowing your scores on these two factors can help you capitalize on your strengths and enhance your potential for management success. While substantial research exists associating some positive managerial behaviors with internal locus of control and tolerance of ambiguity, possessing these orientations is neither an assurance of success as a manager nor a solution to the problems that managers face. By knowing your scores, however, you will be able to choose situations in which you are more likely to feel comfortable, perform effectively, and understand the point of view of those whose perspectives differ from yours. Self-understanding is a prerequisite to self-improvement and change.

CORE SELF-EVALUATION

Every person has a distinct personality. This concept of *personality* refers to the relatively enduring combination of traits that makes an individual unique and at the same time produces consistencies in his or her thoughts and behaviors. There is much disagreement about how much of our personality is learned as opposed to being biologically or genetically determined. Some explanation for what makes us unique can certainly be attributed to the genetic predispositions we bring with us when we are born. Yet a sizable portion of our behavioral makeup is learned and can be changed. We focus on factors over which we have some control and can change if we decide to do so.

In the field of personality psychology, there has been a gradual convergence around a few major dimensions of personality. A review of the psychological literature, for example, found that more than 50,000 studies had been conducted on just three attributes of personality—self-esteem, locus of control, and neuroticism or emotional stability (Bono & Judge, 2003). More than 100 studies a month are published on the topic of self-esteem alone!

It has become popular in psychology to refer to the "Big Five" personality attributes as the most important aspects of personality, although there is insufficient scientific evidence that such a conclusion is merited. These Big Five attributes are the most researched, however, and they include *extroversion* (the extent to which people are inclined toward gregariousness and sociability instead of being quiet and reserved); *agreeableness* (the extent to which people are friendly and affable as opposed to being disagreeable and aggressive); *conscientiousness* (the extent to which people are careful, task oriented, and orderly as opposed to being disorganized, flexible, and unreliable); *neuroticism* (the extent to which people are emotionally fragile, negative, and fearful as opposed to being optimistic, positive, and emotionally stable); and *openness* (the extent to which people are curious and open to new ideas as opposed to being rigid or dogmatic). Individuals tend to differ on these five attributes, and scores on these five factors have been used to predict a wide variety of outcomes, including behavioral performance, life success, job satisfaction, interpersonal attraction, and intellectual achievement.

Tim Judge and his colleagues have found, however, that the Big Five personality attributes can be collapsed into a more foundational personality factor. In combination, these personality dimensions create a single, powerful factor that lies at the core of personality (Judge, et al., 2002, 2003, 2005). It is referred to as *core self-evaluation*, or the fundamental evaluation each person has developed about himself or herself. Core self-evaluation is as predictive of behavior as are the Big Five measured separately (Gardner & Pierce, 2010). Core self-evaluation is composed of four components: (1) *self-esteem*, or the extent to which people see themselves as capable, successful, and worthy; (2) *generalized self-efficacy*, or the sense of one's ability to perform capably across a variety of circumstances; (3) *neuroticism*, which is reverse-scored, or the tendency to have a negative outlook and pessimistic approach to life; and (4) *locus of control*, which has been discussed earlier, referring to a person's beliefs about the extent to which he or she can control his or her own experiences.

The commonalties among the four factors that make up core self-evaluation are not difficult to understand. That is, when people view themselves in a positive way, or when they possess high self-esteem, they also tend to feel capable of performing effectively across a variety of situations (generalized self-efficacy), they feel in control of their circumstances (locus of control), and they feel emotionally stable (the opposite of neuroticism). Each of these factors has a slightly different meaning, of course, but the overlap and shared meaning among them is the thing being measured by the Core Self-Evaluation Survey you completed in the Skill Assessment section.

Of course, we have all met people who are self-centered, braggarts, or narcissists. They seem to possess an abundance of positive self-regard, and we might be tempted to think of them as having very high scores in core self-evaluation. However, these people also are likely to be insensitive to their abrasive impact on others. When threatened, they emphasize winning or getting their way. They tend to look in the mirror more often than others, spend more time thinking about themselves and the impressions they convey, and work to make themselves look good or be in the spotlight. They tend to be manipulative in their relationships with others.

They are, in a word, selfish. This is not the same as having a positive core self-evaluation. Rather, a positive core self-evaluation includes sensitivity to others and to the environment so that relationships with others are strengthened rather than weakened, developed rather than destroyed. As summarized in Figure 1.2, strong, confident people are better able to lead, manage, and form supportive relationships with others.

Evidence for this fact comes from the studies of the relationships between core self-evaluation and the effectiveness of individuals at work. Individuals with high core self-evaluations tend to be more satisfied with their jobs. They tend to select more challenging jobs, and they tend to find the work in which they are engaged to be more intrinsically fulfilling. They make their work more rewarding and more stimulating to themselves.

In addition to job satisfaction, core self-evaluation is also strongly related to job performance. That is, people who score higher in core self-evaluation tend to perform more successfully at work as employees and as managers. They tend to earn higher salaries, achieve leadership positions more frequently, and have less career plateauing than others (Judge & Kammeyer-Mueller, 2011; Simsek, Heavey, & Veiga, 2010).

In summary, core self-evaluation scores tend to be a very important predictor of personality differences, job satisfaction, job performance, leadership success, and life happiness. When people have developed a positive self-regard—when they feel valuable, capable, stable, and in control—they tend to function better at work, in relationships, and in life. Developing management skills and acquiring the competency to perform effectively in work settings is one way to enhance feelings of positive self-regard.

Summary

Corporations increasingly have begun to discover the power of developing self-awareness in their managers. Each year, millions of executives around the globe complete instruments designed to increase

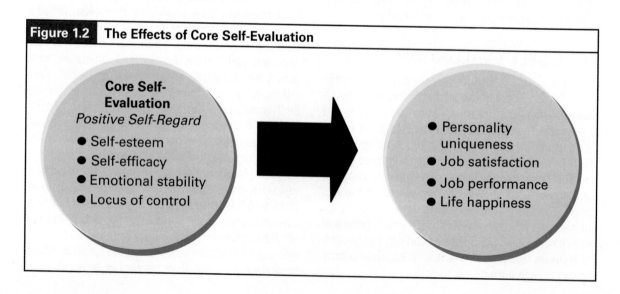

Figure 1.2 The Effects of Core Self-Evaluation

Core Self-Evaluation
Positive Self-Regard
- Self-esteem
- Self-efficacy
- Emotional stability
- Locus of control

- Personality uniqueness
- Job satisfaction
- Job performance
- Life happiness

self-awareness in a large number of name-brand private and public-sector organizations. An awareness of how individuals differ in their emotional maturity, values priorities and values maturity, character strengths, cognitive style, orientation toward change, and personality (core self-evaluation) has helped many companies cope better with interpersonal conflicts, botched communications, breakdowns in trust, and misunderstandings. For example, not only does self-awareness training assist you in your ability to understand and manage yourself, but it also is important in helping you develop understanding of the differences in others. You will regularly encounter individuals who possess different styles, different sets of values, and different perspectives than you do. Most workforces are becoming more, not less, diverse. Self-awareness, therefore, can be a valuable tool in helping you develop empathy and understanding for other people as well as to more successfully manage yourself. The relationship between the five critical areas of self-awareness and these management outcomes is summarized in Figure 1.3.

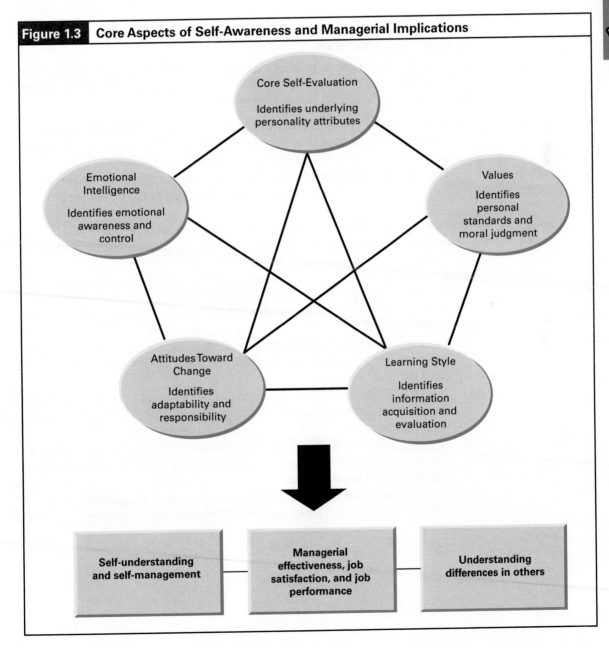

Figure 1.3   Core Aspects of Self-Awareness and Managerial Implications

Core Self-Evaluation

Identifies underlying personality attributes

Emotional Intelligence

Identifies emotional awareness and control

Values

Identifies personal standards and moral judgment

Attitudes Toward Change

Identifies adaptability and responsibility

Learning Style

Identifies information acquisition and evaluation

Self-understanding and self-management

Managerial effectiveness, job satisfaction, and job performance

Understanding differences in others

Most of the following chapters in this book intend to help you develop and improve your skills in interpersonal or group interaction as well as enhance your employability skills. But, remember that an important paradox exists in developing management skills: *We can know others only by knowing ourselves, but we can know ourselves only by knowing others.* Our knowledge of others, and therefore our ability to manage or interact successfully with them, comes from connecting what we see in them to our own experience. If we are not self-aware, we have no foundation for knowing certain things about others. Self-recognition leads to recognition and understanding of others. As Harris (1981) puts it:

> *Nothing is really personal that is not first interpersonal, beginning with the infant's shock of separation from the umbilical cord. What we know about ourselves comes only from the outside, and it is interpreted by the kind of experiences we have had. What we know about others comes only from analogy with our own network of feelings.*

Behavioral Guidelines

Following are the behavioral guidelines relating to the improvement of self-awareness. These guidelines will be helpful to you as you engage in analysis, practice, and application activities designed to improve your self-awareness.

A. Identify your sensitive line. When was it crossed? What kinds of feedback about yourself caused you to become defensive or depressed? Determine what information about yourself you are most likely to defend against.

B. Use the seven dimensions of national culture to diagnose differences between your own values orientation and that of individuals from other cultures, age categories, or ethnic groups.

C. Develop a comprehensive, consistent, and universal set of principles on which you will base your behavior. Identify your signature character strengths and find ways to display them more frequently.

D. Expand your cognitive style, your tolerance of ambiguity, and your internal locus of control by increasing your exposure to new information and engaging in activities with which you are unfamiliar and that will stretch you. Seek ways to expand and broaden yourself.

E. Enhance your emotional intelligence by consciously monitoring your own emotional responses, working to enhance self-control, and practicing the diagnosis of others' emotional cues.

F. Develop a healthy core self-evaluation and positive self-regard by consciously capitalizing on your personal strengths and by highlighting and building on your successful accomplishments.

G. Engage in honest self-disclosure with someone who is close to you and accepting of you. Check out aspects of yourself about which you are uncertain. Ask for feedback from people who know you well.

H. Keep a journal, and make time regularly to engage in self-analysis. Balance life's activities with some time for self-renewal and self-awareness development.

CASES INVOLVING SELF-AWARENESS

The Case of Heinz

To understand the different levels of values maturity, consider the following well-known story used by Kohlberg (1969). It will help you better understand levels of values maturity.

In Europe a woman was near death from a rare form of cancer. There was one drug that the doctors thought might save her. It was a form of radium that a druggist in the same town had recently discovered. The drug was expensive to make, but the druggist was charging 10 times what it cost him to make the drug. He paid $200 for radium and charged $2,000 for a small dose of the drug. The sick woman's husband, Heinz, went to everyone he knew to borrow the money, but he could get together only about $1,000. He told the druggist that his wife was dying and begged him to sell the drug at a lower price or let him pay later. But the druggist said, "No, I discovered the drug and I'm going to make money from it." So Heinz grew desperate and began to think about breaking into the store to steal the drug for his wife.

Now, answer the following questions in reaction to the story:

YES	NO	
_____	_____	1. Would it be wrong for Heinz to break into the store?
_____	_____	2. Did the druggist have the right to charge that much for the product?
_____	_____	3. Did Heinz have an obligation to steal the drug for his wife?
_____	_____	4. What if Heinz and his wife did not get along and were planning a divorce? Should Heinz steal the drug for her?
_____	_____	5. Suppose Heinz's best friend was dying of cancer, rather than Heinz's wife. Should Heinz steal the drug for his friend?
_____	_____	6. Suppose the person dying was not personally close to Heinz but lived in the neighborhood. Should Heinz steal the drug for a neighbor?
_____	_____	7. Suppose Heinz read in the newspaper about a woman dying of cancer. Should he steal the drug for her?
_____	_____	8. Would you steal the drug to save your own life?
_____	_____	9. Suppose Heinz was caught breaking into the store and was brought before a judge. Should he be sentenced to jail?

A discussion regarding these alternatives as they relate to values maturity is available at the end of the chapter.

Computerized Exam

Graduate business school students were all required to take a one-credit-hour current events course. Like other courses in the business school, the final exam was administered on a computer. From a memory bank containing 350 questions, the computer was programmed to select 40 questions for each student, flashing them on the screen one at a time. Students could take the exam any time after the course began in January, whenever they felt ready.

Unfortunately, problems arose. When the test was computerized, a "skip feature" was added to the computer program. This feature was designed so that students could pass over a question they didn't want to answer immediately. The question, theoretically, would return to the screen at a later time, simulating the way in which students skip over and then return to questions on a written exam. However, the skip feature didn't work correctly. Instead of recycling skipped questions back to the student, the computer simply threw them out. Thus, the skip feature became a way for students to avoid any questions they couldn't answer.

Another snafu in the program was that when a certain number of questions were skipped during the exam—between 6 and 10—the computer automatically ended the test. Scores were immediately flashed to the student and recorded in the computer memory. Scores were calculated on a percentage basis, only counting the questions that the student answered. Skipped questions were not counted as correct or incorrect. Therefore, a student who answered 10 questions, 9 of them correctly, and skipped enough other questions to trigger the automatic computer shutoff, received a score of 90 percent.

Knowledge of the skip command was widely distributed well before the end of the term. One person estimated that at least half the students knew about it. Upon review, it was discovered that 77 out of 139 members of the graduating class answered fewer than the required 40 questions when they took the exam. When questioned, some students said they didn't realize a programming error had occurred and didn't keep track of how many questions were asked in total. Others argued that it is like filling out an income tax form. People hire accountants all the time to find loopholes that they can use. That is not illegal, even if the government doesn't advertise the loopholes. The computer program allowed for this loophole, and we did what we did.

1.6. *If you were one of the students in the class, would you:*
   a. Tell the instructor about the programming error before the end of the term?
   b. Report the names of the other students you knew who cheated?
   c. Admit that you cheated?

1.7. *If you were the instructor of the course, which of the following would you do?*
   a. Flunk the 77 students who did not complete 40 questions.
   b. Require the 77 students to retake the exam, but let them graduate.
   c. Require all 139 students to retake the course since no student reported the problem, a violation of the student ethical code.
   d. Change the computer program, but do nothing to the students.
   e. Select another alternative.

1.8. *What is your rationale for the decisions you made in questions 1.6 and 1.7 above? Discuss your rationale with your colleagues.*

1.9. *What level of values maturity is displayed by each alternative? What ethical principles are demonstrated?*

Decision Dilemmas

For each of the five scenarios below, select the choice you would make if you were in the situation.

1. A young manager in a technology firm was offered a position by the firm's chief competitor for almost double her salary. Her firm sought to prevent her from changing jobs, arguing that her knowledge of certain specialized manufacturing processes would give the competitor unfair advantage. Because she had acquired that knowledge through special training and unique opportunities in her current position, the firm argued that it was unethical for her to accept the competitor's offer. What should the young manager do?

   _____ Accept the offer

   _____ Reject the offer

2. A consumer advocate organization conducted a survey to determine whether Indeed.com was really the world's most utilized job recruitment website, as they advertised in the media. After testing a variety of job recruitment websites and businesses, the consumer advocate firm concluded that no single firm could make such a claim because of the variety of different criteria used to measure the number of companies using the websites and the number of applications being processed. The consumer group advocated that Indeed.com not advertise itself as the world's largest job recruiter. The company indicated that its own tests showed no single firm could make this claim. Should these advertisements cease or not?

   _____ Cease to advertise

   _____ Continue to advertise

3. After several profitable years, the Bob Cummings Organic Vitamin Company was put up for sale. Bob's escalating commitments for movie and TV appearances precluded him from having the time to manage such a large company. It became apparent that to persevere the firm, new management and/or new ownership would be necessary. Several firms were interested in purchasing the company for the asking price, but one firm was particularly aggressive. It sponsored several parties and receptions in Bob's honor, a 35-foot yacht was made available for his use during the summer, and several gifts for family members arrived during the holidays. Bob's wife questioned the propriety of these activities. Was it appropriate for Bob to accept the gifts? Should he sell to that firm?

   _____ Proper to accept

   _____ Not proper to accept

   _____ Should not sell

   _____ Should sell

4. Kwame Waller was hired as head coach of a college football team. After two seasons, he was so successful that he was named Coach of the Year by UPI, *Sporting News*, and ESPN. He was also very vocal about the need to clean up cheating in college athletics, especially among competitor schools in his own conference. He heard rumors about inappropriate alumni gifts to some of his own athletes, but after confronting those involved, he received assurances that the rumors weren't true. At the beginning of the next season, however, he received conclusive evidence that seven of the starters on his team, including an All-American player, had received financial benefits from a wealthy booster. What should Kwame do?

_____ Kick them off the team

_____ Suspend them for several games

_____ Warn them but do nothing

_____ Do something else

5. Keiko's company had been battered by competition from Asian firms. Not only were Asian products selling for less money, but their quality was substantially higher. By investing in some high-technology equipment and fostering better union–management relations, Keiko was relatively certain that the quality gap could be overcome. But her overhead rate was more than 40 percent above that of the competitor firms. She reasoned that the most efficient way to lower costs would be to close one of her older plants, lay off the employees, and increase production in the newer plants. She knew just which plant would be the one to close. The trouble was, the community was dependent on that plant as its major employer and had recently invested a great deal of money for highway repair and streetlight construction around the plant. The workforce was composed mainly of older people who had lived in the area most of their lives. It was improbable that they could obtain alternative employment in the same area. Should Keiko close the plant or not?

_____ Close the plant

_____ Do not close the plant

Discussion Questions

Form a small group and discuss the following questions regarding these five scenarios:

1.10. Why did you make the choices you did in each case? Justify each answer.
1.11. What principles or basic values for decision-making did you use in each case?
1.12. What additional information would you need in order to be certain about your choices?
1.13. What circumstances might arise to make you change your mind about your decision? Could there be a different answer to each case in a different circumstance?
1.14. What do your answers tell you about your own emotional intelligence, values, cognitive style, attitude toward change, and core self-evaluation?

EXERCISES FOR IMPROVING
SELF-AWARENESS THROUGH
SELF-DISCLOSURE

Shipping the Part

Form a team or a discussion group, and read the following case together. Then discuss your decision with one another. Is your decision to ship the product, call the customer, or refuse to ship? Each group member should explain his or her decision and rationale. Then, after sharing with one another, turn to the end of the chapter and read what the company actually did. Discuss whether you agree or disagree with the company's strategy and why. The point is to examine your own values and the cognitive style you tend to prefer. Practice articulating your point of view to others.

Maxine Hong, a top manufacturing manager at a satellite telecommunications company, walked into the office of Neville Lobo, the head of quality control. Maxine was carrying an assembled part that was to be shipped to a customer on the West Coast. Maxine handed Neville the part and said, "Look, Neville, this part is in perfect shape electronically, but the case has a gouge in it. I've seen engineering and they say that the mark doesn't affect form, fit, or function. Marketing says the customer won't mind because they are just going to bury the unit anyway. We can't rework it, and it would cost $75,000 to make new cases. We will only do 23 units, and they're already made. The parts are due to be shipped at the end of the week." Neville responded, "Well, what do you want from me?" "Just sign off so we can move forward," said Maxine. "Since you're the one who needs to certify acceptable quality, I thought I'd better get this straightened out now rather than wait until the last minute before shipping."

If you were Neville, what would you do? You must select one of the alternatives below.

_____ Ship the part to the customer as planned

_____ Call the customer

_____ Refuse to ship the part

Discuss with your group members what decision you would make and why.

Through the Looking Glass

The concept of "looking-glass self" was developed in the nineteenth century to describe the process used by people to develop self-awareness. It means that other people serve as a looking glass for each of us. They mirror back our actions and behaviors. In turn, we form our opinions of ourselves as a result of observing and interpreting this mirroring. The best way to form accurate self-perceptions, therefore, is to become vulnerable to others. This usually involves sharing your thoughts, attitudes, feelings, actions, or plans with others. This exercise helps you do that by asking you to analyze your own styles and inclinations and then share and discuss them with others. This sharing exercise will provide insights that you haven't recognized before.

Assignment

In a group of three or four, share your scores on the Skill Assessment instruments. Determine what similarities and differences exist among group members. Do systematic ethnic or gender differences exist? Now read aloud the 10 statements listed below. Each person should respond to each statement, but take turns going first. The purpose of your completing the statements aloud is to help you articulate aspects of your self-awareness and to receive reactions to them from others.

1. In taking the assessment instruments, I was surprised by...

2. Some of my dominant characteristics captured by the instruments are...

3. Among my greatest strengths are...

4. The areas in which I need the most development are...

5. The time I felt most successful was...

6. The time I felt least competent was...

7. My three highest priorities in life are...

8. The way in which I differ most from other people is...

9. I get along best with people who...

10. From what the others in this group have shared, here is an impression I have formed about each of you:

Diagnosing Managerial Characteristics

This exercise is designed to give you practice in diagnosing differences in others' styles and inclinations. Being aware of the styles, values, and attitudes of others will help you manage them more effectively. Below are brief descriptions of four successful managers. They differ in values, learning styles, orientations toward change, and interpersonal orientation. After reading the scenarios, form small groups to discuss the questions that follow.

Michael Dell

Michael Dell is the kind of guy people either love or hate. He is worth more than $13 billion, loves to go to work each day, and is as likely to tear a computer apart and put it back together again as to read a financial report. Several decades after he started assembling computers in his dorm room, Michael is still fascinated with the hardware. Despite his billionaire status, "if anyone believes that he is not the chief technologist in this company, they are naive," says Robert McFarland, former vice president of Dell's federal sales group. Although Dell Computer is the quintessential lean-and-mean company, Michael does not play the part of the whip-cracker. After recently receiving an award from the Austin, Texas, Chamber of Commerce, for example, Michael and his wife stayed long after the program was over to chat with everyone who wanted to meet him. He has been described as shy and quiet and not inclined toward public hyperbole. "Michael has a genuine shyness...he is a genuinely mild-mannered, low-key person who was very focused on reaching his objectives," says Brian Fawkes, a former Dell employee. Admittedly, Dell has experienced several missteps and losses, but Michael has been unafraid to learn from missteps. "Michael makes mistakes. He just never makes the same mistake twice," says Mark Tebbe, former president of a firm that Dell acquired.

SOURCE: *Adapted from Darrow, 1998.*

Patrick M. Byrne

As president and chairman of Overstock.com in Salt Lake City, Utah, Byrne was a Marshall Scholar who received his PhD in philosophy from Stanford University. His management style, personality, and core values are illustrated in his interview with *Fast Company*: "Learning philosophy has been useful in teaching me how to get to the heart of things—to be able to deconstruct what the real issues are. People think we're endless debaters, but what we're really doing is refining concepts in order to reach agreement. With negotiations, instead of trying to fight someone on every one of the issues, most of the time it turns out he cares about a whole bunch of things that you don't care about. Make those trade-offs, and he'll think you're being too generous when in fact you're just giving him the sleeves off your vest. Ultimately, philosophy is about values, and that definitely has its place in business. I consider myself a far outsider to Wall Street. There's a whole lot of obfuscation involved. In August, I spoke out on how the Wall Street system was corrupt and how the financial press was co-opted. Because of it I got called a buffoon and wacky; then a lot of lies came out about my being gay, taking cocaine, and hiring a stripper. That's sort of the fifth-grade level we're operating on. It doesn't bother me. When you decide to stand for things, you have to be prepared to face criticism, mockery, and derision."

SOURCE: *Adapted from* Fast Company, *2005.*

Jack Ma

As founder and executive chairman of Alibaba Group, Jack Ma is among the world's most successful entrepreneurs. He indicated that he earned this status "by walking positively upon the pillars of failure." Jack faced a life full of struggle and failures. He passed his college exams in four attempts and was rejected for 30 different jobs. He was the only candidate among 24 who was rejected by KFC. He was refused admission to Harvard University 10 times. All these rejections led Jack to become one of the most influential businessmen and entrepreneurs in the world. As an introvert, Jack capitalized on strong leadership skills and charisma to acquire multiple accolades, such as being named one of the world's most influential people by *Time* magazine, one of the 30 best CEOs in the world by *Barron's*, and No. 2 on the list of the World's Greatest Leaders by *Fortune*. His company, Alibaba, set a record as the world's largest stock offering in its IPO in 2014. Among his 30,000 employees, 47 percent are women—including 33 percent of senior management. Before the booming growth of Alibaba, he was distributing equity to the high school students who worked for him. This inclusive growth mind-set continued as Alibaba grew into an e-commerce giant. Jack is described by one Harvard professor as "embodying the global intelligence that is needed for today's global leaders." Global intelligence means that one is able to adapt to diversity at a global level. This mind-set is partly translated into Jack's statement about ethics: "I would say in the past 70 years we are the leader of anti-piracy (counterfeit goods). Last year alone, we have put 400 people in jail, and we deleted 370 million product listings."

Steve Jobs

Charismatic, passionate, risk oriented, and *nontraditional* are terms that have frequently been used to describe Steve Jobs. Some have described him as a born leader exhibiting confidence, determination, and passion. Still others emphasized strong-headedness, narcissism, insensitiveness, and domination. Steve was among the most successful entrepreneurs and business executives in history. He started the NeXT company after being fired from Apple the first company he founded. Apple hired him back a few years later, and by the time of his death in 2011, Steve had led Apple to be the most valuable company in the world. He was notoriously abrasive by nature. He possessed a rude and obnoxious personality that often led him to yell at his colleagues and his team when things didn't go according to his expectations. One of his mantras was: "Stay Hungry, Stay Foolish." What he meant by "stay hungry" was to never be satisfied with what you have because there may be a chance to make things better. What he meant by "stay foolish" was that if you remain foolish enough, there is still a lot to learn and you can always be better than you were yesterday. An example of his never-ending pursuit of quality and innovation was his rejection of the first prototype of the iPod. He insisted that his engineers make it smaller and lighter, but the engineers told him that it was impossible to make it smaller than the prototype. Steve dropped the prototype iPod into an aquarium, and the moment it touched the bottom, he could see bubbles floating to the top of the tank. "See there," he said. "Those are air bubbles, and that means there is space in there. Make it smaller." And they did.

Discussion Questions

1.15. Rank these individuals from highest to lowest in terms of:
   - ❑ Emotional intelligence
   - ❑ Values maturity

❑ Tolerance of ambiguity

❑ Core self-evaluation

Justify your evaluations in a discussion with your colleagues, and compare your rankings.

1.16. What is your prediction about the dominant cognitive styles of each of these individuals? What data do you use as evidence?

1.17. If you were assigned to hire a senior manager for your organization and this was your candidate pool, what questions would you ask in order to identify the following attributes?

❑ Cognitive styles

❑ Values orientations

❑ Character strengths

❑ Orientation toward change

❑ Core self-evaluation

Which one of these people would you hire if you wanted a CEO for your company? Why?

1.18. Assume each of these individuals is a member of your team. What would be the greatest strengths and weaknesses of your team? What kinds of attributes would you want to add to your team to ensure that it is optimally heterogeneous?

An Exercise for Identifying Aspects of Personal Culture: A Learning Plan and Autobiography

The purpose of this exercise is to assist you in articulating your key goals and aspirations as well as in identifying a personal learning plan to facilitate your success. Because continuous learning is so important for you to succeed throughout your life, we want to help you identify some specific ambitions and to develop a set of procedures to help you reach your potential.

This exercise is accomplished in three steps:

Step 1 (Aspirations): Write an autobiographical story that might appear in *Fortune, Fast Company*, or the *Wall Street Journal* on this date 15 years from now. This story should identify your notable accomplishments and your newsworthy successes. What will you have achieved that will fulfill your dreams? What outcomes would make you ecstatically happy? What legacy do you want to be known for?

Step 2 (Characteristics): Review your scores on the skill assessment instruments. Using Figure 1.4, identify the extent to which you are satisfied with your scores on these various instruments. The vertical axis in the figure ranges from Very Satisfied to Very Dissatisfied. The horizontal axis identifies the five areas of self-awareness being assessed in this chapter. For each of the seven instruments, plot your satisfaction level with how you scored. By joining those points together, you will have created a *Self-Awareness Satisfaction Profile*. This will help you highlight areas in which you want to improve.

Based on that plot, identify your distinctive competencies, your strengths, and your unique attributes. What are the values, styles, and attitudes that will assist you in achieving the aspirations you identified in Step 1? In what areas do you want to focus improvement efforts?

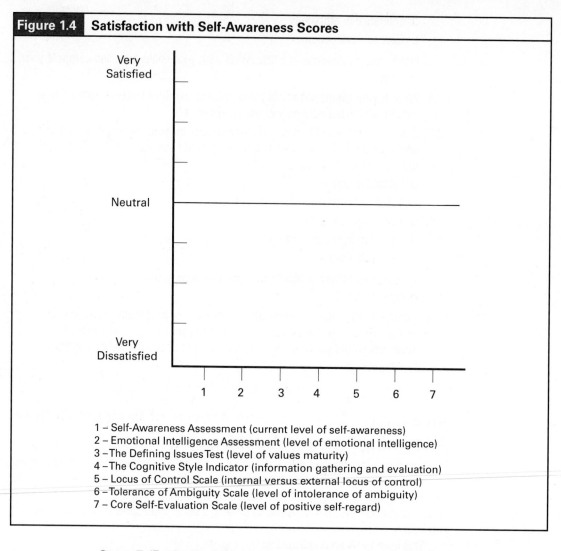

Figure 1.4 Satisfaction with Self-Awareness Scores

Very Satisfied

Neutral

Very Dissatisfied

1 2 3 4 5 6 7

1 – Self-Awareness Assessment (current level of self-awareness)
2 – Emotional Intelligence Assessment (level of emotional intelligence)
3 – The Defining Issues Test (level of values maturity)
4 – The Cognitive Style Indicator (information gathering and evaluation)
5 – Locus of Control Scale (internal versus external locus of control)
6 – Tolerance of Ambiguity Scale (level of intolerance of ambiguity)
7 – Core Self-Evaluation Scale (level of positive self-regard)

Step 3 (Feedback): Interview a member of your family or someone who knows you very well. Ask that person to describe what they see as your unique strengths and capabilities. What does he or she predict for you in your future? Include the following questions in your interview:

- ❏ Who do you admire a great deal because of their success in life? What capabilities and attributes do they possess?
- ❏ Who do you know that has failed to achieve their potential? What do you see as the most significant causes of their failure?
- ❏ What do you see as the distinctive and notable capabilities that I possess?
- ❏ In what areas do you think I should focus my improvement and development efforts?
- ❏ What do you see me doing in 15 years?

Step 4 (Planning): Now identify the developmental activities in which you will engage if you are to achieve your aspirations. With the insight you have gained from Steps 2 and 3, identify the things you must do to help you achieve what you hope to accomplish. Consider the following activities.

- ❏ What courses will you take?
- ❏ What people will you get to know?

❑ In what extracurricular or life-balance activities will you engage?

❑ What will you read?

❑ What spiritual activities will be most meaningful?

This written product should be handed in to your instructor, or it should be given to a family member for safekeeping. Open and reread this document in five years to determine the extent to which you are on track.

ACTIVITIES FOR DEVELOPING SELF-AWARENESS

Suggested Assignments

1.19. Keep a journal for at least the remainder of this course. Record significant discoveries, insights, learnings, and personal recollections—not daily activities. Write in your journal at least twice a week. Give yourself some feedback.

1.20. Ask someone you know well to complete the assessment instruments by rating you on each item. Compare your own scores with those of this other person. Discuss differences, strengths, and areas of confusion. The goal is to help you increase your self-awareness by getting a picture of yourself from someone else's standpoint.

1.21. Write down the comprehensive, consistent, and universal principles that guide your behavior under all circumstances. What core principles will you rarely violate? Share the list with someone with whom you have a close relationship.

1.22. In considering your own values and character strengths, consider answering any two of the following questions. Explain your answers to your colleagues, to your family, or to your close friends, or merely write answers in a journal. In so doing, you will reveal some of your closely held character strengths based on your core values.

1. If you won $1 million, what would you do with the money? How would it affect who you are and how you see yourself?
2. If you could award a *Time* magazine Person of the Year Award to the person you most admire, to whom would you give the award? Why?
3. If you could choose one superpower, what would you pick? Why?
4. If you learned that you had only three weeks to live, how would you spend the time? What would you do week by week?
5. If the entire world would listen to you for one minute, what would you say?
6. If you could meet one person you most admire from the past or present, who would you want to meet? Why? What would you say?

1.23. Spend an evening with a close friend or relative discussing your emotional intelligence, values, cognitive style, attitude toward change, and core self-evaluation. You may want to have that person complete the instruments, giving his or her impressions of you, so you can compare and contrast your scores. Discuss implications for your future and for your relationship.

1.24. Teach someone else the value of self-awareness in managerial success and explain the relevance of emotional intelligence, values maturity, cognitive style, attitudes toward change, and core self-evaluation. Describe the experience in your journal.

Application Plan and Evaluation

The intent of this exercise is to help you apply this cluster of skills in a real-life, out-of-class setting. Now that you have become familiar with the behavioral guidelines that form the basis of effective skill performance, you will improve most by trying out those guidelines in an everyday context. Unlike a classroom activity, in which feedback is immediate and others can assist you with their evaluations, this skill application activity is one you must accomplish and evaluate on your own. There are two parts to this activity. Part 1 helps prepare you to apply the skill. Part 2 helps you evaluate and improve on your experience. Be sure to write down answers to each item. Don't short-circuit the process by skipping steps.

Part 1. Planning

1. Write down the two or three aspects of this skill of self-awareness that are most important to you. These may be areas of weakness, areas you most want to improve, or areas that are most salient to a problem you face right now. Identify the specific aspects of this skill that you want to apply.

2. Now identify the setting or the situation in which you will apply this skill of self-awareness. Establish a plan for performance by actually writing down a description of the situation. Who else will be involved? When will you do it? Where will it be done?
   Circumstances:
   Who else?
   When?
   Where?

3. Identify the specific behaviors in which you will engage to apply this skill. Operationalize your skill performance.

4. What are the indicators of successful performance? How will you know you have been effective? What will indicate you have performed competently?

Part 2. Evaluation

5. After you have completed your implementation, record the results. What happened? How successful were you? What was the effect on others?

6. How can you improve? What modifications can you make next time? What will you do differently in a similar situation in the future?

7. Looking back on your entire skill practice and application experience, what have you learned? What has been surprising? In what ways might this experience help you in the long term?

⭐ Go to www.pearson.com/mylab/management for scoring keys and comparison data for the following instruments:

Self-Awareness Assessment
Emotional Intelligence Assessment
Locus of Control Scale

The Defining Issues Test

The possibility of misusing and misinterpreting this instrument is high enough that its author, James Rest, maintains control over the scoring procedure associated with its use. Some people may interpret the results of this instrument to be an indication of the degree of a person's inherent morality, honesty, or personal worth, none of which the instrument is intended to assess. A scoring manual may be obtained from James Rest, Minnesota Moral Research Center, Burton Hall, University of Minnesota, Minneapolis, MN 55455.

The most difficult moral decisions are experienced as dilemmas. Our purpose is to help you become aware of the moral standards you apply when facing these difficult choices. These standards have been codified by scholars as "stages" of moral development. The stage of the 12 questions you rated for each of the three stories is shown below. Looking for patterns across the three sets of four statements you selected as most important will help you better understand the stage of moral development you most often use.

Escaped Prisoner

1. Hasn't Mr. Thompson been good enough for such a long time to prove he isn't a bad person? (Stage 3)
2. Every time someone escapes punishment for a crime, doesn't that just encourage more crime? (Stage 4)
3. Wouldn't we be better off without prisons and the oppression of our legal system? (Indicates antiauthoritarian attitudes.)
4. Has Mr. Thompson really paid his debt to society? (Stage 4)
5. Would society be unfairly treating Mr. Thompson? (Stage 6)
6. What benefits would prison be apart from society, especially for a charitable man? (Nonsense alternative, designed to identify people picking high-sounding alternatives.)
7. How could anyone be so cruel and heartless as to send Mr. Thompson back to prison? (Stage 3)
8. Would it be fair to all the prisoners who had to serve out their full sentences if Mr. Thompson was let off? (Stage 4)
9. Was Ms. Jones a good friend of Mr. Thompson? (Stage 3)
10. Wouldn't it be a citizen's duty to report an escaped criminal, regardless of circumstances? (Stage 4)
11. How would the will of the people and the public good best be served? (Stage 5)
12. Would going to prison do any good for Mr. Thompson or protect anybody? (Stage 5)

The Doctor's Dilemma

1. Is the woman's family is in favor of giving her an overdose? (Stage 3)
2. Is the doctor obligated to follow the same laws as everybody else if giving her an overdose would be the same as killing her? (Stage 4)
3. Would people be much better off without society regimenting their lives and even their deaths? (Indicates antiauthoritarian attitudes.)
4. Should the doctor could make it appear like an accident? (Stage 2)
5. Does the state have the right to force continued existence on those who don't want to live? (Stage 5)
6. What is the value of death prior to society's perspective on personal values? (Nonsense alternative, designed to identify people picking high-sounding alternatives.)
7. Should the doctor have sympathy for the woman's suffering, or should he care more about what society might think? (Stage 3)
8. Is helping to end another's life ever a responsible act of cooperation? (Stage 6)
9. Should only God decide when a person's life should end? (Stage 4)
10. What values has the doctor has set for himself in his own personal code of behavior? (Stage 5)
11. Can society afford to let everybody end their lives when they want to? (Stage 4)
12. Can society allow suicides or mercy killing and still protect the lives of individuals who want to live? (Stage 5)

The Newspaper

1. Is the principal more responsible to the students or to the parents? (Stage 4)
2. Did the principal give his word that the newspaper could be published for a long time, or did he promise to approve the newspaper one issue at a time? (Stage 4)
3. Would the students start protesting even more if the principal stopped the newspaper? (Stage 2)
4. When the welfare of the school is threatened, does the principal have the right to give orders to students? (Stage 4)
5. Does the principal have the freedom of speech to say no in this case? (Nonsense alternative, designed to identify people picking high-sounding alternatives.)
6. If the principal stopped the newspaper, would he be preventing full discussion of important problems? (Stage 5)
7. Would the principal's order make Rami lose faith in the him? (Stage 3)
8. Is Rami really loyal to his school and patriotic to his country? (Stage 3)
9. What effect would stopping the paper have on the students' education in critical thinking and judgment? (Stage 5)
10. Is Rami in any way violating the rights of others in publishing his own opinions? (Stage 5)
11. Should the principal be influenced by some angry parents when it is the principal who knows best what is going on in the school? (Stage 4)
12. Is Rami using the newspaper to stir up hatred and discontent? (Stage 3)

Cognitive Style Indicator

Scoring Key

DIMENSIONS	ITEMS	AVERAGE SCORES
Knowing Style	5, 8, 11, 14	Add scores and divide by 4: _____
Planning Style	1, 3, 6, 9, 12, 15, 17	Add scores and divide by 7: _____
Creating Style	2, 4, 7, 10, 13, 16, 18	Add scores and divide by 7: _____

Comparison Data (N = 11,000 students)

DIMENSION SCORES (AVERAGES)	MEAN	BOTTOM QUARTILE	SECOND QUARTILE	THIRD QUARTILE	TOP QUARTILE
Knowing Style	4.14	3.75 or below	3.76–4.25	4.26–4.5	4.51 or above
Planning Style	4.20	3.86 or below	3.87–4.28	4.29–4.71	4.72 or above
Creating Style	3.92	3.57 or below	3.58–3.99	4.0–4.29	4.30 or above

Tolerance of Ambiguity Scale

Scoring Key

High scores indicate an intolerance of ambiguity. Having high intolerance means that you tend to perceive situations as threatening rather than promising, and lack of information or uncertainty would tend to make you uncomfortable. Ambiguity arises from three primary sources: novelty, complexity, and insolubility.

In scoring the instrument, the *even-numbered* items must be reversed. That is, 7 becomes 1, 6 becomes 2, 5 becomes 3, 3 becomes 5, 2 becomes 6, and 1 becomes 7.

1. _____ An expert who doesn't come up with a definite answer probably doesn't know too much.
2. _____ I would like to live in a foreign country for a while. **(reverse)**
3. _____ There is really no such thing as a problem that can't be solved.
4. _____ People who fit their lives to a schedule probably miss most of the joy of living. **(reverse)**
5. _____ A good job is one where what is to be done and how it is to be done are always clear.
6. _____ It is more fun to tackle a complicated problem than to solve a simple one. **(reverse)**
7. _____ In the long run it is possible to get more done by tackling small, simple problems rather than large and complicated ones.
8. _____ Often the most interesting and stimulating people are those who don't mind being different and original. **(reverse)**
9. _____ What we are used to is always preferable to what is unfamiliar.
10. _____ People who insist upon a yes or no answer just don't know how complicated things really are. **(reverse)**
11. _____ A person who leads an even, regular life in which few surprises or unexpected happenings arise really has a lot to be grateful for.

12. _____ Many of our most important decisions are based upon insufficient information. **(reverse)**
13. _____ I like parties where I know most of the people more than ones where all or most of the people are complete strangers.
14. _____ Teachers or supervisors who hand out vague assignments give one a chance to show initiative and originality. **(reverse)**
15. _____ The sooner we all acquire similar values and ideals the better.
16. _____ A good teacher is one who makes you wonder about your way of looking at things. **(reverse)**

Total of odd-numbered items: _____

Total of reverse-scored even-numbered items: _____

Total: _____

    After reversing the even-numbered items, compute your score for three dimensions, or kinds, of ambiguous situations.

N = Novelty score (questions 2, 9, 11, 13): _____

C = Complexity score (questions 4, 5, 6, 7, 8, 10, 14, 15, 16): _____

I = Insolubility score (questions 1, 3, 12): _____

Comparison Data (N = 5,000 students)

SCORES	MEAN	FIRST QUARTILE	SECOND QUARTILE	THIRD QUARTILE	FOURTH QUARTILE
Total Dimensions	56.47	49 or below	50–56	57–62	63 or above
Novelty	XX.X	Total or Dim			
Complexity	XX.X				
Insolubility	XX.X				

Core Self-Evaluation Scale

Scoring Key

Reverse your scores for entries 2, 4, 6, 8, 10, and 12. That is, for these entries, 1 becomes 5, 2 becomes 4, 4 becomes 2, and 5 becomes 1. Divide the sum of all entries by 12 to produce an average CSES score.

1. _____ I am confident I get the success I deserve in life.
2. _____ Sometimes I feel depressed. **(reverse)**
3. _____ When I try, I generally succeed.
4. _____ Sometimes when I fail, I feel worthless. **(reverse)**
5. _____ I complete tasks successfully.
6. _____ Sometimes, I do not feel in control of my work. **(reverse)**
7. _____ Overall, I am satisfied with myself.
8. _____ I am filled with doubts about my competence. **(reverse)**
9. _____ I determine what will happen in my life.

10. _____ I do not feel in control of my success in my career. **(reverse)**
11. _____ I am capable of coping with most of my problems.
12. _____ There are times when things look pretty bleak and hopeless to me.
   (reverse)
   _____ **Total Score**

÷12 _____ **Average Score**

Next, compute your average score for each dimension, or component, of self-evaluations, by dividing your total for each by 3.

DIMENSIONS	ENTRIES	AVERAGE SCORE
Self-esteem	1–3 ÷ 3	____
Self-efficacy	4–6 ÷ 3	____
Emotional stability	7–9 ÷ 3	____
Locus of control	10–12 ÷ 3	____

Comparison Data (N = 5,000 students)

SCORES (AVERAGES)	MEAN	FIRST QUARTILE	SECOND QUARTILE	THIRD QUARTILE	FOURTH QUARTILE
Total Dimensions	3.73	3.3 or below	3.4–3.8	3.9–4.2	4.3 or above
Self-esteem	X.XX	Total or Ave.?			
Self-efficacy	X.XX	Instruct	To compute Ave.		
Emotional stability	X.XX				
Locus of control	X.XX				

Discussion Regarding the Case of Heinz

For individuals in the self-centered level of maturity, stealing the drug might be labeled as wrong—period. No violation of the law is justified. On the other hand, one might determine that Heinz would be justified in stealing the drug for his wife because she has instrumental value for him. She could provide companionship, help raise the children, provide emotional support, and so on. A stranger, however, would not have the same instrumental value for Heinz, so it would be inappropriate for him to steal the drug for a stranger. Fear of punishment is a major motivator in this stage.

Individuals in the conformity level base their judgments on the closeness of the relationship and on the law and authority. The closer the relationship, the more obligation Heinz should feel to steal the drug. Heinz has an obligation to steal for family members, according to this reasoning, but not for nonfamily members. People have a different obligation regarding family members than they do for others. Another governing principle for individuals in the conformity level is whether or not an action is against the law (or society's expectations). If the probability of getting caught is low, or if no harm is done to society, stealing the drug is justified.

Principle-level individuals base their judgments on a set of universal, comprehensive, and consistent principles. They may answer any question yes or no, but their reasoning is based on their own internal principles, not on externally imposed standards or expectations.

These principles are universal and applicable for every circumstance. For example, they might feel an obligation to steal the drug for anyone because they value human life more than property. Or they may determine that regardless of the threat to one's wife, upholding society's values is necessary to maintain social order, and stealing is a threat to the social order.

Discussion Regarding the Shipping the Part Case

Here is what happened in this company. Neville's reply to the request by Maxine was as follows:

- ❏ We will refuse to ship the part.
- ❏ We will refuse to call the customer.

Here is our rationale:

1. "We will not dump our quality-control problems in the lap of the customer. We will never ask our customer to decide about compromised quality. We promise our customers to get it right, and we will always keep our word."

2. "We are at least as interested in the long-term image of our firm as we are in the immediate sale or profits from one transaction. We will do nothing to compromise our image of quality over the long run. Next time it could be merely a soldering joint, compromised material, or a million-dollar order or serious safety issue. Never will any customer have to worry about our integrity."

3. "We have many people inside and outside this firm watching us make these kinds of decisions. We never want to give the message to any of them that we are willing to settle for second best. No employee should ever be given an excuse for compromising integrity and commitments."

4. "We aspire to be a world-class company. We believe world-class companies just don't compromise on some things. The best in the world would not send customers something that was not their very best. We won't either."

The company actually scheduled an extra shift, reproduced the part at a cost above the original estimate of $75,000, and shipped it to the customer on time.

Discuss your opinions about your agreement or disagreement with this decision. Explain why.

SKILL *ASSESSMENT*

- Stress Management Assessment
- Time Management Assessment
- Social Readjustment Rating Scale
- Sources of Personal Stress
- Flourishing Scale

SKILL *LEARNING*

- Improving the Management of Stress and Time
- Major Elements of Stress
- Managing Stress
- Eliminating Stressors
- Developing Resiliency and Well-Being
- Temporary Stress-Reduction Techniques
- Summary
- Behavioral Guidelines

SKILL *ANALYSIS*

- The Turn of the Tide
- The Case of the Missing Time
- Stress and the Millennial Generation

SKILL *PRACTICE*

- The Small-Wins Strategy
- Life-Balance Analysis
- Deep Relaxation
- Monitoring and Managing Time
- Reciprocity Exercise

SKILL *APPLICATION*

- Suggested Assignments
- Application Plan and Evaluation

SCORING KEYS AND *COMPARISON DATA*

MyLab Management

Go to www.pearson.com/mylab/management to complete the exercises marked with this icon ✪.

2

Managing Stress and Well-Being

LEARNING OBJECTIVES

1. Eliminate stressors
2. Develop resiliency
3. Cope with stress in the short term
4. Enhance personal well-being

DIAGNOSTIC SURVEYS FOR MANAGING STRESS AND WELL-BEING

MyLab Management Personal Inventory Assessments

PERSONAL
INVENTORY
ASSESSMENT

The assessment instruments in this chapter are briefly described below. The assessments appear either in your text or in MyLab. The assessments marked with ✪ are available only in MyLab. If assigned, go to www.pearson.com/mylab/management to complete these assessments. The assessments without the ✪ appear only in the text.

All assessments should be completed before reading the chapter material.

After completing the first assessment, save your response to your hard drive. When you have finished reading the chapter, re-take the assessment and compare your responses to see what you have learned.

- ✪ ❏ The *Stress Management Assessment* measures the extent to which you effectively manage the various sources of stress in your life and the degree to which you have developed stress management skills.
- ✪ ❏ The *Time Management Assessment* evaluates the degree to which you effectively manage your time and the extent to which you implement effective time management principles.
- ❏ The *Social Readjustment Rating Scale* (SRRS) identifies the relative importance of events that have occurred in your life in the past year. The weightings associated with these events help identify the impact of stress.
- ❏ The *Sources of Personal Stress* instrument personalizes your ratings on the *Social Readjustment Rating Scale* by identifying unique stressors occurring in your life right now.
- ❏ The *Flourishing Scale* measures the extent to which you are experiencing well-being in your life at the present time.

MANAGING STRESS AND WELL-BEING

Assessment Section

SOCIAL READJUSTMENT RATING SCALE

The SRRS self-assessment helps you identify stressful experiences in your life and understand the level of stress associated with each event, according to research conducted by the authors of the scale.

Rating Scale

Circle any of the following you have experienced in the past year. Using the weightings at the left, total up your score.

Mean Value	Life Event
87	1. Death of spouse/partner
79	2. Death of a close family member
78	3. Major injury to/illness of self

Mean Value	Life Event
76	4. Detention in jail or other institution
72	5. Major injury to/illness of a close family member
71	6. Foreclosure on loan/mortgage
71	7. Divorce
70	8. Being a victim of crime
69	9. Being a victim of police brutality
69	10. Infidelity
69	11. Experiencing domestic violence/sexual abuse
66	12. Separation from or reconciliation with spouse/mate
64	13. Being fired/laid off/unemployed
62	14. Experiencing financial problems/difficulties
61	15. Death of a close friend
59	16. Surviving a disaster
59	17. Becoming a single parent
56	18. Assuming responsibility for a sick or elderly loved one
56	19. Loss of or major reduction in health insurance/benefits
56	20. Self/close family member being arrested for violating the law
53	21. Major disagreement over child support/custody/visitation
53	22. Being involved in an auto accident
53	23. Being disciplined or demoted at work
51	24. Dealing with unwanted pregnancy
50	25. Adult child moving in with parent/parent moving in with adult child
49	26. Child develops behavior or learning problem
48	27. Experiencing employment discrimination or sexual harassment
47	28. Attempting to modify addictive behavior of self
46	29. Discovering/attempting to modify addictive behavior of close family member
45	30. Employer reorganization/downsizing
44	31. Dealing with infertility/miscarriage
43	32. Getting married
43	33. Changing employers/careers
42	34. Failure to obtain/qualify for a mortgage
41	35. Pregnancy of self/spouse/partner
39	36. Experiencing discrimination/harassment outside the workplace
39	37. Release from jail
38	38. Spouse/partner begins/ceases work outside the home
37	39. Major disagreement with boss/coworker
35	40. Change in residence
34	41. Finding appropriate childcare/day care
33	42. Experiencing a large unexpected monetary gain
33	43. Changing positions at work (transfer, promotion)
33	44. Gaining a new family member

Mean Value	Life Event
32	45. Changing work responsibilities
30	46. Child leaving home
30	47. Obtaining a home mortgage
30	48. Obtaining a major loan other than home mortgage
28	49. Retirement
26	50. Beginning/ceasing formal education
22	51. Receiving a ticket for violating the law
_____	Total score for circled items

SOURCE: *Social Readjustment Rating Scale, Hobson, Charles Jo, Joseph Kaen, Jane Szotek, Carol M. Nethercutt, James W. Tiedmann and Susan Wojnarowicz (1998), "Stressful Life Events: A Revision and Update of the Social Readjustment Rating Scale,"* International Journal of Stress Management, 5: 1–23.

SOCIAL READJUSTMENT RATING SCALE

College and high school students might find this version of the SRRS more relevant.

Mean	Value	Life Event
1	100	Death of parent
2	100	Unplanned pregnancy/abortion
3	95	Getting married
4	90	Divorce of parents
5	80	Acquiring a visible deformity
6	70	Fathering a child
7	70	Jail sentence of parent for over one year
8	69	Marital separation of parents
9	68	Death of a brother or sister
10	67	Change in acceptance by peers
11	64	Unplanned pregnancy of sister
12	63	Discovery of being an adopted child
13	63	Marriage of parent to stepparent
14	63	Death of a close friend
15	62	Having a visible congenital deformity
16	58	Serious illness requiring hospitalization
17	56	Receiving a failing grade in school
18	55	Not making an extracurricular activity
19	55	Hospitalization of a parent
20	53	Jail sentence of parent for over 30 days
21	53	Breaking up with boyfriend or girlfriend
22	51	Beginning to date
23	50	Suspension from school

Mean Value	Life Event	
24	50	Becoming involved with drugs or alcohol
25	50	Birth of a brother or sister
26	47	Increase in arguments between parents
27	46	Loss of job by parent
28	46	Outstanding personal achievement
29	45	Change in parent's financial status
30	43	Accepted at college of choice
31	42	Being a senior in high school
32	41	Hospitalization of a sibling
33	38	Increased absence of parent from home
34	37	Brother or sister leaving home
35	34	Addition of third adult to family
36	31	Becoming a full-fledged member of a church
37	27	Decrease in arguments between parents
38	26	Decrease in arguments with parents
39	26	Mother or father beginning work
_____		Total score for circled items _____

SOURCE: *Pastorino, E. & Doyle-Portillo, S. (2009):* What Is Psychology?
2nd Ed. Belmont, CA: Thompson Higher Education.

SOURCES OF PERSONAL STRESS

This stress assessment is designed to complement the SRRS. Please complete that instrument before beginning this one. Adding the stressors you are experiencing at this time to those identified in the SRRS provides a more comprehensive assessment of your current stress level. Consider both the stressors you marked in the SRRS instrument as well as your current experiences right now as you discuss and practice the stress management principles presented in this chapter.

1. Identify the factors that produce the most stress for you right now. What is it that creates feelings of stress in your life?
2. Now give each of these entries a "stress rating," from 1 to 100, indicating the level of stress they are producing. Refer to the weightings used in the SRRS as a guide. A rating of 100, for example, might be associated with the death of a spouse or child, while a rating of 10 might be associated with an annoying "backseat driver" in your carpool.

Source of Stress	Rating
_____	_____
_____	_____
_____	_____
_____	_____
_____	_____
_____	_____
_____	_____

FLOURISHING SCALE

Researchers have identified several benefits of living a life characterized as "flourishing" (psychological well-being). Through this self-assessment you will better understand the extent to which the following eight attributes of flourishing characterize your current life experience. It is important to respond candidly to this self-diagnostic assessment.

Rating Scale

Below are eight statements with which you may agree or disagree. Using a scale of 1 (strongly disagree) to 7 (strongly agree), indicate your agreement with each item.

1 Strongly disagree
2 Disagree
3 Slightly disagree
4 Neither disagree nor agree or mixed
5 Slightly agree
6 Agree
7 Strongly agree

_____ 1. I lead a purposeful and meaningful life.

_____ 2. My social relationships are supportive and rewarding.

_____ 3. I am engaged and interested in my daily activities.

_____ 4. I actively contribute to the happiness and well-being of others.

_____ 5. I am competent and capable in the activities that are important to me.

_____ 6. I am a good person and live a good life.

_____ 7. I am optimistic about my future.

_____ 8. People respect me.

_____ **Total**

SOURCE: © *Used with permission of Ed Diener and Robert Biswas-Diener. In Diener, E., Wirtz, D., Tov, W., Kim-Prieto, C., Choi. D., Oishi, S., & Biswas-Diener, R. (2009). New measures of well-being: Flourishing and positive and negative feelings.* Social Indicators Research, *39, 247–266.*

SKILL *LEARNING*

Our goal in this chapter is to help you manage two personal challenges—one is a major inhibitor of effective management, and one is a key facilitator of effective management. The first part of the chapter highlights a common and serious problem for us all—experiencing negative stress. It is difficult to flourish in our activities when we are facing major stressors in our lives, such as overload, anxiety, conflict, tension in relationships, uncertainty, failure, and regret. We highlight ways in which stress can be minimized or eliminated. In the process, we highlight ways in which personal well-being can be fostered. We provide some guidelines for achieving extraordinary personal effectiveness by focusing on enhancements to well-being.

Managing Stress and Fostering Well-Being

Managing stress is a crucial skill in a competent manager's repertoire. Here is why: The American Psychological Association estimates that the problem of stress on the job siphons off more than $500 billion from the nation's economy. More than 50 percent of workers admit to being less productive at work because of stress, and the median number of days missed at work due to stress is 25—significantly above the six days per year missed due to illness or accident. Between 75 and 90 percent of all visits to primary care physicians are for stress-related complaints or disorders.

And things are getting worse. The percentage of workers who report feeling "highly stressed" has more than quadrupled in the past two decades and now exceeds 80 percent.

Stress is the single biggest factor in producing such a devastating and costly effect on workers, managers, and organizations. When we experience stress, it is difficult to pay attention to almost anything else.

Research on the physiological effects of stress shows widespread and devastating effects, including negative impact on the cardiovascular system, the respiratory system, the endocrine system, the gastro-intestinal tract, the female reproductive system, reproductive hormones, male reproductive functioning, immunodepression, neurological disorders, addictions, malignancy immune functions with HIV-1, dental pathology, pain, anxiety disorders, and even suicide (Hubbard & Workman, 2002). Almost no part of life or health is immune from the effects of stress.

As an illustration of the effects of job-related stress, consider the following true story reported in Baltimore, Maryland:

The stress of the job was getting to the ambulance attendant, not to mention the stress of troubles at home. Long shifts, recurring tragedies, and a dominating boss made his job seem like a boiling cauldron.

One night it all blew up.

He was riding in the back of the ambulance while his partner drove. Their first call was for a man whose arm had been mangled in a machine shop. His screaming and agony were horrifying, but the second call was worse. It was severe child abuse. As the attendant treated the youngster's bruised body and snapped bones, he thought of his own child at home and his anger escalated. In contrast to the first call, the child only whimpered but bridled at the slightest touch. He wanted to cradle the child in his arms, but he couldn't.

Immediately after dropping off the child at the emergency room, they received another call to assist a heart attack victim seen lying in a street. When they arrived, however, they found not a cardiac patient but a drunk. As they lifted the man into the ambulance, their frustration and anger came to a head. They decided to give this guy the ride of his life, a reminder that he was taking up valuable time and resources.

They sped down the road, vaulting over railroad tracks at high speed, and taking corners as fast as they could. The drunk wasn't strapped in tightly, so he was flung from side to side in the back. To the attendants, it was all a joke.

Suddenly, however, the old man began having a real heart attack. Neither attendant cared. Whatever discomfort he was experiencing, he deserved it. They didn't stop or slow down, and they didn't administer CPR. They simply watched the old man shutter and die. By the time they reached the hospital, they had their stories straight. Dead on arrival, they said. Nothing they could do.

The attendant, who must remain anonymous, talked about that night at a recent counseling session on "professional burnout"—a growing problem in high-stress jobs.

As this story graphically illustrates, when we face substantial stress in our lives, normal behavior and normal decision-making are frequently set aside, and we suffer debilitating effects (Blasco-Fontecilla, et al., 2012; Contrada & Baum, 2011; Ganster & Tosen, 2013; O'Neill & Rothbart, 2015; Staw, Sandelands, & Dutton, 1981). Consequently, we spend the first part of this chapter highlighting the major types of negative stress that we all encounter, and then we share ways to cope with and minimize negative stress as well as highlight ways in which personal well-being and resiliency can be enhanced.

We begin our discussion by presenting a framework for understanding stress and identifying the strategies to cope with it. This model explains the major types of stressors, the primary reactions to stress, and the reasons some people experience more negative reactions than others. Then we provide specific examples and behavioral guidelines for eliminating and reducing the negative effects of stress and enhancing psychological and social well-being and resilience.

Major Elements of Stress

One way to understand stress is to think of it as the product of a "force field" (Lewin, 1951). Kurt Lewin suggested that all individuals and organizations exist in an environment filled with reinforcing or opposing forces. These forces act to stimulate or inhibit the performance desired by the individual. As illustrated in Figure 2.1, a person's level of performance in an organization results from factors that may either complement or contradict one another. Certain forces drive

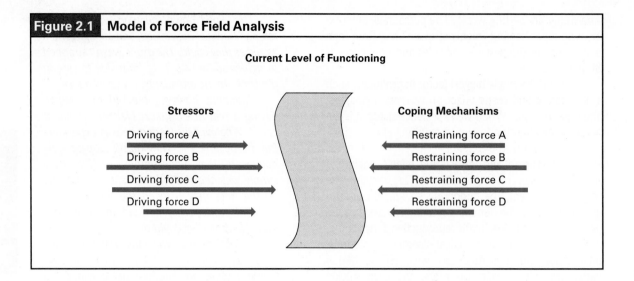

Figure 2.1 **Model of Force Field Analysis**

Current Level of Functioning

Stressors

Driving force A

Driving force B

Driving force C

Driving force D

Coping Mechanisms

Restraining force A

Restraining force B

Restraining force C

Restraining force D

or motivate changes in behavior, while other forces restrain or block those changes.

According to Lewin's theory, the forces affecting individuals are normally balanced in the force field. The strength of the driving forces is exactly matched by the strength of the restraining forces. (In the figure, longer arrows indicate stronger forces.) A person's performance changes when the forces become imbalanced. That is, if the driving forces become stronger than the restraining forces, or more numerous or enduring, behavioral change occurs. Conversely, if restraining forces become stronger or more numerous than driving forces, change occurs in the opposite direction, or else people become more and more resistant to change.

Think of stress as represented as driving forces in the model. That is, driving forces exert pressure on the individual to change present levels of performance physiologically, psychologically, and interpersonally. Unrestrained, those forces can lead to pathological results (e.g., anxiety, heart disease, depression, and mental breakdown).

However, most people have developed a certain amount of resiliency—represented by the restraining forces—to counter stressors and inhibit pathological results. These restraining forces include behavior patterns, psychological characteristics, and supportive social relationships. Strong restraining forces lead to low heart rates, good interpersonal relationships, emotional stability, and effective stress management. An absence of restraining forces leads to burnout.

Of course, stress produces positive as well as negative effects. In the absence of any stress, people feel completely bored and lack any inclination to act. Stress is needed to motivate action. However, we are discussing only negative, unproductive stressors in this chapter.

Even when high levels of stress are experienced, equilibrium can be restored quickly if there is sufficient resiliency. In the case of the ambulance attendant, for example, multiple stressors overpowered the available restraining forces, and burnout occurred.

Figure 2.2 identifies the major categories of **stressors** (driving forces) that managers experience as well as the major attributes of resiliency (restraining forces) that inhibit the negative effects of stress. Each of these forces is discussed in this chapter, so it will become clear how to identify stressors, how to eliminate them, how to develop more resiliency, and how to cope with stress on a temporary basis.

COPING WITH STRESS

Using a hierarchy of approaches has been found most effective in managing stress (Eliot, 2010; Kahn & Byosiere, 1992; Lehrer, 1996). First, the best way to manage stress is to eliminate or minimize stressors with **enactive strategies**. These create, or enact, a new environment for the individual that does not contain the stressors. The second most effective approach is for individuals to enhance their overall capacity to handle stress by increasing their personal resiliency. These are called **proactive strategies** and are designed to initiate action that resists the negative effects of stress. Finally, developing short-term techniques for coping with stressors is necessary when an immediate response is required. These are **reactive strategies**, and they are applied as on-the-spot remedies to temporarily reduce the effects of stress.

Individuals are better off if they can eliminate harmful stressors and the potentially negative effects

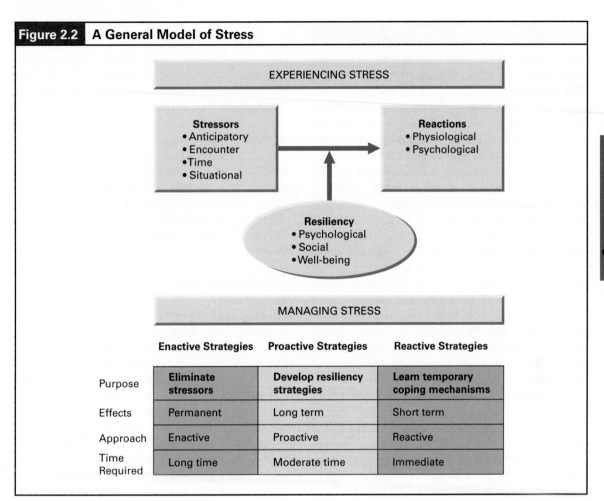

Figure 2.2 | **A General Model of Stress**

EXPERIENCING STRESS

Stressors
- Anticipatory
- Encounter
- Time
- Situational

Reactions
- Physiological
- Psychological

Resiliency
- Psychological
- Social
- Well-being

MANAGING STRESS

	Enactive Strategies	**Proactive Strategies**	**Reactive Strategies**
Purpose	Eliminate stressors	Develop resiliency strategies	Learn temporary coping mechanisms
Effects	Permanent	Long term	Short term
Approach	Enactive	Proactive	Reactive
Time Required	Long time	Moderate time	Immediate

of frequent, potent stress reactions. However, because most individuals do not have complete control over their environments or their circumstances, they can seldom eliminate all harmful stressors. Their next-best alternative, therefore, is to develop a greater capacity to withstand the negative effects of stress and to mobilize the energy generated by stressors. This is done by enhancing personal resiliency and well-being. Finally, on a temporary basis, individuals can respond to a negatively stressed state by using constructive strategies such as temporary relaxation techniques and contemplative practices. These reactive strategies can also foster resiliency and enhance well-being if used properly.

Unfortunately, most people reverse the order of these three coping strategies. They rely first on temporary reactive methods to cope with stress because these actions can be implemented immediately. But reactive strategies have to be repeated whenever stressors are encountered, because their effects are short-lived. Moreover, some common reactive strategies,

such as drinking, taking sleeping pills, or letting off steam through anger can become habit-forming and harmful themselves. It's important to employ longer-term strategies, because relying on repetitive reactive strategies can create a vicious or addictive cycle.

It takes more effort to develop proactive resiliency strategies and the effects are more long lasting, but resiliency strategies can take time to implement, so the payoff is usually not immediate. The best and most permanent strategies are those that eliminate negative stressors altogether. They require the longest time to implement, but because stress is abolished, the payoff is enduring (Stranks, 2013).

MyLab Management Watch it!
If your instructor has assigned this activity, go to www.pearson.com/mylab/management to complete the video exercise.

Managing Stressors

Table 2.1 lists the four main types of stressors illustrated in the story of the ambulance attendant. The first, **time stressors**, generally result from having too much to do in too little time. These are the most common and most pervasive sources of stress faced by managers in corporations (Eliot, 2010; Robinson & Godbey, 2010). As might be expected, significant relationships exist between the presence of time stressors and job dissatisfaction, tension, perceived threat, increased heart rate, high cholesterol levels, skin resistance, and other factors (Contrada & Baum, 2011).

As mentioned in Chapter 1, time stressors are experienced differently in different national cultures (Trompenaars, 2011; Trompenaars & Hampden-Turner, 1998), so some cultures, such as those in Australia, Brazil, India, Ireland, the Philippines, and the United States, experience more time stress because of their emphasis on a short time horizon. In cultures with a longer time horizon (e.g., Austria, Czech Republic, Hong Kong, Portugal, and Sweden), the immediacy of time demands is less prevalent.

Encounter stressors are those that result from interpersonal interactions. Most people have experienced the debilitating effects of a quarrel with a friend, roommate, or spouse; of trying to work with an employee or supervisor with whom there has been an interpersonal conflict; or of trying to accomplish a task in a group divided by lack of trust.

Each of these stressors results from some kind of conflictual interpersonal encounter. Our own research has revealed that encounter stressors in organizations have significant negative effects on productivity and satisfaction (Bright, Cameron, & Caza, 2006; Cameron, Bright, & Caza, 2004; Cameron, et al., 2011), and encounter stressors have been found by other researchers to be at the very heart of most organizational dysfunction (Pfeffer & Sutton, 2006). Differences have also been discovered among national cultures with regard to encounter stressors (Trompenaars & Hampden-Turner, 2004) in that *egalitarian* cultures that emphasize interpersonal relationships as a way to accomplish work (e.g., Finland, Ireland, Norway, and the United States) and *affectivity* cultures that emphasize the public display of emotions (e.g., Iran and Mexico rather than China and Japan) have more encounter stress in the workplace.

The third category of stressors, **situational stressors**, arises from the environment in which a person lives or from an individual's circumstances. One of the most common forms of situational stress is unfavorable working conditions. For the ambulance attendant, these included continual crises, long hours, and isolation from colleagues.

One of the well-researched links between situational stressors and negative consequences involves rapid change, particularly the effects of changes in life events (Blasco-Fontecilla, et al., 2012; Holmes & Rahe, 1970). The Social Readjustment Rating Scale tracks the number of changes individuals have experienced over the past 12 months. Since some life-event changes are more stressful than others, a scaling method is used to assign weights to each life event. Hobson and colleagues (1998) revised the SRRS so that the weightings of individual items have been updated to match the modern environment, and we included the revised instrument in the Assessment section of this chapter. More than 5,000 studies have been published just since 1995 among a variety of cultures, age groups, and occupations using this SRRS instrument (Goldberger & Breznitz, 2010). (You will note that two different versions of the SRRS are reproduced in the Assessment section—one for adults, and one for nonadults. You should have completed the appropriate version(s) of the instrument in the Assessment section.)

Statistical relationships between the amount of life-event change and physical illness and injury have been found consistently among a wide variety of individuals. High scores are strongly associated with illness and/or injury, whereas people with low scores are much less

Table 2.1	Four Key Sources of Stress

Time Stressors

- Work overload
- Lack of control

Encounter Stressors

- Role conflicts
- Issue conflicts
- Action conflicts

Situational Stressors

- Unfavorable working conditions
- Rapid change

Anticipatory Stressors

- Unpleasant expectations
- Fear

likely to experience illness or injury. For example, in the general population, a score of 150 points or below results in a probability of less than 37 percent that the person will suffer a serious illness or injury in the next year, but the probability increases to about 50 percent with scores of 150–300. Those who score over 300 on the SRRS have an 80 percent chance of serious illness or injury (Blasco-Fontecilla, et al., 2012; Holmes & Rahe, 1967; Kobasa, 1979; Miller & Rasmussen, 2010; Scully, Tosi, & Banning, 2000).

Several studies have been conducted using college and high school athletes to determine if life-event change is related to injury as well as to illness. One study found that college athletes with the lowest scores on the SRRS had a rate of injury (causing them to miss three or more practices) of 35 percent. Those with medium scores had an injury rate of 44 percent, and those with high scores were injured at a rate of 72 percent. Another study showed an athlete injury rate five times as great for high scorers on the SRRS as for low scorers. Still another study found a significant increase in minor physiological symptoms such as headache, nausea, fever, backache, eyestrain, and so forth among high scorers on the SRRS (Andersen & Williams, 1999; Bramwell, et al., 1975; Coddington & Troxell, 1980; Cordes and Dougherty, 1993; Scully, Tosi, & Banning, 2000).

We must point out, of course, that scoring high on the SRRS does not necessarily guarantee that a person is going to become ill or be injured. A variety of coping skills and personal characteristics may counteract those tendencies. The point is that situational stressors are important factors to consider in learning to manage stress skillfully.

Anticipatory stressors, the fourth category, include potentially disagreeable events that threaten to occur—unpleasant things that have not yet happened, but might happen. Stress results from the anticipation or fear of the event. In the case of the ambulance attendant, the constant threat of anticipating having to witness more human suffering or death served as an anticipatory stressor. Anticipatory stressors need not be highly unpleasant or severe to produce stress. Investigators have induced high levels of stress by telling individuals that they would experience a loud noise or a mild shock or that someone else might become uncomfortable because of their actions (Milgram, 1963). Fear of failure or fear of embarrassment in front of peers is a common anticipatory stressor. Anxieties about losing a job or not being accepted or liked by colleagues have been identified as common stress producers as well.

Table 2.2	Management Strategies for Eliminating Stressors	
Type of Stressor	**Elimination Strategy**
Time	Effective time management
	Efficient time management
Encounter	Building community
	Contributing
	Emotional and social intelligence
Situational	Work redesign
Anticipatory	Goal setting
	Small wins

Eliminating Stressors

Because eliminating **stressors** is a permanent stress reduction strategy, it is by far the most desirable. Although it is impossible, and even undesirable, for individuals to eliminate all the stressors they encounter, they can effectively eliminate those that are harmful. Table 2.2 outlines several ways to eliminate each of the four types of stressors.

ELIMINATING TIME STRESSORS THROUGH TIME MANAGEMENT

As pointed out earlier, time is usually the greatest source of stress for managers. With a proliferation of books about time management, organizers, consultants, efficiency enhancers, and technological time-savers, you'd expect most of us to be pretty good at managing our time. We certainly have all the gadgets and advice we can use. The trouble is, most of us are getting worse. Just look around you. Who do you know that is a terrific time manager, who isn't overloaded, or who doesn't complain about being stressed because of time?

It's no surprise that time stress is escalating because of the rapidity of change and the overwhelming amounts of information that people encounter in the twenty-first century. In one study, two-thirds of the respondents indicated a desire to put more emphasis on "having free time" (Davidson, 1995). Time stress is an almost universal complaint of practicing managers who face between 237 and 1,073 separate incidents in a day.

Two sets of skills are important for effectively managing time and for eliminating time stressors. One set focuses on *efficiently* using time each day. The other set focuses on *effectively* using time over the long term. Because the effectiveness approach to time management serves as the foundation for the efficiency approach, we explain it first. Then we review some techniques for achieving efficiency in time use.

Effective Time Management

Almost everyone suffers now and then from a pervasive feeling of time stress. Somehow, no matter how much time is available, it seems to get filled up and squeezed out. Currently, the most commonly prescribed solutions for attacking problems of time stress are to use calendars and planners, generate to-do lists, and learn to say no. Almost all of us have tried such tactics but continue to experience enormous time stress. This is not to say that calendars, lists, and saying no are not useful. They are examples, however, of an efficiency approach to time management rather than an effectiveness approach. In eliminating time stressors, efficiency without effectiveness is fruitless.

Managing time with an effectiveness approach means that (1) we spend our time on important matters, not just urgent matters; (2) we are able to distinguish clearly between what is important and what is merely urgent; (3) results, rather than methods, are the objectives; and (4) we have a reason not to feel guilty when we must say no.

A number of time management experts have pointed out the usefulness of a "time management matrix" in which activities are categorized in terms of their relative importance and urgency (Covey, 1989; Lakein, 1989). *Important* activities are those that produce a desired result. They accomplish a valued end, or they achieve a meaningful purpose. *Urgent* activities are those that demand immediate attention. They are associated with a need expressed by someone else, or they relate to an uncomfortable problem or situation that requires a solution as soon as possible. Figure 2.3 outlines this matrix and provides examples of types of activities that fit in each quadrant.

Activities such as handling employee crises or customer complaints are both urgent and important (Cell 1). A ringing telephone or the arrival of emails, texts, or unscheduled interruptions might be examples of urgent but potentially unimportant activities (Cell 2). Important but nonurgent activities include developmental opportunities, innovating, planning, and so on (Cell 3). Unimportant and nonurgent activities are escapes and routines that people may pursue but that produce little valuable payoff: for example, small talk, daydreaming, shuffling paper, or arguing (Cell 4).

Activities in the Important/Urgent quadrant (Cell 1) usually dominate our lives. The trouble is, these activities require us to merely react. They are usually controlled by someone else, and they may or may not lead to a result we want to achieve.

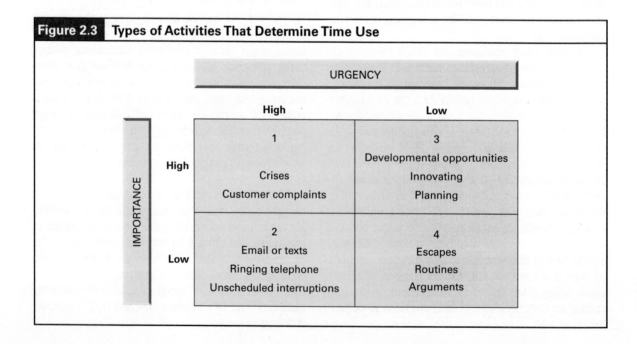

Figure 2.3   Types of Activities That Determine Time Use

	URGENCY	
	High	**Low**
IMPORTANCE High	1 Crises Customer complaints	3 Developmental opportunities Innovating Planning
IMPORTANCE Low	2 Email or texts Ringing telephone Unscheduled interruptions	4 Escapes Routines Arguments

The problem is even worse in the Unimportant/Urgent quadrant (Cell 2). Demands by others that serve only as deflections or interruptions to our own agenda only escalate a sense of time stress. Because these demands may not achieve results that are meaningful, purposeful, and important, feelings of overload and loss of control can be guaranteed. When such time stressors are experienced over an extended period of time, we often try to escape into Unimportant/Nonurgent activities (Cell 4) to relieve the stress. We put everything on hold to escape, but, by doing so, often exacerbate our time stress.

A more effective alternative is to focus on activities in the Important/Nonurgent quadrant (Cell 3). Activities that are Important/Nonurgent might be labeled "opportunities" instead of "problems." They are oriented toward accomplishing high-priority results. By focusing on these activities you may prevent problems from occurring rather than just being forced to react to them. Preparation, preventive maintenance, planning, personal development, providing support to another person, and organizing are all "non-have-to" activities that are crucial for long-term success. Because they are not urgent, however, they often get driven out of our schedules. Important/Nonurgent activities should be the top priority on the time management agenda. By ensuring that these kinds of activities get priority, you can reduce the number of urgent problems you encounter. Time stressors can be eliminated.

One of the most difficult, yet crucially important, decisions you must make in managing time effectively is determining what is important to you and what is urgent. There are no rules for dividing all activities, demands, or opportunities into those neat categories. Problems don't come with an "Important/Nonurgent" tag attached. In fact, every problem or time demand is important to someone. But if you let others determine what is and is not important, you will never effectively manage your time.

Barry Sullivan, former CEO at First Chicago, for example, reorganized the way he managed his time. Instead of leaving his appointments calendar in the control of his secretary, he personally determined what activities he wanted to accomplish, then he allocated specific blocks of time to work on those activities. Only then did he make his calendar available to his secretary to schedule other appointments.

Jan Timmer, former CEO of Philips Electronics, assigned an auditor to keep track of the way he used his time. He reported quarterly to the entire company the percent of his time he spent on key company objectives, ensuring that important priorities got the greatest amount of his time.

Priorities and Core Values

The question remains, however: How can we make certain that we focus on activities that are important, not just urgent? To help you clarify your important priorities, consider the following questions:

❑ What do I stand for? What am I willing to die (or live) for?

❑ What do I care passionately about?

❑ What legacy would I like to leave? What do I want to be remembered for?

❑ What do I want to have accomplished 20 years from now?

❑ What are my signature character strengths, and how do I want to demonstrate them?

Answering these questions can help you create a personal principles statement. This is an articulation of the criteria you use for evaluating what is important in your life. Other people generally help determine what is urgent. But judging importance must be done in relation to a set of personal principles and values. Table 2.3 presents two different types of personal principles statements. They are provided as examples of the kinds of principles statements you can write for yourself.

Basing time management on core principles that serve to determine the importance of activities is also the key to being able to say no without feeling guilty. When you have decided what it is that you care about passionately, what it is you most want to accomplish, and what legacy you want to leave, you can more easily say no to activities that aren't congruent with those principles. Effectiveness in time management, then, means that you accomplish what you *want* to accomplish with your time. *How* you achieve those accomplishments relates to efficiency of time use, to which we now turn.

Efficient Time Management

In addition to approaching time management from the point of view of effectiveness (i.e., aligning time use with core personal principles), it is also important to adopt an efficiency point of view (i.e., accomplishing more by reducing wasted time). Many techniques are available to help managers more efficiently utilize the time they have each day.

Table 2.3	Examples of Personal Principles Statements

From Mahatma Gandhi

Let then our first act every morning be to make the following resolve for the day:

- I shall not fear anyone on Earth.

- I shall fear only God.

- I shall not bear ill will toward anyone.

- I shall not submit to injustice from anyone.

- I shall conquer untruth by truth.

- And in resisting untruth I shall put up with all suffering.

From William Rolfe Kerr

Prime Personal and Professional Principles:

- Succeed at home first.

- Seek and merit Divine help.

- Never compromise with honesty.

- Remember the people involved.

- Plan tomorrow today.

- Develop one new proficiency a year.

- Attain visibility by productivity.

- Hustle while I wait.

- Facilitate the success of my colleagues.

- Pursue excellence in all my endeavors.

- Be sincere and gentle yet decisive.

- Be a creative and innovative person.

- Don't fear mistakes.

- Concentrate all abilities on the task at hand.

- Obtain the counsel of others.

- Defend those who are absent.

- Listen twice as much as I speak.

- Be orderly in work and person.

- Maintain a positive attitude and sense of humor.

One way to enhance efficient time use is to be alert to your own tendencies to use time inefficiently. The list of propositions in Table 2.4 shows general patterns of behavior for most individuals in their use of time. In many situations, these tendencies may represent appropriate responses. In others, they may get in the way of efficient time management and increase time stressors unless individuals are aware of them and their possible consequences.

To help you identify your own time management practices and to help you determine the efficiency with which you use your time, we included in the Assessment section an instrument to help you diagnose your time management competency: the Time Management Survey. The principles in the survey have all been derived from research on time management, and the scoring information will show you how well you manage your time compared to others. The rules set forth below correspond to the item numbers in the assessment survey.

Of course, no individual can or should implement all of these time management techniques at once. It would be overwhelming. Therefore, it is best to select just a few of these techniques that will lead to the most improvement in your use of time. Saving just 10 percent more time or using an extra 30 minutes a day more wisely can produce astounding results over months and years, in addition to reducing your time stress.

Rule 1 Read selectively. Most reading should be done the way you read a newspaper; that is, skim most of it, but stop to read what seems most important. If you underline or highlight what you find important, you can review it quickly when you need to.

Rule 2 Make a list of things to accomplish today. Focus on what you want to achieve, not just on what you want to do.

Rule 3 Have a place for everything, and keep everything in its place. Letting things get out of place robs you of time in two ways: You need more time to find something when you need it, and you are tempted to interrupt the task you are doing to do something else.

Rule 4 Prioritize your tasks. Each day you should focus first on important tasks, and then deal with urgent tasks.

Rule 5 Do one important thing at a time but several trivial things simultaneously. You can accomplish a lot by doing more than one thing at a time when tasks are routine, trivial, or require little thought.

Rule 6 Make a list of some 5- or 10-minute discretionary tasks. This helps you make good use of the small bits of time almost everyone has during his or her day (waiting for something to begin, between meetings or events, talking on the telephone, etc.).

Table 2.4	Typical Patterns of Time Use

- We do what we like to do before we do what we don't like to do.
- We do the things we know how to do before the things we do not know how to do.
- We do the things that are easiest before things that are difficult.
- We do things that require a little time before things that require a lot of time.
- We do things for which the resources are available.
- We do things that are scheduled (e.g., meetings) before nonscheduled things.
- We sometimes do things that are planned before things that are unplanned.
- We respond to demands from others before demands from ourselves.
- We do things that are urgent before things that are important.
- We readily respond to crises and to emergencies.
- We do interesting things before uninteresting things.
- We do things that advance our personal objectives or that are politically expedient.
- We wait until a deadline before we really get moving.
- We do things that provide the most immediate closure.
- We respond on the basis of who wants it.
- We respond on the basis of the consequences to us of doing or not doing something.
- We tackle small jobs before large jobs.
- We work on things in the order of arrival.
- We work on the basis of the squeaky-wheel principle (the squeaky wheel gets the grease).
- We work on the basis of consequences to the group.

LEARNING

Rule 7 Divide up large projects. This helps you avoid feeling overwhelmed by large, important, urgent tasks.

Rule 8 Determine the critical 20 percent of your tasks. Pareto's law states that only 20 percent of your time produces 80 percent of your results.

Rule 9 Save your best time for important matters. Do routine work when your energy level is low, your mind is not sharp, or you aren't on top of things. Reserve your high-energy time for accomplishing the most important and urgent tasks.

Rule 10 Reserve some time during the day when others don't have access to you. Use this time to accomplish Important/Nonurgent tasks, or spend it just thinking.

Rule 11 Don't procrastinate. If you do certain tasks promptly, they will require less time and effort than if you put them off.

Rule 12 Keep track of your time. This is one of the best time management strategies. Write down how you use your time each hour over a sustained period.

Rule 13 Set deadlines. Work always expands to fill the time available, so if you don't specify a termination time, tasks tend to continue longer than they need to.

Rule 14 Do something productive while waiting. Try reading, planning, preparing, rehearsing, reviewing, outlining, or memorizing.

Rule 15 Do busywork at only one set time during the day. Reserve your best time for nontrivial tasks.

Rule 16 Reach closure on at least one thing every day. Finishing a task, even a small one, produces a sense of relief and releases stress.

Rule 17 Schedule some personal time. You need some time when no interruptions will occur, when you can get off the "fast track" for a while and be alone.

Rule 18 Allow yourself to worry only at a specified time and avoid dwelling on a worrisome issue at other times.

Rule 19   Write down long-term objectives. You can be efficient and organized but still accomplish nothing unless you have a clear direction in mind.

Rule 20   Be on the alert for ways to improve your management of time. Read a list of time management hints periodically.

Efficient Time Management for Managers

The following list of rules applies to managers at work. The first nine rules deal with conducting meetings, since managers report that approximately 50 to 70 percent of their time is spent in meetings (Dockweiller, 2018; Mintzberg, 1973; Panko, 1992).

Rule 1   Hold routine meetings at the end of the day. Energy and creativity levels are highest early in the day and shouldn't be wasted on trivial matters. Furthermore, an automatic deadline—quitting time—will set a time limit on the meeting.

Rule 2   Hold short meetings standing up. This guarantees that meetings will be kept short.

Rule 3   Set a time limit. Identify when the meeting will end at the beginning of every meeting and appointment.

Rule 4   Cancel meetings once in a while. Meetings should be held only if they can achieve a specific objective.

Rules 5, 6, and 7   Have agendas, stick to them, and keep track of time. Keep track of assignments so that they are not forgotten, so that that follow-up and accountability occur, and so that everyone is clear about expectations.

Rule 8   Start meetings on time. Starting on time rather than waiting for laggards rewards people who are prompt.

Rule 9   Prepare minutes of the meeting and follow up. Commitments and expectations made public through minutes are more likely to be fulfilled.

Rule 10   Insist that subordinates suggest solutions to problems. This eliminates the tendency toward upward delegation, or for subordinates to pass along their problems to you, and it allows you to choose among subordinates' alternatives rather than generate your own.

Rule 11   Meet visitors in the doorway. It is easier to keep a meeting short if you are standing in the doorway rather than sitting in your office.

Rule 12   Go to subordinates' offices for brief meetings if it is practical. This helps you control the length of a meeting by being free to leave when you choose.

Rule 13   Don't overschedule the day. You should stay in control of at least some of your time each workday.

Rule 14   Have someone else answer telephone calls and scan email, or set your computer filters so that you do not receive irrelevant messages.

Rule 15   Have a place to work uninterrupted. This helps guarantee that when a deadline is near, you can concentrate on your task without disruption.

Rule 16   Do something definite with every piece of paperwork handled. Sometimes this means throwing it away.

Rule 17   Keep your workspace clean. This minimizes distractions and reduces the time it takes to find things.

Rules 18, 19, and 20   Delegate work, identify the amount of initiative recipients should take with the tasks they are assigned, and give others credit for their successes. These rules all relate to effective delegation, a key time management technique. These last three rules are also discussed in the Empowering and Engaging Others chapter in this text.

Remember that these techniques for managing time are a means to an end, not the end itself. If trying to implement techniques creates more, rather than less, stress, they should not be applied. However, research has indicated that managers who use these kinds of techniques have better control of their time, accomplish more, have better relations with subordinates, and eliminate many of the time stressors most managers ordinarily encounter (Allen & Fallows, 2015; Robinson & Godbey, 2010; Sitzmann & Johnson, 2012). Saving just 30 minutes a day amounts to one full year of extra free time during your working lifetime. That's 8,760 hours of free time! You will find that as you select a few of these hints to apply in your own life, the efficiency of your time use will improve and your time stress will decrease.

ELIMINATING ENCOUNTER STRESSORS THROUGH COMMUNITY, CONTRIBUTION, AND EMOTIONAL INTELLIGENCE

Dissatisfying relationships with others, particularly with a direct manager or supervisor, are prime causes of job stress among workers. (This topic is discussed in more depth in Chapter 4.) Encounter stressors result directly from abrasive, conflictual, nonfulfilling relationships. Even when work is going smoothly, if encounter stress is present, everything else can seem wrong. It is difficult to maintain positive energy when you are at odds with someone, when you feel offended, or when feelings of acceptance and amiability aren't typical of your important relationships at work.

Community

One important factor that helps eliminate encounter stress is a closely knit group or community. When people feel a part of a group, or accepted by someone else, stress is relieved. For example, 35 years ago Dr. Stewart Wolf found that in the town of Roseto, Pennsylvania, residents were completely free from heart disease and other stress-related illnesses. He suspected that their protection sprang from the town's uncommon social cohesion and stability. The town's population consisted entirely of descendants of Italians who had moved there 100 years earlier from Roseto, Italy. Few married outside the community, the firstborn was always named after a grandparent, conspicuous consumption and displays of superiority were avoided, and social support among community members was a way of life.

Wolf predicted that residents would begin to display the same level of stress-related illnesses as the rest of the country if the modern world intruded. It did, and they did. Residents in Roseto purchased Cadillacs and ranch-style homes, produced mixed marriages, introduced new names, and engaged in competition with one another, and their rate of coronary disease increased until it was the same as any other town's (Farnham, 1991). They had ceased to be a cohesive, collaborative clan and instead had become a community of selfishness and exclusivity. Self-centeredness, it was discovered, is dangerous to one's health.

A similar discovery was made when military practices in the Vietnam War and the Persian Gulf War were compared. In Vietnam, teams of soldiers did not stay together and did not form strong bonds. The constant injection of new personnel into squadrons and the constant transfer of soldiers from one location to another made soldiers feel isolated, without loyalty, and vulnerable to stress-related illnesses. In the Persian Gulf, by contrast, soldiers were kept in the same unit throughout the campaign, were brought home together, and were given lots of time to debrief together after the battle. Using a closely knit group to provide interpretation of, and social support for, behavior was found to be the most powerful deterrent to post-battle trauma. According to David Marlowe, former chief of the department of military psychiatry at Walter Reed

Army Institute of Research, "Squad members are encouraged to use travel time en route home from a war zone to talk about their battlefield experience. It helps them detoxify. That's why we brought them back in groups from Desert Storm. Epistemologically, we know it works" (Farnham, 1991).

Developing close relationships with others is a powerful deterrent to encounter stress. One way of developing this kind of relationship is by applying a concept described by Stephen Covey (1989)—an emotional bank account. Covey used this metaphor to describe the trust or feeling of security that one person develops for another. The more "deposits" made in an emotional bank account, the stronger and more resilient the relationship becomes. Conversely, too many "withdrawals" from the account weaken relationships by destroying trust, security, and confidence.

"Deposits" are made through treating people with kindness, courtesy, honesty, and consistency. The emotional bank account grows when people feel they are receiving love, respect, and caring. "Withdrawals" are made by not keeping promises, not listening, not clarifying expectations, showing irritation, crossing the "sensitive line," or not allowing choice. Because disrespect and autocratic rule devalue people and destroy a sense of self-worth, relationships are ruined because the bank account becomes overdrawn.

The more interactions between people, the more deposits must be made in the emotional bank account. When you see an old friend after years of absence, you can often pick up right where you left off, because the emotional bank account has not been touched. But when you interact with someone frequently, the relationship is constantly fed or depleted. Cues from everyday interactions are interpreted as either deposits or withdrawals. When the emotional account is well stocked, mistakes, disappointments, and minor abrasions are easily forgiven and ignored. But when no reserve exists, those incidents may become creators of distrust, contention, and stress.

One of the most important ways to make deposits into the emotional bank account is by making contributions to the well-being of others. This principle can be illustrated by studies conducted at the University of Michigan.

Contribution

In one study, Crocker and Park (2004) followed entering freshmen at the university for a year. At the beginning of the first semester, students were asked to identify their goals for the year. Students identified goals that could be categorized into two types. Most people possess both kinds of goals, but one or the other type tends to predominate. One type of goal is called an achievement goal. This is an emphasis on achieving desired outcomes, obtaining rewards, accomplishing something that brings self-satisfaction, enhancing self-esteem, or creating a positive self-image in the eyes of others (e.g., getting good grades, making the team, and being popular).

The other type of goal focused on providing a benefit to others or on making a contribution. This type of goal centers on what individuals can give compared to what they can get (assisting others, helping to make something better, fostering improvement in something). Contribution goals are motivated more by benevolence than by a desire for acquisition. The researchers found that goals focused on contributing to others produced a growth orientation in individuals over time, whereas self-interest goals produced a proving orientation over time (Crocker, et al., 2006).

These students were monitored for one academic year in terms of how well they got along with roommates, how many times they missed class, how many minor physiological symptoms occurred (e.g., headache, nausea, cramps), how many leadership positions they attained, their grade point averages, and so forth. On every outcome, contribution goals led to higher performance than achievement goals. The study found that contribution goals led to significantly more learning and development; higher levels of interpersonal trust; more supportive relationships; and less stress, depression, and loneliness than did achievement or self-interest goals (Crocker, et al., 2006).

These findings are reinforced by a study by Brown and colleagues (2003, 2006) of patients being treated with kidney dialysis machines. The study focused on two different factors. One was the extent to which the patients were receiving love, support, and encouragement from others (such as family members). The other was the extent to which the patients were providing love, support, and encouragement to others. Even though they were immobile and could not physically respond, patients enjoyed better health when they felt they were contributing to the well-being of others through support, love, and encouragement compared to when they were receiving these things. Contribution-focused goals produced significantly more mental, emotional, and physiological benefits than achievement-focused goals (also see Koopman, Lanaj, & Scott, 2015).

In studies of the language that people use to describe their work experiences, Pennebaker (2002) found that a predominance of the word *we* was associated with less stress, more meaningful relationships, and higher levels of satisfaction in work than the predominance of

the word *I*. In other words, by shifting our focus from achievement to contribution we can combat and overcome encounter stress. We make deposits in the emotional bank account of relationships when we focus on offering contributions to others' well-being rather than focusing mainly on getting what we want.

Social and Emotional Intelligence

As we mentioned in Chapter 1, *emotional intelligence* has become the catchall phrase that incorporates multiple intelligences—for example, practical intelligence, abstract intelligence, moral intelligence, interpersonal intelligence, spiritual intelligence, mechanical intelligence, and social intelligence (Gardner, 1993; Mayer, Roberts, & Barsade, 2008; Sternberg, 1997). Emotional intelligence consists of a recognition and control of one's own emotions (personal) and the recognition and appropriate response to the behaviors and responses of others (social). Not surprisingly, emotional and social intelligence represent important skills in helping people manage the stresses that arise from interpersonal encounters (Joseph & Newman, 2010; O'Boyle, et al., 2011).

The social aspect of emotional intelligence refers to the ability to effectively manage relationships with other people. It consists of four main dimensions:

1. An accurate perception of others' emotional and behavioral responses.
2. The ability to cognitively and emotionally understand and relate to others' responses.
3. Social knowledge, or an awareness of what is appropriate social behavior.
4. Social problem-solving, or the ability to manage interpersonal difficulties.

The form of intelligence with which most people are familiar is cognitive intelligence, also known as IQ. By and large, cognitive intelligence is beyond our control, especially after the first few years of life. It is a product of the gifts with which we were born or our genetic code. Above a certain threshold level, the correlation between IQ and success in life (e.g., achieving high occupational positions, accumulated wealth, luminary awards, satisfaction with life, performance ratings by peers and superiors) is essentially zero. Very smart people have no greater likelihood of achieving success in life or of achieving personal happiness than people with low IQ scores (Goleman, 1998; Spencer & Spencer, 1993; Sternberg, 1997). On the other hand, social and emotional intelligence have strong positive correlations to success in life and to reduced encounter stress (Goleman, 1994; Joseph & Newman, 2010; O'Boyle, et al., 2011).

For example, in a study at Stanford University, four-year-old children were involved in activities that tested aspects of their emotional intelligence. In one study, a marshmallow was placed in front of them, and they were given two choices: eat it now, or wait until the adult supervisor returned from running an errand, then the child would get two marshmallows. A follow-up study with these same children 14 years later, upon graduation from high school, found that students who demonstrated more emotional intelligence (i.e., controlled their own desires and postponed gratification in the marshmallow task) were less likely to fall apart under stress, became less irritated and less stressed by interpersonally abrasive people, were more likely to accomplish their goals, and scored an average of 210 points higher on the SAT college entrance exam (Shoda, Mischel, & Peake, 1990). The IQ scores of the students did not differ significantly, but the emotional intelligence scores were considerably different. In findings that were consistent with other studies, emotional and social intelligence predicted success in life for these students as well as the ability to handle encounter stress.

In another study, when managers were able to accurately identify others' emotions and respond to them, they were found to be more successful in their personal lives as well as in their work lives (Lusch & Serpkenci, 1990; Rosenthal, 1977), and were evaluated as the most desired and competent managers (Pilling & Eroglu, 1994).

So how does one develop social and emotional intelligence? The answer is neither simple nor simplistic. Each chapter in this book contains some suggested answers to this question. The skills we help you develop are among the most important competencies that comprise social and emotional intelligence. In other words, by improving your abilities in the management skills covered in this book—for example self-awareness, problem-solving, supportive communication, motivating self and others, managing conflict, empowering others, team-building, and so on—your social and emotional competence scores will increase.

This is important, because a national survey of workers found that employees who rated their manager as supportive and interpersonally competent had lower rates of burnout, lower stress levels, lower incidence of stress-related illnesses, higher productivity, more loyalty to their organizations, and more efficiency in work than employees with nonsupportive and interpersonally incompetent managers (Cote & Miners, 2006; NNL, 1992). The impact of managers on their employees is profound and In his book, *Dying for a Paycheck* (2018), Jeff Pfeffer reports voluminous data indicating that the incidence of chronic illness, workplace violence, debilitating anxiety, life expectancy, and suicide rates all can be traced directly to the supportiveness of managers and the relationships they form with their employees.

ELIMINATING SITUATIONAL STRESSORS THROUGH WORK REDESIGN

For decades, researchers in the area of occupational health have examined the relationship between job strain and stress-related behavioral, psychological, and physiological outcomes.

A review of this research suggests that the single most important contributor to stress that arises from the job is lack of freedom (Greenberger & Stasser, 1991; Lin, et al., 2013; Wheatley, 2017). One study found that lack of autonomy at work was a stronger predictor of coronary heart disease than any other factor (Mammot, et al., 1997). In a study of administrators, engineers, and scientists at the Goddard Space Flight Center, researchers found that individuals provided with more discretion in making decisions about assigned tasks experienced fewer time stressors (e.g., role overload), situational stressors (e.g., role ambiguity), encounter stressors (e.g., interpersonal conflict), and anticipatory stressors (e.g., job-related threats). Individuals without discretion and participation experienced significantly more stress.

In response to these dynamics, Hackman and colleagues (1975) proposed a model of job redesign that has proved effective in reducing stress and in increasing satisfaction and productivity. A detailed discussion of this job redesign model is provided in Chapter 5. The model identifies ways to design work so that people flourish and avoid situational stress. It consists of five factors: **skill variety** (the opportunity to use multiple skills in performing work), **task identity** (the opportunity to complete a whole task), **task significance** (the opportunity to see the impact of the work being performed), **autonomy** (the opportunity to choose how and when the work will be done), and **feedback** (the opportunity to receive information on the success of task accomplishment). That is, to eliminate situational stressors at work, foster these five factors in these ways:

Combine Tasks When individuals are able to work on a whole project and perform a variety of related tasks (e.g., programming all components of a computer software package) rather than being restricted to working on a single repetitive task or subcomponent of a larger task, they are more satisfied and committed.

Form Identifiable Work Units Building on the first step, when teams of individuals performing related tasks are formed and can decide how to complete the work, stress decreases dramatically (for example, assembling an entire component from start to finish, rather than doing separate tasks as on an assembly line). Workers learn one another's jobs, rotate assignments, and experience a sense of completion in their work.

Establish Customer Relationships One of the most enjoyable parts of a job is seeing the fruits of one's labor. In most organizations, people who do the work are not given a chance to interact with customers or end users, but they perform much better if they do so (Oldham, 2012).

Increase Decision-Making Authority Being able to influence the what, when, and how of work increases an individual's feelings of control. Cameron, Freeman, and Mishra (1991) found a significant decrease in experienced stress in firms that were downsizing when workers were given authority to make decisions about how and when to do the extra work required of them.

Open Feedback Channels A major source of stress is not knowing what is expected and how task performance is being evaluated. As managers communicate their expectations more clearly and give timely and accurate feedback, subordinates' satisfaction and performance improve and stress decreases. Providing more information to people on how they are doing almost always reduces stress.

Evidence that these practices are effective has been reported in several studies that found productivity increases, less absenteeism, fewer errors, and lower levels of stresses experienced by managers as a result of job redesign (Hackman & Oldham, 1980; Oldham, 2012; Parker, 2014; Singh, 1998).

ELIMINATING ANTICIPATORY STRESSORS THROUGH PRIORITIZING, GOAL SETTING, AND SMALL WINS

Almost everyone experiences anticipatory stressors. We have all been worried about a presentation, an upcoming exam, an important interview, or what the future will bring. This kind of stress can be good for us by increasing our alertness and preparation. But sometimes it can be almost paralyzing. How can we eliminate or minimize the negative effects of anticipatory stress? Two simple practices can help.

Goal Setting Establishing a short-term goal can help eliminate or minimize anticipatory stressors by focusing attention on an immediate action or accomplishment instead of on an uncertain future. To be effective, certain action steps are needed if short-term goals are to lead to achievement and the elimination of stress (Locke & Latham, 2013). Figure 2.4 outlines the four-step process associated with successful short-term goal setting.

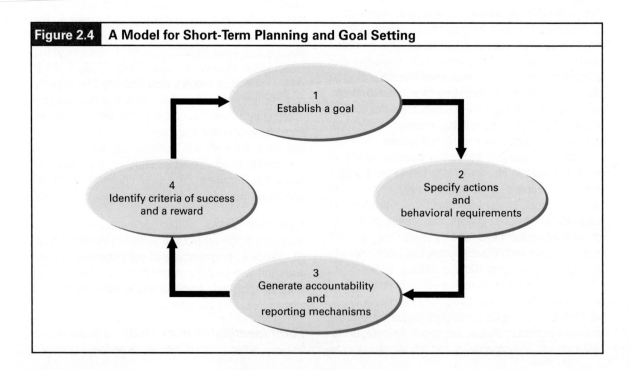

Figure 2.4 **A Model for Short-Term Planning and Goal Setting**

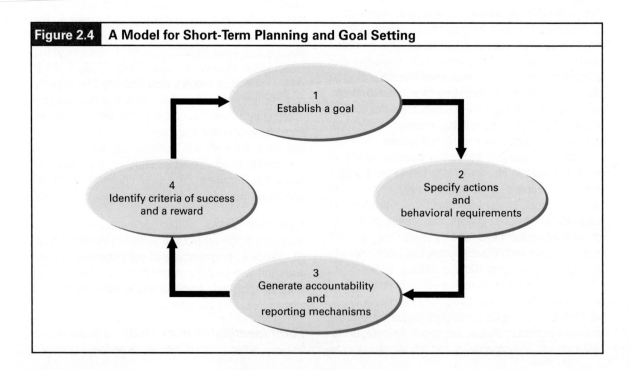

1
Establish a goal

2
Specify actions
and
behavioral requirements

3
Generate accountability
and
reporting mechanisms

4
Identify criteria of success
and a reward

The first step is easy: Just specify a desired goal or objective. The best goals are characterized by five well-known attributes, which are summarized by the acronym SMART:

S = specific (not general)
M = measurable (not subjective)
A = aligned (not unrelated or conflicting)
R = realistic (not fantasy)
T = time bound (not open-ended)

Unfortunately, this first step alone is not likely to lead to goal achievement or stress elimination. Most of us identify New Year's resolutions, for example, but never follow through. Step 2, therefore, is to identify, as specifically as possible, the activities and behaviors that will lead to accomplishing the goal. The principle is: The more difficult the goal is to accomplish, the more numerous and specific these behaviors and activities should be.

Several years ago friend approached us with a problem. She was a wonderfully sensitive, caring, competent single woman in her late 20s who was experiencing a high degree of anticipatory stress because of her size. She had weighed over 350 pounds for more than 10 years. She was afraid of both the health consequences and the social consequences of not being able to lose weight. With the monitoring of a physician, she set a goal to lose 100 pounds in the next 12 months (Step 1). Because it was such a difficult goal to reach, however, she asked us for help in achieving her ambitious objective.

We first identified a dozen or so specific actions and guidelines that would facilitate the attainment of the goal (Step 2). These action steps included, for example, never going grocery shopping alone or without a menu plan, never carrying more than 50 cents in her purse (in order to avoid the temptation to buy a doughnut or another unhealthy snack), exercising with friends each day at 5:30 p.m., forgoing TV at night to reduce the temptation to snack, keeping a food log, and going to bed by 10:30 p.m. The behaviors were rigid, but the goal was so difficult that they were necessary to ensure progress. Because the action steps were specific and short-term, she experienced multiple successes each day as she followed her plan.

Step 3 involves establishing accountability. If no one else will know if the goal was achieved, chances are it will not be. The key principle is: "Make it more difficult to stay the same than to change." This is done by involving others in ensuring accountability for adherence to the plan, establishing a social support network to obtain encouragement from others, and instituting penalties for nonconformance.

In addition to announcing to coworkers, friends, and a church group that she would lose 100 pounds, our friend renegotiated her work contract so that she would take a cut in salary if she did not achieve her goal. Her doctor registered her for a hospital stay at the end of the 12-month period, so that if she did not achieve the goal on her own, she was to go on an intravenous feeding schedule in the hospital to lose the weight, at a cost of over $250 per day. She made it more difficult and more costly to fail than to succeed.

Step 4 involves establishing an evaluation and reward system. This means identifying the evidence that the goal has been accomplished and the benefits that will be produced with success. This step is crucial because many desirable goals—such as being a better leader, a more empathetic friend, a more patient parent—are not achieved without specific indicators of success. How do I know I have achieved the goal? Identify objective indicators of success.

The purpose of this short-term planning model is to eliminate anticipatory stress by establishing a focus and direction for activity. The anxiety associated with uncertainty and potentially negative events is dissipated when mental and physical energy are concentrated on purposeful activity. (By the way, the last time we saw our friend, her weight was well below 200 pounds.)

Small Wins Another principle related to eliminating anticipatory stressors is the small-wins strategy (Weick, 1984). By "small win," we mean a tiny but definite change made in a desired direction. Begin by changing something that is easy to change. Then, change a second thing that is easy to change, and so on. Although each individual success may be relatively modest when considered alone, the multiple small gains eventually mount up, generating a sense of momentum that creates movement toward a desired goal.

When we focus on a small, concrete outcome—giving us a chance to enjoy visible success—we develop heightened confidence and optimism, which motivates the pursuit of another small win. By itself, a small win may seem unimportant. A series of wins at seemingly insignificant tasks, however, reveals a pattern that tends to attract allies, deter opponents, and lower resistance to further action. The fear associated with anticipatory change is eliminated as we build self-confidence through small wins. We also gain the support of others as they see progress being made (Amabile & Kramer, 2011).

In the case of our friend who was trying to lose weight, one key was to begin changing what she could change, a little at a time. Tackling the loss of 100 pounds all at once would have been too overwhelming a task.

But she could change her grocery shopping habits, her bedtime, and what she ate for breakfast. Each successful change generated more and more momentum that, when combined, led to the larger change that she desired. Her ultimate success was a product of multiple small wins.

In summary, the rules for instituting small wins are simple: (1) identify a small, easy-to-change activity that is under your control; (2) change it in a way that leads toward your desired goal; (3) find another small thing to change, and change it; (4) keep track of the changes you are making; and (5) maintain the small gains you have made. Anticipatory stressors are eliminated because the dreaded unknown is replaced by a focus on immediate successes.

Developing Resiliency and Well-Being

Now that we have examined various causes of stress and outlined a series of preventive measures, we turn our attention to a second major strategy for managing negative stress, as shown in Figure 2.2: the development of **resiliency** to handle the stress that cannot be eliminated. This means not only developing the capacity to effectively manage the negative effects of stress, to bounce back from adversity, and to endure difficult situations (Wright, Masten, & Narayan, 2013), but also finding ways to thrive and flourish even in difficult circumstances—that is, to enhance well-being (Diener, et al., 2011; Spreitzer, et al., 2005). The Flourishing Scale in the Assessment section of this chapter measures the level of your personal well-being, or the extent to which you are flourishing in life. Flourishing provides the resilience you need to cope effectively with stress.

The first studies of resiliency emerged from investigations of children living in poverty or with abusive, alcoholic, or mentally ill parents. Some of these children surprised researchers by rising above their circumstances and developing into healthy, well-functioning adolescents and adults. They were referred to as highly resilient individuals (Masten & Reed, 2002).

People differ widely in their ability to cope with stress. Some individuals seem to crumble under pressure, while others appear to thrive. A major predictor of which individuals cope well with stress and which experience well-being is the amount of resiliency that they have developed. In this section, we highlight several key factors that help individuals develop and enhance personal resiliency and find ways to thrive in the presence of stressful situations.

LIFE BALANCE

The wheel in Figure 2.6 represents the types of activities most people spend their time doing. Each segment in the figure identifies an important aspect of life that must be developed in order to achieve resiliency and well-being. The most resilient individuals are those who have achieved a certain degree of balance in their life.

Assume the center of the figure represents the zero point of involvement and the outside edge of the figure represents maximum involvement. Shading in a portion of the area in each of the seven segments would represent the amount of time spent on each area. (This exercise is included in the Skill Practice section.)

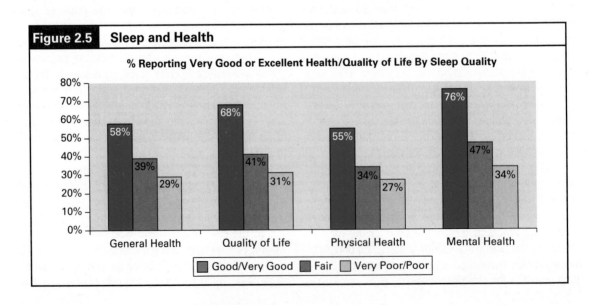

Figure 2.5 Sleep and Health

% Reporting Very Good or Excellent Health/Quality of Life By Sleep Quality

General Health: Good/Very Good 58%, Fair 39%, Very Poor/Poor 29%
Quality of Life: Good/Very Good 68%, Fair 41%, Very Poor/Poor 31%
Physical Health: Good/Very Good 55%, Fair 34%, Very Poor/Poor 27%
Mental Health: Good/Very Good 76%, Fair 47%, Very Poor/Poor 34%

Legend: Good/Very Good, Fair, Very Poor/Poor

Figure 2.6   Balancing Life Activities

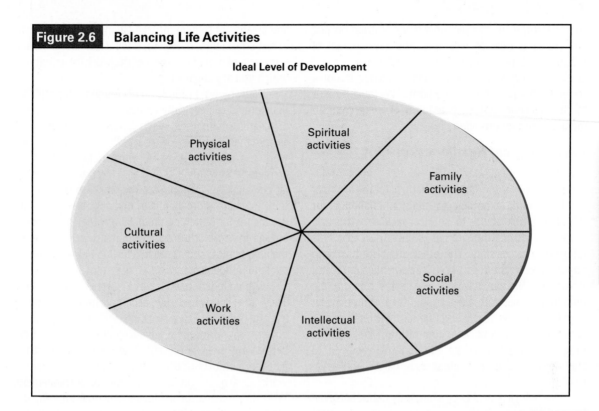

Individuals who are best able to cope with stress would shade in a substantial portion of each segment, indicating they have spent time or energy developing a variety of dimensions of their lives. Overemphasizing one or two areas to the exclusion of others often creates more stress than it eliminates. Life balance is key (Hill, et al., 2001; Lehrer, 1996; Murphy, 1996; Rostad & Long, 1996; White, et al., 2003).

This prescription, of course, seems counterintuitive. Generally, when we are feeling stress in one area of life, such as an overloaded work schedule, we respond by devoting more time and attention to it. While this is a natural reaction, it is counterproductive for several reasons. First, the more we concentrate exclusively on work, the more restricted and less creative we become. We lose perspective, cease to take fresh points of view, and become overwhelmed more easily. That is why several major corporations send senior managers on high-adventure wilderness retreats, foster volunteer community service, or encourage engagement in completely unrelated activities outside of work.

Second, refreshed and relaxed minds think better. More and more companies, including Adobe, Netflix, and Twitter, are requiring employees to take vacation time and to stop working at a certain time each day. They have become convinced by abundant research that employees are more productive and healthier when they are not consumed and overwhelmed by work demands. Productivity as well as employee well-being increase as much as 33 percent when employees are given incentives to obtain more balance in their lives (Alterman, et al., 2013).

In addition, a large number of recent studies show that getting sufficient sleep is an important predictor of physiological well-being, mental and emotional well-being, and productivity at work. On average, people in America rack up 30+ hours of sleep deficit each month.

Third, the cost of stress-related illness decreases markedly when employees participate in well-rounded wellness programs. A study by the Association for Fitness in Business concluded that companies receive an average return of $3 to $4 on each dollar invested in health and wellness promotion. AT&T, for example, expects to save $72 million in the next 10 years as a result of investment in wellness programs for employees.

Well-developed individuals who give time and attention to cultural, physical, spiritual, family, social, and intellectual activities in addition to work are more productive and less stressed than those who are workaholics (Adler & Hillhouse, 1996; Alterman, et al., 2013; Hepburn, McLoughlin, & Barling, 1997; White, et al., 2003). A great deal of literature is available on physical fitness, spiritual development, strengthening families, and so forth, so in this section we concentrate on just two common areas of well-being: the development of psychological resiliency, or grit (Duckworth, et al., 2007). Achieving life balance and resiliency is not a competency that can be accomplished by lunchtime or by the weekend. Rather, it requires ongoing commitment and continuous effort.

Psychological Resiliency, or Grit

Psychological resiliency refers to two types of attributes. One is the ability to return to the original condition after experiencing trauma, challenge, or threat. It is the ability to bounce back or withstand negative stressors. In materials science this capacity is referred to as *tensility*. The other attribute has been popularized by the terms *grit* (Duckworth, 2016) and *hardiness* (Maddi, 2006). These terms refer to the tendency to maintain a determination and motivation over long periods despite experiences with failure and adversity. Persistence and commitment toward the long-term objective create the stamina required to stay the course amid challenges, setbacks, and negative stress.

Psychological resiliency is not only about persevering and surviving; it also includes the idea of flourishing in the presence of negative stress. This is similar to "post-traumatic growth," or excelling as a result of facing negative or difficult conditions. Psychological resiliency has been the focus of a great deal of research (for example, see Duckworth, 2016; Reich, Zautra, & Hall, 2010; Sutcliffe & Vogus, 2003; Wadey, et al., 2012), and the prescriptions for developing resiliency are relatively consistent across studies and populations (Ungar, 2008). They include access to supportive, loving relationships; development of self-awareness, self-confidence, and self-efficacy; involvement in spiritual or religious activities; and the establishment of personal goals (Bandura, 2012; Maddi, 2013; Masten & Obradovic, 2006).

These topics are addressed in other chapters in this book, but here we highlight three practices that have been found to produce resiliency as well as flourishing in the presence of stress. They include meaningfulness in work, reciprocity, and gratitude.

Meaningfulness in Work

A well-established relationship exists between engagement in meaningful work and positive outcomes, including reductions in stress, depression, turnover, absenteeism, dissatisfaction, and cynicism, as well as increases in well-being, resiliency, commitment, effort, engagement, empowerment, happiness, satisfaction,

and a sense of fulfillment (see Chen, 2007). One way to foster resiliency, therefore, is to identify the profound purpose and meaningfulness of the work (or activity) in which you are engaged.

Wrzesniewski (2003, 2012) found in her research that individuals typically associate one of three kinds of meaning with their work. They define their work as a *job*, as a *career*, or as a *calling*. Those who see work as a *job* do their work primarily for the financial or material rewards it provides. They gain no particular personal satisfaction from the work, so they pursue their interests and passions in nonwork settings. Work is a means for obtaining financial or other resources to engage in some other activity (for instance, "Give me the assignment, and I'll do it. This job helps me pay off my student loans").

Other individuals have a *career* orientation. They are motivated by accomplishment, popularity, and success. They work to achieve the prestige, power, recognition, and advancement that come from performing their work well. They desire to be distinguished members of their organizations, and they use work to acquire promotion, title, or advancement. Work is a means for achieving personal growth, recognition, and capability development (e.g., "I want to reach a senior leadership position in this organization. I want to improve my skills").

The third orientation, the sense of work as a *calling*, characterizes individuals who are driven by the meaningfulness associated with the work itself. The actual tasks involved in their work provide intrinsic motivation and profound purpose. They consider their work inherently fulfilling, and they seek a greater good, regardless of the material rewards offered by the work. Their work possesses significance that reaches beyond personal benefit or the acquisition of reward (e.g., "I care deeply about what I am doing at work. This is more important than my own reward").

High levels of meaningfulness in work relieve stress by providing a positive goal or aspiration that serves as the focus of attention. Moreover, meaningfulness is associated with positive outcomes and extraordinary individual and organizational performance (Grant, 2008). For example, workers with a calling orientation reported fewer negative effects of stress, higher levels of trust and confidence in management, higher levels of commitment to the organization, less conflict, more satisfactory relationships with coworkers, higher levels of satisfaction with the tasks themselves, and higher levels of organizational performance compared to those with career or job orientations (Wrzesniewski, et al., 1997; Cook & Wall, 1980; Mowday, Steers, &

Porter, 1979; Taylor & Bowers, 1972; Wrzesniewski & Landman, 2000).

One interesting study of meaningfulness in work was conducted by Grant and colleagues (2007, 2008), in which telephone solicitors (mostly students working in part-time jobs) were placing calls to university alumni and requesting donations. These callers experienced almost universal rejection from the recipients of their calls and had little motivation to produce. They read a standardized script and received little information about the impact of their work. The voluntary turnover rate among the callers was approximately 350 percent.

In the study, half of the callers were exposed for just five minutes to a scholarship student who benefited from the solicitations. This student simply thanked the callers for their efforts and explained that he or she would not have been able to attend the university had these solicitors not raised the money that provided the scholarship funds. This had made a profound difference in his or her life. The other half of the callers was not exposed to a scholarship student and received no such message.

The results of the studies were startling (Grant, 2007, 2008; Grant, et al., 2007). Student callers exposed to a scholarship student increased their productivity (number of calls made) and effectiveness (amount of money raised) by a factor of three compared to callers who received no information about meaningfulness. Not only were the results seen immediately after the intervention (a week later), but the consequences could be seen more than a month later. Even in a stressful, boring job, identifying the meaningfulness associated with the work produced dramatically higher performance.

It is important to remember that a sense of calling is not dependent on the type of work performed. Rather, it is associated with the positive meaning inherent in the work (Bellah, et al., 1985; Wrzesniewski, 2003). Any kind of work—even work that is typically thought of as physically, socially, or morally tainted—can be reframed and recrafted in a more positive light (Ashforth & Kreiner, 1999; Wrzesniewski, et al., 2013). Put another way, exactly the same task may be viewed as a job or as a calling depending on the perspective of the individual. Even the most noxious and unpleasant of tasks can be reinterpreted as a calling that has a profound purpose (Pratt & Ashforth, 2003).

To enhance the meaningfulness of work, it should possess one or more of the attributes summarized in Table 2.5. Each one of these attributes can be enhanced by managers in order to enhance meaningfulness.

Table 2.5	Enablers of Meaningfulness in Work

1. The work has an important positive impact on the well-being of other people.

2. The work is associated with an important virtue or a personal value.

3. The work has an impact that extends beyond the immediate time frame or creates a ripple effect.

4. The work is re-crafted to align with and reinforce individuals' values, strengths, and passions.

5. The work builds supportive relationships and fosters generalized reciprocity.

(1) *The work has an important positive impact on the well-being of other people* (Brown, et al., 2003; Grant, 2008; Grant, et al., 2007).

Some companies, such as Medtronic, Google, and Huffy, regularly post letters from customers or patients whose lives have been transformed by the company's product or service, or reach out and invite them to give speeches at employee gatherings.

(2) *The work is associated with an important virtue or a personal value* (Bright, Cameron, & Caza, 2006; Weber, 1992). The CEO at Timberland, for example, in order to reduce migrant workers' exposure to carcinogens, decided to substantially increase the percentage of organically grown cotton in the clothes the company manufactures—even though no customer had asked that this be done (Schwartz, 2001).

(3) *The work has an impact that extends beyond the immediate time frame or creates a ripple effect* (Cameron & Lavine, 2006; Crocker, et al., 2006). Cameron and Lavine (2006) described the cleanup and closure of the Rocky Flats Nuclear Arsenal—60 years ahead of schedule, $30 billion under budget, and 13 times cleaner than required by federal standards because employees found profound meaningfulness in what they believed to be a multigenerational impact of their efforts. Creating a ripple effect means that when a person displays a virtuous behavior—assisting someone in need, expressing thanks, displaying kindness, showing courage—the tendency is for other people to follow suit.

(4) *The work is re-crafted to align with and reinforce individuals' values, strengths, and passions* (Berg, Wrzesniewski, & Dutton, 2010; Wrzesniewski, et al., 2013). Job crafting has become an oft-implemented tool in organizations to create an optimal fit between individuals and their jobs. This has been

found to significantly boost happiness, well-being, and effectiveness at work. Three kinds of job re-crafting are involved: re-crafting the tasks, re-crafting relationships, and re-crafting cognitions (or the way individuals think about their work). (See www.centerforpos.com/job-crafting.)

(5) *The work builds supportive relationships and fosters generalized reciprocity* (Baker, 2012, 2013; Polodny, Khurana, & Hill-Popper, 2005). A meta-analytic review of 148 scientific studies representing more than 300,000 individuals concluded that interpersonal relationships are a better predictor of mortality rates, cardiovascular disease, cancer, and various infections than were smoking, excessive alcohol consumption, obesity, and lack of physical exercise (Holt-Lunstad, Smith, & Layton, 2010).

Whereas developing strong interpersonal relationships is the topic of Chapter 4, here we discuss a second important technique for developing resilience when encountering negative stress. The technique centers on *generalized reciprocity*.

Reciprocity

All human beings have an inherent tendency toward reciprocity. All economic and exchange systems are based on the principle of reciprocity. For example, if you give something to another person and he or she does not reciprocate, or at least say thank you, you would probably label that person selfish, insensitive, and inappropriate. Taking something from a store without giving something in return is called stealing. We have all been taught that our social order is based on reciprocity. If someone gives you something, an obligation exists to at least acknowledge it, if not to reciprocate. So, merely saying thank you, acknowledging someone else's service to you, and recognizing someone for their positive impact has a tendency to foster resilience in coping with stress (Park, et al., 2017).

On the other hand, *generalized reciprocity* is the term used to describe what occurs when a person contributes something to another person that is not directly connected to receiving something in return (Baker, 2014; Baker & Bulkley, 2014). No benefit is received as a result of giving. The contribution occurs merely because it will be good for someone else. Making contributions, demonstrating generosity, and helping other people flourish all are ways that also engender psychological resilience. Rand, Greene, and Nowak (2012) demonstrated in several carefully controlled scientific studies that human beings have an inherent inclination toward generosity, altruism, and assisting other people;

that is, that people have a biological tendency to be generous even if they receive no reward.

This tendency toward reciprocity, as well as toward generalized reciprocity, fosters psychological resiliency because, as pointed out in several studies by Park and colleagues (2017), the body and the brain are activated in ways that enhance well-being and happiness. Specifically, the ventral striatum in the brain is activated when a person behaves generously and when he or she acknowledges the contributions of others (i.e., reciprocity). This area of the brain produces resilience, well-being, and feelings of happiness.

It is also interesting to note, as a side benefit of generalized reciprocity, that people rate others as more effective leaders, more desirable friends, and higher performers at work when those others contribute to others unselfishly (Putnam, 2013).

This practice was illustrated by former Prudential CEO Jim Mallozzi during his first meeting as CEO, with 2,500 sales personnel in a large auditorium. He asked participants to take out their iPhones and Blackberries, turn them on instead of turn them off, and text or email one great idea for how to get a new client, how to close a sale, or how to keep a customer for life. The objective was to help someone else in the company be more successful. More than 2,200 ideas were shared, and Mallozzi reported several years later that some of these ideas were still being actively used.

One practice for fostering generalized reciprocity is discussed in the Skill Practice section of this chapter. It was introduced by Wayne Baker at the University of Michigan and helps identify new ideas and previously unrecognized resources among individuals (see www.humaxnetworks.com). A reciprocity network is created when each individual in a group makes a personal request ("I need a person to feed my dog while I'm out of town") or a work-related request ("I would like to know how to motivate my sales team"). Other individuals in the group then respond to these requests with resources, knowledge, or connections that may provide value. A network is created when people with requests are linked up to people with resources or assistance.

Gratitude

A third seemingly simple but powerful tool for building resiliency and personal well-being is the practice of gratitude. Feelings and expressions of gratitude have dramatic effects on individuals and groups. For example, Emmons (2003) induced feelings of gratitude in students by assigning them to keep journals as part of a semester-long experiment. Some of the students were required to keep "gratitude journals" on a daily or weekly basis. They wrote down events or incidents that happened during the day (or week) for which they were grateful. Other students were assigned to write down events or incidents that were frustrating, and still other students were assigned to write down events or incidents that were merely neutral.

The students who kept gratitude journals, compared to the students who kept track of frustrating or neutral incidents, had higher levels of well-being; experienced fewer physical symptoms such as headaches and colds; felt better about their lives as a whole; were more optimistic about the coming week; had higher states of alertness, attentiveness, determination, and energy; reported fewer hassles and less stress in their lives; engaged in more helping behavior toward other people; experienced better sleep quality; and had a sense of being more connected to others. In addition, they were absent and tardy less often and had higher grade point averages. Feelings of gratitude had significant impact on students' classroom performance as well as on their personal lives (Emmons, 2008).

Individuals experiencing gratitude demonstrate a more consistent and healthy heart rhythm than individuals experiencing frustration. Physiological health, cognitive functioning, and performance at work are substantially higher when gratitude is fostered, at least partly because of the harmonious pattern adopted by the body.

Emmons (2008) also found that expressions of gratitude by one person tended to motivate others to express gratitude, so a self-perpetuating, virtuous cycle occurred when gratitude was expressed. Gratitude elicited positive behavior on the part of other people (e.g., they were more likely to loan money or provide compassionate support) as well as reciprocal behavior. A handwritten "thank you" on a restaurant bill by the server, for example, elicited about 11 percent higher tips, and visits by case workers and social workers were 80 percent higher if they were thanked for coming (McCullough, Emmons, & Tsang, 2002).

Engaging in gratitude visits (e.g., simply visiting another person in order to express gratitude), writing gratitude letters (e.g., sharing feelings of thanks with another person), keeping gratitude journals (e.g., writing down three things daily for which you are grateful), and distributing daily gratitude cards (e.g., handing out some written expressions of appreciation to coworkers each day) all have been shown in empirical investigations to produce important positive impacts on individuals and organizations (see Emmons, 2008; Seligman, et al., 2005). Despite being easy to implement, their effects are powerful and significant in fostering resiliency and helping to enhance well-being.

Temporary Stress-Reduction Techniques

Thus far, we have emphasized eliminating sources of stress and developing resiliency to stress. These are the most desirable stress-management strategies because they have a permanent or long-term effect on your well-being. However, the occurrence of stressors is sometimes beyond your control, so it may be impossible to eliminate them. Moreover, developing resiliency often takes time, so on occasion we must use temporary reactive mechanisms in order to maintain equilibrium. Although increased resilience can buffer the harmful effects of stress, we must sometimes take immediate action in the short term to cope with the stress we encounter.

Implementing short-term strategies reduces stress temporarily so that longer-term stress-elimination or resiliency strategies can be implemented. Short-term strategies are largely reactive and must be repeated whenever stressors are encountered, because, unlike other strategies, their effects are only temporary. On the other hand, they are especially useful for immediately calming feelings of anxiety or apprehension. You can use them when you are asked a question you can't answer, when you become embarrassed by an unexpected event, when you are faced with a presentation or an important meeting, or almost any time you are suddenly stressed and must respond in a short period of time. More than 150,000 books on temporary stress-reduction techniques have been published since 1990; we review six of the best-known and easiest to learn techniques here. The first two are physiological; the last four are psychological.

Muscle relaxation involves easing the tension in successive muscle groups. Each muscle group is tightened for five or 10 seconds and then completely relaxed. Starting with the feet and progressing to the calves, thighs, stomach, arms, neck, and face, one can relieve tension throughout the entire body. All parts of the body can be included in the exercise. One variation is to roll the head around on the neck several times, shrug the shoulders, or stretch the arms up toward the ceiling for five to 10 seconds, then release the position and relax the muscles. The result is a state of temporary relaxation that helps eliminate tension and refocus energy.

A variation of muscle relaxation involves **deep breathing**. This is done by taking several successive slow, deep breaths, holding them for five seconds, and exhaling completely. You should focus on the act of breathing itself, so that your mind becomes cleared for a brief time while your body relaxes. After each deep breath, muscles in the body should consciously be relaxed.

A third technique uses **imagery and fantasy** to eliminate stress temporarily by changing the focus of your thoughts. Imagery involves visualizing an event using "mind pictures." An increasingly common practice for athletes is to visualize a successful performance or to imagine themselves achieving their goal. Research has confirmed both the stress-reduction advantages of this technique and the performance enhancement benefits (see, for example, Andersen & Williams, 1999; Deepak, 1995). In addition to visualization, imagery also can include recollections of sounds, smells, and textures. Your mind focuses on pleasant experiences from the past (e.g., a fishing trip, family vacation, visit with relatives, or day at the beach) that can be recalled vividly. Fantasies, on the other hand, are not past memories but make-believe events or images. It is especially well known, for example, that children often construct imaginary friends, make-believe occurrences, or special wishes that are comforting to them when they encounter stress. Adults also use daydreams or other fantasy experiences to get them through stressful situations. The purpose of this technique is to relieve anxiety or pressure temporarily by focusing on something pleasant so that other, more productive stress-reducing strategies can be developed for the longer term.

A similar practice is referred to as **reframing**. Reframing is merely a way of viewing events, ideas, concepts, and emotions differently in order to find more positive alternatives. In a study of students preparing for a test, those who practicing cognitive reframing experienced significant improvement in memory compared to those who did not practice reframing. Similarly, depression, anxiety, and stress were significantly reduced through the process of cognitive reframing (Ray, et al., 2005). Some of the cues that can motivate reframing are below. Simply concentrate on one or more of these cues.

- ❏ "I understand this situation."
- ❏ "I've solved similar problems before."
- ❏ "Other people are available to help me get through this situation."
- ❏ "Others have faced similar situations and made it through."
- ❏ "In the long run, this really isn't so critical."
- ❏ "I can learn something from this situation."
- ❏ "There are several good alternatives available to me."

Reframing is similar to various forms of **meditative practices**. These include contemplative practices such as loving kindness meditation, transcendental meditation, guided visualization, mantra meditation, and so forth. Loving kindness meditation, for example, is a well-developed contemplative practice that focuses on self-generated feelings of love, compassion, and goodwill toward oneself and others. Essentially, people focus on their feelings of positive regard for people close to them. Similar practices include writing and contemplating gratitude journal entries, engaging in personal prayer, and pondering spiritual inspiration. These practices put people into a reflective and peaceful condition.

The results of recent research on these kinds of practices are compelling. Studies show that engaging in contemplative practices, reframing, and visualization diminish stress-related cortisol, insomnia, symptoms of autoimmune illnesses, PMS, asthma, falling back into depression, general emotional distress, anxiety, and panic. They help control blood sugar in type 2 diabetes and detachment from negative reactions. They help enhance self-understanding and general well-being. Engaging in these practices has also been shown to have a positive effect on heart rate, oxytocin levels, vagal nerve tone, blood pressure, obesity, incidence of cancer, heart disease, various infections, and, surprisingly, the actual cortical thickness of the brain (Fredrickson, et al., 2008; Hozel, et al., 2010; Kok, et al., 2014).

The sixth technique is called **rehearsal**. Using this technique, people work themselves through potentially stressful situations, trying out different scenarios and alternative reactions. Appropriate reactions are rehearsed, either in a safe environment before stress occurs, or "offline," in private, in the middle of a stressful situation. Removing oneself temporarily from a stressful circumstance and working through dialogue or reactions, as though rehearsing for a play, can help one regain control and reduce the immediacy of the stressor.

Summary

We began this chapter by explaining stress in terms of a relatively simple model. Four kinds of stressors—time, encounter, situational, and anticipatory—cause negative physiological, psychological, and social reactions in individuals. These reactions are moderated by the resiliency that individuals have developed for coping with stress. The best way to manage stress is to eliminate it through effective and efficient time management, fostering a sense of community, making contributions, enhancing emotional and social intelligence, work re-design, prioritizing, goal setting, and small wins. These strategies have permanent benefits, but they often take an extended period of time to implement.

The next most effective stress management strategy is improving one's resiliency. Physiological resiliency is strengthened through increased cardiovascular conditioning and improved diet. Psychological resiliency, grit, hardiness, and personal well-being are improved by focusing on meaningfulness in work, reciprocity, and gratitude. These strategies produce long-term benefits, but they often cannot be implemented on the spot. They are medium-term strategies that enhance resiliency over time.

When circumstances make it impossible to apply longer-term strategies for reducing stress, short-term relaxation techniques can temporarily alleviate the symptoms of stress. These strategies have short-term benefits, but they can be applied immediately and repeated over and over again.

Behavioral Guidelines

Following are specific behavioral guidelines for improving your stress-management skills and fostering personal well-being.

A. Address stress by first trying to eliminate the stressors, then focus on developing resiliency and personal well-being to create hardiness and grit in stressful situations, and finally learn temporary stress coping methods to reduce stress in the short term.

B. Use proven time management practices. Make sure to use time effectively as well as efficiently by generating your own personal mission statement. Make sure low-priority tasks do not drive out time to work on high-priority activities. Make better use of your time by using the guidelines in the Time Management Survey in the Assessment section. Give important activities priority over urgent ones.

C. Build collaborative relationships with individuals based on mutual trust, respect, honesty, and kindness. Make "deposits" into the "emotional bank accounts" of other people. Form close, stable relationships with your coworkers.

D. Reaffirm priorities and short-term goals that provide direction and focus to activities. Make your goals SMART.

E. Increase your psychological resiliency through life balance, especially by consciously engaging in physical, intellectual, cultural, social, family, and spiritual activities.

F. Increase your resilience by implementing a small-wins strategy. Identify and celebrate the small successes that you and others achieve.

G. Learn at least one relaxation technique and practice it regularly, such as muscle relaxation, deep breathing, imagery and fantasy, cognitive reframing, contemplative practices, or rehearsal.

H. Increase your resiliency by forming an open, trusting, sharing relationship with at least one other person. Find someone who can genuinely affirm your worth as a person and provide support during periods of stress.

I. Identify the meaningfulness of your work that is more important than your own personal reward.

J. Identify a contribution you can provide to someone without expecting recognition or reward in return. Find one way this week to demonstrate generalized reciprocity.

K. Implement at least one gratitude practice, such as a gratitude journal, gratitude visits, or gratitude cards.

LEARNING

CASES INVOLVING STRESS MANAGEMENT

The Turn of the Tide

Not long ago I came to one of those bleak periods that many of us encounter from time to time, a sudden drastic dip in the graph of living when everything goes stale and flat, energy wanes, enthusiasm dies. The effect on my work was frightening. Every morning I would clench my teeth and mutter: "Today life will take on some of its old meaning. You've got to break through this thing. You've got to!"

But the barren days went by, and the paralysis grew worse. The time came when I knew I had to have help. The man I turned to was a doctor. Not a psychiatrist, just a doctor. He was older than I, and under his surface gruffness lay great wisdom and compassion. "I don't know what's wrong," I told him miserably, "but I just seem to have come to a dead end. Can you help me?"

"I don't know," he said slowly. He made a tent of his fingers and gazed at me thoughtfully for a long while. Then, abruptly, he asked, "Where were you happiest as a child?"

"As a child?" I echoed. "Why, at the beach, I suppose. We had a summer cottage there. We all loved it."

He looked out the window and watched the October leaves sifting down. "Are you capable of following instructions for a single day?"

"I think so," I said, ready to try anything.

"All right. Here's what I want you to do."

He told me to drive to the beach alone the following morning, arriving not later than nine o'clock. I could take some lunch; but I was not to read, write, listen to the radio, or talk to anyone. "In addition," he said, "I'll give you a prescription to be taken every three hours."

He then tore off four prescription blanks, wrote a few words on each, folded them, numbered them, and handed them to me. "Take these at nine, twelve, three, and six."

"Are you serious?" I asked.

He gave a short bark of laughter. "You won't think I'm joking when you get my bill!"

The next morning, with little faith, I drove to the beach. It was lonely, all right. A northeaster was blowing; the sea looked gray and angry. I sat in the car, the whole day stretching emptily before me. Then I took out the first of the folded slips of paper. On it was written: LISTEN CAREFULLY.

I stared at the two words. "Why," I thought, "the man must be mad." He had ruled out music and newscasts and human conversation. What else was there? I raised my head and I did listen. There were no sounds but the steady roar of the sea, the creaking cry of a gull, the drone of some aircraft high overhead. All these sounds were familiar. I got out of the car. A gust of wind slammed the door with a sudden clap of sound. "Am I supposed to listen carefully to things like that?" I asked myself.

I climbed a dune and looked out over the deserted beach. Here the sea bellowed so loudly that all other sounds were lost. And yet, I thought suddenly, there must be sounds beneath sounds—the soft rasp of drifting sand, the tiny wind-whisperings in the dune grasses—if the listener got close enough to hear them.

On an impulse I ducked down and, feeling fairly ridiculous, thrust my head into a clump of sea-oats. Here I made a discovery: If you listen intently, there is a fractional moment in which everything seems to pause, wait. In that instant of stillness, the racing thoughts halt. For a moment, when you truly listen for something outside yourself, you have to silence the clamorous voices within. The mind rests.

I went back to the car and slid behind the wheel. LISTEN CAREFULLY. As I listened again to the deep growl of the sea, I found myself thinking about the white-fanged fury of its storms.

I thought of the lessons it had taught us as children. A certain amount of patience: You can't hurry the tides. A great deal of respect: The sea does not suffer fools gladly. An awareness of the vast and mysterious interdependence of things: Wind and tide and current, calm and squall and hurricane, all combine to determine the paths of the birds above and the fish below. And the cleanness of it all, with every beach swept twice a day by the great broom of the sea.

Sitting there, I realized I was thinking of things bigger than myself—and there was relief in that.

Even so, the morning passed slowly. The habit of hurling myself at a problem was so strong that I felt lost without it. Once, when I was wistfully eyeing the car radio, a phrase from the philosopher Thomas Carlyle jumped into my head: "Silence is the element in which great things fashion themselves."

By noon, the wind had polished the clouds out of the sky, and the sea had merry sparkle. I unfolded the second "prescription." And again I sat there, half amused and half exasperated. Three words this time: TRY REACHING BACK.

Back to what? To the past, obviously. But why, when all my worries concerned the present or the future?

I left the car and started tramping reflectively along the dunes. The doctor had sent me to the beach because it was a place of happy memories. Maybe that was what I was supposed to reach for: the wealth of happiness that lay half-forgotten behind me.

I decided to experiment: to work on these vague impressions as a painter would, retouching the colors, strengthening the outlines. I would choose specific incidents and recapture as many details as possible. I would visualize people complete with dress and gestures. I would listen (carefully) for the exact sound of their voices, the echo of their laughter.

The tide was going out now, but there was still thunder in the surf. So I chose to go back 20 years to the last fishing trip I made with my younger brother. (He died in the Pacific during World War II and was buried in the Philippines.) I found that if I closed my eyes and really tried, I could see him with amazing vividness, even the humor and eagerness in his eyes that far-off morning.

In fact, I could see it all: the ivory scimitar of beach where we were fishing; the eastern sky smeared with sunrise; the great rollers creaming in, stately and slow. I could feel the backwash swirl warm around my knees, see the sudden arc of my brother's rod as he struck a fish, hear his exultant yell. Piece by piece I rebuilt it, clear and unchanged under the transparent varnish of time. Then it was gone.

I sat up slowly. TRY REACHING BACK. Happy people were usually assured, confident people. If, then, you deliberately reached back and touched happiness, might there not be released little flashes of power, tiny sources of strength?

This second period of the day went more quickly. As the sun began its long slant down the sky, my mind ranged eagerly through the past, reliving some episodes, uncovering others that had been completely forgotten. For example, when I was around 13 and my brother 10, Father had promised to take us to the circus. But at lunch there was a phone call: Some urgent business required his attention downtown. We braced ourselves for disappointment. Then we heard him say, "No, I won't be down. It'll have to wait."

When he came back to the table, Mother smiled. "The circus keeps coming back, you know."

"I know," said Father. "But childhood doesn't."

Across all the years I remembered this and knew from the sudden glow of warmth that no kindness is ever wasted or ever completely lost.

ANALYSIS

By three o'clock the tide was out and the sound of the waves was only a rhythmic whisper, like a giant breathing. I stayed in my sandy nest, feeling relaxed and content—and a little complacent. The doctor's prescriptions, I thought, were easy to take.

But I was not prepared for the next one. This time the three words were not a gentle suggestion. They sounded more like a command. REEXAMINE YOUR MOTIVES.

My first reaction was purely defensive. "There's nothing wrong with my motives," I said to myself. "I want to be successful—who doesn't? I want to have a certain amount of recognition—but so does everybody. I want more security than I've got—and why not?"

"Maybe," said a small voice somewhere inside my head, "those motives aren't good enough. Maybe that's the reason the wheels have stopped going around."

I picked up a handful of sand and let it stream between my fingers. In the past, whenever my work went well, there had always been something spontaneous about it, something uncontrived, something free. Lately it had been calculated, competent—and dead. Why? Because I had been looking past the job itself to the rewards I hoped it would bring. The work had ceased to be an end in itself, it had been merely a means to make money, pay bills. The sense of giving something, of helping people, of making a contribution, had been lost in a frantic clutch at security.

In a flash of certainty, I saw that if one's motives are wrong, nothing can be right. It makes no difference whether you are a mailman, a hairdresser, an insurance salesman, a housewife—whatever. As long as you feel you are serving others, you do the job well. When you are concerned only with helping yourself, you do it less well. This is a law as inexorable as gravity.

For a long time I sat there. Far out on the bar I heard the murmur of the surf change to a hollow roar as the tide turned. Behind me the spears of light were almost horizontal. My time at the beach had almost run out, and I felt a grudging admiration for the doctor and the "prescriptions" he had so casually and cunningly devised. I saw, now, that in them was a therapeutic progression that might well be of value to anyone facing any difficulty.

LISTEN CAREFULLY: To calm a frantic mind, slow it down, shift the focus from inner problems to outer things.

TRY REACHING BACK: Since the human mind can hold but one idea at a time, you blot out present worry when you touch the happiness of the past.

REEXAMINE YOUR MOTIVES: This was the hard core of the "treatment," this challenge to reappraise, to bring one's motives into alignment with one's capabilities and conscience. But the mind must be clear and receptive to do this—hence the six hours of quiet that went before.

The western sky was a blaze of crimson as I took out the last slip of paper. Six words this time. I walked slowly out on the beach. A few yards below the high water mark I stopped and read the words again: WRITE YOUR TROUBLES ON THE SAND.

I let the paper blow away, reached down and picked up a fragment of shell. Kneeling there under the vault of the sky, I wrote several words on the sand, one above the other. Then I walked away, and I did not look back. I had written my troubles on the sand. And the tide was coming in.

SOURCE: *"The Day at the Beach." Copyright by Arthur Gordon, 1959.*

Discussion Questions

2.1. What is effective about these strategies for coping with stress, and why did they work?

2.2. What troubles, challenges, or stressors do you face right now to which these prescriptions might apply?

2.3. Are these prescriptions effective coping strategies or merely escapes?

2.4. What other prescriptions could the author take besides the four mentioned here? Generate your own list based on your own experiences with stress.

The Case of the Missing Time

At approximately 7:30 A.M. on Tuesday, June 23, Ebony Ellsworth, manager of the Norris Company's Central Plant, swung her car out of the driveway of her suburban home and headed toward the plant located some six miles away, just inside the Midvale city limits. It was a beautiful day. The sun was shining brightly and a cool, fresh breeze was blowing. The trip to the plant took about 20 minutes and gave Ebony an opportunity to think about plant problems without interruption.

The Norris Company owns and operates computer chip manufacturing plants. It is a closely held company with some 350 employees, nearly half of whom are employed at the Central Plant, the largest of the three Norris manufacturing operations. The company's main offices are also located in the Central Plant building.

Ebony had started with the Norris Company as an expediter in its Eastern Plant, was promoted to production supervisor, and two years later was made assistant to the manager of the Eastern Plant. She was transferred to the Central Plant as plant manager when the former manager retired.

Today she said to herself, "This is going to be the day to really get things done."

She began to run through the day's work, first one project, then another, trying to establish priorities. After a few minutes she decided that the open-end unit scheduling was probably the most important, certainly the most urgent. She frowned for a moment as she recalled that on Friday the vice president and general manager had casually asked her if she had given the project any further thought. Ebony realized that she had not been giving it much thought lately. She had been meaning to get to work on this idea for over three months, but something else always seemed to crop up. "I haven't had much time to sit down and really work it out," she said to herself. "I'd better get going and hit this one today for sure." With that she began to break down the objectives, procedures, and installation steps of the project. She reviewed the principles involved and roughly calculated the anticipated savings. "It's about time," she told herself. "This idea should have been followed up long ago." Ebony remembered that she had first conceived of the open-end unit scheduling idea nearly a year and a half ago, just prior to her leaving Norris's Eastern Plant. She had spoken to her boss, Jim Quince, manager of the Eastern Plant, about it then, and both agreed that it was worth looking into. The idea was temporarily shelved when she was transferred to the Central Plant a month later.

She started to think through a procedure for simpler transport of precious metals to and from the Eastern Plant. Visualizing the notes on her desk, she thought about the inventory analysis she needed in order to identify and eliminate some of the slow-moving stock items, the packing controls that needed revision, and the need to design a new special-order form. She also decided that this was the day to settle on whether to upgrade some equipment in the clean room. There were a few other projects she couldn't recall offhand, but she could tend to them after lunch, if not before. "Yes, ma'am," she said to herself, "this is the day to really get rolling."

When she arrived at work and entered the plant Ebony knew something was wrong as she met Al Noren, the stockroom foreman, who appeared troubled. "A great morning, Al," Ebony greeted him cheerfully.

"Not so good, Ebony; my new man isn't in this morning," Al growled.

"Have you heard from him?" asked Ebony.

"No, I haven't," replied Al.

Ebony frowned as she commented, "These stock handlers assume you take it for granted that if they're not here, they're not here, and they don't have to call in and verify it. Better ask Human Resources to call him."

Al hesitated for a moment before replying, "Okay, Ebony, but can you find me a man? I have two cars to unload today."

As Ebony turned to leave she said, "I'll call you in half an hour, Al, and let you know."

Making a mental note of the situation, Ebony headed for her office. She greeted the group of workers huddled around Marilyn, the office manager, who was discussing the day's work schedule with them. As the meeting broke up, Marilyn picked up a few samples, showed them to Ebony, and asked if they should be shipped as is or if it would be necessary to inspect them. Before Ebony could answer, Marilyn went on to ask if she could suggest another clerical operator for the sterilization equipment to replace the regular operator, who was home ill. She also told Ebony that Renaldo, the industrial engineer, had called and was waiting to hear from Ebony.

After telling Marilyn to go ahead and ship the samples, Ebony made a note of the need for a sealer operator for the office and then called Renaldo. She agreed to stop by Renaldo's office before lunch, and then she started on her routine morning tour of the plant. She asked each foreman the types and volumes of orders they were running, the number of people present, how the schedules were coming along, and the orders to be run next; helped the dock foreman find temporary storage space for consolidating a carload shipment; discussed quality control with an operator who had been running poor work; arranged to transfer four people temporarily to different departments, including two for Al in the stockroom; and talked to the shipping foreman about pickups and special orders to be delivered that day.

As she continued through the plant, she saw to it that reserve stock was moved out of the forward stock area, talked to another auditor about her requested change of vacation schedule, had a "heart-to-heart" talk with a new employee who seemed to need frequent reassurance, and approved two orders for customized chips for different customers.

Returning to her office, Ebony reviewed the production reports on the larger orders against her initial productions and found that the plant was running behind schedule. She called in the folding-room foreman and together they went over the lineup of machines and made several necessary changes.

During this discussion, the chief engineer stopped in to discuss several changes, and the routing foreman telephoned for approval of a revised schedule for one customer. The production foreman called twice: first to inform her that inventory of two standard, fast-moving stock items was dangerously low, and later to advise her that the final specifications for the urgent Dillion job had finally arrived. Ebony made the necessary subsequent calls to inform those concerned.

She then began to put delivery dates on important and difficult inquiries received from customers and salespeople. (The routine inquiries were handled by Marilyn.) While she was doing this, she was interrupted twice: once by a sales correspondent calling from the West Coast to ask for a better delivery date than originally scheduled, and once by the personnel vice president asking her to set a time when she could hold an initial training and induction interview with a new employee.

After dating the customer and sales personnel inquiries, Ebony headed for her morning conference in the executive offices. At this meeting she answered the sales

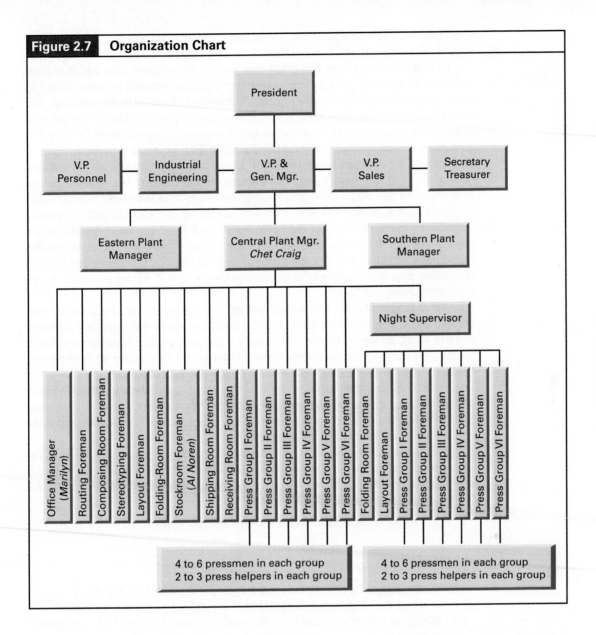

Figure 2.7   Organization Chart

vice president's questions regarding "hot" orders, complaints, and the status of large-volume orders and potential new orders. She then met with the general manager to discuss a few ticklish policy matters and to answer questions on several specific production and personnel problems.

On the way back to her own office, Ebony conferred with Renaldo about two current engineering projects about which he had called earlier. When she reached her desk, she looked at her watch. It was 10 minutes before lunch, just time enough to make a few notes of the details she needed to check in order to answer the knotty questions raised by the sales manager that morning.

After lunch Ebony started again. She began by checking the previous day's production reports, did some rescheduling to get out urgent orders, placed appropriate delivery dates on new orders and inquiries received that morning, and consulted with

ANALYSIS

a foreman on a personal problem. She spent 20 minutes on a Skype call going over mutual problems with the Eastern Plant.

By midafternoon Ebony had made another tour of the plant, after which she met with the personnel director to review with him a touchy personal problem raised by one of the clerical employees, the vacation schedules submitted by her foremen, and the pending job-evaluation program. Following this conference, Ebony hurried back to her office to complete the special statistical report for Oracle, one of Norris's best customers. As she finished the report, she discovered that it was 10 minutes after six and she was the only one left in the office. Ebony was tired. She put on her coat and headed through the plant toward the parking lot. On the way she was stopped by both the night supervisor and night foremen for approval of the production schedule.

With both eyes on the traffic, Ebony reviewed the day she had just completed. "Busy?" she asked herself. "So, did I accomplish anything?" Her mind raced over the day's activities. "Yes and no" seemed to be the answer. "There was the usual routine, the same as any other day. The plant kept going and I think it must have been a good production day. Any creative or special-project work done?" Ebony grimaced as she reluctantly answered, "No."

With a feeling of guilt, she probed further. "Am I an executive? I'm paid like one, respected like one, and have a responsible assignment with the necessary authority to carry it out. Yet one of the greatest values a company derives from an executive is her creative thinking and accomplishments. What have I done about it? An executive needs some time for thinking. Today was a typical day, just like most other days, and I did little, if any, creative work. The projects that I so enthusiastically planned to work on this morning are exactly as they were yesterday. What's more, I have no guarantee that tomorrow or the next day will bring me any closer to their completion. This is the real problem, and there must be an answer."

By this time Ebony had turned onto the side street leading to her home. The problem still uppermost in her mind was: "How can I become a more effective manager of my time?" Her thoughts were interrupted as she saw her son running toward the car calling out, "Daddy, Mommy's home."

SOURCE: *Based on Prod. #: KEL071-PDF-ENG, Kellogg School of Management, 1973.*

Discussion Questions

2.5. What principles of time and stress management are violated in this case?

2.6. What are the most important organizational problems?

2.7. Which of Ebony's personal characteristics inhibit her effective management of time?

2.8. If you were hired as a consultant to Ebony, what would be your advice? Help her become more capable of managing her stress.

Stress and the Millennial Generation

Numerous studies have shown that millennials suffer from anxiety at a much higher rate than generations that preceded them. What's wrong with this group, anyway?

A lot, actually. They're the first generation raised with the internet. They're the first generation to experience "helicopter" parenting. They're at once constantly exposed on social media and also permanently sheltered by overbearing parents.

They're not the first generation to experience a rough economy, but they certainly act as if they are. Marriages happen later or not at all, and the definition of the family, not to mention family structure, is changing dramatically. Freedom of movement has made it easy for people to leave families far behind, and more than 50 percent do. (Studies have shown that having limited family in close proximity can lead to reductions in anxiety and depression.) The endless choices millennials face have also proven paralyzing. While money is the biggest stressor for millennials between the ages of 18 and 35, severe fatigue and personal health concerns are also top issues causing a mental burden. More than half of millennials say they typically begin their workday already fatigued, and the average millennial wakes up tired four days a week. One in six worries about the lack of progress in their romantic relationships, with 15 percent of single millennials worrying they won't ever find a suitable partner. In a poll taken of millennials, the top 10 stressors were identified as:

- Money/finances
- Being tired/lack of sleep
- Health
- Workload
- Future of the country
- Student loans
- Parents' health
- Recent argument with partner
- Relationship with boss/supervisor
- Lack of progress in a romantic relationship

The top 10 coping strategies used by millennials were identified as:

- Become impatient with others
- Nap/sleep
- Try to ignore it
- Cry
- Withdraw from friends
- Eat a favorite snack/food
- Withdraw from family
- Talk to a friend
- Exercise
- Change in sexual activity

Discussion Questions

2.9. What are the major driving forces and restraining forces faced by millennials? What undergirds these stressors?

2.10. What forces could be strengthened or weakened? How would one go about that task?

2.11. What are some specific recommendations for your millennial peers? What strategies do you recommend to help eliminate, adapt to, and/or temporarily cope with these stressors?

EXERCISES FOR LONG-TERM AND SHORT-TERM STRESS MANAGEMENT AND WELL-BEING

In this section, we provide five exercises to help you practice good stress management. We strongly urge you to complete the exercises with a partner who can give you feedback and who will monitor your progress in improving your skill. Because managing stress is a personal skill, most of your practice will be done in private. But having a partner who is aware of your commitment will help foster substantial improvement. The reciprocity exercise requires that you perform it in a group.

The Small-Wins Strategy

An ancient Chinese proverb states that long journeys are always made up of small steps. In Japan, the feeling of obligation to make small, incremental improvements in one's work is known as *kaizen*. In this chapter the notion of small wins is explained as a way to break apart large problems and identify small successes in coping with them. Each of these approaches represents the same basic philosophy—to recognize incremental successes—and each helps an individual build up psychological resilience to stress.

Assignment

Answer the following questions. An example is given to help clarify each question, but your response need not relate to the example.

1. What major stressor do you currently face personally? What creates anxiety or discomfort for you? (For example, "I have too much to do.")

2. What are the major attributes or components of the situation? Divide the major problem into smaller parts, or subproblems. (For example, "I have said yes to too many things. I have deadlines approaching. I don't have the resources I need to complete all my commitments right now.")

3. What are the subcomponents of each of those subproblems? Divide them into yet smaller parts. (For example, "I have the following deadlines approaching: a report due, a large amount of reading to do, a family obligation, an important

presentation, a need to spend some personal time with someone I care about, a committee meeting that requires preparation.")

Component 1:

Component 2:

Component 3:

And so on:

4. What actions can I take that will affect any of these subcomponents? (For example, "I can engage the person I care about in helping me prepare for the presentation. I can write a shorter report than I originally intended. I can carry the reading material with me wherever I go.")

5. What actions have I taken in the past that have helped me cope successfully with similar stressful circumstances? (For example, "I have found someone else to share some of my tasks. I have gotten some reading done while waiting, riding, and eating. I have prepared only key elements for the committee meeting.")

6. What small thing should I feel good about as I think about how I have coped or will cope with this major stressor? (For example, "I have accomplished a lot when the pressure has been on in the past. I have been able to use what I had time to prepare to its best advantage.")

PRACTICE

Repeat this process when you face major stressors. The six specific questions may not be as important to you as (1) breaking the problem down into incremental parts and then breaking those parts down again, and (2) identifying actions that can be done that will be successful in coping with components of the stressor.

Life-Balance Analysis

The prescription to maintain a balanced life seems both intuitive and counterintuitive. On the one hand, it makes sense that life should have variety and that each of us should develop multiple aspects of ourselves. Narrowness and rigidity are not highly valued by anyone. On the other hand, the demands of work, school, or family, for example, can be so overwhelming that we don't have time to do much except respond to those demands. Work could take all of our time. So could school. So could family. The temptation for most of us, then, is to focus on only a few areas of our lives that demand our attention and leave the other areas undeveloped. This exercise helps you discover which areas those might be and which areas need more attention.

Assignment

Use Figure 2.8 below to complete this exercise. In responding to the four items in the exercise, think of the amount of time you spend in each area, the amount of experience and development you have had in the past in each area, and the extent to which development in each area is important to you.

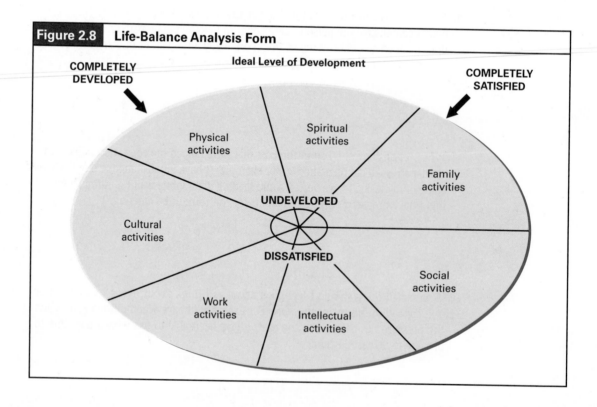

Figure 2.8   Life-Balance Analysis Form

1. In Figure 2.8, shade in the portion of each section that represents the extent to which that aspect of your life has been well developed. In other words, rate how satisfied you are that each aspect is adequately cultivated.

2. Now write down at least one thing you can start doing to improve your development in the areas that need it. For example, you might do more outside reading to develop culturally, invite a foreign visitor to your home to develop socially, engage in regular prayer or meditation to develop spiritually, begin a regular exercise program to develop physically, and so on.

3. Because the intent of this exercise is not to add more pressure and stress to your life but to increase your resiliency through life balance, identify the things you will *stop* doing in various areas that will make it possible to achieve better life balance.

4. To make this a practice exercise and not just a planning exercise, do something today that you have on your list for items 2 and 3 above. Write down specifically what you'll do and when. Don't let the rest of the week go by without implementing something you've written.

PRACTICE

Deep Relaxation

To engage in deep relaxation, you need to reserve time that can be spent concentrating on relaxation. Cognitive control and physiological control are involved. By focusing your mind, you can positively affect both your mental and physical states. This exercise describes one technique that is easily learned and practiced.

The deep-relaxation technique presented below combines key elements of several well-known formulas. It is recommended that this technique be practiced for 10 minutes a day, three times a week. Reserve at least 20 minutes to engage in this exercise for the first time.

Find a quiet spot with a partner. You may want to do this in the classroom itself the first time. Have your partner read the instructions below. Do not rush through the instructions. Allow time to complete each step unrushed. When you have finished, switch roles. (Since you will be practicing this exercise later in a different setting, you may want to make an audio recording of these instructions. Alternatively, agree to do the exercise regularly with a friend or a spouse.)

Assignment

Step 1: Assume a comfortable position. You may lie down. Loosen any tight clothing. Close your eyes and be quiet. Slow down and let go.

Step 2: Focus on your body and on relaxing specific muscles. Tune out all other thoughts. Assume a passive attitude.

Step 3: Now tense and relax each of your muscle groups one at a time for five to 10 seconds each. Do it in the following order:

Forehead. Wrinkle your forehead. Try to make your eyebrows touch your hairline for five seconds, then relax.

Eyes and nose. Close your eyes as tightly as you can for five seconds, then relax.

Lips, cheeks, and jaw. Draw the corners of your mouth back and grimace for five seconds, then relax.

Hands. Extend your arms in front of you. Clench your fists tightly for five seconds, then relax.

Forearms. Extend your arms out against an invisible wall and push forward for five seconds, then relax.

Upper arms. Bend your elbows and tense your biceps for five seconds, then relax.

Shoulders. Shrug your shoulders up to your ears for five seconds, then relax.

Back. Arch your back off the floor for five seconds, then relax.

Stomach. Tighten your stomach muscles by lifting your legs about two inches off the ground for five seconds, then relax.

Hips and buttocks. Tighten your hip and buttock muscles for five seconds, then relax.

Thighs. Tighten your thigh muscles by pressing your legs together as tightly as you can for five seconds, then relax.

Feet. Bend your ankles toward your body as far as you can for five seconds, then point your toes for five seconds, then relax.

Toes. Curl your toes as tightly as you can for five seconds, then relax.

Step 4: Focus on any muscles that are still tense. Repeat the exercise for that muscle group three or four times until it relaxes.

Step 5: Now focus on your breathing. Do not alter it artificially, but focus on taking long, slow, deep breaths. Breathe through your nose and exhale through your mouth. Concentrate exclusively on the rhythm of your breathing until you have taken at least 45 breaths.

Step 6: Now focus on the heaviness and warmth of your body. Let all the energy in your body seep away. Let go of your normal tendency to control your body and mobilize it toward activity.

Step 7: With your body completely relaxed, relax your mind. Picture a person for whom you have loving feelings, feelings of gratitude, or feelings of reverence. Concentrate fully on the person and on your feelings for him or her for at least three minutes without letting any other thoughts enter your mind. Begin now.

Step 8: Now open your eyes, slowly get up, and return to your workday better prepared to cope with it effectively.

Monitoring and Managing Time

Time management is the problem identified most often by managers and business school students. Most people feel overwhelmed at least sometimes with having too much to accomplish in too little time. It is interesting, however, that even though people may be extremely busy, if they feel that their time is *discretionary*—that is, it can be used in any way that they choose, such as in recreation, playing with friends or family, or by themselves—they feel less stress. Increasing discretionary time, therefore, is a key to effective time management.

This exercise helps you identify and better manage your discretionary time. It takes one full week to complete. It requires that you record how you spend your time for the next seven days. Virtually every executive who is a good time manager has completed this exercise and, in fact, regularly repeats this exercise.

Assignment

Complete the following five steps, then use a partner to get feedback and ideas for improving and refining your plans.

Step 1: Beginning today, keep a time log for one full week. Record how you spend each 30-minute block in the next seven 24-hour periods. Using the following format, record the log in your own notebook, diary, or journal. Simply write down what you did during the 30-minute period. If you did multiple things, record them one above the other.

TIME	ACTIVITY	REQUIRED/ DISCRETIONARY	PRODUCTIVE/ UNPRODUCTIVE
12:00–12:30			
12:30-1:00			
1:00–1:30			
1:30–2:00			
2:00–2:30			
.			
.			
.			
23:00–23:30			
23:30–24:00			

Step 2: Beneath the heading "Required/Discretionary," write whether the time spent in each 30-minute block was required by someone or something else (R) or was discretionary (D). That is, to what extent did you have a choice about whether or not you would engage in this activity? You don't have a choice about a certain amount of sleep, for example, or attending class. But you do have a choice about watching TV or spending time socializing.

Step 3: Beneath the heading "Productive/Unproductive," rate the extent to which each activity was productive. That is, identify the extent to which the activity achieved what it was intended to achieve. To what extent did the activity accomplish your own goals or lead to improvements of some kind? Use the following scale for your rating:

4 Time was used productively

3 Time was used somewhat productively

2 Time was used somewhat unproductively

1 Time was used unproductively

Step 4: Draw up a plan for increasing the amount of discretionary time you have during the week. Refer to the Time Management Survey in the Assessment section for suggestions. Write down the things you will *stop* doing and the things you will *start* doing.

Step 5: Identify ways in which you can use your discretionary time more productively, especially any blocks of time you rated 1 or 2 in step 3. What will you do to make sure the time you control is used for more long-term benefit? What will you stop doing that impedes your effective use of time?

Generalized Reciprocity

Creating a reciprocity network requires that you are a member of a participating group or organization. The network is formed among members of this group. The purpose of the exercise is to enhance relationships; provide a way for you to contribute to one another; and build a network of resources, relationships, and goodwill (see Baker, 2012).

Reciprocity networks are created among individuals in a group by having members identify needs or requests and then having others in the group respond to those needs or requests with resources or contacts. Building a reciprocity network occurs in four steps:

Step 1: Write down the name of each of the people in the group in a row at the top of a board. This could be done across the top of a whiteboard or on flip chart pages. Post the pages displaying the names on a wall.

Step 2: Each individual in the group writes down a specific request, a need, or an issue with which he or she needs help. These issues may be personal or work-related. The requests must have characteristics described as SMART. These attributes are not the same as SMART goals but are applicable to requests from others. In this exercise, SMART requests refer to:

S – Specific: A resource or resolution to the request must be available.

M – Meaningful: It is not trivial or irrelevant but refers to something important.

A – Action-oriented: There must be action that can be taken in response to the request.

R – Real need: The request must be tied to a genuine need.

T – Time bound: A time frame is given for when the request is needed.

Examples of work-related requests might be: "I need to find an expert who can assist me with some Excel spreadsheets"; "I need a new IT software system to streamline our inventory control"; "I need to become more recognized as a potential leader in my organization"; or "I need to determine how to downsize my unit by 15 percent."

Examples of personal requests might be: "I need tickets to the game in two weeks"; "I need to get in better physical shape"; "I need to find a great gift for my spouse"; or "I need help with my statistics class."

Step 3: The individual stands up and publicly describes the request to his or her colleagues and posts it below his or her name. An easy way to do this is to write the request on a Post-it Note.

Step 4: Colleagues listen to each person's verbalized request. Each colleague writes down a resource, a contact, or some assistance that might address these requests. Again, this can easily be done on a Post-it Note. Be sure that each person writes his or her name on the Post-it Note so that follow-up connections can be made. Group members will not be able to respond to every request, but the more responses each person can make, the better. Two kinds of contributions may be made. One kind of contribution is that you have the resource, such as knowledge, information, expertise, budget, product, emotional support, and so forth. Another kind of contribution is that you have contacts, such as someone you know who has the resource. You can provide a referral so that the requestor can connect to this person.

Step 5: After taking time to write contributions on separate notes, each person takes time to publicly explain his or her contribution to the requests for which he or she can add value. Each response is posted below the note containing the request. Sharing these contributions aloud tends to stimulate the thinking of others who may also realize some additional resource or contribution.

Step 6: After everyone has had a chance to explain aloud their contributions to the requests with which they can help, provide time for each person to connect with each resource provider associated with their request. The network is formed when requesters and resource providers connect and exchange valuable information.

An important outcome of this practice is to uncover new ideas and new resources that were previously unknown or unrecognized. Baker (2012) found that individuals who offer the most contributions tend to be rated as more competent leaders, more interpersonally effective, and higher performers in their organizations than others. That is, people who are willing to demonstrate generalized reciprocity—to contribute without expecting a personal benefit in return—are more successful leaders.

SKILL **APPLICATION**

ACTIVITIES FOR MANAGING STRESS

Suggested Assignments

2.12. Do a systematic analysis of the stressors you face in your job, family, school, and social life. List the types of stressors you face, and identify strategies to eliminate or sharply reduce them. Record this analysis in your journal.

2.13. Find someone you know well who is experiencing a great deal of stress. Teach him or her how to manage that stress better by applying the concepts, principles, techniques, and exercises in this chapter. Describe what you taught, and record the results in your journal.

2.14. Implement at least three of the time management techniques suggested in the Time Management Survey that you are not currently using and that you think you might find helpful. In your time log, keep track of the amount of time these techniques save you over a one-month period. Be sure to use that extra time productively.

2.15. With a coworker or colleague, identify ways in which your work at school, job, or home can be re-crafted or redesigned to reduce stress, better align with your core values, and increase productivity. Use the hints provided in the chapter to guide your redesign.

2.16. Establish a SMART, short-term goal or plan that you wish to accomplish this year. Make it compatible with the top priorities in your life. Specify the behavioral action steps, the reporting and accounting mechanisms, and the criteria of success and rewards. Share this plan with others you know so that you have an incentive to pursue it even after you finish this class.

2.17. Identify at least one or two ways that you can demonstrate generalized reciprocity. This means that you will contribute to the well-being of someone else without any expectation of recognition or reward.

2.18. Pick at least one relaxation technique. Learn it and practice it on a regular basis. Record your progress in your journal.

2.19. Start keeping a gratitude journal.

2.20. Identify the profound purpose or meaningfulness associated with your work or your major activities in life. That is, identify your calling.

Application Plan and Evaluation

The intent of this exercise is to help you apply this cluster of skills in a real-life, out-of-class setting. Now that you have become familiar with the behavioral guidelines that form the basis of effective skill performance, you will improve most by trying out those guidelines in an everyday context. Unlike a classroom activity, in which feedback is immediate and others can assist you with their evaluations, this skill application activity is one you must accomplish and evaluate on your own. There are two parts to this activity: Part 1 helps prepare you to apply the skill, and Part 2 helps you evaluate and improve on your experience. Be sure to write down answers to each item. Don't short-circuit the process by skipping steps.

Part 1: Planning

2.21. Choose a particular skill that is most important to you or most relevant to your current circumstances. These may be areas of weakness, areas you most want to improve, or areas that are most salient to a problem you face right now. Identify the specific skill that you want to apply.

2.22. Now identify the setting or the situation in which you will apply this skill. Establish a plan for performance by actually writing down a description of the situation. Who else will be involved? When will you do it? Where will it be done?

   Circumstances:
   Who else?
   When?
   Where?

2.23. Identify the specific behaviors in which you will engage to apply this skill. Operationalize your skill performance.

2.24. What are the indicators of successful performance? How will you know you have been effective? What will indicate you have performed competently?

Part 2: Evaluation

2.25. After you have completed your implementation, record the results. What happened? How successful were you? What was the effect on others?

2.26. How can you improve? What modifications can you make next time? What will you do differently in a similar situation in the future?

2.27. Looking back on your whole skill practice and application experience, what have you learned? What has been surprising? In what ways might this experience help you in the long term?

SCORING KEYS AND COMPARISON DATA

✪ Go to www.pearson.com/mylab/management for scoring keys and comparison data for the following instruments:

Stress Management
Time Management Assessment

Social Readjustment Rating Scale

Comparison Data (N = 5,000 students)

TOTAL SCORE	MEAN	BOTTOM QUARTILE	SECOND QUARTILE	THIRD QUARTILE	TOP QUARTILE
	257.76	122 or below	123–221	222–346	347 or above

According to the authors of these instruments, scores of 150 points or below resulted in a probability of less than 37 percent that a serious illness would occur in the next year, but the probability increased to about 50 percent with scores of 150–300. Those who scored over 300 on the SRRS had an 80 percent chance of serious illness. Research results also show an injury rate among athletes five times as great for high scorers on the SRRS as for low scorers.

Sources of Personal Stress

This exercise does not have a solution or scoring data. However, inasmuch as this instrument was designed to complement SRRS, the explanations of scores for that assessment are relevant.

Flourishing Scale

Comparison Data

The range of scores for this instrument is between 8 and 56. Below are the percentiles associated with each score, as reported by the authors of the instrument.

Score	Percentile	Score	Percentile
25	1	45	44
29	3	46	53
32	5	47	60
34	7	48	70
36	10	49	77
37	13	50	83
38	15	51	87
39	18	52	90
40	21	53	93
41	24	54	96
42	28	55	90
43	33	56	100
44	39		

SKILL *ASSESSMENT*

- Problem-Solving, Creativity, and Innovation
- How Creative Are You?
- Innovative Attitude Scale
- Creative Style Assessment

SKILL *LEARNING*

- Problem-Solving, Creativity, and Innovation
- Steps in Analytical Problem-Solving
- Limitations of the Analytical Problem-Solving Model
- Impediments to Creative Problem-Solving
- Multiple Approaches to Creativity
- Conceptual Blocks
- Conceptual Blockbusting
- International Caveats
- Hints for Applying Problem-Solving Techniques
- Fostering Creativity in Others
- Summary
- Behavioral Guidelines

SKILL *ANALYSIS*

- Chip and Bin
- Creativity at Apple

SKILL *PRACTICE*

- Individual Assignment—Analytical Problem-Solving
- Team Assignment—Creative Problem-Solving
- Moving Up in the Rankings
- Elijah Gold and His Restaurant
- Creative Problem-Solving Practice

SKILL *APPLICATION*

- Suggested Assignments
- Application Plan and Evaluation

SCORING KEYS AND *COMPARISON DATA*

MyLab Management

Go to www.pearson.com/mylab/management to complete the exercises marked with this icon ✪.

3

Solving Problems Analytically and Creatively

LEARNING OBJECTIVES

1. Increase proficiency in analytical problem-solving
2. Recognize personal conceptual blocks
3. Enhance creativity by overcoming conceptual blocks
4. Foster innovation among others

DIAGNOSTIC SURVEYS FOR CREATIVE PROBLEM-SOLVING

MyLab Management Personal Inventory Assessments

PROBLEM-SOLVING, CREATIVITY, AND INNOVATION

The assessment instruments in this chapter are briefly described below. The assessments appear either in your text or in MyLab. The assessments marked with ✪ are available only in MyLab. If assigned, go to www.pearson.com/mylab/management to complete these assessments. The assessments without the ✪ appear only in the text.

All assessments should be completed before reading the chapter material.

After completing the first assessment, save your response to your hard drive. When you have finished reading the chapter, re-take the assessment and compare your responses to see what you have learned.

✪ ❑ The *Problem-Solving, Creativity, and Innovation Assessment* measures the extent to which you effectively solve analytic problems and creative problems and the degree to which you have developed a competency for creativity and innovation.

❑ The *How Creative Are You? Assessment* evaluates the degree to which you are characterized by the attitudes, values, and motivations associated with creativity.

❑ The *Innovative Attitude Scale* identifies the extent to which you practice innovation in your daily activities.

❑ The *Creative Style Assessment* measures your personal style as it relates to creativity.

SOLVING PROBLEMS ANALYTICALLY AND CREATIVELY

Assessment Section

HOW CREATIVE ARE YOU?©

How creative are you? The following test helps you determine if you have the personality traits, attitudes, values, motivations, and interests that characterize creativity. It is based on several years' study of attributes possessed by men and women in a variety of fields and occupations who think and act creatively.

Be as frank as possible. Try not to second-guess how a creative person might respond. Turn to the end of the chapter to find the answer key and an interpretation of your scores.

Rating Scale

For each statement, write in the appropriate letter:

A Agree
B Undecided or Don't Know
C Disagree

_____ 1. I always work with a great deal of certainty that I am following the correct procedure for solving a particular problem.

_____ 2. It would be a waste of time for me to ask questions if I had no hope of obtaining answers.

_____ 3. I concentrate harder on whatever interests me than do most people.

_____ 4. I feel that a logical step-by-step method is best for solving problems.

_____ 5. In groups, I occasionally voice opinions that seem to turn some people off.

_____ 6. I spend a great deal of time thinking about what others think of me.

_____ 7. It is more important for me to do what I believe to be right than to try to win the approval of others.

_____ 8. People who seem uncertain about things lose my respect.

_____ 9. More than other people, I need to have things interesting and exciting.

_____ 10. I know how to keep my inner impulses in check.

_____ 11. I am able to stick with difficult problems over extended periods of time.

_____ 12. On occasion, I get overly enthusiastic.

_____ 13. I often get my best ideas when doing nothing in particular.

_____ 14. I rely on intuitive hunches and the feeling of "rightness" or "wrongness" when moving toward the solution of a problem.

_____ 15. When problem solving, I work faster when analyzing the problem and slower when synthesizing the information I have gathered.

_____ 16. I sometimes get a kick out of breaking the rules and doing things I am not supposed to do.

_____ 17. I like hobbies that involve collecting things.

_____ 18. Daydreaming has provided the impetus for many of my more important projects.

_____ 19. I like people who are objective and rational.

_____ 20. If I had to choose from two occupations other than the one I now have, I would rather be a physician than an explorer.

_____ 21. I can get along more easily with people if they belong to about the same social and business class as myself.

_____ 22. I have a high degree of aesthetic sensitivity.

_____ 23. I am driven to achieve high status and power in life.

_____ 24. I like people who are sure of their conclusions.

_____ 25. Inspiration has nothing to do with the successful solution of problems.

_____ 26. When I am in an argument, my greatest pleasure would be for the person who disagrees with me to become a friend, even at the price of sacrificing my point of view.

_____ 27. I am much more interested in coming up with new ideas than in trying to sell them to others.

_____ 28. I would enjoy spending an entire day alone, just "chewing the mental cud."

_____ 29. I tend to avoid situations in which I might feel inferior.

_____ 30. In evaluating information, the source is more important to me than the content.

_____ 31. I resent things being uncertain and unpredictable.

_____ 32. I like people who follow the rule "business before pleasure."

_____ 33. Self-respect is much more important than the respect of others.

_____ 34. I feel that people who strive for perfection are unwise.

_____ 35. I prefer to work with others in a team effort rather than solo.

_____ 36. I like work in which I must influence others.

_____ 37. Many problems that I encounter in life cannot be resolved in terms of right or wrong solutions.

_____ 38. It is important for me to have a place for everything and everything in its place.

_____ 39. Writers who use strange and unusual words merely want to show off.

_____ 40. Below is a list of terms that describe people. Choose 10 words that best characterize you.

energetic	persuasive	observant
fashionable	self-confident	persevering
original	cautious	habit-bound
resourceful	egotistical	independent
stern	predictable	formal
informal	dedicated	forward-looking
factual	open-minded	tactful
inhibited	enthusiastic	innovative
poised	acquisitive	practical
alert	curious	organized
unemotional	clear-thinking	understanding
dynamic	self-demanding	polished
courageous	efficient	helpful
perceptive	quick	good-natured
thorough	impulsive	determined
realistic	modest	involved
absent-minded	flexible	sociable
well-liked	restless	retiring

SOURCE: _Excerpted from_ How Creative Are You? _by Eugene Raudsepp._
Copyright ©1981 by Eugene Raudsepp. Used by permission.
Published by Perigee Books/G.P. Putnam's Sons, Inc.

INNOVATIVE ATTITUDE SCALE

This self-assessment helps you assess certain attitudes that have been shown to foster innovation. While there are many factors that influence innovative behavior, relevant attitudes are good predictors. Candid, realistic responses are essential in order for this diagnostic tool to be effective.

Indicate the extent to which each of the following statements is true of either your actual behavior or your intentions at work. That is, describe the way you are or the way you intend to be on the job. Use the scale for your responses.

Rating Scale

5 Almost always true
4 Often true
3 Not applicable
2 Seldom true
1 Almost never true

____ 1. I am always trying to do things in different ways.

____ 2. I love to dissect problems into pieces in order to see the whole picture.

____ 3. I have an open-door policy at work; anyone can come talk to me about anything.

____ 4. I am always the one people turn to for a creative way to look at old problems.

____ 5. I am more willing to take risks than my coworkers or fellow students.

____ 6. I provide a unique perspective in group work.

____ 7. I believe in not judging others' ideas until we have considered multiple alternatives.

____ 8. I am willing to ask questions to gain as many different perspectives as possible.

____ 9. I always try to carve out time in my schedule to develop new ideas and work on projects that may only be of interest to me.

____ 10. I hardly ever make it through a meeting or class without making a comment.

____ **Total**

SOURCE: *Innovative Attitude Scale, John E. Ettlie & Robert D. O'Keefe (1982),*
"Innovative Attitudes, Values, and Intentions in Organizations,"
Journal of Management Studies, *19: 163–182.*

CREATIVE STYLE ASSESSMENT

Research has identified four creativity styles. These can be thought of as forms of, or approaches to, creativity. This self-assessment helps you identify your preferred style. Candid, realistic responses are essential in order for this diagnostic tool to be effective.

Rating Scale

Four alternatives exist in each of the items below. You should divide 100 points among each of the four alternatives, depending on which alternative is most similar to you. Rate yourself as you are right now, not as you would like to be or as you think you should be. There are no correct or incorrect answers, so be as accurate as you can. For example, in question 1, if you think alternative A is very similar to you, B is somewhat similar, and C and D are hardly similar at all, you might give 50 points to A, 30 points to B, and 10 points each to C and D. Any combination of numbers is acceptable, including 100, 0, 0, 0, or 25, 25, 25, 25. **Just be sure that for each question, the total points add up to 100.**

1. I usually approach difficult problems by:

   _____ a. Brainstorming solutions

   _____ b. Carefully evaluating alternatives

   _____ c. Engaging other people

   _____ d. Responding quickly

   100

2. My friends and colleagues usually think of me as:

_____ a. Creative

_____ b. Systematic

_____ c. Collaborative

_____ d. Competitive

100

3. I am good at:

_____ a. Experimenting

_____ b. Administering

_____ c. Empowering people

_____ d. Meeting challenges

100

4. When I complete a project or an assignment, I am likely to:

_____ a. Come up with a new project

_____ b. Review the results to see how I might be able to improve them

_____ c. Share what I have learned with others

_____ d. Determine the grade or the evaluation of the results

100

5. I would describe myself as:

_____ a. Flexible

_____ b. Organized

_____ c. Supportive

_____ d. Driven

100

6. I like to work on projects that:

_____ a. Let me invent something new

_____ b. Create practical improvements

_____ c. Get other people involved

_____ d. Can be completed quickly

100

7. When solving a problem, I:

_____ a. Enjoy exploring a lot of options

_____ b. Collect a lot of data

_____ c. Communicate a lot with others

_____ d. Emphasize getting the job done

100

SOURCE: *Adapted from "Creative Style Assessment," J. DeGraff and K.A. Lawerence (2002).*
Creativity at Work. San Francisco: Jossey-Bass, pp. 46–49. © by John Wiley and Sons.

Problem-Solving, Creativity, and Innovation

Problem-solving is a skill required of every person in almost every aspect of life. Seldom does an hour go by without the need to solve some kind of problem. The manager's job, in particular, is inherently a problem-solving job. If there were no problems in organizations, there would be no need for managers. Therefore, it is hard to conceive of an incompetent problem solver succeeding as a manager.

In this chapter, we offer specific guidelines and techniques for improving problem-solving skills. Two kinds of problem-solving—analytical and creative—are addressed. Effective managers are able to solve problems both analytically and creatively, even though different skills are required for each type of problem.

First, we discuss analytical problem-solving—the kind of problem-solving managers use many times each day. Then we turn to creative problem-solving, a kind of problem-solving that occurs less frequently, yet this creative problem-solving ability often separates career successes from career failures, heroes from goats, and achievers from derailed executives. It can also produce a dramatic impact on organizational effectiveness. A great deal of research has highlighted the positive relationship between creative problem-solving and successful organizations (Csikszentmihalyi, 2013; Sternberg, 1999). This chapter provides guidelines for how you can become a more effective problem solver, both analytical and creative, and concludes with a brief discussion of how managers can foster creative problem-solving and **innovation** among the people with whom they work.

Steps in Analytical Problem-Solving

Most people, including managers, don't particularly like problems. Problems are time consuming, they create stress, and they never seem to go away.

Malcolm Gladwell, in his intriguing book, *Blink* (2005), argued that people are able to make decisions and reach conclusions on very little data—thin slices of behavior—because of their intuitive sense. In one or two seconds, people can reach a conclusion as valid as the one made after studying a problem for a long time. First impressions count, he argued, and are valid a lot of the time. These first impressions and instantaneous

judgments are valid, however, mainly when problems are not complex, when people have experience with the issue they are judging, and when they have developed an attunement to their own internal cues (that is, they have developed adequate self-awareness and emotional intelligence) (Gigerenzer & Gaissmaier, 2011).

Most of the time, the problems we face are complicated, multifaceted, and ambiguous. In such instances, effective problem-solving techniques are required, and they rely on a systematic and logical approach. This approach involves at least four steps.

DEFINING THE PROBLEM

The most widely accepted model of analytical problem-solving is summarized in Table 3.1. This method is well known and widely utilized in almost all firms. Many large organizations (e.g., Apple, Ford Motor Company, General Electric, Hewlett-Packard, and Microsoft) spend millions of dollars to teach their managers this type of problem-solving as part of their productivity and improvement process. Variations on this four-step approach have been implemented (e.g., Ford uses an eight-step approach), but all the steps are merely derivations of the standard model we discuss here.

The first step is to *define* a problem. This involves diagnosing a situation so that the focus is on the real problem, not just its symptoms. For example, suppose you must deal with an employee who consistently fails to get work done on time. Slow work might be the problem, or it might be only a symptom of another underlying problem, such as bad health, low morale, lack of training, or inadequate rewards. Defining the problem, therefore, requires a wide search for information. The more relevant the information that is acquired, the more likely it is that the problem will be defined accurately. As Charles Kettering put it, "It ain't the things you don't know that'll get you in trouble, but the things you know for sure that ain't so."

Following are some attributes of good problem definition:

1. Factual information is differentiated from opinion or speculation. Objective data are separated from perceptions and suppositions.
2. All individuals involved are tapped as information sources. Broad participation is encouraged in order to capture as much information as possible.

Table 3.1	A Model of Problem-Solving
Step	**Characteristics**
1. Define the problem.	• Differentiate fact from opinion.
	• Specify underlying causes.
	• Tap everyone involved for information.
	• State the problem explicitly.
	• Identify what standard is violated.
	• Determine whose problem it is.
	• Avoid stating the problem as a disguised solution.
2. Generate alternative solutions.	• Postpone evaluating alternatives.
	• Be sure all involved individuals generate alternatives.
	• Specify alternatives that are consistent with goals.
	• Specify both short-term and long-term alternatives.
	• Build on others' ideas.
	• Specify alternatives that solve the problem.
3. Evaluate and select an alternative.	• Evaluate relative to an optimal standard.
	• Evaluate systematically.
	• Evaluate relative to goals.
	• Evaluate main effects and side effects.
	• State the selected alternative explicitly.
4. Implement and follow up on the solution.	• Implement at the proper time and in the right sequence.
	• Provide opportunities for feedback.
	• Engender acceptance of those who are affected.
	• Establish an ongoing monitoring system.
	• Evaluate the results of your problem solution.

3. The problem is stated or written down explicitly. This often helps reveal ambiguities in the definition.
4. The problem definition clearly identifies what standard or expectation has been violated. Problems, by their very nature, involve the violation of some standard or expectation.
5. The problem definition must address the question "Whose problem is this?" No problems are completely independent of people. Identify for whom this is a problem.
6. The definition is not simply a disguised solution. Saying "The problem is that we need to motivate slow employees" is inappropriate because the problem is stated as a solution. The problem should be described, not resolved.

A common problem is that managers often propose a solution before an adequate definition of a problem has been given. This may lead to solving the wrong problem or to reaching conclusions that are misleading or inadequate. Effectively identifying the problem is usually the single most important step in problem-solving.

GENERATING ALTERNATIVES

The second step is to generate alternative solutions. This requires postponing the selection of any one solution until several alternatives have been proposed. Much research on problem-solving (e.g., March, 1999, 2006) supports the prescription that the quality of solutions can be significantly enhanced by considering multiple alternatives.

The problem with evaluating and selecting an alternative too early is that we may rule out some good ideas by just not getting around to thinking about them. We hit on an idea that sounds good and we go with it, thereby never even thinking of alternatives that may be better in the long run.

Some rules of thumb for good alternative generation are:

1. The evaluation of each proposed alternative is postponed. As many relevant alternatives as possible should be proposed before evaluation is allowed.
2. Alternatives are proposed by all individuals involved in the problem. Broad participation in proposing alternatives improves solution quality and group acceptance.
3. The alternative solutions being proposed are consistent with the organization's or the group's goals or desired outcomes.
4. Alternatives take into consideration both short- and long-term consequences.
5. Alternatives build on one another. Bad ideas may become good ones if they are combined with or modified by other ideas.
6. Alternatives solve the problem that has been defined. Another problem may also be important, but it should be ignored if it does not directly affect the problem being considered.

EVALUATING ALTERNATIVES

The third problem-solving step is to evaluate and select an alternative. This step involves carefully weighing the advantages and disadvantages of the proposed alternatives before making a final selection. In selecting the best alternative, skilled problem solvers make sure that alternatives are judged in terms of the extent to which they will solve the problem without causing other, unanticipated problems; the extent to which all individuals involved will accept the alternative; the extent to which implementation of the alternative is likely; and the extent to which the alternative fits within organizational constraints (e.g., is consistent with policies, norms, and budget limitations).

The classic description of the difficulty with problem-solving—made more than 60 years ago—still remains as a core principle in problem-solving (March & Simon, 1958):

Most human decision making, whether individual or organizational, is concerned with the discovery and selection of satisfactory alternatives; only in exceptional cases is it concerned with the discovery and selection of optimal alternatives. To optimize requires processes several orders of magnitude more complex than those required to satisfy. An example is the difference between searching a haystack to find the sharpest needle in it and searching the haystack to find a needle sharp enough to sew with.

Some attributes of good evaluation are:

1. Alternatives are evaluated relative to an optimal, rather than a satisfactory, standard. Determine what is best rather than just what will work.
2. Adequate time for evaluation and consideration is allowed so that each alternative is given due consideration.
3. Alternatives are evaluated in terms of the goals of the organization and the needs and expectations of the individuals involved. Organizational goals should be met, but individual preferences should also be considered.
4. Alternatives are evaluated in terms of their probable effects. Both side effects and direct effects on the problem are considered as well as long- and short-term effects.
5. The selected alternative is stated explicitly. This ensures that everyone involved understands and agrees with the same solution and prevents disagreements later.

IMPLEMENTING THE SOLUTION

The final step is to implement and follow up on the solution. A surprising amount of the time, people faced with a problem will try to jump to step 4 before having gone through steps 1 through 3. That is, they react to a problem by trying to implement a solution before they have defined the problem, analyzed it, or evaluated alternative solutions. It is important to remember, therefore, that "getting rid of the problem" by solving it will not occur successfully without the first three steps in the process.

Chapter 10 in this book discusses rules of thumb for successfully implementing solutions, including overcoming resistance, generating commitment from others, and ensuring that the solution is sustainable.

An important reminder is exemplified by former United States president Calvin Coolidge's well-known quotation:

Nothing in the world can take the place of perseverance. Talent will not; nothing is more common than unsuccessful people with talent. Genius will not; unrewarded genius is almost a proverb. Education will not; the world is full of educated derelicts. Persistence and determination alone are omnipotent.

Of course, any implementation requires follow-up to prevent negative side effects and ensure solution of the problem. Follow-up not only helps ensure effective implementation, but it also serves a feedback function by providing information that can be used to improve future problem-solving.

Some attributes of effective implementation and follow-up are:

1. Implementation occurs at the right time and in the proper sequence. It does not ignore constraining factors, and it does not come before steps 1, 2, and 3 in the problem-solving process.
2. Implementation occurs using a "small-wins" strategy—one small action at a time—in order to discourage resistance and engender support.
3. The implementation process includes opportunities for feedback. How well the solution works is communicated, and recurring information exchange occurs.
4. Participation by individuals affected by the problem solution is fostered in order to create support and commitment.
5. An ongoing measurement and monitoring system is set up. Long-term as well as short-term effects are assessed.
6. Evaluation of success is based on problem solution, not on side benefits. Although the solution may provide some positive outcomes, it is unsuccessful unless it solves the problem being considered.

Limitations of the Analytical Problem-Solving Model

Most experienced problem solvers are familiar with the preceding steps in analytical problem-solving, which are based on empirical research results and sound rationale (Eisenfuhr, Weber, & Langer, 2010; Hastie & Dawes, 2009; March, 1994; Mitroff, 1998).

Unfortunately, most of us do not always practice these steps. The demands of our lives often pressure us into circumventing some steps, and problem-solving suffers as a result. When these four steps are followed, however, effective problem-solving is markedly enhanced.

On the other hand, simply learning about and practicing these four steps does not guarantee that an individual will effectively solve all types of problems. These problem-solving steps are most effective mainly when the problems faced are straightforward, when alternatives are readily definable, when relevant information is available, and when a clear standard exists against which to judge the correctness of a solution.

The main tasks are to agree upon a single definition, gather the accessible information, generate alternatives, and make an informed choice. But many managerial problems do not conform to this model. Definitions, information, alternatives, and standards are often ambiguous or not readily available. In a complex, fast-paced, digital world, these conditions appear less and less frequently. Hence, knowing the steps in problem-solving and being able to implement them are not necessarily the same thing.

It may not be clear how much information is needed, what the complete set of alternatives is, or how one knows if the information being obtained is accurate. Analytical problem-solving may help, but something more is needed to address these problems successfully. Tom Peters said, in characterizing the modern world faced by managers: "If you're not confused, you're not paying attention."

Table 3.2 summarizes some reasons why analytical problem-solving is not always effective in day-to-day managerial situations. Some problems are simply not amenable to systematic or rational analysis. Sufficient and accurate information is not always available. Outcomes may not be predictable. Means-ends connections may not be evident. In order to solve such problems, a new way of thinking may be required, and we refer to this as creative problem-solving.

Impediments to Creative Problem-Solving

As mentioned at the beginning of the chapter, analytical problem-solving is focused on getting rid of problems. Creative problem-solving is focused on generating something new (DeGraff & DeGraff, 2011; DeGraff & Lawrence, 2002). The trouble is, most people have trouble solving problems creatively. There are two reasons why.

Table 3.2 Some Constraints on the Analytical Problem-Solving Model

Step	Constraints
1. Define the problem.	• There is seldom consensus as to the definition of the problem.
	• There is often uncertainty as to whose definition will be accepted.
	• Problems are usually defined in terms of the solutions already possessed.
	• Symptoms get confused with the real problem.
	• Confusing information inhibits problem identification.
2. Generate alternative solutions.	• Solution alternatives are usually evaluated one at a time as they are proposed.
	• Few of the possible alternatives are usually known.
	• The first acceptable solution is usually accepted.
	• Alternatives are based on what was successful in the past.
3. Evaluate and select an alternative.	• Limited information about each alternative is usually available.
	• Search for information occurs close to home—in easily accessible places.
	• The type of information available is constrained by factors such as primacy versus recency, extremity versus centrality, expected versus surprising, and correlation versus causation.
	• Gathering information on each alternative is costly.
	• Preferences of which is the best alternative are not always known.
	• Satisfactory solutions, not optimal ones, are usually accepted.
	• Solutions are often selected by oversight or default.
	• Solutions are often implemented before the problem is defined.
4. Implement and follow up on the solution.	• Others' acceptance of the solution is not always forthcoming.
	• Resistance to change is a universal phenomenon.
	• It is not always clear what part of the solution should be monitored or measured in follow-up.
	• Political and organizational processes must be managed in any implementation effort.
	• It may take a long time to implement a solution.

First, most of us misinterpret creativity as being one-dimensional—that is, creativity is limited to generating new ideas. We are often not aware of the multiple strategies available for being creative, so our repertoire is restricted. Second, all of us have developed certain conceptual blocks in our problem-solving activities, and we are largely unaware of these blocks. They inhibit us from solving certain problems effectively. These blocks are largely personal, as opposed to interpersonal or organizational, so skill development is required to overcome them.

In this chapter, we focus primarily on the skills involved in helping you become a better creative problem solver. A large literature exists on how managers and leaders can foster creativity in organizations, but this is not our focus (see for example, Mumford, 2011; Zhou & Shalley, 2008). Rather, we are interested in helping you strengthen and develop your personal skills and expand your repertoire of creative problem-solving alternatives.

Multiple Approaches to Creativity

One of the most sophisticated approaches to creativity identifies four distinct methods for achieving it: imagination, improvement, investment, and incubation. This approach is based on the Competing Values Framework (Cameron, et al., 2014), which identifies competing or conflicting dimensions that describe people's attitudes, values, and behaviors. Figure 3.1 describes the four different types of creativity and their relationships. These four types have been developed by our colleague Jeff DeGraff (DeGraff & DeGraff, 2017; DeGraff & Lawrence, 2002).

Achieving creativity through **imagination** refers to the *creation* of new ideas, breakthroughs, and radical approaches to problem-solving. People who pursue creativity in this way tend to be experimenters, speculators, and entrepreneurs, and they define creativity as exploration, new product innovation, or developing unique possibilities. When facing difficult problems in need of problem-solving, their approach is focused on coming up with untested possibilities and unique solutions. These kinds of people—people such as Steve Jobs, Stephen Hawking, and Walt Disney—approach problem-solving by generating radically new ideas and products that create entirely new industries or points of view.

However, people may also achieve creativity through opposite means—that is, by developing incrementally better alternatives, *improving* on what already exists, or clarifying the ambiguity that is associated with the problem. Rather than being revolutionaries and risk-takers, they are systematic, careful, and thorough. Creativity comes by finding ways to improve processes or functions.

An example is Ray Kroc, the visionary behind McDonald's remarkable success. As a salesman in the 1950s, Kroc bought out a restaurant in San Bernardino, California, from the McDonald brothers and, by creatively changing the way hamburgers were made and served, he created the largest food service company in the world. He didn't invent fast food—White Castle and Dairy Queen had long been established—but he changed the processes. Creating a limited, standardized menu; uniform cooking procedures; consistent service quality; clean facilities; and inexpensive food—no matter where in the world you eat—demonstrated

---

Figure 3.1 | **Four Types of Creativity**

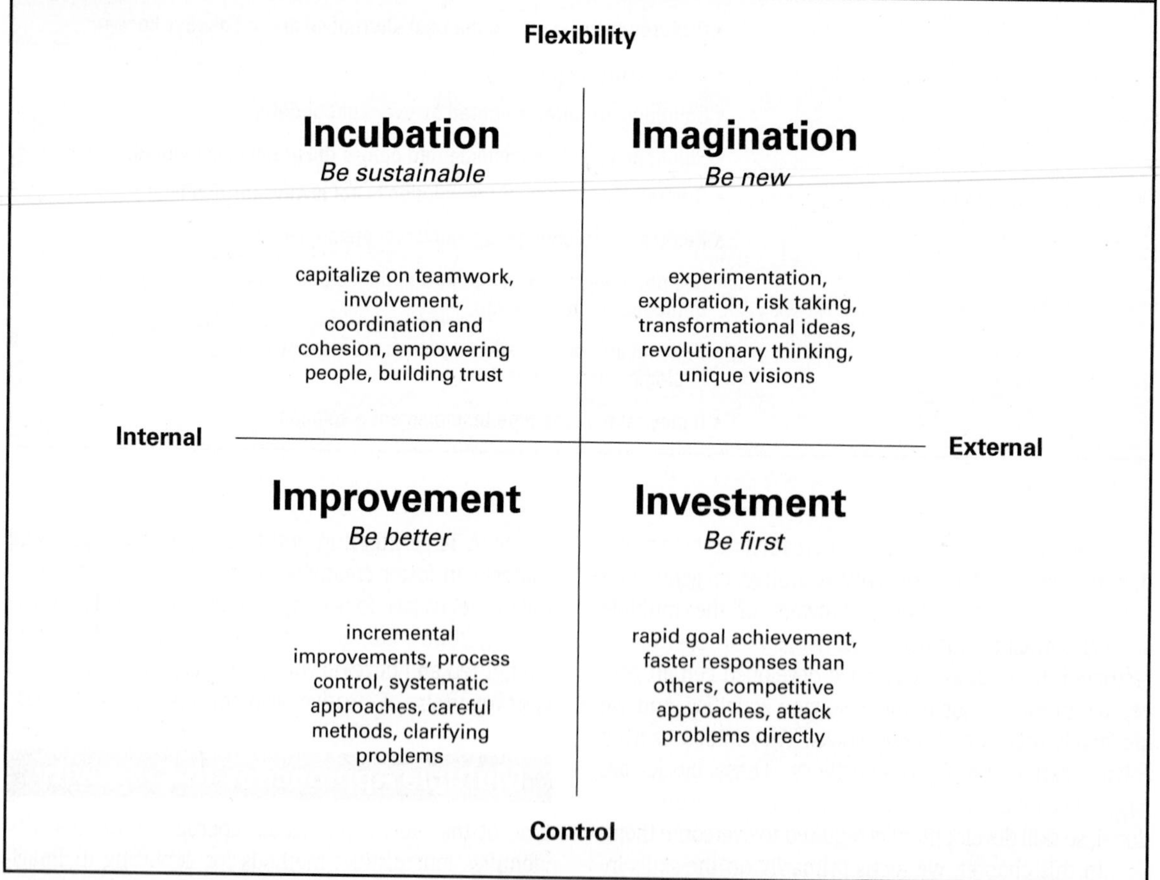

Flexibility

Incubation
Be sustainable

capitalize on teamwork, involvement, coordination and cohesion, empowering people, building trust

Imagination
Be new

experimentation, exploration, risk taking, transformational ideas, revolutionary thinking, unique visions

Internal ——————————————————————— External

Improvement
Be better

incremental improvements, process control, systematic approaches, careful methods, clarifying problems

Investment
Be first

rapid goal achievement, faster responses than others, competitive approaches, attack problems directly

Control

SOURCE: *Adapted from DeGraff & Lawrence, 2002.*

a very different approach to creativity. Instead of breakthrough ideas, Kroc's secret was incremental improvements on existing ideas. This type of creativity is referred to as **improvement**.

A third type of creativity is called **investment**, or the pursuit of rapid goal achievement and *competitiveness*. People who approach creativity in this way meet challenges head-on, adopt a competitive posture, and focus on achieving results faster than others. People achieve creativity by working harder than the competition; exploiting others' weaknesses; and being first to offer a product, service, or idea, even if it is not their own. The advantages of being a "first mover" company are well known.

This kind of creativity is illustrated by Honda president Kiyoshi Kawashima in the "Honda–Yamaha Motorcycle War." Honda became the industry leader in motorcycles in Japan in the 1960s but decided to enter the automobile market in the 1970s. Yamaha saw this as an opportunity to overtake Honda in motorcycle market share in Japan. In public speeches at the beginning of the 1980s, Yamaha president Yoshikazu Koike promised that Yamaha would soon overtake Honda in motorcycle production because of Honda's new focus on automobiles. Honda's president replied: "As long as I am president of this company, we will surrender our number one spot to no one... *Yamaha wo tsubusu*!"—meaning, we will crush (or smash, break, annihilate, or destroy) Yamaha.

In the next year, Honda introduced 81 new models of motorcycles and discontinued 32 models, for a total of 113 changes to its product line. In the following year, Honda introduced 39 additional models and added 18 changes to the 50cc line. Yamaha's sales plummeted 50 percent and the firm endured a loss of 24 billion yen for the year. Yamaha's president conceded: "I would like to end the Honda-Yamaha war....From now on we will move cautiously and ensure Yamaha's relative position as second to Honda." Approaching creativity through investment—rapid response, competitive maneuvering, and being the first mover—characterized Honda president Kawashima's approach to creativity.

The fourth type of creativity is **incubation**. This refers to an approach to creative activity through teamwork, involvement, and coordination among individuals. Creativity occurs by unlocking the potential that exists in interactions among networks of people. Individuals who approach creativity through incubation encourage people to work together, foster trust and cohesion, and empower others. Creativity arises from a collective mind-set and sharing ideas.

For example, Mahatma Gandhi is probably the only person in modern history who has single-handedly

stopped a war. Lone individuals have started wars, but Gandhi was creative enough to stop one. He did so by mobilizing networks of people to pursue a clear vision and set of values. Gandhi would probably have been completely noncreative and ineffective had he not been adept at capitalizing on incubation dynamics. By mobilizing people to march to the sea to make salt, or to burn passes that demarcated ethnic group status, Gandhi was able to engender creative outcomes that had not been considered possible. He was a master at incubation by connecting, involving, and coordinating people.

The same can be said for Bill Wilson, the founder of Alcoholics Anonymous, whose 12-step program is the foundation for almost all addiction treatment organizations around the world—gambling addiction, drug addiction, eating disorders, and so on. To cure his own alcoholism, Wilson began meeting with others with the same problem and, over time, developed a very creative way to help himself as well as other people overcome their dependencies. The genius behind Alcoholics Anonymous is the creativity that emerges when human interactions are facilitated and encouraged.

Figure 3.2 helps put these four types of creativity into perspective. You will note that imagination and improvement emphasize opposite approaches to creativity. They differ in the *magnitude* of the creative ideas being pursued. Imagination focuses on new, revolutionary solutions to problems. Improvement focuses on small, incremental solutions. Investment and incubation are also contradictory and opposing in their approach to creativity. They differ in *speed* of response. Investment focuses on fast, competitive responses to problems, whereas incubation emphasizes more developmental and deliberate responses.

It is important to point out that no one approach to creativity is best. Different circumstances call for different approaches. For example, Ray Kroc and McDonald's would not have been successful with an imagination strategy (revolutionary change), and Walt Disney would not have been effective with an incubation strategy (group consensus). Kawashima at Honda could not afford to wait for an incubation strategy (slow, developmental change); likewise, it would have made no sense for Gandhi to approach creativity using investment (a competitive approach). Figure 3.3 lists a number of circumstances in which each of these four approaches to creativity would be most effective.

This figure shows that imagination is the most appropriate approach to creativity when breakthroughs are needed and when original ideas are necessary—*being new*. The improvement approach is most appropriate when incremental changes or tightening up processes

Figure 3.2   Key Dimensions of Four Types of Creativity

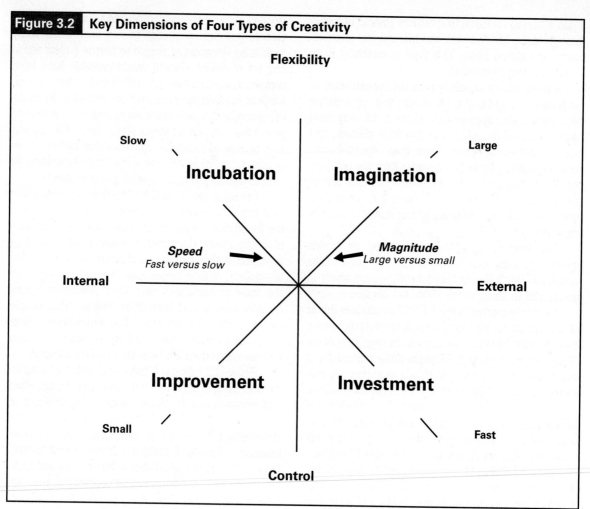

SOURCE: *Adapted from DeGraff & Lawrence, 2002.*

are necessary—*being better.* The investment approach is most appropriate when quick responses and goal achievement take priority—*being first.* And the incubation approach is most appropriate when collective effort and involvement of others are important—*being sustainable.*

The Creativity Assessment survey that you completed in the Assessment section helps identify your own preferences regarding these different approaches to creativity. You were able to create a profile showing the extent to which you are inclined toward imagination, improvement, investment, or incubation as you approach problems calling for creativity. Your profile will help you determine which kinds of problems you are inclined to solve when creativity is required. Of course, having a preference is not the same as having ability or possessing competence in a certain approach, so the remainder of this chapter will help with your creative competence development.

MyLab Management Watch it!
If your instructor has assigned this activity, go to www.pearson.com/mylab/management to complete the video exercise.

Conceptual Blocks

The trouble is, each of these different approaches to creativity can be inhibited. That is, in addition to being unaware of the multiple ways in which we can be creative, most of us have difficulty solving problems creatively because of the presence of **conceptual blocks**. Conceptual blocks are mental obstacles that constrain the way problems are defined, and they can inhibit us

Figure 3.3 | Examples of Situations in Which Each Approach Is Effective

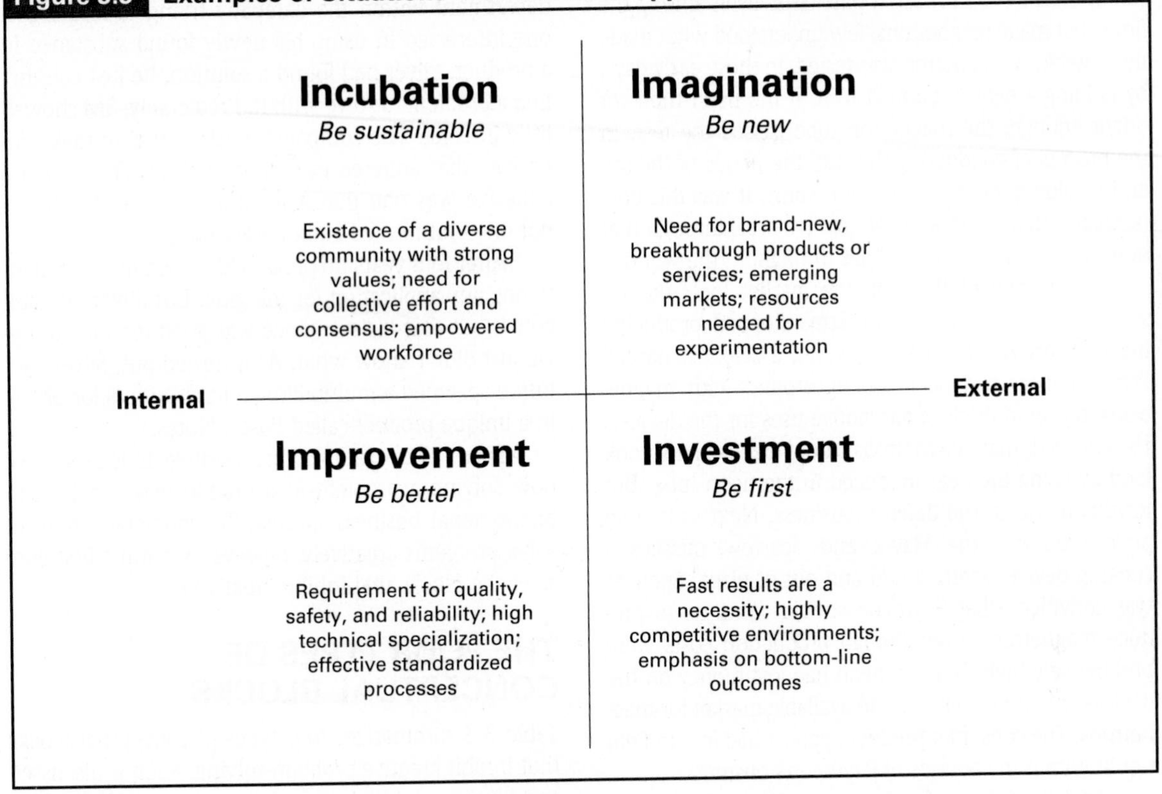

Incubation
Be sustainable

Existence of a diverse community with strong values; need for collective effort and consensus; empowered workforce

Imagination
Be new

Need for brand-new, breakthrough products or services; emerging markets; resources needed for experimentation

Internal ————————————————————— External

Improvement
Be better

Requirement for quality, safety, and reliability; high technical specialization; effective standardized processes

Investment
Be first

Fast results are a necessity; highly competitive environments; emphasis on bottom-line outcomes

LEARNING
ⓘ

SOURCE: *Adapted from DeGraff & Lawrence, 2002.*

from being effective in any of the four types of creativity. Conceptual blocks limit the number of alternative solutions that people think about (Adams, 2001; Tan & Parnell, 2013). Every individual has conceptual blocks, but some people have more numerous and more intense blocks than others. These blocks are largely unrecognized or unconscious, so the only way individuals can be made aware of them is to be confronted with problems that are unsolvable because of them. Conceptual blocks result largely from the thinking processes that problem solvers use when facing problems. Everyone develops some conceptual blocks over time. In fact, we need some of them to cope with everyday life. Here's why.

At every moment, each of us is bombarded with far more information than we can possibly absorb. For example, you are probably not conscious right now of the temperature of the room, the color of your skin, the level of illumination overhead, or how your toes feel in your shoes. All of this information is available to you and is being processed by your brain, but you have tuned out some things and focused on others. Over time, you must develop the habit of mentally filtering out some of the information to which you are exposed;

otherwise, information overload would drive you crazy. These filtering habits eventually become conceptual habits, or blocks. Though you are not conscious of them, they inhibit you from registering some kinds of information and, therefore, from solving certain kinds of problems.

In this section, we focus on problems that require creative rather than analytical solutions. We introduce some tools and techniques that help overcome conceptual blocks and unlock problem-solving creativity. First consider these two examples that illustrate creative problem-solving and breaking through conceptual blocks.

PERCY SPENCER'S MAGNETRON

During World War II, the British developed one of the best-kept military secrets of the war, a special radar detector based on a device called a magnetron. This radar was credited with turning the tide of battle in the war between Britain and Germany and helping the British withstand Hitler's blitzkrieg. In 1940, Raytheon was one of several U.S. firms invited to produce magnetrons for the war effort.

The workings of magnetrons were not well understood, even by sophisticated physicists. Even among the firms that made magnetrons, few understood what made them work. A magnetron was tested, in those early days, by holding a neon tube next to it. If the neon tube got bright enough, the magnetron tube passed the test. In the process of conducting the test, the hands of the scientist holding the neon tube got warm. It was this phenomenon that led to a major creative breakthrough that eventually transformed lifestyles throughout the world.

At the end of the war, the market for radar essentially dried up, and most firms stopped producing magnetrons. At Raytheon, however, a scientist named Percy Spencer had been fooling around with magnetrons, trying to think of alternative uses for the devices. He believed that magnetrons could be used to cook food by using the heat produced in the neon tube. But Raytheon was in the defense business. Next to its two prize products—the Hawk and Sparrow missiles—cooking devices seemed odd and out of place. Spencer was convinced that Raytheon should continue to produce magnetrons, even though production costs were prohibitively high. But Raytheon had lost money on the devices, and now there was no available market for magnetrons. The consumer product Spencer had in mind did not fit within the bounds of Raytheon's business.

As it turned out, Spencer's solution to Raytheon's problem produced the microwave oven and a revolution in cooking methods throughout the world. Later, we will analyze several problem-solving techniques illustrated by Spencer's creative triumph.

SPENCE SILVER'S GLUE

A second example of creative problem-solving began with Spence Silver's assignment to work on a temporary project team within the 3M company. The team was searching for new adhesives, so Silver obtained some material from AMD Inc. that had potential for a new polymer-based adhesive. He described one of his experiments in this way: "In the course of this exploration, I tried an experiment with one of the monomers in which I wanted to see what would happen if I put a lot of it into the reaction mixture. Before, we had used amounts that would correspond to conventional wisdom" (Nayak & Ketteringham, 1986).

The result was a substance that failed all the conventional 3M tests for adhesives. It didn't stick. It preferred its own molecules to the molecules of any other substance. It was more cohesive than adhesive. It sort of "hung around without making a commitment." It was a "now-it-works, now-it-doesn't" kind of glue.

For five years, Silver went from department to department within the company trying to find someone interested in using his newly found substance in a product. Silver had found a solution; he just couldn't find a problem to solve with it. Predictably, 3M showed little interest. The company's mission was to make adhesives that adhered ever more tightly. The ultimate adhesive was one that formed an unbreakable bond, not one that formed a temporary bond.

After four years no progess had been made in identifying any application for the glue. But Silver was still convinced that his substance was good for something. He just didn't know what. As it turned out, Silver's solution spawned a multibillion-dollar business for 3M—in a unique product called Post-it Notes.

These two examples are positive illustrations of how solving a problem in a unique way can lead to phenomenal business success. To understand how to solve problems creatively, however, we must first consider the blocks that inhibit creativity.

THE FOUR TYPES OF CONCEPTUAL BLOCKS

Table 3.3 summarizes four types of conceptual blocks that inhibit creative problem-solving. Each is discussed and illustrated with problems or exercises. We encourage you to complete the exercises and solve the problems as you read the chapter, because doing so will help you become aware of your own conceptual blocks. Later, we shall discuss in more detail how you can overcome those blocks.

Constancy

One type of conceptual block occurs because individuals become wedded to one way of looking at a problem or using one approach to define, describe, or solve it. It is easy to see why **constancy** is common in problem-solving. Being constant, or consistent, is a highly valued attribute for most of us. We like to appear at least moderately consistent in our approach to life, and constancy is often associated with maturity, honesty, and even intelligence. People who lack constancy are often viewed as untrustworthy, peculiar, or airheaded.

Some prominent psychologists theorize, in fact, that a need for constancy is the primary motivator of human behavior (Festinger, 1957; Guadagno & Cialdini, 2010; Heider, 1946; Newcomb, 1954). Many psychological studies have shown that once individuals take a stand or employ a particular approach to a problem, they are highly likely to pursue that same course without deviation in the future (see Cialdini, 2008, for multiple examples).

Table 3.3	Conceptual Blocks That Inhibit Creative Problem-Solving	
1. *Constancy*		
• Vertical thinking	Defining a problem in only one way without considering alternative views	
• One thinking language	Not using more than one language to define and assess the problem	
2. *Commitment*		
• Stereotyping based on past experience	Present problems are seen only as the variations of past problems	
• Ignoring commonalities	Failing to perceive commonalities among elements that initially appear to be different	
3. *Compression*		
• Distinguishing figure from ground	Not filtering out irrelevant information or finding needed information	
• Artificial constraints	Defining the boundaries of a problem too narrowly	
4. *Complacency*		
• Noninquisitiveness	Not asking questions	
• Nonthinking	A bias toward activity in place of mental work	

On the other hand, constancy can inhibit the solution of some kinds of problems. Consistency sometimes drives out creativity. Two illustrations of the constancy block are vertical thinking and using only one thinking language.

Vertical Thinking The term **vertical thinking** was coined by Edward de Bono (1968, 2015b). It refers to defining a problem in a single way and then pursuing that definition without deviation until a solution is reached. No alternative definitions are considered. All information gathered and all alternatives generated are consistent with the original definition. De Bono contrasted lateral thinking (de Bono, 2015a) with vertical thinking in the following ways: Vertical thinking focuses on continuity, lateral thinking focuses on discontinuity; vertical thinking chooses, lateral thinking changes; vertical thinking is concerned with stability, lateral thinking is concerned with instability; vertical thinking searches for what is right, lateral thinking searches for what is different; vertical thinking is analytical, lateral thinking is provocative; vertical thinking is concerned with where an idea came from, lateral thinking is concerned with where the idea is going; vertical thinking moves in the most likely directions, lateral thinking moves in the least likely directions; vertical thinking develops an idea, lateral thinking discovers the idea.

Plenty of examples exist of creative solutions that occurred because an individual refused to get stuck with a single problem definition. Alexander Graham Bell was trying to devise a hearing aid when he shifted definitions and invented the telephone. Harland Sanders was trying to sell his recipe to restaurants when he shifted definitions and developed his Kentucky Fried Chicken business. Karl Jansky was studying telephone static when he shifted definitions, discovered radio waves from the Milky Way galaxy, and developed the science of radio astronomy.

In developing the microwave oven industry, Percy Spencer shifted the definition of the problem from "How can we save our military radar business at the end of the war?" to "What other applications can be made for the magnetron?" Other problem definitions followed, such as: "How can we make magnetrons cheaper?" "How can we mass-produce magnetrons?" "How can we convince someone besides the military to buy magnetrons?" "How can we enter a consumer products market?" "How can we make microwave ovens practical and safe?" And so on. Each new problem definition led to new ways of thinking about the problem, new alternative approaches, and, eventually, to a new microwave oven industry.

Spence Silver at 3M began with "How can I get an adhesive that has a stronger bond?" but switched to "How can I find an application for an adhesive that doesn't stick firmly?" Eventually, other problem definitions followed: "How can we get this new glue to stick to one surface but not another?" "How can we replace staples, thumbtacks, and paper clips in the workplace?" "How can we manufacture and package a product that uses nonadhesive glue?" "How can we get anyone to pay $1.00 a pad for scratch paper?" And so on.

Shifting definitions is not easy, of course, because it is not natural. It requires you to deflect your tendency toward constancy. Later, we will discuss some hints and tools that can help you overcome the constancy block while avoiding the negative consequences of inconsistency.

A Single Thinking Language   A second manifestation of the constancy block is the use of only one **thinking language**. Most people think in words—that is, they think about a problem and its solution in terms of verbal language. **Analytical problem-solving** reinforces this approach. Some writers, in fact, have argued that thinking cannot even occur without words (Feldman, 1999; Vygotsky, Hanfmann, & Vakar, 1962). Other thought languages are available, however, such as nonverbal or symbolic languages (e.g., mathematics), sensory imagery (e.g., smelling or tactile sensation), feelings and emotions (e.g., happiness, fear, or anger), and visual imagery (e.g., mental pictures). The more languages available to problem solvers, the better and more creative their solutions will be.

Percy Spencer at Raytheon is a prime example of a visual thinker:

> One day, while Spencer was lunching with Dr. Ivan Getting and several other Raytheon scientists, a mathematical question arose. Several men, in a familiar reflex, pulled out their slide rules, but before any could complete the equation, Spencer gave the answer. Dr. Getting was astonished. "How did you do that?" he asked. "The root," said Spencer shortly. "I learned cube roots and squares by using blocks as a boy. Since then, all I have to do is visualize them placed together." (Scott, 1974, p. 287)

The microwave oven depended on Spencer's command of multiple thinking languages. Furthermore, the new oven would never have gotten off the ground without a critical incident that illustrates the power of visual thinking.

By 1965, Raytheon was just about to give up on any consumer application of the magnetron when a meeting was held with George Foerstner, president of the recently acquired Amana Refrigeration Company. In the meeting, costs, applications, manufacturing obstacles, and production issues were discussed. Foerstner galvanized the entire microwave oven effort with the following statement, as reported by a Raytheon vice president.

> George says, "It's no problem. It's about the same size as an air conditioner. It weighs about the same. It should sell for the same.

> So we'll price it at $499." Now you think that's silly, but you stop and think about it. Here's a man who really didn't understand the technologies. But there is about the same amount of copper involved, the same amount of steel as an air conditioner. And these are basic raw materials. It didn't make a lot of difference how you fit them together to make them work. They're both boxes; they're both made out of sheet metal; and they both require some sort of trim. (Nayak & Ketteringham, 1986, p. 181)

In several short sentences, Foerstner had taken one of the most complicated military secrets of World War II and translated it into something no more complex than a room air conditioner. He had painted a picture of an application that no one else had been able to capture by describing a magnetron visually, as a familiar object, not as a set of calculations, formulas, or blueprints.

A similar occurrence in the Post-it Note chronology also led to a breakthrough. Spence Silver had been trying for years to get someone in 3M to adopt his unsticky glue. Art Fry, another scientist with 3M, had heard Silver's presentations before. One day while singing in North Presbyterian Church in St. Paul, Minnesota, Fry was fumbling around with the slips of paper that marked the various hymns in his book. Suddenly, a visual image popped into his mind.

> I thought, "Gee, if I had a little adhesive on these bookmarks, that would be just the ticket." So I decided to check into that idea the next week at work. What I had in mind was Silver's adhesive.... I knew I had a much bigger discovery than that. I also now realized that the primary application for Silver's adhesive was not to put it on a fixed surface like bulletin boards. That was a secondary application. The primary application concerned paper to paper. I realized that immediately." (Nayak & Ketteringham, 1986, pp. 63–64)

Years of verbal descriptions had not led to any applications for Silver's glue. Tactile thinking (handling the glue) also had not produced many ideas. However, thinking about the product in visual terms, as applied to what Fry initially called "a better bookmark," led to the breakthrough that was needed.

To illustrate the differences among thinking languages, consider the following simple problem:

> Figure 3.4 shows seven matchsticks. By moving only one matchstick, make the figure into a true

Figure 3.4 The Matchstick Configuration

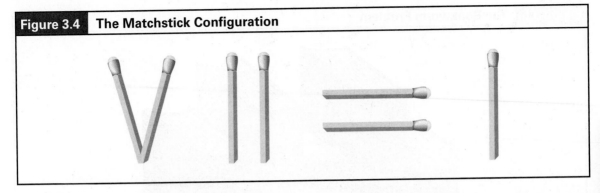

equality (i.e., the value on one side equals the value on the other side). Before looking up the answers in www.mylabmanagement.com, try defining the problem by using different thinking languages. What thinking language is most effective?

Commitment

Commitment can also serve as a conceptual block to creative problem-solving. Once individuals become committed to a particular point of view, definition, or solution, it is likely that they will follow through on that commitment. Cialdini (2008) reported a study, for example, in which researchers asked Californians to put a large, poorly lettered sign on their front lawns saying DRIVE CAREFULLY. Only 17 percent agreed to do so. However, after signing a petition expressing support for "keeping California beautiful," the people were again asked to put the DRIVE CAREFULLY sign on their lawns, and 76 percent agreed to do so. Once they had committed to being active and involved citizens (i.e., to keeping California beautiful), it was consistent for these people to agree to the large, unsightly sign as visible evidence of their commitment. Most people have the same inclination toward being consistent and maintaining commitments.

Two forms of commitment that produce conceptual blocks are stereotyping based on past experiences and **ignoring commonalities**.

Stereotyping Based on Past Experiences

Nobel laureate Daniel Kahneman (2013) pointed out that a major obstacle to innovative problem-solving is that individuals tend to define present problems in terms of problems they have faced in the past. Current problems are usually seen as variations on some past situation, so the alternatives proposed to solve the current problem are ones that have proven successful in the past. Both problem definitions and proposed solutions are therefore restricted by past experience. This restriction is referred to as **perceptual stereotyping** (Adams, 2001).

When individuals receive an initial cue regarding the definition of a problem, all subsequent problems are frequently framed in terms of the initial cue. Of course, this is not all bad, because perceptual stereotyping helps organize problems on the basis of a limited amount of data, and the need to consciously analyze every problem encountered is eliminated. On the other hand, perceptual stereotyping prevents individuals from viewing a problem in novel ways.

The creation of Post-it Notes provides an example of overcoming stereotyping based on past experiences. Spence Silver at 3M described his invention in terms of breaking stereotypes based on past experience.

> The key to the Post-It adhesive was doing the experiment. If I had sat down and factored it out beforehand, and thought about it, I wouldn't have done the experiment. If I had really seriously cracked the books and gone through the literature, I would have stopped. The literature was full of examples that said you can't do this. (Nayak & Ketteringham, 1986, p. 57)

Of course, one should try to learn from past experience and failing to learn the mistakes of history will not necessarily doom us to repeat them. However, commitment to a course of action based on past experience can sometimes inhibit viewing problems in new ways, and can even prevent us from solving some problems at all. Consider the following example.

Assume there are five volumes of medieval literature on the shelf (see Figure 3.5). Assume that the pages of each volume are exactly two inches thick and the front and back cover of each volume is each one-fourth of an inch thick. Assume that a bookworm began eating at page 1 of Volume I, and it ate straight through to the last page of Volume V. What distance did the worm cover? Solving this problem is relatively simple, but it requires that you overcome a stereotyping block to get the correct answer. (Why is 8 inches the correct answer?)

Figure 3.5 The Bookworm Problem

Ignoring Commonalities A second manifestation of the commitment block is failure to identify similarities among seemingly disparate pieces of data. This is among the most commonly identified blocks to creativity. It means that a person becomes committed to a particular point of view, to the fact that elements are different, and, consequently, becomes unable to make connections, identify themes, or perceive commonalities.

The ability to find one definition or solution for two seemingly dissimilar problems is a characteristic of creative individuals (see Sternberg, 1999). The inability to do this can overload a problem solver by requiring that every problem encountered be solved individually.

The discovery of penicillin by Sir Alexander Fleming resulted from his seeing a common theme among seemingly unrelated events. Fleming was working with some cultures of staphylococci that had accidentally become contaminated. The contamination, a growth of fungi, and isolated clusters of dead staphylococci led Fleming to see a relationship no one else had ever seen previously and thus to discover a wonder drug.

The famous chemist Friedrich Kekule saw a conection between his dream of a snake swallowing its own tail and the chemical structure of organic compounds. This creative insight led him to the discovery that organic compounds such as benzene have closed rings rather than open structures.

For Percy Spencer at Raytheon, seeing a link between the heat of a neon tube and the heat required to cook food was the creative connection that led to his breakthrough in the microwave oven industry. One of Spencer's colleagues recalled: "In the process of testing a bulb [with a magnetron], your hands got hot. I don't know when Percy really came up with the thought of microwave ovens, but he knew at that time—and that was 1942. He [remarked] frequently that this would be a good device for cooking food" (Nayak & Ketteringham, 1986, p. 184). Another colleague described Spencer this way: "The way Percy Spencer's mind worked is an interesting thing. He had a mind that allowed him to hold an extraordinary array of associations on phenomena and relate them to one another" (Nayak & Ketteringham, 1986, p. 205). Similarly, the connection Art Fry made between a glue that wouldn't stick tightly and marking hymns in a choir book was the final breakthrough that led to the development of the revolutionary Post-it Note business.

To test your own ability to see commonalities, try the following activity: What are some common terms that apply to both the substance water and the field of finance? (For example, "financial float.") (Some answers are in www.mylabmanagement.com.)

Compression

Conceptual blocks also occur as a result of **compression** of ideas. Looking too narrowly at a problem, screening out too much relevant data, and making assumptions that inhibit problem solving are common examples. Two especially cogent examples of compression are artificially constraining problems and not distinguishing figure from ground.

Artificial Constraints Sometimes people place boundaries around problems, or constrain their approach to them, in such a way that the problems become impossible to solve. Such constraints arise from hidden assumptions people make about problems they encounter. People assume that some problem definitions or alternative solutions are off-limits, so they ignore them. For an illustration of this conceptual block, look at Figure 3.6. This is a problem you have probably seen before. Without lifting your pencil from the paper, draw four straight lines that pass through all nine dots. Complete the task before reading further.

By thinking of the figure as more constrained than it actually is, the problem becomes impossible to solve. It is easy if you break out of your own limiting assumptions on the problem. Now that you have been cued, can you do the same task with only three lines? What limiting constraints are you placing on yourself?

If you are successful, now try to do the task with only one line. Can you determine how to put a single straight line through all nine dots without lifting your pencil from the paper? Both the three-line solution and some one-line solutions are provided in www.mylabmanagement.com.

Artificially constraining problems means that the problem definition and the possible alternatives are limited more than the problem requires. Creative problem-solving requires that individuals become adept at recognizing their hidden assumptions and expanding the alternatives they consider—whether they imagine, improve, invest, or incubate.

Separating Figure from Ground Another illustration of the compression block is the reverse of artificial constraints. It is the inability to constrain problems sufficiently so that they can be solved. Problems almost never come clearly specified, so problem solvers must determine what the real problem is. They must filter out inaccurate, misleading, or irrelevant information in order to define the problem correctly and generate appropriate alternative solutions. The inability to separate the important from the unimportant, and to compress problems appropriately, serves as a conceptual block because it exaggerates the complexity of a problem and inhibits a simple definition.

How well do you filter out irrelevant information and focus on the truly important part of a problem? Can you ask questions that get to the heart of the matter? Consider Figure 3.7. For each pair, find the pattern on

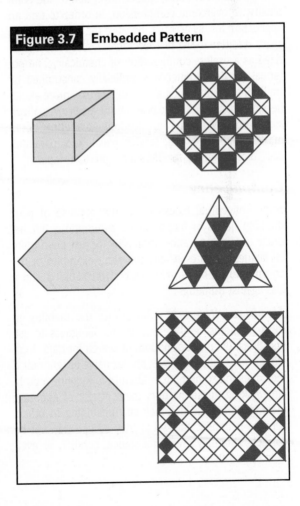

Figure 3.7	Embedded Pattern

Figure 3.6	The Nine-Dot Problem

LEARNING

the left that is embedded in the more complex pattern on the right. On the complex pattern, outline the embedded pattern. Now try to find at least two figures in each pattern. (See www.mylabmanagement.com for some solutions.)

Overcoming this compression block—separating figure from ground and artificially constraining problems—was an important explanation for the microwave oven and Post-it Note breakthroughs. George Foerstner's contribution to the development and manufacture of the microwave oven was to compress the problem, that is, to separate out all the irrelevant complexity that constrained others. Whereas the magnetron was a device so complicated that few people understood it, Foerstner focused on its basic raw materials, its size, and its functionality. By comparing it to an air conditioner, he eliminated much of the complexity and mystery, and, as described by two analysts, "He had seen what all the researchers had failed to see, and they knew he was right" (Nayak & Ketteringham, 1986, p. 181).

On the other hand, Spence Silver had to add complexity, to overcome compression, in order to find an application for his product. Because the glue had failed every traditional 3M test for adhesives, it was categorized as a useless configuration of chemicals. The potential for the product was artificially constrained by traditional assumptions about adhesives—more stickiness, stronger bonding is best—until Art Fry visualized some unconventional applications—a better bookmark, a bulletin board, scratch paper, and, paradoxically, a replacement for 3M's main product, tape.

Complacency

Some conceptual blocks occur not because of poor thinking habits or inappropriate assumptions but because of fear, ignorance, insecurity, or just plain mental laziness. Two especially prevalent examples of the **complacency** block are a lack of questioning and a bias against thinking.

Noninquisitiveness Sometimes the inability to solve problems results from an unwillingness to ask questions, obtain information, or search for data. Individuals may think they will appear naive or ignorant if they question something or attempt to redefine a problem. Asking questions puts them at risk of exposing their ignorance. It also may be threatening to others because it implies that what they accept may not be correct. This may create resistance, conflict, or even ridicule by others.

Creative problem-solving is inherently risky because it potentially involves interpersonal conflict. It is risky also because it is fraught with mistakes. As Linus Pauling, the Nobel laureate, is purported to have said, "If you want to have a good idea, have a lot of them, because most of them will be bad ones." Years of nonsupportive socialization, however, block the adventuresome and inquisitive stance in most people. Most of us are not rewarded for bad ideas. To illustrate, answer the following questions for yourself:

1. Would it be easier to learn a new language when you were five years old or now? Why?
2. How many times in the last month have you tried something for which the probability of success was less than 50 percent?
3. When was the last time you asked three "why" questions in a row?

To illustrate the extent of our lack of inquisitiveness, how many of the following questions can you answer?

❑ Why are people immune to their own body odor?
❑ What happens to the tread that wears off tires?
❑ Why doesn't sugar spoil or get moldy?
❑ Why doesn't a two-by-four measure 2 inches by 4 inches?
❑ Why is a smartphone keypad arranged differently than that of a calculator?
❑ Why do hot dogs come 10 in a package while buns come eight in a package?
❑ How do military cadets find their caps after throwing them in the air at football games and graduation?
❑ Why is Jack the nickname for John?

Most of us don't ask these kinds of questions because we have become complacent in our circumstances, and we don't really seek to find explanations for what is going on around us. We often stop being inquisitive as we get older because we learn that it is good to be intelligent, and being intelligent is interpreted as already knowing the answers, instead of asking good questions. Consequently, we learn less well at 25 years old than at age five, take fewer risks, avoid asking why, and function in the world without really trying to understand it. Creative problem solvers, on the other hand, are frequently engaged in inquisitive and experimental behavior. Spence Silver at 3M described his attitude about the complacency block this way:

People like myself get excited about looking for new properties in materials. I find that very satisfying, to perturb the structure slightly and just see what happens. I have a hard time talking people into doing that—people who are more highly trained. It's been my experience that people are reluctant just to try, to experiment—just to see what will happen. (Nayak & Ketteringham, 1986, p. 58)

Bias Against Thinking A second manifestation of the complacency block is in an inclination to avoid doing mental work. This block, like most of the others, is partly a cultural bias as well as a personal one. For example, assume that you passed by your roommate's or colleague's office one day and noticed him leaning back in his chair, staring out the window. A half hour later, as you passed by again, he had his feet up on the desk, still staring out the window. And 20 minutes later, you noticed that his demeanor hadn't changed much. What would be your conclusion? Most of us would assume that the fellow was not doing any work. We would assume that unless we saw action, he wasn't being productive.

When was the last time you heard someone say, "I'm sorry. I can't go to the ball game [or concert, dance, party, or movie] because I have to think?" Or, "I'll do the dishes tonight. I know you need to catch up on your thinking"? That these statements sound silly illustrates the bias most people develop toward action rather than thought, or against putting their feet up, rocking back in their chair, looking off into space, and engaging in solitary cognitive activity. This does not mean daydreaming or fantasizing, just concentrated thinking.

A particular conceptual block exists in Western cultures against the kind of thinking that uses the right hemisphere of the brain. **Left-hemisphere thinking**, for most people, is concerned with logical, analytical, linear, or sequential tasks. Thinking using the left hemisphere is apt to be organized, planned, and precise. Language and mathematics are left-hemisphere activities. **Right-hemisphere thinking**, on the other hand, is concerned with intuition, synthesis, playfulness, and qualitative judgment. It tends to be more spontaneous, imaginative, and emotional than left-hemisphere thinking. The emphasis in most formal education is toward left-hemisphere thought development even more in Eastern cultures than in Western cultures.

Problem-solving on the basis of reason, logic, and utility is generally rewarded, while problem-solving based on sentiment, intuition, or pleasure is frequently considered tenuous and inferior.

A number of researchers have found that the most creative problem solvers are **ambidextrous** in their thinking. That is, they use both left- and right-hemisphere thinking and easily switch from one to the other (Hermann, 1991; Hudspith, 1985; Martindale, 1999). Creative ideas arise most frequently in the right hemisphere but must be processed and interpreted by the left, so creative problem solvers use both hemispheres equally well.

Try the exercise in Table 3.4. It illustrates this principle of ambidexterity. There are two lists of words. Take about two minutes to memorize the first list. Then, on a piece of paper, write down as many words as you can remember. Now take about two minutes and memorize the words in the second list. Repeat the process of writing down as many words as you can remember.

Most people remember more words from the first list than from the second. This is because the first list contains words that relate to visual perceptions. They connect with right-brain activity as well as left-brain activity. People can draw mental pictures or visualize them. The same is true for creative ideas. The more both sides of the brain are used, the more creative the ideas.

Table 3.4	Exercise to Test Ambidextrous Thinking	
List 1	**List 2**
sunset	decline
perfume	very
brick	ambiguous
monkey	resources
castle	term
guitar	conceptual
pencil	about
computer	appendix
umbrella	determine
radar	forget
blister	quantity
chessboard	survey

LEARNING

Review of Conceptual Blocks

So far, we have suggested that certain conceptual blocks prevent individuals from solving problems creatively and from engaging in the four different types of creativity. These blocks narrow the scope of problem definition, limit the consideration of alternative solutions, and constrain the selection of an optimal solution. Unfortunately, many of these conceptual blocks are unconscious, and only when conceptual blocks make problems unsolvable do individuals become aware that they exist.

We have attempted to make you aware of your own conceptual blocks by asking you to solve some simple problems that require you to overcome these mental barriers. These conceptual blocks are not all bad, of course; not all problems should be addressed with creative problem-solving. But research has shown that individuals who have developed creative problem-solving skills are far more effective with complex problems that require a search for alternative solutions than others who are conceptually blocked (Collins & Amabile, 1999; DeGraff & DeGraff, 2017; Kaufman & Sternberg, 2010; Sternberg, 1999).

In the next section, we provide some techniques and tools that help overcome these blocks and improve creative problem-solving skills.

Conceptual Blockbusting

Conceptual blocks cannot be overcome all at once because most blocks are a product of years of habit-forming thought processes. Overcoming them requires practice in thinking in different ways over a long period of time. You will not become a skilled creative problem solver just by reading this chapter. On the other hand, research has demonstrated that by becoming aware of your conceptual blocks and practicing the following techniques, you can enhance your **creative problem-solving** skills.

STAGES IN CREATIVE THOUGHT

A first step in overcoming conceptual blocks is recognizing that creative problem-solving is a skill that can be developed. Being a creative problem solver is not an inherent ability that some people naturally have and others do not have. Jacob Rainbow, an employee of the U.S. Patent Office who has more than 200 patents himself, described the creative process as follows:

> *So you need three things to be an original thinker. First, you have to have a tremendous amount of information—a big data base if you like to be fancy. Then you have to be willing to pull the ideas, because you're interested. Now, some people could do it, but they don't bother. They're interested in doing something else. It's fun to come up with an idea, and if nobody wants it, I don't give a damn. It's just fun to come up with something strange and different. And then you must have the ability to get rid of the trash which you think of. You cannot only think of good ideas. And by the way, if you're not well-trained, but you've got good ideas, and you don't know if they're good or bad, then you send them to the Bureau of Standards, National Institute of Standards, where I work, and we evaluate them. And we throw them out. (Csikszentmihalyi, 1996, p. 48)*

In other words, gather a lot of information, use it to generate a lot of ideas, and sift through your ideas and get rid of the bad ones. Researchers generally agree that creative problem-solving involves four stages: *preparation, incubation, illumination,* and *verification* (see Albert & Runco, 1999; Kaufman, 2016; Kaufman & Sternberg, 2010; Nickerson, 1999; Poincare, 1921; Ribot, 1906; Wallas, 1926).

The **preparation stage** includes gathering data, defining the problem, generating alternatives, and consciously examining all available information. The primary difference between skillful creative problem-solving and analytical problem-solving is in how this first step is approached. Creative problem solvers are more flexible and fluent in data gathering, problem definition, alternative generation, and examination of options. In fact, it is in this stage that training in creative problem-solving can significantly improve effectiveness, because the other three steps are not amenable to conscious mental work (Adams, 2001; deBono, 2015b; Eisenfuhr, Weber, & Langer, 2010). The following discussion, therefore, is limited primarily to improving functioning in this first stage.

The **incubation stage** involves mostly unconscious mental activity in which the mind combines unrelated thoughts in pursuit of a solution. Conscious effort is not involved. **Illumination**, the third stage, occurs when an insight is recognized and a creative solution is articulated. **Verification** is the final stage, which involves evaluating the creative solution relative to some standard of acceptability.

In the preparation stage, two types of techniques are available for improving creative problem-solving abilities. One technique helps individuals think about and *define problems more creatively*; the other helps individuals gather information and *generate more alternative solutions* to problems.

One major difference between creative problem solvers and other people is that creative problem solvers are less constrained. They allow themselves to be more flexible in the definitions they impose on problems and the number of solutions they identify (Reiter-Palmon, 2014). They develop a large repertoire of approaches to problem-solving. In short, they engage in what Csikszentmihalyi (1996) described as "playfulness and childishness." They try more things and worry less about their false starts or failures. As Interaction Associates (1971, p. 15) explained:

> *Flexibility in thinking is critical to good problem solving. A problem solver should be able to conceptually dance around the problem like a good boxer, jabbing and poking, without getting caught in one place or "fixated." At any given moment, a good problem solver should be able to apply a large number of strategies [for generating alternative definitions and solutions]. Moreover, a good problem solver is a person who has developed, through his understanding of strategies and experiences in problem solving, a sense of appropriateness of what is likely to be the most useful strategy at any particular time.*

We now present a few tools and hints that we have found to be especially effective and relatively simple to help unfreeze you from your normal skeptical, analytical approach to problems and increase your playfulness. They relate to (1) defining problems and (2) generating alternative solutions.

METHODS FOR IMPROVING PROBLEM DEFINITION

Problem definition is probably the most critical step in creative problem-solving. Once a problem is defined, solving it is often relatively simple. However, as explained in Table 3.2, individuals tend to define problems in terms with which they are familiar. Even well-trained scientists encounter this problem. Good scientists study the most important problems they think they can solve.

When they are presented with a problem that is new or complex or does not appear to have an easily identified solution, the problem either remains undefined or is redefined in terms of something familiar.

Unfortunately, new problems may not be the same as old problems, so relying on past definitions may impede the process of solving current problems or lead to solving the wrong problem. Applying techniques for creative problem definition can help individuals see problems in alternative ways so their definitions are less narrowly constrained. Three such techniques for improving and expanding the definition process are discussed below.

Make the Strange Familiar and the Familiar Strange

One well-known, well-tested technique for improving creative problem-solving is called **synectics** (Gordon, 1961; Nolan & Williams, 2010; Roukes, 1988). The goal of synectics is to help you put something you don't know in terms of something you do know, then reverse the process back again. The point is, by analyzing what you know and applying it to what you don't know, you can develop new insights and perspectives. The process of synectics relies on the use of analogies and metaphors, and it works this way:

First, you form a definition of a problem (make the strange familiar). Then you try to transform that definition so it is made similar to something completely different that you know more about (make the familiar strange). That is, you use analogies and metaphors (synectics) to create this distortion. Postpone the original definition of the problem while you examine the analogy or the metaphor. Then impose this same analysis on the original problem to see what new insights you can uncover.

For example, suppose you have defined a problem as low morale among members of your team. You may form an analogy or metaphor by answering questions such as the following about the problem:

❑ What does this remind me of?

❑ What does this make me feel like?

❑ What is this similar to?

❑ What is this the opposite of?

Your answers, for example, might be: This problem reminds me of trying to get warm on a cold day (I need more activity). It makes me feel like I do when visiting a hospital ward (I need to smile and go out of my way to empathize with people). It is similar to the losing team's locker room after an athletic contest

(I need to find an alternative purpose or goal). This isn't like a well-tuned automobile (I need to do a careful diagnosis). And so on. Metaphors and analogies should connect what you are less sure about (the original problem) to what you are more sure about (the metaphor). By analyzing the metaphor or analogy, you may identify attributes of the problem that were not evident before. New insights may occur and new ideas may come to mind.

Many creative solutions have been generated by such a technique. For example, William Harvey was the first to apply the "pump" analogy to the heart, which led to the discovery of the body's circulatory system. Niels Bohr compared the atom to the solar system and supplanted Ernest Rutherford's prevailing "raisin pudding" model of matter's building blocks. Consultant Roger von Oech (1986) helped turn around a struggling computer company by applying a restaurant analogy to the company's operations. By analyzing the restaurant model rather than the company, von Oech was able to uncover the real problems.

Major contributions in the field of organizational behavior have occurred by applying analogies to other types of organization, such as machines, cybernetic or open systems, force fields, clans, and so on. Probably the most effective analogies (called parables) were used by Jesus to teach principles that otherwise were difficult for individuals to grasp (for example, the prodigal son, the good Samaritan, a shepherd and his flock).

Some hints to keep in mind when constructing analogies are:

❑ Include action or motion in the analogy (e.g., driving a car, cooking a meal, attending a funeral).

❑ Include things that can be visualized or pictured in the analogy (e.g., circuses, football games, crowded shopping malls).

❑ Pick familiar events or situations (e.g., families, kissing, bedtime).

❑ Try to relate things that are not obviously similar (e.g., saying an organization is like a big group is not nearly as rich a simile as saying that an organization is like, say, a psychic prison or a poker game).

Four types of analogies are recommended as part of synectics: **personal analogies**, in which individuals try to identify themselves as the problem ("If I were the problem, how would I feel, what would I like, what could satisfy me?"); **direct analogies**, in which individuals apply facts, technology, and common experience to the problem (e.g., Isambard Kingdom Brunel Brunel solved the problem of underwater construction by watching a shipworm tunneling into a tube); **symbolic analogies**, in which symbols or images are imposed on the problem (e.g., modeling the problem mathematically or diagramming the process flow); and **fantasy analogies**, in which individuals ask the question "In my wildest dreams, how would I wish the problem to be resolved?" (e.g., "I wish all employees would work with no supervision.").

Elaborate on the Definition

There are a variety of ways to enlarge, alter, or replace a problem definition once it has been specified. One way is to force yourself to generate at least two alternative hypotheses for every problem definition. That is, specify at least two plausible definitions of the problem in addition to the one originally accepted. Think in plural rather than singular terms. Instead of asking, "What is the problem?" "What is the meaning of this?" "What will be the result?" instead ask questions such as "What are the problems?" "What are the meanings of this?" "What will be the results?"

As an example, look at Figure 3.8. Select the figure that is different from all the others.

Figure 3.8 | **The Five-Figure Problem**

Of the five figures below, select the one that is different from all of the others.

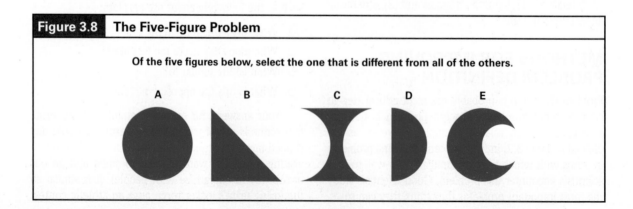

A majority of people select B first. If you did, you're right. It is the only figure that has all straight lines. On the other hand, quite a few people pick A. If you are one of them, you're also right. It is the only figure with a continuous line and no points of discontinuity. Alternatively, C can also be right, with the rationale that it is the only figure with two straight and two curved lines. Similarly, D is the only one with one curved and one straight line, and E is the only figure that is nonsymmetrical or partial. The point is, there can often be more than one problem definition, more than one right answer, and more than one perspective from which to view a problem.

Another way to elaborate definitions is to use a question checklist. This is a series of questions designed to help you think of alternatives to your accepted definitions. Several creative managers have shared with us some of their most fruitful questions, such as:

❑ Is there anything else?

❑ Is the reverse true?

❑ Is this a symptom of a more general problem?

❑ Who sees it differently?

Nickerson (1999) reported an oft-used acronym—SCAMPER—designed to bring to mind questions having to do with **S**ubstitute, **C**ombine, **A**dapt, **M**odify (Magnify–Minimize), **P**ut to other uses, **E**liminate, and **R**earrange.

As an exercise, take a minute now to think of a problem you are currently experiencing. Write it down so it is formally defined. Now manipulate that definition by answering the four questions in the checklist. If you can't think of a problem, try the exercise with this one. "I am not as attractive/intelligent/creative as I would like to be." How would you answer the four questions?

Reverse the Definition

A third tool for improving and expanding problem definition is to reverse the definition of the problem. That is, turn the problem upside down, inside out, or back to front. Reverse the way in which you think of the problem. For example, consider the following problem:

A tradition in Sandusky, Ohio, for as long as anyone could remember was the Fourth of July parade. It was one of the largest and most popular events on the city's annual calendar. Now, in 1988, the city mayor was hit with some startling and potentially disastrous

news. The state of Ohio was mandating that liability insurance be carried on every attraction—floats, bands, majorettes—that participated in the parade. To limit the city's liabilty in the case of an accident or injury of any parade participant, each had to be covered by liability insurance.

The trouble, of course, was that taking out a liability insurance policy for all parade participants would be a much greater expense than the city could afford. The amount of insurance required for that large a number of participants and equipment made it impossible for the city to carry the cost. On the one hand, the mayor hated to cancel an important tradition that everyone in town looked forward to. On the other hand, to hold the event would break the city budget. If you were a consultant to the mayor, what would you suggest?

Commonly suggested alternatives in this problem include the following:

1. Try to negotiate with an insurance company for a lower rate. (However, the risk is merely being transferred to the insurance company.)
2. Hold fundraising events to generate enough money to purchase the insurance policy, or find a wealthy donor to sponsor the parade. (However, this may deflect potential donations away from, or may compete with, other community service agencies, such as the United Way, American Red Cross, or local churches that also sponsor fundraisers and require donations.)
3. Charge a "participation fee" to parade participants to cover the insurance expense. (However, this would likely eliminate most high school, middle school, and elementary school bands and floats. It would also reduce the amount of money float builders and sponsoring organizations could spend on the actual float. Such a requirement would likely be a parade killer.)
4. Charge a fee to spectators of the parade. (However, this would require restricted access to the parade, an administrative structure to coordinate fee collection and ticketing, and the destruction of the sense of community participation that characterized this traditional event.)

Each of these suggestions is good, but each maintains a single definition of the problem. Each assumes

LEARNING

that the solution to the problem is associated with solving the financial problem associated with the liability insurance requirement. Each suggestion, therefore, brings with it some danger of damaging the traditional nature of the parade or eliminating it altogether. If the problem is reversed, other answers normally not considered become evident. That is, the need for liability insurance at all could be addressed.

Here is an excerpt from a newspaper report of how the problem was addressed:

Sandusky, Ohio (AP) *The Fourth of July parade here wasn't canceled, but it was immobilized by liability insurance worries. The band marched in place to the beat of a drum, and a county fair queen waved to her subjects from a float moored to the curb.*

The Reverse Community parade began at 10:00 a.m. Friday along Washington Row at the north end of the city and stayed there until dusk. "Very honestly, it was the issue of liability," said Gene Kleindienst, superintendent of city schools and one of the celebration's organizers. "By not having a mobile parade, we significantly reduced the issue of liability," he said.

The immobile parade included about 20 floats and displays made by community groups. Games, displays, and food booths were in an adjacent park. Parade chairman Judee Hill said some folks didn't understand, however. "Someone asked me if she was too late for the parade, and she had a hard time understanding the parade is here all day," she said.

Those who weren't puzzled seemed to appreciate the parade for its stationary qualities. "I like this. I can see more," said 67-year-old William A. Sibley. "I'm 80 percent blind. Now I know there's something there," he said pointing to a float.

Spectator Emmy Platte preferred the immobile parade because it didn't go on for "what seemed like miles," exhausting participants. "You don't have those little drum majorettes passing out on the street," she commented.

Baton twirler Tammy Ross said her performance was better standing still. "You can throw better. You don't have to worry about dropping it as much," she explained.

Mr. Kleindienst said community responses were favorable. "I think we've started a new tradition," he said.

By reversing the definition, Sandusky not only eliminated the problem without damaging the tradition and without shifting the risk to insurance companies or other community groups; it also added a new dimension that allowed at least some people to enjoy the event more than ever.

This reversal is similar to what Rothenberg (1979, 1991, 2014) referred to as **Janusian thinking**. Janus is the Roman god with two faces that look in opposite directions. Janusian thinking means thinking contradictory thoughts at the same time; that is, conceiving two opposing ideas to be true concurrently. Rothenberg claimed, after studying 54 highly creative artists and scientists (e.g., Nobel Prize winners), that most major scientific breakthroughs and artistic masterpieces are products of Janusian thinking. Creative people who actively formulate antithetical ideas and then resolve them produce the most valuable contributions to the scientific and artistic worlds. Quantum leaps in knowledge often occur as a result of Janusian thinking.

An example is Einstein's account (1919, p. 1) of having "the happiest thought of my life." He developed the concept that, "for an observer in free fall from the roof of a house, there exists, during his fall, no gravitational field . . . in his immediate vicinity. If the observer releases any objects, they will remain, relative to him, in a state of rest. The [falling] observer is therefore justified in considering his state as one of rest." Einstein concluded, in other words, that two seemingly contradictory states could be present simultaneously: motion and rest. This realization led to the development of his revolutionary general theory of relativity.

In another study of creative potential, Rothenberg and Hausman (2000) found that when individuals were presented with a stimulus word and asked to respond with the word that first came to mind, highly creative students, Nobel scientists, and prize-winning artists responded with antonyms significantly more often than did individuals with average creativity. Rothenberg argued, based on these results, that creative people think in terms of opposites more often than other people do. (This finding has been reconfirmed in a variety of studies.)

For our purposes, the whole point is to reverse or contradict the currently accepted definition in order to expand the number of perspectives considered. For instance, a problem might be that morale is

Table 3.5	Techniques for Improving Problem Definition
1. **Make the strange familiar and the familiar strange** (for example, analogies and metaphors).	
2. **Elaborate on the definition** (for example, question checklists and SCAMPER).	
3. **Reverse the definition** (for example, Janusian thinking and opposition).	

Table 3.6	Techniques for Generating More Alternatives
1. **Defer judgment** (for example, brainstorming).	
2. **Expand current alternatives** (for example, subdivision).	
3. **Combine unrelated attributes** (for example, morphological synthesis and relational algorithm).	

too high instead of (or in addition to) too low in our team (we may need more discipline), or maybe employees need less motivation (more direction) instead of more motivation to increase productivity. Opposites and backward looks often enhance creativity in problem definition.

These three techniques for improving creative problem definition are summarized in Table 3.5. Their purpose is not to help you generate alternative definitions just for the sake of alternatives but to broaden your perspectives, to help you overcome conceptual blocks, and to produce more elegant (i.e., high-quality and parsimonious) solutions. They are tools or techniques that you can easily use when you are faced with the need to solve problems creatively.

WAYS TO GENERATE MORE ALTERNATIVES

Because a common tendency is to define problems in terms of available solutions (i.e., the problem is defined as already possessing a certain set of possible solutions; see, for example, Kahneman, 2013), most of us consider a minimal number and a narrow range of alternatives in problem-solving. Most experts agree, however, that the primary characteristics of effective creative problem solvers are their **fluency** and their **flexibility of thought** (Sternberg, 1999).

Fluency refers to the number of ideas or concepts produced in a given length of time. Flexibility refers to the diversity of ideas or concepts generated. While most problem solvers consider a few homogeneous alternatives, creative problem solvers consider many heterogeneous alternatives.

The following techniques are designed to help you improve your ability to generate a large number and a wide variety of alternatives when faced with problems, whether they be imagination, improvement, investment, or incubation. They are summarized in Table 3.6.

Defer Judgment

Probably the most common method of generating alternatives is the technique of **brainstorming** developed by Osborn (1953). This tool is powerful because most people make quick judgments about each piece of information or each alternative solution they encounter. Brainstorming is designed to help people generate alternatives for problem-solving without prematurely evaluating, and hence discarding, them. It is practiced by having a group of people get together and simply begin sharing ideas about a problem— one at a time, with someone recording the ideas that are suggested. Four main rules govern brainstorming:

1. No evaluation of any kind is permitted as alternatives are being generated. Individual energy is spent on generating ideas, not on defending them.
2. The wildest and most divergent ideas are encouraged. It is easier to tighten alternatives than to loosen them up.
3. The quantity of ideas takes precedence over the quality. Emphasizing quality engenders judgment and evaluation.
4. Participants should build on or modify the ideas of others. Poor ideas that are added to or altered often become good ideas.

The idea of brainstorming is to use it in a group setting so individuals can stimulate ideas in one another. Brainstorming often begins with a flurry of ideas that then diminish. After a rush of alternatives is produced at the outset of a brainstorming session, the quantity of ideas often rapidly subsides. But to stop at that point is an ineffective use of brainstorming. Once easily identifiable solutions have been exhausted, that's when the truly creative alternatives are often produced in brainstorming groups. So keep working. Apply some of the tools described in this chapter for expanding definitions and alternatives. If brainstorming continues and members are encouraged to think past that point, breakthrough ideas often emerge as less common or less familiar alternatives are suggested. After that phase has unfolded in brainstorming, it is usually best to terminate the process and begin refining and consolidating ideas.

Recent research has found that brainstorming in a group may be less efficient and more time consuming than alternative forms of brainstorming due to free riders, unwitting evaluations, production blocking, and so on. One widely used alternative brainstorming technique is to have individual group members generate ideas on their own, then submit them to the group for exploration and evaluation (Paulus & Nijstad, 2003). Alternatively, electronic brainstorming, in which individuals use chat rooms or their own computer to generate ideas, has shown positive results as well (Siau, 1995). What is clear from the research is that generating alternatives with others produces more and better ideas than can be produced alone.

The best way to get a feel for the power of brainstorming groups is to participate in one. Try the following exercise based on an actual problem faced by a group of students and university professors. Spend at least 10 minutes in a small group, brainstorming your ideas.

> The business school faculty has become increasingly concerned about the ethics associated with modern business practice. The general reputation of business executives is in the tank. They are seen as greedy, dishonest, and untrustworthy. What could the faculty or the school do to affect this problem?

How do you define the problem? What ideas can you come up with? Generate as many ideas as you can following the rules of brainstorming. After at least 10 minutes, assess the fluency (the number) and flexibility (the variety) of the ideas you generated as a team.

Expand Current Alternatives

Sometimes brainstorming in a group is not possible or is too costly in terms of the number of people involved and hours required. Managers facing a fast-paced twenty-first-century environment may find brainstorming to be too inefficient. Moreover, people sometimes need an external stimulus or way to break through conceptual blocks to help them generate new ideas. One useful and readily available technique for expanding alternatives is **subdivision**, or dividing a problem into smaller parts. This is a well-used and proven technique for enlarging the alternative set.

For example, March and Simon (1958, p. 193) suggested that subdivision improves problem-solving by increasing the speed with which alternatives can be generated and selected.

> *The mode of subdivision has an influence on the extent to which planning can proceed simultaneously on the several aspects of the problem. The more detailed the factorization of the problem, the more simultaneous activity is possible, hence, the greater the speed of problem solving.*

To see how subdivision helps develop more alternatives and speeds the process of problem-solving, consider the problem, common in the creativity literature, of listing alternative uses for a familiar object. For example, in one minute, how many uses can you list for a Ping-Pong ball? Ready . . . go.

The more uses you identify, the greater is your fluency in thinking. The more variety in your list, the greater is your flexibility in thinking. You may have included the following in your list: bob for a fishing line, Christmas ornament, toy for a cat, gearshift knob, model for a molecular structure, wind gauge when hung from a string, head for a finger puppet, miniature basketball. Your list will be much longer.

Now that you have produced your list, apply the technique of subdivision by identifying the specific characteristics of a Ping-Pong ball. That is, divide it into its component attributes. For example, weight, color, texture, shape, porosity, strength, hardness, chemical properties, and conduction potential are all attributes of Ping-Pong balls that help expand the uses you might think of. By dividing an object mentally into more specific attributes, you can arrive at many more alternative uses (e.g., reflector, holder when cut in half, bug bed, ball for lottery drawing, inhibitor of an electrical current, and so on).

One exercise we have used with students and executives to illustrate this technique is to have them write down as many of their leadership or managerial strengths as they can think of. Most people list 10 or 12 attributes relatively easily. Then we analyze the various aspects of the manager's role, the activities in which managers engage, the challenges that most managers face from inside and outside the organization, the different roles they perform, and so on. We then ask these same people to write down another list of their strengths as managers. The list is almost always more than twice as long as the first list. By identifying the subcomponents of any problem, far more alternatives can be generated than by considering the problem as a whole.

Try this by yourself. Divide your life into the multiple roles you play—student, friend, neighbor, leader, brother or sister, and so on. If you list your strengths associated with each role, your list will be much longer than if you just create a general list of personal strengths.

Combine Unrelated Attributes

A third technique focuses on helping problem solvers expand alternatives by forcing the integration of seemingly unrelated elements. Research in creative problem-solving has shown that an ability to see common relationships among disparate factors is a major factor in differentiating creative from noncreative individuals (Feldman, 1999). Two ways to do this are through morphological synthesis (Koberg & Bagnall, 2003; Molina, et al., 2015) and the relational algorithm (Crovitz, 1970).

With **morphological synthesis**, a four-step procedure is involved. First, the problem is written down. Second, attributes of the problem are listed. Third, alternatives to each attribute are listed. Fourth, different alternatives from the attributes list are combined together.

This seems a bit complicated, so let us illustrate the procedure. Suppose you are faced with the problem of an employee who takes an extended lunch break almost every day despite your reminders to be on time. Think of alternative ways to solve this problem. The first solution that comes to mind for most people is to sit down and have a talk with (or threaten) the employee. If that doesn't work, most of us would reduce the person's pay, demote or transfer him or her, or just fire the person. However, look at what other alternatives can be generated by using morphological synthesis (see Table 3.7).

You can see how many more alternatives come to mind when you force together attributes that aren't obviously connected. The matrix of attributes can create a very long list of possible solutions. In more complicated problems—for example, how to improve quality, how to better serve customers, how to improve the reward system, how to land a great job—the potential number of alternatives is even greater, and, hence, more creativity is required to analyze them.

The second technique for combining unrelated attributes in problem-solving, the **relational algorithm**, involves applying connecting words that force a relationship between two elements in a problem. For example, the following is a list of some words that connect other words together. They are called "relational" words.

Table 3.7	Morphological Synthesis

Step 1. Problem statement: The employee takes extended lunch breaks every day with friends in the cafeteria.

Step 2. Major attributes of the problem:

Amount of time	Start time	Place	With whom	Frequency
More than 1 hour	Noon	Cafeteria	Friends	Daily

Step 3. Alternative attributes:

Amount of time	Start time	Place	With whom	Frequency
30 minutes	11:00	Work station	Coworkers	Weekly
90 minutes	11:30	Conference Room	Boss	Twice a Week
45 minutes	12:30	Restaurant	Management Team	Alternate Days

Step 4. Combining attributes:

1. A 30-minute lunch beginning at 12:30 in the conference room with the boss once a week.

2. A 90-minute lunch beginning at 11:30 in the conference room with coworkers twice a week.

3. A 45-minute lunch beginning at 11:00 in the cafeteria with the management team every other day.

4. A 30-minute lunch beginning at 12:00 alone in his or her work station on alternate days.

about	across	after
against	opposite	or
out	among	and
as	at	over
around	still	because
before	between	but
so	then	though
by	down	for
from	through	till
to	if	in
near	not	under
up	when	now
of	off	on
where	while	with

To illustrate the use of this technique, suppose you are faced with the following problem: *Our customers are dissatisfied with our service*. The two major subjects in this problem are *customers* and *service*. They are connected by the phrase *are dissatisfied with*. With the relational algorithm technique, the relational words in the problem statement are removed and replaced with other relational words to see if new ideas for alternative solutions can be identified. For example, consider the following connections when new relational words are used:

- ❑ Customers *among* service (e.g., customers interact with service personnel)

- ❑ Customers *as* service (e.g., customers deliver service to other customers)

- ❑ Customers *and* service (e.g., customers and service personnel work collaboratively together)

- ❑ Customers *for* service (e.g., customer focus groups can help improve service)

- ❑ Service *near* customers (e.g., change the location of the service to be nearer customers)

- ❑ Service *before* customers (e.g., prepare personalized service before the customer arrives)

- ❑ Service *through* customers (e.g., use customers to provide additional service)

- ❑ Service *when* customers (e.g., provide timely service when customers want it)

By connecting the two elements of the problem in different ways, new possibilities for problem solution can be formulated.

International Caveats

The perspective taken in this chapter has a clear bias toward Western culture. It focuses on analytical and creative problem-solving as methods for addressing specific issues. Enhancing creativity has a specific purpose: to solve certain kinds of problems better. Creativity in Eastern cultures, on the other hand, is often defined differently. Creativity is focused less on creating solutions than on uncovering enlightenment, one's true self, or the achievement of wholeness or self-actualization (DeDreu, 2010; Iyanger, Evans, & Abrams, 2006; Morris & Leung, 2010). It is aimed at getting in touch with the unconscious. In both the East and the West, however, creativity is viewed positively. Gods of creativity are worshipped in West African cultures (Olokun) and among Hindus (Vishvakarma), for example, and creativity is often viewed in mystical or religious terms rather than managerial or practical terms.

In fostering creative problem-solving in international settings or with individuals from different countries, Trompenaars and Hampden-Turner's (2012) model is useful for understanding the caveats that must be kept in mind. Countries differ, for example, in their orientation toward *internal control* (e.g., Canada, the United Kingdom, and the United States) versus *external control* (e.g., China, Czech Republic, and Japan). In internal cultures, the environment is assumed to be changeable, so creativity focuses on attacking problems directly. In external cultures, because individuals assume less control of the environment, creativity focuses less on problem resolution and more on achieving insight or oneness with nature. Changing the environment is not the usual objective.

Similarly, cultures emphasizing a *specific orientation* (e.g., Denmark, France, Sweden, and the United Kingdom) are more likely to challenge the status quo and seek new ways to address problems than cultures emphasizing a *diffuse culture* (e.g., China, India, Nigeria, and Singapore) in which loyalty, wholeness, and long-term relationships are more likely to inhibit individual creative effort.

This is similar to the differences that are likely in countries emphasizing *universalism* (e.g., China, India, Korea, and Venezuela) as opposed to *particularism* (e.g., Germany, Sweden, Switzerland, the United Kingdom, and the United States). Cultures emphasizing universalism tend to focus on generalizable outcomes and consistent rules or procedures. Particularistic cultures are more inclined to search for unique aberrations from the norm, thus having more of a tendency toward creative solution finding. Managers encouraging conceptual blockbusting and creative problem-solving, in other words, will find some individuals more inclined toward the rule-oriented procedures of analytical problem-solving and less inclined toward the playfulness and experimentation associated with creative problem-solving than others.

Hints for Applying Problem-Solving Techniques

These techniques and tools for conceptual blockbusting will not work for every problem, of course, nor is every individual equally inclined or skilled. Our intent in presenting these six suggestions is to help you expand the number of options available to you for defining problems and generating additional alternatives. They are most useful with problems that are not straightforward, are complex or ambiguous, or are imprecise in their definitions. All of us have enormous creative potential, but the stresses and pressures of daily life, coupled with the inertia of conceptual habits, tend to submerge that potential. These hints are ways to help unlock it again.

Reading about techniques or having a desire to be creative is not, alone, enough to make you a skillful creative problem solver, of course. Although research has confirmed the effectiveness of these techniques for improving creative problem-solving, they depend on application and practice as well as an environment that is conducive to creativity. Here are six practical hints that will help facilitate your own ability to apply these techniques effectively and improve your creative problem-solving ability.

1. *Give yourself some relaxation time.* The more intense your work, the greater your need for complete breaks. Break out of your routine sometimes. This frees up your mind and gives room for new thoughts.
2. *Find a place (physical space) where you can think.* It should be a place where interruptions are eliminated, at least for a time. Reserve your best time for thinking.
3. *Talk to other people about ideas.* Isolation produces far fewer ideas than does conversation. Make a list of people who stimulate you to think. Spend some time with them.
4. *Ask other people for their suggestions about your problems.* Find out what others think about them. Don't be embarrassed to share your problems, but don't become dependent on others to solve them for you.

5. *Read a lot.* Read at least one thing regularly that is outside your field of expertise. Keep track of new thoughts from your reading.
6. *Protect yourself from idea-killers.* Don't spend time with "black holes"—that is, people who absorb all of your energy and light but give nothing in return. Don't let yourself or others negatively evaluate your ideas too soon.

You'll find these hints useful for enhancing not only creative problem-solving but analytical problem-solving as well. Figure 3.9 summarizes the two problem-solving processes—analytical and creative—and the factors you should consider when determining how to approach each type of problem. In brief, when you encounter a problem that is straightforward—outcomes are predictable, sufficient information is available, and means-ends connections are clear—analytical problem-solving techniques are most appropriate. You should apply the four distinct, sequential steps. On the other hand, when the problem is not straightforward—that is, information is ambiguous or unavailable and alternative solutions are not apparent—you should apply creative problem-solving techniques in order to improve problem definition and alternative generation.

Fostering Creativity in Others

Unlocking your own creative potential is important but insufficient, of course, to make you a successful manager. A major challenge is to help unlock it in other people as well. Fostering creativity among those with whom you work is at least as great a challenge as increasing your own creativity. In this last section of the chapter, we briefly discuss some principles that will help you better accomplish the task of fostering creativity.

MANAGEMENT PRINCIPLES

Neither Percy Spencer nor Spence Silver could have succeeded in their creative endeavors had there not been a support system present that fostered creative problem-solving. In each case, certain characteristics were present in their organizations, fostered by managers around them, which made their innovations possible. In this section, we focus on activities in which individual managers can engage to foster creativity. Table 3.8 summarizes three management principles that help engender creative problem-solving among others.

LEARNING

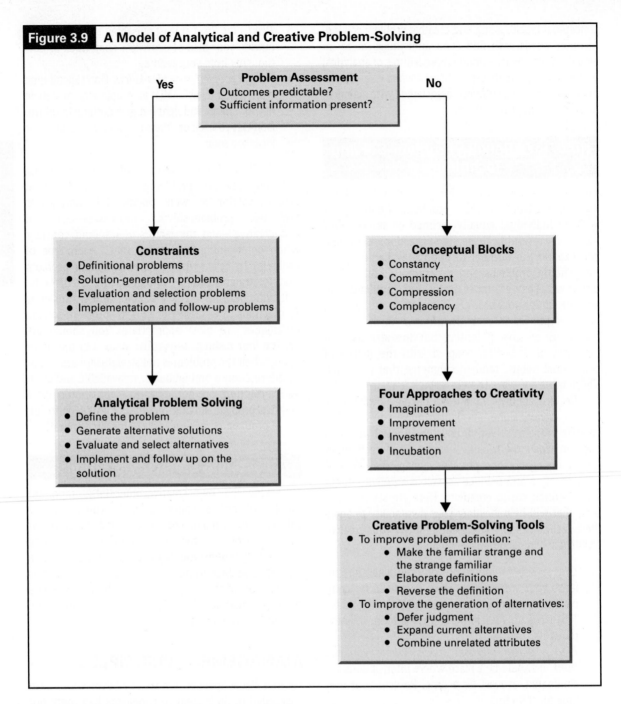

Figure 3.9 A Model of Analytical and Creative Problem-Solving

Problem Assessment
- Outcomes predictable?
- Sufficient information present?

Yes

No

Constraints
- Definitional problems
- Solution-generation problems
- Evaluation and selection problems
- Implementation and follow-up problems

Conceptual Blocks
- Constancy
- Commitment
- Compression
- Complacency

Analytical Problem Solving
- Define the problem
- Generate alternative solutions
- Evaluate and select alternatives
- Implement and follow up on the solution

Four Approaches to Creativity
- Imagination
- Improvement
- Investment
- Incubation

Creative Problem-Solving Tools
- To improve problem definition:
  - Make the familiar strange and the strange familiar
  - Elaborate definitions
  - Reverse the definition
- To improve the generation of alternatives:
  - Defer judgment
  - Expand current alternatives
  - Combine unrelated attributes

Pull People Apart; Put People Together

Percy Spencer's magnetron project involved a consumer product distinct from Raytheon's mainline business of missiles and other defense contract work. Spence Silver's new glue resulted when a polymer adhesive task force was separated from 3M's normal activities. The Macintosh computer was developed by a task force taken outside the company and given space and time to work on an innovative computer.

Many new ideas are the result of individuals being given time and resources and allowed to work apart from the normal activities of the organization. Establishing bullpens, practice fields, or sandlots is as good a way to develop new skills in business as it has proven to be in athletics. Because most businesses are designed to produce the 10,000th part correctly or to service the 10,000th customer efficiently, they do not function well at producing the first part. That

Table 3.8	Three Principles for Fostering Creativity
Principle	**Examples**
1. Pull people apart; put people together.	• Let individuals work alone as well as with teams and task forces.
	• Encourage minority reports and legitimize "devil's advocate" roles.
	• Encourage heterogeneous membership in teams.
	• Separate competing groups or subgroups.
2. Monitor and prod.	• Talk to customers.
	• Identify customer expectations both in advance of and after the sale.
	• Hold people accountable.
	• Use "sharp-pointed" prods.
3. Reward multiple roles.	• Serve as an idea champion.
	• Serve as a sponsor and mentor.
	• Serve as an orchestrator and facilitator.
	• Serve as a rule breaker.

is why pulling people apart is often necessary to foster innovation and creativity. Several innovative organizations, such as 3M, Apple, Facebook, Google, and Microsoft, give employees a certain amount of time each week to work on their own creative projects, outside their regular job assignment.

On the other hand, forming teams (putting people together) is almost always more productive than having people work by themselves. Such teams should be characterized by certain attributes, though. For example, several studies have found that creativity increased markedly when minority influences were present in the team; for example, when "devil's advocate" roles were legitimized, when a formal minority report was always included in final recommendations, and when individuals assigned to work on a team had divergent backgrounds or views. Those exposed to minority views are stimulated to attend to more aspects of the situation, they think in more divergent ways, and they are more likely to detect novel solutions or come to new decisions (DeGraff & DeGraff, 2017; Runco, 2014). Those positive benefits have been found to occur in groups even when the divergent or minority views are wrong.

Similarly, Janis (1971) found that narrow-mindedness in groups (dubbed **groupthink**) was best overcome by establishing competing groups working on the same problem, participation in groups by outsiders, assigning a role of critical evaluator in the group, and having groups made up of cross-functional participants (Sunstein & Hastie, 2015). The most productive groups are those characterized by fluid roles, lots of interaction among members, and flat power structures. On the other hand, too much diversity, too much disagreement, and too much fluidity can sidetrack groups, so devil's advocates must be aware of when to line up and support the decision of the group. Their role is to help groups rethink quick decisions or solutions that have not been considered carefully enough, not to avoid making group decisions or solving problems.

You can help foster creativity among people you manage, therefore, by pulling people apart (e.g., giving them a bullpen, providing them with autonomy, encouraging individual initiative) as well as putting people together (e.g., putting them in teams, enabling minority influence, and fostering heterogeneity).

Monitor and Prod

Neither Percy Spencer nor Spence Silver was allowed to work on their projects without accountability. Both men eventually had to report on the results they accomplished with their experimentation and imagination. At 3M, for example, people are expected to allocate 15 percent of their time away from company business to work on new, creative ideas. They can even appropriate company materials and resources to work on them. However, individuals are always held accountable for their decisions. They need to show results for their "play time."

Holding people accountable for outcomes, in fact, is an important motivator for improved performance. Two innovators in the entertainment industry (Steve Karmen and Nolan Bushnell) captured this principle with these remarks:

> The ultimate inspiration is the deadline. That's when you have to do what needs to be done. The fact that twice a year the creative talent of this country is working until midnight to get something ready for a trade show is very good for the economy. Without this kind of pressure, things would turn to mashed potatoes. (von Oech, 1986, p. 119)

One way Woody Morcott, former CEO at Dana Corporation, held people accountable for creativity was to require that each person in the company submit at least two suggestions for improvement each month. At least 70 percent of the new ideas had to be implemented. Woody admitted that he stole the idea during a visit to a Japanese company where he noticed workers huddled around a table scribbling notes on how some ideas for improvement might work. At Dana, this requirement is part of every person's job assignment. Rewards are associated with such ideas as well. A Dana plant in Chihuahua, Mexico, for example, rewards employees with $1.89 for every idea submitted and another $1.89 if the idea is used. "We drill into people that they are responsible for keeping the plant competitive through innovation," Morcott said (personal communication).

In addition to accountability, creativity is stimulated by what Gene Goodson, formerly of Johnson Controls, called "sharp-pointed prods." After taking over the automotive group at that company, Goodson found that he could stimulate creative problem-solving by issuing certain mandates that demanded new approaches to old tasks. One such mandate was, "There will be no more forklift trucks allowed in any of our plants." At first, that mandate sounded absolutely outrageous. Think about it. You have a plant with tens of thousands of square feet of floor space. The loading docks are on one side of the building, and many tons of heavy raw materials are unloaded weekly and moved from the loading docks to work stations throughout the entire facility. The only way it can be done is with forklifts. Eliminating forklift trucks would ruin the plant, right?

Wrong. This sharp-pointed prod demanded that individuals working in the plant find ways to move the work stations closer to the raw materials, to move the unloading of the raw materials closer to the work stations, and to change the size and amounts of material being unloaded. The innovations that resulted from eliminating forklifts saved the company millions of dollars in materials handling and wasted time; dramatically improved quality, productivity, and efficiency; and made it possible for Johnson Controls to capture some business from their foreign competitors.

One of the best methods for generating useful prods is to regularly monitor customer preferences, expectations, and evaluations. Many of the most creative ideas have come from customers, the recipients of goods and services. Identifying their preferences in advance and monitoring their evaluations of products or services later are good ways to get creative ideas and to foster imagination, improvement, investment, and incubation. All employees should be in regular contact with their own customers, asking questions and monitoring performance.

In summary, you can foster creativity by holding people accountable for new ideas and by stimulating them with periodic prods. The most useful prods generally come from customers.

Reward Multiple Roles

The success of Post-it Notes at 3M is more than a story of the creativity of Spence Silver. It also illustrates the necessity of people playing multiple roles in enabling creativity and the importance of recognizing and rewarding those who play such roles. Without a number of people playing multiple roles, Spence Silver's glue would probably still be on a shelf somewhere.

Four crucial roles for enabling creativity in others include the **idea champion** (the person who comes up with creative problem solutions), the **sponsor** or mentor (the person who helps provide the resources, environment, and encouragement for the idea champion to work on his or her idea), the **orchestrator** or facilitator (the person who brings together crossfunctional groups and necessary political support to facilitate implementation of creative ideas), and the **rule breaker** (the person who goes beyond organizational boundaries and barriers to ensure success of the creative solution). Each of these roles is present in most important innovations in organizations, and all are illustrated by the Post-it Note example.

This story has four major parts.

1. Spence Silver, while fooling around with chemical configurations that the academic literature indicated wouldn't work, invented a glue that wouldn't stick. Silver spent years giving

presentations to any audience at 3M that would listen, trying to pawn off his glue on some division that could find a practical application for it. But nobody was interested.

2. Henry Courtney and Roger Merrill developed a coating substance that allowed the glue to stick to one surface but not to others. This made it possible to produce a permanently temporary glue; that is, one that would peel off easily when pulled but would otherwise hang on forever.

3. Art Fry found a problem that fit Spence Silver's solution. He found an application for the glue as a "better bookmark" and as a note pad. No equipment existed at 3M to coat only a part of a piece of paper with the glue. Fry therefore carried 3M equipment and tools home to his own basement, where he designed and made his own machine to manufacture the forerunner of Post-it Notes. Because the working machine became too large to get out of his basement, he blasted a hole in the wall to get the equipment back to 3M. He then brought together engineers, designers, production managers, and machinists to demonstrate the prototype machine and generate enthusiasm for manufacturing the product.

4. Geoffrey Nicholson and Joseph Ramsey began marketing the product inside 3M. They also submitted the product to the standard 3M market tests. The product failed miserably. No one wanted to pay $1.00 for a pad of scratch paper. But when Nicholson and Ramsey broke 3M rules by personally visiting test market sites and giving away free samples, the consuming public became addicted to the product.

In this scenario, Spence Silver was both a rule breaker and an idea champion. Art Fry was also an idea champion, but more importantly, he orchestrated the coming together of the various groups needed to get the innovation off the ground. Henry Courtney and Roger Merrill helped sponsor Silver's innovation by providing him with the coating substance that would allow his idea to work. Geoff Nicholson and Joe Ramsey were both rule breakers and sponsors in their bid to get the product accepted by the public. In each case, not only did all these people play unique roles, but they did so with tremendous enthusiasm and zeal. They were confident of their ideas and willing to put their time and resources on the line as advocates. They fostered support among a variety of constituencies, both within their own areas of expertise and among outside groups. Most organizations are inclined to give in to those who are sure

of themselves, persistent in their efforts, and savvy enough to make converts of others.

Not everyone can be an idea champion. But when managers recognize and reward those who sponsor and orchestrate the ideas of others, creativity increases in organizations. Teams form, supporters replace competitors, and innovation thrives. Facilitating and rewarding multiple role development is the job of the managers who want to foster creativity. Figure 3.10 summarizes this process.

Summary

In the twenty-first century, almost no manager or organization can afford to stand still, to rely on past practices, and to avoid innovation. In a fast-paced environment in which the half-life of knowledge is about three years and the half-life of almost any technology is counted in weeks and months instead of years, creative problem-solving is increasingly a prerequisite for success. The digital revolution makes the rapid production of new ideas almost mandatory. This is not to

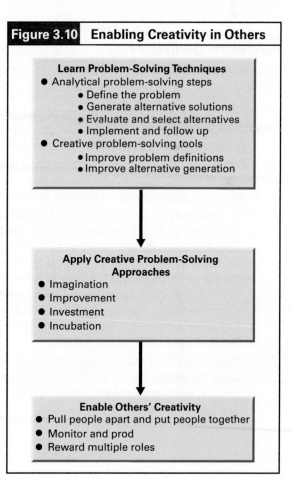

Figure 3.10 Enabling Creativity in Others

Learn Problem-Solving Techniques
- Analytical problem-solving steps
  - Define the problem
  - Generate alternative solutions
  - Evaluate and select alternatives
  - Implement and follow up
- Creative problem-solving tools
  - Improve problem definitions
  - Improve alternative generation

Apply Creative Problem-Solving Approaches
- Imagination
- Improvement
- Investment
- Incubation

Enable Others' Creativity
- Pull people apart and put people together
- Monitor and prod
- Reward multiple roles

LEARNING

negate the importance of analytical problem-solving, of course. The quality revolution of the 1980s and 1990s taught us important lessons about carefully proscribed, sequential, and analytic problem-solving processes. Error rates, response times, and missed deadlines dropped dramatically when analytical problem-solving was institutionalized in manufacturing and service companies.

In this chapter, we have discussed a well-developed model for solving problems. It consists of four separate and sequential stages: defining a problem, generating alternative solutions, evaluating and selecting the best solution, and implementing the chosen solution. This model, however, is mainly useful for solving straightforward problems. Many problems faced by managers are not of this type, and frequently managers are called on to exercise creative problem-solving skills. That is, they must broaden their perspective of the problem and develop alternative solutions that are not immediately obvious.

We have discussed four different types of creativity and encouraged you to consider all four when faced with the need to be creative. However, we have also illustrated eight major conceptual blocks that inhibit most people's creative problem-solving abilities. Conceptual blocks are mental obstacles that artificially constrain problem definition and solution and keep most people from being effective creative problem solvers. Overcoming these conceptual blocks is a matter of skill development and practice in thinking, not a matter of innate ability. Everyone can become a skilled creative problem solver with practice. Becoming aware of these thinking inhibitors helps individuals overcome them.

We also discussed three major techniques for improving creative problem definition and three major techniques for improving the creative generation of alternative solutions. We offered specific suggestions that can help implement these six techniques.

We concluded by offering some hints about how to foster creativity in other people. Becoming an effective problem solver yourself is important, but effective managers can also enhance this activity among those with whom they work.

Behavioral Guidelines

Below are specific behavioral action guidelines to help guide your skill practice in analytical and creative problem-solving.

A. Follow the four-step procedure outlined in Table 3.1 when solving straightforward problems. Keep the steps separate, and do not take shortcuts—define the problem, generate alternative solutions, evaluate the alternatives, and select and implement the optimal solution.

B. When approaching a difficult or complex problem, remember that creative solutions need not be a product of revolutionary and brand-new ideas. Four different types of creativity are available to you—imagination, improvement, investment, and incubation.

C. Try to overcome your conceptual blocks by consciously doing the following:
   ❑ Use lateral thinking in addition to vertical thinking.
   ❑ Use several thought languages instead of just one.
   ❑ Challenge stereotypes based on past experiences.
   ❑ Identify underlying themes and commonalities in seemingly unrelated factors.
   ❑ Delete superfluous information and fill in important missing information when studying the problem.
   ❑ Avoid artificially constraining problem boundaries.
   ❑ Overcome any unwillingness to be inquisitive.
   ❑ Use both right- and left-brain thinking.

D. To enhance creativity, use techniques that elaborate problem definition, such as:
   ❑ Make the strange familiar and the familiar strange by using metaphors and analogies.
   ❑ Develop alternative (opposite) definitions and apply a question checklist.
   ❑ Reverse the definition.

E. To enhance creativity, use techniques that elaborate possible alternative solutions, such as:
   - ❏ Defer judgment.
   - ❏ Subdivide the problem into its attributes.
   - ❏ Combine unrelated problem attributes.

F. Foster creativity among those with whom you work by doing the following:
   - ❏ Provide autonomy, allowing individuals to experiment and try out ideas.
   - ❏ Put people who hold different perspectives into teams to work on problems.
   - ❏ Hold people accountable for innovation.
   - ❏ Use sharp-pointed prods to stimulate new thinking.
   - ❏ Recognize, reward, and encourage multiple roles, including idea champions, sponsors, orchestrators, and rule breakers.

CASES INVOLVING PROBLEM-SOLVING

Chip and Bin

Steven Henderson has some serious concerns about the new "chip and bin" system that Southeast Norfolk District Council has agreed to trial.

As part of the UK's attempts to reduce household waste consigned to landfills, a number of trials were carried out. Steven Henderson, leader of the Southeast Norfolk District Council, found that his council had been chosen to trial microchips on household bins. The trial would include over 50,000 households. Each of the council's 12 refuse trucks was fitted with $40,000 of scanning technology. The idea was that the refuse collectors would be able to identify a household's bin and weigh it. The information captured would be transferred to the truck's onboard computer. Each bin was weighed six times as it was lifted and six times on its way down to ensure accuracy. The council could then accurately bill each address, charging those responsible for excess waste and reducing bills for those not submitting the maximum amount of waste.

This initiative became known as "chip and bin," or "pay as you throw." Many residents, together with environmentalists and the news media, viewed it as a way for the government to collect additional taxes. However, the system was fatally flawed; the technology did not work. Henderson realized that the technology had to be trusted by households; it had to work for every bin on every street on every day of the year. Henderson was also uncomfortable that his refuse collectors were becoming government tax collectors.

The system had electrical, mechanical, hydraulic, and data faults. Numerous times the equipment broke down and the collectors had to carry out repairs or try to override the system. Two weeks into the trial, Henderson attended a meeting with his recycling and refuse collection department, plus representatives from central government. The first devastating news was that there had been a 250 percent increase in "fly tipping." Rubbish was being abandoned at waste sites and along roadsides across the council's area. Residents were choosing to avoid paying higher fees by abandoning their refuse in the countryside. Second, the council's two recycling centers reported a 300 percent increase in the amount of waste material being brought to the sites. There was no charge for items taken to the recycling centers, and residents were choosing this option as an alternative to paying waste fees. Congestion around the recycling centers was becoming a major issue, and the recycling center managers reported that their employees were becoming overwhelmed.

Henderson listened to the problems and complaints his managers and staff were reporting. He considered the additional pressure and stress being placed on his departments. His public relations officer, Beatrice Watkins, summed up Henderson's feelings:

> This is a PR disaster. It is bringing the council into disrepute. If the residents are losing faith with the council and view our carefully considered recycling policies as being a way to tax them more heavily, then we will lose support. We have already seen more rubbish being abandoned in the past few weeks than we did for the whole of the last quarter. I have heard that people in other parts of the country that are to be in stage 2 of the trial are peeling off the bar codes and the chip and pin details from their bins in protest.
>
> I don't think we've told people enough about this. We are losing their trust. I would recommend terminating the trial as soon as possible.

Henderson agreed with her, but he could not say so. He had accepted nearly £1 million in grants and other payments from the central government to run the trial for a year. The contract was legally binding, and Henderson feared the consequences if he were to terminate the program. Before Henderson could comment, the representative from central government raised his hand, and Henderson asked him to speak. The representative said:

> This is not about pay as you throw, more save as you throw. There should be no increase in council taxes. It has public support, and the council has laws to prevent fly tipping. According to the European Union, Britain only recycles 18 percent of its rubbish, compared to 58 percent in Germany. Only Greece and Portugal have worse recycling rates. The UK faces stiff EU penalties for landfill waste, so these tougher targets for everyone are unavoidable.

Henderson sensed the veiled threats. He determined not to make a decision but to reconvene the meeting in a week, after he had talked to his advisers. He needed a way to increase recycling rates; divert waste from the landfills; make the best use of the government-funded technology; and, as a politician, regain the trust of the people in southeast Norfolk. "What we need is an incentive scheme and not a payment scheme. I want a more innovative way to encourage people to recycle rather than charging them money if they don't," he thought to himself.

Before Henderson could meet with his advisers he received a telephone call from the Department for Environment, Food and Rural Affairs. It was a senior adviser to the minister:

> Mr. Henderson, in good faith the government has awarded your council a grant to run this trial on our behalf. We fail to see why you have not acted decisively. You have barely given the trial a chance. There will inevitably be problems in the first few weeks; that is to be expected. Added to this you should be enforcing fly tipping legislation and prosecuting

those dumping rubbish and limit the number of visits that residents can make to recy-
cling centers. By taking their refuse there, they are undermining the whole trial. You
are contractually obliged to run this trial, and the department expects you to give it your
unreserved support and attention.

Henderson simply replied, "I will."

An hour later, Henderson called an emergency meeting with his most trusted advisers. He was deeply concerned about putting the council in this position and that the residents were blaming them for the problems. He listened to various points of view and the fact that the council would have to repay half of the government grant within 30 days if they broke the terms of the contract.

"How much money have we got?" he asked the finance director.

"Enough, but there will be nothing left in the contingency fund," was the reply.

"Do it, terminate the contract," Henderson decided. "But we need an upside to this. There's a new business working alongside councils, providing rewards for re-cycling. Their trials show boosts in recycling rates, and households get redeemable reward points based on how much they recycle. I want to see those people tomorrow and have something to say before we make this public."

At 9:30 the next morning, Henderson and Watkins worked out a deal with the recycling company, Envirobank, to set up a pilot scheme to reward residents for the amount of weekly recycling material collected. It was exactly what Henderson wanted—a reward and not a tax. But it would cost the council $250,000 per year to subsidize. Henderson made the decision without speaking to the finance director.

Afterward, Henderson and Watkins prepared a press release focusing on the posi-tives. For Henderson, the most important thing was that instead of residents paying extra money using the chip and bin system, they would now be rewarded for recycling. The trial scheme would give residents redeemable reward points based on how much they recycled. Like a loyalty program, residents would receive reward points that they could spend at a range of participating retailers in the vicinity. Similar schemes had worked well in the United States and other countries.

Henderson knew that his next telephone call would be difficult. But to stop himself from being dissuaded he had emailed all concerned, stating that at the end of the week the chip and bin trial would be terminated. There was no going back now.

Henderson's contact at the Department of the Environment took the news with calm resignation, but there was something else:

I hope you understand the implications of your decision. In rejecting chip and bin, you
will add at least $160 to every household council tax bill. The country will be fined by
the European Union every time it buries waste in a landfill site. That money has to come
from somewhere; it will be your residents who cover the costs. I don't want you to have
to decide between increasing council tax bills or closing day centers for the elderly, shut-
ting swimming pools, or not having sufficient money to mend roads, but I suppose that
is your decision.

Discussion Questions

3.1. Identify the conceptual blocks illustrated in this case.

3.2. Outline the problem-solving steps followed by Henderson and the council. What steps in analytical problem-solving were skipped or short-circuited?

3.3. If you were Henderson's adviser, knowing what you know about problem-solving, what would you have suggested to help his problem-solving processes? What kinds of conceptual blockbusters could have been useful to Henderson?

3.4. What did you learn from this case that would help you advise Microsoft in its anticompetitive behavior case with the European Commission or the British Airports Authority being told by the Competition Commission to sell two of its London airports? What practical hints, in other words, do you derive from this case of analytical problem-solving gone awry?

Creativity at Apple

Steve Jobs, the lionized former CEO of Apple Inc., proudly described Apple's mission in these terms: "Innovate. That's what we do." And innovate it has. Jobs and his original colleagues Steve Wozniak and Mike Markkula created the personal computer market in 1977 with the introduction of the Apple II. By 1980, Apple was the number one vendor of personal computers in the world.

By 2008 Fortune *magazine had named Apple the most admired company in the United States, and in 2013 Apple surpassed Coca-Cola to become the world's most valuable brand in the Omnicom Group's "Best Global Brands" report. As of December 2017, Apple maintained 499 retail stores in 22 countries as well as the online Apple Store and iTunes Store, the latter of which is the world's largest music retailer. Apple is among the largest publicly traded corporations in the world by market capitalization, with an estimated market capitalization of more than $700 billion at the beginning of 2018. Apple's five-year growth average is above 30 percent for top-line growth and 45 percent for bottom-line growth. Apple is the most financially successful startup company of all time, and astoundingly, in July 2011, due to the American debt-ceiling crisis, Apple's financial reserves were briefly larger than those of the U.S. government.*

This success has occurred as a result of Apple's incredible inventiveness and creativity in developing new products, On the other hand, the market is questioning whether Apple can keep up this pace and remain a world-class innovation factory.

The success of the company, of course, is due to its innovation. Apple created the personal computer market, first with Apple II and then with Macintosh computers and the OS operating system. It created the first computer network with its Macintosh machines—Windows-based PCs did not network until the mid-1990s. Apple introduced the first handheld, pen-based computing device, known as the Newton, and followed that up with a wireless mouse, ambient-lit keyboards for working in the dark, and the fastest computer on the market in 2003. Also in 2003, Apple introduced the first legal digital music store for downloading songs—iTunes—along with its compatible technology, the iPod. This was followed by the Apple Store, iPhone, iTouch, iPad, and iCloud. The company is now rumored to be working on an iCar. In other words, Apple has been at the forefront of product and technological innovation for almost 40 years. Apple has been, hands down, the most innovative company in its industry and one of the most innovative companies on the planet.

The message being declared loudly and prominently in the business press and in the broader global society today is that innovation and creativity are the keys to success. "Change or die." "Innovate or get passed over." "Be creative to be successful."

A key tenet on which progressive, market-based, capitalistic societies are based is the idea of creative destruction. That is, without creativity and innovation, individuals and organizations become casualties of the second law of thermodynamics—they disintegrate, wither, disorganize, and die. New products are needed to keep consumers happy. Obsolescence is ubiquitous. Innovation and creativity, consequently, are touted as being at the very heart of success. For more evidence, just skim over the more than 300,000 book titles that appear when you log onto Amazon and search using the keyword "innovation."

On the other hand, consider some of the most innovative companies in recent history. Xerox Corporation's famed Palo Alto Research Center gave the world laser printing, the Ethernet, Windows-type software, graphical user interfacing, and the mouse, yet it is notorious for not having made any money at all and is on the brink of no longer being an American company. Polaroid introduced the idea of instant images, yet it filed for bankruptcy in 2001. The Internet boom in the late 1990s was an explosion of what is now considered to be worthless innovation. Kodak invented a digital camera in 1974 but did not pursue it, to the detriment of the company's survival. And Enron may have been the most innovative financial company ever but succumbed to innovative practices aimed at implementing unethical practices and illegal activities.

Amazon, Dell, eBay, Southwest Airlines, and Walmart are examples of incredibly successful companies, but these firms did not invent any new products or technologies. They are acknowledged as innovative and creative companies, but they don't hold a candle to Apple in that regard. Instead of new products, they have invented new processes, new ways to deliver products, new distribution channels, and new marketing approaches. Think of Henry Ford, for example. It is well known that he didn't invent the automobile. He simply invented a new way to assemble a car at a cost affordable to his own workers. The person who invented the automobile hardly made a dime.

The trouble is, creativity as applied to business processes—manufacturing methods, sales and marketing techniques, employee incentive systems, or leadership development—is usually seen as humdrum, nitty gritty, uncool, plodding, unimaginative, and boring. Creative people and creative companies that capture headlines are usually those that come up with great new product ideas or splashy features. Scan the list of Fortune 500 companies and judge how many are product champions versus process champions. Decide for yourself which is the driver of economic growth: good innovation or good management.

Discussion Questions

3.5. Consider the four approaches to creativity. What approach(es) has Apple relied on? What alternatives have other firms in the industry pursued? What other alternatives could Apple implement?

3.6. Assume you were a consultant to the CEO at Apple. What advice would you give on how Apple could capitalize on its creativity? How can Apple make money based on its own inclination to pursue creativity in certain ways?

3.7. What are the major obstacles and conceptual blocks that Apple faces right now? What do employees need to watch out for?

3.8. What tools for fostering creative problem-solving are applicable to Apple, and which would not be workable? Which ones do you think are used the most there?

EXERCISES FOR APPLYING CONCEPTUAL BLOCKBUSTING

The purpose of this exercise is to have you practice problem-solving—both analytical and creative. Two actual scenarios are provided below. Both present real problems faced by real managers. They are very likely to be the same kinds of problems faced by your own business school and by many of your local businesses. Your assignment in each case is to identify a solution to the problem. You will approach the problem in two ways: first, using analytical problem-solving techniques; second, using creative problem-solving techniques. You should accomplish the first approach—analytical problem-solving—by yourself. You should accomplish the second approach—creative problem-solving—in a team. Your task is to apply the principles of problem-solving to come up with realistic, cost-efficient, and effective solutions to these problems. Consider each scenario separately. You should take no more than 10 minutes to complete the analytical problem-solving assignment. Then take 20 minutes to complete the creative problem-solving assignment.

Individual Assignment—Analytical Problem-Solving (10 minutes)

1. After reading the first case, write down a specific problem definition. What precisely worded problem are you going to solve? Complete the sentence: The problem I am going to solve is...

2. Now identify at least four or five alternative solutions. What ideas do you have for resolving this problem? Complete this sentence: Possible ways to resolve this problem are...

3. Next, evaluate the alternatives you have proposed. Make sure you don't evaluate each alternative before proposing your complete set. Evaluate your set of alternatives on the basis of these criteria: Will this alternative solve the problem I have defined? Is this alternative realistic in terms of being cost-effective? Can this solution be implemented in a short time frame?

4. Now write down your proposed solution to the problem. Be specific about what should be done and when. Be prepared to share that solution with other team members.

Team Assignment—Creative Problem-Solving (20 minutes)

1. Form teams team of four or five people. Working in teams, each team member should share his or her own definition of the problem. It is unlikely that they will all be the same, so make sure you keep track of them. Now add at least three more plausible definitions of the problem. In doing so, use at least two techniques for expanding problem definition discussed in the text. Each problem definition should differ from the others in what the problem is, not just a statement of different causes of the problem.

2. Examine each of the definitions you have proposed. Select one that the entire team can agree upon. Since it is unlikely that you can solve multiple problems at once, select just one problem definition that you will work on.

3. Share the four or five proposed solutions that you generated on your own, even if they don't relate to the specific problem your team has defined. Keep track of all the different alternatives proposed by team members. After all team members have shared their alternatives, generate at least five additional alternative solutions to the problem you have agreed upon. Use at least two of the techniques for expanding alternatives discussed in the text.

4. Of all the alternatives your team proposed, select the five that you consider to be the most creative and to have the highest probability of success.

5. Select one team member from each team to serve on a judging panel. This panel is charged with selecting the team with the most creative and potentially successful alternatives to the problem. Judges cannot vote for their own team.

6. Each team now shares their five alternatives with the class. The judging panel selects the winner.

PRACTICE

Moving Up in the Rankings

Business schools seem to have lost the ability to evaluate their own quality and effectiveness. With the emergence of rankings of business schools in the popular press, the role of judging quality seems to have been captured by publications such as *Businessweek, U.S. News & World Report*, and the *Financial Times*. The accreditation association for business schools, AACSB, mainly assesses the extent to which a school is accreditable or not, a 0–1 distinction, so a wide range in quality exists among accredited business schools. More refined distinctions have been made in the popular press by identifying the highest-rated 50; the first, second, or third tiers; or the top 20. Each publication relies on slightly different criteria in their rankings, but a substantial portion of each ranking rests on name recognition, visibility, or public acclaim. In some of the polls, more than 50 percent of the weighting is placed on the reputation or notoriety of the school. This is problematic, of course, because reputation can be deceiving. For example, one recent poll rated the Harvard and Stanford undergraduate business programs among the top three in the country, even though neither school has an undergraduate business program. Princeton's law school has been rated in the top five in several polls, even though, you guessed it, no such law school exists.

Other criteria sometimes considered in various ranking services include student selectivity, percent of students placed in jobs, starting salaries of graduates, tuition costs compared to graduates' earnings, faculty publications, percent of international faculty, student satisfaction, recruiter satisfaction, and so on. By and large, however, name recognition is the single most crucial factor. It helps predict the number of student applicants, the ability to hire prominent faculty members, fundraising opportunities, corporate partnerships, and so on.

Many business schools have responded to this pressure to become better known by creating advertising campaigns, circulating internal publications to other business schools and media outlets, and hiring additional staff to market the school. Most business school deans receive an average of 20 publications a week from other business schools, for example, and an editor at *Businessweek* reported receiving more than 100 per week. Some deans begrudge the fact that these resources are being spent on activities other than improving the educational experience for students and faculty. Given constrained resources and tuition increases that outstrip the consumer price index every year, allocating money to one activity precludes it from being spent on others. On the other hand, most deans acknowledge that this is the way the game must be played.

As part of a strategy to increase visibility, one business school hired world-renowned architect Frank Gehry to design a new business school building. It is a $70 million building that houses classrooms, faculty and staff offices, food courts, and student spaces associated with the school. Currently this particular school does not appear in the top 20 on the major rankings lists. However, like about 75 other business schools in the world, it would very much like to reach that level. One problem with this new landmark building is that it is so unusual, so avant-garde, that it is not even recognized as a building. Upon seeing a photograph for the first time, some people don't even know what they're looking at. On the other hand, it presents an opportunity to leapfrog other schools listed higher in the rankings if the institution is creative in its approach. The challenge, of course, is that no one is sure exactly how to make this happen.

Discussion Questions

3.9. Assume that you are hired to serve as a consulting team to the dean of your business school. What counsel would you provide?

3.10. What elements in each step of the analytical problem-solving process are appropriate? Outline them specifically for your dean.

3.11. What creative problem-solving steps are appropriate? Outline them for your dean and provide a recommendation for how to facilitate them.

3.12. Prepare a specific consulting report containing your definition of the problem, alternative solutions, your evaluation of the best ones, your suggestions for creative and innovative alternatives, and at least one out-of-the-box idea for your dean that would increase the ranking of your school.

3.13. What conceptual blocks are getting in the way?

Elijah Gold and His Restaurant

Elijah Gold knew exactly what to expect. He knew how his employees felt about him. That's why he had sent them the questionnaire in the first place. He needed a shot of confidence, a feeling that his employees were behind him as he struggled to build Golden Restaurants Inc. beyond two restaurants and $4 million in annual sales.

Gathering up the anonymous questionnaires, Elijah returned to his tiny corporate office in Ann Arbor, Michigan. With one of his partners by his side, he ripped open the first envelope as eagerly as a Broadway producer checking the reviews on opening night. His eyes zoomed directly to the question where employees were asked to rate the three owners' performance on a scale of 1 to 10.

A zero. The employee had scrawled in a big, fat zero. "Find out whose handwriting this is," he told his partner, Tyrone Laibson.

He ripped open another: zero again. And another. A two. "We'll fire these people," Elijah said to Tyrone coldly. Another zero.

A one.

"Oh, go work for somebody else, you jerk!" Elijah shouted.

Soon he had decided to fire 10 of his 230 employees. "Plenty of people seemed to hate my guts," he says.

Over the next day, though, Elijah's anger subsided. "You think, 'I've done all this for these people and they think I'm a total jerk who doesn't care about them,'" he says. "Finally, you have to look in the mirror and think, 'Maybe they're right.'"

For Elijah, that realization was absolutely shattering. He had started the company three years earlier out of frustration over all the abuse he had suffered while working at big restaurant chains. If Elijah had one overriding mission at Golden's, it was to prove that restaurants didn't have to mistreat their employees.

He thought he had succeeded. Until he opened those surveys, he had believed that Golden's was a place where employees felt valued, involved, and appreciated. "I had no idea we were treating people so badly," he says. Somewhere along the way, in the day-to-day running of the business, he had lost his connection with them and left behind the employee-oriented company he thought he was running.

Elijah's 13-year odyssey through some big restaurant chains left him feeling as limp as a cheeseburger after a day under the heat lamps. After immigrating to the United States 13 years before, he had been employed at Ponderosa in Georgia; Bennigan's in Florida and Tennessee; and TGI Friday's in Texas, Tennessee, and Indiana. Within one six-month period at Friday's, he got two promotions, two bonuses, and two raises; then his boss left, and he got fired. That did it. Elijah was fed up with big chains.

At the age of 29, he moved back to Ann Arbor, where he had attended the University of Michigan as an older undergraduate. There he met Uma Hahn, the general manager of a restaurant, a similarly jaded 29-year-old who, by her own admission, had "begun to lose faith." Uma and Elijah started hatching plans to open their own place, where employees would enjoy working as much as customers enjoyed eating. They planned to target the smaller markets that the chains ignored. With financing from a friend, they opened Golden's.

PRACTICE

True to their people-oriented goals, the partners tried to make employees feel more appreciated than they themselves had felt at the chains. They gave them a free drink and a meal at the end of every shift, let them give away appetizers and desserts, and provided them a week of paid vacation each year.

A special camaraderie developed among the employees. After all, they worked in an industry in which a turnover rate of 250 percent was something to aspire to. The night before Golden's opened, some 75 employees encircled the ficus tree next to the bar, joined hands, and prayed silently for two minutes. "The tree had a special energy," says Elijah.

Maybe so. By the third night of operation, the 230-seat Golden's had a waiting list. The dining room was regularly so crowded that after three months the owners decided to add a 58-seat patio. Then they had to rearrange the kitchen to handle the volume. In its first three and a half months, Golden's racked up sales of about $415,000, ending the year just over $110,000 in the red, mostly because the partners paid back the bulk of their $162,000 debt right away.

Word of the restaurant's success reached Detroit. One auto executive even stopped by to recruit the partners. With almost no market research, they opened the second Golden's 18 months later in Detroit. The first, in Ann Arbor, was still roaring, having broken the $2 million mark in sales in its first year, with a marginal loss of just over $16,000.

By midsummer, the 200-seat Detroit restaurant was hauling in $35,000 a week. The Ann Arbor restaurant, though, was developing some problems. Right after the Detroit Golden's opened, sales at Ann Arbor fell 15 percent. The partners shrugged it off. Some Ann Arbor customers lived closer to Detroit, so one restaurant was probably pulling some of the other's customers. Either way, the customers were still there. "We're just spreading our market a little thinner," Elijah told his partners. When Ann Arbor had lost another 10 percent and Detroit 5 percent, Elijah blamed the fact that the drinking age had been raised to 21 in Ann Arbor, cutting into liquor sales.

By the end of that year, the company recorded nearly $3.5 million in sales, with nominal losses of about $95,000. But the adulation was beginning to cloud the real reason they had started the business. "Golden's was born purely out of frustration," says Elijah. Now, the frustration was gone. "You get pulled in so many directions that you just lose touch," says Tyrone. "There are things that you simply forget."

What the partners forgot, in the warm flush of success, was their roots.

"Success breeds ego," says Elijah, "and ego breeds contempt." He would come back from trade shows or real-estate meetings all pumped up. "Isn't this exciting?" he'd ask an employee. "We're going to open a new restaurant next year." When the employee stared back blankly, Elijah felt resentful. "I didn't understand why they weren't thrilled," he says. He didn't see that while his world was constantly growing and expanding, his employees' world was sliding downhill. They were still busing tables and hustling for tips and thinking, "Forget the new restaurant, you haven't said hello to me in months; and by the way, why don't you fix the tea machine?"

"I just got too good, and too busy, to do orientation," he says. So he decided to tape orientation sessions for new employees, to make a film just like the one he had been subjected to when he worked at Bennigan's. On tape, Elijah told new employees one of his favorite stories, the one about the customer who walks into a chain restaurant and finds herself asking questions of a hostess sign because she can't find a human. The moral: "Golden's will never be so impersonal as to make people talk to a sign." A film maybe, but never a sign.

Since Elijah wasn't around the restaurants all that much, he didn't notice that employees were leaving in droves. Even the departure of Jose Valdez, the kitchen manager in Ann Arbor, wasn't enough to take the shine off his "glowing ego," as he calls it.

Jose had worked as Elijah's kitchen manager at TGI Friday's. When the Detroit Golden's was opening up, Elijah recruited him as kitchen manager. A few months later, Jose marched into Elijah's office and announced that he was heading back to Indianapolis. "There's too much b.s. around here," he blurted out. "You don't care about your people." Elijah was shocked. "As soon as we get this next restaurant opened, we'll make things the way they used to be," he replied. But Jose wouldn't budge. "Elijah," he said bitterly, "you are turning out to be like all the other companies." Elijah shrugged. "We're a big company, and we've got to do big-company things," he replied. Jose walked out, slamming the door. Three months later, Golden's two top managers announced that they were moving to the West Coast to start their own company. Elijah beamed, boasting, "Our employees learn so much, they are ready to start their own restaurants."

Before they left, Elijah sat down with them in the classroom in Ann Arbor. "So," he asked casually, "how do you think we could run the place better?" Three hours later, he was still listening. "The Golden's we fell in love with just doesn't exist anymore," one of them concluded sadly.

Elijah was outraged. How could his employees be so ungrateful? Couldn't they see how everybody was sharing the success? Who had given them health insurance as soon as the partners could afford it? Who had given them dental insurance this year? And who—not that anyone would appreciate it—planned to set up profit sharing next year?

Sales at both restaurants were still dwindling. This time, there were no changes in the liquor laws or new restaurants to blame. With employees feeling ignored, resentful, and abandoned, the restrooms didn't get scrubbed as thoroughly, the food didn't arrive quite as piping hot, the servers didn't smile as often. But the owners, wrapped up in themselves, couldn't see it. They were mystified. "It began to seem like what made our company great had somehow gotten lost," says Tyrone.

Shaken by all the recent defections, Elijah needed a boost of confidence. So he sent out the one-page survey, which asked employees to rate the owners' performance. He was crushed by the results. Out of curiosity, Elijah later turned to an assistant and asked a favor. Can you calculate our turnover rate? Came the reply: "220 percent, sir."

Elijah decided to consult the management gurus through their books, tapes, and speeches. And thus the CUDA (Customer Undeniably Deserves Attention) contest was born. At Detroit and Ann Arbor, he divided the employees into six teams. The winning team would win $1,000, based on talking to customers, keeping the restaurant clean, and collecting special tokens for extra work beyond the call of duty.

Employees came in every morning, donned their colors, and dug in for battle. Within a few weeks, two teams pulled out in front. Managers also seemed revitalized. To Elijah, it seemed like they would do anything, anything, to keep their food costs down, their sales up, their profit margins in line. This was just what all the high-priced consultants had promised.

But after about six months, only one store's managers seemed capable of winning those all-or-nothing bonuses. At managers' meetings and reviews, Elijah started hearing grumblings. "How come your labor costs are so out of whack?" he'd ask. "Heck, I can't win the bonus anyway," a manager would answer, "so why try?" "Look, Elijah," another would say, "I haven't seen a bonus in so long, I've forgotten what they look like." Some managers wanted the bonus so badly that they worked understaffed, didn't fix equipment, and ran short on supplies.

The CUDA contest deteriorated into jealousy and malaise. Elijah was angry. These were the same employees who, after all, had claimed he wasn't doing enough for them.

PRACTICE

But OK, he wanted to hear what they had to say. "Get feedback," the management gurus preached; "find out what your employees think." Elijah announced that the owners would hold informal rap sessions once a month.

"This is your time to talk," Elijah told the employees who showed up—all three of them. That's how it was most times, with three to five employees in attendance, and the owners dragging others away from their jobs in the kitchen. Nothing was sinking in, and Elijah knew it. He decided to hire a consulting team from a university to advise him.

SOURCE: Adapted From: *Inc: The Magazine for Growing Companies by J. Hyatt.*
Copyright © 1989 by Mansueto Ventures LLC. Reproduced with permission of Mansueto Ventures LLC in the format CD-ROM via Copyright Clearance Center.

Assignment

1. Assume that you are hired to serve as a consulting team to Elijah. What counsel would you provide?

2. What elements in each step of the analytical problem-solving process are appropriate? Outline them specifically for Elijah.

3. What creative problem-solving steps are appropriate? Outline them for Elijah and provide a recommendation for how to facilitate them.

4. Prepare a specific consulting report containing your definition of the problem, alternative solutions, your evaluation of the best ones, your suggestions for creative and innovative alternatives, and at least one out-of-the-box idea for Elijah and his team.

5. What conceptual blocks are getting in the way?

Creative Problem-Solving Practice

In a team of colleagues, apply as many of the creative problem-solving tools as you can in developing alternative solutions to any of the following problems. Different teams may take different problems and then report their solutions to the entire class. You may substitute a current pressing issue you are facing instead of one of these problems if you choose. Try consciously to break through your conceptual blocks and apply the hints that can help you expand your problem definition and the alternatives you consider to be relevant. Keep in mind the four different approaches to creativity.

Problem 1: Consumers now have access to thousands of shows on demand, and online entertainment is replacing television as a choice for entertainment and news. Television viewership is declining. How could you address this problem?

Problem 2: At least 20 different rankings of schools appear periodically in the modern press. Students are attracted to schools that receive high rankings, and resources tend to flow to the top schools more than to the bottom schools. What could be done to improve the rankings of your own school?

Problem 3: Self-driving automobiles and the escalation in ridesharing threaten to diminish the number of automobiles sold each year throughout the world. Most countries— including the United States—are dependent on automobile production as a manufacturing base. How would you ensure that automotive companies do not go out of business?

Problem 4: The newspaper industry has been declining over the past several decades. People rely less and less on newspapers to obtain the news. What could be done to reverse this trend?

Have a team of observers watch the analytical and creative problem-solving process as it unfolds. Use the Observers' forms at the end of the chapter to provide feedback to the individuals and the teams on the basis of how well they applied the analytical and creative problem-solving techniques.

SKILL *APPLICATION*

ACTIVITIES FOR SOLVING PROBLEMS CREATIVELY

Suggested Assignments

3.14. Teach someone else how to solve problems creatively. Explain the guidelines and give examples from your own experience. Record everything in your journal.

3.15. Think of a problem that is important to you right now for which there is not an obvious solution. It may relate to your family, your classroom experiences, your work situation, or some interpersonal relationship. Use the principles and techniques discussed in the chapter to work out a creative solution to that problem. Spend the time it takes to do a good job, even if several days are required. Describe the experience in your journal.

3.16. Help direct a group (your family, roommates, social club, church, etc.) in a carefully crafted analytical problem-solving process—or a creative problem-solving exercise—using techniques discussed in the chapter. Record your experience in your journal.

3.17. Write a letter to your dean or a CEO of a firm identifying solutions to some perplexing problem facing his or her organization right now. Write about an issue that you care about. Be sure to offer suggested solutions. This will require that you apply in advance the principles of problem-solving discussed in the chapter.

Application Plan and Evaluation

The intent of this exercise is to help you apply this cluster of skills in a real-life, out-of-class setting. Now that you have become familiar with the behavioral guidelines that form the basis of effective skill performance, you will improve most by trying out those guidelines in an everyday context. Unlike a classroom activity, in which feedback is immediate and others can assist you with their evaluations, this skill application activity is one you must accomplish and evaluate on your own. There are two parts to this activity: Part 1 helps prepare you to apply the skill, and Part 2 helps you evaluate and improve on your experience. Be sure to write down answers to each item. Don't short-circuit the process by skipping steps.

Part 1: Planning

3.18. Write down the two or three aspects of this skill that are most important to you. These may be areas of weakness, areas you most want to improve, or areas that are most salient to a problem you face right now. Identify the specific aspects of this skill that you want to apply.

3.19. Now identify the setting or the situation in which you will apply this skill. Establish a plan for performance by actually writing down a description of the situation. Who else will be involved? When will you do it? Where will it be done?

Circumstances:
Who else?
When?
Where?

3.20. Identify the specific behaviors in which you will engage to apply this skill. Operationalize your skill performance.

3.21. What are the indicators of successful performance? How will you know you have been effective? What will indicate you have performed competently?

Part 2: Evaluation

3.22. After you have completed your implementation, record the results. What happened? How successful were you? What was the effect on others?

3.23. How can you improve? What modifications can you make next time? What will you do differently in a similar situation in the future?

3.24. Looking back on your whole skill practice and application experience, what have you learned? What has been surprising? In what ways might this experience help you in the long term?

SCORING KEYS AND COMPARISON DATA

⭐ Go to www.pearson.com/mylab/management for scoring keys and comparison data for the following instruments:

Problem-Solving, Creativity, and Innovation

How Creative Are You?©

Scoring Key

Circle and add up the values assigned to each item below.

ITEM	A. AGREE	B. UNDECIDED/ DON'T KNOW	C. DISAGREE
1	0	1	2
2	0	1	2
3	4	1	0
4	−2	0	3
5	2	1	0
6	−1	0	3
7	3	0	−1
8	0	1	2

ITEM	A. AGREE	B. UNDECIDED/ DON'T KNOW	C. DISAGREE
9	3	0	−1
10	1	0	3
11	4	1	0
12	3	0	−1
13	2	1	0
14	4	0	−2
15	−1	0	2
16	2	1	0
17	0	1	2
18	3	0	−1
19	0	1	2
20	0	1	2
21	0	1	2
22	3	0	−1
23	0	1	2
24	−1	0	2
25	0	1	3
26	−1	0	2
27	2	1	0
28	2	0	−1
29	0	1	2
30	−2	0	3
31	0	1	2
32	0	1	2
33	3	0	−1
34	−1	0	2
35	0	1	2
36	1	2	3
37	2	1	0
38	0	1	2
39	−1	0	2

40. These words have values of 2:

energetic	perceptive
resourceful	innovative
original	self-demanding
enthusiastic	persevering
dynamic	dedicated
flexible	courageous
observant	curious
independent	involved

These words have values of 1:

self-confident	informal
thorough	alert
restless	forward-looking
	open-minded

The remaining words have a value of 0.

Total Score _____

Comparison Data (N = 5,000 students)

TOTAL SCORE	MEAN	BOTTOM QUARTILE	SECOND QUARTILE	THIRD QUARTILE	TOP QUARTILE
	55.99	47 or below	48–55	56–65	66 or above

Innovative Attitude Scale

Comparison Data (N = 5,000 students)

TOTAL SCORE	MEAN	BOTTOM QUARTILE	SECOND QUARTILE	THIRD QUARTILE	TOP QUARTILE
	36	32 or below	33–35	36–38	39 or above

Creative Style Assessment

Scoring Key

Add up the points you gave to all of the "A" alternatives, the "B" alternatives, the "C" alternatives, and the "D" alternatives. Then divide by 7 to get an average score for each of the alternatives. Plot your score on the profile below, connecting the lines so that you produce some kind of kite-like shape.

Total of As: ____/7   Average score for A: ____ Imagine

Total of Bs: ____/7   Average score for B: ____ Incubate

Total of Cs: ____/7   Average score for C: ____ Invest

Total of Ds: ____/7   Average score for D: ____ Improve

Comparison Data (N = 5,000 students)

DIMENSION SCORES (AVERAGES)	MEAN	FIRST QUARTILE	SECOND QUARTILE	THIRD QUARTILE	FOURTH QUARTILE
Imagination	24.70	20 or below	20.01–24.29	24.30–29.29	29.30 or above
Incubation	25.92	21.43 or below	21.44–25.71	25.72–29.99	30 or above
Investment	25.47	20.71 or below	20.72–25.71	25.72–29.99	30 or above
Improvement	24.04	18.57 or below	18.58–23.99	23.30–28.57	28.58 or above

Part II
Interpersonal Skills

CHAPTERS

SKILL ASSESSMENT

- Communicating Supportively
- Communication Styles

SKILL LEARNING

- Building Positive Interpersonal Relationships
- The Importance of Effective Communication
- What Is Supportive Communication?
- Principles of Supportive Communication
- The Personal Management Interview
- International Caveats
- Summary
- Behavioral Guidelines

SKILL ANALYSIS

- Find Somebody Else
- Rejected Plans

SKILL PRACTICE

- United Chemical Company
- Byron vs. Thomas
- Active Listening Exercise

SKILL APPLICATION

- Suggested Assignments
- Application Plan and Evaluation

SCORING KEYS AND COMPARISON DATA

MyLab Management

Go to www.pearson.com/mylab/management to complete the exercises marked with this icon ✪.

4

Building Relationships by Communicating Supportively

LEARNING OBJECTIVES

1. Build supportive relationships even when delivering negative feedback

2. Avoid defensiveness and disconfirmation in interpersonal communication

3. Improve ability to apply principles of supportive communication

4. Improve relationships by using personal management interviews

DIAGNOSTIC SURVEYS FOR SUPPORTIVE COMMUNICATION

MyLab Management Personal Inventory Assessments

The assessment instruments in this chapter are briefly described below. The assessments appear either in your text or in MyLab. The assessments marked with ✪ are available only in MyLab. If assigned, go to www.pearson.com/mylab/management to complete these assessments. The assessments without the ✪ appear only in the text.

All assessments should be completed before reading the chapter material.

After completing the first assessment, save your response to your hard drive. When you have finished reading the chapter, re-take the assessment and compare your responses to see what you have learned.

- ✪ ❑ The *Communicating Supportively Assessment* measures the extent to which you demonstrate supportive communication, especially when providing negative or corrective feedback.
- ✪ ❑ The *Communication Styles Assessment* helps identify your dominant style of communicating when faced with problems or the need to provide assistance.

SKILL *LEARNING* ⓘ

Building Positive Interpersonal Relationships

A great deal of research supports the idea that **positive interpersonal relationships** are a key to creating positive energy in people's lives (Baker, 2000; Dutton, 2003). When people experience positive interactions—even if they are just temporary encounters—they are elevated, revitalized, and enlivened. Positive relationships create positive energy. All of us have known people who give us energy—they are pleasant to be around, they lift us, and they help us flourish. We also have encountered people who have the reverse effect—we feel depleted, less alive, and emotionally exhausted when we interact with them. Such encounters are personally de-energizing.

The effects of positive relationships are much stronger and more long-lasting than just making people feel happy or uplifted, however. When individuals are able to build relationships that are positive and that create energy, important physiological, emotional, intellectual, and social consequences result. For example, people's physical well-being is significantly affected by their interpersonal relationships. Individuals in positive relationships recover from surgery twice as fast as those in conflicting or negative relationships. They have fewer incidences of cancer and fewer heart attacks, and they recover faster if they experience them. They contract fewer minor illnesses such as colds, flu, or headaches; they cope better with stress; and they actually have fewer accidents (e.g., being in the wrong place at the wrong time). As might be expected, they also have a longer life expectancy. These benefits occur because positive relationships actually strengthen the immune system, the cardiovascular system, and the hormonal system (Dutton, 2003; Heaphy & Dutton, 2008; Reis & Gable, 2003).

Positive relationships also help people perform better in tasks and at work, and learn more effectively. That is, positive relationships help people feel safe and secure, so individuals are more able to concentrate on the tasks at hand (Carmeli, Brueller, & Dutton, 2009). They are less distracted by feelings of anxiety, frustration, or uncertainty that accompany almost all relationships that are nonpositive. People are more inclined to seek information and resources from people who are positively energizing, and they are less likely to obtain what they need to succeed if it means interacting with energy-depleting people. The amount of information exchange, participation, and commitment with other people is significantly higher when relationships are positive, so productivity and success at work are also markedly higher (see Dutton, 2003; Dutton & Ragins, 2007, for a review of studies).

Positive emotions—such as joy, excitement, and interest—are a product of positive relationships, and these emotions actually expand people's mental capacities. Feelings of joy and excitement, for example, create a desire to act, to learn, and to contribute to others. Moreover, the amount of information people pay attention to, the breadth of data they can process, and the quality of the decisions and judgments they make are all enhanced in conditions in which positive relationships are present. People's intellectual capacities are actually broadened (mental acuity expands), they learn more and more efficiently, and they make fewer mental errors when experiencing positive relationships (Fredrickson, 2001, 2009).

Not surprisingly, the presence of positive relationships among employees enhances the performance of organizations. Positive relationships foster cooperation among people, so the things that get in the way of highly successful performance—such as conflict, disagreements, confusion and ambiguity, unproductive competition, anger, or personal offense—are minimized (Cameron, et al., 2011). Employees are more loyal and committed to their work and to the organization when positive relationships exist, and information exchange, dialogue, and knowledge transfer are significantly enhanced. Creativity and innovation, as well as the ability of the system to adapt to change, are substantially higher when positive relationships characterize the workforce (Gittell, 2003; Gittell, Cameron, & Lim, 2006).

HIGH-QUALITY CONNECTIONS

Positive relationships usually imply a lasting or ongoing connection with other people. Our colleague, Jane Dutton, has identified the attributes of *high-quality connections* (Dutton, 2003, 2014). The word *connection* refers to a temporary interaction with another person. This differs from a relationship in that the encounter is momentary, lasting only a very brief period of time, and without any expectation that the interaction will last. Examples of high-quality connections include pleasant interactions with a cashier in a store, a flight attendant, the receptionist in the dentist's office, or a stranger at a social event. Dutton's research demonstrates that high-quality connections are characterized by three attributes: a sense of vitality and energy for both individuals; a sense of responsiveness and cooperation in the interaction; and enhanced physiological changes affecting, for example, heart rhythms, blood pressure, and energy (Dutton & Heaphy, 2003; Heaphy & Dutton, 2008).

That is, the positive effects of these short-term, momentary interactions mirror those of longer-term relationships. High-quality connections also help broaden thinking, heighten the ability to learn, build resilience, improve self-image, enhance coordination, strengthen attachment, increase adaptability, and reduce frustration and irritation.

Four attributes characterize high-quality connections and can help each of us be more effective in these momentary, temporary encounters (Dutton, 2014). Figure 4.1 summarizes these four attributes.

1. ***Respectful engagement.*** Respectful engagement means sending a message to another person to let him or her know that he or she is valued and respected. This can be done by simply making eye contact, using a pleasant tone of voice, and giving complete attention to the conversation. By offering verbal or nonverbal acknowledgment that you are listening, and by conveying interest in what the other person is saying, you send a message that the interaction is worth your time and attention. The way you communicate is a key part of respectful engagement.

2. ***Task enabling.*** Task enabling refers to helping another person solve a problem, achieve a goal, or move forward. This is not always needed if the interaction is limited merely to a temporary social connection. However, everyone can be uplifted and experience thriving as a result of an interaction. Sometimes this means merely communicating helpful information, providing emotional support, or just being open to the other person's concerns. Again, the way you communicate is a key part of task enabling.

3. ***Trusting.*** Conveying trust in another person means sending a message that you believe he or she is being open and honest in the interaction. The interaction is authentic and sincere. Trust is communicated when you ascribe good intentions to the other person and, as a result, you are willing to be open and honest in your own communication. As with the other attributes of high-quality connections, the way you communicate is a key part of conveying trust.

LEARNING

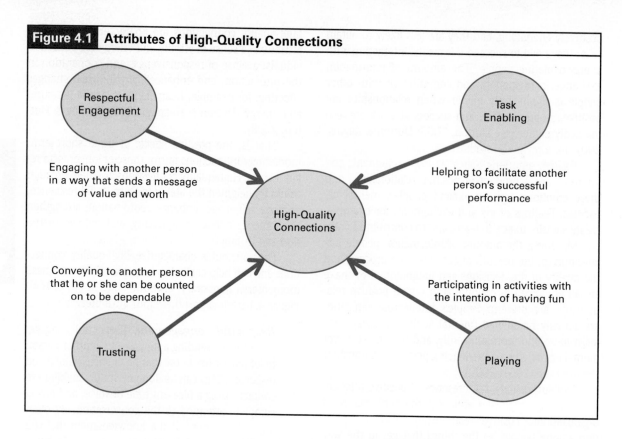

Figure 4.1 **Attributes of High-Quality Connections**

Respectful Engagement

Engaging with another person in a way that sends a message of value and worth

Task Enabling

Helping to facilitate another person's successful performance

High-Quality Connections

Conveying to another person that he or she can be counted on to be dependable

Trusting

Participating in activities with the intention of having fun

Playing

4. *Play.* Playfulness in an interaction can be communicated with humor, smiling, exuding positive energy, and being vulnerable. It involves engaging in spontaneous interchange. Being playful helps the connection feel relaxed and fun. Again, the way you communicate is a key part of fostering playfulness.

THE KEY

It is hard to find a reason why people would *not* want to build high-quality connections and enhance positive relationships. Many advantages and very few liabilities are associated with positive relationships. Creating such relationships sounds simple, of course, because we all engage frequently in momentary connections and enjoy ongoing relationships on a regular basis. However, it is sometimes easier said than done. It is not difficult to build positive relationships with people who are like us, to whom we are attracted, or who behave according to our expectations. But when we encounter people who are abrasive, who are not easy to like, or who make a lot of errors or blunders, it becomes more difficult to build relationships and create high-quality connections. In other words, building positive relationships in negative circumstances or with negative people requires special skill.

Arguably the most important skill in building and strengthening positive relationships, and the most important attribute in fostering high-quality connections, is the ability to communicate with people in a way that enhances feelings of trust, openness, respect, and support. In this chapter we focus on helping you develop and improve this skill.

Of course, all of us communicate constantly, and most of us feel that we do a reasonably good job of it. We haven't gotten this far in life without being able to communicate effectively. On the other hand, in study after study, communication problems are identified as the single biggest impediment to positive relationships and positive connections (Carrell & Willmington, 1996; DaVito, 2015). We focus in this chapter on the most important skill that effective managers must possess: the ability to communicate supportively.

The Importance of Effective Communication

In an age of electronic communication, the most frequently used means of passing messages to other people is electronic technology. Messages containing 280 or fewer characters dominate interpersonal interactions. Yet surveys have consistently shown that the ability to effectively communicate face to face is the characteristic judged by managers to be most critical in determining promotability (see surveys reported by Brownell, 1986, 1990; Furnham, 2008; Goleman, 1998; Hargie, 1997; Steil, Barker, & Watson, 1983). In fact, the increasing reliance on electronic forms of communication (e.g., texting, Twitter) has been found to diminish competency in interpersonal communication (Nie, 2001).

Not surprisingly, the quality of communication between managers and their employees is also fairly low (Madlock, 2008; Yrle, Hartman, & Galle, 2002), yet it is face-to-face, one-on-one communication that dominates all the other types in predicting managerial success. In study after study across all types of organizations and sectors, of all managerial skills, interpersonal communication skills, including listening, were rated as the most important (DeVito, 2015).

At least 80 percent of a manager's waking hours are spent in verbal communication, so it is not surprising that serious attention has been given to a plethora of procedures to improve interpersonal communication. Scholars have written extensively on communicology, semantics, rhetoric, linguistics, cybernetics, syntactics, pragmatics, proxemics, and canalization; and thousands of books have been produced on the physics of the communication process—encoding, decoding, transmission, media, perception, reception, and noise. Similarly, volumes are available on effective public-speaking techniques, making formal presentations, and the processes of organizational communication. Most colleges and universities have academic departments dedicated to the field of speech communication; most business schools provide a business communication curriculum; and many organizations have public communication departments and intraorganizational communication specialists such as newsletter editors and speechwriters. All of this attention is understandable, as illustrated by our own study of major manufacturing organizations undergoing large-scale changes. In the study, we asked two key questions: (1) What is your major problem in trying to get organizational changes implemented? and (2) What is the key factor that explains your past success in effectively managing organizational change? To both questions, a large majority of managers gave the same answer: communication.

COMMUNICATION PROBLEMS

Even with all this available information about the communication process and the dedicated resources in many organizations for fostering better communication, most managers still indicate that poor communication is their biggest problem (McNaughtan, 2012; Schnake, et al.,

1990). One reason is that most people feel they are effective communicators themselves. They tend to think that communication problems are a product of others' weaknesses, not their own (Carrell & Willmington, 1996; Cupach & Spitzberg, 2007; DeVito, 2015). Instead of fostering high-quality connections or positive long-term relationships, communication problems are often the major culprit in inhibiting flourishing relationships.

People still become offended at one another, make insulting statements, and communicate clumsily. Individuals still communicate in abrasive, insensitive, and unproductive ways. Rather than building and enhancing positive relationships, they damage relationships. More often than not, it is the interpersonal aspect of communication that stands in the way of effective message (Cupach & Spitzberg, 2007; Golen, 1990).

Ineffective communication may lead individuals to dislike each other, be offended by each other, lose confidence in each other, refuse to listen to each other, and disagree with each other, as well as cause a host of other interpersonal problems. These interpersonal problems, in turn, generally lead to restricted communication flow, inaccurate messages, and misinterpretations of meanings and motives.

To illustrate, consider the following situation. Latisha is introducing a new goal-setting program to the organization as a way to overcome some productivity problems. After Latisha's carefully prepared presentation in the management council meeting, Jose raises his hand. "In my opinion, this is a naive approach to solving our productivity issues. The considerations are much more complex than Latisha seems to realize. I don't think we should waste our time by pursuing this plan any further."

Jose's opinion may be justified, but the manner in which he delivers the message will probably eliminate any hope of its being dealt with objectively. Instead, Latisha will probably hear a message such as, "You're naive," "You're stupid," or "You're incompetent." Therefore, we wouldn't be surprised if Latisha's response is defensive or even hostile. Any good feelings between the two have probably been jeopardized, and their communication will probably be reduced to self-image protection. The merits of the proposal will be smothered by personal defensiveness. Future communication between the two will probably be minimal and superficial.

What Is Supportive Communication?

In this chapter, we focus on a kind of interpersonal communication that helps you build and strengthen interpersonal relationships, especially in difficult circumstances. It is not hard to communicate supportively—to express confidence and trust in others and to convey compliments—when things are going well and when people are doing what you like. But when you have to correct someone else's behavior, when you have to deliver negative feedback, or when you have to point out shortcomings of another person, communicating in a way that builds and strengthens the relationship is more difficult.

This type of communication is called **supportive communication**. Supportive communication seeks to preserve or enhance a positive relationship between you and another person while still addressing a problem, giving adverse feedback, or tackling a difficult issue. It allows you to communicate information to others that is not complimentary, or to resolve an uncomfortable issue with another person but, in the process, strengthen your relationship. One major benefit of supportive communication is that it builds or strengthens a relationship in the presence of uncomfortable, negative, or offensive circumstances. It is also useful, however, even when problem-solving is not the focus of the interaction.

Supportive communication has eight attributes, which are summarized in Table 4.1. Later in the chapter, we expand on each attribute. When supportive communication is used, the relationship between

---

Table 4.1   The Eight Attributes of Supportive Communication

• Congruent, Not Incongruent

A focus on honest messages in which verbal statements match thoughts and feelings

| *Example:* "Your behavior really upset me." | *Not* | "Do I seem upset? No, everything's fine." |

• Descriptive, Not Evaluative

A focus on describing an objective occurrence, describing your reaction to it, and offering a suggested alternative

| *Example:* "Here is what happened; here is my reaction or the consequences; here is a suggestion that would be more acceptable." | *Not* | "You are wrong or at fault for doing what you did." |

• Problem-Oriented, Not Person-Oriented

A focus on problems and issues that can be changed rather than on people and their characteristics

| *Example:* "How can we solve this problem?" | *Not* | "Because of the way you are, a problem exists." |

• Validating, Not Invalidating

A focus on statements that communicate respect, flexibility, collaboration, and areas of agreement

| *Example:* "I have some ideas, but do you have any suggestions?" | *Not* | "You wouldn't understand, so we'll do it my way." |

• Specific, Not Global

A focus on specific events or behaviors and avoiding general, extreme, or either-or statements

| *Example:* "You interrupted me three times during the meeting." | *Not* | "You're always trying to get attention." |

• Conjunctive, Not Disjunctive

A focus on statements that flow from what has been said previously and facilitate interaction

| *Example:* "Relating to what you just said, I'd like to raise another point." | *Not* | "I want to say something (regardless of what you just said)." |

• Owned, Not Disowned

A focus on taking responsibility for your own statements by using personal ("I") words

| *Example:* "I have decided to turn down your request because..." | *Not* | "You have a pretty good idea, but it wouldn't get approved." |

• Supportive Listening, Not One-Way Listening

A focus on using a variety of appropriate responses, with a bias toward reflective responses

| *Example:* "I believe I heard you say that you prefer to take this approach, is that correct?" | *NOT* | "As I said before, I just don't understand you." |

---

the two communicating parties is strengthened and enhanced by the interchange. Positive feelings and mutual respect result. People feel energized and uplifted, even when the information being communicated is negative. And, even when engaging in temporary connections, feelings of mutuality, respect, and warmth are fostered.

The goal of supportive communication is not merely to be liked by other people or to be judged to be a nice person, nor is it used to produce social acceptance. As pointed out previously, positive interpersonal relationships have practical, instrumental value in organizations. Researchers have found that organizations fostering supportive interpersonal relationships enjoy higher productivity, faster problem-solving, higher-quality outputs, and fewer conflicts and subversive activities than groups and organizations in which relationships are less positive (Huselid, 1995; Stephens, Heaphy, & Dutton, 2012).

Moreover, delivering outstanding customer service is almost impossible without supportive communication. Customer complaints and misunderstandings frequently require supportive communication skills to resolve. Not only must managers be competent in using this kind of communication, but they must also help their subordinates develop this competency.

Hansen and Wernerfelt (1989) found, for example, that the presence of good interpersonal relationships between managers and subordinates was three times more powerful in predicting profitability in 40 major corporations over a five-year period than the four next most powerful variables—market share, capital intensity, firm size, and sales growth rate—combined. Supportive communication, therefore, isn't just a "nice-person technique," but a proven competitive advantage for both managers and organizations.

MyLab Management Watch it!
If your instructor has assigned this activity, go to www.pearson.com/mylab/management to complete the video exercise.

Coaching and Counseling

One of the ways to illustrate the principles of supportive communication is to discuss two common roles performed by managers, parents, friends, and coworkers: coaching and counseling others. In coaching, managers pass along advice and information, or they set standards to help others improve their skills and behaviors. In counseling, managers help others recognize and address problems involving their level of understanding, emotions, or perspectives. Thus, coaching focuses on abilities, counseling on attitudes.

Coaching situations are not the same as counseling situations, and the understanding the differences between the two is crucial for effective management and for building strong, supportive relationships. To introduce the differences between coaching and counseling situations, consider the following two scenarios:

SCENARIO 1: Jagdip Ahwal is the manager of the division sales force in a company that makes and sells components for the aerospace industry. He reports directly to you. Jagdip's division consistently misses its sales projections, its revenues per salesperson are below the firm average, and Jagdip's monthly reports are almost always late. You make an appointment to meet with Jagdip after getting the latest sales figures, but he isn't in his office when you arrive. His secretary tells you that one of Jagdip's sales managers dropped by a few minutes ago to complain that some employees are coming in late for work in the morning and taking extra-long coffee breaks. Jagdip had immediately gone with the manager to his sales department to give the salespeople a "pep talk" and to remind them of performance expectations. You wait for 15 minutes until he returns.

SCENARIO 2: Betsy Christensen has an MBA from a prestigious university and has recently joined your firm in the financial planning group. She came with great recommendations and credentials. However, she seems to be trying to enhance her own reputation at the expense of others in her group. You have heard increasing complaints lately that Betsy acts arrogantly, is self-promotional, and is openly critical of other group members' work. In your first conversation with her about her performance in the group, she denied that there is a problem. She said that, if anything, she was having a positive impact on the group by raising its standards. You schedule another meeting with Betsy after this latest set of complaints from her coworkers.

What are the basic problems in these two cases? Which one is primarily a coaching problem and which is primarily a counseling problem? How would you approach them so that the problems get solved and, at the same time, strengthen your relationships with Jagdip and Betsy? What would you say so that the best possible outcomes result? Although no situation is completely one type versus the other, in the case with Jagdip Ahwal, the basic need is primarily for **coaching**. Coaching situations are those in which managers must pass along advice and information or set standards for others. People are advised on how to do their jobs better and to be coached toward better performance. Coaching problems are usually caused by lack of ability, insufficient information and understanding, or incompetence on the part of individuals. Athletic coaches are prime examples in that their major task is to provide the information and advice that is needed to obtain high performance.

In scenario 1, Jagdip was accepting upward delegation from his subordinates, and he was not allowing them to solve their own problems. By not insisting that his subordinates bring recommendations for solutions to him instead of problems, and by intervening directly in the problems of his subordinate's subordinates, Jagdip became overloaded himself. He didn't allow his subordinates to do their jobs. Productivity almost always suffers in cases in which one person is trying to resolve all the problems and run the whole show. Jagdip appears to need coaching regarding how to avoid upward delegation and how to delegate responsibility as well as authority effectively.

Scenario 2 illustrates primarily a **counseling** problem. Managers need to counsel others instead of coach them when the problem stems from attitudes, personality, defensiveness, or other factors tied to emotions. Betsy's competency or skill is not a problem, but her unwillingness to recognize that a problem exists or that a change is needed requires counseling by the manager. Betsy is highly qualified for her position, so coaching or giving advice would not be a useful approach. Instead, an important goal of counseling is to help Betsy understand that a problem exists, that her attitude is of critical importance, and that alternatives exist to address the problem.

Coaching applies to ability problems, and the manager's approach is, "I can help you do this better." Counseling applies to attitude problems, and the manager's approach is, "I can help you understand the problem more clearly."

Here is the problem. A large majority of the time, people tend to coach or advise others when confronted with a problem. "Here is what I suggest you do." When the person facing the problem is asked what kind of assistance he or she desires, however, counseling focused on enhancing understanding and increased insight is the overwhelming preference. That is, people tend to coach and advise instead of foster understanding and show empathy. Counseling is preferred more than coaching, as we will discuss later in the chapter.

Although many problems involve both coaching and counseling, it is important to recognize the difference between these two types of problems because a mismatch of problem with communication approach can aggravate, rather than resolve, a problem. Giving direction or advice (coaching) in a counseling situation often increases defensiveness or resistance to change.

For example, advising Betsy Christensen about how to do her job or focusing on the behaviors she should not be doing (such as criticizing others' work) will probably only magnify her defensiveness because she doesn't perceive that she has a problem. Similarly, counseling in a situation that calls for coaching simply sidesteps the problem and doesn't resolve it. Jagdip Ahwal knows that a problem exists, for example, but he doesn't know how to resolve it. Coaching, not problem recognition, is needed.

So, how do we effectively coach or counsel another person? What behavioral guidelines help us perform effectively in these situations? Both coaching and counseling rely on the same set of key supportive communication principles summarized in, Table 4.1 which we'll now examine more closely.

DEFENSIVENESS AND DISCONFIRMATION

If principles of supportive communication are not followed when coaching or counseling others, two major obstacles result that lead to a variety of negative outcomes (Burleson, 2009; Cupach & Spitzberg, 2007; Czech & Forward, 2010; Gibb, 1961). These two obstacles are defensiveness and disconfirmation (see Table 4.2).

Defensiveness is an emotional and physical state in which a person is agitated, estranged, angered, and inclined to strike out (Gordon, 1988). Defensiveness arises when a person feels threatened or punished by the communication. If I feel that you are attacking me, I will defend myself. That is, self-protection becomes more important than listening, so defensiveness blocks both the message and the interpersonal relationship. Energy is spent on constructing a defense rather than on listening. Aggression, anger, competitiveness, and avoidance are common reactions.

The second obstacle, **disconfirmation**, occurs when people feel put down, worthless, or insignificant

Table 4.2	Two Major Obstacles to Effective Interpersonal Communication

Supportive communication engenders feelings of support, understanding, and helpfulness. It helps overcome the two main obstacles resulting from poor interpersonal communication:

Defensiveness

- One individual feels threatened or attacked as a result of the communication.
- Self-protection becomes paramount.
- Energy is spent on constructing a defense rather than on listening.
- Aggression, anger, competitiveness, and avoidance are common reactions.

Disconfirmation

- One individual feels incompetent, unworthy, or insignificant as a result of the communication.
- Attempts to reestablish self-worth take precedence.
- Energy is spent trying to portray self-importance rather than on listening.
- Showing off, self-centered behavior, withdrawal, and loss of motivation are common reactions.

because of the communication. They feel that their self-worth is in question, so they feel unworthy or unimportant. They focus on establishing self-worth and self-importance rather than listening. Reactions are often self-aggrandizing or show-off behaviors, loss of motivation, withdrawal, and loss of respect for the offending communicator.

The eight attributes of supportive communication serve as behavioral guidelines for overcoming defensiveness and disconfirmation. They are also guidelines for how to deliver negative feedback and critical messages in ways that build and strengthen relationships. Supportive communication is a key to building high-quality connections and long-term flourishing relationships.

Principles of Supportive Communication

1. SUPPORTIVE COMMUNICATION IS BASED ON CONGRUENCE, NOT INCONGRUENCE

A classic article written many years ago proposed a "general law of interpersonal relationships." This law states that all high-quality connections and all long-lasting relationships are based on the concept of **congruence** (Rogers, 1961). After 40 years of clinical treatment of psychological problems in patients, Rogers concluded that this one law is the fundamental key to all positive interpersonal relationships. The law simply states that what is communicated, verbally and nonverbally, must match what the communicator is

thinking and feeling (Dyer, 1972; Hyman, 1989; Knapp & Vangelisti, 1996; Rogers, 1961; Schnake, et al., 1990). Congruence simply means being honest and authentic in conveying a message.

Two kinds of **incongruence** are possible: One is a mismatch between what the person is experiencing and his or her awareness. For example, an individual may not even be aware that he or she is experiencing anger or hostility toward another person, even though the anger or hostility is really present. In severe cases, therapists are required to help individuals reach greater congruence between experience and awareness. People repress their deep-seated anger, sadness, or fear. They aren't really aware of what is bothering them.

A second kind of incongruence, and the one more closely related to supportive communication, is a mismatch between what a person thinks or feels and what is communicated. For example, a person may be aware of feeling angry but be unwilling to admit that the feeling exists. People sometimes feel guilty about their thoughts or feelings, thinking them to be inappropriate or wrong. More commonly, people think that if they express the way they are really feeling, it will offend the other person.

When building interpersonal relationships, and when coaching and counseling others, genuine, honest, authentic statements are always better than artificial or dishonest statements. People who hold back their authentic feelings or opinions, or who don't express what's really on their minds, create the impression that a hidden agenda exists. Other people sense that there is something else not being said, or that an opinion or thought is not being expressed. Therefore, they trust the communicator less and focus on trying to figure out what the hidden message is, not on listening or trying to improve the relationship. The connection between the two communicators stays superficial and distrusting. So, unless communication is genuine, open, and respectful, and unless it is also *perceived* to be genuine, open, and respectful, false impressions and miscommunication result. Congruence is a prerequisite of trust, and trust lies at the heart of positive relationships.

Striving for congruence, being honest and open, or demonstrating authenticity does not mean, of course, that we should blow off steam immediately upon getting upset, nor does it mean that we cannot repress certain inappropriate feelings (e.g., keeping anger, disappointment, or aggression under wraps). Other principles of supportive communication must also be practiced, and achieving congruence at the expense of all other consideration is not productive.

On the other hand, in problematic interactions, when negative feedback must be given, or when correcting someone else's behavior, we are more likely to express too little congruence than too much. This is because we are afraid to respond in a completely honest way, or we are not sure how to communicate congruently without being offensive. Saying exactly what we feel can sometimes offend the other person. So, the problem is often a matter of not knowing *how* to be congruent.

Consider the problem of a person who is not performing up to expectations and displays a nonchalant attitude even after having been given hints that your team's rating is being negatively affected. What could you say that will strengthen the relationship with this person and still resolve the problem? How can you express honest feelings and opinions and still remain non-judgmental? How can you ever be completely honest without offending other people?

This is even more difficult when you consider how to respond supportively to someone who, for instance, has bad breath or displays poor manners while eating. The more personal or delicate the feedback, the more difficult it is to be completely congruent. This is why the other principles of supportive communication are so important.

2. SUPPORTIVE COMMUNICATION IS DESCRIPTIVE, NOT EVALUATIVE

Being congruent is very challenging in isolation. That is, without using other principles of supportive communication, it is difficult to be effective. If a friend asks,

"How did I do?" and he or she didn't do so well, it is difficult to know how to respond honestly without being offensive. To say "You sucked" is probably not helpful. People worry about hurting other people's feelings, so the key is to separate descriptive from evaluative communication (Czech & Forward, 2013; Harvey & Harris, 2010).

Evaluative communication makes a judgment or places a label on other individuals or on their behavior: "You are doing it wrong." "You are incompetent." "You are the problem." Such evaluation generally makes other people feel attacked or denigrated, and, consequently, to respond defensively. They see the communicator as judgmental. Examples of their responses might be: "I am *not* doing it wrong." "Who are *you* to say?" or even, "I might as well give up." Arguments, bad feelings, or emotional withdrawal lead to deterioration in the interpersonal relationship.

The tendency to evaluate others is strongest when the issue is emotionally charged or when a person feels personally attacked. For example, it is more threatening to provide negative messages when others may be emotionally wounded, as when commenting on a sensitive or personally important issue. Sometimes people try to resolve their own bad feelings or anxieties by placing a label on others: "You are dumb" implies "Therefore, I am smart, so I feel better." Or, they may have such strong feelings that they want to punish the other person for violating their expectations or standards: "What you have done deserves to be punished. You have it coming." Most often, evaluations occur merely because people don't have any other alternatives in mind. They don't know how to be congruent without being judgmental or evaluating the other person.

The problem with evaluative communication is that it is likely to be self-perpetuating. Placing a label on someone else generally leads that person to place a label on the other, and defensiveness escalates. When both are defensive, it is not hard to see why effective communication does not occur. The relationship weakens, and arguments and accusations often ensue.

An alternative to evaluation is **descriptive communication**. Descriptive communication allows a person to be congruent and authentic as well as being helpful. It involves three steps, summarized in Table 4.3.

First, *describe objectively your observation of the event that occurred or the behavior that you think needs to be modified.* As objectively and dispassionately as possible, talk about *what* happened instead of about the person involved. Identify elements of the behavior that can be confirmed by someone else. Behavior should be

Table 4.3	Descriptive Communication

Step 1: Describe objectively the event, behavior, or circumstance.

• Avoid accusations.

• Present data or evidence.

Example: Three clients have complained to me this month that you have not responded to their requests.

Step 2: Focus on the consequences and/or your reaction, not on the other person's attributes.

• Describe your reactions and feelings.

• Describe the objective consequences that have resulted or will result.

Example: I'm worried because each client has threatened to go elsewhere if we aren't more responsive.

Step 3: Focus on solutions.

• Avoid discussing who's right or wrong.

• Suggest an acceptable alternative.

• Be open to other alternatives.

Example: We need to win back their confidence and to show them you are responsive. I suggest you offer to do a free analysis of their systems.

compared to accepted standards rather than to personal opinions or preferences. Subjective impressions or attributions about the motives of another person should be avoided. The description "You have finished fewer projects this month than anyone else in the division" or "I noticed that you made several comments in opposition to JR's proposal" can be confirmed by an objective record. They relate to the observed behaviors or to an objective standard, not to the motives or personal characteristics of the person. There is less likelihood that the other person will feel unfairly treated, since no evaluative label is placed on the behavior or the person. A description of a behavior, as opposed to an evaluation of a behavior, is neutral and impartial.

Second, *describe your (or others') reactions to the behavior, or describe the consequences of the behavior*. Rather than projecting onto another person the cause of the problem, focus instead on the reactions or consequences the behavior has produced. This requires that you are aware of your own feelings and reactions and are able to describe them. Using one-word descriptions for feelings is often an effective method: "I'm concerned about our productivity." "Your level of accomplishment frustrates me." "I was very uncomfortable." Similarly, the consequences of the behavior can be pointed out: "Profits are off this month." "Department quality ratings are down." "Your comments resulted in other participants shutting down."

Describing feelings or consequences lessens the likelihood of defensiveness, because the problem is framed in the context of your feelings or objective consequences, not the attributes of the other person. If those feelings or consequences are described in a nonaccusing way, then the focus can be on problem-solving rather than on defending against evaluations. That is, if *I* am concerned, *you* have less of a reason to feel defensive.

Third, *suggest a more acceptable alternative*. This focuses the discussion on the suggested alternative, not on the person. It also helps the other person save face and avoid feeling personally criticized or denigrated. The individual is separated from the behavior. Self-esteem is preserved because it is the behavior—something controllable—not the person, that can be modified.

Of course, care should be taken not to give the message, "I don't like the way things are, so what are *you* going to do about it?" The change need not be the responsibility of only one of the communicating parties. Instead, the emphasis should be on finding a solution that is acceptable to both people, not on deciding who is right and who is wrong or who should change and who shouldn't. For example, "I suggest that you identify what it would take to complete six more projects than you did last month." "I would like to help you identify the things that are standing in the way of higher performance." "You might want to ask some questions to gather more information before making a final judgment."

One concern that is sometimes expressed regarding descriptive communication is that these steps may not work unless the other person knows the rules too.

We have heard people say that if both people know about supportive communication, it works; otherwise, the person who doesn't want to be supportive can subvert any positive result.

For example, the other person might say "I don't care how you feel," or "I have an excuse for what happened, so it's not my fault," or "It's too bad if this annoys you. I'm not going to change." How might one respond to these responses? Should the principles of descriptive communication be abandoned, and the participant become evaluative and defensive in return? An alternative exists. This display of uncaring, lack of concern, or a defensive reaction now becomes the priority problem. The problem of low performance, for example, will be very difficult to address as long as the more important interpersonal problem between the two people is blocking progress. In effect, the focus must shift from coaching to counseling, from focusing on ability to focusing on attitude. If two people cannot work on the problem together, no amount of communication about the consequences of poor performance will be productive. Instead, the focus of the communication should be shifted to the lack of concern in the relationship, or the obstacles that inhibit working together to improve performance. Staying focused on the problem, remaining congruent, and using descriptive language become critical.

So, the three steps now switch focus. An appropriate response might be: "I'm surprised to hear you say that you don't care how I feel about this problem (step 1: describe the event). Your response is very disconcerting, and I think it might have important implications for the productivity of our team (step 2: articulate the reaction or consequences). I suggest we spend some time trying to identify the obstacles you feel are inhibiting our ability to work together on this problem (step 3: a suggested alternative)." "Or, I suggest that we ask a third party to help us resolve our differences in perspective."

It has been our experience that few individuals are completely recalcitrant regarding the desire to engage in a productive relationship. Few are completely unwilling to work on problem-solving when they believe that their interests are being considered. Most people want to perform successfully, to be a part of a productive and satisfying team, and to be contributors. When using supportive communication principles, not as manipulative devices but as genuine techniques to foster development and improvement, we have found that people usually accept these genuine, authentic, congruent expressions. This applies to cultures all over the world.

It is important to keep in mind that the steps of descriptive communication do not imply that one person should do all the changing. Frequently, a middle ground must be reached on which both individuals are satisfied (e.g., one person becomes more tolerant of deliberate work, and the other person becomes more conscious of trying to work faster). Sometimes, of course, it is necessary to make evaluative statements. When this is the case, the evaluations should be made in terms of an established criteria or standards (e.g., "Your behavior does not meet the prescribed standard"), some probable outcomes (e.g., "Continuation of your behavior will lead to worse consequences"), or some past successes by the same individual (e.g., "This behavior is not as good as your past behavior"). The important point is to avoid disconfirming the other person or arousing defensiveness.

3. SUPPORTIVE COMMUNICATION IS PROBLEM-ORIENTED, NOT PERSON-ORIENTED

Problem-oriented communication focuses on problems and solutions rather than on personal traits. Person-oriented communication focuses on the characteristics of the individual, not the event. "This is the problem" rather than "You are the problem" illustrates the difference between problem and person orientation. Problem-oriented communication is useful even when personal appraisals are called for, because it focuses on behaviors and events. Person-oriented communication, on the other hand, often focuses on personal attributes that rarely can be changed or controlled, and it can send the message that the individual is just plain incompetent.

Statements such as "You are dictatorial" and "You are insensitive" describe the person, while "I was left out of the decision-making" and "Two people complained to me about the tone of the meeting" describe problems. Imputing motives is person-oriented ("It's because you want to control other people"), whereas describing overt behaviors is problem-oriented ("You made several sarcastic comments in the meeting today").

One problem with person-oriented communication is that, while most people can change their behavior, few can change their personality. If I receive feedback about which I can do nothing, or if a label is put on me as a person, I feel helpless to do anything about it. Because I can't change, I will most likely get defensive and my relationship with the feedback giver will deteriorate. Person-oriented messages often try to persuade the other individual that "this is how you should feel" or "this is what kind of person you are." But since most people accept themselves pretty much as they are, their common reaction to person-oriented communication is to defend themselves against it or reject it outright. Even when communication is positive (e.g., "You are a wonderful person"), it may not be viewed as trustworthy if it is not tied to a behavior or an accomplishment (e.g., "I think you are terrific because of the extra-mile service you rendered to our organization"). The absence of a meaningful referent is the key weakness in person-oriented communication.

In building positive, supportive relationships, problem-oriented communication should also be linked to accepted standards or expectations rather than to personal opinions. Personal opinions are more likely to be interpreted as person-oriented and arouse defensiveness than statements in which the behavior is compared to an accepted standard or performance. Supportive communicators need not avoid expressing personal opinions or feelings about the behavior or attitudes of others. When doing so, however, they should keep in mind the following additional principles.

4. SUPPORTIVE COMMUNICATION VALIDATES RATHER THAN INVALIDATES INDIVIDUALS

Validating communication helps people feel recognized, understood, accepted, and valued. Communication that is **invalidating** challenges self-worth, identity, and relationships to others. It denies the presence, uniqueness, or importance of other individuals (Ellis, 2004; Waller, Corstorphine, & Mountford, 2007). For example, when the other person is not allowed to finish a sentence, when a competitive win-or-lose stance is adopted, when messages are confusing or incongruent, or when the other person is disqualified from making a contribution, communication is invalidating. People are invalidated in four main ways: superiority, rigidity, indifference, and imperviousness (Brownell, 1986; Cupach & Spitzberg, 1994).

Superiority: Communication that is superiority oriented gives the impression that one person is informed while others are ignorant, adequate while others are inadequate, competent while others are incompetent, or powerful while others are impotent. It creates a barrier between the person and the other people to whom the message is sent. **Superiority-oriented communication** can take the form of put-downs, in which others are made to look bad so that someone else looks good. Or it can take the form of

"one-upmanship," in which a person tries to elevate him- or herself in the esteem of others. One form of one-upmanship is withholding information, either boastfully ("If you knew what I knew, you would feel differently") or coyly to trip people up ("If you had asked me, I could have told you how to avoid this mistake"). Boasting almost always makes others uncomfortable, mainly because it is designed to convey superiority.

Another common form of superiority-oriented communication is the use of jargon, acronyms, or words in such a way as to exclude others or to create barriers in a relationship. Doctors, lawyers, government employees, military personnel, and many professionals are well known for their use of jargon or acronyms designed to exclude others or to elevate themselves rather than to clarify a message. Speaking a foreign language in the presence of individuals who don't understand it may also be done to create the impression of exclusiveness or superiority. In most circumstances, using words or language that a listener can't understand is bad manners because it invalidates the other person.

Rigidity: **Rigidity in communication** is a second major type of invalidation: The message is portrayed as absolute, unequivocal, or unquestionable. No other opinion or point of view could possibly be considered. Individuals who communicate in dogmatic, "know-it-all" ways often do so in order to minimize others' contributions or to invalidate others' perspectives.

It is also possible to communicate rigidity in other ways. Rigidity is also communicated by:

- ❑ Reinterpreting other viewpoints to conform to one's own
- ❑ Never saying, "I don't know," but having an answer for everything
- ❑ Appearing unwilling to tolerate criticisms or alternative points of view
- ❑ Reducing complex issues to overly simplistic definitions or generalizations
- ❑ Placing exclamation points after statements so the impression is created that the statement is final, complete, or unqualified
- ❑ Being resistant to receiving personal feedback

Indifference: Communicating indifference occurs when the other person's existence or importance is not acknowledged. A person may do this by using silence, by making no verbal response to the other's statements, by avoiding eye contact or any facial expression, by interrupting the other person frequently, by using impersonal words ("people should not" instead of "you should not"), or by engaging in unrelated activity during a conversation. The communicator appears not to care about the other person and gives the impression of being impervious to the other person's feelings or perspectives. To be indifferent is to exclude others or to treat them as if they are not even present.

Imperviousness: To be impervious means that the communicator does not acknowledge the feelings or opinions of the other person. They are either labeled illegitimate—"You shouldn't feel that way" or "Your opinion is incorrect"—or they are labeled as ignorant—"You don't understand," "You've been misinformed," or (worse yet) "Your thinking is naive." Being impervious means to ignore or make unimportant the personal feelings or thoughts of another. It serves to exclude the other person's contribution to the conversation or the relationship, and it makes the other person feel illegitimate or unimportant. Indifference implies "I don't care about you." Imperviousness implies "You are not important enough to be cared about."

Invalidation is even more destructive in interpersonal relationships than criticism or disagreement, because criticism and disagreement do, in fact, validate the other person by recognizing that what was said or done is worthy of correction, response, or notice. As William James (1965) stated, "No more fiendish punishment could be devised, even were such a thing physically possible, than that one could be turned loose in a society and remain absolutely unnoticed by all the members thereof."

Validating communication, on the other hand, helps people feel recognized, understood, accepted, and valued. Validating communication has four attributes: It is *egalitarian, flexible, two-way,* and *based on agreement.*

Egalitarian: **Respectful, egalitarian communication** is the opposite of superiority-oriented communication. It is especially important when a person with a higher status interacts with a person of a lower status. When a hierarchical distinction exists between individuals, it is easy for people of lower status to feel invalidated. Supportive communicators help people of lower status feel that they are important and that they have a stake in identifying problems and resolving them. They treat others as worthwhile, competent, and insightful, and they emphasize joint problem-solving rather than projecting a superior position. They can do this merely by asking for opinions, suggestions, and ideas. Even without hierarchical differences, it is important to communicate respectfully and in an egalitarian way. When people of different nationalities, ethnic groups, or genders are communicating, for example, some people are almost always vulnerable to feeling excluded or inferior. In those circumstances, egalitarian

and inclusive statements are especially important in order to foster supportive relationships.

Flexibility: **Flexibility in communication** refers to a willingness to remain open to other people's points of view or contributions. It means communicating that the other person may possess additional data and other alternatives that may make a contribution to the problem solution or to the relationship. It implies being receptive to other people. It means communicating genuine humility—not self-abasement or weakness—and a willingness to learn and to be open to new experience. It means remaining open to new insights. As Benjamin Disraeli noted, "To be conscious that you are ignorant is a first great step toward knowledge."

In flexible communication, perceptions and opinions are not presented as facts but are stated provisionally. No claim is made for the absolute truthfulness of opinions or assumptions. "I may be wrong, but..." is flexible. "I am right" is inflexible. Flexible communication conveys a willingness to enter into joint problem-solving rather than to control the other person or to assume a master–teacher role. However, being flexible is not synonymous with being wishy-washy. "Gee, I can't make up my mind" is wishy-washy, whereas "I have my own opinions, but what do you think?" suggests flexibility.

Two-way communication: Individuals feel validated when they are asked questions, given "air time" to express their opinions, and encouraged to participate actively in the interpersonal interaction. Two-way interchange communicates the message that the other person is valued, which is a prerequisite for building collaboration and teamwork.

Agreement: Communication also validates another person when it *identifies areas of agreement* and commonality. Identifying what both people can agree on and what they jointly can be committed to pursue is validating to both individuals. Almost all models of effective negotiation, team building, and conflict resolution prescribe finding areas of agreement upon which everyone can concur. One way to express validation is to identify positive behaviors, positive attitudes, and positive consequences upon which everyone can agree. Agreement makes progress possible.

Some examples of ways to positively validate others include noting important points made by the other person before pointing out trivial ones, areas of agreement before areas of disagreement, advantages of the other person's statements before disadvantages, and positive next steps before past mistakes. It means paying compliments before making criticisms. The point is, validating other people helps create feelings of self-worth and self-confidence that can translate into self-motivation and improved performance. Positive relationships result. Invalidation, on the other hand, seldom produces such positive outcomes, yet it is a common form of response when people encounter something that they feel a need to criticize or correct.

5. SUPPORTIVE COMMUNICATION IS SPECIFIC (USEFUL), NOT GLOBAL (NONUSEFUL)

Specific statements are supportive because they identify something that can be easily understood and acted upon. In general, the more specific a statement, the more effective it is in motivating improvement. For example, the statement "You have trouble managing your time" is too general to be useful, whereas "You spent an hour scheduling meetings today when that could have been done by your assistant" provides specific information that can serve as a basis for behavioral change. "Your communication needs to improve" is not nearly as useful as a more specific "In this role-play exercise, you used evaluative statements 60 percent of the time and descriptive statements 10 percent of the time."

Absolutes: Specific statements avoid extremes and absolutes. The following are extreme or global (and nonuseful) statements that lead to defensiveness or disconfirmation:

> A: "You never ask for my advice."
> B: "Yes, I do. I always consult you before making a decision."
>
> A: "You have no consideration for others' feelings."
> B: "I do so. I am always very considerate."
>
> A: "This job stinks."
> B: "You're wrong. It's a great job."

Either–Or: Another common type of global communication is the either–or statement, such as "You either do what I say or I'll fire you," "Life is either a daring adventure or nothing" (Helen Keller), and "Either America reduces its national debt or the next generation will never achieve the standard of living people enjoy today."

The problem with extreme and either–or statements is that they deny any alternatives. The possible responses of the recipient of the communication are severely constrained. To contradict or deny the statement generally leads to defensiveness and arguments.

A statement by Adolf Hitler in 1933 illustrates the point: "Everyone in Germany is a National Socialist; the few outside the party are either lunatics or idiots."

A friend of ours was asked to serve as a consultant to a labor and management committee in a company. As he entered the room and was introduced as a professor, the union president declared: "Either he goes or I go." What would you do in this situation? How would you use supportive communication when the union president has made a global statement that either excludes you or cancels the negotiations? Our friend's reply was, "I hope there are more alternatives than that. Why don't we explore them?" This response provided a way for communication to continue and for the possibility of a supportive relationship to be formed.

Behavioral: Specific statements are more useful in interpersonal relationships because they focus on behavioral events and indicate gradations in positions. More useful forms of the examples above are the following:

> A: "You made that decision yesterday without asking for my advice."
> B: "Yes, I did. While I generally like to get your opinion, I didn't think it was necessary in this case."
>
> A: "By using sarcasm in your response to my request, you gave me the impression you don't care about my feelings."
> B: "You are right. I know I am often sarcastic without thinking about how it affects others."
>
> A: "The pressure to meet deadlines often affects the quality of my work."
> B: "Since deadlines are part of our work, let's discuss ways to manage the pressure."

Specific statements may not be useful if they focus on things over which another person has no control. "I hate it when it rains," for example, may relieve some personal frustration, but nothing can be done to change the weather. Similarly, communicating (even implicitly) "The sound of your voice (or your personality, your weight, your tastes, your ethnicity, etc.) bothers me" only proves frustrating for the interacting individuals. Such a statement is usually interpreted as a personal attack or a bigoted assertion. The reaction is likely to be, "What can I do about that?" "I don't even understand what you mean." or, "You sound very narrow-minded." Specific communication is useful to the extent that it focuses on an identifiable problem or behavior about which something can be

LEARNING

done (e.g., "It bothers me when you talk so loudly in the library that it disturbs others' concentration").

Even when offering compliments to another person, being specific is better than being global or general. For example, providing positive feedback to someone by saying "You are a nice person" is not nearly as helpful as describing an incident or a behavior that created that impression; for example, "You seem to always smile when I see you, and you express interest in my work." Whereas both statements are pleasant to hear, the specific comment is much more helpful than the general comment.

6. SUPPORTIVE COMMUNICATION IS CONJUNCTIVE, NOT DISJUNCTIVE

Conjunctive communication is connected to previous messages that were spoken by someone earlier in the conversation. This kind of communication flows smoothly. **Disjunctive communication** is disconnected from what was stated before.

Communication can become disjunctive in at least three ways. First, there can be a lack of equal opportunity to speak. When a person is interrupted, when one person dominates by controlling "air time," or when two or more people try to speak at the same time, the communication is disjunctive. A smooth transition does not occur between one statement and the next.

Second, extended pauses are disjunctive. When a person pauses for long periods in the middle of his or her statements or when there are long pauses before responding to another, the communication is disjunctive. Pauses need not be total silence; the space may be filled with "umm," "aaah," or a repetition of something stated earlier, but the communication does not progress.

Third, topic control can be disjunctive. When one person decides unilaterally what the next topic of conversation will be without input or others' preferences, the communication is disjunctive. That person may switch topics, for example, with no reference to what was just said. He or she may control the topics discussed by dominating the talk time and not allowing others to make statements. Sieburg (1969) found that more than 25 percent of the statements made in small-group discussions failed to refer to or even acknowledge prior speakers or their statements.

These three factors—taking turns speaking, management of timing, and topic control—contribute to something called "interaction management." In an empirical study of perceived communication competence, Wiemann (1977, p. 104) found that "the smoother the management of the interaction, the more competent the communicator was perceived to be." People who took turns, who did not dominate with pauses or excessive air time, and who connected what they said to what others had said in the past were judged as competent communicators. In fact, interaction management was concluded to be the most powerful determinant of perceived communication competence in his experimental study. Individuals who used conjunctive communication were rated as being significantly more competent in interpersonal communication than were those whose communication was disjunctive.

Conjunctive communication, on the other hand, can be displayed by asking questions based directly on a previous statement, by waiting for a sentence to be completed before beginning a response (e.g., not finishing a sentence for someone else), and by saying only three or four sentences at a time before pausing to give the other person a chance to add input. All of us have been in interactions in which one person goes on and on without allowing others to comment or contribute. Interaction, exchange, and give-and-take are necessary in order for supportive communication to occur. Figure 4.2 illustrates the continuum of conjunctive and disjunctive statements.

7. SUPPORTIVE COMMUNICATION IS OWNED, NOT DISOWNED

Taking responsibility for one's own statements and acknowledging that the source of the ideas is oneself rather than another person or group is called **owned communication**. Using first-person words, such as *I, me*, and *mine*, indicates owned communication. **Disowned communication** is suggested when third-person or first-person-plural language is used: "People think," "They said," or "Someone might say." Disowned communication is attributed to an unknown person, group, or some external source (e.g., "Lots of people said"). This kind of communication avoids taking responsibility for the message and therefore avoids investing in the other person. This may convey the message that the communicator is aloof or uncaring about the other person or is not confident enough in his or her ideas to take responsibility for them. Having a trusting relationship is highly dependent on owned communication.

Glasser (1965, 2000) based his approach to mental health—reality therapy—on the concept of taking responsibility for, or owning, communication and behavior. According to Glasser, healthy people accept responsibility for their statements and behaviors. Unhealthy people

Figure 4.2 | The Continuum of Conjunctive Statements

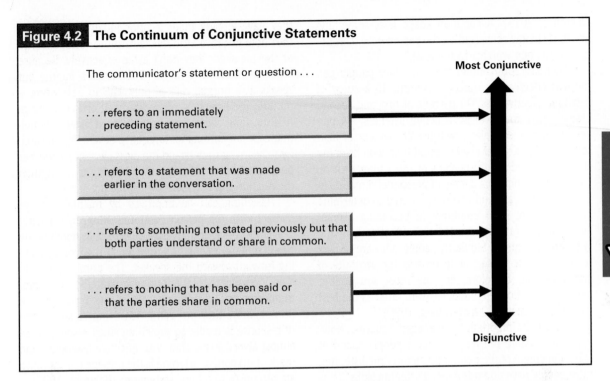

The communicator's statement or question . . .

... refers to an immediately preceding statement.

... refers to a statement that was made earlier in the conversation.

... refers to something not stated previously but that both parties understand or share in common.

... refers to nothing that has been said or that the parties share in common.

Most Conjunctive

Disjunctive

attribute what they feel or say to someone or something else (e.g., "My being cranky isn't my fault because my roommate stayed up all night playing loud music"). One result of disowned communication is that the listener is never sure whose point of view the message represents: "How can I respond if I don't know to whom I am responding?" "If I don't understand the message, who can I ask since the message represents someone else's point of view?" "If you are not willing to take responsibility for your opinions or statements, why should I trust you?"

Moreover, an implicit message associated with disowned communication is "I want to keep distance between you and me." The communicator takes the role of a representative rather than as a person, as a message-conveyer rather than an interested individual. Owned communication, on the other hand, indicates a willingness to invest oneself in a relationship and to act as a colleague or helper.

This last point suggests that when a person acts as a coach or as a counselor, he or she should encourage others to own their own statements as well. This can be done by example but also by asking the other person to restate disowning statements, as in this exchange:

SUBORDINATE: Everyone else says my work is fine.
MANAGER: So no one besides me has ever expressed dissatisfaction with your work or suggested how to improve it?

SUBORDINATE: Well...Mark complained that I took shortcuts and left him to clean up after me.
MANAGER: Was his complaint fair?
SUBORDINATE: Yeah, I guess so.
MANAGER: What led you to take shortcuts?
SUBORDINATE: My work was piling up, and I felt I had too much to do.
MANAGER: Does this happen often, that your work builds up and you look for shortcuts?
SUBORDINATE: More than I'd like.

Here the manager has used conjunctive questions to guide the subordinate away from disowning responsibility and toward acknowledging a behavior that may be affecting others' performance.

8. SUPPORTIVE COMMUNICATION REQUIRES SUPPORTIVE LISTENING, NOT ONE-WAY MESSAGE DELIVERY

The previous seven attributes of supportive communication all focus on message delivery. But a crucial aspect of supportive communication—*listening and responding effectively to someone else's statements*—is at least as important as delivering supportive messages (Bodie, et al., 2012; Imhof & Janusik, 2006; Johnston, Reed, &

Lawrence, 2011). A common adage goes something like this: "In any conversation, the person who talks the most is the one who learns the least."

Nichols (2009) found that the older people get, the less effective they are at listening. In a study of listening effectiveness, 90 percent of first and second graders were found to be effective listeners, 44 percent of middle schoolers, and just 28 percent of high schoolers. Yet Kramer (1997) found that good listening skills accounted for 40 percent of the variance in effective leadership. In a survey of personnel directors in 300 businesses and industries conducted to determine what skills are most important in becoming a manager, Crocker (1978) reported that effective listening was ranked highest. Similarly, people who are judged to be the most "wise," or to possess the attribute of wisdom—and, therefore, are the most sought-after people with whom to interact—were rated as the best listeners (Kramer, 2000; Sternberg, 1990).

Despite its importance in managerial success, however, and despite the fact that most people spend at least 45 percent of their communication time listening, most people have underdeveloped listening skills. Tests have shown, for example, that individuals are usually about 25 percent effective in listening; that is, they listen to and understand only about a fourth of what is being communicated (Bostrom, 1997). Geddie (1999) reported that in a survey across 15 countries, listening was found to be the poorest communication skill.

When individuals are preoccupied with meeting their own needs (e.g., saving face, persuading someone else, winning a point, avoiding getting involved), when they have already made a prior judgment, or when they hold negative attitudes toward the communicator or the message, they don't listen effectively. Because a person listens at a rate of 500 words a minute but speaks at a normal rate of only 125 to 250 words a minute, the listener's mind can dwell on other things half the time. Therefore, being a good listener is neither easy nor automatic. It requires developing the ability to hear and understand the message sent by another person, while at the same time helping to strengthen the relationship between the interacting parties.

Listening can be improved by maintaining eye contact with the person communicating, by regularly providing verbal or nonverbal cues such as nodding the head, smiling, saying "uh-huh" or "I see," or by leaning forward toward the speaker. The point is to be in a position where total attention is riveted on the communicator and distractions are blanked out. People do not know they are being heard unless some type of response is made, so providing small responses are almost always associated with effective listening. One mark of supportive listening is the presence of appropriate responses to others' statements (Bostrom, 1997).

Responding

Figure 4.3 lists four major response types and arranges them on a continuum from most directive and closed to most nondirective and open. Closed responses eliminate discussion and provide direction to individuals. They represent methods by which the listener can control the topic of conversation. They are most frequently associated with coaching. Open responses, on the other hand,

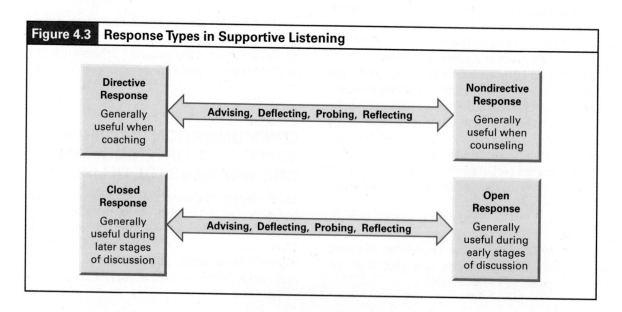

Figure 4.3 Response Types in Supportive Listening

Directive Response

Generally useful when coaching

Advising, Deflecting, Probing, Reflecting

Nondirective Response

Generally useful when counseling

Closed Response

Generally useful during later stages of discussion

Advising, Deflecting, Probing, Reflecting

Open Response

Generally useful during early stages of discussion

allow both the communicator and the listener to control the topic of conversation. They are most frequently associated with counseling. Each of these response types has certain advantages and disadvantages, and none is appropriate all the time under all circumstances.

Most people get in the habit of relying heavily on one or two response types and use them regardless of the circumstances. On average, about 80 percent of most people's responses have been found to be evaluative and directive (Bostrom, 1997; Rogers, 1961). Supportive listening, however, avoids evaluation and judgment as a first response and instead relies on flexibility in response types and the appropriate match of responses to circumstances. The four major types of responses are discussed below.

Advising

Assume that someone comes to you and says: "I am having a real problem with my friend, and I'm not sure how to handle it." An **advising response** provides direction, evaluation, personal opinion, or instructions. Such a response imposes on the other person your point of view, and it allows you to control the direction of the conversation.

The advantages of an advising response are that it provides the other person alternatives that may have been unclear before, it helps identify a solution to a problem, and it can provide clarity about how the other person should act or how they should interpret the problem. It is most appropriate when the listener has expertise that the other person does not possess or when the other person is in need of direction. Supportive listening sometimes means that the listener does the talking, but this is usually appropriate only when advice or direction is specifically requested. Most people have a tendency to offer much more advice and direction than is desired.

Four potential problems are created by an advising response. One is that it can produce dependence. The other person may get used to having someone else generate answers, directions, or clarifications. Rather than figuring out issues and solutions for themselves, he or she may delegate to another person.

A second problem is that advising may create the impression that the communicator is not understood. Rogers (1961) found that most people, even when they seem to be asking for advice, mainly desire understanding and acceptance. They want someone else to understand and empathize, not take control. The problem with advising is that it removes the opportunity for the other person to stay focused on the issue. Advice shifts the control of the conversation away from the communicator.

A third problem with advising is that listeners tend to concentrate more on the legitimacy of their advice or the problem solutions than on simply listening attentively. When listeners are expected to generate advice and direction, they tend to focus more on their own experience than on the communicator's experience. It is difficult to simultaneously be a good listener and a good adviser.

A fourth potential problem with advising is that it can imply that the communicator doesn't have the necessary understanding, expertise, insight, or maturity to solve his or her own problem. Giving advice may provide the impression that the communicator needs help because of his or her incompetence.

When advice is asked for or is an appropriate response, therefore, it should be communicated as one's own opinion or experience (owned, specific, validating), but other alternatives may be available (flexible). Listeners should ask the other person for his or her perspective or for his or her reaction (conjunctive). This way, the person does not feel obligated to accept the advice, but rather may choose to accept it or reject it.

Deflecting

A **deflecting response** switches the focus from the communicator's problem to one selected by the listener. This kind of response deflects attention away from the original problem or the original statement. It is a response that, essentially, changes the subject. The listener substitutes his or her own experience for that of the communicator (e.g., "Let me tell you something similar that happened to me") or introduces an entirely new topic (e.g., "That reminds me of the time that…").

Deflecting responses are most appropriate when an expanded perspective or some reassurance is needed. These responses can provide empathy and support by communicating the message "I understand because of what happened to me (or someone else)." They can also convey the assurance "Things will be fine. Others have also had this experience." Deflection is also often used to avoid embarrassing the other person. Changing the subject or answering a question other than the one asked are common occurrences when the problem discussed is uncomfortable or embarrassing.

The disadvantages of deflecting responses are that they can imply that the other person's problem is not important or that the listener's experience is more significant than that of the communicator. Deflecting responses may produce competitiveness or feelings that the listener is trying to one-up the other person. Deflection can be interpreted as "My experience is more worthy of discussion than yours." Or it may simply change the subject from something that is important and central to the other person to a topic that is not as important. ("I want to talk about something important to me, but you changed the subject to your own experience.")

Deflecting responses are most effective when they are conjunctive—that is, when they are clearly connected to what the other person just said, when the response leads directly back to the other person's concerns, and when the reason for the deflection is made clear. That is, deflecting can produce desirable outcomes if the communicator feels supported and understood, not invalidated, and achieves additional insight by way of examples.

Probing

A **probing response** asks a question about what the other person just said or about the problem he or she has shared. The intent of a probe is to acquire additional information, to help the other person say more about the topic, to help the listener become more empathetic with more insight, or to help the listener develop more appropriate responses. For example, an effective way to avoid being evaluative and judgmental is to continue to ask questions. Questioning helps listeners adopt the communicator's frame of reference so that in coaching situations suggestions can be specific (not global) and in counseling situations statements can be descriptive (not evaluative). Questions tend to be more neutral in tone than direct statements.

A study of top management team communication, for example, found that high-performing teams had a balance between inquiry (asking questions or probing) and advocacy (declaring or advocating a perspective). Questions and probes received equal time and emphasis in the team members' interactions. Low-performing teams were heavily oriented toward advocacy (i.e., telling, advising) and away from inquiry and probing (i.e., asking) (Losada & Heaphy, 2004).

Questioning, however, can sometimes have the unwelcome effect of switching the focus of attention from the other person's statement to the reasons behind it. For example, the questions "Why do you think that way?" or "Why is this a problem for you?" might pressure the other person to justify a feeling or a perception rather than just report it. Similarly, probing responses can serve to deflect attention away from the actual problem and toward a set of factors that are not central to the issue (e.g., "What were the results of the actions of the other people?"). Probing responses can also allow the other person to lose control of the conversation, especially when difficult subjects need to be addressed; for example, "Why are you waiting until now to bring this up?" allows all kinds of other issues to be raised that may or may not be apropos.

Two important hints should be kept in mind to make probing responses more effective. One is that "why" questions are seldom as effective as "what" questions. "Why" questions lead to topic changes, escapes, and speculations more often than to valid information. For example, the question "Why do you feel that way?" can lead to surprising or off-topic statements such as "Because I'm having a bad day," or "Because I'm allergic to cloudy days," or "Because Dr. Phil said so." These are silly examples, but they illustrate how ineffective "why" questions can be. "What do you mean by that?" is likely to be more fruitful is helping trigger insight.

A second hint is to tailor the probes to fit the situation. At least four types of probing responses exist. When the other person's statement does not contain enough information, or if part of the message is not understood, an **elaboration probe** should be used (e.g., "Can you tell me more about that?"). When the message is not clear or is ambiguous, a **clarification probe** is best (e.g., "What do you mean by that?"). A **repetition probe** works best when the communicator is avoiding a topic, hasn't answered a previous question, or a previous statement is unclear (e.g., "Once again, can you say more about this?"). A **reflection probe** is most effective when the communicator is encouraged to keep pursuing the same topic in greater depth (e.g., "So, are you saying that this is how you feel?"). Table 4.4 summarizes these four kinds of questions or probes.

Probing responses are especially effective in turning hostile or conflicting conversations into supportive conversations. Asking questions can often turn attacks into consensus, evaluations into descriptions, general statements into specific statements, disowned statements into owned statements, or person-focused declarations into problem-focused declarations. In other words, probes can often be used to help others use supportive communication when they have not been trained in advance to do so. The questions can foster progress toward understanding and clarity.

Reflecting

The primary purpose of the **reflecting response** is to mirror back to the communicator the message you heard and to communicate understanding and acceptance of the person. Reflecting the message *in different words* allows the speaker to feel listened to, understood, and free to explore the topic in more depth. Reflective responding involves paraphrasing and clarifying the message. Instead of simply mimicking the communication, reflecting responses contribute meaning,

Table 4.4	**Four Types of Probing Responses**
Type of Probe	**Explanation**
Elaboration	Use when more information is needed. ("Can you tell me more about that?")
Clarification	Use when the message is unclear or ambiguous. ("What do you mean by that?")
Repetition	Use when topic drift occurs or statements are unclear. ("Once again, what do you think about this?")
Reflection	Use to encourage more in-depth pursuit of the same topic. ("So, are you saying that you are having difficulty?")

understanding, and acceptance to the conversation while still allowing the other person to pursue topics of his or her choosing.

A large number of writers and therapists argue that this response should be the most frequently used and is most typical in supportive communication (Brownell, 1986; Steil, Barker, & Watson, 1983; Wolvin & Coakley, 1988; Dutton, 2011). It should dominate, say these authors, especially in coaching and counseling situations. It leads to the clearest communication, the most two-way exchanges, and the most supportive relationships. For example:

SUPERVISOR: Jerry, I'd like to hear about any problems you've been having with your job over the last several weeks.

SUBORDINATE: Don't you think they ought to do something about the air conditioning in the office? It gets to be like an oven in here every afternoon! They said they were going to fix the system weeks ago!

SUPERVISOR: It sounds like the delay is really beginning to make you angry.

SUBORDINATE: It sure is! It's just terrible the way maintenance seems to being goofing off instead of being responsive.

SUPERVISOR: So it's frustrating...and discouraging.

SUBORDINATE: Amen. And by the way, there's something else I want to mention....

A potential disadvantage of reflective responses is that the other person may get the feeling that you do not understand, are not listening carefully, or are just mimicking what was just stated. If he or she keeps hearing reflections of what was just said, a response might be "I thought I had made myself clear. Aren't you listening to me?" Reflective responses, in other words,

can be perceived as an artificial technique or as a superficial response to a message.

Therefore, when using reflective responses, keep the following rules:

1. Avoid repeating the same response over and over, such as "So, you feel that...," "Are you saying that...?" or "What I heard you say was...."
2. Avoid mimicking the communicator's words. Instead, restate the message in a way that helps ensure that the communicator knows that you understand or are trying to understand.
3. Avoid an exchange in which you do not contribute equally to the conversation, but serve only as a mimic. (You can use understanding or reflective responses while still taking equal responsibility for the depth and meaning of the communication.)
4. Respond to the personal rather than the impersonal. Responding to individuals is always more important than responding to circumstances or facts.
5. Respond to expressed feelings before responding to content. When people express feelings, they are the most important part of the message. Feelings may stand in the way of the ability to communicate clearly unless they are acknowledged.
6. Respond with empathy and acceptance. Avoid the extremes of complete objectivity, detachment, or distance on the one hand, or overidentification (accepting the feelings as your own) on the other.
7. Avoid expressing agreement or disagreement with the statements. Use listening responses to help the other person explore and analyze the problem and make progress in understanding and in resolving the issue.

The Personal Management Interview

Not only are the eight attributes of supportive communication effective in normal discourse and problem-solving situations, but they can be most effectively applied when specific interactions with direct-reports are planned and conducted frequently. One important difference between effective and ineffective managers is the extent to which they provide their direct-reports with opportunities to receive regular feedback, to feel supported and bolstered, and to be coached and counseled. Providing these opportunities is difficult, however, because of the tremendous time demands most managers face. Many managers want to coach, counsel, train, and develop direct-reports, but they simply never find the time. Therefore, one important mechanism for applying supportive communication and for providing direct-reports with development and feedback opportunities is to implement a **personal management interview (PMI) program** (Cameron, 2012).

This program is probably the most frequently adopted tool that managers employ in the executive education programs we teach when they commit themselves to improving relationships with their direct-reports and team members. We have received more feedback about the success of the PMI program than almost any other management improvement technique we have shared. It is a simple and straightforward technique for implementing supportive communication and building positive relationships in organizations as well as in family settings, community groups, church service, or athletic teams.

A PMI program is a regularly scheduled, one-on-one meeting between a manager and those for whom he or she is responsible. In a study of the performance of working departments and intact teams in a variety of organizations, Boss (1983) found that effectiveness increased significantly when managers conducted regular, private meetings with members on a biweekly or monthly basis. In a study of health care organizations holding these regular personal management interviews compared to those that did not, significant differences were found in organizational performance, employee performance and satisfaction, and personal stress management scores. The organizations that had instituted a PMI program were significantly higher performers on all the personal and organizational performance dimensions. Figure 4.4 compares the performance effectiveness of teams and

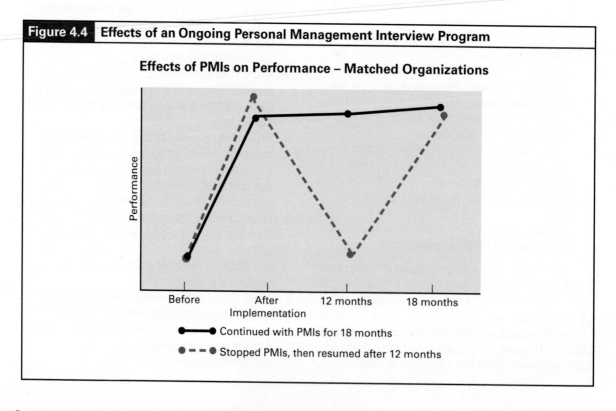

Figure 4.4 | Effects of an Ongoing Personal Management Interview Program

Effects of PMIs on Performance – Matched Organizations

Performance

Before — After Implementation — 12 months — 18 months

━●━ Continued with PMIs for 18 months

●- - -● Stopped PMIs, then resumed after 12 months

departments that implemented the program versus those that did not.

Our own personal experience is also consistent with the empirical findings. We have conducted personal management interviews with individuals for whom we have responsibility in a variety of professional, community, and church organization settings. We also have conducted these sessions with our individual family members. Rather than being an imposition and an artificial means of communication, these sessions—held one-on-one with each child or each member of the organization—have been incredibly productive. Close bonds have resulted, open sharing of information and feelings has emerged, and the meetings themselves are eagerly anticipated by both us and those with whom we have conducted the PMI.

Instituting a PMI program consists of two steps. First, a *role-negotiation session* is held in which expectations, responsibilities, standards of evaluation, reporting relationships, and so on are clarified. If possible, this meeting is held at the outset of the relationship or when a PMI process begins. Unless such a meeting is held, most individuals do not have a crystal clear idea of exactly what is expected of them or on what basis they will be evaluated. Most people have a clear idea of their job responsibilities from formal job descriptions, but the informal expectations, the interpersonal relationships, the values and culture, and the evaluation processes are usually not as clear. In a role-negotiation session, this uncertainty is addressed.

The manager and direct-report negotiate all job-related issues that are not prescribed by policy or by mandate. A written record is made of the agreements and responsibilities that result from the meeting, which can serve as an informal contract between the manager and the direct-report. The goal of a role-negotiation session is to obtain clarity regarding what each person expects from the other, what the goals and standards are, and what the ground rules for the relationship will be. Because this role negotiation is not adversarial but rather focuses on supportiveness and building a positive relationship, the eight supportive communication principles should always characterize the interaction.

When we hold PMIs in our families, these agreements often center on household chores, planned vacations, father–daughter or father–son activities, family rules, values, and so on. This role-negotiation session is simply a meeting to establish ground rules, spell out expectations, and clarify standards. It provides a foundation upon which the relationship can be built and

helps foster better performance on the part of the manager as well as the direct-report.

The second step in a PMI program is to schedule a set of ongoing, one-on-one meetings between the manager and each direct-report. These meetings are held regularly (not just when a mistake is made or a crisis arises) and are private (not overheard by others). This is not a department staff meeting, a family gathering, or an end-of-the-day checkup. The meeting occurs one-on-one. We have never seen this program work when these meetings have been held less frequently than once per month—both in organizations and in families. Many times managers choose to hold them more frequently depending on the work challenges being faced and the time pressures being experienced.

These meetings provide each person with a chance to communicate freely, openly, and collaboratively. They also provide managers with the opportunity to coach and counsel direct-reports and to help them improve their own skills or job performance. Therefore, each meeting lasts from 45 to 60 minutes and focuses on items such as the following: (1) managerial and organizational problems, (2) information sharing, (3) interpersonal issues, (4) obstacles to improvement, (5) training in management skills, (6) individual needs, (7) feedback on job performance and personal capabilities, (8) career aspirations, and (9) personal concerns or issues.

These meetings are not just a time to sit and chat. They have two overarching, crucial objectives: (1) to foster improvement and (2) to strengthen relationships. If improvement does not occur as a result of the meetings, they are not being held correctly. If relationships are not strengthened over time, something is not working as it should. Meetings always lead toward action items to be accomplished before the next meeting, some by the direct-report and others by the manager. Those action items are reviewed at the end of each meeting and reviewed again at the beginning of the next meeting. That is, accountability is maintained for improvement.

This is not a meeting just for the sake of having a meeting. Without agreements as to specific actions that will be taken, and the accountability that will be maintained, it can be a waste of both people's time. This means both people prepare for the meeting, and both bring agenda items to be discussed. It is not a formal appraisal session called by the manager, but a development and improvement session in which both the manager and direct-report have a stake. It does not replace formal performance appraisal sessions, but it supplements them. The purpose of PMIs is not to conduct evaluation or performance appraisals. Rather, they provide a chance for direct-reports to have personal time with the manager to

LEARNING

work out issues, report information, receive coaching and counseling, and improve performance.

PMI sessions help eliminate unscheduled interruptions and long, inefficient group meetings. At each subsequent meeting, action items are reviewed from previous meetings, so that continuous improvement is encouraged. The PMIs, in other words, become an institutionalized continuous improvement activity. They are also a key to building the collaboration and teamwork needed in organizations. Table 4.5 summarizes the characteristics of the personal management interview program.

The major objection to holding these PMI sessions, of course, is lack of time. Most people think that they simply cannot impose on their schedules a group of one-on-one meetings with each of their team members, direct-reports, or children. Boss' research (1983) found, however, that a variety of benefits resulted in teams that instituted this program. It not only increased their effectiveness, but it improved individual accountability, department meeting efficiency, and communication flow. Managers actually found that more discretionary time became available because the program reduced interruptions, unscheduled meetings, mistakes, and problem-solving time. Furthermore, participants defined it as a positive experience in itself. When correction or negative feedback had to be communicated, and when coaching or counseling was called for (which is typical of almost every manager–direct-report relationship at some point), supportive communication helped strengthen the interpersonal relationship at the same time that problems were solved and performance improved. In summary, setting aside time for formal, structured interaction between managers and their direct-reports, in which supportive communication played a part, produced markedly improved bottom-line results in those organizations that implemented the program.

Table 4.5	Characteristics of a Personal Management Interview Program

- The interview is regular and private.
- The chief intent of the meeting is continuous improvement in personal, interpersonal, and organizational performance, so the meeting is action oriented.
- Both the manager and the subordinate prepare agenda items for the meeting. It is a meeting for improving both of them, not just for the manager's appraisal.
- Sufficient time is allowed for the interaction, usually about an hour.
- Supportive communication is used so that joint problem-solving and continuous improvement result (in both task accomplishment and interpersonal relationships).
- The first agenda item is a follow-up on the action items generated by the previous meeting.
- Major agenda items for the meeting might include:
  - Managerial and organizational problems
  - Organizational values and vision
  - Information sharing
  - Interpersonal issues
  - Obstacles to improvement
  - Training in management skills
  - Individual needs
  - Feedback on job performance
  - Personal concerns and problems
- Praise and encouragement are intermingled with problem-solving but are more frequently communicated.
- A review of action items generated by the meeting occurs at the end of the interview.

International Caveats

We point out in other chapters that cultural differences sometimes call for a modification of the skills discussed in this book. For example, Asian managers are often less inclined to be open in initial stages of a conversation, and they consider managers from the United States or Latin America to be a bit brash and aggressive because they may be too personal too soon. Similarly, certain types of response patterns may differ among cultures—for example, deflecting responses are more typical of Eastern cultures than Western cultures. The language patterns and language structures across cultures can be dramatically different, and considerable evidence exists that individuals are most effective interpersonally, and they display the greatest amount of emotional intelligence, when they recognize, appreciate, and capitalize on these differences among others.

On the other hand, whereas stylistic differences may exist among individuals and among various cultures, certain core principles of effective communication are universally associated with effective communication. The research on interpersonal communication among various cultures and nationalities confirms that the eight attributes of supportive communication are effective in all cultures and nationalities (DaVito, 2015; Gudykunst, Ting-Toomey, & Nishida, 1996; Triandis, 1994). These eight factors have almost universal applicability in solving interpersonal problems.

We have used Trompenaars' (1996, 2011) model of cultural diversity to identify key differences among people raised in different cultural contexts. (Chapter 1 in this book provides a more detailed explanation of these value dimensions.) Differences exist, for example, on an *affectivity orientation* versus a *neutral orientation*. Affective cultures (e.g., the Middle East, southern Europe, and the South Pacific) are more inclined to be expressive and personal in their responses than neutral cultures (e.g., East Asia and Scandinavia). Sharing personal data and engaging quickly in sensitive topics may be comfortable for people in some cultures but very uncomfortable in others. The timing and pace of communication will vary, therefore, among different cultures.

Similarly, *particularistic* cultures (e.g., China, Indonesia, and Korea) are more likely to allow individuals to work out issues in their own way compared to *universalistic* cultures (e.g., Norway, Sweden, and the United States), where a common pattern or approach is preferred. This implies that reflective responses may be more common in particularistic cultures and advising responses more typical of universalistic cultures.

When individuals are assumed to have a great deal of individual autonomy, coaching responses (directing, advising, and correcting) are less common than counseling responses (empathizing, probing, and reflecting) in interpersonal problem-solving.

Research by Trompenaars and Hampton-Turner (2011), Gudykunst and Ting-Toomey (1988), and others clearly points out, however, that the differences among cultures are not great enough to negate or dramatically modify the principles of supportive communication. Regardless of the differences in cultural background of those with whom you interact, being problem centered, congruent, descriptive, validating, specific, conjunctive, owned, and supportive in listening are all judged to indicate managerial competence and serve to build strong interpersonal relationships. Sensitivity to individual differences and styles is an important prerequisite to effective communication.

Summary

The most important barriers to effective communication in organizations are interpersonal. Much technological progress has been made in the last two decades in improving the accuracy and volume of message delivery in organizations, but communication problems still persist among people, regardless of their relationships or roles. A major reason for these problems is that a great deal of communication does not support a positive interpersonal relationship. Instead, it frequently engenders distrust, hostility, defensiveness, and feelings of incompetence and low self-esteem. Ask any manager about the major problems being faced in their organizations, and communication problems will most assuredly appear near the top of the list.

Dysfunctional communication is seldom associated with situations in which compliments are given, congratulations are made, a bonus is awarded, or other positive interactions occur. Most people have little trouble communicating effectively in positive or complimentary situations. The most difficult, and potentially most harmful, communication patterns are most likely to emerge when giving feedback on poor performance, saying no to a proposal or request, resolving a difference of opinion between two people, correcting problem behaviors, receiving criticism from others, providing feedback that could hurt another person's feelings, or encountering other negative interactions. Handling these situations in a way that fosters interpersonal growth and engenders stronger positive relationships is one mark of an effective manager. Using supportive communication builds and strengthens the relationship even when delivering negative news.

In this chapter, we pointed out that effective managers adhere to the principles of supportive communication. Thus, they ensure greater clarity and understanding of messages while making other people feel accepted, valued, and supported. Of course, it is possible to become overly concerned with applying a technique or following a rule in trying to incorporate these principles and thereby to defeat the goal of being supportive. A person can become artificial, inauthentic, or incongruent by focusing on technique alone rather than on honest, caring communication. But if the principles are practiced and consciously implemented in everyday interactions, they can become important tools for improving your communication competence.

Behavioral Guidelines

The following behavioral guidelines will help you practice supportive communication:

A. Differentiate between coaching situations—which require giving advice and direction to help foster behavior change—and counseling situations, in which understanding and problem recognition are the desired outcomes.

B. Communicate congruently by acknowledging your authentic feelings and thoughts. Make certain your statements match your feelings and thoughts and that you communicate genuinely.

C. In communicating congruently, especially when providing negative feedback, use the eight rules of supportive communication to avoid creating defensiveness or disconfirmation.

D. Use descriptive, not evaluative, statements. Describe objectively what occurred, describe your reactions to events and their objective consequences, and suggest acceptable alternatives.

E. Use problem-oriented statements rather than person-oriented statements. That is, focus on behavioral referents or characteristics of events, not attributes of the person.

F. Use validating statements that acknowledge the other person's importance and uniqueness. Communicate your investment in the relationship by demonstrating your respect for the other person and your flexibility and humility in being open to new ideas or new data. Foster two-way interchanges rather than dominating or interrupting the other person. Identify areas of agreement or positive characteristics of the other person before pointing out areas of disagreement or negative characteristics.

G. Use specific rather than global (either–or, black-or-white) statements, and, when trying to correct behavior, focus on things that are under the control of the other person rather than factors that cannot be changed.

H. Use conjunctive statements that refer to what was said previously. Ensure equal speaking opportunities for others participating in the interaction. Do not cause long pauses that dominate the time. Be careful not to completely control the topic being discussed. Acknowledge what was said before by others.

I. Own your statements, and encourage the other person to do likewise. Use personal words ("I") rather than impersonal words ("they").

J. Demonstrate supportive listening. Make eye contact and be responsive nonverbally. Use a variety of responses to others' statements, depending on whether you are coaching or counseling someone else. Develop a bias toward the use of reflective responses.

K. Implement a personal management interview program with people for whom you have responsibility, and use supportive communication to coach, counsel, foster personal development, and build strong positive relationships.

SKILL *ANALYSIS*

CASES INVOLVING BUILDING POSITIVE RELATIONSHIPS

Find Somebody Else

Ronnie Davis, the relatively new general manager of the machine tooling group at Parker Manufacturing, was visiting one of the plants. He scheduled a meeting with Mike Leonard, a plant manager who reports to him.

RONNIE: Mike, I've scheduled this meeting with you because I've been reviewing performance data, and I wanted to give you some feedback. I know we haven't talked face-to-face before, but I think it's time we review how you're doing. I'm afraid that some of the things I have to say are not very favorable.

MIKE: Well, since you're the new boss, I guess I'll have to listen. I've had meetings like this before with new people who come in my plant and think they know what's going on.

RONNIE: Look, Mike, I want this to be a two-way interchange. I'm not here to read a verdict to you, and I'm not here to tell you how to do your job. There are just some areas for improvement I want to review.

MIKE: OK, sure, I've heard that before. But you called the meeting. Go ahead and lower the boom.

RONNIE: Well, Mike, I don't think this is lowering the boom. But there are several things you need to hear. One is what I noticed during the plant tour. I think you're too chummy with some of your female personnel. You know, one of them might take offense and level a sexual harassment suit against you.

MIKE: Oh, come on. You haven't been around this plant before, and you don't know the informal, friendly relationships we have. The office staff and the women on the floor are flattered by a little attention now and then.

RONNIE: That may be so, but you need to be more careful. You may not be sensitive to what's really going on with them. But that raises another thing I noticed—the appearance of your shop. You know how important it is in Parker to have a neat and clean shop. As I walked through this morning, I noticed that it wasn't as orderly and neat as I would like to see it. Having things in disarray reflects poorly on you, Mike.

MIKE: I'll stack my plant up against any in Parker for neatness. You may have seen a few tools out of place because someone was just using them, but we take a lot of pride in our neatness. I don't see how you can say that things are in disarray. You've got no experience around here, so who are you to judge?

RONNIE: Well, I'm glad you're sensitive to the neatness issue. I just think you need to pay attention to it, that's all. But regarding neatness, I notice that you don't dress like a plant manager. I think you're creating a substandard impression by not wearing a tie, for example. Casualness in dress can be used as an excuse for workers to come to work in really grubby attire. That may not be safe.

MIKE: Look, I don't agree with making a big separation between the managers and the employees. By dressing like people out on the shop floor, I think we eliminate a lot of barriers. Besides, I don't have the money to buy clothes that might get oil on them every day. That seems pretty picky to me.

RONNIE: I don't want to seem picky, Mike. But I do feel strongly about the issues I've mentioned. There are some other things, though, that need to get corrected. One is the appearance of the reports you send into division headquarters. There are often mistakes, misspellings, and, I suspect, some wrong numbers. I wonder if you are paying attention to these reports. You seem to be reviewing them superficially.

MIKE: If there is one thing we have too much of, it's reports. I could spend three-quarters of my time filling out report forms and generating data for some bean counter in headquarters. We have reports coming out our ears. Why don't you give us a chance to get our work done and eliminate all this paperwork?

RONNIE: You know as well as I do, Mike, that we need to carefully monitor our productivity, quality, and costs. You just need to get more serious about taking care of that part of your responsibility.

MIKE: OK. I'm not going to fight about that. It's a losing battle for me. No one at headquarters will ever decrease their demand for reports. But, listen, Ronnie, I also have one question for you.

RONNIE: OK. What's that?

MIKE: Why don't you go find somebody else to pick on? I need to get back to work.

Discussion Questions

4.1. What principles of supportive communication and supportive listening are violated in this case?

4.2. If you were to change this interaction to make it more productive, what would you change?

4.3. Categorize each of the statements by naming the rule of supportive communication that is either illustrated or violated.

4.4. Conduct a role-play. Discuss the key issues that exist between Ronnie and Mike. Identify the principles you used to make this a productive conversation. If you were Ronnie, what would you do in your follow-up meeting with Mike?

Rejected Plans

The following dialogue occurred between two employees in a large firm. The conversation illustrates several characteristics of supportive communication.

SUSETTE: How did your meeting go with Mr. Schmidt yesterday?

LEONARDO: Well, uh, it went...aaah...it was no big deal.

SUSETTE: It looks as if you're pretty upset about it.

LEONARDO: Yeah, I am. It was a totally frustrating experience. I, uh, well, let's just say I would like to forget the whole thing.

SUSETTE: Things must not have gone as well as you had hoped they would.

LEONARDO: I'll say! That guy was impossible. I thought the plans I submitted were very clear and well thought out. Then he rejected the entire package.

SUSETTE: You mean he didn't accept any of them?

LEONARDO: You got it.

SUSETTE: I've seen your work before, Leonardo. You've always done a first-rate job. It's hard for me to figure out why your plans were rejected by Schmidt. What did he say about them?

LEONARDO: He said they were unrealistic and too difficult to implement, and...

SUSETTE: Really?

LEONARDO: Yeah, and when he said that I felt he was attacking me personally. But, on the other hand, I was also angry because I thought my plans were very good, and, you know, I paid close attention to every detail in those plans.

SUSETTE: I'm certain that you did.

LEONARDO: It just really ticks me off.

SUSETTE: I'll bet it does. I would be upset, too.

LEONARDO: Schmidt has something against me.

SUSETTE: After all the effort you put into those plans, you still couldn't figure out whether Schmidt was rejecting you or your plans, right?

LEONARDO: Yeah. Right. How could you tell?

SUSETTE: I can really understand your confusion and uncertainty when you felt Schmidt's actions were unreasonable.

LEONARDO: I just don't understand why he did what he did.

SUSETTE: Sure. If he said your plans were unrealistic, what does that mean? I mean, how can you deal with a rationale like that? It's just too general—meaningless, even. Did he mention anything specific? Did you ask him to point out some problems or explain the reasons for his rejection more clearly?

LEONARDO: Good point, but, uh, you know...I was so disappointed at the rejection that I was kinda like in outer space. You know what I mean?

SUSETTE: Yeah. It's an incapacitating experience. You have so much invested personally that you try to divest as fast as you can to save what little self-respect is left.

LEONARDO: That's it, all right. I just wanted to get out of there before I said something I would be sorry for.

SUSETTE: Yet, in the back of your mind, you probably figured that Schmidt wouldn't risk the company's future just because he didn't like you personally. But then, well...the plans were good! It's hard to deal with that contradiction on the spot, isn't it?

LEONARDO: Exactly. I knew I should have pushed him for more information, but, uh, I just stood there like a dummy. But what can you do about it now? It's spilled milk.

SUSETTE: I don't think it's a total loss, Leonardo. I mean, from what you have told me—what he said and what you said—I don't think that a conclusion can be reached. Maybe he doesn't understand the plans, or maybe it was just his off day. Who knows? It could be a lot of things. What would you think about pinning Schmidt down by asking for his objections, point by point? Do you think it would help to talk to him again?

LEONARDO: Well, I would sure know a lot more than I know now. As it is, I wouldn't know where to begin revising or modifying the plans. And you're right, I really don't know what Schmidt thinks about me or my work. Sometimes I just react and interpret with little or no evidence.

SUSETTE: Maybe, uh...maybe another meeting would be a good thing, then.

LEONARDO: Well, I guess I should get off my duff and schedule an appointment with him for next week. I am curious to find out what the problem is, with the plans, or me. (Pause) Thanks, Susette, for helping me work through this thing.

Discussion Questions

4.5. Categorize each statement in the case according to the supportive communication characteristic or type of response it represents. For example, the first statement by Leonardo obviously is not very congruent, but the second one is much more so.

4.6. Which statements in the conversation were most helpful? Which were least helpful, or could have produced defensiveness or closed off the conversation?

4.7. If you were the coach of Susette, how would you assist her in being more competent as a supportive communicator? How would you coach Leonardo to be more supportive even though it is he who faces the problem?

SKILL ***PRACTICE***

EXERCISES FOR DIAGNOSING COMMUNICATION PROBLEMS AND FOSTERING UNDERSTANDING

United Chemical Company

The role of manager encompasses not only one-on-one coaching and counseling with an employee but also frequently entails helping other people understand coaching and counseling principles for themselves. Sometimes it means refereeing interactions and, by example, helping other people learn about correct principles of supportive communication. This is part of the task in this exercise. In a group setting, coaching and counseling become more difficult because multiple messages, driven by multiple motives, interact. Skilled supportive communicators, however, help each group member feel supported and understood in the interaction, even though the solution to an issue may not always be the one he or she would have preferred.

Assignment

In this exercise, you should apply the principles of supportive communication you have read about in the chapter. First, you will need to form groups of four people each. Next, read the case and assign the following roles in your group: Max, Marquita, Keeshaun, and an observer. Assume that Max, Marquita, and Keeshaun are having a meeting immediately after the end of the incidents in the following case. Play the roles you have been assigned and try to resolve the problems. The observer should provide feedback to the three players at the end of the exercise. Use the Observer's Feedback Form at the end of the case to provide feedback to each group member.

The Case

The United Chemical Company is a large producer and distributor of commodity chemicals, with five production plants in the United States. The main plant in Baytown, Texas, is not only a production plant but also the company's research and engineering center.

The process design group consists of eight male engineers and their supervisor, Max Kane. The group has worked together steadily for a number of years, and good relationships have developed among all the members. When the workload began to increase, Max hired a new design engineer, Marquita Davis, a recent master's degree graduate from one of the foremost engineering schools in the country. Marquita was assigned to a project that would expand the capacity of one of the existing plant facilities. Three other design engineers were assigned to the project along with Marquita: Keeshaun Keller (age 38, 15 years with the company), Sam Sims (age 40, 10 years with the company), and Lance Madison (age 32, 8 years with the company).

As a new employee, Marquita was very enthusiastic about the opportunity to work at United. She liked her work very much because it was challenging and it offered her a chance to apply much of the knowledge she had gained in her university studies. On the job, Marquita kept mostly to herself and her design work. Her relations with her fellow project members were friendly, but she did not go out of her way to have informal conversations with them during or after working hours.

Marquita was a diligent employee who took her work seriously. On occasions when a difficult problem arose, she would stay after hours in order to come up with a solution. Because of her persistence, coupled with her more current education, Marquita usually completed her portion of the various project stages several days ahead of her colleagues. This was somewhat irritating to her, because on these occasions she had to go to Max to ask for additional work to keep her busy until her coworkers caught up to her. Initially, she had offered to help Keeshaun, Sam, and Lance with their assignments, but each time she was abruptly turned down.

About five months after Marquita had joined the design group, Keeshaun asked to see Max about a problem the group was having. The conversation between Max and Keeshaun went as follows:

MAX: Keeshaun, I understand you want to discuss a problem with me.
KEESHAUN: Yes, Max, I don't want to waste your time, but some of the other design engineers want me to discuss Marquita with you. She is irritating everyone with her know-it-all, pompous attitude. She's just not the kind of person we want to work with.
MAX: I can't understand that, Keeshaun. She's an excellent worker, and her design work is always well done and usually flawless. She's doing everything the company wants her to do.
KEESHAUN: The company never asked her to disrupt the morale of the group or to tell us how to do our work. The animosity in our group could eventually result in lower-quality work for the whole unit.
MAX: I'll tell you what I'll do. Marquita has a meeting with me next week to discuss her six-month performance. I'll keep your thoughts in mind, but I can't promise an improvement in what you and the others believe is a pompous attitude.
KEESHAUN: Immediate improvement in her behavior is not the problem; it's her coaching others when she has no right to. She publicly shows others what to do. You'd think she was lecturing an advanced class in design with all her high-powered, useless equations and formulas. She'd better back off soon, or some of us will quit or transfer.

During the next week, Max thought carefully about his meeting with Keeshaun. He knew that Keeshaun was the informal leader of the design engineers and generally spoke for the other group members. On Thursday of the following week, Max called Marquita into his office for her midyear review. One portion of the conversation went as follows:

MAX: There is one other aspect I'd like to discuss with you about your performance. As I just related to you, your technical performance has been excellent; however, there are some questions about your relationships with the other workers.
MARQUITA: I don't understand. What questions are you talking about?
MAX: Well, to be specific, certain members of the design group have complained about your apparent "know-it-all attitude" and the manner in which you try to tell them how to do their job. You're going to have to be patient with them and not publicly call them out about their performance. This is a good group of engineers, and their work over the years has been more than acceptable. I don't want any problems that will cause the group to produce less effectively.

MARQUITA: Let me make a few comments. First of all, I have never publicly criticized their performance to them or to you. Initially, when I finished ahead of them, I offered to help them with their work but was bluntly told to mind my own business. I took the hint and concentrated only on my part of the work. What you don't understand is that after five months of working in this group I have come to the conclusion that what is going on is a rip-off of the company. The other engineers are goldbricking; they're setting a work pace much slower than they're capable of. They're more interested in the music from Sam's radio, the local football team, and the bar they're going to go to for TGIF. I'm sorry, but this is just not the way I was raised or trained. And finally, they've never looked on me as a qualified engineer, but as a woman who has broken their professional barrier.

SOURCE: *Based on United Chemical Company. Szilagyi, A. D. and M. J. Wallace,*
Organizational Behavior and Performance, Third Edition,
pp. 204–205. © 1983. Glenview, IL: Scott Foresman

Observer's Feedback Form

United Chemical Company

As an observer, provide feedback to each of the other role-players based on your observations. To what extent did each person display the attributes of supportive communication in the exercise? Use the following numerical rating scale for each person. Identify specific statements made that represent strengths, and identify potential areas for improvement.

1 = Strongly Disagree
2 = Disagree
3 = Neither
4 = Agree
5 = Strongly Agree

Supportive Communication Attribute	Role 1	Role 2	Role 3
• Communicated congruently	___	___	___
• Used description vs. evaluative statements	___	___	___
• Used problem- vs. person-focused statements	___	___	___
• Used validating vs. invalidating statements	___	___	___
• Used specific vs. general statements	___	___	___
• Used conjunctive vs. disjunctive statements	___	___	___
• Owned vs. disowned statements	___	___	___
• Listened intensively	___	___	___
• Used appropriate response alternatives	___	___	___

Comments:

Byron vs. Thomas

Effective one-on-one coaching and counseling are skills required in many settings in life, not just in management. It is hard to imagine a parent, roommate, Little League coach, classroom mother, or good friend who would not benefit from training in supportive communication. Because there are so many aspects of supportive communication, however, it is sometimes difficult to remember all of them. That is why practice, with observation and feedback, is so important. These attributes of supportive communication can become a natural part of your interaction approach as you consciously practice and receive feedback from a colleague.

Assignment

In the following exercise, one individual should take the role of Alex Byron, and another should take the role of Julian Thomas. To make the role-play realistic, do not read each other's role descriptions. When you have finished reading, hold a meeting between Alex Byron and Julian Thomas. A third person should serve as the observer. An Observer's Feedback Form to assist in providing feedback is at the end of the case.

Alex Byron, Department Head

You are Alex Byron, head of the operations group—the "back room"—in a large bank corporation. This is your second year on the job, and you have moved up rather quickly in the bank. You enjoy working for this firm, which has a reputation for being one of the finest in the region. One reason is that outside opportunities for management development and training are funded by the bank. In addition, each employee is given an opportunity for a personal management interview each month, and these sessions are usually both productive and developmental.

One of the department members, Julian Thomas, has been in this department for 19 years, 15 of them in the same job. She is reasonably good at what she does, and she is always punctual and efficient. She tends to get to work earlier than most employees in order to peruse the *American Banker* and *USA Today*. You can almost set your watch by the time Julian visits the restroom during the day and by the time she makes her phone call to her daughter every afternoon.

Your feeling about Julian is that although she is a good worker, she lacks imagination and initiative. This has been indicated by her lack of merit increases over the last five years and by the fact that she has had the same job for 15 years. She's content to do just what is assigned, nothing more. Your predecessor must have given hints to Julian that she might be in line for a promotion, however, because Julian has raised this with you more than once. Because she has been in her job so long, she is at the top of her pay range, and without a promotion, she cannot receive a salary adjustment above the basic cost-of-living increase.

The one thing Julian does beyond the basic minimum job requirements is to help train young people who come into the department. She is very patient and methodical with them, and she seems to take pride in helping them learn the ropes. She has not been hesitant to point out this contribution to you. Unfortunately, this activity does not qualify Julian for a promotion, nor could she be transferred into the training and development department. Once you suggested that she take a few courses at the local college, paid for by the bank, but she matter-of-factly stated that she was too old to go to school. You surmise that she might be intimidated because she doesn't have a college degree.

As much as you would like to promote Julian, there just doesn't seem to be any way to do that in good conscience. You have tried putting additional work under her control, but she seems to be slowing down in her productivity rather than speeding up. The work needs to get done, and expanding her role just puts you behind schedule.

This interview coming up is probably the time to level with Julian about her performance and her potential. You certainly don't want to lose her as an employee, but there is not going to be a change in job assignment for a long time unless she changes her performance dramatically.

Julian Thomas, Department Member

You are a member of the operations group in a large bank corporation. You have been with the bank now for 19 years, 15 of them in the same job. You enjoy the company because of its friendly climate and because of its prestigious image in the region. It's nice to be known as an employee of this firm. However, lately you have become more dissatisfied as you've seen person after person come into the bank and get promoted ahead of you. Your own boss, Alex Byron, is almost 20 years your junior. Another woman who joined the bank the same time you did is now a senior vice president. You can't understand why you've been neglected. You are efficient and accurate in your work, you have a near-perfect attendance record, and you consider yourself to be a good employee. You have gone out of your way on many occasions to help train and orient young people who are just joining the bank. Several of them have written letters later telling you how important your help was in getting them promoted. A lot of good that does you!

The only thing you can figure out is that there is a bias against you because you haven't graduated from college. On the other hand, others have moved up without a diploma. You haven't taken advantage of any college courses paid for by the bank, but after a long day at work, you're not inclined to go to class for another three hours. Besides, you only see your family in the evenings, and you don't want to take time away from them. It doesn't take a college degree to do your job, anyway.

Your monthly personal management interview is coming up with your department head, Alex Byron, and you've decided the time has come to get a few answers. Several things need explaining. Not only haven't you been promoted, but you haven't even received a merit increase for five years. You're not getting any credit for the extra contributions you make with new employees, nor for your steady, reliable work. Could anyone blame you for being a little bitter?

Observer's Feedback Form

Byron vs. Thomas

As an observer, provide feedback to each of the other role players based on your observations. To what extent did each person display the attributes of supportive communication in the exercise? Use the following numerical rating scale for each person. Identify specific statements made that represent strengths, and identify potential areas for improvement.

1 = Strongly Disagree
2 = Disagree
3 = Neither
4 = Agree
5 = Strongly Agree

Supportive Communication Attribute	Role 1	Role 2
• Communicated congruently	___	___
• Used descriptive vs. evaluative statements	___	___
• Used problem- vs. person-focused statements	___	___
• Used validating vs. invalidating statements	___	___
• Used specific vs. general statements	___	___
• Used conjunctive vs. disjunctive statements	___	___
• Used owned vs. disowned statements	___	___
• Listened intensively	___	___
• Used appropriate response alternatives	___	___

Comments:

Active Listening Exercise

Form a trio of colleagues who hold differing opinions about any of the following topics. Hold a 10- or 15-minute conversation about any of the topics. Take a position on the issue. Make a case for your point of view. Convince your partners that you are right. When you are finished, complete the short questionnaire below, and discuss the results together. Offer any helpful feedback to your colleagues that you think may be appropriate.

1. Should the United States impose tariffs on foreign goods?
2. Should late-term abortions be performed?
3. Is global warming a critical issue?
4. Should the United States prosecute and deport illegal aliens?
5. Should English become the national language in the United States?
6. Does the international media have a liberal bias, and does it matter either way?
7. Are business school rankings helpful or harmful?
8. Who is the world's most dangerous person?
9. Should professional athletes be allowed to compete in the Olympics?
10. Should the United Nations exist?

Rate your two colleagues' performance in the following categories using this response scale:

1 = Strongly disagree
2 = Disagree
3 = Neither
4 = Agree
5 = Strongly agree

ITEM	COLLEAGUE 1	COLLEAGUE 2
My colleague...		
1. Maintained eye contact and interest	1 2 3 4 5	1 2 3 4 5
2. Displayed useful nonverbal feedback	1 2 3 4 5	1 2 3 4 5
3. Interrupted	1 2 3 4 5	1 2 3 4 5
4. Probed for understanding	1 2 3 4 5	1 2 3 4 5
5. Used a variety of response types	1 2 3 4 5	1 2 3 4 5
6. Used reflective responses	1 2 3 4 5	1 2 3 4 5

PRACTICE

Reverse the scoring for item 3, and add up the scores for each colleague. Provide those scores to one another and discuss the results. Provide helpful feedback to one another.

ACTIVITIES FOR COMMUNICATING SUPPORTIVELY

Suggested Assignments

4.8. Record an interview with someone such as a coworker, friend, or spouse. Focus on an issue or challenge faced right now by that person. Diagnose the situation to determine if you should be a coach or a counselor. (Our bet is that it will be the latter.) Conduct a conversation in which you apply the principles of supportive communication discussed in the chapter. (The Rejected Plans case provides an example of such an interview.) Use the recording to determine how you could improve your own supportive communication skills.

4.9. Teach someone you know the concepts of supportive communication and supportive listening. Provide your own explanations and illustrations so the person understands what you are talking about. Describe your experience in your journal.

4.10. Identify a person with whom you have had a disagreement, some difficulty in the past, or some discomfort in your relationship. This could be a roommate, parent, friend, or instructor. Approach that person and ask to hold a conversation in which you discuss the interpersonal problem. To be successful, you'll discover how crucial supportive communication is in the conversation. When you have finished, write up the experience in as much detail as possible. What did you say and what did the other person say? What was especially effective and what didn't work so well? Identify areas in which you need to improve.

4.11. Write two mini case studies. One should recount an effective coaching or counseling situation. The other should recount an ineffective coaching or counseling situation. The cases should be based on a real event, either from your own personal experience or from the experience of someone you know well. Use principles of supportive communication and listening in your cases.

Application Plan and Evaluation

The intent of this exercise is to help you apply this cluster of skills in a real-life, out-of-class setting. Now that you have become familiar with the behavioral guidelines that form the basis of effective skill performance, you will improve most by trying out those guidelines in an everyday context. Unlike a classroom activity, in which feedback is immediate and others can assist you with their evaluations, this skill application activity is one you must accomplish and evaluate on your own. There are two parts to this activity: Part 1 helps prepare you to apply the skill, and Part 2 helps you evaluate and improve on your experience. Be sure to write down answers to each item. Don't short-circuit the process by skipping steps.

Part 1: Planning

4.12. Write down the two or three aspects of this skill that are most important to you. These may be areas of weakness, areas you most want to improve, or areas that are most salient to a problem or opportunity you face right now. Identify the specific aspects of this skill that you want to apply.

4.13. Now identify the setting or the situation in which you will apply this skill. Establish a plan for performance by actually writing down a description of the situation. Who else will be involved? When will you do it? Where will it be done?

    Circumstances:
    Who else?
    When?
    Where?

4.14. Identify the specific behaviors in which you will engage to apply this skill. Operationalize your skill performance.

4.15. What are the indicators of successful performance? How will you know you have been effective? What will indicate you have performed competently?

Part 2: Evaluation

4.16. After you have completed your implementation, record the results. What happened? How successful were you? What was the effect on others?

4.17. How can you improve? What modifications can you make next time? What will you do differently in a similar situation in the future?

4.18. Looking back on your whole skill practice and application experience, what have you learned? What has been surprising? In what ways might this experience help you in the long term?

SCORING KEYS AND COMPARISON DATA

⊕ Go to www.pearson.com/mylab/management for scoring keys and comparison data for the following instruments:

Communicating Supportively
Communication Styles

5

Gaining Power and Influence

SKILL ASSESSMENT

- Gaining Power and Influence
- Using Influence Strategies

SKILL LEARNING

- Building a Strong Power Base and Using Influence Wisely
- Opportunities for Gaining Power
- Transforming Power into Influence
- Acting Assertively: Neutralizing Influence Attempts

SKILL ANALYSIS

- Dynica Software Solutions

SKILL PRACTICE

- Repairing Power Failures in Management Circuits
- Kalina Ivanov's Proposal
- Cindy's Fast Foods
- 9:00 to 7:30

SKILL APPLICATION

- Suggested Assignments
- Application Plan and Evaluation

SCORING KEYS AND COMPARISON DATA

LEARNING OBJECTIVES

1. Enhance Personal and Positional Power
2. Use Influence Appropriately to Accomplish Exceptional Work
3. Neutralize Inappropriate Influence Attempts

MyLab Management

Go to www.pearson.com/mylab/management to complete the exercises marked with this icon ✪.

MyLab Management Personal Inventory Assessments

PERSONAL
INVENTORY
ASSESSMENT

The assessment instruments in this chapter are briefly described below. The assessments appear either in your text or in MyLab. The assessments marked with ✪ are available only in MyLab. If assigned, go to www.pearson.com/mylab/management to complete these assessments. The assessments without the ✪ appear only in the text.

All assessments should be completed before reading the chapter material.

After completing the first assessment, save your response to your hard drive. When you have finished reading the chapter, re-take the assessment and compare your responses to see what you have learned.

- ✪ ❑ The *Gaining Power and Influence Assessment* measures the extent to which you exhibit competency in gaining power and influence in a work context.
- ✪ ❑ The *Using Influence Strategies Assessment* measures your preferences for three different influence strategies that will be discussed in the chapter.

SKILL *LEARNING*

Building a Strong Power Base and Using Influence Wisely

"The difference between someone who can get an idea off the ground and accepted in an organization and someone who can't isn't a question of who has the better idea. It's a question of who has political competence. Political competence isn't something you're born with, but a skill you learn. It's an out-in-the-open process of methodically mapping the political terrain, building coalitions, and leading them to get your idea adopted." So says Samuel Bacharach, a Cornell University professor who has spent his career negotiating the halls of powerful New York businesses and labor unions (Bacharach, 2005, p. 93).

The skill of political competence is particularly relevant in today's workforce, where young managers are taking positions traditionally reserved for battle-tested pros who understand from experience the ins and outs of gaining power and influence. The challenge might be particularly difficult for the millennial generation (those currently in their 20s and early 30s), who are coming into the workplace with very different views about

how power should work. Millennials, according to researcher and consultant Dan Shawbel, fundamentally reject the idea of strict hierarchies at work and believe they should have as much of a voice as senior people in their organizations (Shawbel, 2012). This may be why some young, inexperienced managers report difficulties managing "up" (getting their bosses to respect them) as well as managing "down" (getting their older subordinates to respect their position) (Leger, 2000).

> **MyLab Management** Watch it!
> If your instructor has assigned this activity, go to www.pearson.com/mylab/management to complete the video exercise.

Nothing is more demoralizing than feeling you have a creative new idea or a unique insight into a significant organizational problem and then coming face-to-face with your organizational impotence. This is often the experience of young college graduates who enter the workplace feeling energetic, optimistic, and supremely confident that their "awesome" ability, state-of-the-art training, and indefatigable energy will rocket them up the corporate ladder. However, many soon become discouraged and embittered. They blame "the old guard" for protecting their turf and not being open to new ideas. One young manager stated dejectedly, "Hell is knowing you have a better solution than someone else but not being able to get the votes."

Despite millennials' disdain for hierarchies, most organizations still rely on status to determine how things get done. Consequently, young managers cannot simply hope that their ideas will speak for themselves. They need to develop skills to influence others if they want to make a difference. Kerry Patterson and his colleagues, authors of *Influencer,* tell a story about a group of employees who had received valuable training and were attempting to transfer it to their workplace. Many were unsuccessful in doing so. But the ones who were able to implement new ideas exhibited a set of skills that allowed them to be influential. They "...skillfully challenged their supervisor. They were candid with peers who weren't carrying their weight. And finally, they were capable of talking to senior management—the same senior managers more cynical peers avoided—about policies or practices that they believed impeded improvements" (Grenny, et al., 2013). Developing the confidence and skills to speak up effectively made all the difference for these employees.

GAINING POWER: POLARIZED PERSPECTIVES

Of all the topics examined in this book, the notion of "gaining power" in organizations is likely the most polarizing. We will first examine the arguments of those who worry about the effects of power on others, as well as on the person exercising power, followed by a more positive perspective, emphasizing the utility of power for doing good. We will conclude with our own views.

Power Corrupts

John Gardner has observed, "In this country—and in most democracies—power has such a bad name that many people persuade themselves they want nothing to do with it" (1990). For these people, power is a "four-letter word," conjuring up images of vindictive, domineering bosses and manipulative, cunning subordinates. It is associated with dirty office politics engaged in by ruthless individuals who use as their handbooks for corporate guerrilla warfare books such as *Winning Through Intimidation*, and who subscribe

to the philosophy of Heinrich von Treitschke: "Your neighbor, even though he may look upon you as a natural ally against another power which is feared by you both, is always ready, at the first opportunity, as soon as it can be done with safety, to better himself at your expense....Whoever fails to increase his power, must decrease it, if others increase theirs" (Mulgan, 1998, p. 68).

Those with a distaste for power argue that teaching managers and prospective managers how to increase their power is tantamount to sanctioning the use of primitive forms of domination. They support this argument by pointing to the devastating tragedies of corporate power abuse in recent decades, such as Jeff Skilling's arrogant deceptions that led to the downfall of Enron and Bernie Madoff's exploitation of trusting friends as he perpetrated one of the most egregious Ponzi schemes in history. And when we add in the seemingly endless revelations of sexual abuse in organizations, giving rise to the #MeToo movement and calls for reform in the Catholic church, it's clear that Lord Acton's well-known dictum, "Power corrupts, and absolute power corrupts absolutely," is not limited to 19th-century British politics.

In the Greek plays of Sophocles, the viewer is confronted with the image of great and powerful rulers transformed by their prior success so that they are filled with a sense of their own worth and importance—hubris—which causes them to be dismissive of the advice of others and unwilling to listen to opinions different from their own. In the end, they are destroyed by events that they discover they cannot control. Oedipus is destroyed soon after the crowds say (and he believes) "he is almost like a God"; King Creon, at the zenith of his political and military power, is brought down as a result of his belief in the infallibility of his judgments.

Headlines of business trade periodicals regularly trumpet examples of modern-day hubris among business elites (Bunker, Kram, & Ting, 2002). One example is Aubrey McClendon, the CEO of Chesapeake Energy, who was near the top of *BusinessWeek*'s list of "Worst CEOs of 2012" (Lavelle, 2012). McClendon took a notoriously cavalier attitude toward the company's finances, using the company jet and employee time for his personal purposes and striking a corporate sponsorship deal for a professional sports team he happened to own. He also borrowed more than $1 billion over a three-year period in undisclosed loans against his stake in the company.

Sophocles warns us never to be envious of the powerful until we see the nature of their endings. Support for the modern-day relevance of this timeless warning is reflected in the results of studies of both

Table 5.1	Characteristics That Derail Managers' Careers

- Lack of sensitivity to others; abrasive and intimidating
- Acting cold, aloof, and arrogant
- Untrustworthiness
- Being overly ambitious; playing politics and always trying to move up
- Inability to delegate to others or to build a team
- Overdependence on others (e.g., a mentor)

SOURCE: Based on Psychology Today, Copyright © 2006 www.psychologytoday.com.

successful and failed corporate executives (McCall & Lombardo, 1983; Shipper & Dillard, 2000). In the first study of its kind, scholars at the Center for Creative Leadership identified approximately 20 executives who had risen to the top of their firms and matched them with a group of 20 executives who had failed to reach their career aspirations. Both groups had entered their respective organizations with equal promise. There were no noticeable differences in their preparation, expertise, education, and so forth. However, over time, the careers of the members of the second group had become "derailed" due to the personal inadequacies shown in Table 5.2.

It is sobering to note how many of these problems relate to the inappropriate use of power in interpersonal relationships. In general, the "derailed" group support Lord Acton's dictum as well as the warnings of Sophocles. They were given a little authority, and they failed to be good stewards of it.

It is noteworthy that a negative view of "seeking power" is especially common in cultures that place a high value on ascription, rather than achievement, and on collectivism, rather than individualism (Triandis, 1994; Trompenaars, 1996). People who value ascription believe power resides in stable, personal characteristics such as age, gender, level of education, ethnic background, or social class. Hence, to them, focusing on "getting ahead," "taking charge," and "making things happen" seems contrary to the natural social order. Those who place a high value on collectivism may worry that placing too much emphasis on increasing a single individual's power might not be in the best interests of the larger group. For these reasons, some might find this chapter's focus on developing individual power overly "American" in its cultural orientation. However, though we acknowledge that our treatment of how to gain power in the corporate world has a strong indi-

vidualistic flavor typical of Western (Euro-American) cultures, our conceptualization of power tempers the value of personal achievement with a strong sense of social responsibility: using one's power for the benefit of others.

Power Enables

But surely it is not inevitable that power corrupts—there are plenty of examples of powerful people who use their influence to benefit others, both in their inner circle and in society at large. Support for this perspective comes from management guru Warren Bennis. Seeking the quintessential ingredients of effective leaders, he interviewed 90 individuals who had been nominated by peers as the most influential leaders in all walks of our society. Bennis found these individuals shared one significant characteristic: They made *others* feel powerful. They were influential because they used their power to help others accomplish exceptional tasks (Bennis & Nanus, 2003).

One of the early scholars to study organizational power, Rosabeth Kanter, pointed out that powerful managers not only can accomplish more personally, but they can also pass on more information and make more resources available to subordinates. For this reason, people tend to prefer bosses with "clout." Subordinates tend to feel they have higher status in an organization and their morale is higher when they perceive that their boss has considerable upward influence. In contrast, Kanter argues, powerlessness tends to foster bossiness, rather than true leadership. "In large organizations, at least," she notes, "it is powerlessness that often creates ineffective, desultory management and petty, dictatorial, rules-minded managerial styles" (1979, p. 65).

Kanter (1979) has identified several indicators of a manager's upward and outward power in an organization. These are shown in Table 5.2. In some respects, these serve as a set of behavioral objectives for our discussion of power and influence.

This line of thought is consistent with the research findings of David McClelland, who has spent many years studying what he considers to be one of the fundamental human needs, the "need for power" (McClelland & Burnham, 2003). According to McClelland, whether leaders maintain their power in the long term or not depends on the motives behind their use of power. Managers who use their power to advance the goals of the organization develop sustainable influence, whereas those who use their power for personal gain tend to succumb to the unwelcome legacy of the power abuser. Recent laboratory research has begun

| Table 5.2 | Indicators of a Manager's Upward and Outward Power |

Powerful managers can:

- Intercede favorably on behalf of someone in trouble.
- Get a desirable placement for a talented subordinate.
- Get approval for expenditures beyond the budget.
- Get items on and off the agenda at policy meetings.
- Get fast access to top decision makers.
- Maintain regular, frequent contact with top decision makers.
- Acquire early information about decisions and policy shifts.

SOURCE: *Reprinted by permission of* Harvard Business Review. *Indicators of a Manager's Upward and Outward Power. From "Power Failures in Management Circuits" by R. Kanter, 57. Copyright © 1979 by the Harvard Business School Publishing Corporation; all rights reserved.*

to paint a fascinating picture of how motives affect people's use of power. Serena Chen and her colleagues have shown that when people who are fundamentally self-interested assume a position of power, they tend to make others do more work. In contrast, people with a strong sense of social responsibility actually take more work upon themselves when they assume a position of power (Chen, Lee-Chai, & Bargh, 2001). These and

other studies suggest that power doesn't so much shape us, as reveal our true motives. Power has the capacity to bring out both the best and the worst in groups and organizations, depending on the motives for its use (Bunderson & Reagans, 2011).

Figure 5.1 depicts the relationship between power and personal effectiveness as we have described it. Both a lack of power and the abuse of power are debilitating and counterproductive. The purpose of this chapter is to help managers "stay on top of the power curve," as represented by the indicators of organizational power reported by Kanter in Table 5.2. This is accomplished with the aid of three interpersonal skills, comprising the three sections of this chapter:

- ❏ Gaining power (overcoming feelings of powerlessness),
- ❏ Converting power into "positive" interpersonal influence, and
- ❏ Acting assertively: neutralizing unwanted, inappropriate attempts to influence you.

We define **power** as the potential to influence the behavior of others. We distinguish power from **authority**, which is the right to influence others, typically associated with a person's position in an organization. As a consequence, this material is equally relevant for those who have been appointed to manage others, and those who aspire to such an appointment. Similarly,

LEARNING

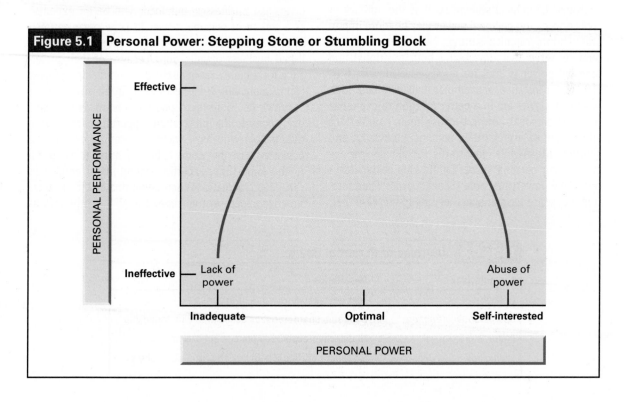

| Figure 5.1 | Personal Power: Stepping Stone or Stumbling Block |

inasmuch as the second and third topics do not accept "Because I am your boss..." as a legitimate form of influence, they are equally relevant for managers and non-managers alike.

Opportunities for Gaining Power

Our discussion to this point should be viewed as an argument that we need not avoid the use of power because of its inherent dangers, but rather that we need to learn how to use it wisely. This is particularly true given the rapid changes taking place in organizations—changes such as telecommuting, which means that leaders must influence people who aren't physically present, and "boundaryless" organizations composed of networks of people who may not have hierarchical relationships with one another. Under these conditions, power is likely to come less from someone's formal position in the organization and more from one's ability to perform. These conditions make the notion of empowerment particularly important for your effectiveness in today's organizations.

Two basic factors determine a person's power in an organization: personal attributes and position characteristics. Naturally, the importance of each factor varies depending on the organizational context. For example, position title is extremely important in a strong hierarchical system, such as the military or civil service, and personal power may be more important in nonhierarchical settings. Nevertheless, experts tend to agree that developing both positional and personal power is vital for managerial success. Burt (1977), for instance, argued that managers with high positional power are in a better position to capitalize on their personal power because their connections allow them to leverage their personal knowledge and abilities. Meanwhile, low-status individuals can increase their personal power by drawing on whatever positional power they hold (Sauer, 2011). Therefore, it makes sense for managers seeking to increase their influence in an organization to increase both sources of power.

SOURCES OF PERSONAL POWER

Four personal characteristics are important sources of power. As Table 5.3 shows, these are *expertise, interpersonal attraction, effort,* and *legitimacy.*

Expertise

It is virtually self-evident that in an era of technological sophistication, expertise is an important source of power. In an e-commerce business environment, in which the most highly sought-after skills are more likely possessed by teenagers who have never had a real job than by their parents, who have been working for decades, and in which the median age of millionaires will soon be closer to 30 than to 60, it is hard to dispute that expertise is the ascending "coin of the realm" in business. Increasingly, what you know is more important than who you know in getting a job, and what you can do technically is the key to what you can become organizationally. **Expertise**, or work-related knowledge, is the great organizational equalizer because it can come from formal education, self-directed learning, or on-the-job experience.

Because most management positions are not in small "dot.com" companies but are in larger, more diversified businesses, our focus will be on expertise as a source of personal power in large organizational settings. Expertise is especially important in established business organizations because of their preference for a highly rationalized decision-making process (Bunderson, 2003; Pfeffer, 1977). In an environment in which decisions are supposed to be made by objectively considering information supporting each alternative, people who have knowledge can quickly accrue power because they come to be seen as reliable experts. At the same time, expertise among junior employees can be problematic. When subordinates clearly have superior expertise, their bosses might become jealous

Table 5.3	Sources of Personal Power
Characteristic	**Description**
Expertise	Task-relevant knowledge or experience
Interpersonal attraction	Desirable characteristics associated with friendship
Effort	Higher-than-expected commitment of time
Legitimacy	Behavior consistent with key organizational values

or feel threatened. The skillful subordinate, therefore, makes knowledge available in a manner that does not threaten the boss's credibility and right to make the final decision.

Expertise is an important way for someone with low positional power to gain influence. People with less formal status in the organization may not be very visible compared to top managers; their jobs are often routine; and their tasks, by themselves, are generally not linked to the most central objectives and concerns of the firm. However, staff members can compensate for weak positional power by developing expertise in a particular aspect of organizational life. This might involve a new accounting system, tax loopholes, safety and pollution regulations, or recent legal precedents in acquisitions, for example.

There is, however, a catch-22 associated with expert power. Becoming an expert on a subject typically requires considerable time and effort, and in organizations using rapidly changing technologies, individuals must continually upgrade their expertise to avoid the "sell-by date" of their knowledge (Grove, 1983). Given the investment required to stay up to date in a particular area of specialization, it is easy to become typecast as a specialist. In fact, becoming an expert can cause you to become "cognitively entrenched," meaning that you become less flexible in problem-solving and generating new ideas (Dane, 2010). If you are interested in moving into a general management position, this can be a hindrance. Given the dynamic environment facing today's organizations, overspecialization may be a recipe for obsolescence. Aspiring young managers must be careful not to limit advancement opportunities by focusing their attention on very narrow aspects of a business's activities. This may be tempting for individuals who are overly anxious to establish a power base. There are always small niches in an organization to which power-hungry novices can quickly lay claim. Only when they have fallen into the specialist trap do they recognize the value of building a broad base of knowledge about a wide variety of organizational activities to enhance their long-term attractiveness for promotion.

Attraction

We will consider three ways in which interpersonal **attraction** is a source of personal power: charisma, agreeable behavior, and physical characteristics.

First, charismatic leadership has been the subject of extensive scholarly study (Yukl, 2002). The Greek origins of the word *charisma* mean favor or grace from God. The idea that charismatic leaders are favored by God stems from the observation that some people have an uncommon ability to engender devotion and enthusiasm—a seemingly mystical quality that cannot be acquired in a skill development workshop. This quality is reflected in comments such as the following: "When she makes a presentation in a management meeting, her presence is so powerful any message sounds good"; "His magnetic personality enables him to attract the most qualified and dedicated people to his department—everyone wants to work for him." These anecdotal comments are consistent with research showing that a leader's charisma is associated with higher positivity among followers (Erez, et al., 2008).

How do we explain which qualities make someone charismatic? Research on this topic (Conger & Kanungo, 1998) has found that leaders are more likely to be considered charismatic if they (1) express a vision that is inspiring; (2) incur personal sacrifice and even risk their personal well-being in pursuing their vision; (3) recommend the use of unconventional, nontraditional approaches to achieving shared goals; (4) have a seemingly uncanny feel for what is possible, including an acute sense of timing; and (5) demonstrate sensitivity to members' needs and concerns. It has also been shown that people tend to attribute charisma to leaders of high-performing organizations (Agle, et al., 2006) and to people who are central in their organization's communication network (Balkundi, et al., 2011). This research implies that it is a mistake to treat charisma as an inborn, inimitable trait. The behaviors and characteristics associated with charismatic leadership are far from mystical.

A related source of interpersonal attraction is much more mundane, but equally powerful. Social psychologists who have done research on interpersonal attraction have isolated several critical behaviors that determine what they call *agreeable behavior.* These behaviors are the kinds one would normally associate with friendship. Studies of this type have identified several major factors that foster interpersonal attraction. Some of these are shown in Table 5.4 (Anderson, et al., 2001; Canfield & LaGaipa, 1970; Furman, 2001).

How can we relate this information on friendship to the supposedly hard-nosed world of management? Must you become good friends with your coworkers, subordinates, or boss? Not necessarily. It is often inappropriate to establish a close friendship with someone in your office. But people who display agreeable behaviors to their coworkers will likely help others feel empowered (Hogg, 2001; Mechanic, 1962).

Table 5.4	Characteristics of Likable People

We like people when we have reason to believe they will:

- Support an open, honest, and loyal relationship.
- Foster intimacy by being emotionally accessible.
- Provide unconditional, positive regard and acceptance.
- Endure some sacrifices if the relationship should demand them.
- Provide social reinforcement in the form of sympathy or empathy.
- Engage in the social exchanges necessary to sustain a relationship.

Source: *Adapted from Canfield and LaGaipa, 1970.*

An impressive amount of evidence supports this idea. For example, research shows that people are more effective persuaders if their audience finds them likable. Likable individuals are viewed as more trustworthy and impartial than disliked individuals. Subordinates who are liked by their supervisor also tend to be given the benefit of the doubt in performance appraisals. Research also shows that bosses use rewards rather than coercion to influence subordinates they like (Allinson, Armstrong, & Hayes, 2001; Tedeschi, 1974). In fact, one study showed that likability completely overwhelms competence when people choose work partners; we would generally rather work with an agreeable person than someone who is good at what they do (Casciaro & Lobo, 2008).

We don't want to overemphasize this point, nor do we mean to suggest "good guys" always win, but there is an impressive amount of evidence that individuals with agreeable personalities become more influential than those with disagreeable personalities. Their arguments are given more credence, their influence attempts are less likely to evoke resistance, and coworkers seem less threatened if these individuals are promoted.

The third basis for interpersonal attraction, *physical appearance,* operates independently of personality or even behavior (Hosoda, Stone-Romero, & Coats, 2003; Langlois, et al., 2000). Studies have shown that we tend to associate socially desirable personality traits with people we judge to have attractive appearances. We tend to assume they lead highly successful lives, hold prestigious jobs, and are successful marriage partners and parents. In addition, attractive individuals are judged to be masters of their own fate—pursuing their own goals, imbued with a sense of mission—rather than being buffeted by environmental forces. In general, people tend to assume that attractive individuals are also virtuous and efficacious.

There is considerable evidence that these are not merely fanciful attributions. In some respects, attractive people *are* more successful. Research has found that, on average, physically attractive people are paid more than their counterparts in organizations (Judge, Hurst, & Simon, 2009). Reflective of a societal double standard, women who make the highest salaries have a below-average body weight, whereas men are paid the most when their body weight is greater than average (Judge & Cable, 2011). In a work setting, the written work of attractive people is more likely to be judged of high quality, and attractive people are more likely to receive high performance appraisals from their supervisors than are other people (Hosoda, et al., 2003; Langlois, et al., 2000).

Findings on personal attraction are somewhat difficult to transform into concrete suggestions for personal development. There is not much one can do as an adult to radically transform one's basic appearance. However, this information is still highly relevant for managers for two reasons. First, in many experimental studies, scholars simply used dress and grooming to distinguish "attractive" research confederates from "unattractive" ones (Thompson, 2001, p. 141). Hence, it appears unnecessary for most people to resort to plastic surgery and other artificial forms of physical enhancement to boost their self-confidence. Personal grooming matters a great deal. Second, people can usually improve the impressions they make on others regardless of their physical features. Conveying a confident, friendly air increases your perceived attractiveness.

Effort

A high level of personal **effort** is one of the most highly prized characteristics of employees because it means they are a dependable, reliable human resource. If individuals can be counted on to stay late to get out a delivery following a technological breakdown, to catch an early-morning flight to visit a promising new customer, or to take a night class to learn a new software program, they earn the trust of their coworkers and their supervisors. Being known as a person who will do "whatever it takes" to get the job done is a valuable personal asset, especially in today's highly uncertain and rapidly changing business climate. As one classic article argues, employees who expend effort at work tend to make their overburdened supervisors look good, thus creating a sense of indebtedness from those higher in the hierarchy (Mechanic, 1962).

In addition to creating indebtedness, high levels of effort enhance other personal characteristics. For example, individuals who work hard at a task tend to increase their knowledge of the subject, and thus their expertise. Therefore, they are more likely to be sought out for advice and to gather information that is relevant to other members of the organization.

The efficacy of personal effort is borne out in the career of George Bodenheimer, the longest-tenured president in the 40-year history of ESPN. Unlike most network executives, who are hired away from other networks, Bodenheimer is a homegrown product of ESPN. As a young man, he was fascinated by the cable television industry and decided he wanted to work for the fledgling sports network. However, the only position he could land was mailroom clerk. Still, he applied himself with great gusto and quickly gained the attention of others in the organization. Over the years, Bodenheimer held 15 different positions, including in marketing, accounts, and sales. His stellar work ethic ultimately led him to executive functions. Under his lead, ESPN expanded to many new creative outlets, and Bodenheimer became known as a pioneer in the cable and media industries.

Before leaving this topic, we want to make a distinction between extraordinary effort and extraordinary image. Some people put forth a lot of effort simply to make a show and impress others. Just putting in face time or drawing inordinate attention to your own effort can backfire, especially if you aren't producing real value for your organization. Based on their intensive examination of effective boss–subordinate relationships in major corporations, Jack Gabarro and John Kotter (2007) suggest several highly relevant guidelines for directing your efforts to the benefit of your boss. As shown in Table 5.5, these include understanding your boss's pressures and priorities as well as assessing your own needs and strengths. This knowledge helps you improve your performance by targeting your efforts to maximize their impact.

Legitimacy

Another important source of personal power is **legitimacy**, which you achieve when your actions are congruent with the prevailing value system of the organization. Legitimacy increases one's acceptance in the organization, and acceptance is a key to personal influence. For instance, employees who contribute to their organization's ideological goals become more influential than employees who simply focus on getting ahead socially (Bingham, et al., 2014).

Organizational leaders tend to be vigilant in defending core organizational values, and they work hard

Table 5.5	Managing the Relationship with Your Boss

Make sure you understand your boss, including:

- Your boss's goals and objectives
- The pressures on him or her
- Your boss's strengths, weaknesses, blind spots
- His or her preferred work style

Assess yourself, including:

- Your own strengths and weaknesses
- Your personal style
- Your predisposition toward dependence on authority figures

Develop and maintain a relationship that:

- Fits the needs and styles of you both
- Is characterized by mutual expectations
- Keeps your boss informed
- Is based on dependability and honesty
- Selectively uses your boss's time and resources

SOURCE: *Adapted and reprinted by permission of* Harvard Business Review. *From J. J. Gabarro & J. P. Kotter, "Managing the Relationship with Your Boss," May–June 1993. Copyright © 1993 by the Harvard Business School Publishing Corporation; all rights reserved.*

to socialize newcomers to the "proper" modes of thinking and acting. Often, new members or outsiders fail to understand the importance of an organization's unique culture. They might find the organization's way of doing things peculiar or overly conventional. But it is vital for new employees to appreciate how important the organization's values and culture are to their own success.

Organizational values are important both historically and strategically. Here's why: Good leaders understand that a precondition for their organization becoming a market leader is to be perceived as a unique player in the market (e.g., not just another computer company). They strive to create distinctiveness that merits attention from the financial community, potential employees, and customers. This may involve placing a premium on quality, economy, value, service, loyalty to employees, civic involvement, or some other core value. This uniqueness is the basis for internal organizational pride and external projections of excellence.

The leader (often the founder) articulates this vision and institutionalizes it as part of the organization's culture (Deal & Kennedy, 1982; Peters, 1978; Schein, 1999). Leaders use culture to expresses the "hows" and "whys" of doing business the "right" way. For example, Harold Geneen at ITT consistently stressed, "Search for the unshakable facts"; Tom Jones at Northrop emphasized, "Everybody at Northrop is in marketing"; John DeButts at AT&T drummed into employees, "The system is the solution"; and Ed Rust at State Farm frequently asked colleagues, "How would a good neighbor handle this?"

New members of an organization are taught what is acceptable behavior through stories (for example, the engineer who worked for 72 hours straight to save a project), rites (graduation or promotion ceremonies), and symbols (uniforms, or no private offices for managers). The savvy newcomer looks beyond formal position statements, probing for answers to questions such as: "What are the organization's 'sacred cows'?" "What is the source of organizational pride?" "Who are the corporate heroes?" "What are the revered traditions?"

Many organizational practices make sense only when viewed as symbolic support for fundamental values. For example, a large insurance firm stipulates that no one can be promoted above a certain level in any department unless he or she has completed the requirements for insurance industry professional certification. Young employees in data processing, accounting, or personnel might chafe under the edict to take classes on the details of the insurance business, but they miss the symbolic meaning of this requirement. The founders of the firm felt that the organization's key to success was a workforce deeply committed to the overarching goal of providing excellent services and products in the insurance business at large, rather than becoming too entrenched in their department's interests. In this organization, taking insurance courses has become synonymous with commitment to the organization's mission, and organizational commitment is a litmus test for organizational advancement.

This does not mean a nonconformist can't get ahead in the corporate world. It simply suggests he or she will be held to a higher standard in terms of other sources of personal power, such as expertise and effort. A conversation during a promotion review meeting in a major corporation reflects this attitude: "Sometimes I don't know where he's coming from, but he is so blasted smart and he works so darn hard, we have no choice but to promote him."

Before leaving the subject of organizational culture and personal legitimacy, it is important to raise an ethical question. We have described how conforming to the organization's culture helps you accrue power, but that doesn't mean strict conformity is morally right or that it is necessarily in the best long-term interests of the firm. In fact, evidence suggests that successful organizations have members who are capable of both gaining power by fitting in and using that power to challenge the prevailing belief where necessary (Pascale, 1985). Unchallenged organizational beliefs often interfere with a company's necessary adaptation to changing competitive and regulatory conditions. However, challenges are most successful when mounted by members whose commitment to the organization has been the most loyal. "Paying your dues" creates legitimacy, and legitimacy is a prerequisite for effective criticism.

In summary, we have highlighted four sources of personal power, all of which are rooted in the individual's characteristics rather than in the positions or titles they hold. These personal characteristics have one thing in common—they are the ingredients of trust (Dirks & Ferrin, 2001; Hosmer, 1995). One meaning of the term *trustworthy* is "being above suspicion." Hence, individuals who are deemed trustworthy by their peers are likely candidates for positions of power and influence in organizations because organizational authority in their hands is less threatening. As shown in Table 5.6, a direct relationship exists between the four bases of personal power we have discussed and the requirements for personal trust.

Table 5.6	The Relationship Between the Sources of Personal Power and Personal Trustworthiness	
Sources of Personal Power	**Related Personal Characteristic**	**Requirements for Personal Trustworthiness**
Expertise	Reliability	Ability: *Can* they make good on their commitments?
Effort	Dependability	
Attraction	Likability	Motivation: *Will* they make good on their commitments?
Legitimacy	Acceptability	

Basically, the trustworthiness of an individual's claims, promises, or commitments is a function of two factors: (1) How likely is it that the person *can* do what he or she says? and (2) How likely is it the person *will* do what he or she says? In other words, questions of trust involve assessment of probable performance informed by judgments about the individual's ability and motivation. This is why organizations place a great deal of emphasis on only putting proven performers in positions of high trust (or, in other words, positions of power).

SOURCES OF POSITIONAL POWER

Not all power stems from personal characteristics. The nature of one's position and task assignments also play an important role. Four important characteristics of a position account for its power potential in an organization: *centrality and brokerage, flexibility, visibility,* and *relevance* (Fiol, O'Connor, & Aguinis, 2001; Kanter, 1979; Pfeffer, 1994). These are shown in Table 5.7.

Social Capital

For our purposes, **social capital** is conceptualized as resources embedded in social networks accessed through network connections, which can be mobilized for productive purposes (Adler & Kwon, 2002; Coleman, 1988). The importance of social ties in organizational settings is highlighted in data collected over more than a dozen years by a consulting firm. They report, "Failure to build strong relationships and teamwork with peers and subordinates is the chief culprit in 61% of new hires and promotions that don't work out" (Fisher, 2005).

Social capital research uses the locations of individuals in social networks as indicators of their social capital. Various terms have been used to describe advantageous network locations. We will explore two: *network centrality* and *bridging structural holes (brokerage).*

Imagine three different network configurations involving seven people: They can be connected as a Circle, a Line, and a Star. Clearly the person serving as the hub of a star with six branches is in the most favorable structural position for garnering social capital. As this imaginary illustration demonstrates, one of the most important ways of gaining power in an organization is by occupying a position of **centrality** in a broad network of relationships. Networks are critical to effective performance for one compelling reason: No one has all the necessary information and resources to accomplish what's expected of him or her. Indeed, one study of effective management concluded that a key factor in distinguishing high and low performers was their ability to establish informal relationships via networks. "Lone wolves" in informal networks were unable to gather the information, resource commitments, and personal support necessary to accomplish unusual, important tasks (Kaplan & Mazique, 1983; Sparrowe, Liden, & Kraimer, 2001). On the other hand, those who have extensive and diverse social networks earn higher salaries and are more successful than those with a narrower set of contacts (Pfeffer & Konrad, 1991; Sparrowe, et al., 2001).

Increasing one's power by becoming more central in a communication or work-flow network represents a very different approach from conventional strategies of power building. Typically, young upward-focused employees think only in terms of increasing their power by moving up the organizational career ladder. They mistakenly assume that power is the exclusive right of hierarchical position. If they are not promoted as quickly as they would like, they assume they have limited power to make change or accomplish extraordinary things. Inexperienced, ineffective organizational members grumble about not having enough formal power to get work done, and they covet the influence wielded on higher levels.

In contrast, savvy organizational members realize that informal network power is available to individuals

Table 5.7	Sources of Position-Power
Social Capital	**Description**
Centrality and Brokerage	Access to resources in a social network
Flexibility	Amount of discretion vested in a position
Visibility	Degree to which task performance is seen by influential people in the organization
Relevance	Alignment of assigned tasks and organizational priorities

at all levels. In fact, simply being able to "read" the social network is associated with power. In a classic study, Krackhardt (1990) found that people who could more accurately describe the advice network in their organization (i.e., they knew who sought advice from whom) were rated by others as more powerful. Numerous studies show that being central in one's organizational network increases not only perceived status, but also salary and long-term career success. It is critical, then, for new organization members to understand that informal personal power generally precedes, rather than follows from, formal organizational power. A promotion is simply a formal recognition by senior management that an individual has demonstrated the ability to get work done using informal networks.

One of the more interesting research findings about network centrality is that the *type* of network one builds matters a lot. Most people develop networks with people who have similar backgrounds and experience as themselves. Their social contacts tend to know their other social contacts, so the network becomes dense and interconnected. As a consequence, one's position in this type of social network provides little advantage, because every person has equal access to other network members.

Ron Burt (1992) and others have argued that the most effective networks, in contrast, are networks that have many *structural holes*. A structural hole exists when two people in your network are not connected to each other. For example, structural holes exist in a social network if it consists of multiple densely connected groups that are not connected with each other. (Think of three departments in an organization that don't interact with each other.) Alternatively, if a person serves as a unique connecting link (bridge) for two or more otherwise isolated groups, this is referred to as *brokerage*. In this position, your value to others increases because you can monitor the flow of information between parties and provide unique value to each of the two people to whom you are connected. It is thus not surprising that research shows that brokerage increases job performance, possibility of promotion, and innovation (Burt, 1992).

Playing this brokerage role does not come naturally for most people. It means branching out to interact with people who may come from a very different background than oneself. In fact, one study showed that being an "organizational misfit" with an atypical career path can actually *strengthen* your influence; an unusual background affords one opportunities to bring unique information to the organization and to broker relationships across structural holes, thus giving more opportunities for influence (Kleinbaum, 2012).

A striking example of the merits of building a diverse network is Adam Rifkin. In the early 1990s, Rifkin was a doctoral student in computer engineering and a fan of the band Green Day. He created a fan website for the band, one of the first of its kind. In 1994, he received a complaint email about his site from someone who disagreed with his labeling Green Day a "punk band." Rifkin decided to take the feedback to heart. He reached out to the complainer and ultimately decided to change his description of the band. Based on the experience, he created a separate website to direct his followers to other punk bands. The author of the email was impressed with Rifkin's response. Five years later, Rifkin was working on some social media start-up ideas. Struggling for direction and resources, he started looking through his old emails to see who might be able to help him. He came across the old email complaining about the Green Day site and decided to reach out to its author, Graham Spencer. Spencer had since founded Excite, a pioneering search engine. He had sold it the year before for $6.7 billion. Spencer remembered Rifkin and offered help. With Spencer's assistance, Rifkin created some of the earliest successful social media ventures. He was the founder of Renkoo, which developed Facebook and MySpace applications used by 36 million people. Rifkin is now the CEO of PandaWhale, a successful social networking website (Grant, 2013).

This example illustrates the merits of having a broad network of contacts. One of the biggest mistakes individuals make at the outset of their management careers is to become isolated. Some people assume that getting ahead in their department is sufficient for getting ahead in the organization. As a result, they concentrate all their attention on accomplishing their narrow work responsibilities or on building strong relations only with their immediate coworkers. If you look at organizations only in terms of vertical structures, you will see how isolated a communication network in a single department can become. In contrast, it is important to become a central actor in the organization's broad communication network, not just the department's. This can be done by going to lunch with people in other departments, reading the annual reports of all the divisions, volunteering for interdepartmental task forces, and seeking out boundary-spanning positions that require you to work with other departments.

It is important that managers seeking to form wide-reaching social networks understand that social relations look very different in different cultural settings. Specifically, research has shown that members of different cultures differ in terms of how many and what types of friendships they are likely to form at work, the extent to which they mix socioemotional and instrumental social ties, and the strength and longevity of their social relations (Morris, Podolny, & Ariel, 2000). For example, American business relationships are characterized by the norms of the marketplace (they must be profitable). In contrast, Chinese business relationships are characterized by a familial orientation (doing whatever is good for the organization), German relationships are characterized by a legal-bureaucratic orientation (play by the rules), and Spanish relationships are characterized by an affiliative orientation (sociability and friendship) (Morris, et al., 2000).

Flexibility

A critical requirement for building a power base is **flexibility**, or discretion—that is, freedom to exercise one's judgment. A person who has little latitude to improvise, innovate, or demonstrate initiative will find it extremely difficult to become powerful. A flexible position has few rules or established routines governing how work should be done. In addition, flexibility means that a manager need not seek a supervisor's approval to make nonroutine decisions. People in flexible positions perform tasks that allow considerable judgment.

Flexibility is correlated with the life cycle of a position. New tasks are less likely to be routinized than old ones. Similarly, the number of rules governing a position tends to be positively related to the number of individuals who have previously occupied it. The same logic applies to the life cycle of a decision-making process. The longer a group has been meeting to discuss an issue, the more difficult it is to have any significant amount of influence over its deliberations. The critical decisions about how discussions will be conducted, what evidence should be examined, and which alternatives are germane are all made early in a group's history. To make a difference, therefore, it is preferable to be a participant from the beginning, or to take on new roles or new tasks.

One indication of the amount of flexibility inherent in a position is the reward system governing it. If an organization rewards people for being reliable and predictable, that suggests the organization will penalize people who use discretion. On the other hand, if organizations reward people for unusual performance and innovation, discretion is encouraged. For example, a company may teach salespeople how to close a deal but at the same time encourage them to figure out better ways to do the task. Individuals with a high need for power should avoid a job that is governed by the reliable performance criterion—no matter how attractive it might appear in other aspects—because it will strip them of a necessary prerequisite of power.

Some managers in low-discretion positions might feel like they are completely stymied in using flexibility as a power source. However, recent research suggests that people with a **proactive personality** can often create their own sense of flexibility. Proactive personality has been defined as a tendency to effect change in one's environment (Bateman & Crant, 1993). Proactive people focus on finding new opportunities, taking initiative, and persisting in the process of making positive changes happen. Scholars have provided strong evidence that proactive people are promoted more quickly and earn higher salaries (Seibert, et al., 1999). They also tend to receive higher performance evaluations from supervisors, but only if they are adept at building their network so that their initiatives have support from others (Thompson, 2005). Achieving flexibility at work may have as much to do with the employee's own behavior as it does with the characteristics of the role. Striving for flexibility by taking personal initiative to add value and solve problems is one technique for increasing one's power in roles that don't naturally afford a lot of discretion.

Visibility

A sage corporate executive once counseled a young, aspiring MBA, "The key formula for promotion is excellent performance multiplied by visibility." Obviously, highly visible but poor performance will not lead to promotion, but the real message of this advice is that an excellent but obscure performance won't either. Of course, no one likes the person who is always showing off and demanding the spotlight. But developing power does require you to achieve **visibility** in your organization, so that people recognize you and see you making contributions.

One way to increase your visibility is to foster frequent contact with senior officials, decision makers, and informal leaders. If your normal work activities don't bring you into contact with important people, you may be able to heighten your visibility through participation in company or outside programs, meetings, and conferences. Many a young career has been advanced by a strong presentation at a trade association convention or board meeting. Volunteering to make presentations, and thus to act as the "face" of your department, is an excellent route to increasing visibility.

Recognizing this point, an enterprising junior executive in a large Chicago conglomerate seized on a chance occurrence to impress the chairman of the board. By a strange set of circumstances, the young executive was asked to fill in for the secretary of the board of directors and take notes at a stockholders' meeting. Making sure he arrived early, he greeted every person who entered the boardroom and then introduced that person to every other member in the room. The fact that this young man was able to put everyone at ease (not to mention remember the names of a large number of strangers) so impressed the chairman, he subsequently provided several opportunities for him to advance rapidly in the organization.

The importance of face-to-face contact in establishing visibility cannot be overemphasized. Inexperienced managers, for instance, often assume they will get credit for writing an excellent report. Unfortunately, this is not always the case. If another member of the team gives a very good presentation of the report to an executive committee, the presenter will likely receive a disproportionately large share of the credit for the work. Busy executives tend to be more impressed by what they see in a meeting than by what they read in their offices, particularly if they observe their fellow executives giving approving nods and smiles during the presentation. The benefits of the positive reaction tend to go to the person who is in front of them at the time.

Another important opportunity for gaining visibility is participation in problem-solving task forces. Being asked to serve in this capacity conveys to others that you have valuable expertise. More importantly, if the task force's report is received well by senior officials, your name will be associated with the group responsible for the "breakthrough," particularly if it comes during a time of uncertainty or change. For example, heads of government whose accomplishments stand out dramatically in a historical perspective are those who proposed remedies during major crises. Consider that Winston Churchill is credited with helping Britain survive World War II. On the smaller scale of a business firm, this is equally true. The power a person gains is directly proportional to his or her visibility in successfully handling change or crisis.

An additional source of visibility is name recognition. Elected officials recognize the value of keeping their names before the electorate, so they place signs at state and city boundaries and entrances to public transportation terminals welcoming travelers. In organizations, there are analogous opportunities for enhancing your visibility. For example, if your office regularly sends information to the public or to other departments, try enclosing a signed cover note. If you are new to an organization, introduce yourself to other members. If you have a good idea, formally communicate it to the appropriate parties in person as well as in a follow-up memo. If someone has recently accomplished something significant, send a note expressing congratulations and appreciation.

Relevance

This leads us to the fourth critical characteristic of powerful positions, **relevance**, which means being associated with activities directly related to central objectives and issues in an organization. As one manager put it, "My peers are responsive to me because the functions that I manage are the lifeblood of the organization...my presence in their office implies that there's a vital concern of one sort or another that needs to be dealt with" (Kaplan & Mazique, 1983, p. 10).

Paul Lawrence and Jay Lorsch (1986) argued for the importance of identifying a company's "dominant competitive issue," which is the organizational activity that most accounts for the firm's competitiveness in its industry. An organization's dominant competitive issue depends on the industry in which it operates. For instance, companies that use a flow-process form of technology, such as oil refineries and chemical plants, are most dependent on effective marketing because of their sizable capital investment and small range of product alternatives. In contrast, companies using a standard mass-production (assembly line) form of technology, with a stable line of products and established customers, are most dependent on the efficiency of their production processes. Finally, high-tech firms, or companies producing custom-designed products, are most successful when they have strong research and development departments. Employees who attach themselves to their particular organization's dominant competitive issue are more likely to develop power based on relevance.

Thinking about relevance may be particularly important for employees who work in departments that aren't directly connected to the organization's dominant competitive issue. For instance, Tony Rucci, former chief administrative officer at Cardinal Health, argues that in today's lean corporate environment, human resource departments have to demonstrate to management how they contribute to the bottom line. As the *Wall Street Journal* argued, "Strong HR departments are now focusing on boosting productivity by helping employees better understand what's expected of them and by showing managers how to be more effective" (Rendon, 2010).

These trends have significant implications for relevance. An individual who seeks influential positions must be sensitive to the relevance of his or her department's activities for the company. For example, a design engineer who works for an oil company is less likely to become influential than one who works for an electronics firm, and operations researchers will have more influence in companies with established product lines and an assembly-line production process. Computer scientists are more likely to feel empowered in a software development firm than if they are working for an insurance company or a public utility. In the latter organization, computer programming is viewed as a support function, with only an indirect effect on profitability.

Of course, it usually isn't easy to change functions just to increase one's relevance. But there are often other ways to increase relevance in one's current position; for instance, assuming an outreach role can connect one to relevant functions or projects. Employees can act as a representative to, or an advocate for, projects and causes that are important to the organization. Another key role is that of evaluator. Positions that serve as checkpoints become powerful by virtue of the fact that they create dependence. The role of trainer or mentor to new members of a work unit is another powerful position. It places you in a critical position to reduce uncertainty for newcomers and substantially enhance their performance. Newcomers are generally apprehensive, and they will appreciate your showing them the ropes. Also, successful performance in this developmental role earns you the respect and admiration of those colleagues who stand to benefit from your effective training.

To summarize, we have discussed four aspects of organizational positions that are critical to the achievement of power. As Table 5.7 shows, centrality and relevance encourage the gaining of power through horizontal relationships. In other words, power stemming from centrality and relevance is based on relationships to other lateral positions and activities in the organization. However, visibility and flexibility are linked to hierarchical power. Flexibility reflects the amount of discretion vested in a position by superiors. A highly visible position has close ties with higher levels of authority, so a noteworthy performance in a visible position receives more recognition, which is an important prerequisite for an individual's upward mobility in an organization.

Transforming Power into Influence

Having discussed the skill of gaining power, we now turn our attention to converting power into influence. This concept requires an understanding of the difference between power and influence. As we stated at the beginning of this chapter, many popular books on this subject suggest power is an end in itself. Our goal here is not to help people gain power for its own sake. When the weak seek power simply because they are tired of being pushed around, tyranny generally follows their ascension. Our interest, instead, is in helping people accomplish the exceptional in organizations, recognizing that this generally requires political clout. The well-meaning but politically naive seldom make major contributions to organizations. Consequently, our focus is on how you can become influential as well as powerful.

Influential people have power, but not all powerful people have influence. Influence entails actually securing the consent of others to work with you in accomplishing an objective. Many powerful people cannot do that, as evidenced by the chronic inability of American presidents to convince Congress to pass what the president considers to be essential legislation. The skill of transforming power into influence hinges on engendering support and commitment from others, rather than resistance and resentment.

INFLUENCE STRATEGIES: THE THREE RS

Power becomes influence when others willingly consent to behave according to the desires of the power holder. The strategies used by managers to influence others fall into three broad categories: *retribution, reciprocity,* and *reason* (Allen, et al., 1979; Kipnis, 1987; Kipnis, Schmidt, & Wilkinson, 1980). Table 5.8 lists these strategies and the corresponding direct and indirect approaches. Specific examples of these strategies are shown in Table 5.9 (Cialdini, 2001; Marwell & Schmitt, 1967).

You may have mixed reactions to these lists. Some strategies will probably strike you as particularly effective; others may seem inappropriate or even manipulative or dishonest. Our purpose in listing these is not to imply that all of these strategies ought to be used. Rather, we present the full arsenal of influence strategies so that you can informatively choose those with which you feel most comfortable and so that you can be aware when others are attempting to influence you.

These three influence strategies rely on different mechanisms for obtaining compliance. **Retribution** is based on personal threat, which typically stems from formal authority. The direct form of this approach, *coercion*, involves an explicit threat to impose sanctions if the manager's will is not obeyed. Recognizing their vulnerability to the boss's sanctions, subordinates generally comply, reluctantly.

Intimidation is an indirect form of retribution because the threat is only implied. The manager's intimidating interpersonal style suggests the possibility of organizationally based sanctions for noncompliance, even if he or she does not make an overt threat.

LEARNING

Table 5.8   Influence Strategies

Strategies	Direct Approach	Indirect Approach
Retribution: Force others to do what you say	1. Coercion (threaten)	2. Intimidation (pressure)
Reciprocity: Help others want to do what you say	3. Bargaining (exchange)	4. Ingratiation (obligate)
Reason: Show others that it makes sense to do what you say	5. Present facts (or needs)	6. Appeal to personal values (or goals)

Table 5.9   Examples of Influence Strategies

Retribution (Coercion and Intimidation)

General form:	"If you don't do X, you will regret it."
Threat:	"If you do not comply, I will punish you."
Social pressure:	"Others in your group have agreed; what's your decision?"
Had enough?:	"I will stop nagging you if you comply."
Perceived scarcity and time pressure:	"If you don't act now, you'll lose this opportunity/cause problems for others."
Avoid causing pain to others:	"If you don't agree, others will be hurt/disadvantaged."

Reciprocity (Exchange and Ingratiation)

General form:	"If you do X, you'll receive Y."
Promise:	"If you comply, I will reward you."
Esteem:	"People you value will think better of you if you comply/worse of you if you do not comply."
Pregiving:	"I will do something you like for you; then will you do this for me?"
Obligation:	"You owe me compliance because of past favors." (Even though I implied, there would be no future obligation.)
Reciprocal compromise:	"I have lowered my initial offer/price, and now I expect you to reciprocate." (No matter how unreasonable my initial position was.)
Escalation of commitment:	"I'm only interested in a small commitment." (But I'll be back later for more.)

Reason (Persuasion Based on Facts, Needs, or Personal Values)

General form:	"I want you to do X, because it's consistent with/good for/necessary to…"
Evidence:	"These facts/experts' opinions demonstrate the merits of my position/request."
Need:	"This is what I need; will you help me out?"
Goal attainment:	"Compliance will enable you to reach a personally important objective."
Value congruence:	"This action is consistent with your commitment to X."
Ability:	"This endeavor would be enhanced if we could count on your ability/experience."
Loyalty:	"Because we are friends/minorities, will you do this?"
Altruism:	"The group needs your support, so do it for the good of us all."

Intimidation can take many forms; for instance, a manager publicly criticizing a subordinate's report, systematically ignoring a subordinate during meetings, or handing out impossible tasks to junior executives.

Acts of intimidation are generally accompanied by emphasis on the power holder's authority. Intimidators tend to give assignments in their own office, in a highly formal manner, and while highlighting the vulnerability of the target (e.g., mentioning his junior grade or short tenure with the organization). This sets the stage for an implicit threat (e.g., "If people aren't willing to work overtime on this project, corporate headquarters is going to pull the plug on our budget and a number of younger employees will get hurt").

Intimidation can also occur through peer pressure. Managers who know that a majority of their subordinates support a controversial action can use group dynamics to secure the compliance of the minority. This is done by telling the majority that a decision must be unanimous and it's their responsibility to demonstrate leadership by securing the commitment of all members. Or, the manager can apply pressure directly to the holdout members of the group by stressing the need for harmony, mutual support, and working for the common good.

The second strategy extracts compliance from others by invoking the norm of **reciprocity**. Reciprocity operates on the principle of satisfying the self-interest of both parties. Reciprocity commonly involves straightforward *bargaining* in which each party gains something from the exchange. In bargaining, both parties are aware of the costs and benefits associated with striking a deal, and their negotiations focus on reaching an agreement that is satisfactory to both. *Ingratiation*, however, is more subtle. It involves using friendliness and favors to compel social obligations. When compliance is required or support is needed, previous benefactors are then reminded of their debts. A recent study shows that ingratiation is most effective when it is subtle rather than overt (Stern & Westphal, 2010). Other research shows that ingratiation has some negative side effects; recipients of ingratiation tend to exhibit overconfidence and an unwillingness to make needed changes (Park, et al., 2011).

Managers use reciprocity in many ways. These include striking deals with influential opinion leaders to support a new program, asking subordinates to work overtime in exchange for an extended weekend, doing small favors for the boss so one can occasionally take longer lunch hours, and formally negotiating with staff members to get them to accept undesirable assignments.

Comparing the strategies of retribution and reciprocity, it should be clear that the former is more ethically suspect than the latter. Retribution strategies ignore the rights of others and the norm of fairness, whereas reciprocity strategies honor both. An emphasis on retribution leads to ignoring the quality of the ongoing relationship between the parties, while reciprocity recognizes the value of strengthening interdependence between people.

The third influence approach is based on the manager's persuasive ability. Instead of seeking compliance by using one's position of authority, this approach appeals to **reason**. The manager uses the inherent merits of the request to convince the influence target to choose compliance themselves. Here, the focus is on helping others to see why your ideas make sense. Direct forms of persuasion rely on articulating compelling *facts or needs* describing why the request is critical for the organization. For example, "If your shift doesn't work overtime tonight, we will lose $5,000 worth of product. Will you pitch in and help us solve this problem?" In the indirect form of reason, the manager appeals to the other person's *personal values or goals*. These might include focusing on the other person's desire to be altruistic, to be a loyal team member, or to be respected as an expert.

Because persuasion is sometimes confused with manipulation, it is important here to distinguish between the two. A persuasive appeal is explicit and direct, while a manipulative act is implicit and deceptive. The persuader respects the autonomy of decision makers and trusts their ability to judge evidence effectively. In contrast, a manipulator has low regard for the abilities of decision makers and doesn't trust them to make good decisions. Manipulators have the same objectives as authoritarian leaders—they simply use more subtle tactics. Manipulative managers, therefore, often appear to the casual observer to be using a democratic leadership style. In fact, they are actually "illusory democrats" because, although their actions may appear democratic, they have no inclination to share power. They use a democratic style only because it makes others less defensive and therefore more vulnerable to their power initiatives (Dyer, 1972).

THE PROS AND CONS OF EACH STRATEGY

As Table 5.10 notes, each approach has advantages and limitations (Cuming, 1984; Mulder, et al., 1986). The retribution strategy produces immediate action and work that conforms to the manager's specifications. But the retribution strategy comes with high costs. Of the three strategies, it is the most likely to engender resistance. Most people do not like to be forced to do something. Effective managers use this approach sparingly, generally reserving it for crises or as a last resort when the other strategies have failed. It is best

LEARNING

Table 5.10	Comparisons Among Influence Strategies			
Influence Strategy	**When to Use it**	**Possible Advantages**	**Possible Disadvantages**	**Possible Complaints**
Retribution	• Unequal power, in influencer's favor • Commitment and quality not important • Tight time constraints • Serious violation • Issue not important to target • If issue is important, retribution not likely • Specific, unambiguous request • Resistance to request is likely	Quick, direct action	• Stifles commitment, creativity • Insecurity of boss • Engenders resentment • Must increase seriousness of threats to maintain pressure	• Violation of rights • Ethical violations
Reciprocity	• Parties mutually dependent • Each party has resources valued by other • Adequate time for negotiating • Established exchange norms exist • Parties viewed as trustworthy • Commitment to broad goals and values not critical • Needs are specific and short-term	• Low incidence of resentment • Justification for request not required	• Engenders instrumental view of work (expectation of specific rewards for specific actions) • Encourages people to feel that the terms of assignments are open for negotiation	• Unfairness, dashed expectations, manipulation
Reason	• Adequate time for extensive discussion • Common goals/values • Parties share mutual respect/credibility • Parties share ongoing relationship	• Need for surveillance reduced	• Considerable time required to build trust (time increases as number of people increases) • Requires common goals and values	• Difference of opinions, conflicting perceptions of priorities

suited to situations in which the goals of the parties are competing or independent. This approach is effective only when the target person perceives that the manager has both the power and the will to follow through on his or her threat. Otherwise, the person being influenced may be tempted to call the manager's bluff. Also, the threatened sanctions must be sufficiently severe that disobedience is unthinkable.

When used repeatedly, the retribution approach produces resentment and alienation, which frequently generates overt or covert opposition. Because these conditions tend to stifle initiative and innovative behavior—even when the individual complies—organizational performance may suffer.

The reciprocity strategy allows the manager to obtain compliance without causing resentment, since both parties benefit from the agreement. It is most appropriate when each party controls some outcomes valued by the other party and there are established rules to govern the transaction, including provisions for adjudication of grievances. Even under these conditions, however, reciprocity requires some degree of trust. If individuals have reneged on past agreements, their credibility as negotiating partners becomes suspect. Reciprocity is also best suited to situations in which the power holder needs the target person to perform specific, unambiguous assignments.

The chief disadvantage of this approach, when used frequently, is that it engenders a highly instrumental view of work. The other person begins to expect that every request is open for negotiation and that every completed assignment will result in a reward of equal value. Consequently, relying solely on reciprocity might undercut employees' commitment levels; they may start to view their work only calculatively and downplay the value of working hard to achieve organizational goals, other than for personal gain.

The assets and liabilities of the third approach—reason—are more complicated. The objective of the rational strategy is a higher form of compliance; that is, internalized commitment. In other words, the goal is for the employee to voluntarily choose to comply. Commitment relies on teaching correct principles and explaining legitimate needs and then trusting the good intent and sound judgment of subordinates to act appropriately. In its ideal form, commitment decreases the need for surveillance and enhances the subordinate's initiative, commitment, and creativity.

The principal disadvantage of the rational, or reason, approach is the amount of time required to build the trust and mutual understanding required to make it operate effectively. The required time increases as the number of involved people expands. Also, because the success of this strategy depends on shared goals and values, persuasion through reason is difficult to implement when the parties have dissimilar backgrounds; subscribe to competing philosophies; or are assigned conflicting responsibilities, such as maintaining quality versus meeting deadlines.

In their classic studies on influence strategies, Schmidt and Kipnis (1987; Kipnis & Schmidt, 1988) provided compelling evidence supporting the superior benefits of the approach based on reason. Individuals who rely primarily on reason and logic to influence others are rated as highly effective by their bosses, and they report low levels of job-related stress and high levels of job satisfaction. In contrast, individuals who persistently use any other approach to get their way tend to receive lower performance ratings and experience higher levels of personal stress and job dissatisfaction.

Overall, it appears that higher-numbered strategies in Table 5.8 are more effective than lower-numbered strategies. This ordering reflects the overall value system portrayed here: Direct is better than indirect; open is better than closed; exchange is better than intimidation; and sincere requests are better than guile.

One justification for this conclusion is that the higher-numbered strategies are more likely to be perceived as fair and just, in part because they usually involve an explanation. Research on organizational change has consistently shown that people are more willing to change when they understand why. For example, in a study of 187 employees in seven business firms that had just been relocated, they rated the process as fair, even though they felt the move was unfavorable, when they understood the reasons behind the action (Daly, 1995).

It is important to point out how cultural preferences need to be factored into your choice of influence strategy. First, your influence strategy needs to be congruent with your personal cultural values. Second, it needs to be congruent with the cultural values of the influence "target." Third, it needs to be congruent with the general context in which your relationship is embedded. As an extreme case of these three situational factors, one might imagine a Japanese manager trying to influence an African employee in an auto plant in Germany. The claims we've made in this chapter about the merits and liabilities of these various influence attempts are clearly rooted in traditional American cultural norms (which include egalitarian relations, direct communication, and individualism). In contrast, members of cultures that place a high value on social obligation may prefer reciprocity influence strategies. In addition, cultures that emphasize indirect communication methods, such as storytelling and inference making, would likely prefer the indirect over the direct strategies. Similarly, individuals who place particular importance on hierarchical relationships may feel more comfortable with the forcing strategies (Thompson, 2001).

EXERCISING UPWARD INFLUENCE UTILIZING THE REASON STRATEGY

One particular form of influence warrants special attention. Our discussion of the "Three Rs" has largely focused on influencing others either "downward" (e.g., subordinates) or laterally (e.g., peers). The role that is obviously missing from this set of influence targets is "the boss." Given Kanter's (1979) notion, discussed earlier in this chapter, that organizational power can be measured in terms of one's control over making "exceptions to the rule," it is important that we examine strategies for getting exceptional requests granted by exerting upward influence. Table 5.1 listed a number of exceptions that subordinates believed were the result of having a "boss with clout." For instance, bosses with clout might be able to intercede on behalf of someone in trouble, get a desirable placement for a talented subordinate, or get approval for expenditures beyond the budget.

Given the weight we've placed on using power to have a positive, constructive influence in an organization, it is important to underscore the merits of managers using their power to benefit their subordinates by exerting upward and outward influence. If subordinates perceive that their unit leader's clout will shield them from outside, disruptive pressures and help them break down artificial organizational barriers to getting the job done right, then they are naturally inclined to strengthen their boss's power base.

One approach to upward influence that has received a great deal of attention is called **issue selling** (Dutton & Ashford, 1993). Issue selling is the process of drawing leaders' attention to those issues or problems that concern you most, notwithstanding the numerous other issues that compete for their attention. Busy leaders tend to devote attention to those issues that they perceive are most consequential. Effectively influencing upward, therefore, means that you need to convince your boss that a particular issue you espouse is so important that it demands his or her timely attention. Table 5.11 contains a summary of the key strategies for exercising upward influence through effective issue selling (Dutton & Ashford, 1993; Dutton & Duncan, 1987).

Table 5.11	Ways to Sell Issues Upward
Principle	**Explanation**
Congruence	The issue must be congruent with your position and role. A person in the marketing department trying to sell an issue relating to computers would be less effective than would be an information specialist.
Credibility	Maintain credibility by being honest, open, non-self-serving, and straightforward. Demonstrate that your interest in the issue is not mere personal gain. Issues that seem self-serving are more difficult to sell.
Communication	Gain or maintain access to a broad communication network. Use multiple communication channels, including face-to-face conversations, written memos, email, conferences, news clippings, and so on.
Compatibility	Select issues that are compatible and in harmony with the organization. Avoid issues that contradict the company culture.
Solvability	The issue must be solvable. Make it clear that the issue can be solved. Show that solution alternatives are available. Unresolvable issues don't capture attention.
Payoff	Clearly point out the long-term payoff, for the organization or the manager, of addressing the issue. The higher the potential payoff appears to be, the more likely the issue will receive attention.
Expertise	Identify the expertise needed to solve the problem. Issues are more likely to capture attention if it is clear that the expertise necessary to resolve them resides in the organization, or better still, under the purview of the top manager or boss.
Responsibility	Point out the responsibility that top managers have to address the issue. Emphasize the negative consequences associated with ignoring the issue or leaving it unresolved.
Presentation	Ensure that the issue is presented succinctly, in emotionally positive terms, with supporting data and novel information. Complex and convoluted information does not capture attention, so the issue must be explained in precise, simple terms.
Bundling	Bundle similar issues together with other important issues that interest top managers. Point out the relationship between your issue and other issues already being addressed.
Coalitions	The issue must be sponsored by other people who will help see the issue. Building coalitions of supporters makes the issue hard to ignore.
Visibility	Present and sell the issue in a public forum rather than in a private meeting. The more individuals who hear about the issue, the more likely it is to reach the boss's agenda.

SOURCE: *Adapted from Dutton and Ashford, 1993.*

Michael Useem, director of the Center for Leadership and Change Management, provides additional perspective on influencing upward. In an interview regarding his book, *Leading Up: How to Lead Your Boss So You Both Win*, Useem says, bluntly, "If people are afraid to help their leaders lead, their leaders will fail" (Breen, 2001). He offers several tips for what he calls "trickle-up leadership." First, you've got to speak up to lead up. He notes that even in the Marine Corps officers are expected to speak up if their superior issues a flawed order. Second, before you lead up, you've got to team up. When the implications of your message will require a major change of course, it is particularly important to work with allies, especially those who add credibility to your argument. Third, lead up, don't argue up. When offering a contrary perspective, disagree without being disagreeable. By modeling open-mindedness, support, and trustworthiness, your example of how you disagree may be your most important message, especially during times of high stress and conflict. Fourth, don't try to be all things to everyone, or else you'll end up being nothing to anybody. Superiors are more willing to hear bad news from subordinates whose judgment they can trust and whose loyalty is unquestioned; simply trying to keep everyone happy will lead others to question your loyalty.

Acting Assertively: Neutralizing Influence Attempts

In general, managers are more effective when they assume that others are reasonable, well meaning, and motivated. Unfortunately, in some cases, these assumptions are proven false. When this happens, it is important to be prepared to protect ourselves from unwanted, inappropriate efforts by others to influence our actions. Recalling Figure 5.1, lack of power is just as harmful to our personal performance as excessive use of power. Therefore, it is just as important to be skillful at resisting unwanted influence attempts as it is to influence the behavior of others. Tables 5.8 and 5.9 contain an impressive arsenal of influence strategies. Is it possible to neutralize the impact of such a highly developed, well-conceived set of tools? Many people succumb to these influence attempts, either because they are unaware of the social dynamics affecting their decisions or because they feel compelled to give in without offering any resistance. The importance of avoiding relationships in which individuals in power positions attempt to foster dependency in others has been the subject of research on the "toxic effects of tyranny in organizations" (Bies & Tripp, 1998). A summary of the characteristics of abusive bosses, from this study, is shown

Table 5.12	Characteristics of Abusive Bosses

- Micromanager—obsessed with details and perfection
- Inexplicit direction with decisive delivery—treats everything as a priority, requiring immediate, careful attention
- Mercurial mood swings—responses are very unpredictable
- Obsession with loyalty and obedience—believes "You are either for me or against me"
- Status derogation—criticizes subordinates in public, to the point of ridicule
- Capricious actions—known for arbitrariness and hypocrisy
- Exercises raw power for personal gain—feels entitled to the "spoils of victory"

SOURCE: *Adapted from Bies and Tripp, 1988.*

in Table 5.12. As you examine the following strategies for neutralizing inappropriate influence attempts, you might find it helpful to use these characteristics of abusive relationships as a frame of reference.

Neutralizing Retribution Strategies Used by Others

Coercive and intimidating actions are intended to create a power imbalance based on dependence. This is the most detrimental form of influence, and therefore it should be resisted most vigorously and directly. You can use several approaches. The following can be thought of as a hierarchy of preferred responses (begin with the first and progress to the next responses, if necessary).

A. **Use countervailing power to shift dependence to interdependence.** The primary reason individuals (particularly bosses) rely heavily on the threat of retribution is to take advantage of a perceived inequality in power. Obviously, the boss has the final say, but the larger the perceived discrepancy in power, the greater the temptation for the boss to exploit the powerless. To resist retribution, focus your boss's attention on your mutual dependence; that is, your interdependence. Explain the negative consequences of failing to respect your rights and acting cooperatively. As part of this discussion, it may be appropriate to discuss more acceptable means of satisfying the boss's demands.

B. **Confront the exploiting individual directly.** All individuals, no matter what their job or organizational status, must protect their personal rights. One of those rights is to be treated as an intelligent, mature, responsible adult. To initiate a complaint effectively, key elements include describing the problem in terms of behaviors, consequences, and feelings; persisting until understood; and making specific suggestions. These techniques can be used to stress the seriousness of your concerns. If necessary, you should specify actions you are willing to take to stop coercive behavior. For example, whistle-blowing involves registering a complaint with an external governing body.

C. **Actively resist.** As a last resort, you should consider "fighting fire with fire." A work slow-down, deliberate disobedience to orders, or reporting the problem to a senior manager might be necessary. Again, this step should be pursued only after all other efforts to counter unwanted threats and demands have failed.

Neutralizing Reciprocity Strategies Used by Others

Many of the persuasion strategies used in sales and advertising fall into this category. In the marketplace, your concern is to avoid being duped. In the workplace, your concern is to avoid being manipulated. The following hierarchically arranged actions should be helpful in either situation. Once again, begin with the first response and follow with others if necessary.

A. **Examine the intent of any gift or favor-giving activity.** When a favor or gift is offered, you should consider the motives of the person, the appropriateness of his or her behavior, and the probable consequences of accepting. You should ask yourself questions such as "Is the giver likely to profit from this?" "Is this transaction inappropriate, unethical, or illegal?" "Is there a stated or implied expectation of reciprocation, and would I feel good about complying if the gift or favor were not offered?" In brief, when in doubt about a benefactor's motives, ask questions or decline the gift.

B. **Confront individuals who are using manipulative bargaining tactics.** Common ploys used in these situations are escalating commitments ("I'm only interested in a small commitment [now]") and reciprocal compromises ("I've lowered my [extreme] initial position; now I expect you [in the spirit of fair play] to also offer a compromise"). The simple

act of drawing attention to these attempts at manipulation will enhance your power in the relationship. State that you do not approve of the manipulative strategy; then propose an alternative exchange, with emphasis on the merits of the case or the true value of the product rather than on the craftiness of the negotiators. You will thus be able to reshape the exchange process and avoid being manipulated.

C. **Refuse to bargain with individuals who use high-pressure tactics.** If steps A and B have failed, refuse to continue the discussion unless high-pressure tactics, such as imposing unrealistic time constraints or emphasizing the limited supply of the commodity or service, are dropped. If you suspect the dynamics of the negotiation process may be clouding your judgment about the value of the object or the importance of the issue, ask yourself, "Would I be interested in this item if there were an unlimited supply and no decision-making deadline?" If the answer is negative, either disengage from the negotiation process or focus your attention on its inequality. By shifting attention from content to process, you neutralize the advantage of a more experienced or powerful bargainer. By refusing to continue unless artificial constraints of time and supply are removed, you can establish fairer terms of trade.

Neutralizing Reason Strategies Used by Others

Although strategies based on reason are the most egalitarian of influence attempts, they can still create or exacerbate conditions of inequity. The following ordered guidelines should help you avoid these situations:

A. **Explain the adverse effects of compliance on performance.** Often, others' pressing priorities are your incidentals. The fact that someone can present a legitimate, convincing case does not mean you should comply with the request. For example, a request may be reasonable, but its timing bad; compliance would mean your having to miss important personal deadlines or neglect your customers. You should discuss these concerns with the influencer. By acknowledging the other person's need, explaining your concerns about personal compliance, and then helping to find alternatives, you avoid becoming overcommitted without giving offense.

B. **Defend your personal rights.** If you have used step A and your petitioner persists, focus the discussion on your personal rights. If individuals frequently come to you for help because they mismanage their time or resources, appeal to their sense of fairness. Ask if it is right to ask you to get behind in your own work in order to bail them out of their predicaments. Coworkers have the right to request your help in a pinch, but you also have the right to say no when even reasonable requests place you at a serious disadvantage or when they stem from the negligence or overdependence of others.

C. **Firmly refuse to comply with the request.** If your efforts to explain why you are unable to comply have not worked, you should firmly restate your refusal and terminate the discussion. Some people believe that their case is so compelling that they have difficulty believing others won't comply. If your coworker still won't take no for an answer, it's probably because your "no" was not firm enough. As a last resort, you may have to seek the support of a higher authority.

THE SPECIAL CASE OF SEXUAL HARASSMENT

It is truly unfortunate that sexual harassment of any kind exists. In organizations it is a particularly heinous example of the abuse of power, either personal or positional. As the global #MeToo movement has revealed, countless women have lived with the emotional scars of sexual harassment for years—hiding their wounds due to fear of retribution. It is no wonder that the incidence of sexual harassment is woefully underreported.

Research has found that factors such as the severity of the incident and perceived consequences can affect the likelihood of reporting (Gruber & Smith, 1995). Aside from incident-specific factors, organizational factors can also affect the likelihood of reporting. Compounding the fear of retribution from the perpetrator, when employees fear backlash from coworkers they are less likely to submit formal complaints (Vijayasiri, 2008). Additionally, if a complaint isn't handled well by the organization, it can lead to a lack of trust in the adjudication procedures, which, in turn, discourages reports of future incidents (Vijayasiri, 2008).

One of the reasons why sexual harassment warrants special attention is because it is against the law in many countries. In the United States, the Equal Employment Opportunity Commission (EEOC) is the federal agency responsible for enforcing laws against sexual harassment. Their website defines sexual harassment in this manner (https://www.eeoc.gov/laws/types/harassment.cfm):

❑ Sexual harassment is a form of sex discrimination that violates *Title VII of the Civil Rights Act of 1964.*
❑ Unwelcome sexual advances, requests for sexual favors, and other verbal or physical conduct of a sexual nature constitute sexual harassment when this conduct explicitly or implicitly affects an individual's employment, unreasonably interferes with an individual's work performance, or creates an intimidating, hostile, or offensive work environment.

This agency also provides guidance for actions to take if you feel you have been harassed in the workplace. (https://www.eeoc.gov/eeoc/newsroom/wysk/harassed_at_work.cfm)

EEOC regulations also make it clear that managers have a responsibility to provide a work environment safe from sexual harassment. They can do this by periodically reminding group members that there is zero tolerance for any form of discrimination, including gender-related. They should also make it clear that what constitutes discrimination is based on the perception of the offended person, not on what others believe is appropriate. Finally, they should invite any who experience or observe gender-related harassment to report it immediately. Managers who turn a blind eye to discrimination, of any kind, are admitting their personal feelings of powerlessness—cowering to the fear of social retribution. For information about the potential legal liability of overlooking this form of illegal behavior, see the EEOC website.

Summary

In Figure 5.2, we highlight the two skills discussed in this chapter: gaining power and translating power into influence. We began by discussing sources of power such as personal attributes and position characteristics. One must develop both of these to maximize one's potential as a power holder. A strong person in a weak position and a weak person in a strong position are both at a disadvantage. Ideally, one should become a strong person in a strong position.

A manager must establish a power base in order to get work accomplished and obtain commitments to important objectives. But power without influence is not sufficient. Consequently, we discussed how to translate power into influence by selecting an appropriate

LEARNING

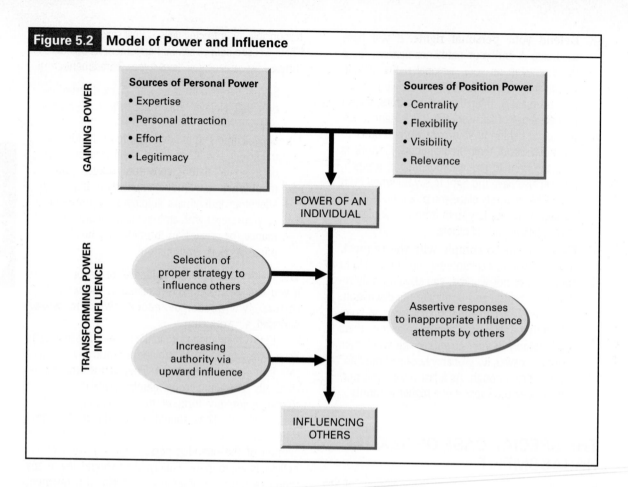

Figure 5.2 | **Model of Power and Influence**

GAINING POWER

Sources of Personal Power
- Expertise
- Personal attraction
- Effort
- Legitimacy

Sources of Position Power
- Centrality
- Flexibility
- Visibility
- Relevance

POWER OF AN INDIVIDUAL

TRANSFORMING POWER INTO INFLUENCE

Selection of proper strategy to influence others

Assertive responses to inappropriate influence attempts by others

Increasing authority via upward influence

INFLUENCING OTHERS

influence strategy and implementing it in a way that minimizes resistance. In general, the higher-numbered strategies in Table 5.8 are the most effective. Persuasion tends to build trust and encourage internalized commitment, while coercion and intimidation erode trust, produce only superficial compliance, and encourage servility.

The unbridled use of power tends to increase resistance among subordinates, which in turn erodes the manager's power base. It also transforms the nature of the manager's stewardship over subordinates. The more a manager dominates subordinates, the more dependent the subordinates become on management's initiatives. As a result, managers tend to overvalue their contribution to their workers' job-performance activities ("Without me, they would be lost"). This inflated sense of self-importance encourages abuse of power that weakens the manager's influence and may even lead others to demand the manager's resignation. Thus, the abuse of power is both organizationally and personally destructive.

Power need not be abused, however. Managers who wield power effectively work within acknowledged constraints, but they figure out ways to do things right. They take full responsibility for their subordinates'

performance, as well as for their commitment to their work and their membership in the organization.

Translating power into influence should not only be directed downward (i.e., toward organizational subordinates) but also upward (i.e., toward organizational superiors). Incompetent attempts to influence upward can quickly derail a manager's career, while competent upward influence can markedly enhance it. By helping to set the agenda of senior managers (issue selling) and by working for senior management's success (benefiting the boss), a manager's influence can increase significantly. When applying these two principles, however, managers should be motivated not by a thirst for mere self-aggrandizement, but by an honest desire to benefit their companies and strengthen their bosses' position.

The counsel of the late A. Bartlett Giamatti, former president of Yale University and commissioner of Major League Baseball, serves as a particularly fitting conclusion to this discussion: "Far better to conceive of power as consisting in part of the knowledge of when not to use all the power you have...Whoever knows how to restrain and effectively release power finds...that power flows back to him" (1981, p. 169).

Behavioral Guidelines

Effective management within an organization includes both gaining power and exercising influence wisely. Key guidelines for gaining power include:

1. Enhance your personal power in the organization by:

   □ Developing your knowledge and skills to the point of becoming an acknowledged expert.
   □ Enhancing your attractiveness to others, for example, by fostering the attributes of friendship (genuineness, intimacy, acceptance, validation of self-worth, tolerance, and social exchange) and by attending to professional appearance.
   □ Being extremely dependable and, when appropriate, putting forth more effort than expected.
   □ Increase your legitimacy by aligning your behaviors and decisions with core organizational values.

2. Increase the centrality of your position by:

   □ Expanding your network of communication contacts.
   □ Staying abreast of relevant information.
   □ Serving as the source of information for others.

3. Increase the latitude and flexibility of your job by:

   □ Reducing the percentage of routine activities.
   □ Expanding task variety and novelty.
   □ Initiating new ideas.
   □ Getting involved in new projects.
   □ Participating in the early stages of decision-making processes.
   □ Seeking unusual and design-oriented jobs, rather than those that are repetitive and maintenance oriented.

4. Increase the visibility of your job performance by:

   □ Expanding the number of contacts you have with senior people.
   □ Making oral presentations of written work.
   □ Participating in problem-solving task forces.
   □ Inviting senior managers to help you recognize important accomplishments within your work group.
   □ Sending personal notes of congratulations or cover notes accompanying reports or useful information.

5. Increase the relevance of your tasks to the organization by:

   □ Becoming an internal coordinator or external representative.
   □ Providing services and information to other units.
   □ Monitoring and evaluating activities within your own unit.
   □ Expanding the domain of your work activities.
   □ Becoming involved in activities central to the organization's top priorities.
   □ Becoming a trainer or mentor for new members.

   The general guidelines for influencing others effectively involve matching your influence strategy to specific situations, acting assertively when others attempt to influence you inappropriately, and empowering others. In general, use reason strategies more often than reciprocity strategies, and reciprocity more than threats of retribution. Use open, direct approaches in preference to indirect, manipulative approaches.

6. Use reason strategies when:

- ❏ There are few time constraints.
- ❏ Initiative and innovation are vital.
- ❏ Interpersonal trust is high.
- ❏ The relationship is long term.
- ❏ Interpersonal conflict is not high.
- ❏ Personal goals are congruent and/or respected by both parties.
- ❏ It is important for the other person to understand why the request is being made.

7. Use reciprocity strategies when:

- ❏ The parties are mutually dependent.
- ❏ There are clearly specified rules governing interpersonal transactions.
- ❏ Long-term commitment to common goals and values is not important.
- ❏ There is sufficient time to reach satisfactory agreements.

8. Use retribution strategies when:

- ❏ There is a substantial imbalance of power between the parties.
- ❏ The ongoing commitment of the other person is not critical.
- ❏ Quality and innovation are not important.
- ❏ Opposition is acceptable (e.g., when personnel replacement is possible, if necessary).
- ❏ Extensive surveillance is possible.
- ❏ No other alternatives exist.

9. To neutralize reason influence strategies of others:

- ❏ Explain the negative consequences of compliance.
- ❏ Defend your rights.
- ❏ Firmly refuse to comply with request.

10. To neutralize reciprocity influence strategies of others:

- ❏ Examine the context of any gift- or favor-giving activity.
- ❏ Confront individuals who are using escalating or compromising tactics.
- ❏ Refuse to bargain with individuals who are using high-pressure tactics.

11. To neutralize retribution influence strategies of others:

- ❏ Use countervailing power to shift dependence to interdependence.
- ❏ Confront the exploitative individual directly.
- ❏ Actively resist.

12. To sell issues to your superiors:

- ❏ Select issues that are congruent with your position or role.
- ❏ Present the issue honestly and without being self-serving.
- ❏ Communicate the issue broadly.
- ❏ Select an issue that is compatible with the culture.
- ❏ Select a solvable issue.
- ❏ Clarify the payoff to be achieved.
- ❏ Identify the needed expertise.
- ❏ Point out senior managers' responsibility for the issue.
- ❏ Be succinct, use emotional imagery, and provide supporting data and novel information.
- ❏ Bundle the issue with other similar important issues.
- ❏ Find like-minded supporters.
- ❏ Use public forums.

CASE INVOLVING POWER AND INFLUENCE

Dynica Software Solutions

Dynica Technologies recently announced plans to construct a new production facility in River Woods. The new facility would replace the company's original production facility, which is adjacent to the company headquarters in Edgemont. In announcing the new facility, the company stated that, to the extent possible, it would be staffed by Edgemont plant personnel and that the excess personnel would be transferred to other Dynica plants in neighboring states.

Dynica management views the River Woods facility as the plant of the future, featuring lower processing costs and staffing requirements, as well as state-of-the art environmental standards. In a recent press release, the Dynica CEO noted they were replacing one of the least environmentally friendly plants in the industry with a facility that will be "greener" than any of their competitors' production plants.

Dynica is also using the River Woods plant to pilot a new decentralized management structure. In the past, the firm's marketing activities were directed from the home office by a vice president. Manufacturing operations and certain other departments were under the control of the company's senior vice president. In this centralized, functional arrangement none of the company's four production facilities had a general manager. Instead, each department in a plant reported on a line basis to its functional counterpart at the home office (e.g., director of production, director of engineering). In contrast, the new River Woods plant manager will be responsible for the management of all functions and personnel, except marketing and sales.

There is general consensus among the top management team that the long-term viability of the firm depends on the success of this initiative. However, some have expressed concerns about the difficulty of the task facing the River Woods general manager. They point to the shift from functional lines of communication and accountability to a plant-level focus, as well as the challenges of upgrading the skills of the Edgemont plant personnel, working out the bugs in new applications of advanced manufacturing processes to design and production, and dealing with the inevitable complaints from employees in a small company town who are not satisfied with their new assignments and who might serve as the catalyst for unionizing the facility.

Discussion Questions

5.1.   If you were part of the selection committee for the River Woods plant manager position, based on what you've learned about the sources of personal power in this chapter, describe what you'd consider to be the ideal candidate's qualifications.

5.2.   If you were offered the new River Woods plant manager position, based on what you've learned about the sources of positional power, what actions would you take to ensure that as the company's first general manager you have the necessary clout to accomplish your assigned duties?

5.3.   Using the information on influence strategies in the second half of this chapter as your guide, strategize how you would address the challenges you are likely to encounter if you were to accept the position of River Woods plant manager.

EXERCISE FOR GAINING POWER

Repairing Power Failures in Management Circuits

Rosabeth Kanter (1979) argues that much of what is labeled "poor management" in organizations is simply individuals protecting their diminished power bases. Instead of criticizing these managers as incompetent, she proposes we bolster their feelings of personal power. If we solve the real problem of perceived lack of power, the undesirable symptoms of poor leadership often evaporate. This point of view is consistent with the principles discussed in this chapter.

Assignment

In this exercise, you are asked to give advice to individuals who feel powerless. For each of the situations below, form groups to explore opportunities for enhancing the power base of these three individuals. Prepare to report your recommendations.

Situation 1: Department Store Manager

Six months ago, Kate Shalene was promoted from her sales associate position to become a manager of the accessories department at an upscale department store. She was proud of her new promotion but was surprised to discover she felt increasingly powerless. Instead of being a stepping stone, this position was feeling more and more like a dead end. Managers above her were about her age, and the hoped-for company expansion was beginning to appear unlikely. She was not a central part of the organization, and she felt no one ever noticed her unless she messed up. She was expected to be supportive of her subordinates, but they never returned the favor. She was expected to absorb their flak without support from above. In general, she felt as though she was constantly "getting it from both ends." Her job was extremely rule-bound, so she had little discretion in what she did or how she did it. She had only modest control over the pay or benefits of her subordinates because their union agreement left very little flexibility. So she felt powerless to reward them or punish them in ways that really mattered.

As a result, she found she was more and more apt to impose rules to get subordinates to do what she wanted. She became increasingly jealous of any successes and recognition achieved by her subordinates, so she tended to isolate them from people higher up in the organization and from complete information. She lost her penchant for informality and became increasingly rigid in following standard operating procedures. Predictably, her subordinates were becoming more resentful and less productive.

Situation 2: Human Resource Professional

Tao Leung joined his organization a year ago as a senior human resources professional. He believed the position might be a way for him to achieve considerable visibility with the top brass, but instead he felt isolated and forgotten. As a staff officer, he had almost no decision-making authority except in his narrow area of expertise. Most of what went on in the organization occurred without his involvement. Innovation and entrepreneurial activity were completely out of his realm. While some of the finance and marketing officers were given opportunities for professional development, no one seemed to care about his becoming more experienced and capable. They saw him only as a specialist. Because his job didn't necessarily require that he interact with people outside of his division, he had little opportunity to cultivate relationships that might lead to contacts with someone near the top.

What hurt was that a consultant had been hired a few times to work on projects that were part of his area. If consultants could be brought in to do his work, he thought, he must not be very important to the organization.

Tao found himself being more and more turf conscious. He didn't want others encroaching on his area of expertise. He tried to demonstrate his competence to others, but the more he did so, the more he became defined as a specialist, outside the mainstream of the organization. Overall, he felt he was losing ground in his career.

Situation 3: Chief Financial Officer

Aadhya Laghari has been her company's CFO for three years. When she obtained the position, she felt that her ultimate career goal had been achieved. Now she was not so sure. Surprisingly, she discovered myriad constraints limiting her discretion and initiative. For example, the job had so many demands and details associated with it that she never had time to engage in any long-term planning. There always seemed to be one more crisis that demanded her attention. Unfortunately, most of the constraints were from sources she couldn't control, such as government regulations, demands for greater accountability made by the board of directors and by stockholders, union relationships, equal opportunity statutes, and so on. She had built her reputation as a successful manager by being entrepreneurial, creative, and innovative, but none of those qualities seemed appropriate for the demands of her current work. Furthermore, because she was so mired in managing financial reporting, she had become more and more out of touch with the information flow in the organization. Some things had to remain confidential with her, but her secrecy made others unwilling to share information with her. She had assistants who were supposed to be monitoring the organization and providing her with information, but she often felt they only told her what she wanted to hear.

Aadhya had begun to hear rumors that certain special-interest groups were demanding her removal from the top job. She responded by becoming more dictatorial and defensive, with the result that the organization was becoming more control-oriented and conservative. She felt that she was in a downward spiral, but she couldn't find a way to reverse the trend. "I always thought the saying 'It's lonely at the top' was just a metaphor," she mused.

EXERCISE FOR USING INFLUENCE EFFECTIVELY

Managers are given formal power in an organization by virtue of their position of authority. However, they often find this authority does not readily translate into actual influence. Particularly when they are working with peers, they find it necessary to develop informal relationships through making deals, persuasive arguments, and so forth. These relationships form the basis of real influence in an organization.

Assignment

After reading the following case, assume the roles of staff members for Ann Lyman, a recently hired marketing executive. Divide into small groups and conduct an informal staff discussion in which you design a plan for influencing Ann's colleagues and superiors to support her proposal. First, decide which general influence strategy (or combination of strategies) is most appropriate for this situation. Second, using Table 5.7, recommend specific actions for implementing your general strategy. Prepare to present your suggestions, including justifications.

Kalina Ivanov's Proposal

Kalina Ivanov was recently hired by the Challenge Products Corporation (CPC) as a senior marketing executive for the electronic housewares division. Her previous experience at Pearces, a major competitor, had earned her a reputation for being a creative and hardworking manager. Her department at Pearces had increased its sales at least 15 percent per year over the past five years, and she had been featured in a lead article in *Contemporary Management*. This combination of competence and visibility was what attracted the attention of John Dilworth, the CEO of CPC. John was troubled about the two-quarter decline in electronics sales. This was the core of CPC's business, and he could not risk losing market share.

In the past, CPC's products had dominated such a large share of the market that, ironically, marketing wasn't considered very important. Production touted its high quality and low costs, purchasing emphasized its contribution to keeping costs low, and engineering stressed the durability of its designs. CPC products, it was argued by many, "sold themselves."

But that was before the cheaper "lookalike" products from Asia flooded the discount stores. No longer could CPC expect high customer loyalty simply because it was the oldest, best-known, most reliable name brand on the shelf. Kalina was convinced that in order for CPC to stay competitive, the company needed to expand its product line, offering more options at different price levels. She felt it also needed to branch out into "trend designs" that appealed to the contemporary lifestyles of young adults.

These changes had far-reaching ramifications for other departments at CPC. For one thing, they meant engineering would have to shorten its design cycle, provide support for a broader range of products, and emphasize customer-oriented, rather than functional, features. These changes would obviously not sit well with the production department, which jealously protected its long production runs based on standard orders and relatively few model changes. It also stressed ease of fabrication and assembly. In addition, purchasing would be required to find new sourcing alternatives for nonstandard parts, which would make it more difficult to get volume discounts and ensure quality.

After three months on the job, Kalina felt she was ready to make her proposal to John. She pushed her staff hard to add the finishing touches before John left on his two-week vacation to Lake Tahoe. She wasn't disappointed—he thought it was a winner. He was excited and ready to "sign on." But he was also realistic about the difficulty they faced convincing others that these changes were necessary. Kalina's counterparts in production, purchasing, and engineering would certainly object. "It'll be a hard sell, but I think you have some good ideas," he concluded. "While I'm away, I'd like you to design a plan for getting the cooperation of the other departments. You can count on me for general support, but the culture in this organization isn't consistent with sending out an edict. You'll have to figure out how to get their support some other way."

EXERCISES FOR NEUTRALIZING UNWANTED INFLUENCE ATTEMPTS

An important aspect of becoming empowered and influential is reducing inappropriate dependence. Obviously, interdependence in both social circles and work circles is essential to healthy organizational life. Most forms of interdependence are natural and healthy. However, sometimes individuals attempt to turn interdependence into dependence by exercising inappropriate influence. Their objective is to increase their power over others by creating a significant imbalance of power.

Assignment

In each of the following role-plays, assume the role of the person who needs to resist unwanted influence (Isabella or Amaliya). Prior to the beginning of the role-play, review the relevant behavioral guidelines guidelines 9 through 11 on page 250, determine which combination is most appropriate, and plan your strategy for dealing with this problem. Do not read the other role descriptions (Bill or Aiko). Following the role-play, an assigned observer will give you feedback using the Observer's Feedback Form (found at the end of the chapter) as a guide.

Cindy's Fast Foods

Isabella Garcia, Assistant Manager

You are the assistant manager of Cindy's, a fast-food franchise in a college town. You are one of the few student employees who has stayed on after graduation. You weren't ready to move away after graduation because of family obligations, and there weren't many other job opportunities locally. The spring before graduation, the owner offered you the job of assistant manager. The timing was perfect because the offer would relieve the pressure on you to pursue teaching jobs in which you really weren't interested. Your work at Cindy's had sparked your interest in business, and your student-teaching experience had not been very successful. Even though your parents weren't too pleased about paying four years' tuition at an expensive private liberal arts college to have you end up "slinging burgers" for a career, their feelings mellowed when you explained the opportunities you would have to advance and possibly purchase a franchise. "Besides," you told them, "I'll only be in this position for three years, and then I can decide whether I want to apply for a manager's position or try again for a teaching job."

It's hard to believe it's been two years since graduation. Your manager, Bill, has done a conscientious job helping you learn the ropes as a manager. He has worked you hard but trained you well. You feel indebted to him for his help. You have become quite close friends, although his occasional dirty jokes and sexist comments with the guys on break in the back room make you feel uncomfortable.

One night after the rest of the crew has gone home, you are finishing your work for the day. These late nights are the one really bad feature of your job. Just as you are about to turn out the lights, Bill comes in. It is not unusual for him to stop by at closing. He is single, likes to bowl after work, and sometimes drops by on his way home. You are just putting on your coat when he asks you to come into his office. He shuts the door and pulls up a chair next to you. "Isabella, I've been watching your performance very closely. You're a hard worker. The employees enjoy your management style. And I've taken a liking to you as well. I think I have a good shot at transferring to a much larger store in Cincinnati. I'll be glad to get out of this one-horse town and gain more visibility closer to corporate headquarters."

You start getting a little nervous as he moves his chair closer to yours. "I think you would be a really good replacement for me, but you haven't completed your full term as assistant. So I'll need to ask for a special exception to the corporate policy. And I'll have to put in a good word for you with the owner. However, there's some risk involved for me, because the regional manager is a real stickler on rules, and I've asked him to recommend me for the Cincinnati job. But I'd be willing to take that risk under certain conditions." As he waits for a response, you know very well where this conversation is headed.

Bill, Manager

You have been attracted to Isabella for some time. You find her very attractive, and you enjoy her company. You have several times manufactured excuses to have personal chats with her or to be alone with her. You think Isabella finds you attractive, also. It seems that she has been extra friendly lately. You figure she's either bucking for your job or sending you signals that she'd like to expand your relationship beyond strictly business—or both.

Besides, you feel she owes you something. You have worked extra hard to train her, and you've been dropping hints to the owner that you think Isabella might be ready to move up.

9:00 to 7:30

Amaliya Petrov, Loan Officer

You are a member of a small consumer loan company. The staff consists of you, another loan officer, and a secretary. Last month, a larger financial institution acquired your firm and made some personnel changes. The other loan officer, with whom you had worked for four years, was replaced by Aiko Sato. Having entered the company at about the same time, you and Aiko have known each other for years. In fact, you worked in the Ann Arbor office together for a year. During that time, you were both single, and together you enjoyed the nightlife of Detroit. You learn Aiko is still single and "living it up." In contrast, you have been married for about three years. You looked forward to working with Aiko again but wondered if your lack of interest in the local night scene would affect your relationship. Aiko has a reputation of being capable but lazy. She's known for taking in lots of loan applications and then striking bargains with or cajoling coworkers into helping out with the dreaded credit-checking process. You wonder if this practice has anything to do with the fact that her uncle was a founding partner in the bank.

After Aiko arrives, you are shocked at the difference in your work attitudes and lifestyles. "Boy, what a difference three years makes!" you think to yourself. You and your previous officemate, Jim, were both married, and both of you favored a vigorous working tempo from 9:00 to 5:15, taking lunch when convenient. You and Jim had a great working relationship, and the loan volume in your office increased steadily. There was even some discussion of expanding the size of the staff. In contrast, Aiko prefers leisurely mornings that begin around 10:30, lunches as long as Mexican siestas, and a flurry of activity between 4:00 and 7:30 p.m.

You and your spouse are experiencing some marital turbulence, and you feel it is very important to be home in the evenings. Your spouse has begun attending night classes and leaves for school at 8:00 p.m. The educational program is an extremely intense three-year ordeal. Unfortunately, the stress level already seems unbearable. When you stay at the office late, you not only miss dinner together, but you don't even see each other until after class, when you are both so tired there is no opportunity for quality time. It seems as though most weekends are devoted to homework.

Because the office staff is so small, the difference in workday rhythms is creating a serious hardship on you. Aiko doesn't function well in the morning and has begun expressing irritation when you rush out the door at closing time. Lately, your relationship has become strained. You handle most of the walk-in business early in the morning, eat lunch at your desk, and have your paperwork done by 5:30 at the latest. In contrast, Aiko is just getting into high gear about 4:00. Because company rules require checking each other's loan approvals, Aiko becomes testy when you say you can't stay after 5:30 to check her work. Some evenings you have relented and stayed until 7:00 or 8:00, but your spouse got upset. When you don't stay late, you are greeted by a stack of paperwork on your desk in the morning, which makes it difficult for you to meet with new customers. Several times Aiko has tried to get you to do the credit checks on her loan applications, saying that the press of new business was too great.

Something has got to change! You decide to go to lunch with Aiko today and tell her how you feel.

Aiko Sato, Loan Officer

You have worked for this firm for 10 years, and you are very good at your work. During that time, you have passed up offers from larger financial institutions because you like the flexibility of working in a small office. Besides, your family is financially well off, so you aren't concerned about making a lot of money.

In every other office, your coworkers have been willing to accommodate your work style. They recognize you are one of the top loan officers in the company—and having the right last name doesn't hurt any—so they make allowances for your quirks.

But your new officemate (and, you thought, old friend) is an exception. Since you arrived, the relationship has been testy because of your different schedules. You don't understand why there can't be more tolerance for your work style. After all, you get the job done, and that's what counts. Besides, your requests for assistance are not that unreasonable; other coworkers have always been willing to comply.

Thinking about the impending discussion, you realize how important it is for you to get Amaliya to change her work habits to conform with yours. You certainly hope you can convince Amaliya to pitch in and help you when you get behind. "I mean, that's what coworkers (and old friends) are for, right?" you muse on the way to work. During the discussion, you plan to stress the reasonableness of your requests. Others have never objected strenuously; why should Amaliya? If that doesn't work, you plan to try to work out a bargain. Maybe you could put in a good word for Amaliya with your uncle, a founder of the company. Amaliya's career hasn't exactly skyrocketed, and she is probably itching to move to a larger office in a metropolitan city. Possibly, her title could be upgraded to Senior Loan Officer.

SKILL *APPLICATION*

ACTIVITIES FOR GAINING POWER AND INFLUENCE

Suggested Assignments

5.4.   Select a friend or associate who has complained to you about feeling powerless in an organizational position. This might be a person who holds a relatively insignificant leadership position in a campus organization or a low-level position in a work organization. Perhaps the individual feels his or her personal abilities do not command respect in that position. Sit down with this person and teach him or her the guidelines for gaining power in an organization. (You might use the Assessment Survey at the beginning of this chapter as a diagnostic instrument.) As part of this conversation, design a specific plan of action for increasing both the positional and personal bases of power. Discuss the outcomes of this plan with your friend and report on his or her success.

5.5.   Using the guidelines for gaining power, develop a plan for increasing your power in an organizational setting. Describe the setting, including the factors you feel account for your feelings of powerlessness. Use your score on the Assessment Survey as a diagnostic aid. Formulate a detailed strategy for increasing your positional and personal power. Report on your results and describe the benefits of becoming more empowered.

5.6. Over time, analyze your efforts to influence other people. Use the "Three Rs" model to catalog your strategies. Consider why you used each strategy. Did you repeatedly rely on one or two strategies, or did you vary your approach according to circumstances? Keep track of the outcome of each attempt. Did you seem to have more success with one of the strategies? Next, select a person you have attempted to influence, one with whom you have a close, ongoing relationship. Discuss the alternative influence strategies with that person and ask him or her what effect the frequent use of each approach might have on your relationship.

5.7. Watch at least two realistic dramas (movies, plays, TV). Observe the influence strategies used by various characters. Which form of influence did they use most frequently, and why? Did certain people demonstrate a preference for a particular strategy? If so, was this based on personality traits, gender roles, authority relationships, or other situational factors? How successful were these influence attempts, and what impact did they have on ongoing relationships?

5.8. Identify a specific relationship in which you are regularly asked to do things that you feel are inappropriate. Using the relevant guidelines for resisting unwanted influence, formulate a strategy for assertively responding to the next attempt. Role-play this approach with a friend or coworker and incorporate his or her suggestions. After you implement your plan, report on the outcome. What was the reaction? Were you successful in communicating your position? Was an understanding reached regarding future interactions that is more fair? Based on this experience, examine other relationships for which this approach might be appropriate.

Application Plan and Evaluation

The intent of this exercise is to help you apply this cluster of skills in a real-life, out-of-class setting. Now that you have become familiar with the behavioral guidelines that form the basis of effective skill performance, you will improve most by trying out those guidelines in an everyday context. Unlike a classroom activity, in which feedback is immediate and others can assist you with their evaluations, this skill application activity is one you must accomplish and evaluate on your own. There are two parts to this activity. Part 1 helps prepare you to apply the skill, and Part 2 helps you evaluate and improve on your experience. Be sure to write down answers to each item. Don't short-circuit the process by skipping steps.

Part 1: Planning

5.9. Write down the two or three aspects of this skill that are most important to you. These may be areas of weakness, areas you most want to improve, or areas that are most salient to a problem you face right now. Identify the specific aspects of this skill that you want to apply.

5.10. Now identify the setting or the situation in which you will apply this skill. Establish a plan for performance by actually writing down a description of the situation. Who else will be involved? When will you do it? Where will it be done?

> Circumstances:
> Who else?
> When?
> Where?

5.11. Identify the specific behaviors you will engage in to apply this skill. Operationalize your skill performance.

5.12. What are the indicators of successful performance? How will you know you have been effective? What will indicate you have performed competently?

Part 2: Evaluation

5.13. After you have completed your implementation, record the results. What happened? How successful were you? What was the effect on others?

5.14. How can you improve? What modifications can you make next time? What will you do differently in a similar situation in the future?

5.15. Looking back on your whole skill practice and application experience, what have you learned? What has been surprising? In what ways might this experience help you in the long term?

SCORING KEYS AND COMPARISON DATA

✪ Go to www.pearson.com/mylab/management for scoring keys and comparison data for the following instruments:

Gaining Power and Influence
Using Influence Strategies

SCORING KEYS AND COMPARISON DATA

SKILL ASSESSMENT

- Motivating Performance Assessment
- Diagnosing Unsatisfactory Performance and Enhancing Motivation

SKILL LEARNING

- Increasing Motivation and Performance
- Understanding the Prerequisites for Successful Task Performance
- Fostering High Performance
- Diagnosing and Correcting the Causes of Unacceptable Performance

SKILL ANALYSIS

- Electro Logic

SKILL PRACTICE

- Joe Chaney
- Motivating Performance Assessment
- Job Design Survey

SKILL APPLICATION

- Suggested Assignments
- Application Plan and Evaluation

SCORING KEYS AND COMPARISON DATA

6

Motivating Performance

LEARNING OBJECTIVES

1. Understand what contributes to task performance
2. Foster high performance
3. Identify and correct the causes of unacceptable performance

SKILL *ASSESSMENT* (?)

MyLab Management Personal Inventory Assessments

**PERSONAL
INVENTORY
ASSESSMENT**

The assessment instruments in this chapter are briefly described below. The assessments appear either in your text or in MyLab. The assessments marked with ✪ are available only in MyLab. If assigned, go to www.pearson.com/mylab/management to complete these assessments. The assessments without the ✪ appear only in the text.

All assessments should be completed before reading the chapter material.

After completing the first assessment, save your response to your hard drive. When you have finished reading the chapter, re-take the assessment and compare your responses to see what you have learned.

- ✪ ❑ The *Motivating Performance Assessment* evaluates your motivation and performance in a current (or recent) work setting.
- ✪ ❑ The *Diagnosing Unsatisfactory Performance and Enhancing Motivation* assessment measures your competency in the management of performance. Use the results of this assessment to tailor your study of this chapter to your specific needs.

SKILL *LEARNING* (i)

Increasing Motivation and Performance

Focus groups at Intermountain Healthcare, a Utah-based health care organization with more than 23,000 employees, revealed that a majority of front-line workers would not leave their jobs unless another employer offered them a 20 percent increase in pay and a 30 percent increase in benefits (interview with Alison Mackey). Such commitment is an extremely valued commodity in our current economy. Most organizations struggle to retain their best employees and to motivate them to high performance. The following comments from three front-line workers at Intermountain Healthcare reveal that a motivating work environment and the organization's clear values are what foster their strong sense of commitment (Intermountain Healthcare Employee Opinion Survey Database).

"I have never worked at a place where people have been so concerned about their employees. And because of that we can turn around and give the same to our customers."

"I think [Intermountain Healthcare] is a system that's concerned about its employees, and as a result it can attract employees with strong technical and people-based knowledge and experience."

"The values that [Intermountain Healthcare] stands for make me never want to leave."

The efforts Intermountain Healthcare has taken to create such a motivating work environment have improved its clinical care and its bottom line. In 2016, Forbes added Intermountain to its "America's Best Employers" list, and they received their 5th award from The Gallup Organization as one of its "Great Workplaces" in the United States. It is also noteworthy that in 2017 Intermountain was the only health care system in the United States to have four of its hospitals included in Truven's "Top 100 Hospitals." In addition, Intermountain's president and CEO was named one of the "50 Most Influential Physician Executives and Leaders" by Modern Healthcare, ranking No. 10 overall in 2017 (https://intermountainhealthcare.org/about/transforming-healthcare/awards-and-recognition/).

Organizations like Intermountain Healthcare, that have highly motivated and committed employees, are well equipped to compete in any market, be it health care or heavy industry. But like any distinctive competence, employee commitment is difficult to achieve; if it were otherwise, it would have no competitive value.

After winning an unprecedented seventh NBA title as a coach, Phil Jackson was asked what his method was for motivating professional basketball players. He responded, "I don't motivate my players. You cannot motivate someone; all you can do is provide a motivating environment and the players will motivate themselves" (Jackson, 2000). We believe the imagery of "manager-as-coach" and "motivation-as-facilitation," as suggested by one of the most successful coaches of our time, provides the appropriate backdrop for our discussion. Whether managers are working with a group of steel workers, computer programmers, artists, or basketball players, their common challenge is to create a work environment in which team members are motivated to do their very best.

The contents of this chapter will help you successfully discharge this fundamental management responsibility. To set the stage, we begin by addressing the fundamental question, "Why do some people perform higher than others?" Following our examination of the predictors of task performance, we zero in on one of them: personal motivation—the central focus of this chapter. We utilize a four-part model to offer insights into the actions managers can take to strengthen the Motivation → Performance link. In the final section, we offer guidance for helping team members whose performance is below expectations by identifying their roadblocks to higher performance.

Understanding the Prerequisites for Successful Task Performance

The fundamental responsibility of managers, generally speaking, is to help those they supervise achieve high levels of performance. Training programs, and related guidebooks, typically focus on a few key ideas and practical suggestions. Our objective is to complement those materials with a broad understanding of the prerequisites for successful task performance.

We begin our discussion of how to effectively manage work performance with the question "What has decades of research revealed about the predictors of work performance?" Several scholars (e.g., Gerhart, 2003; Steers, Porter, & Bigley, 1996; Vroom, 1964) have identified key ingredients of task performance.

According to the formula in Figure 6.1, performance is the product of Expectations multiplied by Ability multiplied by Motivation. The multiplicative function in this formula indicates that all elements are required—they are prerequisites. For example,

Figure 6.1 **The Prerequisites for Successful Task Performance**

$Performance = Expectations \times Ability \times Motivation$
$(Should\ do)\ (Can\ do)\ (Will\ do)$

workers who have 100 percent of the ability required to perform a task and 75 percent of the motivation to perform that task will likely perform at an above-average rate. On the other hand, regardless of how much ability these individuals possess, if they have zero motivation, their performance will be unacceptable. Simply put, individual or group performance (in any walk of life) can be explained using this formula. As we will explore in detail later, this formula is especially useful in diagnosing the causes of unacceptable performance.

Performance expectations refers to the performance requirements associated with a position, role, or job. Expectations specify the standard by which the performance of individuals executing an assignment will be measured. Performance expectations address the subjective question "What *should I do* to satisfy expectations?"

For our purposes, **ability** (i.e., capabilities) pertains to the subjective question "*Can I do* what is expected?" It is a very broad category, covering everything a person needs to do a job well, other than motivation. It includes a person's native aptitude, their task-related training, and relevant organizational resources.

The online Business Dictionary (businessdictionary.com) defines **motivation** as "Internal and external factors that stimulate desire and energy in people to be continually interested and committed to a job, role or subject, or to make an effort to attain a goal." Thus, motivation has two components: the desire to engage in a task and the commitment to stay engaged. In work settings, motivation is commonly equated with what can be observed: task-related effort (high motivation = high effort; that is, working hard). This is in contrast to expressed desires, previous effort, or promises to perform. Motivation is reflected in a third subjective question: "*Will I do* what's expected?"

Before moving on, we need to say this about the manager's role in "motivating others." It is a good idea for managers to assume that employees approach a new job or task assignment with a commitment to work hard and to do well. By implication, a subsequent lack of effort is a "learned response"—meaning it reflects a person's on-the-job experience, not some sort of innate predisposition. While it is thus not the responsibility

LEARNING

of managers to "motivate" those they work with, it is in everyone's best interests if they enhance a person's initial motivation using the practices described in this chapter.

As shown in Figure 6.1, motivation is one of three prerequisites for successful task performance. As suggested by the chapter title, "Motivating Performance," our emphasis is on how managers can enhance the Motivation → Performance connection. Our rationale for focusing on motivation's contribution to performance is threefold: (1) a lack of shared understanding regarding task-specific performance expectations is seldom a problem, plus, misunderstandings can be quickly resolved; (2) if employees don't have what it takes to perform a task, they will generally speak up; and (3) it follows that on a day-to-day basis, motivation has the greatest impact on performance, and what managers do, day to day, has the greatest impact on motivation. But before exploring ways to strengthen the Motivation → Performance link, we need to understand how a third element, Satisfaction, fits in.

One of the authors regularly begins workshops on this topic by asking participants to arrange these three concepts in the causal sequence they believe works best. Invariably some propose the sequence shown in Model 1 in Figure 6.2. Proponents of this perspective are informed that this was the prevailing view among scholars in the mid-1900s. But as researchers in that era tested this model, they discovered that Model 2, not Model 1, fit their results. In this revised conception, a person's motivation is viewed as the primary driver of their performance for reasons, and in ways, we'll examine in detail. Although satisfaction has been

shifted to the other side of performance, its effect on motivation is preserved via a "feedback loop." The final iteration, Model 3, adds "outcomes" so as to clarify that personal satisfaction refers to the personal consequences of performance (e.g., rewards), not to performance, per se. This "four-factor model" will serve as our organizing framework.

Model 3 proposes that individuals are motivated to perform a task if they believe (1) putting forth greater effort will yield higher levels of performance (M → P), (2) their performance will be reflected in the outcomes they receive (P → O), and (3) these outcomes are personally salient because they satisfy important needs (O → S). The question-form of these beliefs are: "If I work hard, how likely is it that my performance will satisfy my and others' expectations?" "If I perform at that level, how likely is it that I will receive the anticipated rewards?" "How likely is it that these rewards will be personally satisfying?"

Fostering High Performance

We are now prepared to address the question "How can managers foster high performance in their work units?" With the adage "a chain is only as strong as its weakest link" in mind, we will identify the factors that can strengthen, or weaken, each connecting link in Model 3. Academics refer to these as moderating conditions or, simply, moderators. These are factors that impact the effect (positive or negative, weak or strong) of an antecedent condition on a specified outcome. Each moderator is depicted as an arrow pointing to a connecting link.

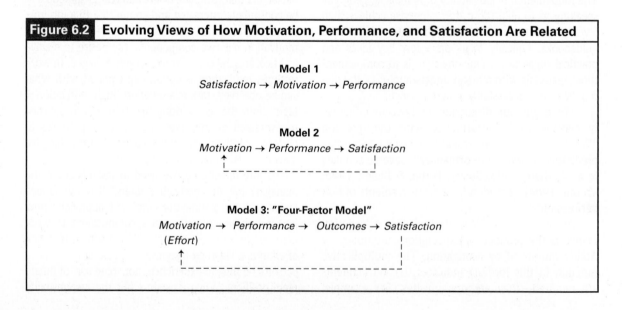

Figure 6.2 | **Evolving Views of How Motivation, Performance, and Satisfaction Are Related**

Model 1
Satisfaction → Motivation → Performance

Model 2
Motivation → Performance → Satisfaction

Model 3: "Four-Factor Model"
Motivation → Performance → Outcomes → Satisfaction
(Effort)

Strengthen the *Motivation → Performance* Link

The Motivation → Performance link signifies a personal estimation of the likelihood that one's efforts will result in the attainment of a performance goal. Figure 6.3 illustrates our use of moderating conditions to strengthen this link. Life experience tells us that the amount of effort we put forth is seldom enough to achieve our performance objectives. Extrapolating from Figure 6.1, we now understand that the effect of motivation on performance depends on two moderating factors: **expectations and goals**, and **ability**.

EXPECTATIONS AND GOALS

Based on data collected since 1993, Right Management Consultants reported that one-third of all managers who change jobs fail in their new positions within 18 months (Fisher, 2005). According to this study, the primary tip for getting off to a good start is to ask your boss exactly what's expected of you and how soon you're supposed to deliver it. Ironically, however, people in managerial positions are less likely to receive a clear job description or detailed performance expectations than people who do entry-level work. Too often, the organization's attitude seems to be: "We pay people to know without being told."

If we imagine a continuum of performance ratings (Unacceptable—Acceptable—Exceptional), **performance expectations** set the standard for acceptable performance. Thus, they specify what must be done to avoid the threat of punishment. One approach managers might use, at least conceptually, to establish appropriate performance expectations for the individuals they supervise is to start with the performance expectations for their work unit. This is what the work unit must produce in order for its manager to receive an acceptable performance rating—to avoid the threat of punishment. Unit-level expectations can then be used to set appropriate performance expectations for individuals, roles, functions, etc., within the unit.

A related concept, **performance goals**, specifies a level of performance above what is expected that, if attained, holds the promise of rewards. Though performance goals can be used to remediate unacceptable performance, they are more commonly used as markers on the path to exceptional performance. It should also be

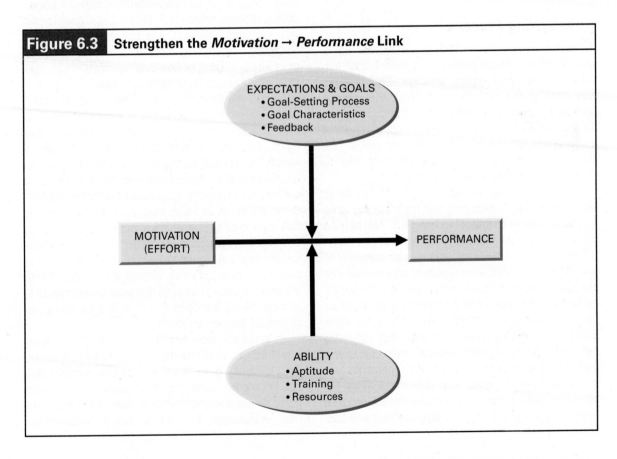

Figure 6.3   **Strengthen the *Motivation → Performance* Link**

noted that performance goals need not be restricted to "the number of widgets produced." To illustrate, when a new vice president of operations was appointed at a major Midwestern steel factory, he announced three goals: reduce finished product rejection by 15 percent (quality); reduce average shipment period by two days (customer satisfaction); and respond to all employee suggestions within 48 hours (employee involvement).

Perhaps no other concept in the field of organizational behavior has received more empirical support than that good goal setting increases individual effort (Latham & Locke, 2006; Locke & Latham, 2002; Latham, 2004). In addition, numerous studies show that groups with goals significantly outperform groups without goals (O'Leary-Kelly, Marocchio, & Fink, 1994). Goal-setting theory suggests that goals enhance performance because they mobilize our efforts, direct our attention, and encourage both persistence and strategy development (Sue-Chan & Ong, 2002). Not all goals work this well, however. Goals have to incorporate particular traits in order to make a difference in our effort and performance. In brief, the effective use of performance goals includes three critical components: a good goal-setting *process*, the right goal *characteristics*, and the consistent use of *feedback and reinforcement*.

Goal-Setting Process

It stands to reason that individuals are more likely to understand and accept performance goals if they participate in the **goal-setting process**. This is likely why work groups perform better when they choose their goals rather than have them assigned (Sue-Chan & Ong, 2002). One way to judge the effectiveness of a goal-setting process is to listen to how people talk about individual and group goals: Do they refer to them as "my/our goals" or as "their goals"?

Participative goal setting, at any level, can be as simple as asking, "Given your past performance, what do you feel would be an appropriate goal?" Not only do questions like this increase the likelihood of goal "buy-in," but they also provide opportunities for managers to gain insights into their team members' personalities. For example, it has been shown that people with the conscientiousness personality trait are more comfortable when they have clear goals (Colbert & Witt, 2009). For these individuals, the question is not whether they use goals, but rather how well their personal goals correspond with what their supervisors believe are appropriate.

Sometimes, however, it is difficult to allow for extensive participation in the establishment of work goals. For example, a computer programming unit may not have any say about which application programs are assigned to the group or what priority is assigned each incoming task. Still, the manager can involve unit members in deciding how much time to allocate to each assignment ("What is a realistic goal for completing this task?") or who should receive which job assignment ("Which type of programs would you find challenging?").

Goal Characteristics

Shifting from process to content, research has shown that **goal characteristics** significantly affect the likelihood of goal achievement (Latham & Locke, 2006; Latham, 2004; Locke & Latham, 2002). Effective goals are *specific, consistent,* and *appropriately challenging*.

Goals that are **specific** are measurable, unambiguous, and behavioral. Specific goals reduce misunderstanding about what behaviors will be rewarded. Admonitions such as "be dependable," "work hard," "take initiative," or "do your best" are too general and too difficult to measure and therefore have limited motivational value.

Here's another aspect of goal specificity. The way goals are framed affects whether individuals will cooperate, compete, or act independently (Latham & Locke, 2006). In cases where individuals might misinterpret your preferred approach, it is important to eliminate ambiguity. The short-term practices of working together or alone, sharing or hoarding information can have long-lasting effects on work-unit culture.

Goals should also be **consistent**. An already hardworking assistant vice president in a large metropolitan bank complains she cannot increase both the number of reports she writes in a week and the amount of time she spends "on the floor," visiting with employees and customers. Goals that are inconsistent—in the sense that they are logically impossible to accomplish simultaneously—create frustration and alienation. A recent study showed that organizations that set many weakly correlated goals can expect a "performance freeze," in which employees are essential paralyzed with confusion about what behavior is most important (Ethiraj & Levinthal, 2009). When subordinates complain that goals are incompatible or inconsistent, managers should be flexible enough to reconsider their expectations.

One of the most important requirements of goals is that they be **challenging** (Knight, Durham, & Locke, 2001). Simply stated, if a person has the requisite skill and knowledge, there is a linear relationship between goal difficulty and performance (Latham & Locke, 2004). One explanation for this is called "achievement motivation" (Atkinson, 1992; Weiner, 2000). According to this perspective, motivated workers size up new tasks in terms of both their chances for success and the significance of the anticipated accomplishment. To complete a goal anyone can reach is not rewarding enough for highly motivated individuals. In order for them to feel successful, they must believe an accomplishment represents a meaningful achievement. Given their desire for success and achievement, it is clear these workers will be most motivated by challenging, but reachable, goals.

Although no single standard of difficulty fits all people, it is important to keep in mind this general rule: High expectations generally foster high performance and low expectations decrease performance (Davidson & Eden, 2000). As one experienced manager said, "We pretty much get what we expect." Warren Bennis, author of *The Unconscious Conspiracy: Why Leaders Can't Lead*, agrees. "In a study of schoolteachers, it turned out that when they held high expectations of their students, that alone was enough to cause an increase of 25 points in the students' IQ scores" (Bennis, 1984, 2003).

Research examining the interaction between goal difficulty and goal setting has shown that holding the difficulty of a goal constant, performance is usually the same, regardless of whether the goal was assigned or set participatively. However, referring to complex tasks, "When working smarter rather than harder, when one's knowledge rather than one's effort (motivation) is required, participation in decision-making leads to higher performance if it increases the probability of finding an appropriate strategy for performing the task, and if it increases the confidence of people that the strategy can be implemented effectively" (Latham, 2004).

Performance Feedback

In addition to selecting the right type of goal, the effective use of goals must also include frequent, accurate, and specific **feedback**. Goal setting and feedback, together, are the essential components of self-management (Latham & Locke, 2006, p. 334). Performance feedback provides opportunities for discussing how performance is assessed, clarifying expectations, adjusting goal difficulty, and identifying obstacles hindering the achievement of performance goals. To achieve the maximum benefit of performance feedback, it should occur frequently. These along-the-way progress reports are particularly critical when the time required to complete an assignment or reach a goal is extensive. For example, feedback is very useful for projects such as writing a large computer program or raising a million dollars for a local charity. In these cases, feedback should be linked to accomplishing intermediate stages or the completion of specific components.

In addition to the timing of feedback, the content of feedback significantly affects its potential for improving performance. As a rule of thumb, to increase the motivational potential of performance feedback, be very specific—including examples whenever possible. Keep in mind that feedback, whether positive or negative, is itself an outcome. The main purpose for giving people feedback on their performance is to reinforce productive behaviors and extinguish counterproductive behaviors. But this can only occur if the feedback focuses on specific behaviors. To illustrate this point, compare the reinforcement value of the following, equally positive, messages: "You are a great member of this team—we couldn't get along without you." "You are a great member of this team. In particular, I've observed that you are willing to do whatever is required to meet a deadline."

It is especially important for managers to provide accurate, honest, and specific feedback when a person's performance is marginal or substandard. It is especially important to have periodic informal conversations prior to the next official performance review in cases of chronic low performance. There are many reasons why managers are reluctant to "tell it like it is" when dealing with unsatisfactory performers. It is unpleasant to deliver bad news of any kind. Therefore, it is easy to justify sugarcoating negative information on the belief that you are doing the recipient a favor. However, it is hard to imagine a case where an unsatisfactory performer is better off not receiving detailed, honest, accurate feedback. Detailed guidance for successfully helping poor performers get back on track is provided in the final section of this chapter.

ABILITY

The role of ability, in Figure 6.3, can be summarized this way: Managers need to enable goal accomplishment by removing personal and organizational ability-related obstacles. Our broad conception of ability includes three components: aptitude, training, and resources.

Components of Ability

Aptitude refers to the native skills and abilities a person brings to a job. These involve physical and mental capabilities, and for many people-oriented jobs, they also include personality characteristics. Most of our inherent abilities can be enhanced by education and training. Indeed, much of what we call native ability in adults can be traced to previous skill-enhancement experiences, such as modeling the social skills of parents or older siblings.

Nevertheless, it is useful to consider *training* as a separate component of ability, since it represents an important mechanism for improving employee performance. Ability should be assessed during the job-matching process by screening applicants against the skill requirements of the job. If an applicant has minor deficiencies in skill aptitude but has many other desirable characteristics, an intensive training program can be used to increase the applicant's qualifications to perform the job.

The third component of ability is task-related organizational *resources*. In some cases, highly capable and well-trained individuals are placed in situations that inhibit their performance because they aren't given the resources (technical, personnel, and/or political) to perform assigned tasks effectively. Resource deficiencies come in many forms, including back-ordered supplies, delays in gearing up for new projects, budget cutbacks, and delays in hiring requests.

Linking goal setting and ability, studies have shown that if individuals lack the knowledge and skill required to achieve a goal, giving them a challenging goal sometimes leads to poorer performance than simply telling them to do their best. In these cases, it is wise to assign high-learning goals—activities that help a person learn how to master the task will likely lead to higher performance (Latham & Locke, 2006).

Our emphasis on making sure employees have what they need to perform well raises the broader subject of managerial involvement, expressed as, "How involved should I be in offering ability-related assistance for team members?" Managers asking this question want to avoid the extremes of "too much" and "too little" involvement, and they intuitively understand that there is not a one-size-fits-all approach.

Appropriate Level of Assistance

For guidance, we turn to the **"path goal" theory of leadership** (House & Mitchell, 1974; see also, Schriesheim & Neider, 1996; Shamir, House, & Arthur, 1993), summarized in Figure 6.4. The research behind this model suggests that the level of a manager's involvement should vary according to three factors: (1) how much help do subordinates actually need, (2) how much do they expect, and (3) how much support is available to them from other organizational sources?

The first condition that influences the appropriate level of managerial involvement is the *nature of the task being performed*, on two dimensions: *structure* and *difficulty*. A task that is highly structured (i.e., that has a lot of built-in order and direction and is easy to complete) does not require extensive management direction. If managers offer too much advice, they will come across as controlling, bossy, or nagging because

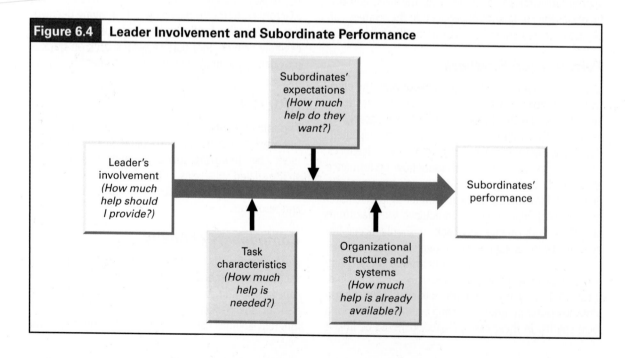

Figure 6.4 Leader Involvement and Subordinate Performance

it is already clear to the subordinates what they should do. On the other hand, for an unstructured (i.e., ambiguous) and difficult (e.g., complex) task, management's direction and strong involvement in problem-solving activities will be seen as constructive and satisfying.

The second factor that should be considered is *subordinates' expectations*. An important factor that affects employees' expectations about management involvement is their *need for autonomy*. Individuals who prize autonomy and independence prefer managers with a highly participative leadership style because it gives them more latitude for controlling what they do.

According to this model, another characteristic that impacts employee expectations regarding managerial involvement is their *ability and experience*. Capable and experienced employees feel they need less assistance from their managers because they are adequately trained, know how to obtain the necessary resources, and can handle political entanglements with their counterparts in other units.

The third component that path-goal theory suggests is important for deciding how involved managers should be is the availability of *organizational support*. Management involvement should complement, rather than duplicate, organizational sources of support. Specifically, managers should become more involved when what an employee needs to do their work well is not available from other team members, training programs, or self-help tools.

In short, the path-goal model encourages managers to tailor their style to employee conditions, as shown in Table 6.1. Managers' direct involvement should be calibrated to the nature of the work and the availability of organizational support as well as the ability and experience of the individuals. If managers are insensitive to these contingencies, some employees may see them as interfering, while others will feel lost.

Strengthen the *Performance → Outcomes* Link

Once managers have helped establish clear goals and cleared the path to goal completion, the next step toward motivating performance is to encourage goal accomplishment by linking performance to extrinsic outcomes (rewards and discipline) and fostering intrinsic outcomes. To strengthen the Performance → Outcomes link, managers can maximize the performance-reinforcing potential of both extrinsic and intrinsic reinforcement by (1) demonstrating that, to the extent possible, extrinsic rewards are tied to the achievement of performance goals, (2) utilizing extrinsic rewards and discipline appropriately, and (3) creating work conditions that are conducive to intrinsic motivation via their daily practices and the design of work assignments. These critical moderating conditions are shown in Figure 6.5.

Before examining these in detail, we must first address the topic of performance measurement. It is important to point out that our discussion of performance, throughout, is predicated on the use of objective, relevant, agreed-upon measures of performance. We earlier warned that if performance expectations are not clear and clearly accepted, employees might challenge low performance ratings by claiming, "That's not what I was told/understood." By comparison, it's far more problematic if employees in this situation respond, "I don't agree with your assessment of my performance." In the first case, managers can clarify their expectations and move on. However, if employees don't accept how their performance was measured,

Table 6.1	Gauging the Appropriateness of Leader Involvement	
Contingencies	**Conditions Appropriate for High Involvement**	**Conditions Appropriate for Low Involvement**
Task structure	Low	High
Task mastery	Low	High
Subordinate's desire for autonomy	Low	High
Subordinate's experience	Low	High
Subordinate's ability	Low	High
Strength of group norms	Low	High
Effectiveness of organization's controls and rewards	Low	High

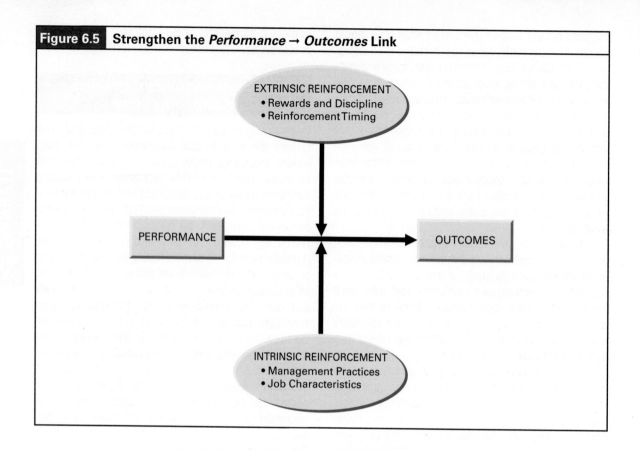

Figure 6.5 Strengthen the *Performance → Outcomes* Link

EXTRINSIC REINFORCEMENT
• Rewards and Discipline
• Reinforcement Timing

PERFORMANCE

OUTCOMES

INTRINSIC REINFORCEMENT
• Management Practices
• Job Characteristics

linking performance ratings to extrinsic outcomes has little chance of strengthening employees' motivation to improve their performance.

EXTRINSIC REINFORCEMENT

Extrinsic motivation refers to behavior that is driven by external rewards, such as money, fame, grades, or praise, or by a desire to avoid punishment. As its name suggests, these outcomes are controlled by someone other than the person performing a task—in our case, a supervising manager. Briefly stated, if high-performing individuals or groups believe they are not rewarded more than others, or if they see little being done to "correct" unsatisfactory behavior, their motivation to achieve performance goals will suffer.

"Performance Matters!"

When managers link rewards to desired behaviors, they reinforce that behavior (Luthans & Stajkovic, 1999; Stajkovic & Luthans, 2001). Reinforcing productive behavior sends a clear message that "performance matters." Ed Lawler, one of the foremost

authorities on reward systems, underscored this point when he said, "Often the early reward systems of an organization are particularly important in shaping its culture. They reinforce certain behavior patterns and signal how highly valued different individuals are by the organization. They also attract a certain type of employee and in a host of little ways indicate what the organization stands for and values" (Lawler, 2000a, p. 39).

Some modern management practices seem to challenge the principle that rewards should be linked to performance. Many companies are minimizing distinctions between workers by providing attractive universal benefits like recreational facilities, library services, day care, and attractive stock option programs for all employees. One aeronautics firm in France tried to help employees foster a stronger personal connection to the company by allowing them to use company tools and time to create personal artifacts (Anteby, 2008). Cognex Corporation provides incentives such as free films and refreshments at the local movie theater or the use of a limo for five hours. The company's CEO, Dr. Robert J. Shillman, says, "Give people $500, they put it in the bank and they won't remember it. We like to do memorable things that get a bang for the buck" (Lublin, 2006).

Although there are obvious motivational benefits for employees receiving life-enhancing "perks," when universal benefits are the center of a motivation program, the organization runs the risk of undermining the motivation of high performers. Although there is evidence that some companies decrease turnover by employing creative incentives, focusing exclusively on incentives that everyone receives may come with a cost. Organizations that overlook the vital link between performance and rewards may find it difficult to attract and retain the strongest performers (Pfeffer, 1995).

It may sound self-evident, but managers seeking to improve performance in their work units must make it clear that "performance matters." Regardless of how closely general (organizational-level) rewards are linked to performance, managers should use local (unit-level) rewards, such as awards and other forms of recognition, to reinforce performance. Speaking of awards, here are some tips for their effective use: (1) give the awards publicly, (2) use awards infrequently, (3) embed them in a credible reward process, (4) use the awards presentation to acknowledge past recipients, and (5) make sure the award is meaningful within the organization's culture (Lawler, 2000a, pp. 72–73).

In addition to formal recognition, managers' daily interactions with subordinates are powerful reinforcers.

Examples include whose opinions you consult when challenging problems arise, who you include in a promotion list, who you select for special projects and to make presentations outside the unit, who you ask to stand in for you in your absence, and even what you focus on during a project report.

Managers who consistently align their actions with high-performance expectations avoid what has been referred to as "the folly of rewarding A while hoping for B" (Kerr, 1995), illustrated by this example. Suppose that a vice president of research and development has a low tolerance for conflict. She might genuinely want her work teams to generate creative breakthroughs. But if she consistently rewards only the teams that avoid disagreement, her employees might think twice before bringing up new and challenging ideas. In a way, rewarding only unity and harmony means that she is unintentionally *punishing* work groups that propose radical ideas. In other words, she is "rewarding A" (conformity) while "hoping for B" (creativity).

Here's a favorite example of how managers' daily behaviors influence the behavior of work-unit members. Let's imagine that a manager would like those he supervises to take more initiative. Instead of bringing every detail to him for approval, he wants them to figure out more things on their own. With this goal in mind, Table 6.2 contains two lists of actions that will positively or negatively reinforce initiative-taking.

Table 6.2	Reinforcing Subordinate Initiative	
Positive	**Negative**
Ask "How are we going to tackle this situation?" "What can I do to help you achieve this result?" "How will we use this result?," thus implying you will both work together to achieve results both will benefit from.	Tell them "This is your responsibility. If you fail, we all fail."
Ask open-ended questions that demonstrate interest and prompt factual information.	Ask questions in an interrogative fashion, only allowing employees to answer "yes" or "no" before moving to the next question.
Allow employees to analyze and evaluate organization issues by using their best judgment.	Take employees' analysis and recommendations as a personal attack on management, thus refusing to take evaluations seriously.
Clearly identify organization goals, allowing employees to suggest improvements.	Command change by using authoritarian tone or intimidation.
Explain that there may be some imbalance in the weight they placed on different points, and ask them to review and revise their plans.	Mark-up their written plans crossing out anything you disagree with.

SOURCE: *Based on* Putting Management Theories to Work *by Marion S. Kellogg, revised by Irving Burstiner. Simon & Schuster Adult Publishing Group Copyright © 1979 by Prentice Hall. All rights reserved.*

As this example demonstrates, actions and reactions that might appear insignificant to the boss often have strong reinforcing effects on subordinates. Hence the truism, "Managers get what they reinforce, not what they want," and its companion, "People do what is inspected, not what is expected." Indeed, the reinforcing potential of managers' reactions to subordinates' behaviors is so strong that it has been argued, "The best way to change an individual's behavior in a work setting is to change his or her manager's behavior" (Thompson, 1978, p. 52).

Rewards and Discipline

The study of behavioral psychology, generally referred to as "behaviorism," was pioneered by B. F. Skinner (1953). Its focus on "things you can observe and measure" was very appealing, and it soon became the dominant paradigm in social science. Central to behaviorism, the term "operant conditioning" is used to describe the process of shaping others' behavior through linking rewards and punishments with behaviors (Miltenberger, 2008). This approach uses a wide variety of motivational strategies that involve the presentation or withdrawal of positive or negative reinforcers. **Reinforcement** refers to anything that increases the frequency of a behavior. **Positive reinforcement** involves adding something that is pleasant; **negative reinforcement** refers to removing something that is unpleasant. A related term, **punishment**, refers to adding something negative when undesired behaviors occur. For our purposes, we will focus on the use of positive reinforcement (*rewards*) to increase the frequency of performance-enhancing behavior and the use of punishment (*discipline*) to decrease the frequency of performance-inhibiting behaviors. Before discussing the use of rewards and discipline, it is important to point out the futility of hoping a "nonresponse" to negative behavior will have the same consequence as punishment. One can think of a nonresponse as *ignoring* (overlooking, not paying attention to) unproductive or socially unacceptable comments and actions.

If a person acts inappropriately because that behavior has been positively reinforced in the past, then consistently ignoring that behavior will eventually lead to its elimination, or "extinction." Think of a parent in a check-out lane at a store with a screaming child who, out of desperation, buys a candy bar to quiet the child. If, in the future, the parent can put up with the screaming in the checkout lane, removing the positive reinforcer will eventually eliminate the negative behavior. In an organizational context, sexist, crude or rude comments might be positively rewarded by smiles, winks, or laughter from similarly minded peers. But what about persistent negative behaviors at work that have not been positively reinforced in the past?

From psychology we learn that humans are compelled to interpret (make sense of, explain) their environment, especially others' responses to our actions, and our tendency is to code these responses as either positive (approval) or negative (disapproval) feedback. In this binary coding scheme, nonresponses are interpreted as negative or positive based on the response the actor expected—more specifically, they are interpreted as the opposite of what was expected. In the case of unproductive or socially unacceptable behaviors, if they ignored by those who have the authority to correct them, the absence of an expected punishment will likely be interpreted as a positive response. ("Because my boss didn't object to what I just said/did, which is not what I expected, it's OK to repeat it.") So as strange as it might seem, ignoring negative behavior can have the same effect as rewarding it. Here are two things to remember about the unintended consequences of ignoring bad behavior: "*Not doing* something is still *doing something*," and more specifically, "There is no such thing as a *neutral* nonresponse to bad behavior."

It is important to note that failure to reward positive behavior can be equally detrimental to performance. In this case, a nonresponse to positive behavior will likely be interpreted as punishment. ("I have voluntarily worked extra hours this week to complete a big project and it's as if no one cared—I haven't heard a single 'Thanks.' You won't see me doing this again.") One fascinating study exhibited how failing to give recognition eroded people's persistence. Student subjects in the study were asked to complete mindless paperwork for minimal financial rewards and were told they could stop participating whenever they wished. Each time the subjects finished a page of work, they handed it to the experimenter, who either acknowledged the sheet (looked at it and nodded before placing it in a pile), ignored it (didn't look at it before placing it on the pile), or shredded it (immediately put it in a shredder without even looking at it). As you might expect, subjects whose work was shredded were the quickest to withdraw from the experiment. But more surprisingly, subjects whose work was ignored quit the experiment almost as quickly (Ariely, Kamenica, & Prelec, 2008). Failing

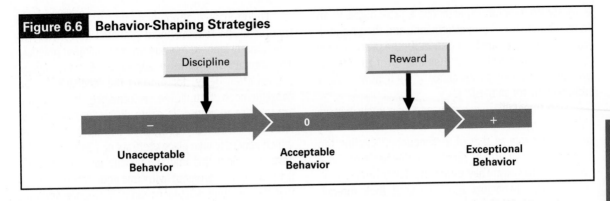

Figure 6.6 | Behavior-Shaping Strategies

Discipline

Reward

−

0

+

Unacceptable
Behavior

Acceptable
Behavior

Exceptional
Behavior

to recognize an employee's good behaviors might extinguish them almost as quickly as if you destroyed his or her work.

In as much as not responding to negative or positive behavior yields unreliable results, we turn our attention to the effective use of disciplining and rewarding strategies, as shown in Figure 6.3. The **disciplining** approach involves responding negatively to an employee's behavior in order to discourage future occurrences. For example, if an employee is consistently late, a supervisor may reprimand him with the hope of decreasing the employee's tardiness. Consistently correcting subordinates when they fail to obey safety regulations is another example.

The **rewarding** approach consists of linking desired behaviors with employee-valued outcomes. When a management trainee completes a report in a timely manner, the supervisor should praise his promptness. If a senior executive takes the initiative to solve a thorny, time-consuming problem on her own, she could be given some extra time to enjoy a scenic location at the conclusion of a business trip. Unfortunately, it appears that even simple rewards like these are rarely given. Dr. Noelle Nelson, the author of a book on the power of appreciation in the workplace (2005), points out that according to U.S. Department of Labor data, the number one reason people leave their job is that they do not feel appreciated. She also points to a Gallup poll report that 65 percent of workers said they didn't receive a single word of praise or recognition during the past year. Elaborating on these data, Nelson argues that even the most energetic and effective employees get worn down when they are rarely acknowledged for their good work and only singled out when they make mistakes.

When used appropriately, disciplining and rewarding are useful tools for fostering performance, and each has its place in the effective manager's motivational repertoire. As Figure 6.6 shows, each is associated with different behavior-shaping goals. Discipline should be used to extinguish unacceptable behaviors. However, once an individual's behavior has reached an acceptable level, negative responses will not push the behavior up to the exceptional level. The left-hand side of Figure 6.6 shows that subordinates work to remove an aversive response rather than to gain a desired reward. In contrast, as portrayed in the right side, positive reinforcement provides employees with what they want and, therefore, the incentive to achieve higher levels of performance.

The emphasis in Figure 6.6 on matching discipline and rewards with unacceptable and acceptable behaviors, respectively, highlights two common misapplications of reinforcement principles. First, top performers frequently get upset because they feel "management is too soft on those guys who are not pulling their load." Thinking it is good management practice always to be upbeat and optimistic and to discourage negative interactions, some managers try to downplay the seriousness of mistakes by ignoring them, by personally fixing errors, or by encouraging the high performers to be more tolerant and patient. Although there is a lot to be said for managers having a positive attitude, their failure to discipline unproductive behavior leads to two undesirable outcomes: The morale of high performers is threatened, and the poor performers' behaviors are not improved. The challenge of using discipline appropriately is examined in detail later.

Just as some managers find it unpleasant to issue reprimands for poor performance, other managers have difficulty praising exceptional performance. As a result, subordinates complain, "Nothing ever satisfies him." This second misapplication of the negative-response behavior-shaping strategy is just as dysfunctional as the indiscriminate use of praise. These managers mistakenly believe the best way to motivate people is by always keeping expectations a little higher than their subordinates' best performance and then reminding them that they are falling short. In the process, they run the risk of burning out their staff or inadvertently encouraging lower performance ("We'll never satisfy him, so why try so hard?").

Unfortunately, many managers genuinely believe this is the best way to manage in all situations. They define their role as that of a "sheepdog," circling the perimeter of the group, nipping at the heels of those who begin to stray. They establish a fairly broad range of acceptable behaviors and then limit their interactions with employees to barking at those who exceed the boundaries. This negative, desultory style of management creates a demoralizing work environment and does not foster exceptional performance. Instead, workers are motivated to stay out of the boss's way and to avoid doing anything unusual or untried. Innovation and involvement are extinguished, and mundane performance becomes not only acceptable but desirable.

Here's a final word on the use of rewards as performance incentives: Be aware of cultural differences regarding the desirability of individual vs. group rewards. Individuals from collectivist cultures, mostly Asia, tend to favor rewards delivered at the group level (Graham & Trevor, 2000; Parker, 2001; Triandis, 1994). So, in addition to all of the factors managers must consider in developing incentives, they must also take into consideration the employees' culturally based assumptions about what is the appropriate unit of analysis (group or individual) for measuring and rewarding performance. If a manager is planning a bonus system for a work unit consisting of a mixture of individuals holding collectivist and individualist value perspectives, the manager should look for ways to factor these conflicting perspectives into the design of the bonus program.

Reinforcement Timing

As a general rule, the longer the delay in the administration of rewards, the less reinforcement value they have. Ironically, in a worst-case situation, the mistiming of a reward may actually reinforce undesirable behaviors. For instance, if a manager gives an employee a long-overdue raise only when she complains about the unfairness of the reward system, the manager may actually be reinforcing complaining rather than good work performance. Moreover, failure to give a reward immediately after a desired behavior makes it difficult for employees to sustain desirable behaviors in the future, since they may lose confidence that rewards will follow their sustained efforts.

Unfortunately, although timing is a critical contributor to the reinforcement potential of a reward, it is frequently ignored in everyday management practice. The formal administrative apparatus of many organizations often delays for months the feedback on the consequences of employee performance. It is customary practice to restrict in-depth discussions of job performance to formally designated appraisal interviews, which generally take place every six or 12 months. ("I'll have to review this matter officially later, so why do it twice?") The problem with this common practice is that the resulting delay between performance and outcomes dilutes the effectiveness of any rewards, or discipline, dispensed as a result of the evaluation process.

By contrast, effective managers understand the importance of immediate, spontaneous rewards. They use the formal performance evaluation process to discuss long-term trends in performance, solve problems inhibiting performance, and set performance goals. But they don't expect these infrequent general discussions to significantly alter an employee's motivation. For this, they rely on brief, frequent, highly visible performance feedback.

Peters and Waterman, in their classic book *In Search of Excellence* (1988), stress the importance of immediacy by relating the following amusing anecdote:

> At Foxboro, a technical advance was desperately needed for survival in the company's early days. Late one evening, a scientist rushed into the president's office with a working prototype. Dumbfounded at the elegance of the solution and bemused about how to reward it, the president bent forward in his chair, rummaged through most of the drawers in his desk, found something, leaned over the desk to the scientist, and said, "Here!" In his hand was a banana, the only reward he could immediately put his hands on. From that point on, the small "gold banana" pin has been the highest accolade for scientific achievement at Foxboro. (pp. 70–71)

The implication for effective management is clear: Effective rewards are spontaneous rewards. Reward programs that become highly routinized, especially those linked to formal performance appraisal systems, lose their immediacy.

There is a second critical aspect of reinforcement timing: the consistency of reward administration. Administering a reward every time a behavior occurs is called

continuous reinforcement. Administering rewards on an intermittent basis (the same reward is always used but is not given every time it is warranted) is referred to as **partial reinforcement**, or **intermittent reinforcement**. Neither approach is clearly superior; both approaches have trade-offs. Continuous reinforcement represents the fastest way to establish new behavior. For example, if a boss consistently praises a subordinate for writing reports using the manager's preferred format, the subordinate will readily adopt that style in order to receive more and more contingent rewards. However, if the boss suddenly takes an extended leave of absence, the learned behavior will be highly vulnerable to extinction because the reinforcement pattern is broken. By contrast, while partial reinforcement results in slow learning, it is very resistant to extinction. The persistence associated with gambling behavior illustrates the addictive nature of a partial reinforcement schedule. Not knowing when the next payoff may come preserves the myth that the jackpot is only one more try away.

It is important to realize that continuous reinforcement systems are rare in organizations unless they are mechanically built into the job, as in the case of a "piece-rate pay plan" (employees are paid for each item they produce or sell). Seldom are individuals rewarded every time they make a good presentation or effectively handle a customer's complaint. When we recognize that most work in organizations is governed by an intermittent reinforcement schedule, we gain new insights into some of the more frustrating aspects of a manager's role. For example, it helps explain why new employees seem to take forever to catch on to how the boss wants things done. It also suggests why it is so difficult to extinguish outdated behaviors, particularly in long-time employees.

INTRINSIC REINFORCEMENT

Our examination thus far of how managers can facilitate high performance has focused on the use of extrinsic outcomes to reinforce performance-enhancing behavior: "When you do A, you will receive B." **Intrinsic motivation**, sometimes referred to as self-motivation, occurs when individuals perform activities because they enjoy doing them, for their own sake, or to receive self-administered rewards pertaining to personal development, such as a sense of accomplishment or mastery. The expression "I enjoy my work so much I would continue doing it even if I wasn't paid" typifies intrinsic motivation. It is worth noting that the early work on intrinsic motivation was viewed as a much-needed antidote to the dominant

paradigm of behaviorism. Appropriately, the most widely cited conception of intrinsic motivation is called self-determination theory (Deci & Ryan, 1985).

Today, it is generally understood that people who engage in intrinsically satisfying activities experience a sense of purpose, feelings of accomplishment, enhanced self-esteem, and the development of new skills and interests (Ryan & Deci, 2000). Due to these beneficial outcomes, coupled with a strong inner desire to control their lives, it has been shown that intrinsically motivated individuals are more successful than those who merely seek external rewards (Ryan & Deci, 2017; Pink, 2017).

Theories of intrinsic motivation argue that it is activated by the fulfillment of certain human needs: *competence (mastery), autonomy, relatedness (social connection),* and a sense of *purpose* (Deci & Ryan, 2017; Pink, 2017). **Competence** refers to the innate desire to be good at the things we do and to excel in something. **Autonomy** refers to the desire for self-governance—the ability to control what we do, as well as when and how we do it. **Relatedness** pertains to our desire to connect with others in meaningful ways, including giving and receiving care and support. **Purpose** pertains to our desire to find meaning in what we do—it's the answer to the question, "Why am I doing this—day after day?"

Some people have stronger needs for intrinsic rewards than others. For example, researchers have discovered that for highly intelligent people, job satisfaction is closely linked to the degree of difficulty they encounter in performing their work (Ganzach, 1998). Younger workers, too, seem to place a greater emphasis on intrinsic rewards and meaningfulness. The millennial generation (people born between 1981 and 1996) has often been described as generally idealistic and focused on doing work that serves a cause.

Adam Grant, the author of *Give and Take*, argues that people perform best at work when they are focused on helping and giving to others—satisfying their need for connection. His research showed, for instance, that students who worked at a university telefund (as cold callers asking for alumni donations) increased their fundraising effectiveness by 400 percent after listening to one scholarship recipient describe how much the alumni donations meant to her personally. The impact of that single conversation was still impacting employee performance three months later (Grant, 2011). Researchers have also found that many workers long for a sense of purpose, or "calling," at work—a belief that they are doing work they were meant to do and that serves an important cause. One example is a study of zookeepers, whose sense of calling propelled them to devote tremendous effort and sacrifice for their animals at work, even with very limited extrinsic rewards (Bunderson & Thompson, 2009).

Management Practices

Managers intuitively understand the importance of intrinsic motivation. No matter how many external rewards managers use, if individuals find their jobs uninteresting and unfulfilling, performance will suffer. Supporting these intuitions, research has shown that, compared with extrinsic motivation, intrinsic motivation is associated with higher performance, stronger persistence in the face of obstacles, and greater creativity (Deci & Ryan, 1985; Ryan & Deci, 2017). In brief, intrinsic motivation is superior to extrinsic motivation. This is partly due to the fact that intrinsic rewards are self-administered.

Given the obvious merits of intrinsic motivation, research conducted by Kinley and Ben-Hur (2015) is a bit puzzling. They asked more than 500 managers from multiple countries what motivates them. The authors report that these responses contain elements linked to autonomy, mastery, connection, and purpose. However, when they asked what these managers did to motivate their subordinates, most mentioned things like merit increases, bonuses, and awards. From a manager's perspective, this finding is not surprising. Compared with managers routinely administering their organization's package of organizational rewards, the challenge of creating work environments that foster intrinsic motivation can seem overwhelming.

The good news is that what effective managers do, on a day-to-day basis, contributes to this type of work environment. It is noteworthy that many of the management practices described in the Interpersonal Skills and Group Skills sections of this book can contribute to the fulfillment of employees' needs for competence/mastery, autonomy, supportive relationships, and a sense of purpose. Here are a few examples of those practices.

❑ *Competence/Mastery:* Provide opportunities for individuals to expand their skill-set through job rotation, participation in interdepartmental projects, and overseas assignments. Encourage skill development through training and education. Acknowledge individuals' expertise by seeking their input on important decisions. Set performance goals that are challenging. Provide timely, accurate, and honest feedback on performance. Celebrate individual accomplishments.

❑ *Autonomy:* Promote self-management by involving others in making decisions and setting goals. Empower subordinates by delegating responsibility and authority. Create a positive work environment, where people feel valued and appreciated. Invite suggestions for improvement, including radical ideas. If necessary, use personal power and influence to "sell" these proposals to higher levels of management. Provide negative feedback in ways that build, rather than undermine, initiative and self-confidence.

❑ *Supportive Relationships:* Help others build supportive social networks through the use of relationship-building roles and assignments. Use supportive communication to foster positive interpersonal relationships with team members. Support unit members by providing resources, both within and outside the work unit, required to achieve performance goals. Manage interpersonal conflicts in such a way that the parties support the outcome and feel they have been fairly treated. Use power and influence to get qualified unit members promoted. Provide incentives for performance that are personally salient and in a manner that is perceived as fair.

❑ *Sense of Purpose:* Seek to understand individuals' values and life-goals. Ask what they find most rewarding about their job and seek to maximize those opportunities. Help individuals understand the importance of their contributions to unit-level performance expectations and goals. Help them understand how their individual job assignments, as well as the work of the unit, contribute to the mission and purpose of the organization.

Job Characteristics

Among the many ways managers can facilitate intrinsic motivation none is more important than organizing work activities in ways that make them enjoyable and fulfilling. **Job design** is the process of matching job characteristics to workers' skills, interests, and needs (Hackman & Oldham, 1980). A variation of job design, **job crafting**, allows workers to redesign their own jobs to promote job satisfaction and enhanced engagement (Wrzesniewski & Dutton, 2001; Berg, Dutton, & Wrzesniewski, 2013).

The most prominent model of job design identifies a set of job characteristics that explain the motivating potential of the job (Hackman & Oldham, 1980; Oldham & Fried, 2016). Although these

Figure 6.7 Designing Highly Motivating Jobs

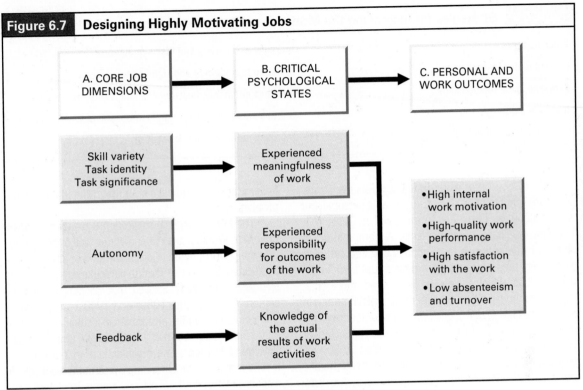

SOURCE: *Hackman/Oldham*, Work Redesign, © 1980. Reprinted by permission of Pearson Education, Inc.

authors use somewhat different terminology than the authors previously cited, this is a proven approach for fostering intrinsic motivation and satisfaction. Figure 6.7 shows the relationship between the three components of their framework: core job dimensions (characteristics), the psychological states they produce in employees, and the resulting personal and work outcomes.

The greater the variety of skills one uses at work, the more one perceives the work as meaningful or worthwhile. Similarly, the more an individual can perform a complete job from beginning to end (task identity) and the more the work has a direct effect on the work or lives of other people (task significance), the more the employee will view the job as meaningful. On the other hand, when the work requires few skills, only part of a task is performed, or there seems to be little effect on others, experienced meaningfulness is low.

In addition, the more autonomy one has at work (i.e., freedom to choose how and when to do particular jobs), the more responsibility one feels for successes and failures. Increased responsibility results in increased commitment to one's work. Managers can increase employee autonomy by such things as instituting flexible work schedules, decentralizing decision-making, or removing formalized controls, such as punching a

time clock. Autonomy appears to be particularly important for employees doing knowledge-intensive work (Haas, 2010).

Finally, the more feedback individuals receive about how well they are doing their jobs, the more knowledge they have about how to improve. Recent research shows that employees invest more time in tasks that provide more and better feedback (Northcraft, Schmidt, & Ashford, 2011). Managers may provide feedback directly to employees or create opportunities for them to gain feedback through direct contact with clients.

One line of research on job design has searched for conditions that moderate the two relationships (A → B, B → C) portrayed in Figure 6.7 (Oldham & Fried, 2016). Promising possibilities include a person's personality, knowledge and skill level, physical work environment and career stage. The authors of the job design movement proposed a moderator they called Growth Need Strength (GNS) (Hackman & Oldham, 1980). GNS refers to the strength of a person's need for personal accomplishment, learning, and development. These "GNS needs" are similar to the needs for self-actualization, growth, and achievement, prominent in broad conceptions of human needs that we will discuss in the next section. It was argued that high/low GNS scores increase/decrease the impact of A → B and B → C.

Table 6.3	Strategies for Increasing the Motivational Potential of Assigned Work		
Combine tasks	$\rightarrow$		Increase skill variety and task significance
Form identifiable work units	$\rightarrow$		Increase task identity and significance
Establish client relationships	$\rightarrow$		Increase autonomy, task identity, and feedback
Increase authority	$\rightarrow$		Increase autonomy, task significance, and task identity
Open feedback channels	$\rightarrow$		Increase autonomy and feedback

This discussion of work design suggests five strategies managers can use to increase desirable personal and work outcomes. These are summarized in Table 6.3. The first one is to *combine tasks*. A combination of tasks is, by definition, a more challenging and complex work assignment. It requires workers to use a wider variety of skills, which makes the work seem more challenging and meaningful. A related managerial principle is to *form identifiable work units* so task identity and task significance can be increased. For example, clerical work in a large insurance firm was handled by 80 employees, organized by functional task. To create higher levels of task identity and task significance, the firm reorganized the clerical staff into eight self-contained groups. Each group handled all business associated with specific clients. As a result, they felt a greater sense of meaningfulness because they were using a greater variety of skills, were engaged in completing an entire task, and could see their contributions more clearly.

The third guideline for enhancing jobs is to *establish client relationships*. A client relationship involves an ongoing personal relationship between an employee (the producer) and the client (the consumer). The establishment of this relationship can increase autonomy, task identity, and feedback. Interacting with the beneficiaries of one's work can have a surprisingly positive impact on employee effort and effectiveness (like it did for the telefund employees mentioned in the previous section). One example of a company taking this principle seriously is Caterpillar Inc., which assigns members of each division's R&D group to make regular contact with their major clients.

The fourth suggestion, *increase authority*, refers to granting more authority for making job-related decisions to workers. As supervisors delegate more authority and responsibility, their subordinates' perceived autonomy, task significance, and task identity increase. Historically, workers on auto assembly lines have had little decision-making authority. However, in conjunction with increased emphasis on quality, many plants now allow workers to adjust their equipment, reject faulty materials, and even shut down the line if a major problem is evident.

The fifth managerial suggestion is to *open feedback channels*. Workers need to know how well or how poorly they are performing their jobs if any kind of improvement is expected. Younger workers in particular expect frequent feedback. One study showed that 85 percent of Generation Y (born in the 1980s and 1990s) workers want "frequent and candid performance feedback," whereas only half of baby boomer (1947–1960) employees do. This trend has led some organizations to seek creative mechanisms for providing employees more feedback. In response to this study, Ernst and Young developed a system called the "feedback zone," which allows employees to request or submit feedback at any time (Hite, 2008).

The overall record of job redesign interventions is impressive. Historically, firms that carefully redesign jobs typically report a substantial increase in productivity, work quality, and worker satisfaction (reflected in lower rates of absenteeism). For example, early results of the job redesign movement included the following: The Social Security Administration increased productivity 23.5 percent among a group of 50 employees; General Electric realized a 50 percent increase in product quality as a result of a job redesign program; and the absenteeism rate among data-processing operators at Travelers Insurance decreased 24 percent (Kopelman, 1985). In addition, a review of 33 job design interventions reports that job crafting contributes to higher job performance and individual well-being (Daniels, et al., 2017).

As a way of gauging the level of intrinsic satisfaction within a work unit, as circumstances permit, managers might openly explore this subject with unit members, possibly as part of a regular performance review discussion, or as the focus of a different conversation devoted to this subject. Through these conversations, managers can better understand (1) the value a person places on intrinsic satisfaction, (2) which aspects of their job are most/least enjoyable, and (3) their level of interest in crafting assigned tasks so they better match the attributes shown in Figure 6.7.

Strengthen the *Outcomes* → *Satisfaction* Link

We now turn our attention to the third component in our framework: one's personal satisfaction with performance-based rewards. As shown in Figure 6.8, there are two moderating conditions that determine the strength of the Outcomes → Satisfaction link. **Reward salience** refers to the extent to which an outcome is personally valued because it satisfies an important need. The second contingency, **perceived equity**, refers to a person's perception that valued outcomes are distributed fairly. We will examine ways in which managers can ensure that these conditions are in place.

HUMAN NEEDS

One of the common mistakes managers make in use of rewards to enhance performance is misunderstanding their subordinates' reward preferences. For example, managers often assume that most people prefer cash incentives. But according to a 2004 study conducted by the University of Chicago, performance improves much faster when it is linked to noncash rewards (14.6 percent increase for cash vs. 38.6 percent increase for noncash)

(Cook, 2005, p. 6). Managers need to develop a sound understanding of their employees' personal needs and motivations before adopting a particular incentive.

A variety of approaches for understanding human needs have been advanced. They can be classified as hierarchical and nonhierarchical. **Hierarchical needs theories** posit that people are motivated to satisfy their most basic unfulfilled need. That is, until a lower-level need has been satisfied, a higher-level need won't become activated. The best-known, and earliest, example of a hierarchical needs theory was proposed by Abraham Maslow (1970, 1954). He posited five levels of needs, beginning with physiological and followed by safety, belongingness, esteem, and self-actualization. Clay Alderfer proposed a more parsimonious hierarchical model (1977) that contains only three levels, or categories: existence (Maslow's physiological), relatedness (social), and growth (self-actualization). A comparison of these hierarchical needs models is shown in Table 6.4. Like Maslow, Alderfer proposed that satisfied needs become dormant unless a dramatic shift in circumstances increases their salience. For example, a middle-level executive who is fired during a hostile takeover may suddenly find that her interest in personal growth is overwhelmed by a pressing need for security.

Figure 6.8 Strengthen the *Outcomes* → *Satisfaction* Link

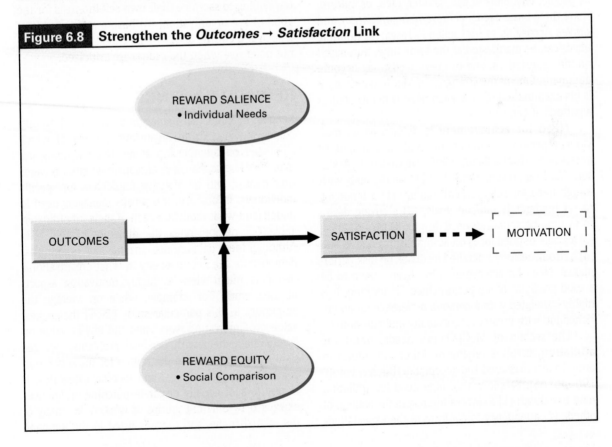

While anecdotal examples such as this lend credibility to hierarchical models, critics argue that research has failed to validate the ranking of these needs or show that a definitive hierarchy exists (Rutledge, 2011). For example, it is argued that social connections are required for the accomplishment of any human need. Hence, despite the popularity of hierarchical theories, managers should use caution in using them to predict the active needs of others.

> **MyLab Management** Watch it!
>
> If your instructor has assigned this activity, go to www.pearson.com/mylab/management to complete the video exercise.

An alternative to these hierarchical theories was proposed by David McClelland (1988). In contrast to hierarchical models, in which needs are categorized based on their inherent strength (hunger is a stronger need than self-actualization), McClelland argues that all people, regardless of age, gender, race, or culture, share three basic needs: *achievement, affiliation,* and *power.* According to McClelland's research, multiple needs can be manifested at the same time, but, based on life experiences, one of these needs may become dominant. One of the strengths of McClelland's work is his examination of how each need is manifested as a pattern of behavior.

Need for achievement is defined as an individual's personal "competition with a standard of excellence" (McClelland, 1965; McClelland, Arkinson, Clark, & Lowell, 1953, p. 111). Individuals with a high need for achievement exhibit: (1) a tendency to set moderately difficult goals, (2) a strong desire to assume personal responsibility for work activities, (3) a single-minded focus on accomplishing a task, and (4) a strong desire for detailed feedback on task performance. Need for achievement has been shown to be a good predictor of job performance. In addition, it is highly correlated with a person's preference for an enriched job with greater responsibility and autonomy.

The second of McClelland's needs, **need for affiliation**, involves relying on other individuals in order to feel reassured and acceptable (Birch & Veroff, 1966, p. 65). People with a high need for affiliation tend to exhibit: (1) a sincere interest in the feelings of others; (2) a tendency to conform to the expectations of others, especially those whose affiliation they value; and (3) a strong desire for reassurance and approval from others. In contrast to the need for achievement, the need for affiliation does not seem to be strongly correlated with job performance.

Rounding out McClelland's model is the **need for power**, which represents a desire to influence others and to control one's environment. Individuals with a high need for power seek leadership positions and tend to influence others in a fairly open, direct manner. McClelland and Burnham (2003) suggest two manifestations of the need for power. Individuals with a high need for personal power tend to seek power and influence for its own sake. To them, control, dominance, and conquest are important indicators of personal efficacy. These leaders inspire their subordinates to perform heroic feats, but for the sake of the leader, not the organization. By contrast, individuals with high institutional power needs are more oriented toward using their influence to advance the goals of the group or organization. According to McClelland, these people: (1) are organization minded, feeling personally responsible for advancing the purposes of the organization; (2) enjoy work and accomplishing tasks in an orderly fashion; (3) are often willing to sacrifice their own self-interests for the good of the organization; (4) have a strong sense of justice and equity; and (5) seek expert advice and are not defensive when their ideas are criticized.

REWARD SALIENCE

Keeping in mind that managers don't control all outcomes provided in an organization, many of which are based on membership alone, understanding human needs helps managers anticipate whether rewards they control will be effective reinforcers for specific individuals. In practice, this means managers need to understand what motivates each of their subordinates. Table 6.5 demonstrates the difficulty of this task. Although these data are not current, they nonetheless demonstrate the heterogeneity in what organizational members might view as highly motivating aspects of their work. For example, while on average the employees in this particular study placed the highest value on "interesting work" and the lowest value on "sympathetic help with personal problems," we see significant differences in the ratings for these two outcomes across gender, age, and income categories. It is easy to spot equally disparate outcome preferences expressed by different groups of workers for many of the other benefits and rewards listed in the left-hand

Table 6.4	Comparison of Hierarchical Needs Theories	
Maslow	**Alderfer**	
Self-actualization	Growth	
Esteem		
Belongingness	Relatedness	
Safety		
Physiological	Existence	

column, which are commonly used by business firms to attract, retain, and motivate employees.

Scanning the data in Table 6.5, one sees the folly of stereotyping individuals based on a single attribute. We always need to keep in mind that data showing differences in preferences based on gender, age, income, job classification, or organizational position are "average responses" for each subgroup. Thus, while we see differences within each subgroup's preferences, the salience that individuals attach to performance-related rewards is not fully explained by any one of these attributes.

In the abstract, it is not surprising to learn that individuals with different demographic and economic profiles have different needs and, thus, bring different expectations to the workplace. But at least one research study suggests that managers are not particularly good at predicting how their subordinates would rank outcomes, such as those shown in Table 6.5 (LeDue, 1980). More particularly, this research suggests that managers tend to base their answers to the question "What motivates your subordinates?" on two faulty assumptions. First, they assume the outcome preferences among their subordinates are fairly homogenous, and second, they assume their personal outcome preferences are similar to those held by their subordinates. Knowing this, the data shown in Table 6.5 illustrate how easy it is for managers with a certain gender, age, and income profile to systematically misread the salient needs of subordinates representing a different profile. Furthermore, it is not difficult to imagine individual circumstances that would result in a person's preferences being significantly different from those of others with a similar demographic and economic profile. In summary, this data underscores the importance of managers getting to know their subordinates well enough that they can effectively match individual and group performance expectations with personally salient outcomes.

The importance of gaining this person-specific information is illustrated in the case of a stockbroker who was promoted to office manager because upper management in the home office felt he was "the most qualified and most deserving." Unfortunately, they failed to ask him if he wanted to be promoted. Because they had worked hard to qualify for their management positions, they assumed that all hard workers were similarly motivated. Two weeks after receiving his "reward" for outstanding performance, the super-stockbroker-turned-manager was in the hospital with a stress-related illness.

One way that managers can gain information about salient needs and personal values is through informal discussions with their subordinates about expectations, responsibilities, challenges, and opportunities. When engaging in such discussions, it is important to keep in mind that there are always trade-offs between the rewards employees might value. Thus, it might be particularly instructive to see how an employee responds to a discussion about how a colleague's new job provides opportunities for more pay, but at the expense of being away from home three nights a week. Similarly, the opportunity to be involved with the design of a new product line also might mean longer hours at work, higher levels of personal stress, and the possibility that the failure to meet high expectations may reflect negatively on the team members.

The data reported in Table 6.5 are also relevant for individuals in a position to shape the pay and benefits package for an entire organization. Scanning these results, it is easy to discern differences between the ratings of blue-collar and white-collar, unskilled and skilled, lower- and higher-level employees. Recognizing the wide disparity in outcome preferences within the employee ranks of most large businesses, many firms, ranging from investment banks to manufacturing firms, have experimented with "cafeteria-style" incentive systems (Abbott, 1997; Lawler, 1987). This approach takes much of the guesswork out of linking an individual's organizational membership and work performance with personally salient outcomes by allowing employees some say in the matching process. Using this approach, employees receive a certain number of work credits based on performance, seniority, or task difficulty, and they are allowed to trade those in for a variety of benefits, including upgraded insurance packages, financial planning services, disability income plans, extended vacation benefits, tuition reimbursement for educational programs, and so forth.

	All Employees	Men	Women	Under 30	31–40	41–50	Over 50	Under $25,000	$25,001–$40,000	$40,001–$50,000	Over $50,000	Blue-Collar Unskilled	Blue-Collar Skilled	White-Collar Unskilled	White-Collar Skilled	Lower Nonsupervisory	Middle Nonsupervisory	Higher Nonsupervisory
Interesting work	1	1	2	4	2	3	1	5	2	1	1	2	1	1	2	3	1	1
Full appreciation of work done	2	2	1	5	3	2	2	4	3	3	2	1	6	3	1	4	2	2
Feeling of being in on things	3	3	3	6	4	1	3	6	1	2	4	5	2	5	4	5	3	3
Job security	4	5	4	2	1	4	7	2	4	4	3	4	3	7	5	2	4	6
Good wages	5	4	5	1	5	5	8	1	5	6	8	3	4	6	6	1	6	8
Promotion and growth in organization	6	6	6	3	6	8	9	3	6	5	7	6	5	4	3	6	5	5
Good working conditions	7	7	10	7	7	7	4	8	7	7	6	9	7	2	7	7	7	4
Personal loyalty to employees	8	8	8	9	9	6	5	7	8	8	5	8	9	9	8	8	8	7
Tactful discipline	9	9	9	8	10	9	10	10	9	9	10	7	10	10	9	9	9	10
Sympathetic help with personal problems	10	10	7	10	8	10	6	9	10	10	9	10	8	8	10	10	10	9

*Ranked from 1 (highest) to 10 (lowest).

SOURCE: *Courtesy of George Mason University. Results are from a study of 1,000 employees conducted in 1995.*

REWARD EQUITY

The satisfaction associated with managers' best efforts to match reinforcers with each individual's salient needs may be undermined if work-unit members perceive that valued outcomes are not fairly distributed (Cropanzano & Folger, 1996). Whereas reward salience pertains to receiving desired outcomes, perceived equity pertains to receiving deserved outcomes.

More specifically, **equity** refers to workers' perceptions of whether rewards are distributed fairly (Adams, 1963; Walster, Walster, & Bershcheid, 1978; Lawler, 1968). Evaluations of equity are based on a social comparison process in which workers individually compare what they are getting out of the work relationship (outcomes) to what they are putting into the work relationship (inputs). Outcomes include such items as pay, fringe benefits, increased responsibility, and prestige, and inputs include hours worked and work quality as well as education and experience. Employees compare the ratio of their outcomes to inputs with the corresponding ratios of other

individuals, judged to be an appropriate comparison group. The results of these comparisons inform their beliefs about reward equity.

If workers perceive inequity when they compare their outcome/input ratio with that of similar others, they will be motivated to restore equity in some way. One way they can seek to restore equity is through behavioral changes. For instance, they might request a pay raise (seek to increase their outcomes) or they can decrease their effort at work or find excuses not to do difficult assignments (decrease their inputs). Employees might also restore equity through cognitive adjustments. For instance, they may rationalize that their inputs are not as valuable as they thought (e.g., that their talents or training lag behind that of their peers) or that their coworkers are actually working harder (or more effectively) than they thought they were.

The strength of people's yearning for fairness underscores the need for managers to closely monitor subordinates' perceptions of equity (Janssen, 2001). In some cases, a manager might learn through conversations with employees that their comparison processes are faulty. For example, employees might misunderstand the value placed on certain inputs, such as experience versus expertise or quantity versus quality; or they might have unrealistic views of their own or others' performance. Since most people tend to believe that their leadership skills are better than average, these discrepancies are common.

However, just as often these discussions uncover real inequities. For example, the hourly rate of a worker may not be keeping up with recent skill upgrades or increased job responsibilities. The act of identifying and correcting legitimate inequities generates commitment and loyalty among employees. For example, a manager in the computer industry felt he had been unfairly passed over for promotion by a dishonest rival. Utilizing the company's open-door policy, he took his case to a higher level in the firm. After a thorough investigation, the decision was reversed and the rival reprimanded. The individual's response was, "After they went to bat for me, I could never leave the company."

The important thing to keep in mind about equity and fairness is that we are dealing with perceptions. Consequently, whether the employees' beliefs are accurate or distorted, legitimate or ill-founded, to the employees themselves, they are both accurate and legitimate until proven otherwise. A basic principle of social psychology states: "That which is perceived as being real is real in its consequences." Therefore, effective managers should constantly perform "reality checks" on their subordinates' perceptions of equity, using questions such as: "What criteria for promotions, pay raises, and so on do you feel management should be placing more/less emphasis on?" "Relative to others similar to you in this organization, do you feel your job assignments, promotions, and so on are appropriate?" "Why do you think Alice was recently promoted over Jack?"

To conclude our examination of how to motivate high performance, Figure 6.8 includes a feedback loop (dotted line) from Satisfaction to Motivation. This connection reminds us that satisfaction, per se, does not increase performance. Instead, it's the impact of satisfaction on motivation that increases or decreases the level of effort individuals expend in achieving performance goals.

Diagnosing and Correcting the Causes of Unacceptable Performance

Now that we've explored ways to foster high performance, we return to one of the most difficult challenges managers face—giving negative performance feedback in a manner that both improves performance and demonstrates genuine respect and support for the individual. Our approach to this challenge emphasizes the need to correctly diagnose the underlying causes of substandard performance before exploring possible remedies. As we will see, a manager's diagnosis pretty much determines whether the unacceptable performance will be corrected. Following the diagnostic phase, managers can utilize the material in the previous section to motivate acceptable performance.

DIAGNOSTIC FRAMEWORK

The formula for performance introduced in the beginning (Figure 6.1) is used here as a diagnostic tool (Figure 6.9). Whereas earlier we used this formula to explain performance, in the abstract, the arrows added in Figure 6.9 suggest its use as a guide for discovering

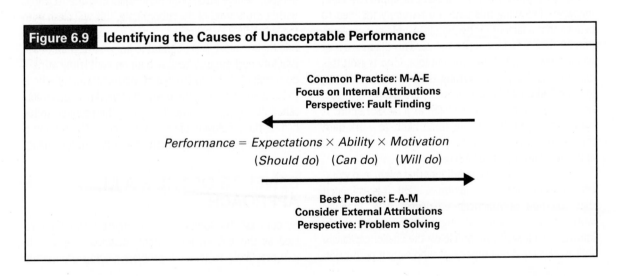

Figure 6.9 | **Identifying the Causes of Unacceptable Performance**

Common Practice: M-A-E
Focus on Internal Attributions
Perspective: Fault Finding

$$Performance = Expectations \times Ability \times Motivation$$
$$(Should\ do) \quad (Can\ do) \quad (Will\ do)$$

Best Practice: E-A-M
Consider External Attributions
Perspective: Problem Solving

why a person's (or group's) performance is substandard. When there is mutual agreement on the causes of unacceptable performance, the material in previous sections can be used to correct the problem.

Humans are programmed to seek explanations for why something happens. Young children are notorious for asking lots of "why" questions as they seek to make sense of their environment. In psychology, the explanations we formulate for behavior are called **attributions**. **External attributions** interpret someone's behavior as being caused by situational conditions, including cultural values and social norms, poverty, and education. **Internal attributions** assign causes to the attributes of individuals, such as intelligence, personality, interests, and motivation (Heider, 1958; Choi, Nisbett, & Norenzayan, 1999; Sanderson, 2010).

Psychologists studying attributions have identified a common bias in the attribution process (Ross, 1977, 2017). What is known as the **fundamental attribution error** refers to the human tendency to explain another person's behavior based on internal, dispositional factors and to underestimate the effects of external, situational conditions. This is likely because when a behavior occurs, the attention of observers naturally focuses on the individual, rather than the actor's less-visible life experiences and situational influences (Heider, 1958).

True to form, research shows that when employees fail to meet performance expectations supervisors tend to blame the individual for simply not working hard enough—not being fully committed or having a bad attitude (Bitter & Gardner, 1995). In Figure 6.9, this tendency is illustrated as an M-A-E, "right-to-left" diagnosis—beginning, and typically ending, with a motivation-deficiency explanation.

As we alluded to earlier, there are dual dangers posed by adopting the M-A-E diagnostic approach. First, managers following this path are naturally inclined to believe that a lack of motivation is a sufficient explanation for unsatisfactory performance. This diagnosis is at worst wrong, and at best incomplete. One reason this diagnosis is likely to be wrong is that, to an observer, low motivation and a lack of ability are easily confused, because they are both manifested as a lack of effort. It stands to reason that people aren't likely to work hard if they don't want to or if they don't have the requisite aptitude, training, or resources.

Consider some work conditions that might lead workers to not put forth their maximum effort. It is estimated that one-third of American employees have irregular work schedules (often involving night work), commonly known as shift work. An article on the challenges facing shift workers told of a supervisor who sought permission from the human resources department to fire a worker because he didn't "stay on task"; he often walked around talking to others and occasionally fell asleep on the job. The supervisor concluded that the employee lacked the motivation for the job. However, research on shift workers challenges the simplistic notion that unsatisfactory performance is symptomatic of low motivation and commitment. For example, shift workers sleep two to three hours less per night than day workers. They are four to five times more likely to experience digestive disorders due to eating the wrong foods at the wrong times. Chronic fatigue affects 80 percent of shift workers, while 75 percent report feeling isolated on the job. Drug and alcohol abuse are three times greater among permanent shift workers than among those with traditional work hours (Perry, 2000). Clearly, it is likely there is much more to the story here than poor motivation.

The second problem with the M-A-E inquiry is that it invariably yields harmful consequences. Imagine a performance review in which, after informing an employee that their performance is below par, the manager proceeds to, directly or indirectly, blame the problem on the person's lack of effort, possibly due to a lack of interest, commitment, or a bad attitude. From the perspective of the employee, this can feel overwhelming and unfair. Although they may have sensed that the performance feedback would be negative, it is unlikely they would have anticipated this problem becoming "personal"—finding fault with them.

Here's where a second finding about attributions is relevant. Studies have shown that when explaining our own behavior, situational factors are exaggerated for negative outcomes and dispositional factors are exaggerated for positive outcomes (Lillenfield, Jay, & Woolf, 2010; Malle, 2004; Heider, 1958.) As a consequence, if a supervisor believes that poor performance is due to things within the control of the subordinate, this will clash with the subordinate's belief that it was caused by things outside their control. It is not hard to imagine how an unsatisfactory performance review built on conflicting attributions will likely be obstructed by arguments about who is to blame (the worker, the boss, other workers, impossible schedules, etc.) and how to remedy the problem (rehabilitate the employee, offer more support). Contention is unlikely to produce constructive plans for improvement.

BENEFITS OF THE E-A-M APPROACH

By contrast, the lower arrow in Figure 6.9, characterized as the E-A-M, left-to-right, diagnostic approach, is more likely to foster a problem-solving orientation focused on solutions, not blame—making improvements and planning for a positive future, not finding fault for a regrettable past. Regardless of which of the three factors is mostly contributing to an unsatisfactory performance rating, the E-A-M diagnostic process is the best way to arrive at a mutually agreeable plan for performance improvement. Here's why.

Signaling, up front, a willingness to consider causes outside the control of the individual focuses the conversation on a shared problem, not on how to fix the person. One way to signal this intention is for supervisors to begin the discussion by openly considering the possibility that something about their performance expectations may have contributed to the problem. For example, supervisors might seek feedback on whether their expectations were both understood and accepted. A lack of understanding might suggest the expectations were not clearly laid out; a lack of acceptance might be due to the inappropriate application of what is generally expected of this particular person or task. Following the trajectory of this arrow, the diagnosis process would next explore whether the employee has the ability (personal and organizational capabilities) necessary to perform their work satisfactorily. This second line of inquiry further signals a willingness to look at this negative outcome from the subordinate's perspective—looking first for possible external causes.

Recalling the research on attributions, the E-A-M sequence has two clear benefits: It forces supervisors to set aside their natural tendency to make internal attributions, and it signals that supervisors are open to considering subordinates' natural preference for external attributions. Regardless of whether subordinates' attributions are accurate, giving them the benefit of the doubt reflects a manager's concern for their welfare over and above their performance. This "charitable" perspective is reflected in the language and tone of a manager's diagnostic questions: "Have I been clear about what is expected of you?" "Have I overlooked something you need to satisfy these expectations?" "Are you enjoying your work?" "Do you have suggestions for how I can better support you and your work activities?"

It is to be expected that in some cases the first two diagnostic inquiries ("Is this an expectations problem?" and "Is it an ability problem?") will not yield satisfactory explanations. In these cases, the third diagnostic question, "Is this a motivation problem?" is brought forward. When this is presented as the only remaining possibility, employees are more likely to explore it in an open and collaborative manner. It is hard to be upset with someone who has been willing to explore your attributions, rather than forcing theirs.

To avoid misunderstandings of our proposed approach for diagnosing and correcting unacceptable performance, let us offer some clarifications and additions. First, we hope this brief introduction to "attribution theory" helps managers understand that the proclivity of low performers to explain this negative outcome using external attributions is no more a sign of a questionable character than is a manager's natural tendency to invoke internal attributions.

Second, we are not recommending that a joint exploration into the causes of poor performance rigidly follow the E-A-M sequence: "If it wasn't caused by that, then what about this...?" Obviously, the best way to initiate this joint investigation is to ask the employee why they believe their recent performance has fallen. Our primary objective in recommending the E-A-M approach is to sensitize managers to their natural tendency to enter such an investigation having already decided that the employee is at fault. In addition to its utility as a counterweight, using the E-A-M orientation to guide the conversation helps signal, early on, a willingness to consider, without prejudice, external attributions that may be put forth.

Third, it is best if all proposed explanations, internal and external alike, are viewed as hypotheses—possibilities that require testing. For example, how long has an individual received unsatisfactory performance ratings? In cases of chronic poor performance, internal attributions are likely applicable. To ascertain the validity of proposed external attributions, managers might ask fact-finding questions such as the following: "Can you recall specific incidences in which [a lack of necessary resources] impeded your performance?" "Are you aware of others who have experienced this problem while performing similar tasks?" "When did you first become aware of this obstacle?" "What have you done to correct it?" "What remedies do you propose?" And finally, "If we were to adopt this proposed remedy, how confident are you that your next performance review will be positive?"

Summary

Our discussion of how managers can facilitate performance began by identifying the prerequisites for performance: expectations, ability, and motivation. We posited that each of these elements is required, and together they constitute the necessary conditions, for satisfactory performance. From a subjective perspective, expectations answer the question "What should I do?" the perceived ability to satisfy these expectations informs the question, "Can I do it?" which, in turn, informs the motivational question, "Will I do it?" From our examination of these building blocks of performance, it was determined that, from a manager's perspective, motivation is the most important prerequisite.

Adding to this foundational knowledge, the next section traced the evolution of academics' understanding of the relationships between motivation, performance, and satisfaction, culminating in the four-factor model, used here as an organizing framework. This framework posits that a person's motivation to perform a task is determined by the perceived strength of the connecting links between: motivation, performance, outcomes, and satisfaction. Employees' subjective assessments of the strength of the three connecting links can be expressed as a set of questions:

1. "If I work hard, how likely is it that I will achieve the intended level of performance?" ($M \rightarrow P$).
2. "If I perform at that level, how likely is it that I will receive the anticipated rewards?" ($P \rightarrow O$).
3. "How likely is it that these rewards will be personally satisfying?" ($O \rightarrow S$).

The model summarizing our discussion, Figure 6.10, shows the complete four-factor model and the moderating factors that regulate the strength of each link. Skilled managers incorporate all components of this model into their motivational efforts, rather than concentrating on a favorite subset, or the parts that are most easily implemented. There are no shortcuts to, or simplistic recommendations for, motivating employees to perform at a consistently high level. Here's an example. There is a tendency for managers to overlook the motivating consequences of what happens *after* the completion of a performance review cycle—depicted as the right two-thirds of Figure 6.10: $P \rightarrow O$ and $O \rightarrow S$. How management responds to employees' past performance sets the tone for how hard they will work to achieve future performance targets.

Beginning on the left side of the model, the strength of the Motivation → Performance link depends on two factors: expectations/goals and ability. The effectiveness of expectations and goals rests on three moderating factors: (1) a participative goal-setting process that promotes both understanding and acceptance of the goals; (2) goals that are specific enough to guide behavior, appropriately challenging, and consistent with other goals; and (3) frequent, specific, and accurate feedback—what we might think of as progress reports. Finally, the effect of motivation on performance depends on a person's ability: aptitude, training, and resources. From a manager's perspective, the "path goal" theory of leadership offers guidance on the appropriate level of supervisory involvement—assisting subordinates' efforts to perform well.

The next section of the model, Performance → Outcomes, focuses on linking both positive and negative outcomes with performance. The effectiveness of efforts to enhance extrinsic motivation depends on the appropriate use of discipline and rewards and their timely administration. Intrinsic motivation can be enhanced via the fulfillment of individuals' needs for autonomy, competence, social connection, and purpose. Management practices that promote employee involvement and engagement, as well as meaningful relationships, work best. The greatest contribution managers can make to intrinsic motivation is to work with their employees to design work that fulfills these needs.

Proceeding to the final component of the model, the contributions of reward salience and perceived reward equity to the strength of the Outcomes → Satisfaction link are paramount. Reward salience refers to the subjective value individuals attach to incentives for performance based on the extent to which they satisfy personal needs. While the list of human needs seems infinite, within the field of management the needs for achievement, affiliation, and power stand out. The point here is that rewards with little personal value have low motivational potential. The second moderating condition, perceived reward equity, refers to the perceived fairness of how rewards are distributed. This judgment is based on the perceived outputs/inputs of an individual compared with others. When individuals conclude that they have been treated unfairly they bring their output/inputs in balance by reducing their inputs, most notably the level of their effort.

Based on the perceived value and equity of the performance-based outcomes they receive, individuals experience varying degrees of satisfaction. High satisfaction creates a positive feedback loop, increasing the individual's motivation, as manifested by increased effort. Low satisfaction, on the other hand, results in decreased effort and, therefore, lower performance and rewards. If uncorrected, this pattern may ultimately result in absenteeism or turnover.

In the final section, the challenge managers face when giving negative performance feedback was singled out for special attention. What psychologists refer to as the fundamental attribution error was introduced and the bias it introduces into how managers explain poor performance in others examined. In Figure 6.9, this biased approach to diagnosing the causes of poor performance was characterized as the M-A-E diagnostic sequence, emphasizing internal attributions. The alternative E-A-M sequence helps managers avoid this bias by considering the possibility of external attributions. Regarding the E-A-M model, it is noteworthy that with the exception of "Aptitude," the summary model, Figure 6.10, focuses on external attributions for unacceptable performance.

Behavioral Guidelines

The behavioral guidelines suitable for motivating performance are organized according to the major sections of this chapter. To aid in their implementation, illustrative diagnostic questions are included.

Foster High Performance

A. *Strengthen the Motivation → Performance Link*

Performance Expectations/Goals

- ❑ Establish clear, realistic performance expectations that are both understood and accepted.
- ❑ Formulate goals collaboratively, if possible.
- ❑ Establish goals that are specific, consistent, and challenging.
- ❑ Provide frequent, specific, and accurate feedback on performance.

Ability

- ❑ Match assignments with individuals' aptitude, based on their mastery of related tasks.
- ❑ Match assignments with individuals' training, or make provisions for the required training.
- ❑ Make sure individuals have the organizational resources required to perform their assignments, such as technical information, financial support, personnel, and clearances to work with other units.
- ❑ Gear your level of involvement as a leader to how much help a person expects, your assessment of what is needed, and how much help is otherwise available.

B. *Strengthen the Performance → Outcomes Link*

- ❑ Use rewards to reinforce performance-enhancing behaviors and the accomplishment of specific performance goals.
- ❑ Use discipline to correct performance-distracting behavior and unacceptable levels of performance.
- ❑ Never assume that a nonresponse to unacceptable behavior will be interpreted by the actor as negative feedback.
- ❑ Administer rewards and discipline in a timely manner.
- ❑ Foster intrinsic motivation via management practices and job attributes that contribute to the fulfillment of employees' needs for competence (mastery), autonomy, relatedness (social connection), and a sense of purpose.

C. *Strengthen the Outcomes → Satisfaction Link*

- ❑ Utilize rewards that individuals view as personally salient.
- ❑ Distribute rewards in ways that are perceived to be fair.

Diagnose and Correct Unacceptable Performance

A. Jointly investigate what caused the downturn in performance.

- ❑ Invite the employee's explanation for their low performance rating.
- ❑ Use the E-A-M line of inquiry to nullify the harmful effects of the "universal attribution error."

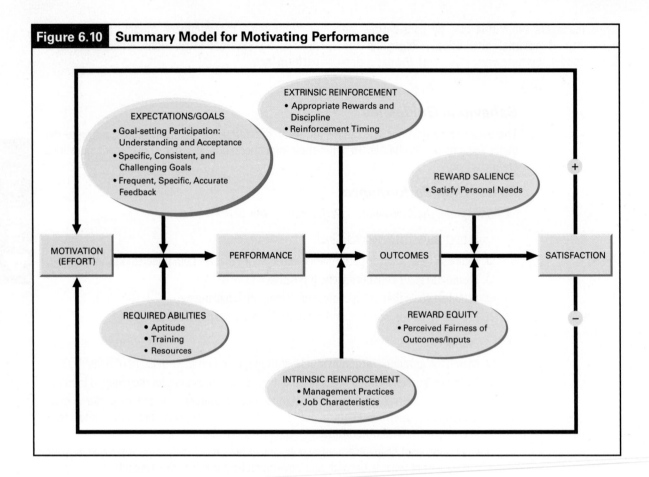

Figure 6.10 | Summary Model for Motivating Performance

- ☐ Foster a problem-solving approach by seeking to understand the person's perspective, including giving due consideration to their external attributions.
- ☐ Treat all attributions as hypotheses to be tested against relevant facts.

B. Make corrections and plan for performance improvement.

- ☐ Utilize the practices set forth in the "Fostering Exceptional Performance" section, and the corresponding Behavioral Guidelines.

CASE INVOLVING MOTIVATION PROBLEMS

Electro Logic

Electro Logic (EL) is a small R&D firm located in a Midwestern college town adjacent to a major university. Its primary mission is to perform basic research on, and development of, a new technology called "Very Fast, Very Accurate" (VFVA). Founded four years ago by Steve Morgan, an electrical engineering professor and inventor of the technology, EL is primarily funded by government contracts, although it plans to market VFVA technology and devices to nongovernmental organizations within the year.

The government is very interested in VFVA, as it will enhance radar technology, robotics, and a number of other important defense applications. EL recently received the largest small-business contract ever awarded by the government to research and develop this or any other technology. Phase I of the contract has just been completed, and the government has agreed to Phase II contracting as well.

The organizational chart of EL is shown in Figure 6.11. There are currently 75 employees, with roughly 88 percent in engineering. The hierarchy of engineering titles and requirements for each are listed in Table 6.6. Heads of staff are supposedly appointed based on their knowledge of VFVA technology and their ability to manage people. In practice, the president of EL handpicks these people based on what some might call arbitrary guidelines: Most of the staff leaders were or are the president's graduate students. There is no predetermined time frame for advancement up the hierarchy. Raises are directly related to performance appraisal evaluations.

Working directly with the engineers are the technicians. Technicians generally have a high school degree, and some also have a college degree. They are trained on the job, although some have gone through a local community college's program on microtechnology fabrication. The technicians perform the mundane tasks of the engineering department: running tests, building circuit boards, manufacturing VFVA chips, and so on. Most are full-time, hourly employees.

The administrative staff is composed of the staff head (who has an MBA from a major university), accountants, a personnel director, graphic artists, a purchasing agent, a project controller, technical writers/editors, and secretaries. Most of the people in the administrative staff are women. All are hourly employees except the staff head, personnel director, and project controller. The graphic artists and technical writer/editor are part-time employees.

The facilities staff is composed of the staff head and maintenance personnel. EL is housed in three different buildings, and the primary responsibility of the facilities

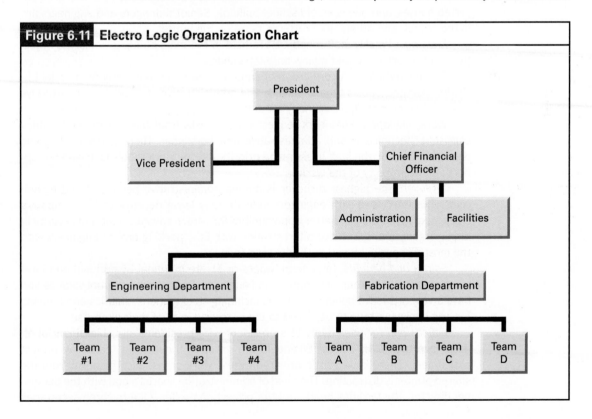

Figure 6.11   Electro Logic Organization Chart

Table 6.6	Engineering Titles and Requirements
Title	**Requirement**
Member of Technical Staff	BSEE, MSEE
Senior Member of Technical Staff	PhD, MSEE with 2 years of industrial experience; BSEE with 5 years of industrial experience
Research Engineer	PhD with 2 years of industrial experience
	BSEE or MSEE with 7 years of industrial experience
Research Scientist	PhD with appropriate experience in research
Senior Research Scientist	PhD with appropriate industrial and research experience

staff is to ensure that the facilities of each building are in good working order. Additionally, the facilities staff is often called on to remodel parts of the buildings as the staff continues to grow.

EL anticipates a major recruiting campaign to enhance the overall staff. In particular, it is looking for more technicians and engineers. Prior to this recruiting campaign, however, the president of EL hired an outside consultant to assess employee needs as well as the morale and overall effectiveness of the firm. The consultant has been observing EL for about three weeks and has written up some notes of her impressions and observations of the company.

Consultant's Notes from Observations of Electro Logic

Facilities: Electro Logic (EL) is housed in three different buildings. Two are converted houses, and one is an old school building. Senior managers and engineers are in the school, and others are scattered between the houses.

Meetings: Weekly staff meetings are held in the main building to discuss objectives and to formulate and review milestone charts.

Social interaction: A core group of employees interact frequently on a social basis; for example, sports teams, parties. The administrative staff celebrates birthdays at work. The president occasionally attends.

Work allocation: Engineers request various tasks from the support staff, which consists of technicians and administrative unit personnel. There is obviously some discretion used by the staff in assigning priorities to the work requests, based on rapport and desirability of the work.

Turnover: The highest turnover is among administrative personnel and technicians. Exit interviews with engineers indicate they leave because of the company's crisis-management style, better opportunities for career advancement and security in larger organizations, and overall frustration with EL's "pecking order." Engineers with the most responsibility and authority tend to leave.

Salary and benefits: In general, wages at EL are marginal by national and local standards. A small group of scientists and engineers do make substantial salaries and have a very attractive benefits package, including stock options. Salaries and benefits for new engineers tend to be linked to the perceived level of their expertise.

Offices and facilities: Only EL's president, vice president, and chief financial officer have their own offices. Engineers are grouped together in "pods" by project assignment. There is very little privacy in these work areas, and the noise from the shared printer is distracting. The head of administration shares a pod with the personnel director, the facilities head, and the project controller. One to three secretaries per building are located in or near the reception areas. The large building has an employee lounge with three vending machines. There is also a coffee and tea station. The smaller buildings have only a soft-drink vending machine in the reception area.

Consultant's Interviews with Employees

After making these observations, the consultant requested interviews with a cross section of the staff for the purpose of developing a survey to be taken by all employees. Presented below are excerpts from those interviews.

Pat Klausen, Senior Member of the Technical Staff

CONSULTANT: What is it about Electro Logic (EL) that gives you the most satisfaction?

PAT: I really enjoy the work. I mean, I've always liked to do research, and working on VFVA is an incredible opportunity. Just getting to work with Steve (EL's president and VFVA's inventor) again is exciting. I was his graduate student about six years ago, you know. He really likes to work closely with his people—perhaps sometimes too closely. There have been times when I could have done with a little less supervision.

CONSULTANT: What's the least satisfying aspect of your work?

PAT: Probably the fact that I'm never quite sure we'll be funded next month, given the defense budget problems and the tentativeness of our research. I've got a family to consider, and this place isn't the most stable in terms of its financial situation. Maybe it'll change once we get more into commercial production. Who knows?

CONSULTANT: You've offered some general positives and negatives about EL. Can you be more specific about day-to-day dealings? What's good and bad about working here on a daily basis?

PAT: You're sure this isn't going to get back to anyone? Okay. Well, in general I'm not satisfied with the fact that too often we end up changing horses in the middle of the stream, if you know what I mean. In the past seven months, three of my engineers and four of my techs have been pulled off my project onto projects whose deadlines were nearer than mine. Now I'm faced with a deadline, and I'm supposed to be getting more staff. But I'll have to spend so much time briefing them that it might make more sense for me to just finish the project myself. On the other hand, Steve keeps telling me that we have to be concerned with EL's overall goals, not just our individual concerns—you know, we have to be "team players," "good members of the family." It's kind of hard to deal with that, though, when deadlines are bearing down and you know your butt's on the line, team player or not. But if you go along with this kind of stuff and don't complain, the higher-ups treat you well. Still, it seems to me there's got to be a better way to manage these projects.

CONSULTANT: What are the positive aspects of your daily work?

PAT: Well, the people here are all great to work with. They know their stuff or can learn quickly. I tend to be a social person and I really like socializing with these people. We play softball and basketball together and do happy hours and stuff. I like that. I've got some good friends here, which helps get my work orders filled quickly, if you know what I mean.

Bob Christensen, Member of the Technical Staff

CONSULTANT: You said earlier that Steve was your adviser for your MS. So you've known him a long time.

BOB: Yes, that's right. I've known Professor Morgan—Steve—for about eight years. I had him for a few undergraduate classes; then, of course, he was my adviser for my two-year master's program, and now I've worked at Electro Logic for two years.

CONSULTANT: It seems as if you enjoy working with Steve.

BOB: Oh, yeah. But I really don't get to work directly with him anymore. I'll see him at meetings and such, but that's about it.

CONSULTANT: So he's not your immediate supervisor?

BOB: No, but for the amount of time I spend with my supervisor, Steve might as well be. My boss and I meet maybe once every three weeks for about an hour to see if all is well. And that's it. The rest of the time, I'm on my own. I used to talk to Steve when I had questions, but he's gotten so busy now that it's hard to see him—you need to make an appointment a few days in advance.

CONSULTANT: Do you think your supervisor treats all his staff this way?

BOB: To be honest, I have heard some complaints. In fact, about six months ago, the situation was so bad, some other people and I had a meeting with him. He promised that he would be more available to us and was, for about a month. Then we got involved in a new proposal, so he made himself scarce again. So nothing's really changed. We're coming up on finalizing the proposal now, and it's important that I see him, ask him questions. The last few drafts I've submitted to him, he's returned, rewritten in his own way, and with no explanation of the changes. Sometimes I think he treats me like somebody who doesn't know anything, as if I had no training what-soever. I realize his neck is on the line with this project, but sometimes it seems that he uses being busy to avoid talking to me.

Chris Chen, Research Scientist

CONSULTANT: What kind of characteristics should a person have if he/she wants to work as a research scientist at Electro Logic?

CHRIS: Well, certainly technical knowledge is important. When I've interviewed recent college grads for entry-level positions, I am always concerned with their GPA. I like to see straight-A averages, if possible. But for experienced research scientists, technical knowledge shows up in their publication records, mostly. So I'll read their papers. I also think a research scientist has to be highly self-motivated, not look to others for praise and such. Particularly here. If you want someone to tell you you've done a good job, you'll be waiting a long time. It's not clear to me that research scientists really get the support we need from the rest of the staff here. Work orders are often lost or put off for one reason or another. Senior members seem to get more techs than scientists do, and they certainly get more attention from Steve. The rumor is that these guys also get higher raises than the scientists; allegedly, this is to keep pay at an equitable rate—you know, they're supposedly more valuable to the company. Of course, everybody knows that most of the senior members are Steve's old graduate students, and so he takes care of them really well. One of the things that really galls me is that I need to keep up my publication record to maintain my career options. But publishing is frowned on because it takes time away from your work. I've even been told that my work can't be published because of proprietary rights or that the defense department consid-ers the information classified. However, if somebody important is working with me and needs the publication, then it's full steam ahead.

CONSULTANT: You sound pretty disgruntled with your work.

CHRIS: It's not my work so much. I'm really very happy doing this work—it's cutting-edge, after all. The problem is I'm never quite sure where the work is going. I do my part of a project, and unless I go out of my way to talk to other people, I never find out the final results of the total project. That's just something you learn to live with around here—being part of a system that's not particularly open.

Meg Sanchez, Assistant to the Head of Administration

CONSULTANT: You've only been here a short time, is that correct?

MEG: That's right—just a little over a year.

CONSULTANT: Why did you take the job?

MEG: Well, I was in my last semester of college and was looking for a job, like most college seniors. My fiancé at the time—now he's my husband—was already working for Electro Logic and found out that there was an opening. So I applied.

CONSULTANT: So you were a business major in school?

MEG: Oh, no. I was a history major.

CONSULTANT: Do you like your job?

MEG: It has a lot to offer. I get paid pretty well for what I'm doing. And I'm learning a lot. I just wish the company would let me take some classes in administration, like accounting. The auditors ask some pretty tough questions. Steve says we should hire that expertise, but I'd still be responsible for supervising the people.

CONSULTANT: Is there any particular aspect about your job that you really find satisfying?

MEG: Well, let me think. I guess I like the fact that I get to do a lot of different tasks so that things don't get so boring. I would hate to have to do the same thing, day in and day out. A lot of times, I go to the library to do research on different things, and that's nice because it gets me out of the office.

CONSULTANT: What don't you like about your job?

MEG: Well, I often get the feeling that administration isn't taken seriously. You know, the engineers could get along without us quite nicely, or so they seem to think. The whole structure of the department shows that we're the catchall department: If you don't fit anywhere else, they put you in here. Perhaps some of that is because our department is primarily women—in fact, I've been told that 95 percent of all the female employees are in administration. Sometimes it's hard to work with the engineers because they treat you like you don't know anything, and they always want things to be done their way. Clearly, the engineers get the money and consideration and yet, well, we do contribute quite a lot to the whole team, as Steve would say. But words of praise just aren't as impressive as actions. Sure, we get our birthday parties, but that still seems to be a little patronizing. We rarely get to see what's going on in the research area. I've asked a number of engineers specific questions, and they just kind of look at me with a blank stare and give me some really simplified answer. It seems to me if you want to build a family, like the president says, you can't treat administration like a bad relation.

P. J. Ginelli, Technician

CONSULTANT: I gather you've just been through your semiannual performance appraisal. How did it go?

P. J.: Like I expected. No surprises.

CONSULTANT: Do you find these appraisals useful?

P. J.: Sure. I get to find out what he thinks of my work.

CONSULTANT: Is that all?

P. J.: Well, I suppose it's a nice opportunity to understand what my supervisor wants. Sometimes he's not so clear during the rest of the year. I suppose he's been given specific goals from higher-ups before he talks with me, so he's clear and then I'm clear.

ANALYSIS

CONSULTANT: Do you like what you're doing?

P. J.: Oh yeah. The best part is that I'm not at the main building and so I don't have to put up with the "important" people, you know? I've heard from other techs that those guys can be a real pain—trying to be nice and all, but really just being a bother. I mean, how can you get your stuff done when the president's looking over your shoulder all the time? On the other hand, if the president knows your name, I suppose that's a good thing when it comes to raises and promotions. But my boss sticks up for his techs; we get a fair deal from him.

CONSULTANT: Do you think you'll be able to get ahead at Electro Logic?

P. J.: Get ahead? You mean become an engineer or something? No, and I really don't want to do that. Everyone around here keeps pushing me to move up. I'm afraid to tell people how I really feel for fear they'll decide I don't fit into this high-tech environment. I don't want to be the "black sheep of the family." I like where I am, and if the raises keep coming, I'll keep liking it. One of my kids is starting college next year, and I need the money to help her out. I get a lot of overtime, particularly when contract deadlines are near. I suppose the rush toward the end of contracts gives some people big headaches, but for me, I don't mind. The work is pretty slow otherwise, and so at least I'm working all the time and then some. But my family wishes my schedule was more predictable.

CONSULTANT: Do you think you'll continue working for EL?

P. J.: I'm not sure I want to answer that. Let's just say that my ratings on the performance appraisal were good, and I expect to see an improvement in my pay. I'll stay for that.

Chalida Montgomery, Technician

CONSULTANT: In general, what are your feelings about the work you do for Electro Logic?

CHALIDA: Well, I feel my work is quite good, but I also feel that I perform rather boring, tedious tasks. From what my supervisor says, the kinds of things I do are what electrical engineering students do in their last year of classes. I gather their final project is to make a circuit board, and that's what I do, day in and day out.

CONSULTANT: What is it that you would like to do?

CHALIDA: Well, it would be nice to be able to offer some input into some of the designs of these boards. I know I don't have a PhD or anything, but I do have lots of experience. But because I'm a tech, the engineers don't really feel I've got much to offer—even though I build the boards and can tell from the design which one will do what the designer wants it to do. I also would like to maybe supervise other technicians in my department. You know, some kind of advancement would be nice. As it is, lots of techs ask me how to do things, and of course I help, but then they get the credit. Around here, you have to have a piece of paper that says you're educated before they let you officially help other people.

Discussion Questions

6.1. Using the behavioral guidelines and Figure 6.10 as diagnostic aids, what are the strengths and weaknesses of Electro Logic from a motivational perspective?

6.2. What are the high-priority action items you would include in a consulting report to Steve Morgan, president of EL? Focus on specific actions he could initiate that would better use the abilities of the staff and foster a more motivating work environment.

EXERCISES FOR DIAGNOSING WORK PERFORMANCE PROBLEMS

Proper diagnosis is a critical aspect of effective motivation management. Often, managers become frustrated because they don't understand the causes of observed performance problems. They might experiment with various "cures," but the inefficiency of this trial-and-error process often only increases their frustration level. In addition, the accompanying misunderstanding adds extra strain to the manager–subordinate relationship. This generally makes the performance problem even more pronounced, which in turn prompts the manager to resort to more drastic responses, and a vicious downward spiral ensues.

Our approach to this subject assumes that employees will work hard and be good performers if the work environment encourages these actions. Consequently, rather than jumping to conclusions about poor performance stemming from deficiencies in personality traits or a bad attitude, this diagnostic process focuses attention on improving management practices and other aspects of the work environment.

Joe Chaney

Assignment

Read the case "Joe Chaney" and privately use Figures 6.9 and 6.10 to identify plausible performance problems. Next, discuss in small groups your individual assessments and list specific questions you should ask Joe in order to accurately identify, from his point of view, the obstacles to his high performance. Finally, brainstorm ideas for plausible solutions. Prepare to represent your group in role-playing a problem-solving interview with Joe.

Joe Chaney joined your architectural firm two years ago as a draftsman. He is 35 years old and has been a draftsman since graduating from a two-year technical school right after high school. He is married and has four children. He has worked for four architectural firms in 12 years.

Joe came with mediocre recommendations from his previous employer, but you hired him anyway because you needed help desperately. Your firm's workload has been extremely high due to a local construction boom. The result is that a lot of the practices that contribute to a supportive, well-managed work environment have been overlooked. For instance, you can't remember the last time you conducted a formal performance review or did any career counseling. Furthermore, the tradition of closing the office early on Friday for a social hour was dropped long ago. Unfortunately, the tension in the office runs pretty high some days due to unbearable time pressures and the lack of adequate staff. Night and weekend work have become the norm rather than the exception.

Overall, you have been pleasantly surprised by Joe's performance. Until recently, he worked hard and consistently produced high-quality work. Furthermore, he frequently volunteered for special projects, made lots of suggestions for improving the work environment, and has demonstrated an in-depth practical knowledge of architecture and the construction business. However, during the past few months, he has definitely slacked

MOTIVATING PERFORMANCE CHAPTER 6 **295**

off. He doesn't seem as excited about his work, and several times you have found him daydreaming at his desk. In addition, he has gotten into several heated arguments with architects about the specifications and proper design procedures for recent projects.

After one of these disagreements, you overheard Joe complaining to his officemate, "No one around here respects my opinion. I'm just a lowly draftsman. I know as much as these hotshot architects, but because I don't have the degree, they ignore my input, and I'm stuck doing the grunt work. Adding insult to injury, my wife has had to get a job to help support our family. I must be the lowest-paid person in this firm." In response to a question from a coworker regarding why he didn't pursue a college degree in architecture, Joe responded, "Do you have any idea how hard it is to put bread on the table, pay a Seattle mortgage, work overtime, be a reasonably good father and husband, plus go to night school? Come on, be realistic!"

Motivating Performance Assessment

Assignment

1. Complete the Motivating Performance Assessment for a current or former job.

Assessment

Respond to the following statements, based on your current or previous job.

Rating Scale

1 Strongly disagree

2 Disagree

3 Neutral

4 Agree

5 Strongly agree

_____ 1. I believe my boss plays favorites in allocating rewards.

_____ 2. I could do a much better job if I had more training.

_____ 3. I generally don't enjoy my work.

_____ 4. I believe that my native skills and abilities are matched very well with my job responsibilities.

_____ 5. I believe my boss's expectations are unclear and unrealistic.

_____ 6. The rewards and opportunities available to me if I perform well are attractive to me personally.

_____ 7. I feel I have adequate training to perform my current job assignments.

_____ 8. My supervisor indicates that I am not performing as well as I should, but I disagree.

_____ 9. I believe that I have adequate resources to do my job well.

_____ 10. I believe that my job is too difficult for my ability level.

_____ 11. I understand my boss's expectations and generally feel they are realistic.

_____ 12. I do not find the rewards and opportunities available to high performers very appealing.

_____ 13. My work is generally enjoyable and fulfilling.

_____ 14. I believe that rewards are distributed fairly, on the basis of performance.

_____ 15. My supervisor and I agree on the quality of my performance.

_____ 16. I believe that my job performance is hindered by a lack of resources.

2. Score your responses using instructions in the Scoring Key and Comparison Data section at the end of the chapter.

3. With the job you used to complete this assessment in mind, on a scale of 1 (Low) to 5 (High) rate your motivation (desire, commitment, effort) to perform at a high level. _____ What score do you believe your supervisor would give you? _____

4. **Score Analysis**
   A. In small groups, compare your Motivating Performance Assessment score totals, and your highest and lowest scores for the eight requirements. Using Figures 6.9 and 6.10 as guides, discuss specific work conditions that might account for your scores (e.g., the type of work performed in your unit, the experience level of your supervisor and coworkers, organizational policies and procedures).
   B. In small groups, report your two Motivation scores. If the two scores are significantly different, discuss why you believe this is the case and what you could do to resolve the discrepancy in perceptions. Compare your Motivation score with your scores for the eight requirements. Discuss how your high/low scores are related to your Motivation score, highlighting those that seem to contribute the most to your Motivation score.
   C. Summarize what your group has learned from these discussions about how managers can effectively motivate others to achieve high performance goals.

EXERCISE FOR ASSESSING JOB CHARACTERISTICS

Job Diagnostic Survey

On the following pages [of this survey (short form)], you will find several different kinds of questions about your job. Specific instructions are given at the start of each section. Please read them carefully. It should take no more than 10 minutes to complete the entire questionnaire. Please move through it quickly.

The questions are designed to obtain your perceptions of your job and your reactions to it.

Job Characteristics—I

This part of the questionnaire asks you to describe your job, as *objectively* as you can.

Please do *not* use this part of the questionnaire to show how much you like or dislike your job. Questions about that will come later. Instead, try to make your descriptions as accurate and as objective as you possibly can.

A sample question is given below.

A. To what extent does your job require you to work with mechanical equipment?

1_____ 2 _____ 3 _____ 4 _____ 5 _____ ⑥ _____ 7

Very little; the job requires almost no contact with mechanical equipment of any kind.

Moderately

Very much; the job requires almost constant work with mechanical equipment.

You are to circle the number that is the most accurate description of your job.

If, for example, your job requires you to work with mechanical equipment a good deal of the time—but also requires some paperwork—you might circle the number six, as was done in the above example.

1. How much *autonomy* is there in your job? That is, to what extent does your job permit you to decide *on your own* how to go about doing the work?

1_____ 2 _____ 3 _____ 4 _____ 5 _____ 6 _____ 7

Very little; the job gives me almost no personal "say" about how and when the work is done.

Moderate autonomy; many things are standardized and not under my control, but I can make some decisions about the work.

Very much; the job gives me almost complete responsibility for deciding how and when the work is done.

2. To what extent does your job involve doing a *"whole" and identifiable piece of work*? That is, is the job a complete piece of work that has an obvious beginning and end? Or is it only a small *part* of the overall piece of work, which is finished by other people or by automatic machines?

1_____ 2 _____ 3 _____ 4 _____ 5 _____ 6 _____ 7

My job is only a tiny part of the overall piece of work; the results of my activities cannot be seen in the final product or service.

My job is a moderate-sized "chunk" of the overall piece of work; my own contribution can be seen in the final outcome.

My job involves doing the whole piece of work, from start to finish; the results of my activities are easily seen in the final product or service.

3. How much *variety* is there in your job? That is, to what extent does the job require you to do many different things at work, using a variety of your skills and talents?

1_____ 2 _____ 3 _____ 4 _____ 5 _____ 6 _____ 7

Very little; the job requires me to do the same routine things over and over again.

Moderate variety.

Very much; the job requires me to do many different things, using a number of different skills and talents.

4. In general, how *significant or important* is your job? That is, are the results of your work likely to significantly affect the lives or well-being of other people?

1 _____ 2 _____ 3 _____ 4 _____ 5 _____ 6 _____ 7

Not very significant; the outcomes of my work are not likely to have important effects on other people.	Moderately significant.	Highly significant; the outcomes of my work can affect other people in very important ways.

5. To what extent does *doing the job itself* provide you with information about your work performance? That is, does the actual *work itself* provide clues about how well you are doing—aside from any "feedback" coworkers or supervisors may provide?

1 _____ 2 _____ 3 _____ 4 _____ 5 _____ 6 _____ 7

Very little; the job itself is set up so I could work forever without finding out how well I am doing.	Moderately; sometimes doing the job provides "feedback" to me; sometimes it does not.	Very much; the job is set up so that I get almost constant "feedback" as I work about how well I am doing.

Job Characteristics—II

Write a number in the blank beside each statement, based on the following scale: Listed below are a number of statements that could be used to describe a job.

You are to indicate whether each statement is an *accurate* or an *inaccurate* description of *your* job.

Once again, please try to be as objective as you can in deciding how accurately each statement describes your job—regardless of whether you like or dislike your job.

How accurate is the statement in describing your job?

1	2	3	4	5	6	7
Very Inaccurate	Mostly Inaccurate	Slightly Inaccurate	Uncertain	Slightly Accurate	Mostly Accurate	Very Accurate

_____ 1. The job requires me to use a number of complex or high-level skills.

_____ 2. The job is arranged so that I do *not* have the chance to do an entire piece of work from beginning to end.

_____ 3. Just doing the work required by the job provides many chances for me to figure out how well I am doing.

_____ 4. The job is quite simple and repetitive.

_____ 5. This job is one where a lot of other people can be affected by how well the work gets done.

_____ 6. The job denies me any chance to use my personal initiative or judgment in carrying the work.

_____ 7. The job provides me the chance to completely finish the pieces of work I begin.

_____ 8. The job itself provides very few clues about whether or not I am performing well.

_____ 9. The job gives me considerable opportunity for independence and freedom in how I do the work.

_____ 10. The job itself is *not* very significant or important in the broader scheme of things.

Section III

Listed below are a number of characteristics that could be present on any job. People differ about how much they would like to have each one present in their own jobs. We are interested in learning *how much you personally would like* to have each one present in your job.

Using the scale below, please indicate the *degree* to which you *would like* to have each characteristic present in your job.

NOTE: The numbers on this scale are different from those used in previous scales.

4	5	6	7	8	9	10
Would like having this only a moderate amount (or less)			Would like having this very much			Would like having this <u>extremely</u> much

_____ 1. High respect and fair treatment from my supervisor.

_____ 2. Stimulating and challenging work.

_____ 3. Chances to exercise independent thought and action in my job.

_____ 4. Great job security.

_____ 5. Very friendly coworkers.

_____ 6. Opportunities to learn new things from my work.

_____ 7. High salary and good fringe benefits.

_____ 8. Opportunities to be creative and imaginative in my work.

_____ 9. Quick promotions.

_____ 10. Opportunities for personal growth and development in my job.

_____ 11. A sense of worthwhile accomplishment in my work.

SKILL *APPLICATION*

ACTIVITIES FOR MOTIVATING PERFORMANCE

Suggested Assignments

6.3. Identify a situation in which you have some responsibility for another person whose performance is significantly below your expectations. Using the Motivating Performance Assessment included in the Skill Practice section, collect information on the individual's perceptions of the situation. Using the diagnostic model (decision tree) in that section, specifically identify the perceived performance problems. Compare these results with your own views of the situation. Conduct an interview with the individual and discuss the results, focusing on discrepancies in your scores. Based on this discussion, formulate a plan of action that both parties accept. Implement this plan for a period of time and then report on the results.

6.4. Focus on some aspect of your own work in which you feel performance is below your (or others') expectations. Using the Motivating Performance Assessment, included in the Skill Practice section, identify the specific obstacles to improved performance. Then formulate a plan for overcoming these obstacles, including getting commitments from others. Discuss your plan with individuals affected by it and arrive at a set of actions all parties accept. Implement the plan for a period of time and report on your results. How successful were you in making the changes? Did your performance improve as expected? Based on this experience, identify other aspects of your work that you could improve on in a similar fashion.

6.5. Teach what you learned about the importance of intrinsic reinforcement to several individuals who are employed. Explain that intrinsic satisfaction comes from work conditions that satisfy the needs for mastery, autonomy, supportive relationships, and a sense of purpose. Discuss the management practices described in this chapter that can contribute to the fulfillment of these needs. Ask them to rate their supervisor according to the presence or absence of these practices. Invite them to formulate a list of suggested changes they might discuss with their supervisor.

6.6 Administer the Job Diagnostic Survey to several individuals. Use their scores to teach them the fundamentals of job design, using Figure 6.7 and Table 6.3 as visual aids. Introduce the idea of job crafting and invite them to compile a list of specific changes in their job assignments that would increase their Motivational Potential Score. Help them develop a plan for discussing their suggestions with their supervisor.

Application Plan and Evaluation

The intent of this exercise is to help you apply this cluster of skills in a real-life, out-of-class setting. Now that you have become familiar with the behavioral guidelines that form the basis of effective skill performance, you will improve most by trying out those guidelines in an everyday context. Unlike a classroom activity, in which feedback is immediate and others can assist you with their evaluations, this skill application activity is one you must accomplish and evaluate on your own. There are two parts to this activity. Part 1 helps prepare you to apply the skill, and Part 2 helps you evaluate and improve on your experience. Be sure to write down answers to each item. Don't short-circuit the process by skipping steps.

Part 1: Planning

6.7. Write down the two or three aspects of this skill that are most important to you. These may be areas of weakness, areas you most want to improve, or areas that are most salient to a problem you face right now. Identify the specific aspects of this skill that you want to apply.

6.8. Now identify the setting or the situation in which you will apply this skill. Establish a plan for performance by actually writing down a description of the situation. Who else will be involved? When will you do it? Where will it be done?

> Circumstances:
> Who else?
> When?
> Where?

6.9. Identify the specific behaviors you will engage in to apply this skill. Operationalize your skill performance.

6.10. What are the indicators of successful performance? How will you know you have been effective? What will indicate you have performed competently?

Part 2: Evaluation

6.11. After you have completed your implementation, record the results. What happened? How successful were you? What was the effect on others?

6.12. How can you improve? What modifications can you make next time? What will you do differently in a similar situation in the future?

6.13. Looking back on your whole skill practice and application experience, what have you learned? What has been surprising? In what ways might this experience help you in the long term?

SCORING KEYS AND **COMPARISON DATA**

⭐ Go to www.pearson.com/mylab/management for scoring keys and comparison data for the following instruments:

Motivating Performance Assessment (Scoring key below, comparison data in MyLab Management.)
Diagnosing Poor Performance and Enhancing Motivation

Scoring Key

1. Record your scores for each item and the total below. Reverse your scores for items 1, 2, 3, 5, 8, 10, 12, 16. For these items, if you scored a 5, change it to a 1, change a 4 to a 2, 3 stays the same, change a 2 to a 4, and a 1 to a 5.
2. Sum the total of your scores. The maximum score is 80.

1. _____ (R)
2. _____ (R)
3. _____ (R)
4. _____
5. _____ (R)
6. _____
7. _____
8. _____ (R)
9. _____
10. _____ (R)
11. _____
12. _____ (R)
13. _____
14. _____
15. _____
16. _____ (R)

TOTAL: _____

3. Combine your scores for the "requirements for high performance" items in this assessment.

PERFORMANCE REQUIREMENTS:	ITEMS:		COMBINED SCORES:
Performance Expectations	11. _____	5. _____	_____
Ability/Aptitude	4. _____	10. _____	_____
Ability/Training	7. _____	2. _____	_____
Ability/Resources	9. _____	16. _____	_____
Performance Quality	15. _____	8. _____	_____
Reward Equity	14. _____	1. _____	_____
Reward Salience	6. _____	12. _____	_____
Intrinsic Reinforcement	13. _____	3. _____	_____

Scoring Key

Example: Imagine that your scores were as follows for the three items that measure Skill Variety:

Section I, Item #4	6
Section II, Item #1	5
Section II, Item #4	2

Here is a worked-out computation of your Skill Variety score, given those item responses.

Section I, Item #4 + ____ 6
plus Section II, Item #1 + ____ 5
minus Section II, Item #4 − ____ 2
Sum   9
Adjustment + 8
Total   17 ÷ 3 = 5.67

This is the Skill Variety Score.

I. JOB CHARACTERISTICS

A. Skill Variety

Section I, Item #3 + ____
plus Section II, Item #1 + ____
minus Section II, Item #4 − ____
Sum   ☐
Adjustment   + 8
Total   ☐ ÷ 3 = ☐

B. Task Identity

Section I, Item #2 + ____
plus Section II, Item #7 + ____
minus Section II, Item #2 − ____
Sum   ☐
Adjustment   +8
Total   ☐ ÷ 3 = ☐

C. Task Significance

Section I, Item #4 + _____

plus Section II, Item #5 + _____

minus Section II, Item #10 − _____

Sum   □

Adjustment   + 8

Total   □ ÷ 3 = □

D. Autonomy

Section I, Item #1+ _____

plus Section II, Item #9 + _____

minus Section II, Item #6 − _____

Sum   □

Adjustment   + 8

Total   □ ÷ 3 = □

E. Feedback from the Job Itself

Section I, Item #5 + _____

plus Section II, Item #3 + _____

minus Section II, Item #8 − _____

Sum   □

Adjustment   + 8

Total   □ ÷ 3 = □

F. Motivating Potential Score (MPS)

$$MPS = \left[\frac{\text{Skill Variety} + \text{Task Identity} + \text{Task Significance}}{3.0} \right]$$

$$\times \text{ Autonomy} \times \text{Feedback from job}$$

$$MPS = \left[\frac{\Box + \Box + \Box}{3.0} \right] \times \Box \times \Box$$

$$MPS = \Box$$

II. INDIVIDUAL GROWTH NEEDS STRENGTH

Section III, Item #2 + _____

plus Section III, Item #3 + _____

plus Section III, Item #6 + _____

plus Section III, Item #8 + _____

plus Section III, Item #10 + _____

plus Section III, Item #11 + _____

Sum ☐

Adjustment − 18

Total ☐ ÷ 6 = ☐

Comparison Data

Scores	Mean
Skill Variety	4.7
Task Identity	4.7
Task Significance	5.5
Autonomy	4.9
Feedback	4.9
MPS	128
GNS	5.0

These norms are based on JDS results from approximately 6,930 employees working on 876 heterogenous jobs in 56 diverse organizations, located throughout the United States (Hackman & Oldham, 1980).

7

Negotiating and Resolving Conflict

LEARNING OBJECTIVES

1. Negotiate Effectively
2. Diagnose the Focus and Source of Conflicts
3. Utilize Appropriate Conflict Management Strategies
4. Resolve Interpersonal Confrontations Through Collaboration

MyLab Management

Go to www.pearson.com/mylab/ management to complete the exercises marked with this icon ✪.

MyLab Management **Personal Inventory Assessments**

The assessment instruments in this chapter are briefly described below. The assessments appear either in your text or in MyLab. The assessments marked with ✪ are available only in MyLab. If assigned, go to www.pearson.com/mylab/management to complete these assessments. The assessments without the ✪ appear only in the text.

All assessments should be completed before reading the chapter material.

After completing the first assessment, save your response to your hard drive. When you have finished reading the chapter, re-take the assessment and compare your responses to see what you have learned.

✪ ❑ The *Managing Interpersonal Conflict Assessment* measures the extent to which you exhibit competency in managing conflict in a work context.

✪ ❑ The *Strategies for Handling Conflict Assessment* measures your preferences for five different conflict management strategies that will be discussed in the chapter.

SKILL *LEARNING*

The Pervasiveness of Organizational Conflict

Conflict in organizations is inevitable. It has been esti-mated that managers spend 20 to 40 percent of their time dealing with conflict (Runde & Flanagan, 2012, p. 17). But not all conflicts are unproductive. Clarifying issues, exploring options, and developing solutions are essential and productive responses to organizational conflicts. And some organizations, especially those in which creativity is essential to survival, actually foster conflict between competing ideas or solutions. Also, some forms of strategic decision-making include the use of a devil's advocate—someone assigned to argue against the adoption of a proposal.

There is considerable evidence that poorly man-aged or dysfunctional conflict hurts organizational pro-ductivity, escalates out-of-pocket costs, increases risks, degrades decision-making, and impedes an organiza-tion's ability to achieve strategic goals. These are the conclusions of Daniel Dana (2014, 1984; see also *The Cost of Conflict*), who studies the costs of conflict in organizations. Dana has identified four key unproduc-tive consequences of conflict, at the individual level: wasted time, lower motivation, increased grievances and turnover, and disruptive restructuring—in order to spatially separate employees with unresolved conflicts.

The well-known American psychologist Abraham Maslow observed that people generally have a high degree of ambivalence regarding the value of conflict (1965). On one hand, managers acknowledge the value of conflict and competition. They agree it is a necessary ingredient of the free-enterprise system. On the other hand, their actions often demonstrate an emotional distaste for con-flict, leading them to avoid it whenever possible.

In the best-selling book *Crucial Conversations* (Patterson, et al., 2012), we learn why interpersonal conflict is so difficult to resolve. Conflict causes an esca-lation of emotion that produces a physiological flight-or-fight response, or what the authors refer to as "silence or violence." Silence can be perceived as weakness, and violence is expressed as intimidation and bullying. Nei-ther response is likely to resolve disagreements, and both leave a toxic residue on individuals and relationships.

As testimony to the pervasiveness of interpersonal conflict and the challenges people face in resolving it, the Internet is bursting with recommended remedies, often in the form of lists. We are sympathetic to the concerns of those seeking help for resolving disruptive conflicts from these sources. Our skill-based approach is broader and more comprehensive. We begin by examining the process of **negotiation**, useful in forging agreements in-tended to prevent conflict. In the second section of this chapter we examine **conflict** and **conflict resolution**, including the various forms of conflict, likely causes, and approaches for resolving it. As you will see, the literature on negotiation and conflict resolution shares foundational principles, objectives, and some vocabulary. One major difference between negotiation and conflict resolution is that whereas negotiation is typically used to resolve conflicts involving issues, such as the distribution of tangible assets, conflict resolution is used to resolve both issue-focused and person-focused (interpersonal) conflicts.

Following this broad overview, the third section provides guidance for resolving a particularly challenging form of interpersonal conflict—one that is known for triggering silence or violence. Interpersonal confrontations are initiated by personal complaints about the harmful consequences of another's actions. Here, you will learn how to channel a highly contentious conversation into a collaborative problem-solving process.

Negotiating Effectively

Negotiation is the process by which multiple parties come to agreements. Basic negotiations may occur between two people, while complicated negotiations take place all the way up to a global scale, such as when the United Nations meets for discussions. Most negotiations are extremely minor—practically every interaction with another person can be seen as a sort of negotiation.

Think about walking down a hallway or a sidewalk and seeing someone in your path, walking toward you. To avoid crashing into him, you move to the left. Unfortunately, at the same time he moves to his right. So you switch course and head to the right, but wouldn't you know it, he goes to his left. Still walking toward each other at a steady pace, you make eye contact with each other, both go to your respective right, and pass without consequence. This is a nonverbal negotiation that occurs every day, everywhere. Both parties want to reach a positive outcome. Each makes some initial movements indicating their preferred direction, and finally a decision is reached that suits both parties involved.

Most negotiations are merely conversations we have with those around us. When your manager gives you an assignment and you ask for a small team to help accomplish the project, that's a negotiation. Asking a coworker to cover your shift so you can go to the dentist is a negotiation—they may ask for something in return, or they may just be happy to get the extra hours.

Most people will go through multiple negotiations every day, and negotiations are generally divided into two categories—win-lose (distributive) or win-win (integrative)—although there is often crossover between the two types.

TYPES OF NEGOTIATION

Distributive negotiation, or win-lose negotiation, seems to be what most people think about when asked about negotiations—there is a winner and a loser, and what one person gets must come from the other in the negotiation. There is a set amount of something, usually money, and whatever one party doesn't get is what the other party receives. This type of negotiation often feels like a battle between two individuals. This makes a distributive approach better suited to nonrepeated negotiations in which the relationship is not important. When you will continue to work with the other party or parties after the negotiation, an integrative approach is almost always better.

Integrative negotiation, also known as win-win negotiation or interest-based negotiation, focuses on getting each party the best possible outcome. Often, each party expresses their interests and priorities. For example, a construction company might negotiate with an electrical company for a lower price per unit with an exclusivity contract. That way, the construction company can save money and the electrical company has a guaranteed future revenue stream. The companies can also build a better working relationship.

Integrative negotiations strive to find the best solutions for all the involved parties. Through this type of negotiation, the involved parties work to find a solution that can meet everyone's needs. While some points might be distributive, the overall effect is that the parties are willing to cede less important items to gain ground in more important areas.

For example, a new employee's contract will offer a base salary. The negotiation around this money is almost always distributive in nature; however, the contract as a whole does not need to be distributive if both parties have an integrative lens. For example, many companies are willing to negotiate issues such as more vacation days, better benefits, and paid moving expenses. A starting bonus can be added with a claw-back clause, in which the new hire must pay back the bonus if he or she leaves the company before two years. This helps lower the company's turnover and puts more money in the employee's pocket. The company may offer performance incentives, such as bonuses or perks dependent on the employee's performance. By negotiating employment contracts that address other issues in addition to salary, both parties can walk away from the negotiation with an integrative, win-win agreement.

THE BASICS OF NEGOTIATION

We will examine integrative negotiation in more detail after introducing some general terms and principles.

ZOPA & BATNA

The **Zone of Possible Agreement (ZOPA)** refers to the range in which an agreement might be met that would satisfy the needs of both parties involved in the negotiation (Fisher & Ury, 2011; D. Malhotra & M. Bazerman, 2008). For example: Mark is looking to purchase a car, and his budget is $18,000. Jane is looking to sell her car, and she is not willing to sell it for less than $12,000. The ZOPA in this situation is $12,000 to $18,000—any dollar amount within that range would satisfy both parties' requirements. If Jane were looking to sell her car for at least $20,000, there wouldn't be an immediate ZOPA—Mark would have to buy a different car or convince Jane to take a lower price, or Jane would have to find someone willing to pay $20,000 or convince Mark to increase his budget.

The **Best Alternative to a Negotiated Agreement (BATNA)** refers to the best outcome you can reach if the other party refuses to negotiate (Fisher & Ury, 2011; D. Malhotra & M. Bazerman, 2008.) If you enter a negotiation at a car dealership, what will you do for transportation if you don't buy a car? If your car was just totaled and you have no transportation, your BATNA is to continue renting a car, riding the bus, getting rides, or walking. If you are looking into buying a second car for pleasure, your BATNA could be staying with one car, waiting for a more compliant salesperson, or going to another dealership. Your BATNA is what you deem the most desirable of your options should the negotiation fail.

When you have a stronger BATNA, you have more power in the negotiation. In the previous example, the individual seeking a second car has more power in any potential negotiation—he or she can walk away without any difficulty. The first person is probably on a tight deadline and has less power in the negotiation. He or she must find a car or face severe inconvenience. A savvy salesperson may try to assess the buyer's BATNA to know how to best negotiate with that individual; this is why the first question you will often hear from salespeople is "What brings you in today?" They are trying to figure out how strong your BATNA is and, thus, how strong your negotiating power.

Due to the power associated with your BATNA, you should be strategic about when you share it or how much of it you share. We never advocate lying. However, it can be helpful at times to withhold certain information. For example, in the totaled car situation, there is no reason to tell the salesperson that your car is totaled—you can just say you are looking for a new car. On the other hand, in the situation of buying a second car, letting the salesperson know that you don't need to buy and that you're just looking around will make them work harder for your sale and may help you achieve greater savings.

Again, we never advocate lying or implying false information. We firmly state that you should only enter into negotiations in good faith and that you should never misrepresent information. Negotiations are not moral gray areas—there is an ethical way to negotiate and an unethical way. Intentionally misleading is not ethical.

Reservation Price

Before going into a negotiation, have a **reservation price**. Know when you will walk away from the negotiation. The reservation price is often related to your BATNA, but it helps to put it in terms of the negotiation.

The reservation price should be decided before entering any negotiation and should be agreed by all individuals within the negotiating party—if you are negotiating as a team, everyone should be aware of the reservation price. Trying to decide how high or low you can go in the middle of a negotiation will leave you prone to making mistakes and agreeing to deals that aren't beneficial for you.

Consider the person purchasing a second car, for example. He or she should come in with reservation prices for several aspects of the purchase, such as an interest rate below 2.5 percent and a discount of at least 10 percent off MSRP. If the dealership isn't willing to meet these two thresholds, the buyer will walk away.

Anchoring

An important aspect of almost every negotiation is **anchoring**, which is setting an expectation for what an acceptable offer is for you. Research suggests that aggressive and more precise anchors tend to provide an advantage for the person who offers the anchor (Agndal, et al., 2017; Loscheldera, et al., 2017; Caputo, 2013.) If you are selling a car, you should have a realistic expectation of its worth. If it is worth $5,000, you might post the listing price at $5,500 or even $6,000 with the intent to lower the price for interested parties. If you need to earn at least $4,000 from the sale, don't set the anchor at $4,000. It leaves you no room to give ground.

Anchoring allows you to set the stage on which the negotiation will take place. A question many recruiters ask potential employees is how much money they were making at their last job. The recruiter will then use this figure as an anchor to offer potentially less money than authorized for the position because the recruiter knows it will still be better for the potential employee.

If the other party anchors the conversation, and you are not comfortable with where that anchor, re-anchoring can be effective. In the above situation, for example, if the recruiter is using your previous salary as the basis for the offer, you could bring in market research for what the position generally earns at similar companies and use that number to re-anchor the discussion. While not always effective, re-anchoring can serve as a way to stay focused on your goals during a negotiation.

Goals

Another way to stay focused during negotiations is to make sure that you have clearly defined your goals for the negotiation. With distributive negotiation, the goal can be fairly simple—sell for as much as possible or buy for as low as possible. The more specific you are able to be, however, the more focused you can be during the negotiation. The goal you select will affect your behavior during the negotiation, which will affect the outcome of the negotiation. Research shows that more aggressive goals (indirectly) result in better outcomes for the goal-setting negotiator (Agndal, et al., 2017).

With integrative negotiation, goals can become more complicated. Maintaining the relationship is often more important than any individual negotiation, so it is imperative to include that as a goal. And because integrative negotiations are interest-based, trying to get the absolute lowest price often isn't most beneficial to you, especially if it sours the relationship or causes the other party to walk away, leaving you without a supplier or client.

Goals in all negotiations should be a best-case reasonable scenario. A goal of cutting your supplier's price by 99 percent is, in almost every case, not reasonable, and thus your actions based on that goal won't be reasonable. However, if your goal is to gain a 2 to 5 percent cost reduction by adding a new product from the supplier, you are more likely to gain that because you have a specific plan to attain a reasonable goal.

KEYS TO EFFECTIVE INTEGRATIVE NEGOTIATION

As we noted earlier, integrative negotiation differs from distributive negotiation in several ways, the biggest

being that all parties are trying to "grow the pie" instead of "split the pie" (Fisher & Ury, 2011; D. Malhotra & M. Bazerman, 2008). In distributive negotiations, each party is trying to gain as much money or spend as little money as possible so that they keep as much of the pie as possible. In integrative negotiation, all of the parties are actively looking for ways to make the pie bigger. Each party wants every party to get more from the negotiation than each would have received without an agreement.

Because the focus of integrative negotiation is on creating benefit for all involved parties, the process of integrative negotiations differs greatly from that of distributive negotiations. The first difference is the focus on the relationship. Interest-based negotiations often involve a working relationship with the other parties and have the potential for future negotiations. Because of this, it is prudent to take measure of the importance of the relationship before entering negotiations. If the relationship is important, more care should be taken to make sure that the negotiations do not sour the relationship.

One way to achieve a positive view of the negotiation is to ask questions to understand the other parties' interests. This is best accomplished with a give-and-take communication, where good information is given to build trust. As all parties share and ask for information, they build trust, and the likelihood of a positive agreement increases.

Of course, there will be integrative negotiations in which one party is unwilling or unable to provide information. We are not suggesting that you should openly share all of your information without receiving any in return—trust must be built, and giving trust to someone who is unwilling to reciprocate can be dangerous. Also, some ways of sharing information are safer than others. We recommend a conservative approach to information sharing that shows you are willing to build trust without compromising your interests.

Of course, asking questions is always paired with listening to the responses. In order to build trust, you must pay attention to what the other parties in the negotiation tell you. Asking the same question multiple times because you forgot the response shows that you aren't engaged in the negotiation.

Finding out what is important to each involved party will allow you to come up with solutions that accommodate the importance the parties assign to different interests. Rarely will everyone in a negotiation care about every aspect of the negotiation to the same degree; therefore, listening to what issues the other parties bring up, how frequently they bring these issues up, and their willingness to make concessions on different issues will help you learn what is most important to each party.

Once you know the importance assigned to each issue by each party, you can begin the "log rolling" process. This is the process by which you concede on issues that are less important to you to gain concessions on issues that are more important. If contract length is less important to you but very important to the other party, for example, that is an area where you can concede to make sure you get something else that is more important to you, such as delivery times. The following proven practices will aid your efforts to reach mutually agreeable outcome.

Focus on interests, not positions.   Positions are demands or assertions; interests constitute the reasons behind the demands. Experience shows that it is easier to establish agreement on interests, given that they tend to be broader and multifaceted. This step involves redefining and broadening problems to make them more tractable. It involves asking "why" questions to get to the heart of the other person's needs.

Establish overarching, shared goals.   In order to foster a climate of collaboration, both parties need to focus on their shared interests in the negotiation. For instance, the parties might agree that the shared goal is increased productivity and lower costs, or improved customer support for new buyers. Starting with shared goals makes the parties aware of the mutual benefits of reaching an agreement.

Use objective criteria for evaluating alternative agreements.   No matter how agreeable parties may be, there are bound to be some incompatible interests. Rather than seizing on these as opportunities for rejecting an agreement, it is far more productive to present alternative agreements that are still fair. A shift in thinking from "getting what I want" to "deciding what makes most sense" fosters an open, reasonable attitude. It encourages parties to avoid overconfidence or overcommitment to their initial position. Using objective measurements of any presented agreements will help keep you from rejecting them if they don't line up perfectly with what you want.

Define success in terms of real gains, not imaginary losses.   If a manager seeks a 10 percent raise and receives only 6 percent, that outcome can be viewed as either a 6 percent improvement or a 40 percent shortfall. The first interpretation focuses on gains, the second on losses (in this case, unrealized expectations). The outcome is the same, but the manager's satisfaction with it varies substantially. It is important to recognize that our satisfaction with an outcome is affected by the standards we use to judge it. Recognizing this, the collaborative negotiator facilitates agreement by judging the value of proposed solutions against reasonable standards.

Invent options for mutual gains.   This step focuses on generating creative solutions. By focusing both parties' attention on brainstorming novel, mutually agreeable solutions, the interpersonal dynamics naturally shift from competitive to collaborative. In addition, the more options and combinations there are to explore, the greater the probability of finding common ground. This step can be summarized as "Now that we better understand each other's underlying concerns and objectives, let's brainstorm ways to satisfy both our needs."

Sometimes negotiations will reach a point at which no one is willing to concede, and the atmosphere gets heated. One technique to counteract this is to "go to the balcony." Physically stepping out of the room and taking a short break can ease the tension built up in the room and allow all parties a chance to catch their breath and to rein in emotions.

These are excellent ways to come to an agreeable solution in win-win negotiations, and they all come down to one basic tenet: Help everyone get what they want the most. When everyone can accept the outcome, agreeing that any other outcome would lead to lower overall satisfaction, the negotiation has reached **Pareto efficiency**.

Pareto efficiency is the goal for most integrative negotiations, but it is rarely reached. An example: A negotiation has just concluded between Company A, Company B, and Company C. They met to discuss a collaborative project, which included issues X, Y, and Z. The three companies were able to reach an agreement in which Company A was 97 percent satisfied, Company B was 94 percent satisfied, and Company C was 88 percent satisfied, giving an average satisfaction of 93 percent. However, if the groups had negotiated a 1 percent increase on issue Y, Company B's total satisfaction would have increased to 95 percent and Company C's satisfaction to 91 percent, while Company A's satisfaction would have remained the same at 97 percent. This solution would have been closer to Pareto efficiency because the overall satisfaction would have increased to 94 percent.

One way to more often reach Pareto efficiency is with post-negotiation negotiation. After an agreement has been agreed to by all parties, you may opt to partake in post-negotiation negotiations, where creativity is allowed to flow more freely. The original agreement stays in force, but everyone can put their heads together to see if there is a better solution for all parties involved. If a better solution is found, the original agreement can be nullified in favor of the better agreement; if a better solution isn't found, the agreement remains in force, no harm done.

Post-negotiation negotiation can be a valuable tool if the involved parties are willing to continue to negotiate. Once the stress of finding an agreeable solution has been removed from the negotiation, parties are often more willing to look for creative solutions that may address everyone's interests better than the original solution. Because addressing each party's interest is the point of interest-based negotiation, post-negotiation negotiations can be an extremely valuable tool.

Detailed suggestions for planning and conducting negotiations are included in the Behavioral Guidelines at the end of the Skill Learning section and in the Negotiation Planning Document in the Skill Practice section.

Resolving Conflicts Successfully

Conflict is a constant in organizations, and how well it is managed is an increasingly important predictor of organizational success (Memeth, 2004). Unresolved conflict, whether it involves issues related to globalization and joint ventures, workforce diversity, or localized conflicts within work units, predictably produces

harmful results. And although some conflicts, such as personality clashes, ideological differences, and arguments over things that can't be changed, are very difficult to resolve, most can be, with the aid of the right tools. Generally speaking, two of the essential tools are: 1) understanding the focus and source of a particular conflict, and 2) selecting the appropriate approach, or strategy, for conflict resolution.

> **MyLab Management** Watch it!
> If your instructor has assigned this activity, go to www.pearson.com/mylab/management to complete the video exercise.

UNDERSTANDING DIFFERENT TYPES OF CONFLICT

Because interpersonal conflicts come in many varieties, our first skill-building task involves the art of diagnosis. In any type of clinical setting, from medicine to management, it is common knowledge that effective intervention is predicated upon accurate diagnosis. Figure 7.1 presents a categorizing device for diagnosing the *type of conflict*, based on two critical identifying characteristics: focus and source. By understanding the *focus of the conflict*, we gain an appreciation for the substance of the dispute (what is fueling the conflict),

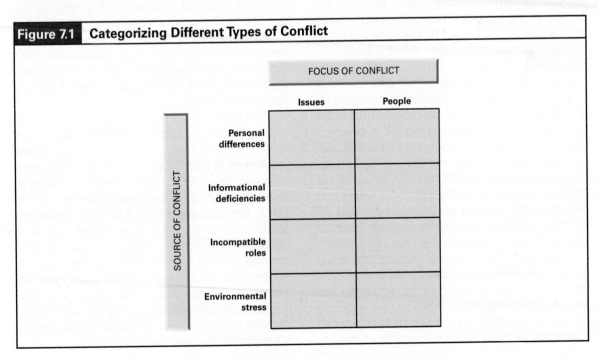

Figure 7.1   Categorizing Different Types of Conflict

and by learning more about the origins, or *source of the conflict*, we better understand how it got started (the igniting spark). As with medicine, a correct diagnosis is essential for effective treatment.

Conflict Focus

We can categorize conflicts as primarily focused on either *issues* or *people* (Eisenhardt, et al., 1997; Jehn & Mannix, 2001). In other words, conflicts can be about competing ideas, proposals, interests, or resource needs, or about relationships between specific individuals (e.g., tensions over personality or value differences, hard feelings over past events, taking offense at something another person said). The distinction between issue-focused and people-focused conflicts helps us understand why some managers believe that conflict is the lifeblood of their organization while others believe that each and every conflict episode sucks life from their organization. Research has shown that people-focused conflicts threaten effectiveness, whereas issue-based conflicts actually enhance performance as long as people feel psychologically safe at work (Bradley, et al., 2012) and have the skills to manage the conflict effectively and openly (Bradley, et al., 2013; de Dreu & Weingart, 2002; Jehn, 1997). So, when people talk about the benefits of productive conflict, they are generally referring to issue-focused conflict.

Issue-focused conflicts are likely to take the form of negotiations, which can be thought of as "an interpersonal decision-making process by which two or more people agree how to allocate scarce resources" (Thompson, 2001, p. 2). In issue-based conflicts, manager-negotiators are typically acting as agents, representing the interests of their department, function, or project. Although negotiators may have conflicting priorities for the way in which scarce resources should be utilized, most negotiators recognize the need to find an amicable settlement that appears fair to all parties. This desire for fairness at least partly reflects the fact that a particular issue-based conflict is seldom the last word on the matter. Said differently, knowing that parties must periodically resolve differences arising from their inherently different perspectives and needs, for example, different product lines or business functions, tends to mitigate against a winner-takes-all mentality.

Of course, all interpersonal conflicts involve people, but **people-focused conflict** refers to in-your-face confrontations in which emotions run high because one or both of the parties believe they have been personally harmed by the actions of the other. These disputes are often fueled by moral indignation and characterized by accusations of harm, demands for justice, and feelings of resentment. In short, in people-focused conflicts it is the other party, not the group or role they represent, that is the subject of the conflict. While some of these altercations can be resolved quickly by correcting misperceptions about who did what and for what reasons, most personal disputes are extremely difficult to resolve, and the long-term effects of the dispute on interpersonal relations can be devastating. It follows that the longer this type of dispute goes on, the larger the gulf between the parties becomes.

The material in this section, focusing on understanding the sources and types of conflict and the use of this information to select the appropriate conflict management approach, is, generally speaking, relevant for both types of conflict. Building on this general discussion of conflict management, the final section focuses more specifically on resolving people-focused conflicts with the aid of proven behavioral guidelines.

Conflict Source

We now shift our diagnostic lens from understanding the focus, or content, of a conflict ("What's this about?") to the source, or origin, of the conflict ("How did it get started?"). Managers, especially those who feel uncomfortable with conflict, often behave as though interpersonal conflict is the result of personality defects. They label people who are frequently involved in conflicts as troublemakers or bad apples and attempt to transfer or dismiss them as a way of resolving disagreements. While some individuals seem to have a propensity for making trouble and appear to be disagreeable under even the best of circumstances, sour dispositions actually account for only a small percentage of organizational conflicts (Hines, 1980; Schmidt & Tannenbaum, 1965).

This proposition is supported by research on performance appraisals (Latham & Wexley, 1994). It has been shown that managers generally attribute poor performance to personal deficiencies in workers, such as laziness, lack of skill, or lack of motivation. However, when workers are asked the causes of their poor performance, they generally explain it in terms of problems in their environment, such as insufficient supplies or uncooperative coworkers. While some face-saving is obviously involved here, this line of research suggests that managers need to guard against the reflexive tendency to assume that bad behaviors imply bad people. In fact, people who express aggressive or harsh behaviors often have good intentions but are simply unskilled in handling intense, emotional experiences.

Table 7.1	Sources of Conflict
Personal differences	Perceptions and expectations
Informational deficiencies	Misinformation and misrepresentation
Role incompatibility	Goals and responsibilities
Environmental stress	Resource scarcity and uncertainty

In contrast to the personality-defect theory of conflict, we list four sources of interpersonal conflict in Table 7.1. **Personal differences** are a common source of conflict because individuals bring different backgrounds to their roles in organizations. Their values and needs have been shaped by different socialization processes, based on their cultural and family traditions, level of education, breadth of experience, and so forth. As a result, people's interpretations of events and their expectations about relationships with others in the organization vary considerably. Conflicts stemming from incompatible personal values and needs are some of the most difficult to resolve. They often become highly emotional and take on moral overtones. Under these conditions, a disagreement about what is *factually correct* can easily turn into a bitter argument over *who is morally right*.

At first glance, it might appear that personal differences and people-focused conflict are the same thing. They are not. It might help to think of personal differences as a set of lenses that each member of an organization uses to make sense of daily experiences and to make value judgments in terms of what is good and bad, appropriate and inappropriate. When someone has used a particular lens or perspective for a long time, it becomes a strongly held belief that the individual may never question. It is easy to see how challenges to these strongly held interpretations of the world could spark interpersonal conflicts. However, that does not necessarily mean that the conflict will become personal. Even when one's deeply held beliefs are challenged, one still has choices regarding what path their dispute will take. Will they focus on the issues (e.g., the fact that you and I have differing views or values) or the people (e.g., I question your competence, intent, acceptance, understanding, etc.)?

This question is particularly relevant for managers working in an organizational environment characterized by demographic and value diversity. On the one hand, a diverse workforce can be a strategic organizational asset (Cox, 1994), but on the other, very different people have the potential to experience intense conflicts—which can become an organizational liability (Lombardo & Eichinger, 1996; Pelled, Eisenhardt, & Xin, 1999). Some of the consistently cited benefits of an effectively managed, diverse workforce (Cox & Blake, 1991; Morrison, 1996) include:

- ❑ Cost savings from reducing turnover rates among minority employees
- ❑ Improved creativity and problem-solving capabilities due to the broader range of perspectives and cultural mind-sets
- ❑ Perceptions of fairness and equity in the workplace
- ❑ Increased flexibility that positively affects motivation and minimizes conflict between work and nonwork demands (e.g., family, personal interests, leisure)

Research suggests that diverse groups might have less confidence in their performance than homogenous groups, but they actually perform better (Phillips, Liljenquist, & Neale, 2009). The benefits of diversity don't come without challenges, however. Consider the old saying: "To create a spark, strike two unlike substances together." The spark of creativity in groups might also require some collisions between diverse perspectives and ideas. For example, imagine a team that includes one member who is extremely laid back and casual by nature, and who enjoys generating imaginative ideas. By contrast, another member of the team is highly formal, anxious, and detail-oriented. There are obvious ways in which these two members could develop person-based conflict stemming from annoyance around differing styles. On the other hand, if these two team members can learn to manage their differences with each other, they could experience great synergy; the detail-oriented teammate may have exactly the right demeanor to help the creative teammate see her ideas through to execution.

Interpersonal collisions also happen when people from different ethnic and cultural groups have different views about the value of, and justifications for, interpersonal disputes (Adler, 2002; Trompenaars, 1994, 1996). In other words, our cultural background shapes our views of what is worth fighting for and what constitutes a fair fight (Sillars & Weisberg, 1987; Weldon & Jehn, 1995; Wilmot & Hocker, 2001). The potential for harmful conflict is even greater when confrontations involve members of majority and minority groups within an organization. This is where diversity-sensitive managers can help out by considering questions such as: Are both participants from the majority culture of the organization? If one is from a minority culture, to what extent is diversity valued in the organization? To what extent do members of these minority and majority cultures understand and value the benefits of a diverse workforce for our organization? Has this particular minority group or individual had a history of conflict within the organization? If so, are there broader issues regarding the appreciation of personal differences that need to be addressed?

Another source or cause of conflict among members of an organization is **informational deficiencies**. An important message may not be received, a boss's instructions may be misinterpreted, or decision makers may arrive at different conclusions because they use different databases. Conflicts based on misinformation or misunderstanding tend to be factual; hence, clarifying previous messages or obtaining additional information generally resolves the dispute. This might entail rewording the boss's instructions, reconciling contradictory sources of data, or redistributing copies of misplaced messages. This type of conflict is common in organizations, but it is also easy to resolve. Because these confrontations do not necessarily challenge value systems, they tend to be less emotional. Once the breakdown in the information system is repaired, disputants are generally able to resolve their disagreement with minimal resentment. For example, one employee felt deeply hurt when a project she expected to supervise was entrusted to another coworker. Assuming that her manager was somehow unhappy with her, she kept her distance and began interpreting everything her boss did as evidence of his dissatisfaction with her. Only later did she discover that her boss had withheld the project because he knew she was in line for a promotion that would prevent her from seeing the project through. Her resentment evaporated, of course, and she apologized to her supervisor for contributing to a conflict based on incomplete information. Her apology was readily reciprocated.

A third source of conflict is **role incompatibility**, which is inherent in complex organizations in which employees' tasks are highly interdependent. This type of conflict is exemplified by the classic goal conflicts between line and staff, production and sales, and marketing and R&D. Each unit has different responsibilities in the organization, and, as a result, each places different priorities on organizational goals (e.g., customer satisfaction, product quality, production efficiency, compliance with government regulations). It is also typical of firms whose multiple product lines compete for scarce resources.

Another major source of conflict is **environmentally induced stress**. When an organization is forced to operate on an austere budget, for example, its members are more likely to become embroiled in disputes over domain claims and resource requests. Scarcity tends to lower trust, increase ethnocentrism, and reduce participation in decision-making. These are ideal conditions for incubating interpersonal conflict (Cameron, Kim, & Whetten, 1987).

When a large Eastern bank announced a major downsizing, the threat to employees' security was so severe that it disrupted longtime close working relationships. Even friendships were not immune to the effects of the scarcity-induced stress. Long-standing golf foursomes and carpools were disbanded because tension among members was so high.

Another environmental condition that fosters conflict is uncertainty. When individuals are unsure about their status in an organization, they become anxious and prone to conflict. This type of frustration conflict often stems from rapid, repeated change. If task assignments, management philosophy, accounting procedures, and lines of authority are changed frequently, members find it difficult to cope with the resulting stress, and sharp, bitter conflicts can easily erupt over seemingly trivial problems. This type of conflict is generally intense, but it dissipates quickly once a change becomes routinized and individuals' stress levels are lowered.

When a major pet food manufacturing facility announced that one-third of its managers would have to support a new third shift, the feared disruption of personal and family routines prompted many managers to think about sending out their résumés. In addition, the uncertainty of who was going to be required to work at night was so great that even routine management work was disrupted by posturing and infighting.

Before we conclude our discussion of the sources of interpersonal conflict, it is useful to point out that people from particular cultural backgrounds might tend to be drawn into particular types of conflict. For example, one of the primary dimensions of cultural values emerging from Geert Hofstede's (1980) seminal research was tolerance for uncertainty. Some cultures, such as Japan's, have a high uncertainty avoidance, whereas other cultures, like the United States, are much more uncertainty tolerant. Extrapolating from these findings, if an American firm and a Japanese firm have created a joint venture in an industry known for highly volatile sales (e.g., memory chips), one would expect that the Japanese managers would experience a higher level of uncertainty-induced conflict than their American counterparts. By contrast, because American culture places an extremely high value on individualism (another of Hofstede's key dimensions of cultural values), one would expect that the U.S. managers in this joint venture would experience a higher level of conflict stemming from their role interdependence with their Japanese counterparts.

SELECTING AN APPROPRIATE CONFLICT MANAGEMENT APPROACH

Now that we have examined different types of conflict in terms of their focus and sources, we shift our attention to strategies for managing conflicts of any type. As you saw in the skill assessment survey, people's responses to interpersonal confrontations tend to fall into five categories: *forcing, accommodating, avoiding, compromising,* and *collaborating* (Volkema & Bergmann, 2001). These responses can be organized along two dimensions, as shown in Figure 7.2 (Ruble & Thomas, 1976). These five approaches to conflict reflect different degrees of cooperativeness and assertiveness. A cooperative response focuses on the concerns of the other person; an assertive approach focuses on one's own concerns. The cooperativeness dimension

reflects the importance of the relationship, and the assertiveness dimension reflects the importance of the issue. As you will see in the following discussion, cooperativeness and assertiveness are not mutually exclusive.

Conflict Management Approaches

The **forcing response** (assertive, uncooperative) is an attempt to satisfy one's own needs at the expense of the needs of the other individual. This can be done by using formal authority, physical threats, or manipulation ploys, or by ignoring the claims of the other party. The blatant use of the authority of one's office ("I'm the boss, so we'll do it my way") or other forms of intimidation reflect an egoistic leadership style that may actually reflect a lack of self-confidence on the leader's part. Managers who rely on forcing strategies may simply ignore proposals that threaten their personal interests and may use manipulative tactics to get their way, even while striving to appear democratic in their leadership style.

The problem with the repeated use of this conflict management approach is that it breeds hostility and resentment. While observers may intellectually admire

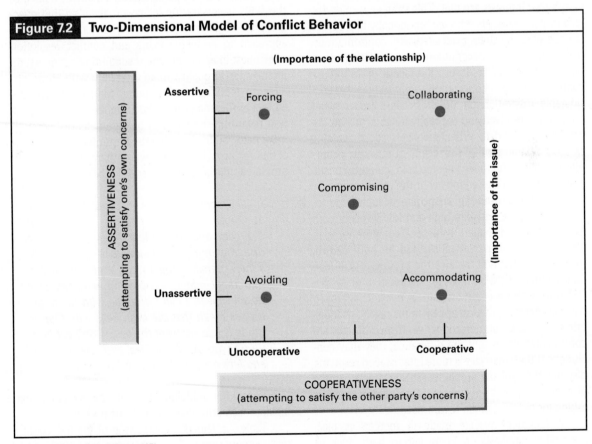

Figure 7.2 Two-Dimensional Model of Conflict Behavior

SOURCE: *Adapted from Ruble & Thomas, 1976.*

authoritarian or manipulative leaders because they appear to accomplish a great deal, their management styles generally produce a backlash in the long run as people become increasingly unwilling to absorb the emotional costs. Often, followers will actively work to undermine the power base of the authoritarian leader.

The **accommodating approach** (cooperative, unassertive) satisfies the other party's concerns while neglecting one's own. Unfortunately, some boards of directors take an accommodating approach in their interactions with management of failing firms, and thus neglect their vital oversight responsibilities. The difficulty with habitual use of the accommodating approach is that it emphasizes preserving a friendly relationship and ignores the need to critically appraise issues and protect personal rights. This may result in others taking advantage of you, which lowers your self-esteem as you observe yourself being used by others to accomplish their objectives while you fail to make any progress toward your own.

The **avoiding response** (uncooperative, unassertive) neglects the interests of both parties by sidestepping the conflict or postponing a solution. Avoiding is a lose-lose alternative because it ensures that neither party's true interests are met. This strategy is often the response of managers who are emotionally ill-prepared to cope with the stress associated with confrontations, or it might reflect recognition that a relationship is not strong enough to absorb the fallout of an intense conflict. The repeated use of this approach causes considerable frustration for others because issues never seem to get resolved and the really tough problems are consistently avoided. When managers adopt avoiding as their default conflict management strategy, people often rush in to fill the leadership void, creating considerable confusion and animosity in the process.

The **compromising response** occupies the intermediate space between high and low levels of both assertiveness and cooperativeness. A compromise is an attempt to obtain partial satisfaction for both parties, in the sense that both receive the proverbial half loaf. To accomplish this, both parties are asked to make sacrifices to obtain a common gain. While this approach has considerable practical appeal to managers, its indiscriminate use is counterproductive. If subordinates are continually told to split the difference, they may conclude that their manager is more interested in resolving disputes than solving problems. This creates a climate of expediency that encourages game playing, such as asking for twice as much as you need.

A common mistake made in mergers is placing undue emphasis on being fair to both sides by compromising on competing corporate policies and practices. When decisions are made on the basis of "spreading the pain evenly" or "using half of your procedures and half of ours," rather than on the basis of merit, then harmony takes priority over value. Ironically, actions taken in the name of keeping peace in the merged companies often end up being so illogical and impractical that the emerging union is doomed to operate under a pall of constant internal turmoil and conflict.

Similar to the integrative form of negotiation, the **collaborating approach** (cooperative, assertive) is an attempt to fully address the concerns of both parties. It is often referred to as the problem-solving mode. In this mode, the intent is to find solutions that are satisfactory to both parties rather than to find fault or assign blame. In this way, both parties can feel that they have won. This is the only win-win strategy among the five. Although the collaborative approach is not appropriate for all situations, when used appropriately, it has the most beneficial effect on the involved parties. It encourages norms of collaboration and trust while acknowledging the value of assertiveness. It encourages individuals to focus their disputes on problems and issues rather than on personalities. Finally, it cultivates the skills necessary for self-governance, so that effective problem solvers feel empowered. The collaborative approach to problem-solving and conflict resolution works best in an environment supporting openness, directness, and equality. In an interview with Steve Jobs after he founded the computer company NeXT, the editors of *Inc.* magazine asked him the following question regarding the perils of being a celebrity boss: "It must help you in attracting the best minds to your new computer firm, but once they're there, aren't they intimidated, working for a legend?" Jobs's response was:

> It all depends on the culture. The culture at NeXT definitely rewards independent thought, and we often have constructive disagreements—at all levels. It doesn't take a new person long to see that people feel fine about openly disagreeing with me. That doesn't mean I can't disagree with them, but it does mean that the best ideas win. Our attitude is that we want the best. Don't get hung up on who owns the idea. Pick the best one, and let's go. (Gendron & Burlingham, 1989)

Behavioral guidelines for utilizing the collaborating approach are provided in the next section.

Table 7.2 shows a comparison of the five conflict management approaches. In this table, the fundamentals

Table 7.2

Table 7.2 A Comparison of Conflict Management Approaches

Approach	Objective	Point of View	Supporting Rationale	Likely Outcome
Forcing	Get your way.	"I know what's right. Don't question my judgment or authority."	It is better to risk causing a few hard feelings than to abandon an issue you are committed to.	You feel vindicated, but the other party feels defeated and possibly humiliated.
Avoiding	Avoid having to deal with conflict.	"I'm neutral on that issue." "Let me think about it." "That's someone else's problem."	Disagreements are inherently bad because they create tension.	Interpersonal problems don't get resolved, causing long-term frustration that manifests in a variety of ways.
Compromising	Reach an agreement quickly.	"Let's search for a solution we can both live with, so we can get on with our work."	Prolonged conflicts distract people from their work and engender bitter feelings.	Participants become conditioned to seek expedient, rather than effective, solutions.
Accommodating	Don't upset the other person.	"How can I help you feel good about this encounter?" "My position isn't so important that it is worth risking bad feelings between us."	Maintaining harmonious relationships should be our top priority.	The other person is likely to take advantage of you.
Collaborating	Solve the problem together.	"This is my position. What is yours?" "I'm committed to finding the best possible solution." "What do the facts suggest?"	The positions of both parties are equally important (though not necessarily equally valid). Equal emphasis should be placed on the quality of the outcome and the fairness of the decision-making process.	The problem is most likely to be resolved. Also, both parties are committed to the solution and satisfied that they have been treated fairly.

of each approach are laid out, including its objective, how that objective is reflected in terms of an expressed point of view, and a supporting rationale. In addition, the likely outcomes of each approach are summarized.

SELECTION CRITERIA

Each approach has its place in organizational life. The question for good conflict managers, therefore, is not "Which strategy is the best one?" but rather "Which strategy should I use in *this* situation?" The appropriateness of a management strategy depends on its congruence with both personal preferences and situational factors.

PERSONAL PREFERENCES

As reflected in the "Strategies for Handling Conflict" survey in the Skill Assessment section of this chapter, it is important that we understand our own personal preferences for managing conflict. Someone who does not feel comfortable with a particular approach is not likely to use that approach, no matter how convinced

they are that it is the best available tool for a particular conflict situation. Although there are numerous factors that affect our personal preferences for how we manage conflict, including basic personality differences, two are worth particular note: ethnic culture and gender.

Research suggests that *ethnic culture* strongly affects individual preferences for the five conflict management strategies (Seybolt, et al., 1996; Weldon & Jehn, 1995). For example, individuals from Asian cultures tend to prefer the nonconfrontational styles of accommodating and avoiding (Rahim & Blum, 1994; Ting-Toomey, et al., 1991; Xie, Song, & Stringfellow, 1998), whereas, by comparison, Americans and South Africans prefer the forcing approach (Rahim & Blum, 1994; Seybolt, et al., 1996; Xie, et al., 1998). In general, compromise is the most commonly preferred approach across cultures (Seybolt, et al., 1996), possibly because compromising may be viewed as the least costly alternative and the approach that most quickly reaches acceptable levels of fairness to both parties.

The research on the relationship between preferred conflict management style and *gender* is less clear-cut. Some studies report that males are more likely to use the forcing response, whereas females tend to select the compromising approach (Kilmann & Thomas, 1977; Ruble & Schneer, 1994). However, other studies found gender to have little influence on an individual's preferred responses to conflict (Korabik, Baril, & Watson, 1993). Overall, it appears that gender is probably not a strong predictor of one's preference for conflict management styles, but that people still cling to sex-role expectations about conflict management preferences (Keashly, 1994).

SITUATIONAL FACTORS

Even though people have preferences for particular conflict management strategies, it is important to point out that those preferences are just general tendencies. Most people are able to draw upon more than just one conflict management style. This is important because, given the variety of causes or forms of conflict, effective conflict management requires the use of a variety of strategies.

Table 7.3 identifies four important situational attributes that can be used to select the appropriate conflict management approach.

A. How important is the disputed issue? (In the table, "High" signifies extremely important; "Low" signifies not very important.)

B. How important is the relationship? ("High" signifies a critical, ongoing, one-of-a-kind partnership; "Low" signifies a one-time transaction, for which there are readily available alternatives.)

C. What is the relative level of power, or authority, between the disputants? ("High" signifies that the actor has higher status than the conflict partner; "Equal" signifies that the two parties are peers; "Low" signifies that the actor has a lower status than the conflict partner.)

D. To what extent is time a significant constraint in resolving the dispute? ("High" signifies that the dispute must be resolved quickly; "Low" signifies that time is not a salient factor.)

This table allows you to quickly assess a situation and decide if a particular conflict management approach is suitable. As noted in the following descriptions, it is important to keep in mind that not all of the situational factors are equally important for selecting a particular approach.

The forcing approach is most appropriate when a conflict involves core values or policies and one feels compelled to defend the "correct" position; when maintaining a close, supportive relationship is not critical; and when there is a sense of urgency. An example of such a situation might be a manager insisting that a summer intern follow important company safety regulations.

The accommodating approach is most appropriate when the importance of maintaining a good working relationship outweighs all other considerations. The nature of the issues and the amount of time available play a secondary role in determining the choice of this strategy. Accommodation becomes especially appropriate when the issues are not vital to your interests and the problem must be resolved quickly.

Trying to reach a compromise is most appropriate when the issues are complex and moderately important, there are no simple solutions, and both parties have a strong interest in different facets of the problem. The other essential situational requirement is adequate time for negotiation. The classic case is a bargaining session between representatives of management and labor to avert a scheduled strike. Experience has shown that a compromising approach works best between parties with equal power who are committed to maintaining a good long-term relationship.

The collaborating approach is most appropriate when the issues are critical, maintaining an ongoing supportive relationship between peers is important, and time constraints are not pressing. When a conflict involves

Table 7.3	Matching the Conflict Management Approach with the Situation				
SITUATIONAL FACTORS	**CONFLICT MANAGEMENT APPROACH**				
	Forcing	**Accommodating**	**Compromising**	**Collaborating**	**Avoiding**
Issue Importance	High	Low	Med.	High	Low
Relationship Importance	Low	Highv	Med.	High	Low
Relative Power	High	Low	Equal	Low-High	Equal
Time Constraints	Med.-High	Med.-High	Low	Low	Med.-High

peers, the collaborative mode is more appropriate than either the forcing or accommodating approach. Collaboration can also be an effective approach for resolving conflicts between a superior and subordinate.

The avoidance approach is most appropriate when one's stake in an issue is not high and there is not a strong interpersonal reason for getting involved, regardless of whether the conflict involves a superior, subordinate, or peer. Although other strategies, such as compromise and collaboration, have a better chance of resolving problems without damaging relationships, sometimes the amount of time required to pursue these strategies is too great to justify using them. Occasionally, extreme time pressures make avoidance the best strategy.

Admittedly, this is a very rational view of how to select the appropriate approach(es) for resolving a conflict. You might wonder if it is realistic to believe that in the heat of an emotional confrontation a person is likely to step back and make this type of deliberate, systematic assessment of the situation. We have observed that the best conflict managers learn to conduct this analysis very quickly, and to respond almost instinctively with a strategy that is well-suited to the occasion.

Although we are encouraging you to take a thoughtful, analytical approach to resolving disputes, that doesn't mean you can count on the other parties to the dispute adopting the same strategy. For example, when conflicts involve individuals from dissimilar cultural traditions, it is not uncommon for them to disagree about how to resolve their differences, or even about whether the conflict should be resolved at all. If parties to a conflict hold opposing views regarding time, power, ambiguity, the rule of norms, or the importance of relationships, one can expect they will have difficulty agreeing on the appropriate course of action for resolving their dispute (Trompenaars, 1994). Put simply: If you don't agree on *how* you are going to reach an agreement, it doesn't do you much good to discuss *what* that agreement might look like. Consequently, good conflict managers must strive to clarify assumptions, interpretations, and expectations early in the conflict management process.

Regardless of your personal preferences for conflict management styles, it is important to stretch your comfort zone and become proficient in the application of the full range of choices. It is also important to match your choice with relevant situational factors, including issue and relationship importance, relative power, and time constraints. Finally, especially when parties to a dispute come from different backgrounds, it is advisable to discuss their assumptions regarding the appropriate process for resolving their differences.

Using Collaboration to Resolve People-Focused Confrontations

Thus far, our discussion of conflict management has been fairly broad and analytical. Our goal has been to help you correctly identify various types of conflict and select the appropriate approach for resolving conflicts. In this final section we speak in practical terms about how to implement the collaborative approach. We have chosen this focus for two reasons. First, as noted throughout our discussion, collaboration is most likely to generate positive results in terms of the parties' satisfaction with the conflict resolution process and the outcome. For these reasons, effective managers treat collaboration as their default option for resolving conflicts—what they use unless circumstances dictate an alternative approach. Second, it is also the hardest approach to implement effectively. In a classic study by Kipnis and Schmidt (1983) most managers expressed general support for the collaborative approach, but when it appeared that things were not going their way they reverted to a more directive approach. From our observation, one reason for this pattern is that some managers lack confidence in their ability to resolve conflicts in a collaborative manner. Managers often think a collaborative approach sounds good, but to pull it off well may be the most severe test of a manager's interpersonal skill proficiency.

With that observation in mind, we situate the following in-depth presentation of how to effectively utilize the collaborative approach in possibly the most challenging type of conflict to resolve: Person A (complaint-initiator) accuses Person B (complaint-responder) of causing personal harm to Person A. From our experience, unless either the initiator or the responder chooses to adopt a collaborative approach to resolving this type of people-focused conflict, it is unlikely the issue will be resolved to the satisfaction of both parties. In addition to initiating or responding to personal complaints, managers are sometimes called upon to mediate conflicts of this type among unit members.

To emphasize the problem-solving nature of the collaborative approach to resolving conflicts, our presentation of relevant behavioral guidelines is organized using a four-phase problem-solving process: (1) *problem identification*, (2) *solution generation*, (3) *action plan formulation and agreement*, and (4) *implementation and follow-up*. (Additional information on problem-solving is included in: Solving Problems Analytically and Creatively.) In the midst of a heated exchange, the first two phases are the most critical steps, as well as the most difficult to implement effectively. If you are able to achieve agreement on what the problem is and how you intend to resolve it, the details of the agreement, including a follow-up plan, should follow naturally. We are, therefore, placing our skill-building emphasis where skillful implementation is most critical.

We have also organized our guidelines around specific roles, or parts, in a dispute: *initiator, responder*, and *mediator*. For each role, your goal should be to foster a collaborative approach regardless of what the other party says or does. If you are the initiator of a personal complaint, you have time to rehearse your lines, so to speak. Most often, the subject of a complaint has little warning prior to a scheduled appointment or a spontaneous emotional eruption. Managers might use the initiator guidelines when giving negative performance feedback or correcting negative behavior. The responder guidelines help managers avoid responding negatively to personal complaints. Because it is difficult to think straight when someone bursts into your office complaining about things you've done, we suggest committing the responder guidelines to memory. Mediation is a private, voluntary process in which an impartial person facilitates communication between the parties to promote a mutually agreeable solution. When members of a work-unit are unable to resolve a conflict, their manager may decide to mediate the impasse. In this role, managers can utilize the mediator guidelines and/or coach the individuals embroiled in conflict on how to resolve their issues using the initiator and responder guidelines.

INITIATOR

The manner in which a complaint is initiated influences how it will be received. It is therefore important to wait until your emotions aren't in control of what you say. Using the initiator guidelines to frame what you will say helps maintain a problem-solving focus and increases the odds that the responder will follow suit.

Problem Identification

A. Maintain Personal Ownership of the Problem
It is important to recognize that when you are upset and frustrated, this is your problem, not the other person's. You may feel that your boss or co-worker is the source of your problem, but the first step in addressing your concern is acknowledging accountability for your feelings. Suppose someone uses a pungent cologne. The fact that your office is going to stink all day may infuriate you, but the odor does not present a problem for your suave guest. One way to determine ownership of a problem is to identify whose needs are not being met. In this case, your need for a clean working environment is not being met, so the smelly office is your problem.

The advantage of taking ownership of a problem when registering a complaint is that it reduces defensiveness (Adler, Rosenfeld, & Proctor, 2001; Alder & Rodman, 2003). In order to resolve your problem, the respondent must not feel threatened by your initial statement of that problem. By beginning the conversation with a request for help in solving your problem, you immediately establish a problem-solving atmosphere. For example, you might say, "Bill, do you have a few minutes? I have a problem I need to discuss with you."

B. Succinctly Describe Your Problem in Terms of Behaviors, Consequences, and Feelings
A useful model for stating your problem effectively has been prescribed by Gordon (2000): *"I have a problem. When you do X, Y results, and I feel Z."* Although we don't advocate the memorization of set formulas for improving communication skills, keeping this model in mind will help you implement three critical elements in your "problem statement."

First, describe the specific behaviors (X) that present a problem for you. This will help you avoid the reflexive tendency when you are upset to give feedback that is evaluative and not specific. One way to do this is to specify the expectations or standards that have been violated. For example, a subordinate may have missed a deadline for completing an assigned task, your boss may gradually be taking over tasks previously delegated to you, or a colleague in the accounting department may have repeatedly failed to provide you with data required for an important presentation.

Second, outline the specific, observable consequences (Y) of these behaviors. Simply telling others that their actions are causing you problems is often sufficient stimulus for change. In fast-paced work environments, people generally become insensitive to the impact of their actions. They don't intend to cause offense, but they become so busy meeting deadlines associated with getting the product out the door that they tune out subtle negative feedback from others. When this occurs, bringing to the attention of others the consequences of their behaviors will often prompt them to change.

Unfortunately, not all problems can be resolved this simply. At times, offenders are aware of the negative consequences of their behaviors, yet they persist in them. In such cases, this approach is still useful in stimulating a problem-solving discussion because it presents concerns in a nonthreatening manner. Possibly, the responders' behaviors are constrained by the expectations of their boss or by the fact that the department is currently understaffed. Responders may not be able to change these constraints, but this approach will encourage them to discuss them with you so you can work on the problem together.

Third, describe the feelings (Z) you experience as a result of the problem. It is important that the responder understand that the behavior is not just inconvenient. You need to explain how it is affecting you personally by engendering feelings of frustration, anger, or insecurity. Explain how these feelings are interfering with your work. They may make it more difficult for you to concentrate, to be congenial with customers, to be supportive of your boss, or to be willing to make needed personal sacrifices to meet deadlines.

We recommend using this three-step model as a general guide. The order of the components may vary, and you should obviously not use the same words every time. Observe how the key elements in the XYZ model are used in different ways in Table 7.4.

C. Avoid Drawing Evaluative Conclusions and Attributing Motives to the Respondent

When exchanges between two disputing parties become vengeful, each side often has a different perspective about the justification of the other's actions. Typically, each party believes that he or she is the victim of the other's aggression. In international conflicts, opposing nations often believe they are acting defensively rather than offensively. Similarly, in smaller-scale conflicts, each side may have distorted views of its own hurt and the motives of the "offender" (Kim & Smith, 1993). Therefore, in presenting your problem, avoid the pitfalls of making accusations, drawing inferences about motivations or intentions, or attributing the responder's undesirable behavior to personal inadequacies. Statements such as "You are always interrupting me," "You haven't been fair to me since the day I disagreed with you in the board meeting," and "You never have time to listen to our problems and suggestions because you manage your time so poorly" are ineffective for initiating a problem-solving process.

Another key to reducing defensiveness is to delay proposing a solution until both parties agree on the nature of the problem. When you become so upset with someone's behavior that you feel it is necessary to initiate a complaint, it is often because the person has seriously violated your expectations. For example, you might feel that your manager should have been less dogmatic and listened more during a goal-setting interview. Consequently, you might be tempted to offer immediate prescriptions for a more democratic or sensitive style.

In addition to creating defensiveness, the principal disadvantage to initiating problem-solving with a suggested remedy is that it hinders the problem-solving process. Before completing the problem-articulation phase, you have immediately jumped to the solution-generation phase, based on the assumption that you know all the reasons for, and constraints on, the other person's behavior. You will jointly produce better, more acceptable, solutions if you present your statement of the problem and discuss it thoroughly before proposing potential solutions.

Table 7.4	Examples of the XYZ Approach to Stating a Problem

Model:

"I have a problem. When you do X (behavior), Y results (consequences), and I feel Z."

Examples:

I have to tell you that I get upset [feelings] when you make jokes about my bad memory in front of other people [behavior]. In fact, I get so angry so that I find myself bringing up your faults to get even [consequences].

I have a problem. When you say you'll be here for our date at six and don't show up until after seven [behavior], the dinner gets ruined, we're late for the show we planned to see [consequences], and I feel hurt because it seems as though I'm just not that important to you [feelings].

The employees want to let management know that we've been having a hard time lately with the short notice you've been giving when you need us to work overtime [behavior]. That probably explains some of the grumbling and lack of cooperation you've mentioned [consequences]. Anyhow, we wanted to make it clear that this policy has really caused a lot of the workers to feel resentful [feeling].

SOURCE: *Adapted from Adler, 1977.*

D. Persist Until Understood There are times when the respondent will not clearly receive or acknowledge even the most effectively expressed message. Suppose, for instance, that you share the following problem with a coworker:

> Something has been bothering me, and I need to share my concerns with you. Frankly, I'm uncomfortable [feeling] with your heavy use of profanity [behavior]. I don't mind an occasional "damn" or "hell," but the other words bother me a lot. Lately I've been avoiding you [consequences], and that's not good because it interferes with our working relationship, so I wanted to let you know how I feel.

When you share your feelings in this nonevaluative way, it's likely that the other person will understand your position and possibly try to change their behavior to suit your needs. On the other hand, there are a number of less satisfying responses that could be made to your comment:

> Listen, these days everyone talks that way. And besides, you've got your faults, too, you know! [Your coworker becomes defensive, rationalizing and counterattacking.]
>
> Yeah, I suppose I do swear a lot. I'll have to work on that someday. [Gets the general drift of your message but fails to comprehend how serious the problem is to you.]
>
> Listen, if you're still angry about my forgetting to tell you about that meeting the other day, you can be sure that I'm really sorry. I won't do it again. [Totally misunderstands.]
>
> Speaking of avoiding, have you seen Chris lately? I wonder if anything is wrong with him. [Is discomfited by your frustration and changes the subject.]

In each case, the coworker does not understand or does not wish to acknowledge the problem. In these situations, you must reiterate your concern until the other party acknowledges it as a problem to be solved. Otherwise, the problem-solving process will terminate at this point and nothing will change. Repeated assertions can take the form of restating the same phrase several times or reiterating your concern with different words or examples that you feel may improve comprehension. To avoid introducing new concerns or shifting from a descriptive to an evaluative mode, keep in mind the XYZ formula for feedback.

E. Encourage Two-Way Discussion by Inviting Respondent to Ask Questions and Express Their Point of View You can establish a better problem-solving climate by encouraging the other party to ask clarifying questions and to express their understanding of the issue. There may be a reasonable explanation for another's disturbing behavior. Or the person may have a radically different view of the problem. The sooner this information is introduced into the conversation, the more likely you can resolve the issue.

As a rule of thumb, an initiator should keep his or her opening statement brief. The longer the opening statement of the problem, the more likely it is to encourage a defensive reaction. The longer we talk, the more worked up we get, and the more likely we are to violate principles of supportive communication. As a result, the other party begins to feel threatened, starts mentally outlining a rebuttal or counterattack, and stops listening empathetically to our concerns. Once these dynamics enter the discussion, the collaborative approach is usually discarded in favor of the accommodating or forcing strategies, depending on the circumstances. When this occurs, it is unlikely that the actors will be able to reach a mutually satisfactory solution to their problem without third-party intervention.

F. Focus on One Problem at a Time: Build Rapport and Understanding One way to shorten your opening statement is to approach complex problems incrementally. Rather than raising a series of issues all at once, focus initially on a simple or rudimentary problem. Then, as you gain greater appreciation for the other party's perspective and share some problem-solving success, you can discuss more challenging issues. This is especially important when trying to resolve a problem with a person who is important to your work performance but who does not have a long-standing relationship with you. The less familiar you are with the other's opinions and personality, as well as the situational constraints influencing his or her behaviors, the more you should approach a problem-solving discussion as a fact-finding and rapport-building mission. This is best done by focusing your introductory statement on a specific manifestation of a problem and then opening the conversation to the responder. For example, "Bill, we had difficulty getting that work order processed on time yesterday. What seemed to be the problem?"

Solution Generation

A. Focus on Commonalities as the Basis for Requesting Changes
Once both parties clearly understand the problem, the discussion should shift to the solution-generation phase. Most disputants share at least some personal and organizational goals, believe in many of the same fundamental principles of management, and operate under similar constraints. These commonalities can serve as a useful starting point for generating solutions. The most straightforward approach to changing another's offensive behavior is to make a request. The legitimacy of a request will be enhanced if it is linked to common interests. These might include shared values, such as treating coworkers fairly and following through on commitments, or shared constraints, such as getting reports in on time and operating within budgetary restrictions. Pointing out how a change in the respondent's behavior would positively affect your shared fate will reduce defensiveness: "Jane, one of the things we have all worked hard to build in this audit team is mutual support. We are all pushed to the limit getting this job completed by the third-quarter deadline next week. Will you reconsider your position on not working overtime, at least until we can all get through this crisis together?"

RESPONDER

Now we shift our attention to the responder role—the person who is supposedly the source of the problem. In a work setting, you could find yourself as the responder if one of your employees tells you that you are making unrealistic demands, a supervisor claims you are not following proper procedures, or if a coworker accuses you of claiming credit for ideas she generated. The following guidelines show how to respond to the initiator's behavior so you can have a productive problem-solving experience.

Problem Identification

A. Establish a Climate for Joint Problem-Solving by Showing Genuine Interest and Concern
When a person complains to you, do not treat that complaint lightly. While this may seem self-evident, managers often make the mistake of trying to quickly brush a concern under the rug because they are so busy with other demands. Consequently, unless the other person's emotional condition necessitates dealing with the problem immediately, it is sometimes better to set up a time for another meeting if your current time pressures will make it difficult to give the complaint the attention it deserves.

In most cases, the initiator will be expecting you to set the tone for the meeting. You will quickly undermine collaboration if you overreact or become defensive. Even if you disagree with the complaint and feel it has no foundation, you need to respond empathetically to the initiator's statement of the problem. This is done by conveying an attitude of interest and receptivity through your posture, tone of voice, and facial expressions.

One of the most difficult aspects of establishing the proper climate for your discussion is responding appropriately to the initiator's emotions. Sometimes you may need to let a person blow off steam before trying to address the substance of a specific complaint. In some cases, the therapeutic effect of being able to express negative emotions to the boss will be enough to satisfy a subordinate. This occurs frequently in high-pressure jobs in which tempers flare easily as a result of intense stress.

However, an emotional outburst can be detrimental to problem-solving. If an employee begins verbally attacking you or someone else, and it is apparent that the individual is more interested in getting even than in solving an interpersonal problem, you may need to interrupt and interject some ground rules for collaborative problem-solving. By explaining calmly to the other person that you are willing to discuss a genuine problem but that you will not tolerate personal attacks or scapegoating, you can quickly determine the initiator's true intentions. In most instances, he or she will apologize, emulate your emotional tenor, and begin formulating a useful statement to explain the problem.

B. Seek Additional, Clarifying Information About the Problem by Asking Questions
As shown in Figure 7.3, untrained initiators typically present complaints that are so general and evaluative that they aren't useful problem statements. It is difficult to understand how you should respond to a general, vague comment like "You never listen to me during our meetings," followed by an evaluative, critical comment like "You obviously aren't interested in what I have to say." If you and the initiator are going to transform a personal complaint into a joint problem, you must redirect the conversation from general and evaluative accusations to descriptions of specific behaviors.

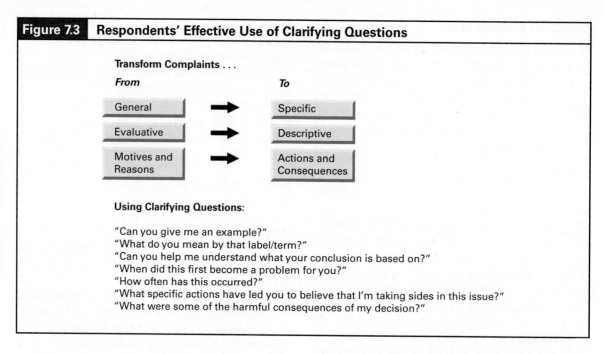

Figure 7.3   Respondents' Effective Use of Clarifying Questions

Transform Complaints . . .

From

General

Evaluative

Motives and Reasons

To

Specific

Descriptive

Actions and Consequences

Using Clarifying Questions:

"Can you give me an example?"
"What do you mean by that label/term?"
"Can you help me understand what your conclusion is based on?"
"When did this first become a problem for you?"
"How often has this occurred?"
"What specific actions have led you to believe that I'm taking sides in this issue?"
"What were some of the harmful consequences of my decision?"

The problem is that when you are getting steamed up over what you believe are unfair and unjustified accusations, it is difficult to avoid fighting back. ("Oh yeah, well I haven't wanted to say this about you before, but since you've brought up the subject...") The single best way to keep your mind focused on transforming a personal attack into a jointly identified problem is to limit your responses to questions. As the authors of the book *Crucial Conversations* put it, "at the very moment when most people become furious, we need to become curious" (Patterson, et al., 2012, p. 157). If you stick with asking clarifying questions, you are going to get better-quality information and you are going to demonstrate your commitment to joint problem-solving.

As shown in Figure 7.3, one of the best ways of doing this is to ask for examples ("Can you give me an example of what I did during a staff meeting that led you to believe I wasn't listening to what you had to say?"). Building on our discussion of the XYZ model in the initiator's guidelines, you might find it useful to ask for examples of your offending actions and their harmful consequences, including damaged feelings ("Can you give me a specific example of my behavior that concerns you?" "When I did that, what were the specific consequences for your work?" "How did you feel when that happened?").

C. Agree with Some Aspect of the Complaint

This is an important point that is difficult for some people to accept because they wonder how it is possible to agree with something they don't believe is true. They may also be worried about reinforcing complaining behavior. In practice, this step is probably the best test of whether a responder is committed to using the collaborative approach to conflict management rather than the avoiding, forcing, or accommodating approach. People who use the forcing mode will grit their teeth while listening to the initiator, just waiting to find a flaw they can use to launch a counterattack. Or they will simply respond, "I'm sorry, but that's just the way I am. You'll simply have to get used to it." Accommodators will apologize profusely and ask for forgiveness. People who avoid conflicts will acknowledge and agree with the initiator's concerns, but only in a superficial manner because their only concern is how to terminate the awkward conversation quickly.

By contrast, collaborators will demonstrate their concerns for both cooperation and assertiveness by looking for points in the initiator's presentation with which they can genuinely agree. It is usually possible to validate the other person's viewpoint without conceding your own position. Even in the most blatantly malicious and hostile verbal assault (which may be more a reflection of the initiator's insecurity than evidence of your inadequacies), there is generally a grain of truth. For example, a few years ago, a junior faculty member in a business school who was being reviewed for promotion received a very unfair appraisal from one of his senior colleagues. Since the junior member knew that the critic was going through a personal crisis, he could have dismissed the criticism as irrelevant and tendentious. However, one particular phrase—"You are stuck on a narrow line of research"—kept coming back to his mind. There was something there that couldn't be ignored. Rather than taking the feedback as simply a vindictive reproach, he considered whether it had some validity. Ultimately, the junior faculty member took this small idea (which had been buried amid the senior faculty's unfair ranting) and made a major career decision that produced very positive outcomes. Furthermore, by publicly giving the senior colleague credit for the suggestion, he substantially strengthened the interpersonal relationship.

There are a number of ways to agree with a message without accepting all of its ramifications (Adler, et al., 2001). You can find an element of truth, as in the incident related above. Or you can agree in principle with the argument: "I agree that managers should set a good example" or "I agree that it is important for salesclerks to be at the store when it opens." If you can't find anything substantive with which to agree, you can always agree with the initiator's perception of the situation: "Well, I can see how you would think that. I have known people who deliberately shirked their responsibilities." Or you can agree with the person's feelings: "It is obvious that our earlier discussion greatly upset you."

In none of these cases are you necessarily agreeing with the initiator's conclusions or evaluations, nor are you conceding your position. You are trying to understand, to foster a problem-solving, rather than argumentative, discussion. Generally, initiators prepare for a complaint session by mentally cataloguing all the evidence supporting their point of view. Once the discussion begins, they introduce as much evidence as necessary to make their argument convincing; that is, they commit themselves to keep arguing until you agree. Consequently, establishing a basis of agreement early on is the key to moving toward the problem-solving stage.

Solution Generation

A. Ask for Suggestions of Acceptable Alternatives
Once you are certain you fully understand the initiator's complaint, move on to the solution-generation phase by asking the initiator for recommended solutions. This triggers an important transition in the discussion by shifting attention from the negative to the positive and from the past to the future. It also communicates your regard for the initiator's opinions. Some managers listen patiently to a subordinate's complaint, say they will rectify the problem, and then terminate the discussion. This leaves the initiator guessing about the outcome of the meeting. Will you take the complaint seriously? Will you really change? If so, will the change resolve the problem? It is important to eliminate this ambiguity by agreeing on

a plan of action. If the problem is particularly serious or complex, it is useful to write down specific agreements, including assignments and deadlines, as well as follow-up conversations to check progress.

MEDIATOR

Managers sometimes find it necessary to mediate disputes between coworkers. The following guidelines are intended to help mediators avoid the common pitfalls associated with this role, shown in Table 7.5.

Problem Identification

A. Acknowledge That a Conflict Exists and Propose a Collaborative Problem-Solving Approach for Resolving It
When a mediator is called in, it means the disputants have failed as problem solvers. Therefore, the first step for an effective mediator is to establish a problem-solving framework for the purpose of crafting a mutually acceptable resolution. To do this, the mediator must first take seriously the problems between conflicting parties, and not belittle them. While you might wish that your subordinates could have worked out their disagreement without bothering you, this is not the time to lecture them on self-reliance. A lecture will make both parties defensive and will interfere with any serious problem-solving efforts. Seldom are lectures conducive to problem-solving.

One early decision a mediator has to make is whether to convene a joint problem-solving session or meet separately with the parties first. The diagnostic criteria shown in Table 7.6 should help you weigh the trade-offs. First, what is the current position of the disputants? Are both aware that a problem exists? Are they equally motivated to work on solving the problem? The more similar the awareness and motivation of the parties, the more likely it is that a joint session will be productive. If there is a serious discrepancy in awareness and motivation, the mediator should work to reduce that discrepancy through one-on-one meetings before bringing the disputants together.

Second, what is the current relationship between the disputants? Does their work require them to interact frequently? Is a good working relationship critical for their individual job performance? What has their relationship been in the past? What is the difference in their formal status in the organization? As we discussed earlier, joint problem-solving sessions are most productive between individuals of equal status who are required to work together regularly. This does not mean that joint meetings should not be held between a supervisor and subordinate, only that greater care

Table 7.5	Ten Mistakes to Avoid as a Mediator

1. After you have listened to the argument for a short time, don't begin to nonverbally communicate your discomfort with the discussion (e.g., sit back, begin to fidget).

2. Don't signal your agreement with one of the parties (e.g., through facial expressions, posture, chair position, reinforcing comments).

3. Don't say it is inappropriate talking about this kind of thing at work or where others can hear you.

4. Don't discourage the expression of emotion. Suggest that the discussion would better be held later after both parties have cooled off.

5. Don't suggest that both parties are wrong. Point out the problems with both points of view.

6. Don't suggest partway through the discussion that possibly you aren't the person who should be helping solve this problem.

7. Don't see if you can get both parties to attack you.

8. Don't minimize the seriousness of the problem.

9. Don't change the subject (e.g., ask for advice to help you solve one of your problems).

10. Don't express displeasure that the two parties are experiencing conflict (e.g., imply that it might undermine the solidarity of the work group).

SOURCE: *Adapted from Morris & Sashkin, 1976.*

needs to be taken in preparing for such a meeting. Specifically, if a department head becomes involved in a dispute between a worker and a supervisor, the department head should make sure that the worker does not feel this meeting will serve as an excuse for two managers to gang up on an hourly employee.

Separate fact-finding meetings with the disputants prior to a joint meeting are particularly useful when the parties have a history of recurring disputes, especially if these disputes should have been resolved without a mediator. Such a history often suggests a lack of conflict management or problem-solving skills on the part

Table 7.6	Choosing a Format for Mediating Conflicts		
Factors		**Hold Joint Meetings**	**Hold Separate Meetings First**
Awareness and Motivation			
• Both parties are aware of the problem.		Yes	No
• They are equally motivated to resolve the problem.		Yes	No
• They accept your legitimacy as a mediator.		Yes	No
Nature of the Relationship			
• The parties hold equal status.		Yes	No
• They work together regularly.		Yes	No
• They have an overall good relationship.		Yes	No
Nature of the Problem			
• This is an isolated (not a recurring) problem.		Yes	No
• The complaint is substantive in nature and easily verified.		Yes	No
• The parties agree on the root causes of the problem.		Yes	No
• The parties share common values and work priorities.		Yes	No

of the disputants, or it might stem from a broader set of issues that are beyond their control. In these situations, individual coaching sessions prior to a joint meeting will increase your understanding of the root causes and improve the individuals' abilities to resolve their differences. Following up these private meetings with a joint problem-solving session in which the mediator coaches the disputants through the process for resolving their conflicts can be a positive learning experience.

Third, what is the nature of the problem? Is the complaint substantive in nature and easily verifiable? If the problem stems from conflicting role responsibilities and the actions of both parties in question are common knowledge, then a joint problem-solving session may be preferable. However, if the complaint stems from differences in managerial style, values, personality traits, and so forth, bringing the parties together immediately following a complaint may seriously undermine the problem-solving process because it may pose threats to the participants' self-image. To prevent individuals feeling as though they are being ambushed in a meeting, you should discuss serious personal complaints with them ahead of time, in private.

B. Make It Clear that the Disputants "Own" Their Problem; Avoid the Role of Judge
It is important that the mediator avoid being seduced into rendering a "verdict" by comments from the disputants such as "Well, you're the boss; tell us which one is right." A key aspect of effective mediation is helping disputants explore multiple alternatives in a nonjudgmental manner; the problem with a mediator assuming the role of judge is that it sets in motion processes antithetical to effective interpersonal problem-solving. The parties focus on persuading the mediator of their innocence and the other party's guilt rather than striving to improve their working relationship with the assistance of the mediator. The disputants work to establish facts about what happened in the past rather than trying to reach an agreement about what ought to happen in the future.

C. While Seeking to Understand the Perspective of Both Parties, Maintain a Neutral Posture Regarding the Disputants—If Not the Issues
Effective mediation requires impartiality. If a mediator shows personal bias in favor of one party in a joint problem-solving session, the other party may simply walk out. However, such personal bias is more likely to emerge in private conversations with the disputants. Statements such as "I can't believe he really did that!" and "Everyone seems to be having trouble working with Charlie these days" imply that the media-

tor is taking sides, and any attempt to appear impartial in a joint meeting will seem like mere window dressing to appease the other party. No matter how well-intentioned or justified these comments might be, they destroy the credibility of the mediator in the long run. By contrast, effective mediators respect both parties' points of view and make sure that both perspectives are expressed adequately.

Occasionally it is not possible to be impartial on issues. One person may have violated company policy, engaged in unethical competition with a colleague, or broken a personal agreement. In these cases, the challenge of the mediator is to separate the offense from the offender. If a person is clearly in the wrong, the inappropriate behavior needs to be corrected, but in such a way that the individual doesn't feel his or her image and working relationships have been permanently marred. This can be done most effectively when correction occurs in private.

D. Manage the Discussion to Ensure Fairness—Keep the Discussion Issue Oriented, Not Personality Oriented
It is important that the mediator maintain a problem-solving atmosphere throughout the discussion. This is not to say that strong emotional statements don't have their place. People often associate effective problem-solving with a calm, highly rational discussion of the issues. However, placid, cerebral discussions may not solve all problems, and impassioned statements don't have to be insulting. The critical point about process is that it should be centered on the issues and the consequences of continued conflict on performance. Good mediators focus the discussion on specific behaviors, not on personality quirks. Attributions of motives and overgeneralizing about each other's proclivities distract participants from the problem-solving process. It is important that the mediator establish and maintain these ground rules.

It is also important for a mediator to ensure that neither party dominates the discussion. A relatively even balance in the level of input improves the quality of the final outcome. It also increases the likelihood that both parties will accept the final decision, because there is a high correlation between feelings about the problem-solving process and attitudes about the final solution. If one party is dominating a discussion, the mediator can help balance the exchange by asking the less talkative individual direct questions: "Now that we have heard Bill's view of that incident, how do you see it?" "That's an important point, Brad, so let's make sure Brian agrees. How do you feel, Brian?"

Solution Generation

A. Explore Options by Focusing on Common Interests, Not Disparate Positions
As noted earlier in this section, positions are demands, whereas interests are the underlying needs, values, goals, or concerns behind the demands. Focusing only on positions may cause disputants to feel that they have irreconcilable differences. Mediators can help by examining the interests behind the positions.

The mediator's job is to help disputants bring their unspoken interests to the surface and to discover where they intersect and where they conflict. In order to flesh out each party's interests, ask "why" questions: "Why have they taken this position?" "Why does this matter to them?" Understand that there is probably no one simple answer to these questions. Each side may represent a number of constituents, each with special interests.

After each side has articulated its underlying interests, help the parties identify areas of agreement and reconcilability. It is common for participants in an intense conflict to feel that they are on opposite sides of all issues—that they have little in common. Helping them recognize that there are areas of agreement and reconcilability often represents a major turning point in resolving long-standing feuds.

B. Use the Dispute as an Opportunity to Teach Problem-Solving Skills and to Establish Protocols for Dispute Resolution
When parties with a history of chronic interpersonal problems must work closely together, it is often more important to teach problem-solving skills than to resolve a specific dispute. The guidelines for initiators and respondents can be used as teaching tools. In addition, it is advisable for managers to establish guidelines for the kinds of issues that should be brought to their attention, leaving the rest to be resolved by coworkers. This understanding will help managers avoid unintentionally reinforcing negative behavior, by agreeing to hear, or worse resolve, every disagreement.

ALL ROLES

Action Plan and Follow-Up

A. Make Sure All Parties Understand and Support the Agreed-Upon Solution and Establish Follow-Up Procedures
The last two phases of the proposed conflict problem-solving process are (1) agreement on an action plan, and (2) follow-up. We will discuss these within the context of the mediator's role, but they are equally relevant to the other roles.

A common mistake of ineffective mediators is terminating discussions prematurely, on the supposition that once a problem has been solved in principle, the disputants can be left to work out the details on their own. Or a mediator may assume that because one party has recommended a solution that appears reasonable and workable, the second disputant will be willing to implement it.

To avoid these mistakes, it is important to stay engaged in the mediation process until both parties have agreed on a detailed plan of action. You might consider using the familiar planning template—who, what, how, when, and where—as a checklist for making sure the plan is complete. Carefully explore any hesitancy on the part of either disputant ("Tom, I sense that you are somewhat less enthusiastic than Sue about this plan. Is there something that bothers you?").

When you are confident that both parties support the plan, check to make sure they are aware of their respective responsibilities and then propose a mechanism for monitoring progress. For example, you might schedule another formal meeting, or you might stop by both individuals' offices to get a progress report. As you go forward, be open to good-faith modifications of the proposal to accommodate unforeseen implementation issues. Consider using a follow-up meeting to celebrate the successful resolution of the dispute and to discuss lessons learned for future applications.

Summary

Conflict is a difficult and controversial topic. In most cultures, it has negative connotations because it runs counter to the notion that we should get along with people by being kind and friendly. Although many people intellectually understand the value of conflict, they feel uncomfortable confronting it. Their discomfort may result from a lack of understanding of the conflict process as well as from a lack of training in how to handle interpersonal confrontations effectively. In this chapter, we have addressed these issues by introducing both analytical and behavioral skills.

Negotiations, both formal and informal, are a key component of conflict management. Conflict management comes into play after a conflict arises, whereas negotiation is used to prevent conflicts from arising. Successful negotiations produce agreement, but along the way conflict-resolution tools may be needed.

A summary model of conflict management, the central focus of this chapter, is shown in Figure 7.4.

Figure 7.4 **Summary Model of Conflict Management**

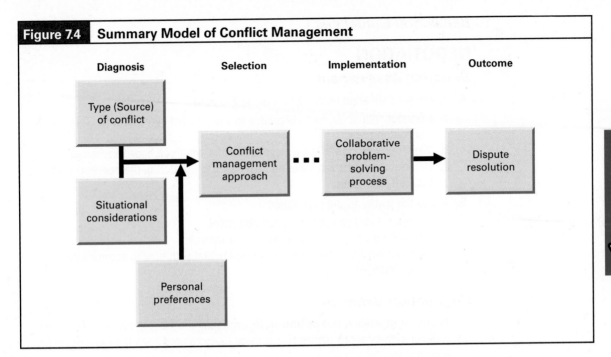

The model contains four elements: (1) diagnosing the sources of conflict; (2) selecting an appropriate conflict management strategy; (3) effectively implementing the strategy, using a collaborative problem-solving process when possible; and (4) successfully resolving the dispute. Note that the final outcome of our model is successful dispute resolution. Given our introductory claim that conflict plays an important role in organizations, our concluding observation is that the objective of effective conflict management is the successful resolution of disputes, not the elimination of conflict altogether.

The diagnostic element of our summary model contains two important components. First, assessing the source or type of conflict provides insights into the whys behind a confrontation. We have considered four common causes of conflict: personal differences, discrepancies in information, role incompatibilities, and environmentally induced stress. These types of conflict differ in both frequency and intensity. For example, information-based conflicts occur frequently, but they are easily resolved because disputants have low personal stakes in the outcome. By contrast, conflicts grounded in differences of perceptions and expectations are generally intense and difficult to defuse.

The second important component of the diagnostic process is assessing the relevant situational factors, so as to determine the feasible set of responses.

Important contextual factors that we considered include the importance of the issue, the importance of the relationship, the relative power of the disputants, and the degree to which time is a limiting factor.

The purpose of the diagnostic phase of the model is to choose wisely between the five conflict management approaches: avoiding, compromising, collaborating, forcing, and accommodating. These reflect different degrees of assertiveness and cooperativeness, or the priority given to satisfying one's own concerns versus the concerns of the other party.

As shown in Figure 7.4, personal preferences, reflecting a person's ethnic culture, gender, and personality, play a key role in our conflict management strategies. If we feel comfortable with an approach, we are likely to use it effectively. However, because effective problem solvers use a variety of tools, we shouldn't pass over an appropriate tool because we feel discomfort about it. For this reason, it is important for conflict managers to stretch their natural comfort zone through skill development activities.

That is why, as shown in the figure, we elected to focus on the implementation of one conflict management approach that is generally the most effective but also often the most challenging—collaborative problem-solving. The behavioral guidelines provided below reflect our emphasis on collaborative problem-solving as the preferred conflict management strategy when circumstances permit it.

Behavioral Guidelines

NEGOTIATION
Situation Assessment

A. Assess your situation entering into the negotiation.
   a. Consider your goals, best alternative to a negotiated agreement (BATNA), and reservation price.
   b. Write out your power in the negotiation and what you hope to accomplish.
   c. Determine negotiation styles and strategies to use during the negotiation that best suit your goals.

B. Assess the parties in the negotiation.
   a. Consider their goals, BATNA, and objectives.
   b. Estimate how important each issue is for them.
   c. Consider what strategies they may employ, and plan how to accommodate those strategies.

Negotiation Behavior

A. **Focus on interests, not positions.** By switching the focus to interests, you allow collaboration between parties that is more likely to produce a favorable result for everyone involved.

B. **Invent options for mutual gains.** Instead of focusing on winning a negotiation, which often leads to poor business or personal relations, focus on improving the situation for all of the parties.

C. **Work toward the Pareto efficiency.** Working toward the optimum solution can help reach a more favorable outcome for the current negotiation and can lay the groundwork for more favorable future negotiations.

D. **Establish overarching, shared goals.** Setting goals at the beginning of a negotiation helps frame the conversation and keeps each party's priorities in the forefront of discussion.

E. **Use objective criteria for evaluating alternative agreements.** It is easy to take negotiations personally, so having objective measures can help individuals to not reject good agreements without thought.

F. **Define success in terms of real gains, not imaginary losses.** Entering a negotiation with the mind-set of it being a clean slate can help keep the focus on what is actually occurring in the negotiation, not on what could have or might have been.

CONFLICT RESOLUTION
Conflict Assessment and Conflict Resolution Approach

A. Understand the type of conflict at hand by identifying its focus (issue-focused, people-focused) and source (personal differences, information deficiency, role incompatibility, environment-induced stress).

B. Select the appropriate conflict management approach:
   Examine relevant situational factors, including the importance of the issue, the importance of the relationship, the relative power of the disputants, and the degree to which time is a factor.

C. Take into consideration your personal preferences for using the various conflict management approaches. These preferences tend to reflect important elements of your personal identity, including ethnic culture, gender, and personality.

D. Utilize the collaborative approach for managing conflict unless specific conditions dictate the use of an alternative approach.

USE COLLABORATION TO RESOLVE PERSONAL CONFRONTATIONS

INITIATOR

Problem Identification

A. Maintain personal ownership of the problem. ("I have a problem, that I'd like to discuss.")
B. Succinctly describe your problem in terms of behaviors, consequences, and feelings. ("When you do X, Y happens, and I feel Z.")
C. Avoid drawing evaluative conclusions and attributing motives to the respondent.
D. Persist until understood.
E. Encourage two-way discussion by inviting the respondent to ask questions and express their perspective.
F. Focus on one issue at a time; build rapport and understanding.

Solution Generation

A. Focus on the things you share in common (principles, goals, constraints) as the basis for requesting changes.

RESPONDER

Problem Identification

A. Establish a climate for joint problem-solving.
   - ❑ Show genuine concern and interest. Respond empathetically, even if you disagree with the complaint.
   - ❑ Respond appropriately to the initiator's emotions. If necessary, let the person blow off steam before addressing the complaint.
B. Seek additional information about the problem.
   - ❑ Ask questions that channel the initiator's statements from general to specific and from evaluative to descriptive.
C. Agree with some aspect of the complaint.
   - ❑ Signal your willingness to consider making changes by agreeing with facts, perceptions, feelings, or principles.

Solution Generation

A. Ask for suggestions and recommendations.
   - ❑ To avoid debating the merits of a single suggestion, brainstorm multiple alternatives.

MEDIATOR

Problem Identification

A. Acknowledge that a conflict exists and propose a problem-solving approach for resolving it.
B. While seeking to understand the perspective of both parties, maintain a neutral posture regarding the disputants, if not the issues.

C. Assume the role of facilitator, not judge.

D. Manage the discussion to ensure fairness. Keep the discussion issue oriented, not personality oriented.

Solution Generation

A. Explore options by focusing on common interests, not disparate positions.

B. Use the dispute as an opportunity to teach problem-solving skills and to establish protocols for dispute resolution.

ALL ROLES

Action Plan and Follow-Up

A. Ensure that all parties understand and support the agreed-upon plan and establish follow-up procedures.

CASE INVOLVING INTERPERSONAL CONFLICT

Educational Pension Investments

Educational Pension Investments (EPI), located in New York, invests pension funds for educational institutions. It employs approximately 75 people, 25 of whom are responsible for actual investment activities. The company manages about $5 billion of assets and derived an income of about $10 million.

The firm was incorporated almost 30 years ago by a group of academic professionals who wanted to control the destiny of their retirement years by pursuing investments that would be consistent and safe. The firm has weathered rapid technological change and economic volatility. Leadership has consistently resisted opportunities to make it big and instead stayed with less profitable but relatively secure investments.

Dan Richardson, one of the founders of EPI, has an MBA from Wharton. He started out working in the research department and has worked in every department since then. The other partners, comfortable with Dan's conservative yet flexible nature, elected him to the position of CEO 13 years ago. After that, Dan became known as "the great equalizer." He works hard to make sure that all the partners are included in decisions. Over the years, he has become the confidant of the other seniors and the mentor of the next generation. EPI's employees look to Dan for leadership and direction. Dan's management philosophy is built on the concept of loyalty. As he is fond of saying, "My dad was a small-town banker. He told me, 'Look out for the other guys and they'll look out for you.' Sounds corny, I know, but I firmly believe in this philosophy."

Given Dan's practice of consistent and safe investing, EPI's growth has not kept pace with other investment opportunities. As a result, Dan has reluctantly begun to consider the merits of a more aggressive investment approach. Part of Dan's reconsideration is that several of the younger analysts are beginning to refer to EPI as "stodgy." Some are leaving EPI for positions in more aggressive firms.

One evening, Dan talked about his concern with his racquetball partner and longtime friend, Mike Roth. Mike was an investment broker in another firm. An MBA graduate from the University of Illinois, Mike's accomplishments in research had brought him widespread recognition. Everyone respected him for his knowledge, his work ethic, and his uncanny ability to predict trends.

When Mike heard Dan's concerns about EPI's image and need for an aggressive approach, he suggested to his friend that what EPI needed was some fresh blood, someone who could infuse enthusiasm into the organization—someone like him. He told Dan, "I can help you get things moving. In fact, I've been developing some concepts that would be perfect for EPI."

Dan brought up the idea of hiring Mike at the next staff meeting, but the idea was met with caution and skepticism. "Sure, he's had a brilliant career on paper," said one senior partner. "But he's never stayed in one place long enough to really validate his success. Look at his résumé. During the past seven years, he's been with four different firms, in four different positions."

"That's true," said Dan, "but his references all check out. In fact, he's been described as a rising star, aggressive, productive. He's just what we need to help us explore new opportunities."

Another partner responded, "A friend of mine worked with Mike a while back and said that while he is definitely good, he's a real maverick—in terms of both investment philosophy and lifestyle. Is that what we really want at EPI?"

Throughout the discussion, Dan defended Mike's work record. He repeatedly pointed out Mike's impressive performance. He deflected concerns about Mike's reputation by saying that he was a loyal and trusted friend. Largely on Dan's recommendation, the other partners agreed, although somewhat reluctantly, to hire Mike. When Dan offered Mike the job, he promised Mike the freedom and flexibility to operate a segment of the fund as he desired.

Mike took the job and performed his responsibilities at EPI in a superior manner. Indeed, he was largely responsible for increasing the managed assets of the company by 150 percent. However, this increase came at a price. From the day Mike moved in, junior analysts enjoyed working with him very much. They liked his fresh, new approach, and were encouraged by the spectacular results. This caused jealousy among the other partners, who thought Mike was pushing too hard to change the tried-and-true traditions of the firm. It was not uncommon for sharp disagreements to erupt in staff meetings, with one or another partner coming close to storming out of the room. Throughout this time, Dan tried to soothe ruffled feathers and maintain an atmosphere of trust and loyalty.

Mike seemed oblivious to all the turmoil he was causing. He was optimistic about potential growth opportunities. He believed that voice-activated technology, 3D printing, and cloud databases were the wave of the future, and he wanted to direct the focus of his portfolio toward these emerging technologies. "Investments in small firm stocks in these industries, coupled with an aggressive market timing strategy, should yield a 50 percent increase in performance," Mike said. He rallied support for this idea not only among the younger members of EPI, but also with the pension fund managers who invested with EPI. Mike championed his position and openly questioned the traditional philosophy. "We should compromise on conservatism and achieve some real growth while we can," Mike argued. "If we don't, we'll lose the investors' confidence and ultimately lose them."

Most of the senior partners disagreed with Mike, stating that the majority of their investors emphasized security above all else. They also disagreed with the projected profits, stating that "We could go from 8 to 12 percent return on investment (ROI); then again, we could drop to 4 percent. A lot depends on whose data you use." They reminded Mike, "The fundamental approach of the corporation is to provide safe and moderate-income mutual funds for academic pension funds to invest in. That's the philosophy we used to solicit the investments originally, and that's the approach we are obligated to maintain."

Months passed, and dissension among the managers grew. Mike began to criticize his detractors openly as he talked with younger EPI employees. In addition, he assigned research department employees to focus on high-tech investments, distracting them from investigating more traditional investments. This disrupted the operations of other EPI managers because their funds relied on timely input from the researchers and other support staff. Amid a rapidly spreading undercurrent of tension, one of the founding partners, Tom Watson, approached Dan one day. Conservative in his ways, Watson was the partner who walks the office and always has time to stop and chat. He began the conversation.

"Dan, I speak for most of the senior staff when I say that we are very troubled by Mike's approach. We've expressed ourselves well enough for Mike to understand, but his actions defy everything we've said. He's a catastrophe just waiting to happen."

"I can understand your concern, Tom," replied Dan. "I'm troubled, too. We have an opportunity to attract new business with some of Mike's new ideas. And the younger staff love working on his projects. But he has stirred up a lot of turmoil."

Tom agreed. "The real issue is that EPI is no longer presenting a unified image. Mike is willfully defying the stated objectives of our organization. And some of our oldest clients don't like that."

"That's true, Tom. On the other hand, some of our newer clients are really encouraged by Mike's approach—and his track record is extremely impressive."

"Come on, Dan. You and I both know that many experts feel the market is overheating. Mike's paper profits could quickly be incinerated if the budget and trade deficits don't turn around. We can't stake the reputation of the firm on a few high-flying technology stocks. Dan, the other senior partners agree. Mike must either conform to the philosophy and management practices of this organization or else resign."

Reflecting on the situation, Dan realized he faced the most difficult challenge of his career. He felt a strong personal investment in helping Mike succeed. Not only had he hired Mike over the objections of several colleagues; he had personally helped him learn the ropes at EPI. Beyond that, Dan was haunted by his promise to Mike that he would have the freedom and flexibility to perform the requirements of the position as he pleased. However, this flexibility had clearly caused problems within EPI.

Finally, bowing to the pressure of his peers, Dan called Mike in for a meeting, hoping to find some basis for compromise. Their conversation proceeded as follows:

DAN: I gather you know the kinds of concerns the senior partners have expressed regarding your approach.

MIKE: I guess you've talked with Tom. Well, we did have a small disagreement earlier this week.

DAN: The way Tom tells it, you're willfully defying corporate objectives and being insubordinate.

MIKE: Well, it's just like Watson to see progressive change as an attempt to take away his power.

DAN: It's not quite that simple, Mike. When we founded EPI, we all agreed that a conservative stance was best. And right now, with the economic indicators looking soft, many experts agree that it may still be the best alternative.

MIKE: Dan, what are you going to rely on—predictions or performance? These concerns are just smokescreens to deflect attention away from the subpar records of other portfolio managers. Old views need to be challenged and ultimately discarded. How else are we going to progress and keep up with our competitors?

DAN: I agree we need to change, Mike—but gradually. You have great ideas and terrific instincts, but you can't change a 30-year-old firm overnight. You can help me promote change, but you're pushing so fast, others are digging in their heels. The rate of change is just as important as the direction.

MIKE: You're telling me. And at this rate, it doesn't make much difference which direction we're headed in.

DAN: Come on, Mike. Don't be so cynical. If you'd just stop rubbing people's noses in your performance record and try to see things from their perspective, we could calm things down around here. Then maybe we could start building consensus. (*Mike's emotions betray his impatience with the pace of the organization; he becomes agitated.*)

MIKE: I've always admired your judgment, and I value your friendship, but I honestly think you're kidding yourself. You seem to think you can get this firm to look like it's progressive—shrugging off its stodgy image—without taking any risks or ruffling any feathers. Are you interested in appearance or substance? If you want appearance, then hire a good PR person. If you want substance, then back me up and we'll rewrite the record book. Get off the fence, Dan, before your butt's full of slivers.

DAN: Mike, it simply isn't that easy. I'm not EPI, I'm simply its caretaker. You know we make decisions around here by consensus; that's the backbone of this organization. To move ahead, the confidence of the others has to be won, especially the confidence of the seniors. Frankly, your reputation as a maverick makes it hard to foster confidence in, and loyalty to, your plans.

MIKE: You knew my style when you hired me. Remember how you made it a point to promise me flexibility and autonomy? I'm not getting that anymore, Dan. All I'm getting is grief, even though I'm running circles around your conservative cronies.

DAN: Well, that may be true. But your flamboyance...

MIKE: Oh, yeah. The sports car, the singles lifestyle, the messy office. But, again, that's appearance, Dan, not substance. Performance is what counts. That's what got me this far, and that's my ticket out. You know I could walk into any firm in town and write my own plan.

DAN: Well, there's no reason to be hasty.

MIKE: Do you honestly believe this can be salvaged? I think not. Maybe it's time for me to be moving on. Isn't that why you called me in here anyway? (*Dan, feeling uncomfortable, breaks eye contact and shifts his gaze to the New York skyline. After a long pause, he continues, still gazing out of the window.*)

DAN: I don't know, Mike. I feel I've failed. My grand experiment in change has polarized the office; we've got two armies at war out there. On the other hand, you really have done a good job here. EPI will no doubt lose a good part of its customer base if you leave. You have a loyal following with both customers and staff. If you go, so do they—along with our shot at changing our image.

MIKE: It's just like you to take this problem personally, Dan. Blast it, you take everything personally. Even when I beat you at racquetball. Your heart's in the right place—you just can't ever seem to make the cutthroat hit. You know and I know that EPI needs a change in image. But it doesn't appear to be ready for it yet. And I'm certainly not willing to move slowly.

DAN: Yeah. Maybe. It's just hard to give up... [long pause]. Well, why don't we talk more about this after the reception tonight? Come on over and see Joanie and the kids. Besides, I'm dying to show off my new boat.

MIKE: What you see in sailing is beyond me. It's a waste of time, lazily drifting on gentle breezes.

DAN: Save it for later, "Speed King." I've got to get ready for tonight.

ANALYSIS

Discussion Questions

7.1. What are the sources of conflict in this case?

7.2. What approaches to conflict management are used by the actors in this situation? How effective is each?

7.3. Based on the behavioral guidelines for the collaborative approach, how could Dan have managed this conflict more effectively?

EXERCISE FOR NEGOTIATING

DeTienne and Associates Publishing
Reprinted by permission of copyright owner.
No further copying permitted without express
permission from publisher.

Case Number 1-2014-1
February 19, 2016

KRISTEN BELL DeTIENNE Kristen_DeTienne@byu.edu

A Home by the Sea

Assignment

The following exercise, based on a real situation, is a negotiation between a builder who is selling a condominium and a person interested in buying the condominium. You will play the buyer or seller role, as assigned to you by your instructor. Before negotiating, complete the planning document to assist you as you prepare for the negotiation. Use the Negotiations section in this chapter to help you determine your BATNA, Reservation Price, and so on.

Confidential Role Information for Joan (BUYER)

This case involves the sale of a condominium home for sale in Sunset Beach, CA. This case is based on a real situation that occurred in 2012.

Ken is the seller of the condo. He is a new real estate developer and has built two attached units/homes on one lot two doors from the ocean in Orange County, CA. Each home is 4800 square feet and includes a 2-car garage. Ken has also purchased two more lots he plans to build four units on. He wants to sell for as much as possible because the sale will set the comparative sales (comps) for the other four units he is planning to sell on the other lots on the street.

As happened in much of the nation, Sunset Beach real estate decreased in value in the period around 2008. Prior to the crash, similar units to the one Ken is selling sold for 2.5M. Real estate prices in this area are expected to rise in the next two years.

Joan is the estranged wife of an MLB team owner. She is planning to move to a home by the beach in California. She just bought the other attached unit three weeks ago for 1.4 million dollars. That unit is 4800 square feet and is on the street side. Joan is interested in buying this attached unit for her son, Stephen, to live in. This unit is almost identical; 4800 sq. ft., but is on the alley side of the lot.

The following information is known only to you: You really want to buy this unit for your son. It's the only one close to the one you just bought for yourself. You did your "due diligence" before buying the first unit; you know that 1.9M is a fair market value for the second unit. Also, your net worth with your estranged husband is 2.7B. Thus, while you want to do your best to get a great deal, and you don't want to pay any more than you have to, price is not a big issue for you. You are a private person and you are not thrilled with the prospect of sharing walls with a stranger, so you'd rather not see it sold to someone else. **You have the 1.9M cash that you are willing to pay. Your goal in this negotiation is to buy the condo for the lowest possible price.**

Kristen Bell DeTienne

Confidential Role Information for Ken (Builder/SELLER)

This case involves the sale of a condominium home for sale in Sunset Beach, CA. This case is based on a real situation that occurred in 2012.

Ken is the seller of the condo. He is a new real estate developer and has built two attached units/homes on one lot two doors from the ocean in Orange County, CA. Each home is 4800 square feet and includes a 2-car garage. Ken has also purchased two more lots he plans to build four units on. He wants to sell for as much as possible because the sale will set the comparative sales (comps) for the other four units he is planning to sell on the other lots on the street.

Due to the 2008 US Real Estate crash, Sunset Beach real estate decreased in value. Prior to the crash, similar units to the one Ken is selling sold for 2.5M. Real estate prices in this area are expected to rise over the next two years.

Joan is the estranged wife of an MLB team owner. She is planning to move to a home by the beach in California. She just bought the other attached unit three weeks ago for 1.4 million dollars. That unit is 4800 square feet and is on the street side. Joan is interested in buying this attached unit for her son, Stephen, to live in. This unit is almost identical; 4800 sq. ft., but is on the alley side of the lot.

The following information is known only to you: You have already purchased three lots next to each other; each lot cost you $624,000. Your cost to build the two units on each lot is $950,000. Thus, your net cost to build each unit including land is $787,000. Your construction costs were higher than expected and you ended up cash poor at this time. Because you are cash poor, you stopped making payments on the third lot about six months ago. You lender has started the process of foreclosing on you. You can stop the foreclosure by catching up on your payments to the lender on that third lot.

You bought the third lot for $624,000 and put down $300,000 of your own money. You paid down $8,000 of the loan balance in the first few months after purchase. Now the lender is about to sell the third lot for the loan balance ($316,000), interest, and late fees next week (total $398,000); it is expected to sell immediately for that price. For that lot, you have paid $624,000 and are expecting $950,000 for construction costs. Thus, your cost is 1.5M to build both units. If the units sell for 1.4M each, your profit is around 1.3M. If your lender forecloses, you lose the $300,000 you put down and you do not make the 1.3M profit you expect to make on the sale of the two units on that third lot.

PRACTICE

Sunset Beach was recently purchased by Huntington Beach, so you are expecting to save $200,000 in foundation costs. Thus, construction costs for that third lot may be as low as $750,000 for two units.

If you lose your third building lot, the only other lot for sale by the beach is listed at $875,000. That lot has not yet had a geological inspection; it may not be buildable. Also, if the lender forecloses on you, it's unlikely that another bank will lend to you, so you'd really like to hold on to your third lot.

Joan is the only interested buyer today. Unfortunately, your other buyers fell through and you're quickly running out of time with the lender on the third lot. Basically, you must sell this condo to her in order to keep that lot. **It's still in your best interest to sell it for a price as low as $350,000, because you can restore your credit and make the $1.3M on the two units if you can keep the lot that is up for foreclosure. Your goal in this negotiation is to sell this condo for the highest possible price.**

Negotiation Planning Document

Name: _____   Negotiation: _____

Role: _____   Name of student(s) in other role (if known): _____

What issues are important to you? Please list all issues you care about, beginning with most important as the first item; add rows as needed.

Name of Issue & Position	Priority (Rank)	Interest (Why do you want it?)
1.		
2.		
3.		
4.		
5.		

What is your BATNA?

Reservation price?

Goal?

What are your sources of power?

What issues are most important to your opponent? Make your best estimate about all of the things your opponent will care about, listing in order with the highest-priority item first.

Name of Issue & Position	Priority (Rank)	Interest (Why do they want it?)
1.		
2.		
3.		
4.		
5.		

What is your opponent's BATNA?

Reservation price?

Goal?

What are your opponent's sources of power?

What is your opening move?

What strategies do you plan to implement?

What are the main questions you have for your opponent, and what is the best way to ask them?

EXERCISE FOR DIAGNOSING TYPES OF CONFLICT

SSS Software Management Problems

In order to manage conflict between others effectively, it is important to be aware of early warning signs. It is also important to understand the underlying causes of disagreements. Conflict that is unmanaged, or managed ineffectively, interferes with workgroup performance. A key to managing conflict effectively is recognizing it in its early stages and understanding its roots.

Assignment

Read the memos, faxes, voice mail, and email messages that follow. As you examine each of these documents, look for evidence of organizational conflicts. Identify the two conflicts that you think are most significant for you to address in your role as Chris Perillo. Begin your analysis of these conflicts by identifying their likely sources or causes. Use Figure 7.1 as a diagnostic tool for identifying the type of conflict, based on its source and focus. Prepare to present your analysis, along with supporting evidence from the memos. Also, share your ideas regarding how this analysis of the causes of conflict would influence your approach to resolving the conflict.

SSS Software In-Basket Memos, Emails, Faxes, and Voice Mails

ITEM 1 – EMAIL

TO: All Employees
FROM: Roger Steiner, Chief Executive Officer
DATE: October 15

I am pleased to announce that Chris Perillo has been appointed as Vice President of Operations for Health and Financial Services. Chris will immediately assume responsibility for all operations previously managed by Michael Grant. Chris will have end-to-end responsibility for the design, development, integration, and maintenance of custom software for the health and finance/banking industries. This responsibility includes all technical, financial, and staffing issues. Chris will also manage our program of software support and integration for the recently announced merger of three large health maintenance organizations (HMOs). Chris will be responsible for our recently announced project with a consortium of banks and financial firms operating in Tanzania. This project represents an exciting opportunity for us, and Chris's background seems ideally suited to the task.

Chris comes to this position with an undergraduate degree in computer science from the California Institute of Technology and an MBA from the University of Virginia. Chris began as a member of our technical/professional staff six years ago and has most recently served for three years as a group manager supporting domestic and international projects for our airlines industry group, including our recent work for the European Airbus consortium.

I am sure you all join me in offering congratulations to Chris for this promotion.

ITEM 2 – EMAIL

TO: All Managers
FROM: Hal Harris, Vice President, Community and Public Relations
DATE: October 15

For your information, the following article appeared on the front page of the business section of Thursday's *Los Angeles Times*.

In a move that may create problems for SSS Software, Michael Grant and Janice Ramos have left SSS Software and moved to Universal Business Solutions Inc. Industry analysts see the move as another victory for Universal Business Solutions Inc. in their battle with SSS Software for share of the growing software development and integration business. Both Grant and Ramos had been with SSS Software for over seven years. Grant was most recently Vice President of Operations for all SSS Software's work in two industries: health and hospitals, and finance and banking. Ramos brings to Universal Business Solutions Inc. her special expertise in the growing area of international software development and integration.

Hillary Collins, an industry analyst with Merrill Lynch, said, "The loss of key staff to a competitor can often create serious problems for a firm such as SSS Software. Grant and Ramos have an insider's understanding of SSS Software's strategic and technical limitations. It will be interesting to see if they can exploit this knowledge to the advantage of Universal Business Solutions Inc."

ITEM 3 – EMAIL

TO: Chris Perillo
FROM: Paula Sprague, Executive Assistant to Roger Steiner
DATE: October 15

Chris, I know that in your former position as a group manager in the Airline Services Division you probably have met most of the group managers in the Health and Financial Services Division, but I thought you might like some more personal information about them. These people will be your direct reports on the management team.

Group #1: Bob Miller, 55-year-old white male, married (Anna) with two children and three grandchildren. Active in local Republican politics. Well regarded as a "hands-off" manager heading a high-performing team. Plays golf regularly with Mark McIntyre, John Small, and a couple of VPs from other divisions.

Group #2: Wanda Manners, 38-year-old white female, single with one school-age child. A fitness "nut" and has run in several marathons. Some experience in Germany and Japan. Considered a hard-driving manager with a constant focus on the task at hand. Will be the first person to show up every morning.

Group #3: William Chen, 31-year-old male of Chinese descent, married (Harriet), two young children from his first marriage. Enjoys tennis and is quite good at it. A rising star in the company, he is highly respected by his peers as a "man of action" and a good friend.

Group #4: Leo Jones, 36-year-old white male, married (Janet) with an infant daughter. Recently returned from paternity leave. Has traveled extensively on projects since he speaks three languages. Has liked hockey ever since the time he spent in Montreal. Considered a strong manager who gets the most out of his people.

Group #5: Mark McIntyre, 45-year-old white male, married (Mary Theresa) to an executive in the banking industry. No children. A lot of experience in Germany and Eastern Europe. Has been writing a mystery novel. Has always been a good "team player," but several members of his technical staff are not well respected and he hasn't addressed the problem.

Group #6: John Small, 38-year-old white male, recently divorced. Three children living with his ex-wife. A gregarious individual who likes sports. He spent a lot of time in Mexico and Central America before he came to SSS Software. Recently has been doing mostly contract work with the federal government. An average manager; has had some trouble keeping his people on schedule.

Group #7: This position vacant since Janice Ramos left. Roger thinks we ought to fill this position quickly. Get in touch with me if you want information on any in-house candidates for any position.

Group #8: Marcus Harper, 42-year-old African American male, married (Tamara) with two teenage children. Recently won an award in a local photography contest. Considered a strong manager who gets along with peers and works long hours.

Customer Service: Armand Marke, 38-year-old male, divorced. A basketball fan. Originally from Armenia. Previously a group manager. Worked hard to establish the Technical Services Phone Line, but now has pretty much left it alone.

Office Administrator: Michelle Harrison, 41-year-old white female, single. Grew up on a ranch and still rides horses whenever she can. A strict administrator.

There are a number of good folks here, but they don't function well as a management team. I think Michael played favorites, especially with Janice and Leo. There are a few cliques in this group, and I'm not sure how effectively Michael dealt with them. I expect you will find it a challenge to build a cohesive team.

ITEM 4 – EMAIL

TO: Chris Perillo
FROM: Wanda Manners, Group 2 Manager
DATE: October 15

CONFIDENTIAL AND RESTRICTED

Although I know you are new to your job, I feel it is important that I let you know about some information I just obtained concerning the development work we recently completed for First National Investment. Our project involved the development of asset management software for managing their international funds. This was a very complex project due to the volatile exchange rates and the forecasting tools we needed to develop.

As part of this project, we had to integrate the software and reports with all their existing systems and reporting mechanisms. To do this, we were given access to all of their existing software (much of which was developed by Universal Business Solutions Inc.). Of course, we signed an agreement acknowledging that the software to which we were given access was proprietary and that our access was solely for the purpose of our system integration work associated with the project.

Unfortunately, I have learned that some parts of the software we developed actually "borrow" heavily from complex application programs developed for First National Investment by Universal Business Solutions Inc. It seems obvious to me that one or more of the software developers from Group 5 (that is, Mark McIntyre's group) inappropriately "borrowed" algorithms developed by Universal Business Solutions Inc. I am sure that doing so saved us significant development time on some aspects of the project. It seems very unlikely that First National Investment or Universal Business Solutions Inc. will ever become aware of this issue.

Finally, First National Investment is successfully using the software we developed and is thrilled with the work we did. We brought the project in on time and under budget. You probably know that they have invited us to bid on several other substantial projects.

I'm sorry to bring this delicate matter to your attention, but I thought you should know about it.

ITEM 5A – EMAIL

TO: Chris Perillo
FROM: Paula Sprague, Executive Assistant to Roger Steiner
DATE: October 15
RE: Letter from C.A.R.E. Services (copies attached)

Roger asked me to work on this C.A.R.E. project and obviously wants some fast action. A lot of the staff are already booked solid for the next couple of weeks. I know that Elise Soto and Chu Hung Woo have the expertise to do this system, and when I checked with them, they were relatively free. I had them pencil in the next two weeks and wanted to let you know. Hopefully, it will take a "hot potato" out of your hands.

ITEM 5B – COPY OF FAX

C.A.R.E.
Child and Adolescent Rehabilitative and Educational Services
A United Way Member Agency
200 Main Street
Los Angeles, CA 90230

DATE: October 11
Roger Steiner, CEO
SSS Software
13 Miller Way
Los Angeles, CA 90224

Dear Roger,

This letter is a follow-up to our conversation after last night's board meeting. I appreciated your comments during the board meeting about the need for sophisticated computer systems in nonprofit organizations and I especially appreciate your generous offer of help to have SSS Software provide assistance to deal with the immediate problem with our accounting system. Since the board voted to fire the computer consultant, I am very worried about getting our reports done in time to meet the state funding cycle.

Thanks again for your offer of help during this crisis.

Sincerely yours,

Janice Polocizwic

Executive Director

PRACTICE

ITEM 5C – COPY OF A LETTER

SSS SOFTWARE
13 Miller Way
Los Angeles, CA 90224

DATE: October 12

Janice Polocizwic
Executive Director, C.A.R.E. Services
200 Main Street
Los Angeles, CA 90230

Dear Janice,

I received your fax of October 11. I have asked Paula Sprague, my executive assistant, to line up people to work on your accounting system as soon as possible. You can expect to hear from her shortly.

Sincerely,

Roger Steiner

Roger Steiner

cc: Paula Sprague, Executive Assistant

ITEM 6 – EMAIL

TO: Michael Grant
FROM: Harry Withers, Group 6 Technical Staff
DATE: October 12

PERSONAL AND CONFIDENTIAL

Our team is having difficulty meeting the submission deadline of November 5 for the Halstrom project. Kim, Fred, Peter, Kyoto, Susan, Mala, and I have been working on the project for several weeks, but we are experiencing some problems and may need additional time. I hesitate to write this letter, but the main problem is that our group manager, John Small, is involved in a relationship with Mala. Mala gets John's support for her ideas and brings them to the team as required components of the project. Needless to say, this has posed some problems for the group. Mala's background is especially valuable for this project, but Kim and Fred, who have both worked very hard on the project, do not want to work with her. In addition, one member of the team has been unavailable recently because of childcare needs. Commitment to the project and team morale have plummeted. However, we'll do our best to get the project finished as soon as possible. Mala will be on vacation the next two weeks, so I'm expecting that some of us can complete it in her absence.

ITEM 7 – VOICE MAIL MESSAGE

Hello, Michael. This is Jim Bishop of United Hospitals. I wanted to talk with you about the quality assurance project that you are working on for us. When Jose Martinez first started talking with us, I was impressed with his friendliness and expertise. But recently, he doesn't seem to be getting much accomplished and has seemed distant and on-edge in conversations. Today, I asked him about the schedule and he seemed very defensive and not entirely in control of his emotions. I am quite concerned about our project. Please give me a call.

ITEM 8 – VOICE MAIL MESSAGE

Hi, Michael. This is Armand. I wanted to talk with you about some issues with the Technical Services Phone Line. I've recently received some complaint letters from Phone Line customers whose complaints have included long delays while waiting for a technician to answer the phone, technicians who are not knowledgeable enough to solve problems, and, on occasion, rude service. Needless to say, I'm quite concerned about these complaints.

I believe that the overall quality of the Phone Line staff is very good, but we continue to be understaffed, even with the recent hires. The new technicians look strong, but are working on the Phone Line before being fully trained. Antolina, our best tech, often brings her child to work, which is adding to the craziness around here.

I think you should know that we're feeling a lot of stress here. I'll talk with you soon.

ITEM 9 – VOICE MAIL MESSAGE

Hi, Chris, it's Pat. Congratulations on your promotion. They definitely picked the right person. It's great news—for me, too. You've been a terrific mentor so far, so I'm expecting to learn a lot from you in your new position. How about lunch next week?

ITEM 10 – VOICE MAIL MESSAGE

Chris, this is Bob Miller. Just thought you'd like to know that John's joke during our planning meeting has disturbed a few of the women in my group. Frankly, I think the thing's being blown out of proportion, especially since we all know this is a good place for both men and women to work. Give me a call if you want to chat about this.

ITEM 11 – VOICE MAIL MESSAGE

Hello. This is Lorraine Adams from Westside Hospital. I read in today's *Los Angeles Times* that you will be taking over from Michael Grant. We haven't met yet, but your division has recently finished two large million-dollar projects for Westside. Michael Grant and I had some discussion about a small conversion of a piece of existing software to be compatible with the new systems. The original vendor had said that they would do the work, but they have been stalling, and I need to move quickly. Can you see if Harris Wilson, Chu Hung Woo, and Elise Soto are available to do this work as soon as possible? They were on the original project and work well with our people.

Um...(long pause) I guess I should tell you that I got a call from Michael offering to do this work. But I think I should stick with SSS Software. Give me a call.

ITEM 12 – VOICE MAIL MESSAGE

Hi, Chris, this is Roosevelt Moore calling. I'm a member of your technical/professional staff. I used to report to Janice Ramos, but since she left the firm, I thought I'd bring my concerns directly to you. I'd like to arrange some time to talk with you about my experiences since returning from six weeks of paternity leave. Some of my major responsibilities have been turned over to others. I seem to be out of the loop and wonder if my career is at risk. Also, I am afraid that I won't be supported or seriously considered for the opening created by Janice's departure. Frankly, I feel like I'm being screwed for taking my leave. I'd like to talk with you this week.

ITEM 13 – EMAIL

TO: Michael Grant
FROM: Jose Martinez, Group 1 Technical Staff
DATE: October 12

I would like to set up a meeting with you as soon as possible. I suspect that you will get a call from Jim Bishop of United Hospitals and want to be sure that you hear my side of the story first. I have been working on a customized system design for quality assurance for them using a variation of the J-3 product we developed several years ago. They had a number of special requirements and some quirks in their accounting systems, so I have had to put in especially long hours. I've worked hard to meet their demands, but they keep changing the ground rules. I keep thinking, this is just another J-3 I'm working on, but they have been interfering with an elegant design I have developed. It seems I'm not getting anywhere on this project. Earlier today, I had a difficult discussion with their controller. He asked for another major change. I've been fighting their deadline and think I am just stretched too thin on this project. Then Jim Bishop asked me if the system was running yet. I was worn out from dealing with the controller, and

I made a sarcastic comment to Jim Bishop. He gave me a funny look and just walked out of the room.

I would like to talk with you about this situation at your earliest convenience.

ITEM 14 – EMAIL

TO: Chris Perillo
FROM: John Small, Group 6 Manager
DATE: October 15

Welcome aboard, Chris. I look forward to meeting with you. I just wanted to put a bug in your ear about finding a replacement for Janice Ramos. One of my technical staff, Mala Abendano, has the ability and drive to make an excellent group manager. I have encouraged her to apply for the position. I'd be happy to talk with you further about this, at your convenience.

ITEM 15 – EMAIL

TO: Chris Perillo
FROM: Paula Sprague, Executive Assistant to Roger Steiner
DATE: October 15

Roger asked me to let you know about the large contract we have gotten in Tanzania. It means that a team of four managers will be making a short trip to determine current needs. They will assign their technical staff the tasks of developing a system and software here over the next six months, and then the managers and possibly some team members will be spending about 10 months on-site in Tanzania to handle the implementation. Roger thought you might want to hold an initial meeting with some of your managers to check on their interest and willingness to take this sort of assignment. Roger would appreciate an email of your thoughts about the issues to be discussed at this meeting, additional considerations about sending people to Tanzania, and about how you will put together an effective team to work on this project. The October 15 memo I sent to you will provide you with some information you'll need to start making these decisions.

ITEM 16 – EMAIL

TO: Chris Perillo
FROM: Sharon Shapiro, VP of Human Resources
DATE: October 15
RE: Upcoming meeting

I want to update you on the rippling effect of John Small's sexual joke at last week's planning meeting. Quite a few women have been very upset and have met informally to talk about it. They have decided to call a meeting of all people concerned about this kind of behavior throughout the firm. I plan to attend, so I'll keep you posted.

ITEM 17 – EMAIL

TO: All SSS Software Managers
FROM: Sharon Shapiro, VP of Human Resources
DATE: October 15
RE: Promotions and External Hires

Year-to-Date (January through September) Promotions and External Hires

Level		Race					Sex		
	White	African American	Asian	Hispanic	Native American		M	F	Total
Hires into Executive Level	0 (0%)	0 (0%)	0 (0%)	0 (0%)	0 (0%)		0 (0%)	0 (0%)	0
Promotions to Executive Level	0 (0%)	0 (0%)	0 (0%)	0 (0%)	0 (0%)		0 (0%)	0 (0%)	0
Hires into Management Level	2 (67%)	1 (33%)	0 (0%)	0 (0%)	0 (0%)		2 (67%)	1 (33%)	3
Promotions to Management Level	7 (88%)	0 (0%)	1 (12%)	0 (0%)	0 (0%)		7 (88%)	1 (12%)	8
Hires into Technical/ Professional Level	10 (36%)	6 (21%)	10 (36%)	2 (7%)	0 (0%)		14 (50%)	14 (50%)	28
Promotions to Technical/ Professional Level	0 (0%)	0 (0%)	0 (0%)	0 (0%)	0 (0%)		0 (0%)	0 (0%)	0
Hires into Non-management Level	4 (20%)	10 (50%)	2 (10%)	4 (20%)	0 (0%)		6 (30%)	14 (70%)	20
Promotions to Non-management Level	NA	NA	NA	NA	NA		NA	NA	NA

SSS Software Employee (EEO) Classification Report as of June 30

Level		Race					Sex		
	White	African American	Asian	Hispanic	Native American		M	F	Total
Executive Level	11 (92%)	0 (0%)	1 (8%)	0 (0%)	0 (0%)		11 (92%)	1 (8%)	12
Management Level	43 (90%)	2 (4%)	2 (4%)	1 (2%)	0 (0%)		38 (79%)	10 (21%)	48

PRACTICE

SSS Software Employee (EEO) Classification Report as of June 30 (continued)

Level	White	African American	Asian	Hispanic	Native American	M	F	Total
			Race				Sex	
Technical/ Professional Level	58	20	37	14	1	80	50	130
	(45%)	(15%)	(28%)	(11%)	(1%)	(62%)	(38%)	
Non-management Level	29	22	4	4	1	12	48	60
	(48%)	(37%)	(7%)	(7%)	(2%)	(20%)	(80%)	
Total	141	44	44	19	2	141	109	250
	(56%)	(18%)	(18%)	(8%)	(1%)	(56%)	(44%)	

EXERCISES FOR SELECTING AN APPROPRIATE CONFLICT MANAGEMENT STRATEGY

Not all conflicts are alike; therefore, they cannot all be managed in exactly the same way. Effective managers are able to accurately assess the true causes of conflict and to match each type of conflict with an appropriate management strategy.

Assignment

For each of the following brief scenarios, select the most appropriate conflict management strategy. Refer to Table 7.3 for assistance in matching situational factors with strategies.

The Red Cow Grill

During an extended holiday overseas, you have decided to take your family to a local restaurant, to celebrate your son's birthday. You are a single parent, so getting home from work in time to prepare a nice dinner is very difficult. Knowing that local regulations require restaurants to provide separate nonsmoking areas, you ask the hostess to seat you in the nonsmoking section because your daughter, Shauna, is allergic to tobacco smoke. On your way to your seat, you notice that the restaurant seems crowded for a Monday night.

After you and your children are seated and have placed your orders, your conversation turns to family plans for the approaching holiday. Interspersed in the general conversation is a light banter with your son about whether or not he is too old to wear "the crown" during dinner—a family tradition on birthdays.

Suddenly, you become aware that your daughter is sneezing and her eyes are beginning to water. You look around and notice a lively group of businesspeople seated at the table behind you; they are all smoking. Your impression is that they are celebrating some type of special occasion. Looking back at Shauna, you realize that something has to be done quickly. You ask your son to escort Shauna outside while you rush to the front of the restaurant and find the hostess.

7.4. What are the salient situational factors?

7.5. What is the most appropriate conflict management strategy?

Avocado Computers

When the head of Avocado Computers ran into operational problems at his production facility, he hired you away from a competitor. It meant a significant increase in pay and the opportunity to manage a state-of-the-art production facility. What's more, there were very few other female production managers in Silicon Valley. Now you've been on the job a year, and it's been exciting to see your staff start working together as a team to solve problems, improve quality, and finally get the plant up to capacity. In general, Bill, the owner, has also been a plus. He is energetic, fair, and a proven industry leader. You feel fortunate to be in a coveted position, in a "star" firm, in a growth industry.

However, there is one distraction that bugs you. Bill is a real stickler about cleanliness, order, and appearance. He wants the robots all painted the same color, the components within the computer laid out perfectly on a grid, the workers wearing clean smocks, and the floor "clean enough to eat off." You are troubled by this compulsion. "Sure," you think, "it might impress potential corporate clients when they tour the production facility, but is it really that important? After all, who's ever going to look for symmetrical design inside their computer? Why should customers care about the color of the robot that built their computers? And who, for Pete's sake, would ever want to have a picnic in a factory?"

Today is your first yearly performance appraisal interview with Bill. In preparation for the meeting, he has sent you a memo outlining "Areas of Strength" and "Areas of Concern." You look with pride at the number of items listed in the first column. It's obvious that Bill likes your work. But you are a bit miffed at the single item of concern: "Needs to maintain a cleaner facility, including employee appearance." You mull over this "demerit" in your mind, wrestling with how to respond in your interview.

Discussion Questions

7.6. What are the salient situational factors?

7.7. What is the most appropriate conflict management strategy?

Phelps Inc.

You are Philip Manual, the head of sales for an office products firm, Phelps Inc. Your personnel sell primarily to small businesses in the Los Angeles metropolitan area. Phelps is doing about average for this rapidly growing market. The firm's new president, Jose Ortega, is putting a lot of pressure on you to increase sales. You feel that a major obstacle is the firm's policy on extending credit. Celeste, the head of the credit office, insists that all new customers fill out an extensive credit application. Credit risks must be low; credit terms and collection procedures are tough. You can appreciate her point of view, but you feel it is unrealistic. Your competitors are much more lenient in their credit examinations; they extend credit to higher risks; their credit terms are more favorable; and they are more lenient in collecting overdue payments. Your sales personnel frequently complain that they aren't "playing on a level field" with their competition. When you brought this concern to Jose, he said he wanted you and Celeste to work things out. His instructions didn't give many clues to his priorities on this matter. "Sure, we need to increase sales," he said, "but the small-business failure in this area is the highest in the country, so we have to be careful we don't make bad credit decisions."

You decide it's time to have a serious discussion with Celeste. A lot is at stake.

Discussion Questions

7.8.　What are the salient situational factors?

7.9.　What is the most appropriate conflict management strategy?

EXERCISES FOR RESOLVING PEOPLE-FOCUSED CONFLICT

At the heart of conflict management is the ability to resolve intense, emotionally charged confrontations. We have discussed guidelines for utilizing the collaborative problem-solving approach to conflict management in these situations. Assuming that the collaborative approach is appropriate for a particular situation, we have provided general guidelines for the roles of initiator, responder, and mediator.

Assignment

Following are three situations involving interpersonal conflict and disagreement. After you have finished reading the assigned roles, review the appropriate behavioral guidelines. Do not read any of the role descriptions except those assigned to you.

In the first exercise (Sabrina Moffatt), students assigned to play Sabrina will practice applying the guidelines for the initiator's role. In the second exercise (Can Larry Fit In?), students assigned to play the role of Larry's boss, Melissa, will practice the guidelines for the respondent's role. In the third exercise (Meeting at Hartford Manufacturing Company), students assigned to play the role of Lynn Smith will practice the guidelines for resolving conflicts among subordinates. For each exercise, an observer will be assigned to give students playing the roles of Sabrina, Melissa, or Lynn feedback on their performance, using the Observer's Feedback Form at the end of the chapter as their guide.

Sabrina Moffatt

Sabrina Moffatt, Production Manager, Sunburst Solutions

Sabrina Moffatt was born the fourth of seven children in a low-income African American family in the deep South. When Sabrina was 14, her parents moved the family to rural Wisconsin, hoping for better educational opportunities for their children. The Moffatts chose a neighborhood where the vast majority of the students in the schools were Caucasian. They wanted their children to feel proud of their heritage, but they also wanted them to learn to excel in an environment where they were an ethnic minority. Sabrina's parents struggled to care for the family while they both worked multiple jobs. They doggedly emphasized the importance of education and insisted on outstanding schoolwork.

Sabrina flourished at her high school, earning one of the top GPAs in her class. She also found a group of supportive friends who were like-minded in their commitment to go to college. Even though she was the only African American in her class, she felt accepted by her peers. But Sabrina often sensed that her teachers and school administrators treated her differently. She felt that some of them talked down to her, while others treated her with superficial kindness—as if they had to handle her delicately. In one instance, a school counselor advised Sabrina to think about going to a technical college rather than applying for a four-year university because, as he said, "You might find that you fit in better in that sort of environment." The comment infuriated Sabrina, because she felt the counselor was judging her by her race. But her parents advised her to let it slide off her back and prove her abilities through her work.

Sabrina was accepted to several top universities, and she decided to stay close to home and attend the University of Wisconsin, majoring in mathematics. Toward the end of her first year of school, and after much personal angst, she decided to openly declare her homosexuality. Sabrina's parents initially responded with shock and disappointment, which caused her great emotional turmoil. She was surprised and hurt that some of her new friends seemed no longer to want to associate with her. The following semester, Sabrina's grades plummeted, and she found that she had lost interest in her studies. She spent one semester on academic probation, and then changed her major two times. She considered dropping out of school altogether. However, she remembered her parents' commitment to education, and all the sacrifices that they had made for her. Even though they were struggling with her sexual orientation, she wanted to honor her parents' values and pursue her education to forge a better life than her parents had.

With a renewed resolve, Sabrina turned her attention back to her studies. She discovered a passion for business and changed her major (yet again) to management. Over time, Sabrina's parents became more understanding and supportive. After five years of college, Sabrina graduated with a 3.4 GPA, a far cry from her original goals, but an accomplishment that she was proud of, considering the adversity she had faced.

After graduating, Sabrina considered several job offers, including a fast-track management development program for a major corporation in Chicago. She couldn't stop thinking about her parents, though, and decided that the most important thing she could do was to rebuild her relationship with them. She rejected her lucrative job offers and instead moved back to her hometown and found work in human resources at a small production facility there. It was a healing time with her family, but frustrating professionally. Working in a unionized environment, Sabrina struggled to gain the respect of the blue-collar workforce. She suspected that both her gender and her skin color had something to do with the fact that employees referred to her as "uppity" and "in over her head." And although she kept her sexual orientation to herself in this rather conservative town, she wondered if the occasional snicker meant that people suspected she was gay.

After four years of professional frustration, and at the urging of her parents, Sabrina decided to get an MBA. After acing the GMAT, Sabrina was accepted into the MBA program at the Kellogg School of Management at Northwestern University in Chicago. She was invigorated by the intellectual environment of the program and felt a sense of direction that she had been lacking for years. That first year, Sabrina met Jocelyn Walker, an African American doctoral student in chemistry at Northwestern. They became close confidantes, and within a year they had moved in together and entered into a long-term committed relationship. The two graduated together, and Jocelyn received an offer to teach at a college in the Phoenix area. Sabrina was thrilled when she landed a position at Sunburst Solutions, a high-growth technology firm in Phoenix. She was hired as the manager of one of several production departments, with direct supervision over eight entry-level technicians.

Sabrina was surprised to learn that she was the first African American to assume a managerial position in the young firm. She was also the only member of the LGBT community in the management ranks. She found herself being very guarded at work about her sexual orientation, and she rarely mentioned Jocelyn to others. Over time, she learned that there was a handful of junior-level technicians who were gay. Two of them told her that it was best not to bring up sexual orientation at Sunburst, however, because of thinly veiled prejudice. This made Sabrina all the more cautious about discussing her personal life at work, and she naturally found herself gravitating toward her gay colleagues on a social level. After six months in the office, however, the director of Sabrina's division, Kyle Huang, began making subtle comments to Sabrina that suggested he thought she wasn't blending well with her managerial-level colleagues. For instance, one day he said in passing, "So, I guess you'll be having lunch with all your blue-collar friends again today?"

Sabrina's relationship with Kyle, who was her direct supervisor, had been strained from the very beginning. Kyle was a hard-driven 37-year-old "corporate climber" type. He was also openly proud of his conservative social views, and he relished political debate. Kyle had the ear of Sunburst's president, who viewed Kyle as a protégé. Sabrina felt that Kyle communicated differently with her than he did with the other office managers in his division. He was quicker to correct her, and he seemed to second-guess her decisions—sometimes challenging her plans in front of her own employees. Sabrina felt that, yet again, she had to go beyond usual standards in order to prove herself.

Sabrina's best sounding board about her frustrations was Jocelyn. "I'm so tired of always being second-guessed," Sabrina said to Jocelyn one evening. "I feel like I've spent my entire life trying to overcome stereotypes. It's exhausting. I can't just be myself at work. And Kyle treats me like I'm incompetent even though my results are as good as any other manager in the company. His prejudice is so obvious. Today, he announced that he's asking Dale Westlund to be the liaison with a big new client from Texas. Dale was hired at Sunburst the same time as I was, but he has less experience than me. He manages another production department, but my department's product is far more important to the client than his is. And, get this: most of the new client's management team is black. I would have been the obvious choice to represent the company, so it's a slap in the face that he didn't choose me. I have to believe that he's uncomfortable having someone who is gay represent the firm."

"I know what you are talking about," said Jocelyn. "I don't think people always mean to be disrespectful, but they can be pretty transparent about their rejection. Just the other day, I mentioned to one of my senior colleagues that I'm living with my girlfriend. He got this shocked look on his face and then said, 'I wish you hadn't told me that.' I don't think he meant to belittle me, but it felt really hurtful."

"I had something hurtful happen yesterday too," said Sabrina pensively. "I was having coffee in the break room and I heard one of my fellow managers talking to someone out in the hall. She was complaining that she had just gotten a bad haircut and was saying her hair was now 'as bad as Sabrina's—all edgy and butch.' Then she said, 'Maybe she should just have a sex change and get it over with.' I sat there in the break room trying not to cry and wondering if I was back in junior high school. She has no idea I heard her, but still, I'm not sure I'm going to be able to look her in the face now."

"I'm not sure it would do much good to confront her about it anyway," Jocelyn sympathized. "I figure that all I can do is to stay above the fray . . . treat others with the respect I think we all deserve, and hope that people come to respect me for it. I don't have time to be a successful scholar *and* crusade against every piece of prejudice I see."

Sabrina seemed dubious. "But Kyle's biases are holding me back. If I don't confront him about the way he talks down to me, how will other people see me as credible? And it really feels like discrimination to me that he chose Dale over me for the client assignment. I mean, he's using my sexuality as a factor in my career opportunities. At what point do I have to speak up to defend myself?"

Kyle Huang, Director of Production, Sunburst Solutions

Kyle Huang is a 37-year-old lifelong Arizonan who is the director overseeing several production departments at Sunburst Solutions in Phoenix. He supervises the manager of each department, who in turn supervises anywhere from eight to 12 entry-level technicians. Kyle has worked at Sunburst for nearly a decade and has thrived there. The president of the company is a friend of his father and has treated Kyle as a promising protégé. Kyle expects a promotion to vice president level in the next year or two. One of the objectives he is pursuing to improve his chances for promotion is to increase the diversity of the production division's staff. Sunburst has received complaints from some of its clients, as well as several employees, that the culture of Sunburst is too homogenous. Although Kyle, as a staunch political conservative, chose Sunburst in part because so many people there share his values, he also feels convinced that the company needs to embrace more diverse perspectives to maintain its creativity and competitive edge.

Hiring Sabrina Moffatt out of Northwestern University's MBA program was a coup. She is the first African American hired into the management level at Sunburst, and only the second woman. It wasn't until a couple of months into her employment that Kyle realized Sabrina is gay and living with a same-sex partner—another first in the management ranks. Kyle's conservative upbringing hasn't equipped him to appreciate Sabrina's lifestyle. He feels a little uncomfortable around her and worries about what he will do if she becomes vocal about gay rights in Sunburst's conservative environment. So far, Sabrina has never brought this issue up, and he has decided that Sabrina's personal life should be a nonissue in the workplace as long as she does her job and doesn't make waves.

Sabrina's introduction to Sunburst has been rocky, however. Kyle has noticed that Sabrina seems timid and withdrawn in meetings with her fellow managers. Rather than socialize with management, she prefers to spend time with a handful of technicians, some of whom he believes are also gay. Kyle's concern is that Sabrina is missing opportunities to network with her colleagues, which means that she hasn't built the level of trust with them that is so important for interdepartmental collaboration.

Kyle has also found that Sabrina is difficult to coach. When he gives her constructive advice, she invariably averts her eyes, which makes Kyle wonder if she is rejecting his advice, or not understanding it. He feels like he has to repeat his suggestions to her several times just to make sure it's registering. A couple of times, he has actually lost his cool and expressed impatience toward her in public. He has felt bad about that, but Sabrina has never brought it up to him.

Kyle was having a conversation with the vice president of production, Howard Graham, when the "Sabrina problem" came up (as it often does). "Look Howard, I still would hire Sabrina in a second. I know she's one of the smartest managers we have. She wasn't just a token hire. The problem is that she seems to have come with a chip on her shoulder, and I have no idea how to knock it off."

Howard responded, "I agree. There is untapped potential there. We really need her to be a success story to show that we have a welcoming culture. Are you sure there's nothing more you could be doing to get her out of her shell? Frankly, I was a little surprised that you didn't ask her to be the contact point for our new client in Texas. That might have been a turning point for her if we showed her that sort of trust."

"You know, Howard," Kyle said after some reflection, "I thought long and hard about that one. Sabrina does manage a product that matters a lot to the client, so it would have made sense in some ways to assign her. But the reason I asked Dale to do it instead is that I know he can put people at ease. Dale is probably not as bright as Sabrina, and he certainly has less supervisory experience, but he does a great job of building relationships across departments. And then there is the fact that Sabrina is gay. Our Texas client is a privately owned firm that wears its conservative values on its sleeve. I just don't think Sabrina will be able to connect with them."

PRACTICE

"I get that, Kyle," Howard responded. "But we are possibly setting a precedent here. This assignment could mean that Dale will advance more quickly than Sabrina in the organization. If Sabrina feels that she is more qualified—and in some ways she is—then she could interpret this decision as discriminatory because of her race...or maybe even her sexual preference."

"That isn't the case at all. I'm making a business decision here." Kyle said adamantly. "I have other plans to help Sabrina advance. In fact, I have a special project in mind for her. It will just take me a couple of months before I am ready to go public with it. In the meantime, I need a diplomat for the Texas client. That's why I chose Dale. If Sabrina turns this into a race issue—or sexual orientation issue—then she is way off base."

Can Larry Fit In?

Melissa, Office Manager

You are the manager of an auditing team sent to Bangkok, Thailand, to represent a major international accounting firm headquartered in New York. Larry, an auditor in your group, was sent there with you. Larry is about seven years older than you and has five more years of seniority in the firm. Your relationship has become strained since you were recently designated the office manager. You feel you were given the promotion because you have established an excellent working relationship with the Thai staff as well as a broad range of international clients. However, Larry has told other members of the staff that your promotion simply reflects the firm's heavy emphasis on affirmative action. He has tried to isolate you from the all-male accounting staff by focusing discussions on sports, local night spots, and so forth.

You are sitting in your office reading some complicated new reporting procedures that have just arrived from the home office. Your concentration is suddenly interrupted by a loud knock on your door. Without waiting for an invitation to enter, Larry bursts into your office. He is obviously upset, and it is not difficult for you to surmise why he is in such a nasty mood.

You recently posted the audit assignments for the coming month, and you scheduled Larry for a job you knew he wouldn't like. Larry is one of your senior auditors, and the company norm is that they get the choice assignments. This particular job will require him to spend two weeks away from Bangkok in a remote town, working with a company whose records are notoriously messy.

Unfortunately, you have had to assign several of these less desirable audits to Larry recently because you are short of personnel. But that's not the only reason. You have received several complaints from the junior staff (all Thais) recently that Larry treats them in a condescending manner. They feel he is always looking for an opportunity to boss them around, as if he were their supervisor instead of an experienced, supportive mentor. As a result, your whole operation works more smoothly when you can send Larry out of town on a solo project for several days. It keeps him from coming into your office and telling you how to do your job, and the morale of the rest of the auditing staff is significantly higher.

Larry slams the door and proceeds to express his anger over this assignment.

Larry, Senior Auditor

You are really ticked off! Melissa is deliberately trying to undermine your status in the office. She knows that the company norm is that senior auditors get the better jobs. You've paid your dues, and now you expect to be treated with respect. And this isn't the first time this has happened. Since she was made the office manager, she has tried to keep you out of the office as much as possible. It's as if she doesn't want her rival for leadership of the office around. When you were asked to go to Bangkok, you assumed that you would be made the office manager because of your seniority in the firm. You are certain that the decision to pick Melissa is yet another indication of reverse discrimination against white males.

In staff meetings, Melissa has talked about the need to be sensitive to the feelings of the office staff as well as the clients in this multicultural setting. "Where does she come off preaching about sensitivity! What about my feelings, for heaven's sake?" you wonder. This is nothing more than a straightforward power play. She is probably feeling insecure about being the only female auditor in the office and being promoted over someone with more experience. "Sending me out of town," you decide, "is a clear case of 'out of sight, out of mind.'"

Well, it's not going to happen that easily. You are not going to roll over and let her treat you unfairly. It's time for a showdown. If she doesn't agree to change this assignment and apologize for the way she's been treating you, you're going to register a formal complaint with her boss in the New York office. You are prepared to submit your resignation if the situation doesn't improve.

Meeting at Hartford Manufacturing Company

Hartford Manufacturing Company is the largest subsidiary of Connecticut Industries. Since the end of World War I, when it was formed, Hartford Manufacturing has become an industrial leader in the Northeast. Its sales currently average approximately $25 million a year, with an annual growth of approximately 6 percent. There are more than 850 employees in production, sales and marketing, accounting, engineering, and management.

Lynn Smith is general manager. He has held his position for a little over two years and is well respected by his subordinates. He has a reputation of being firm but fair. Lynn's training in college was in engineering, so he is technically minded, and he frequently likes to walk around the production area to see for himself how things are going. He has also been known to roll up his sleeves and help work on a problem on the shop floor. He is not opposed to rubbing shoulders with even the lowest-level employees. On the other hand, he tries to run a tight company, and employees pretty well stick to their assigned tasks. He holds high expectations for performance, especially from individuals in management positions.

Richard Hooton is the director of production at Hartford Manufacturing. He has been with the company since he was 19 years old, when he worked on the dock. He has worked himself up through the ranks and now, at age 54, is the oldest of the management personnel. Richard has his own ideas of how things should be run in production, and he is reluctant to tolerate any intervention from anyone, even Lynn Smith. Because he has been with the company so long, he feels he knows it better than anyone else, and he believes he has had a hand in making it the success that it is. His main goal is to keep production running smoothly and efficiently.

Barbara Price is the director of sales and marketing. She joined the company about 18 months ago, after completing her MBA at Dartmouth. Before going back to school for a graduate degree, she held the position of assistant manager of marketing at Connecticut Industries. Price is a conscientious employee and is anxious to make a name for herself. Her major objective, which she has never hesitated to make public, is to be a general manager someday. Sales at Hartford Manufacturing have increased in the past year to near-record levels under her guidance.

Chuck Kasper is the regional sales director for the New York region. He reports directly to Barbara Price. The New York region represents the largest market for Hartford Manufacturing, and Chuck is considered the most competent salesperson in the company. He has built personal relationships with several major clients in his region, and it appears that some sales occur as much because of Chuck Kasper as because of the products of Hartford Manufacturing. Chuck has been with the company for 12 years, all of them in sales.

This is Friday afternoon, and tomorrow Lynn Smith leaves for Copenhagen at noon to attend an important meeting with potential overseas investors. He will be gone for two weeks. Before he leaves, there are several items in his in-box that must receive attention. He calls a meeting with Richard Hooton and Barbara Price in his office. Just before the meeting begins, Chuck Kasper calls and asks if he may join the meeting for a few minutes, since he is in town and has something important to discuss that involves both Lynn Smith and Richard Hooton. Lynn gives permission for him to join the meeting, since there may not be another chance to meet with Chuck before the trip. The meeting convenes, therefore, with Lynn, Richard, Barbara, and Chuck all in the room.

Assignment

Groups of four individuals should be formed. Each person should take the role of one of the characters in the management staff of Hartford Manufacturing Company. A fifth person should be assigned to serve as an observer to provide feedback at the end of the meeting, using the Observer's Feedback Form at the end of the chapter as a guide. The letters described in the case that were received by Lynn Smith are shown in Figures 7.5, 7.6, and 7.7 Only the person playing the role of Lynn Smith should read the letters, and no one should read the instructions for another staff member's role. (The letters will be introduced by Lynn Smith during the meeting.)

Lynn Smith, General Manager

Three letters arrived today, and you judge them to be sufficiently important to require your attention before you leave on your trip. Each letter represents a problem that requires immediate action, and you need commitments from key staff members to resolve these problems. You are concerned about this meeting because these individuals don't work as well together as you'd like.

For example, Richard Hooton is very difficult to pin down. He always seems suspicious of the motives of others and has a reputation for not making tough decisions. You sometimes wonder how a person could become the head of production in a major manufacturing firm by avoiding controversial issues and blaming others for the results.

By contrast, Barbara Price is very straightforward. You always know exactly where she stands. The problem is that sometimes she doesn't take enough time to study a problem before making a decision. She tends to be impulsive and anxious to make a decision, whether it's the right one or not. Her general approach to resolving disagreements between departments is to seek expedient compromises. You are particularly disturbed by her approach to the sales incentive problem. You felt strongly that something needed to be done to increase sales during the winter months. You reluctantly agreed to the incentive program because you didn't want to dampen her initiative. But you aren't convinced this is the right answer, because, frankly, you're not yet sure what the real problem is.

Chuck Kasper is your typical forceful, "take no prisoners" sales manager. He is hard-charging and uncompromising. He is great in the field because he gets the job done, but he sometimes ruffles the feathers of the corporate staff with his uncompromising, "black-and-white" style. He is also fiercely loyal to his sales staff, so you're sure he'll take the complaint about Sam St. Clair hard.

In contrast to the styles of these others, you have tried to use an integrating approach to problem-solving: focusing on the facts, treating everyone's inputs equally, and keeping conversations about controversial topics problem-focused. One of your goals since taking on this position two years ago is to foster a "team" approach within your staff.

Figure 7.5

T. J. Koppel, Inc.
General Accountants
8381 Spring Street
Hartford, Connecticut 06127

February 10, 2015

Mr. Lynn Smith
General Manager
Hartford Manufacturing Company
7450 Central Avenue
Hartford, CT 06118

Dear Mr. Smith:

As you requested last month, we have now completed our financial audit of Hartford Manufacturing Company. We find accounting procedures and fiscal control to be very satisfactory. A more detailed report of these matters is attached. However, we did discover during our perusal of company records that the production department has consistently incurred cost overruns during the past two quarters. Cost per unit of production is approximately 5 percent over budget. While this is not a serious problem given the financial solvency of your company, we thought it wise to bring it to your attention.

Respectfully,

T. J. Koppel

TJK: srw

[*Note*: For more information about how you might approach the issues raised by these letters in your staff meeting, review the collaborating approach in Table 7.2 as well as the mediator's behavioral guidelines at the end of the Skill Learning section of this chapter.]

Richard Hooton, Director of Production

The only times you have had major problems in production were when the young know-it-alls fresh from college have come in and tried to change things. With their progressive management concepts, coupled with fuzzy-headed "interpersonal effectiveness" training,

Figure 7.6

ZODIAK INDUSTRIES
6377 Atlantic Avenue
Boston, Massachusetts 02112

February 8, 2015

Mr. Lynn Smith
General Manager
Hartford Manufacturing Company
7450 Central Avenue
Hartford, CT 06118

Dear Mr. Smith:

We have been purchasing your products since 1975, and we have been very satisfied with our relations with your sales personnel. However, we have had a problem of late that requires your attention. Your sales representative for the Boston region, Sam St. Clair, has appeared at our company the last three times looking and smelling like he was under the influence of alcohol. Not only that, but our last order was mistakenly recorded, so we received the wrong quantities of products. I'm sure you don't make it a practice to put your company's reputation in the hands of someone like Sam St. Clair, so I suggest you get someone else to cover this region. We cannot tolerate, and I'm sure other companies in Boston cannot tolerate, this kind of relationship. While we judge your products to be excellent, we will be forced to find other sources if some action is not taken.

Sincerely yours,

Miles Andrew
Chief of Purchasing

:ms

they have more often made a mess of things than helped to improve matters. The best production methods have been practiced for years in the company, and you have yet to see anyone who could improve on your system.

On the other hand, you have respect for Lynn Smith as the general manager. Because he has experience and the right kind of training, and is involved in the production part of the organization, he often has given you good advice and has shown special interest. He mostly lets you do what you feel is best, however, and he seldom dictates specific methods for doing things.

Figure 7.7

HARTFORD MANUFACTURING COMPANY
7450 Central Avenue
Hartford, Connecticut 06118

"A subsidiary of CONNECTICUT INDUSTRIES"

<u>Memorandum</u>

TO: Lynn Smith, General Manager
FROM: Barbara Price, General Supervisor, Sales and Marketing
DATE: February 11, 2007

Mr. Smith:

In response to your concerns, we have instituted several incentive programs among our sales force to increase sales during these traditionally slow months. We have set up competition among regions, with the salespeople in the top region being honored in the company newsletter and given engraved plaques. We have instituted a "vacation in Hawaii" award for the top salesperson in the company. And we have instituted cash bonuses for any salesperson who gets a new customer order. However, in the last month these incentives have been in operation, sales have not increased at all. In fact, in two regions they have decreased by an average of 5 percent.

What do you suggest now? We have advertised the incentives as lasting through this quarter, but they seem to be doing no good. Not only that, but we cannot afford to provide the incentives within our current budget, and unless sales increase, we will be in the red.

Regretfully, I recommend dropping the program.

PRACTICE

Your general approach to problems is to avoid controversy. You feel uncomfortable when production is made the scapegoat for problems in the company. Because this is a manufacturing business, it seems as if everyone tries to pin the blame for problems on the production department. You've felt for years that the firm was getting away from what it does best: mass producing a few standard products. Instead, the trend has been for marketing and sales to push for more and more products, shorter lead times, and greater customization capability. These actions have increased costs and caused significant production delays as well as higher rejection rates.

[*Note*: During the upcoming meeting, you should adopt the avoidance approach shown in Table 7.2. Defend your turf, place blame on others, defer taking a stand, and avoid taking responsibility for making a controversial decision.]

Barbara Price, Director of Sales and Marketing

You are anxious to impress Lynn Smith because you have your eye on a position that is opening up at the end of the year in the parent company, Connecticut Industries. It would mean a promotion for you. A positive recommendation from Lynn Smith would carry a lot of weight in the selection process. Given that both Hartford Manufacturing and Connecticut Industries are largely male dominated, you are pleased with your career advancement so far, and you are hoping to keep it up.

One current concern is Lynn Smith's suggestion some time ago that you look into the problem of slow sales during the winter months. You implemented an incentive plan that was highly recommended by an industry analyst at a recent trade conference. It consists of three separate incentive programs: (1) competition among regions in which the salesperson in the top region would have his or her picture in the company newsletter and receive an engraved plaque, (2) a vacation in Hawaii for the top salesperson in the company, and (3) cash bonuses for salespeople who obtained new customer orders. Unfortunately, these incentives haven't worked. Not only have sales not increased for the company as a whole, but sales for two regions are down an average of 5 percent. You have told the sales force that the incentives will last through this quarter, but if sales don't improve, your budget will be in the red. You haven't budgeted for the prizes, since you expected the increased sales to more than offset the cost of the incentives.

Obviously, this was a bad idea—it isn't working—and it should be dropped immediately. You are a bit embarrassed about this aborted project. But it is better to cut your losses and try something else rather than continue to support an obvious loser.

In general, you are very confident and self-assured. You feel that the best way to get work done is through negotiation and compromise. What's important is making a decision quickly and efficiently. Maybe everyone doesn't get exactly what he or she wants, but at least they can get on with their work. There are no black and whites in this business—only "grays" that can be traded off to keep the management process from bogging down with "paralysis by analysis." You are impatient over delays caused by intensive studies and investigations of detail. You agree with businessman Tom Peters's views: Action is the hallmark of successful managers.

[*Note*: During this meeting, use the compromise approach shown in Table 7.2. Do whatever is necessary to help the group make a quick decision so you can get on with the pressing demands of your work.]

Chuck Kasper, Regional Sales Director

You don't get back to company headquarters often because your customer contacts take up most of your time. You regularly work 50 to 60 hours a week, and you are proud of the job you do. You also feel a special obligation to your customers to provide them with the best product available in the timeliest fashion. This sense of obligation comes not only from your commitment to the company but also from your personal relationships with many of the customers.

Lately, you have been receiving more and more complaints about late deliveries of Hartford Manufacturing's products to your customers. The time between their ordering and delivery is increasing, and some customers have been greatly inconvenienced by the delays. You have made a formal inquiry of production to find out what the problem is. They replied that they are producing as efficiently as possible, and they see nothing wrong with past practices. Richard Hooton's assistant even suggested that this was just another example of the sales force's unrealistic expectations.

Not only will sales be negatively affected if these delays continue, but your reputation with your customers will be damaged. You have promised them that the problem will be quickly solved and that products will begin arriving on time. Since Richard Hooton is so rigid, however, you are almost certain that it will do no good to talk with him. His subordinate probably got his negative attitude from Richard.

In general, Richard is a 1980s production worker who is being pulled by the rest of the firm into the new age. Competition is different, technology is different, and management is different, but Richard is reluctant to change. You need shorter lead times, a wider range of products, and the capacity to do more customized work. Sure, this makes production's work harder, but other firms are providing these services with high-tech applications. Hartford Manufacturing is clearly behind the curve.

Instead of getting down to the real problems, the home office, in their typical high-handed fashion, announced an incentives plan. This implies that the problem is in the field, not the factory. It made some of your people angry to think they were being pressed to increase their efforts when they weren't receiving the backup support in Hartford to get the job done. Sure, they liked the prizes, but the way the plan was presented made them feel as if they weren't working hard enough. This isn't the first time you have questioned the judgment of Barbara, your boss. She certainly is intelligent and hardworking, but she doesn't seem very interested in what's going on out in the field. Furthermore, she doesn't seem receptive to "bad news" about sales and customer complaints.

Note: During this meeting, use the forcing approach to conflict management and negotiations shown in Table 7.2. However, don't overplay your part, because you are the senior regional sales manager, and if Barbara continues to move up fast in the organization, you may be in line for her position.

ACTIVITIES FOR RESOLVING CONFLICT

Suggested Assignments

7.10. Select a specific conflict with which you are very familiar. Using the framework for identifying the sources of conflict discussed in this chapter, analyze this situation carefully. It might be useful to compare your perceptions of the situation with those of informed observers. What type of conflict is this? Why did it occur? Why is it continuing? Next, using the guidelines for selecting an appropriate conflict management strategy, identify the general approach that would be most appropriate for this situation. Consider both the personal preferences of the parties involved and the relevant situational factors. Is this the approach the parties have been using? If not, attempt to introduce a different perspective into the relationship and explain why you feel it would be more productive. If the parties have been using this approach, discuss with them why it has not been successful thus far. Share information on specific behavioral guidelines or negotiation tactics that might increase the effectiveness of their efforts.

7.11. Select three individuals who are from diverse cultural backgrounds and have work experience outside of their native culture. Discuss with them the sources (especially the personal differences) of previous conflicts they have experienced at work. Ask them about their preferences in dealing with conflict situations. What strategies do they prefer to use? How do they generally attempt to resolve disputes? What relevant situational factors influence the way they manage conflict situations with individuals from other cultures and with individuals of their own culture? With the help of these three people, identify specific behavioral guidelines for managing conflict more effectively with other people from their respective cultures.

7.12. Identify a situation in which another individual is doing something that needs to be corrected. Using the respondent's guidelines for collaborative problem-solving, construct a plan for discussing your concerns with this person. Include specific language designed to state your case assertively without causing a defensive reaction. Role-play this interaction with a friend and incorporate any suggestions for improvement. Make your presentation to the individual and report on your results. What was the reaction? Were you successful in balancing assertiveness with support and responsibility? Based on this experience, identify other situations you feel need to be changed, and follow a similar procedure.

7.13. Volunteer to serve as a mediator to resolve a conflict between two individuals or groups. Using the guidelines for implementing the collaborative approach to mediation, outline a plan of action prior to your intervention. Be sure to consider carefully whether or not private meetings with the parties prior to your mediation session are appropriate. Report on the situation and your plan. How did you feel? Which specific actions worked well? What was the outcome? What would you do differently? Based on this experience, revise your plan for use in related situations.

7.14. Identify a difficult situation involving negotiations. This might involve transactions at work, at home, or in the community. Review the guidelines for integrative bargaining and identify the specific tactics you plan to use. Write down specific questions and responses to likely initiatives from the other party. In particular, anticipate how you might handle the possibility of the other party's using a distributive negotiation strategy. Schedule a negotiation meeting with the party involved, and implement your plan. Following the session, debrief the experience with a coworker or friend. What did you learn? How successful were you? What would you do differently? Based on this experience, modify your plan and prepare to implement it in related situations.

Application Plan and Evaluation

The intent of this exercise is to help you apply this cluster of skills in a real-life, out-of-class setting. Now that you have become familiar with the behavioral guidelines that form the basis of effective skill performance, you will improve most by trying out those guidelines in an everyday context. Unlike a classroom activity, in which feedback is immediate and others can assist you with their evaluations, this skill application activity is one you must accomplish and evaluate on your own. There are two parts to this activity. Part 1 helps prepare you to apply the skill, and Part 2 helps you evaluate and improve on your experience. Be sure to write down answers to each item. Don't short-circuit the process by skipping steps.

Part 1: Planning

7.15. Write down the two or three aspects of this skill that are most important to you. These may be areas of weakness, areas you most want to improve, or areas that are most salient to a problem you face right now. Identify the specific aspects of this skill that you want to apply.

7.16. Now identify the setting or the situation in which you will apply this skill. Establish a plan for performance by actually writing down a description of the situation. Who else will be involved? When will you do it? Where will it be done?

      Circumstances:
      Who else?
      When?
      Where?

7.17. Identify the specific behaviors you will engage in to apply this skill. Operationalize your skill performance.

7.18. What are the indicators of successful performance? How will you know you have been effective? What will indicate you have performed competently?

Part 2: Evaluation

7.19. After you have completed your implementation, record the results. What happened? How successful were you? What was the effect on others?

7.20. How can you improve? What modifications can you make next time? What will you do differently in a similar situation in the future?

7.21. Looking back on your whole skill practice and application experience, what have you learned? What has been surprising? In what ways might this experience help you in the long term?

SKILL PRACTICE
Exercises for Resolving People-Focused Conflict

Observer's Feedback Form

RATING

 1 = Low
 5 = High

Initiator

_____ Maintained personal ownership of the problem, including feelings

_____ Avoided making accusations or attributing motives; stuck to the facts

_____ Succinctly described the problem (behaviors, outcomes, feelings)

_____ Specified expectations or standards violated

_____ Persisted until understood

_____ Encouraged two-way interaction

_____ Approached multiple issues incrementally (proceeded from simple to complex, easy to hard)

_____ Appealed to what the disputants had in common (goals, principles, constraints)

_____ Made a specific request for change

Respondent

_____ Established a climate for joint problem-solving

_____ Showed genuine concern and interest

_____ Responded appropriately to the initiator's emotions

_____ Avoided becoming defensive or overreacting

_____ Sought additional information about the problem (shifted general to specific, evaluative to descriptive)

_____ Focused on one issue at a time, gradually broadened the scope of the discussion, searched for integrative solution

_____ Agreed with some aspect of the complaint (facts, perceptions, feelings, or principles)

_____ Asked for suggestions for making changes

_____ Proposed a specific plan of action

Mediator

_____ Acknowledged that a conflict exists; treated the conflict and disputants seriously

_____ Broke down complex issues, separated the critical from the peripheral; began with a relatively easy problem

_____ Helped disputants avoid entrenched positions by exploring underlying interests

_____ Remained neutral (facilitator, not judge) and impartial toward issues and disputants

_____ Kept the interaction issue-oriented (e.g., pointed out the effect of the conflict on performance)

APPLICATION

_____ Made sure that neither party dominated conversation, asked questions to maintain balance

_____ Kept conflict in perspective by emphasizing areas of agreement

_____ Helped generate multiple alternatives, drawn from common goals, values, or principles

_____ Made sure that both parties were satisfied and committed to the proposed resolution

Comments:

SCORING KEYS AND COMPARISON DATA

✪ Go to www.pearson.com/mylab/management for scoring keys and comparison data for the following instruments:

Managing Interpersonal Conflict
Strategies for Handling Conflict

Part III

Group Skills

CHAPTERS

SKILL ASSESSMENT

- Effective Empowerment and Engagement
- Personal Empowerment Assessment

SKILL LEARNING

- Empowering and Engaging Others
- The Meaning of Empowerment
- Dimensions of Empowerment
- How to Develop Empowerment
- Inhibitors to Empowerment
- Fostering Engagement
- International Caveats
- Summary
- Behavioral Guidelines

SKILL ANALYSIS

- Minding the Store
- Changing the Portfolio

SKILL PRACTICE

- Executive Development Associates
- Empowering Ourselves
- Deciding to Engage Others

SKILL APPLICATION

- Suggested Assignments
- Application Plan and Evaluation

SCORING KEYS AND COMPARISON DATA

8

Empowering and Engaging Others

LEARNING OBJECTIVES

1. Empower others
2. Empower yourself
3. Engaging others effectively

MyLab Management

Go to www.pearson.com/mylab/management to complete the exercises marked with this icon ✪.

MyLab Management Personal Inventory Assessments

The assessment instruments in this chapter are briefly described below. The assessments appear either in your text or in MyLab. The assessments marked with ✪ are available only in MyLab. If assigned, go to www.pearson.com/mylab/management to complete these assessments. The assessments without the ✪ appear only in the text.

All assessments should be completed before reading the chapter material.

After completing the first assessment, save your response to your hard drive. When you have finished reading the chapter, re-take the assessment and compare your responses to see what you have learned.

✪ ❑ *Effective Empowerment and Engagement Instrument* assesses your competency in empowering others with whom you work and the extent to which you can effectively engage other people in the work.

✪ ❑ *The Personal Empowerment Assessment* measures the extent to which you experience an empowering environment in your role at work or as a student.

SKILL *LEARNING* ⓘ

Empowering and Engaging Others

Many management books are focused on helping managers know how to control others' behavior. They emphasize how managers can increase employees' performance, engender conformity, or motivate employees to achieve certain objectives. This book, too, includes skills that will help you motivate people to do what you want them to do (see the chapter on Motivating Others) or achieve power and influence over others (see the Gaining Power and Influence chapter). This chapter, however, focuses on a skill called **empowerment** and how it differs from power. Its purpose is to effectively engage others in their work and in the organization.

Empowerment is based on assumptions that are different from those associated with motivating others or influencing others (see Chapters 5 and 6). Empowerment provides freedom for people to successfully do what *they want* to do, rather than getting them to do what *you want* them to do. This means that a manager's challenge is to ensure that what others want to do matches what the organization needs to be done. Managers who empower people remove controls, constraints, and boundaries for them instead of motivating, directing, or influencing their behavior. Rather than being a "push" strategy, in which managers induce employees to respond in desirable ways through incentives and influence techniques, empowerment is a "pull" strategy. It focuses on finding ways managers can design a work situation so that it energizes and encourages employees to pursue something meaningful that they care about. In the context of such a strategy, workers accomplish tasks because they are intrinsically attracted by them, not because of an extrinsic reward system or influence technique.

Empowering others, however, can lead to a dilemma. On the one hand, evidence shows that empowered employees are more productive, more satisfied, and more innovative, and that they create higher-quality products and services than unempowered employees (Babakus, et al., 2003; Lee, Willis, & Tian, 2017; Spreitzer, 2008). Organizations are more effective when an empowered workforce exists (Pieterse, et al., 2010; Seibert, Wang, & Courtright, 2011).

On the other hand, empowerment means giving up control and letting others make decisions, set goals, accomplish results, and receive rewards. It means that other people probably will get credit for success. Managers with high needs for power and control (see McClelland, 1975) face a challenge when they are expected to sacrifice their needs for someone else's gain. They may ask themselves: "Why should others get the credit when I am in charge? Why should I allow others to exercise power, and even help them obtain more power, when I naturally want to receive rewards and recognition myself?"

The answer is that you don't need to sacrifice desired rewards, recognition, or effectiveness in order to be a skillful empowering manager. On the contrary, through real empowerment, managers actually multiply their own effectiveness. They and their organizations become more successful than they could have been otherwise (Maynard, Gilson, & Mathieu, 2012). Nevertheless, for most managers, empowerment is a skill that must be developed and practiced, because despite the high visibility of the concept of empowerment in popular literature, its actual practice is all too rare in modern management. Survey after survey has reported that a large majority of employees do not feel empowered, are not engaged, and do not believe that they make a difference at work (e.g., Asplund & Blacksmith, 2012; Gallup, 2018). Globally, this includes more than 80 percent of employees!

In this chapter, we begin by discussing the core dimensions of empowerment and, in particular, how to effectively empower other people. In the second part of the chapter, we discuss a special situation in which empowerment is essential: fostering high levels of engagement in work. We conclude with a summary model and a list of behavioral guidelines for successfully empowering and engaging others.

The Meaning of Empowerment

To empower means to enable. It means to help people develop a sense of self-confidence. It means to help people overcome feelings of powerlessness or helplessness. It means to energize people to take action. It means to mobilize intrinsic motivation to accomplish a task. Empowered people not only possess the wherewithal to accomplish something, but they also think of themselves differently than they did before they were empowered. They feel more capable and confident.

It is important to note that empowerment and power are not the same. Creating empowerment is not merely giving power to someone. Both concepts connote the ability to get things done, but Table 8.1 contrasts these concepts and highlights their differences. For example, you can give someone else power, but people must accept empowerment for themselves. It cannot be bestowed on someone. I cannot empower you; I can only create the circumstances in which you can empower yourself.

As explained in the chapter on gaining power and influence, the acquisition of power is based on several personal and positional factors. In each case, other people need to acknowledge your power, follow your lead, and acquiesce to your influence in order for you to have power. The underlying source of your power is other people.

For example, you may have power because you have more resources or political support than someone else. Thus, you can reward others and have *reward power*. Alternatively, you may have the ability to penalize or sanction others as a result of your strength or support, so you have *sanctioning power*. Your title or position may give you power over others, thus giving you *traditional power*. You may possess more knowledge or information than others, giving you *expertise power*. Or, you may be personally attractive or charismatic, thus having *referent power*. French and Raven (1960) identified these five factors as the primary bases of power. Regardless of whether these are the five factors that create power or whether there are others, each can be conveyed to another person. Each depends on others acknowledging it. Each can be bestowed on someone else.

In the case of empowerment, however, people can be empowered even if no one acknowledges their personal attributes or positions. Viktor Frankl, Nelson Mandela, and Mahatma Gandhi are examples of individuals who, despite the absence of the attributes of power, maintained complete empowerment in dismal circumstances (i.e., in prison and in bigoted environments). This is because the source of empowerment is internal. You accept and create empowerment for yourself.

In addition, if I become more powerful, that generally means you become less powerful. If I have the power

Table 8.1	The Difference Between Power and Empowerment	
Power	**Empowerment**
The capacity to get others to do what you want	The capacity to get others to do what they want
To get more implies taking it away from someone else	To get more does not affect how much others have
Comes from an external source	Comes from an internal source
Ultimately, few people have it	Ultimately, everyone can have it
Leads to competition	Leads to cooperation

to get someone to do what I want, but that differs from what you want, my power and your power come into conflict. That is why, ultimately, relatively few people have power. Power gets concentrated among a few people in most organizations. Furthermore, power struggles are almost universal in organizations and even in small groups. Determining who has enough power to have his or her way is a common problem, and it almost always leads to conflict.

On the other hand, every person can be empowered without affecting any other person's position or stature. It merely leads to each of us being enabled to accomplish what we choose. Empowerment, in fact, is more likely to lead to cooperation and collaboration than to conflict.

A key to successfully enable empowerment is to understand its core components. In the next section, we summarize the five key dimensions of empowerment, and provide guidelines for how to foster them. Think of these five dimensions as a formula. A multiplication sign goes between each of the dimensions. That is, if any one dimension is absent or zero, then empowerment is zero. All five must be present for empowerment to be present.

> **MyLab Management** Watch it!
> If your instructor has assigned this activity, go to **www.pearson.com/mylab/management** to complete the video exercise.

Dimensions of Empowerment

In one of the best empirical studies of empowerment, Spreitzer (1992) identified four dimensions of empowerment. We have added one dimension to her model, based on the research of Mishra (1992). Subsequent research has confirmed that in order for you to empower others successfully, you must engender these five qualities in those they intend to empower. Skillful empowerment means producing (1) a sense of *self-efficacy*, (2) a sense of *self-determination*, (3) a sense of *personal consequence*, (4) a sense of *meaning*, and (5) a sense of *trust* (see Table 8.2). When these five dimensions of empowerment are present, empirical evidence is clear: Individuals and organizations perform better than normal (also see Maynard, Gilson, & Mathieu, 2012).

Fostering an environment where these five factors are present makes it highly likely that people will accept empowerment for themselves. Empowered people

Table 8.2	Five Core Dimensions of Empowerment
Dimension	**Explanation**
Self-efficacy	A sense of personal competence
Self-determination	A sense of personal choice
Personal consequence	A sense of having impact
Meaning	A sense of value in activity
Trust	A sense of security

are more confident; they feel more freedom; they feel more important; and they feel more comfortable in their work and work setting.

SELF-EFFICACY

When people are empowered, they have a sense of **self-efficacy**, or the feeling that they possess the capability and competence to perform a task successfully. Empowered people not only feel *competent*, they also feel *confident* that they can perform adequately. They are self-assured. They feel a sense of personal mastery and believe they can learn and grow to meet new challenges (see Bandura, 1989, 1997, 2012; Bowles & Pearlman, 2017). Some writers believe this is the most important element in empowerment because having a sense of self-efficacy determines whether people will try and persist in attempting to accomplish a difficult task (Biron & Bamberger, 2010).

> *The strength of people's conviction in their own effectiveness is likely to affect whether they would even try to cope with given situations.... They get involved in activities and behave assuredly when they judge themselves capable of handling situations that would otherwise be intimidating.... Efficacy expectations determine how much effort people will expend and how long they will persist in the face of obstacles and aversive experiences. (Bandura, 1977, pp. 193–194)*

Our colleague Roger Goddard and his associates found that a sense of efficacy among students in a classroom—what he referred to as "collective efficacy"—is a more powerful predictor of success in school than any other single factor (Goddard, Hoy, & Hoy, 2002). That is, when students have collective efficacy—they believe in themselves, they have confidence that they can succeed, and they have faith that a successful outcome will occur—their grades are higher, their test scores are higher in math and reading, and their absenteeism and tardiness are lower than normal students. Collective efficacy is a more important factor in determining these outcomes than race; gender; socioeconomic status; attending a large or small, inner-city or suburban school; or ethnic makeup of the class. (Also see Bowles & Pearlman, 2017; Caprara, et al., 2011.)

A great deal of additional research has been done on the consequences of self-efficacy and its opposite, powerlessness, in relation to physical and psychological health (Bandura, 2012; Xanthopoulou, Bakker, & Fischbach, 2013). For example, self-efficacy has been found to be a significant factor in overcoming phobias and anxieties, alcohol and drug abuse, eating disorders, smoking addiction, and depression, and in increasing tolerance for pain. Recovery from illness and injury and coping with job loss or disruptions is more effective and more rapid among people who have developed a strong sense of self-efficacy because they are more physically and psychologically resilient and better able to change negative behaviors (Brouwer, et al., 2010; Bandura, 1997, 2012; Lee, Willis, & Tian, 2017; Peterson, Maier, & Seligman, 1995; Seligman, 1975, 2012). We will provide some guidelines for enhancing self-efficacy later in the chapter.

SELF-DETERMINATION

Empowered people also have a sense of **self-determination**, meaning that they have a sense of *having choices*. "To be self-determining means to experience a sense of choice in initiating and regulating one's own actions" (Deci, Connell, & Ryan, 1989, p. 580). People feel self-determined when they can voluntarily and intentionally involve themselves in tasks rather than being forced to or prohibited from involvement (Deci & Ryan, 2012). Their actions are a consequence of personal freedom and autonomy. Self-determination theory, in fact, is one of the best-known and well-researched theories on human motivation (Deci & Ryan, 2012; Ryan & Deci, 2017).

Empowered individuals have alternatives and a sense of freedom; therefore, they develop a sense of responsibility for and ownership of their activities. They are able to take initiative on their own accord, make independent decisions, and try out new ideas. Rather than feeling that their actions are predetermined, externally controlled, or inevitable, they experience an internal locus of control (see Chapter 1).

Research shows that a strong sense of self-determination is associated with a variety of positive outcomes in the workplace—for example, less alienation in the work environment, more work satisfaction, higher levels of work performance, more entrepreneurial and innovative activity, high levels of job involvement, greater work motivation, and less job strain. In medical research, recovery from severe illness has been found to be associated with having the patient "reject the traditional passive role and insist on being an active participant in his own therapy" (Gecas, 1989, p. 298). People who are helped to feel that they can have personal impact on what happens to them, even with regard to the effects of disease, are more likely to experience positive outcomes than those who lack this feeling (Deci & Ryan, 2012; Gagne & Deci, 2005; Maddux, 2002; Ryan & Deci, 2002; Weinstein & Deci, 2011).

Self-determination is associated most directly with having choices about the *methods* used to accomplish a task, the amount of *effort* to be expended, the *pace* of the work, and the *time frame* in which it is to be accomplished. Empowered individuals have a feeling of ownership for tasks because they can determine how tasks are accomplished, when they are accomplished, and how quickly they are completed. Clearly, having a choice is the critical component of self-determination. Later, we will offer specific suggestions for fostering self-determination.

PERSONAL CONSEQUENCE

Empowered people have a sense that when they act, their action produces a result. Think of an assembly-line job where a worker screws a nut on a bolt. If he makes an error, someone down the line will correct it. Such a person will have little sense that his actions have a meaningful effect on the outcome of the product or that he has control over the outcome. Someone else down the line will correct any mistakes.

On the other hand, people with a sense of personal consequence believe that expending effort will produce an outcome. Personal consequence refers to "an individual's beliefs at a given point in time in his or her ability to effect a change in a desired direction" (Greenberger, et al., 1989, p. 165). It is the conviction that through your own actions, you can influence what happens. You have a sense of control, and you can have *impact*.

Empowered individuals do not believe that obstacles in the external environment control their actions; rather, they believe that those obstacles can be overcome (Hoffman, Friese, & Strack, 2009; Thornton & Tizard, 2010). They have a feeling of *active control*—which allows them to bring their environment into alignment with their wishes—as opposed to *passive control*—in which their wishes are brought into alignment with environmental demands (see Casey, et al., 2011; Diamond, 2013; Greenberger & Stasser, 1991; Peterson, Maier, & Seligman, 1995). Instead of being reactive to what they see around them, people with a sense of personal consequence try to influence what they see. For you to feel empowered, you must not only perceive that what you do produces an effect but that you can produce the effect yourself.

Having a sense of personal consequence is related to internal locus of control discussed in the chapter on Self-Awareness, but it is not exactly the same thing. (You completed the Locus of Control instrument in Chapter 1.) Most people have developed an orientation toward internal or external locus of control, which characterizes their general approach to life. Helping people experience empowerment, however, means helping others develop a sense that they can produce a desired result, regardless of their personality dimension. Some ideas for how to foster a sense of consequence are discussed later.

Research suggests that people are intrinsically motivated to seek personal consequence or a feeling of control (Ryan & Deci, 2017; Spreitzer, 2008). We all strive to maintain a sense of control of ourselves and our situations. In fact, even small losses of personal control can be harmful physically and emotionally. For example, loss of control has been found to lead to depression, stress, anxiety, low morale, loss of productivity, burnout, learned helplessness, and even increased death rates (see Xanthopoulou, Bakker, & Fischbach, 2013). Having a sense of personal control over outcomes or consequences, then, appears necessary for health as well as for empowerment.

On the other hand, even the most empowered people are not able to completely control everything that happens to them. No one can produce all the results he or she desires. Nevertheless, empowerment helps people increase the number of personal outcomes that they can impact.

MEANING

Empowered people also have a sense of meaning. They value the purpose or outcomes of the activity in which they are engaged. Their own ideals and values are perceived as consistent with what they are doing. Not only do they feel that they can produce a result (i.e., personal consequence), but they believe in and care about what they produce (Bunderson & Thompson, 2009; Quinn & Thakor, 2018; Strecher, 2016; Wrzesniewski,

2012). Meaningfulness, then, refers to a perception that what is being done produces *value*.

Activities infused with meaning create a sense of purpose, passion, or mission for people. They provide a source of energy and enthusiasm, rather than draining energy and enthusiasm from people. Merely getting paid, helping an organization earn money, or just doing a job does not create a sense of meaning for most people. Something more fundamental, more personal, and more value-laden must be linked to the activity. Almost all people want to feel that they are spending their time on something that will produce lasting benefit, that will make the world a better place, or that is more important than just a paycheck (Bunderson & Thompson, 2009).

Involvement in activities without meaning often produces disengagement, boredom, or exhaustion. Other incentives—such as perks or extra pay—are required to get people to invest in the work. Unfortunately, these extra incentives are costly to organizations and represent nonvalue-added expenses that constrain organizational efficiency and effectiveness. It costs companies a lot of money to require work that has little or no meaning to workers.

Research on meaningfulness in work has found that when individuals engage in work that they feel is meaningful, they are more committed to it and more involved in it (Wrzesniewski, 2012). They have a higher concentration of energy and are more persistent in pursuing desired goals than when a sense of meaningfulness is low. People feel more excitement and passion for their work and have a greater sense of personal significance and self-worth because of their association with activities that are meaningful. Individuals empowered with a sense of meaningfulness also are more innovative, upwardly influential, and personally effective than those with low meaningfulness scores (Pratt & Ashforth, 2003; Vogt & Murrell, 1990; Wrzesniewski, 2003).

TRUST

Finally, empowered people have a sense of trust (Helliwell & Huang, 2011). They are confident that they will be treated fairly and equitably. They maintain an assurance that even if they are in subordinate positions, the ultimate outcome of their actions will be justice and goodness as opposed to harm or damage. Usually, this means they have confidence that those holding authority or power positions will not harm or injure them, and that they will be treated honestly. However, even in circumstances in which individuals holding power positions do not demonstrate integrity and fairness, empowered people can still maintain a sense of *personal security*. Their trust is placed in principles, not in people. Trust also implies that individuals are willing to place themselves in a position of vulnerability and have faith that, ultimately, no harm will come to them as a result of their trust (Castaldo, Premazzi, & Zerbini, 2010; Covey, 2008; Mishra & Mishra, 2013).

How can a person maintain trust and a sense of security even when caught in a circumstance that seems unfair, inequitable, or even dangerous? In his attempts to gain independence for minorities in South Africa, for example, Gandhi determined that he would burn the passes that the British government required be carried by all people of color but not by white South African citizens. Gandhi called a meeting and publicly announced his intent to resist this law by burning the passes of each of his supporters. In a now-famous incident, after Gandhi burned several of the passes, the British police intervened by clubbing him with nightsticks. Despite the beating, Gandhi continued to burn passes.

Where is the trust or sense of security in this case? How can Gandhi be empowered in the process of being beaten by the police? In what did Gandhi have trust? Was Gandhi empowered or not?

The answer is: Gandhi's sense of security and trust came not from the British authorities but from his trust in the principles that he espoused. His sense of security was associated with his belief that doing the right thing always leads, ultimately, to the right consequence. Acting humanely will ultimately motivate humane responses.

Research on trust has also found a great deal of positive outcomes (Lau, Lam, & Wen, 2013). For example, individuals with high levels of trust are more apt to replace superficiality and facades with directness and intimacy. They are more apt to be open, honest, and congruent rather than deceptive or shallow. They are more search-oriented and self-determining, and more self-assured and willing to learn. They have a larger capacity for interdependent relationships, and they display a greater degree of cooperation and risk-taking in groups than do those with low trust.

Trusting people are more willing to try to get along with others and to be a contributing part of a team. They are also more self-disclosing, more honest in their own communication, and more able to listen carefully to others. They have less resistance to change and are better able to cope with unexpected traumas than are those with low levels of trust. Individuals who trust others are more likely to be trustworthy themselves and to maintain high personal ethical standards (see Covey, 2008; Mishra & Mishra, 2013).Trusting others,

in other words, allows people to act in a confident and straightforward manner, without wasting energy on self-protection, trying to uncover hidden agendas, or playing politics (Chan, Taylor, & Markham, 2008). In brief, a sense of trust empowers people by helping them feel secure.

REVIEW OF EMPOWERMENT DIMENSIONS

The main point of our discussion thus far is to convince you that fostering the five attributes of empowerment in individuals produces positive outcomes. Research findings associated with each of the five dimensions of empowerment—*self-efficacy* (a sense of competence), *self-determination* (a sense of choice), *personal consequence* (a sense of impact), *meaning* (a sense of value), and *trust* (a sense of security)—strongly support the fact that both personal and organizational advantages result when people feel empowered. Negative consequences occur, on the other hand, when people experience the opposite of empowerment, such as powerlessness, helplessness, and alienation.

Some cynical students (and a few practicing managers) have argued that empowering people is unnecessary and a waste of time in many situations because there are always "free riders." Some people, they say, are not inclined to want empowerment. They just want to get by on as little as possible. They don't want to put forth effort in teams or classes. They shy away from taking initiative. They would rather just let someone else do the work.

This occurs, however, when people do not value the outcome that has been assigned (absence of a sense of value), when they believe that someone else will produce the result without their input (absence of a sense of personal consequence), when they don't trust that their contribution will be valued (absence of trust), or when they don't believe that they have anything to contribute (absence of self-efficacy). When the five dimensions of empowerment are present, on the other hand, almost all people will become actively engaged and pursue empowerment.

Research by Hackman and Oldham (1980) found that more than 80 percent of workers have high "growth need strength," or a desire to grow and contribute in their jobs. Helping to foster the five dimensions of empowerment responds to this inherent need for growth and contribution.

The next section of this chapter discusses specific actions managers can take to facilitate empowerment in others.

How to Develop Empowerment

People tend to experience empowerment in environments that help them flourish, when they can produce success, and when they experience satisfaction in their work. They are especially in need of empowerment, however, when things aren't going well—as when they are faced with situations they perceive to be threatening, unclear, overly controlled, coercive, or isolating; when they feel stifled in their ability to do what they would like to do; when they are uncertain about how to behave; when they feel that some negative consequence is imminent; and when they feel unrewarded and unappreciated.

Research by a variety of scholars (Bandura, 2012; Daniels, et al., 2017; Hackman & Oldham, 1980) has produced at least nine specific prescriptions for fostering empowerment. These prescriptions help produce a sense of competence, choice, impact, value, and security. They include: (1) articulating a clear vision and goals, (2) fostering personal mastery experiences, (3) modeling, (4) providing support, (5) creating emotional arousal, (6) providing necessary information, (7) providing necessary resources, (8) connecting to outcomes, and (9) creating confidence. Figure 8.1 illustrates the relationships of these prescriptions to the five core dimensions of empowerment.

Some of these prescriptions are similar to the guidelines found in the chapters on Building Relationships by Communicating Supportively, Gaining Power and Influence, and Motivating Others. Because a completely separate and unique set of managerial skills does not exist for communicating with, influencing, and motivating others, some commonality and overlap is inevitable. On the other hand, the context of empowerment sheds a different light on some of the guidelines you have read about before.

A CLEAR GOAL

Creating an environment in which individuals can feel empowered requires that they be guided by a clear goal of what is to be achieved and how they can contribute. A great deal of research confirms that having goals

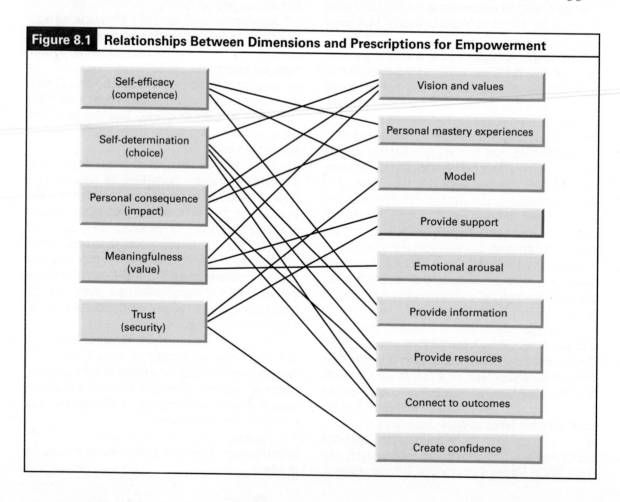

Figure 8.1 Relationships Between Dimensions and Prescriptions for Empowerment

motivates individuals to achieve higher performance than if they have no goals (Locke & Latham, 2012; Ryan & Deci, 2000).

It makes sense that if you are assigned a task but are given no targets or standards for performance, you are unlikely to perform as well as if you are clear about the objective and the level of performance expected of you. Goal setting is a common strategy for helping individuals improve their performance. If we want high performance, we almost always establish goals as a way to attain it. Locke and Latham (2006) identified the attributes of the most effective goals, and the acronym **SMART** best summarizes the attributes of these goals.

- ❏ *S - Specific goals*—goals that are identifiable, behavioral, and observable, with tangible targets (rather than general goals).
- ❏ *M - Measurable goals*—goals that can be assessed objectively and where the degree of successful accomplishment can be determined (rather than unmeasurable goals).
- ❏ *A - Aligned goals*—goals that are congruent with the overall purposes of the organization or that are consistent with the person's values (rather than unattached or superfluous goals).
- ❏ *R - Realistic goals*—goals that are capable of being achieved (rather than mere fantasy goals or those considered to be nonsense). Realistic does not mean easily achieved, because difficult, stretch goals are better motivators and predict higher levels of accomplishment than do easy goals (Locke & Latham, 2006).
- ❏ *T - Time-bound goals*—goals where a deadline for accomplishing the goals is specified. (Goals that have no ending point are not effective.)

The point is that individuals are empowered when they are provided SMART goals that help clarify how they achieve a valued outcome.

FOSTERING PERSONAL MASTERY EXPERIENCES

Bandura (2012) found that the single most important thing you can do to empower other people is to help them experience personal mastery over a challenge or problem. By successfully accomplishing a task, reaching a goal, or resolving a problem, people develop a sense of mastery. Personal mastery can be fostered by providing people with the opportunity to accomplish tasks that progress successively from easy to more difficult, eventually leading to the accomplishment of larger, more robust goals. The key is to start with easy tasks and then progress by small steps to more difficult tasks until the person experiences a sense of mastery over an entire challenge (also see Paglis, 2010).

Think of teaching children to swim. You don't throw them into the water and command them to swim. You begin by teaching them small, easy tasks—putting their face in the water, teaching them to kick, helping them to paddle with their arms, and so forth. Personal mastery begins by dividing complex tasks into small parts. This is the equivalent of adopting a **small-wins strategy** (Weick, 1984).

Each small win or incremental achievement may seem insignificant by itself, but it generates a sense of movement, progress, and success. The recognition and celebration of small wins generate momentum that leads people to feel empowered, capable, and successful.

MODELING

Another way to empower people is to model or demonstrate the correct behavior that they are to perform. Observing someone else succeed at challenging activities provides a forceful impetus for others to believe that they, too, can succeed. It helps people presume that a task is doable, that a job is within their capabilities, and that success is possible.

Because it may not be possible for you to model desired behaviors personally for every single person you want to empower, you may draw people's attention to other individuals who have been successful in similar circumstances.

Think of what happens when a difficult-to-achieve barrier is broken. In track and field athletics, for example, once John Thomas broke the seven-foot high jump mark and Roger Bannister broke the four-minute mile record, a host of other athletes quickly exceeded that standard. But before the first person broke those barriers, they were considered insurmountable. It took someone to demonstrate that the standard could be exceeded in order for others to experience the empowerment necessary to replicate the accomplishment themselves.

PROVIDING SUPPORT

A fourth technique for helping others experience empowerment is providing them with social and emotional support. If people are to feel empowered, they need to be praised, encouraged, approved, and reassured. This can be as simple as praising what they do well on a regular basis, writing notes to them or to their families about the valuable contributions they are making, or providing feedback to them in a supportive way. You can provide opportunities for them to become part of a team or include them in social gatherings, or hold formal or informal ceremonies where achievements are recognized. It may simply be a matter of listening to people and empathizing with their feelings and points of view.

You can empower others, in other words, by engendering a feeling that they are accepted, that they are a valued asset, that you care about them, and that they are an integral part of the overall organizational mission or objective. This support can come from you or from colleagues with whom they work (Gallup, 2018).

EMOTIONAL AROUSAL

Emotional arousal means replacing negative emotions such as fear, anxiety, or crabbiness with positive emotions such as excitement, passion, or anticipation. To empower people, managers help make the work environment fun and attractive. They ensure that the purpose behind the work is clear. They ensure that people's right brain (the side that controls emotions and passions) is involved in the work as well as their left brain (the side that controls logic and analysis). They provide positive energy to people, and as a result, both empowerment and performance increase (Esmaeili, et al., 2011).

Bandura (2012) found that the absence of positive emotional arousal makes it difficult, if not impossible, for individuals to feel empowered. However, emotional arousal doesn't simply mean tooting horns, increasing the decibel levels, clapping for speeches, or superficially creating excitement. Instead, emotional arousal is most likely to occur when what individuals are doing is connected to the values they hold dear. To feel a sense of empowerment, workers must see how what they are doing every day is associated with something that is important to them. Employees get more excited, for example, about working for the betterment of humankind, for the improvement of the quality of people's lives, and for personal growth and development, than they do for a 10 percent increase in salary or for hitting a profit target. This is not to say that attaining financial goals is unimportant. But emotional arousal is associated more with personal values than with organizational profitability.

Emotional arousal is also associated with the attributes of the work people do. This connection is best illustrated by the following truism: *"People are willing to pay for the privilege of working harder than they will work when they are paid."* (Coonradt, 2007). Consider what happens around mid-November in Utah and Colorado when the first major snowfall graces the ski resorts. Work and school absenteeism skyrocket. People sacrifice

a day's pay, don their $400 skis, their $300 boots, and their $500 ski outfit; buy $100 in gasoline to drive to the nearest ski resort; pay $115 for a lift ticket; eat a $35 lunch; and return at the end of the day completely exhausted—paying for the privilege of working harder than they would work when they are paid.

The question is, why? Why will people spend more money to work harder, exhausting themselves, to endure uncomfortable environmental conditions, and to put their bodies at risk than they would possibly tolerate at work? The answer is obvious: "Because it's fun. It's recreation. It provides energy and enjoyment. People feel empowered."

The attributes that create this kind of emotional arousal can be applied to work settings as well. These attributes make activities fun and recreational, and they can be as typical of work as they are of leisure (Duckworth, et al., 2007). For example, almost all fun, recreational activity has a clear *goal* (e.g., winning, exceeding a personal best). Without a clearly defined objective, we don't get excited. This goal is almost always pitted against a standard that we care about (e.g., winning the NCAA championship, bowling a 300 game). In addition, the *scorekeeping* and *feedback* systems are objective, self-administered, and continuous. In a basketball game, for example, we all know that a free throw always counts one point, that the winner is the team that makes the most baskets, and that there is never a time when we cannot find out the exact score of the game. One reason why we get excited watching athletic events is because we know the score all the time. This is, unfortunately, rare in most workplaces and classrooms. When we know the score, emotional arousal is increased.

Furthermore, in recreation, the *out of bounds* is clearly identified. We know the consequence of kicking a soccer ball over the end line, of hitting a groundball on the left side of third base, or standing too long in the keyhole in basketball. They are all out of bounds, and we are very clear that out-of-bounds behavior stops action.

You can help empower people through emotional arousal, not just by being a cheerleader, delivering charismatic speeches, and keeping the work climate fun, but also by capitalizing on some of the principles of recreation that create excitement: clear goals; objective, self-administered, and continuous scorekeeping and feedback; and clearly defined out-of-bounds behavior.

PROVIDING INFORMATION

Information is one of the most crucial of the managerial "power tools." When you provide your people with more, rather than less, information, those people gain a sense of empowerment and are more likely to work productively, successfully, and in harmony with your wishes. You actually enhance your power base by involving others in the pursuit of desirable outcomes. With more information, people tend to experience more self-determination, personal control, and trust. When others feel empowered, the probability is enhanced that they will support you and try to assist you (Cameron, 2012; Gilbert, Laschinger, & Leiter, 2010).

To be sure, it is possible to overload people with information and to create anxiety and burnout with too much data. But our experience has been that most people suffer from too little information instead of too much. Block (1987, p. 90) argued:

Sharing as much information as possible is the opposite of the military notion that only those who "need to know" should be informed. Our goal is to let people know our plans, ideas, and changes as soon as possible.... If we are trying to create the mindset that everyone is responsible for the success of this business, then our people need complete information.

Our own research confirms the importance of providing information to enhance empowerment. In one of our studies, for example, we interviewed CEOs of large, well-known companies every six months to assess organizational changes and strategies they were using to cope with declining revenues. In one firm, not much progress was being made in improving the financial outlook. The CEO was careful to share information on financial, productivity, cost, and climate indicators in the company only with his senior management team. No one else in the firm had access to that information. A change of CEO, however, led to a dramatic change in information-sharing policy. The new CEO began to provide information to every single employee in the firm. No data were treated as the sole possession of senior management. The floor sweepers had the same access as the vice presidents.

The resulting empowerment that employees experienced led to dramatic results. Employee-initiated improvements increased markedly, morale and commitment surged, and the resulting financial turnaround made the CEO look like a genius. He attributed his success to his willingness to empower employees by sharing the information they needed to know to improve (Cameron, 2013; Cameron, Freeman, & Mishra, 1993).

PROVIDING RESOURCES

In addition to providing information, empowerment is also fostered when people are provided with other kinds of resources that help them accomplish their tasks (Zhang & Bartol, 2010). When you empower others, your primary mission is to help them accomplish their objectives.

This means ensuring that they receive, for example, adequate training and development experiences; technical and administrative support; needed space, time, people, or equipment; access to communication and interpersonal networks; and discretion to pursue activities in the way they consider best. This does not mean, of course, that empowered people get everything they want. It is unrealistic to assume that unlimited resources are available—including your own time and attention.

On the other hand, the most important resources that you can provide are those that help people achieve control over their own work and lives; that is, to foster a sense of self-efficacy and self-determination. When individuals feel that they have what they need to be successful and that they have the freedom to pursue what they want to accomplish, performance is significantly higher than when these types of resources are not available (Spreitzer, Porath, & Gibson, 2012).

Watch a YouTube video or two about Google (https://www.youtube.com/watch?v=sFZeSLCagpQ), Southwest Airlines (https://www.youtube.com/watch?v=8_CeFiUkV7s), or Zappos (https://www.youtube.com/watch?v=50eCVVwEjno). You will see companies completely dedicated to empowering their employees to take care of customers, of work, and of one another. Former Marriott International CEO Bill Marriott has a saying that "Customers Come Second. Employees Come First." He is convinced that if he empowers his workforce with the necessary resources, he doesn't need to worry about customers. Employees will ensure spectacular customer service.

CONNECTING TO OUTCOMES

A great deal of research confirms that empowerment is markedly enhanced when employees have information about the outcomes of their work (Mesmer-Magnus & DeChurch, 2009). Many firms (e.g., Huffy, LG, REI) encourage employees to regularly visit customers in their homes or places of business, regularly observing how the products the workers produced and the services they deliver are used. The intent is to receive feedback directly from end users. This connection to the ultimate customer helps workers feel more empowered in addition to providing a valuable source of improvement ideas (Dorio & Shelley, 2011). People are motivated at work when they can interact with ultimate customers in order to see the effects of their work.

A related idea is to provide employees with the authority to resolve problems on the spot. When employees are given discretion to resolve a problem, respond immediately to a customer's complaint, or fix the error instantly, without having to get approvals and sign-offs, not only is customer satisfaction dramatically increased (an average improvement of 300 percent), but workers feel far more empowered as well.

Another of the highly effective ways to enhance employee motivation and satisfaction is to create **task identity**; that is, provide people with the opportunity to accomplish a whole task (Hackman, Oldham, Janson, & Purdy, 1975). Individuals become frustrated and lack a sense of empowerment when they work on only part of a task, never see the end result of their work, and are blocked from observing the impact that their job creates. Having task identity means that individuals can plan, implement, and evaluate the complete job and the success of their efforts. Knowing that you successfully completed a job and that it made any difference markedly enhances a sense of empowerment.

CREATING CONFIDENCE

An additional technique for creating empowerment is to engender people's confidence in you as the leader. Rather than being on guard or suspicious, workers feel secure that you and the organization are honorable and that you have their best interests at heart. This confidence helps drive out uncertainty, insecurity, and ambiguity, and it creates an environment of safety, security, and trust.

There are at least two reasons why individuals feel more empowered as they develop greater confidence in you as their leader or manager. First, the wasteful, unproductive behaviors associated with mistrust and suspicion are avoided. When people distrust one another, they don't listen, they don't communicate clearly, they don't try hard, and they don't collaborate. On the other hand, when trust exists, individuals are free to experiment, to learn, and to contribute without fear of retribution.

Second, individuals who are trustworthy and honorable create positive energy for others as well as a sense of empowerment. In creating this sense of confidence and trustworthiness, five factors are especially important: *reliability*, *fairness*, *caring*, *openness*, and *competence*. You create confidence, and thereby engender empowerment in others, as you display these five characteristics (Mishra & Mishra, 2013).

- *Reliability.* If you want people to have confidence in you, you must be reliable. This means being consistent, dependable, and stable. Do what you

promise. Your actions must be congruent with your words and attitudes.

- *Fairness.* You must be impartial and fair. When you make judgments, workers need to be clear about the criteria you use and the standards by which you make judgments. These judgments must be seen as unbiased and equitable.

- *Caring.* You must show a sense of personal concern for others and help each person feel important. You can do this by pointing out strengths and contributions of others and by using supportive communication when correcting mistakes or providing negative feedback (see Chapter 4).

- *Openness.* You build confidence as you remain open and accessible. This means that you share information openly and honestly and you don't keep secrets that could harm others. This does not suggest that you violate confidences, because keeping confidences is crucial. Rather, it means that other people should not have to worry about hidden agendas that could negatively affect them.

- *Competence.* People need to be aware of your competence. They need to be assured that you have the necessary ability, experience, and knowledge to lead and to solve problems. Without flaunting your expertise, you should inspire a feeling on the part of employees that their confidence in your expertise and proficiency is not misplaced.

The power of creating confidence in others is illustrated by our interviews with several CEOs. The key role of trust and confidence in management is hard to miss.

If they don't believe what I'm telling them, if they think it's all a bunch of bull, they will never go out there and work a little harder. They won't work a little better. They're not going to be receptive to change unless they understand and trust the things that we're talking about are true. I think trust is the biggest single issue.

What's most important in my organization is this: being truthful. Don't b.s. anyone. Tell them what it is. Right or wrong or different. Tell them the truth.

My people are all 150 percent dedicated to helping one another. Because not one of them can do it alone, and they need each other badly. But here comes the openness and trust. You have to talk straight. You have to be open and honest. You have to create trust. (see Cameron, 2013; Mishra & Mishra, 2013)

Successful managers create confidence by being authentic, honorable, and trustworthy.

REVIEW OF EMPOWERMENT PRINCIPLES

Table 8.3 summarizes the list of actions that we have discussed in relation to the nine prescriptions for empowerment. It provides a list of things you can do to empower other people. Not all of these suggestions are relevant in every circumstance or with every person, of course, but developing the skill of empowerment at least partly depends on knowing what alternatives are available as well as knowing how to implement them.

This list is not comprehensive; other activities may also be effective in empowering people. But the nine prescriptions and the suggestions associated with each of them represent actions that you will want to practice. The Skill Practice section of this chapter provides an opportunity for you to do this.

Research suggests that empowered individuals are most inclined to empower others (Lee, Willis, & Tan, 2018). For that reason, we included an Assessment instrument at the beginning of this chapter that measures the extent to which you experience empowerment in your own work. Your scores on the instrument titled Personal Empowerment Assessment indicate how much your own work is empowering in terms of

Table 8.3	Practical Suggestions for Empowering Others
Articulate a Clear Vision and Goals	
• Create a picture of a desired future.	
• Use word pictures and emotional language to describe the vision.	
• Identify specific actions and strategies that will lead to the vision.	
• Establish SMART goals.	
• Associate the vision and goals with personal values.	
Foster Personal Mastery Experiences	
• Break apart large tasks and assign one part at a time.	
• Assign simple tasks before difficult tasks.	
• Highlight and celebrate small wins.	
• Incrementally expand job responsibilities.	
• Give increasingly more responsibility to solve problems.	
Model Successful Behaviors	
• Demonstrate successful task accomplishment.	
• Point out other people who have succeeded.	
• Facilitate interaction with other role models.	
• Find a coach.	
• Establish a mentor relationship.	
Provide Support	
• Praise, encourage, express approval, and reassure.	
• Send letters or notes of praise to family members or coworkers.	
• Regularly provide feedback.	
• Foster informal social activities to build cohesion.	
• Supervise less closely and provide time-slack.	
• Hold recognition ceremonies.	

(continued)

Table 8.3	Continued

Arouse Positive Emotions

- Foster activities to encourage friendship formation.
- Periodically send lighthearted messages.
- Use superlatives in feedback.
- Highlight compatibility between important personal values and organizational goals.
- Clarify impact on the ultimate customer.
- Foster attributes of recreation in work: clear goals, effective scorekeeping and feedback systems, and out-of-bounds behavior.

Provide Information

- Provide all task-relevant information.
- Continuously provide technical information and objective data.
- Pass along relevant cross-unit and cross-functional information.
- Provide access to information or people with senior responsibility.
- Provide access to information from its source.
- Clarify effects of actions on customers.

Provide Resources

- Provide training and development experiences.
- Provide technical and administrative support.
- Provide needed time, space, or equipment.
- Ensure access to relevant information networks.
- Provide more discretion to commit resources.

Connect to Outcomes

- Provide a chance to interact directly with those receiving the service or output.
- Provide authority to resolve problems on the spot.
- Provide immediate, unfiltered, direct feedback on results.
- Create task identity, or the opportunity to accomplish a complete task.
- Clarify and measure effects as well as direct outcomes.

Create Confidence

- Exhibit reliability and consistency.
- Exhibit fairness and equity.
- Exhibit caring and personal concern.
- Exhibit openness and honesty.
- Exhibit competence and expertise.

self-efficacy, self-determination, personal control, meaning, and trust. Knowing what provides a sense of empowerment for you can be helpful as you consider ways in which you, in turn, can help others to experience empowerment. The other instrument that you completed in the Skill Assessment section (Effective Empowerment and Engagement) identified the extent to which you behave in ways that empower people with whom you work and the extent to which you are effective in engaging other people in work. How much you actually demonstrate the behaviors discussed above is measured by these assessments.

Inhibitors to Empowerment

If the evidence is clear that empowering people produces superior results, and if techniques for enhancing empowerment are clear, why then is empowerment in organizations so rare? Why do a majority of people feel that they are alienated from their work, unengaged, and languishing (Cameron, Dutton, & Quinn, 2003; Gallup, 2018)?

In a classic book on managerial empowerment, Peter Block (1987, p. 154) noted that empowerment is difficult to accomplish:

> Many managers have tried repeatedly to open the door of participation to their people, only to find them reluctant to walk through it. [In a study of managers who were offered total responsibility for their work areas], about 20 percent of the managers took the responsibility and ran with it, about 50 percent of the managers cautiously tested the sincerity of the offer and then over a period of six months began to make their own decisions. The frustrating part of the effort was that the other 30 percent absolutely refused to take the reins. They clutched tightly to their dependency and continued to complain that top management did not really mean it, they were not given enough people or resources to really do their job, and the unique characteristics of their particular location made efforts at participative management unreasonable.

Many managers and employees are reluctant to accept empowerment, but they are even more reluctant to offer empowerment. Several surveys have examined the reasons managers have for not being willing to empower their employees (Babakus, et al., 2003; Lee, Willis, & Tian, 2017; Pieterse, et al., 2010; Seibert, Wang, & Courtright, 2011), and these reasons can be organized into three broad categories.

ATTITUDES ABOUT SUBORDINATES

People who avoid empowering others often believe that their workers are not competent enough to accomplish the work, that they aren't interested in taking on more responsibility, that they are already overloaded and unable to accept more responsibility, that training would require too much time, or that they shouldn't be involved in tasks or responsibilities typically performed by someone else. These managers feel that the problem of non-empowerment lies with their workers, not with themselves. Their rationale is: I'm willing to empower my people, but they just won't accept the responsibility.

These negative attitudes toward employees, however, are seldom typical of workers in organizations. A great deal of research confirms that a large majority of individuals will seek empowerment with a conducive work environment (Gallup, 2018; Kanter, 2008).

PERSONAL INSECURITIES

Some people fear they will lose the recognition and rewards associated with successful task accomplishment if they empower others. They are unwilling to share their expertise or "trade secrets" for fear of losing power or position. Or, they have an intolerance for ambiguity, which leads them to feel that they personally must know all the details about projects assigned to them. Or, they prefer working on tasks by themselves rather than getting others involved, or they are unwilling to absorb the consequences associated with subordinates making mistakes.

Their rationale is: I'm willing to empower people, but when I do, they either mess things up or try to grab all the glory. Unfortunately, when people try to be the heroes, obtain all the recognition for themselves, or avoid involving other people, they almost never accomplish what they could have by capitalizing on the expertise and energy of others. The empirical data are abundant showing that empowered teams do better than even the most competent individual (see Chapter 9, Building Effective Teams and Teamwork).

NEED FOR CONTROL

People unwilling to empower others often have a high need to be in charge and to direct and govern what is going on. They presume that an absence of clear direction and goals will lead to confusion, frustration, and failure on the part of employees. They feel that direction from the top is mandatory. Their rationale is: I'm willing to empower people, but they require clear directions and a clear set of guidelines; otherwise, the lack of instructions leads to confusion. I know how to do this job better than they do.

Although it is true that clear goals and specific directions enhance performance, self-established goals are always more motivating than those prescribed by someone else. Thus, people will perform better if they are empowered to establish their own goals and methods rather than to have someone else superimpose them as a prerequisite to success.

OVERCOMING INHIBITORS

The rationale associated with each of these inhibitors may be partially true, of course, but they nevertheless inhibit you from achieving the success that is associated with skillful empowerment. Even if you demonstrate the willingness and courage to empower others, success still requires skillful implementation. Incompetent empowerment, in fact, can undermine rather than enhance the effectiveness of an organization and its employees. It can actually create a sense of frustration, ambiguity, or cynicism.

For example, giving employees freedom without clear directions or resources has been found to lead to psychological casualties among individuals, as manifested by increased depression, heightened stress, decreased performance and job satisfaction, lowered alertness, and even increased mortality (Baltes & Baltes, 2014; Glasser, 1999; Mills, 2000). Of course, these negative consequences are not solely associated with incompetent empowerment, but they have been noted in situations in which attempted empowerment was ineffective and unskillful. The point is, the guidelines we provided are not just interesting ideas but are necessary for capturing the value that effective empowerment can produce.

Fostering Engagement

The situation in which empowerment is most needed, of course, is when other people must become completely engaged in accomplishing work. The trouble is, more than 70 percent of all workers in the United States indicate that they do not feel engaged at work, and in some countries the percentages are substantially higher. Almost 80 percent of senior managers report feeling somewhat burned out at work, with only a fifth feeling completely engaged and thriving (Gallup, 2018; Spreitzer, Porath, & Gibson, 2012). Empowering employees is an important way to enhance feelings of engagement and thriving by enhancing confidence and competence, choice, impact, meaningfulness, and trust.

Engagement has become a popular topic in the last decade or so, but its meaning has become more and more ambiguous. The word *engagement* is sometimes used synonymously with *morale*, *satisfaction*, *loyalty*, *commitment*, and *self-motivated actions*. Sometimes authors have equated engagement with "servant leadership" or helping other people flourish in a work context (Greenleaf, 2002; Lee, Willis, & Tian, 2017). Engagement also refers simply to the involvement of individuals in work, as in determining when to engage and involve others and when to reduce or eliminate the involvement and engagement of others.

In this chapter we focus on a narrow definition of engagement, equating it with involving people in the work to be accomplished. The question is, when should you involve others in work, and when should you do it yourself? When should you make decisions alone, and when should you get others involved? We rely on a long-standing, empirically validated framework of engagement to help make these decisions. This framework addresses three questions: *when*, *with whom*, and *how* you engage others in getting work done.

The skillful engagement of others has a variety of advantages in addition to merely accomplishing more work. As shown in Table 8.4, it also provides important benefits to those who are highly engaged.

Specifically, empowered engagement can help develop subordinates' capabilities and knowledge, so that

Table 8.4	Advantages of Engaging Others
Advantage	**Explanation**
Time	Increases the discretionary time of the manager
Development	Develops knowledge and capabilities of those being engaged
Trust	Demonstrates trust and confidence in those being engaged
Commitment	Enhances the commitment of those being engaged
Information	Improves decision-making with better information
Efficiency	Enhances efficiency and timeliness of decisions
Coordination	Fosters work integration among those being engaged

their personal efficacy is increased. It can encourage the development of personal mastery experiences. Engagement can demonstrate trust and confidence in the person involved in task accomplishment. Research has consistently demonstrated a positive relationship between engagement in work and subsequent satisfaction, productivity, commitment, acceptance of change, and desire for more work (Lorinkova, Pearsall, & Sims, 2013).

Enhancing engagement can also be used to improve the quality of decision-making by bringing to bear more information closer to the source of the problem than the manager has alone. Engaging those who have direct access to relevant information can enhance efficiency (i.e., require less time and fewer resources) as well as effectiveness (i.e., result in a better decision).

Finally, fostering empowered engagement can increase the coordination and integration of work by ensuring that information and final accountability are shared and not the sole responsibility of one person. In other words, engagement is not only enhanced by the five dimensions of empowerment, but it also can enhance all five dimensions of empowerment in turn. Empowerment and engagement, therefore, are reciprocally beneficial.

We now present some guidelines for deciding *when* to engage others, *whom* you should engage, and, finally, *how* to most effectively engage other people in accomplishing work.

DECIDING WHEN TO ENGAGE OTHERS

Fostering engagement involves deciding, first of all, when to involve others in work and when to perform it yourself. This may seem to be a simple decision, but as you will see in the Skill Practice section of this chapter, this decision may not be so straightforward after all. To determine when engagement is most appropriate, you should ask five basic questions (Vroom, 1994; Vroom & Yetton, 2010). Vroom's research indicates that when you follow the guidelines provided by these questions, successful results are four times more likely than when these questions are not considered. These questions are helpful guidelines to determine whether you should engage a single other person or whether you should engage many others.

1. *Do other people have the necessary (or superior) information or expertise?* In many cases, other people may actually be better qualified than you are to make decisions and to perform tasks because they are more familiar with customer preferences, hidden costs, work processes, and so forth. They may be closer to the action than you are.

2. *Is the commitment of other people critical to successful implementation?* Participation in the decision-making process increases commitment to the final decision. When employees have some latitude in performing a task (i.e., what work they do, how they do it, and when they do it), they generally must be involved in the decision-making process to ensure their cooperation. Whereas participation usually increases the time required to make a decision, it substantially decreases the time required to implement it.

3. *Will other peoples' capabilities be expanded by this assignment?* Engagement can quickly get a bad name in a work team if it is viewed as a mechanism used by the boss to get rid of his or her undesirable tasks. Therefore, engaging others should be consistent, not just when overloads occur. It should reflect an overall management philosophy emphasizing employee development and support. Enhancing the abilities and interests of others should be a central motive in involving others.

4. *Do other people have the same values and perspectives as you and each other?* If others do not share a similar point of view with one another and with you, unacceptable solutions, inappropriate means, and outright errors may be perpetuated. This produces a need for closer supervision and frequent monitoring. Articulating a clear mission and objective for people you want to engage is crucial. Coonradt (2007) found that important people are always told why, but less important people are merely told what, how, or when. Telling others why the work is meaningful shows respect.

5. *Is there sufficient time to do an effective job of engaging others?* It takes time to save time. To avoid misunderstanding, you must spend sufficient time explaining the task and discussing acceptable procedures and options. Time must be available for adequate training, for questions and answers, and for opportunities to check on progress.

Enhancing engagement depends on a positive answer to each of these five questions. If any of these conditions is not present when engagement is being considered, the probability is greater that it will not be effective. More time will be required, lower quality will result, more frustration will be experienced, and less empowerment will occur.

DECIDING WHOM TO ENGAGE

If you have decided to engage others in a task, you must now consider whether to involve only a single individual or a team of people. If the decision is made to form a team, it is also important to decide how much authority to give the members of the team. For example, you should determine if the team will only investigate the problem and explore alternatives or if it will make the final decision. You must also outline whether or not you will participate in the team's deliberations. Figure 8.2 presents a model for helping you decide who should be engaged in tasks—individuals or teams—and whether you should be an active participant in a team if it is formed.

Figure 8.2 is constructed as a "tree diagram" that allows you to ask questions and, based on the answer to each question, move along a path until a final alternative is identified (Huber, 1980; Vroom & Jago, 1974). Here is how it works:

If you are a manager determining whether to involve others in accomplishing a task or making a decision, you should look over the considerations below the boxed question "Should I engage others in the task or the decision?" If you decide that others do not possess relevant information or skills, that their acceptance is not important, that no personal development can occur for members of the team, that time is tight, or that conflicts will arise among the other people, you should answer no to this question. The tree then prescribes that you perform the task or make the decision yourself. However, if you answer yes to this question, you then move on to the next question: "Should I direct other people to form a team?"

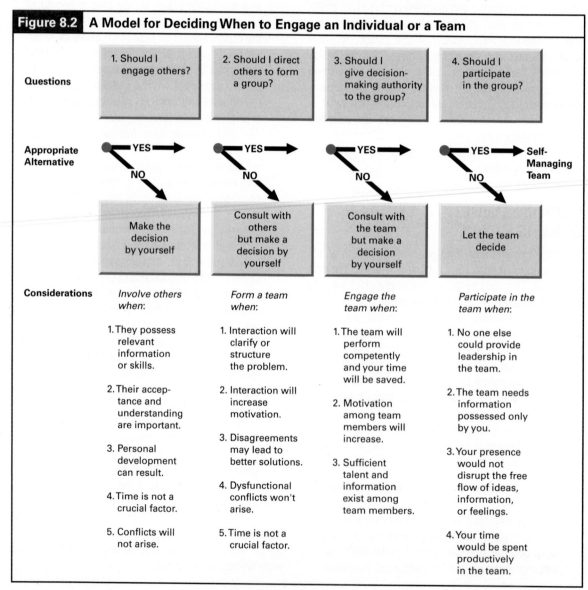

Figure 8.2 A Model for Deciding When to Engage an Individual or a Team

Questions	1. Should I engage others?	2. Should I direct others to form a group?	3. Should I give decision-making authority to the group?	4. Should I participate in the group?
Appropriate Alternative	YES →	YES →	YES →	YES → Self-Managing Team
	NO ↓	NO ↓	NO ↓	NO ↓
	Make the decision by yourself	Consult with others but make a decision by yourself	Consult with the team but make a decision by yourself	Let the team decide
Considerations	*Involve others when:*	*Form a team when:*	*Engage the team when:*	*Participate in the team when:*
	1. They possess relevant information or skills.	1. Interaction will clarify or structure the problem.	1. The team will perform competently and your time will be saved.	1. No one else could provide leadership in the team.
	2. Their acceptance and understanding are important.	2. Interaction will increase motivation.	2. Motivation among team members will increase.	2. The team needs information possessed only by you.
	3. Personal development can result.	3. Disagreements may lead to better solutions.	3. Sufficient talent and information exist among team members.	3. Your presence would not disrupt the free flow of ideas, information, or feelings.
	4. Time is not a crucial factor.	4. Dysfunctional conflicts won't arise.		4. Your time would be spent productively in the team.
	5. Conflicts will not arise.	5. Time is not a crucial factor.		

Look over the five considerations below each question and then continue through the model. Any of the considerations below a question can result in a "no" answer. The most participative and empowering alternative is to engage others in a team and then participate as an equal member of the team. The least empowering response, of course, is to do the work yourself. Remember, making decisions consistent with this model results in a 400 percent improvement in decision quality.

DECIDING HOW TO ENGAGE OTHERS

When a decision has been made to engage others in a task, and the appropriate people to engage have been identified, engagement has just begun. Positive outcomes of engagement are contingent upon your following 10 proven principles throughout the process. They are highlighted here because effective empowered engagement is so rare in real companies.

1. *Begin with the end in mind.* You must articulate clearly the desired results you intend to occur by involving others. Be clear about what is to be accomplished, why it is important, and what benefits will result. Unless people know why a task is important and what is to be achieved by performing it, they are unlikely to act at all.

2. *Identify boundaries.* In addition to the desired ends, you must clearly specify the constraints under which the tasks will be performed. Every organization has rules and procedures, resource constraints, or boundaries that limit the kind of action that can be taken. These should be clarified when engaging others. For example, be clear about deadlines, the time frame for reporting back, what is not included in the assignment, and to whom accountability should be reported.

3. *Specify level of initiative.* People need to know the level of initiative expected. No other oversight causes more confusion than the failure to delineate clear expectations regarding the level of initiative expected or permitted. At least five levels of initiative are possible, each of which may vary in terms of the amount of empowerment expected of others. The five alternatives are:

   ❏ *Wait to be told what to do.* Take action only after specific directions are given. This alternative is the least engaging because it permits no initiative on the part of other people. There is no control over when the task is to be accomplished, or content; that

is, what is to be done. On the other hand, when people do not have the talent or the information to accomplish the task, this is a preferred alternative.

   ❏ *Ask what to do before acting.* Sometimes people need to receive clearance before undertaking a task because you may not be certain of their level of competence or understanding, or because necessary preparation has yet not occurred. This alternative is appropriate when individuals have some control over the timing of the task but not its content. They may formulate their own ideas for approaching the task, but no action can be taken until you give approval.

   ❏ *Recommend, then take action.* This alternative has three different levels of engagement. One is for individuals to gather information and present it to you, and you decide what needs to be done (for example, a teaching assistant finds relevant material for class but you need to decide whether to use it). Another is for individuals to determine alternative courses of action for each part of the task, leaving you to choose which course will be followed (for example, the teaching assistant provides two different approaches for covering certain material). Still another possibility is to outline a course of action for accomplishing the entire task and have the whole package approved at once (for example, the teaching assistant outlines the entire syllabus and teaching approach). Progressively more engagement is associated with each of these three recommendation types.

   ❏ *Act, then report results immediately.* Individuals are given the freedom to act on their own initiative, but they are required to report to you immediately upon completion to ensure that their actions are compatible with your objectives. They may be permitted to perform only one part of a task at a time, reporting the results of each individual step. Or, they may be given the discretion to perform the entire task, reporting only when the final result has been accomplished. The latter alternative, of course, is the most engaging, but it depends on others possessing the necessary ability, information, experience, or maturity.

   ❏ *Initiate action, and report only routinely.* Individuals receive complete control over timing and over content of the tasks assigned.

Reporting occurs only in a routine fashion to maintain coordination. When others have sufficient ability, information, experience, and maturity, this level of initiative is not only the most engaging but also the likeliest to produce high satisfaction and motivation among others (Hackman & Oldham, 1980; Wangrow, Schepker, & Barker, 2014).

The important point for you to remember is that you must be clear about which of these levels of initiative you expect of those you involve in the work.

4. *Allow participation.* Other people are more likely to engage willingly, perform tasks competently, and experience empowerment when they help decide what tasks are to be assigned to them and when. Often, you cannot allow complete choice about such matters, but providing opportunities to decide when tasks will be completed, how accountability will be determined, when work will begin, or what methods and resources will be used in task accomplishment increases employees' engagement. You should encourage others to ask questions and seek information regarding assignments.

5. *Match authority with responsibility.* It is important to match the amount of responsibility given with the amount of authority provided. Nothing is more frustrating, and disengaging, than to be given responsibility but not have the authority to accomplish the task. An important part of developing a sense of self-determination and a sense of personal control—both critical dimensions of empowerment—is ensuring a match between responsibility and authority.

Although you cannot delegate *ultimate* accountability, you can delegate *prime* accountability. This means that "the buck stops," eventually, at your desk. Final blame for failure cannot be given away. This is ultimate accountability. On the other hand, you can delegate prime accountability, which means that others can be given responsibility for producing desired results, but you maintain ultimate responsibility for success or failure.

6. *Provide adequate support.* When you engage other people in work, you must provide as much support to them as they require. This involves presenting clearly stated expectations, providing relevant information, and ensuring that adequate resources are available. This support not only aids task accomplishment but also communicates interest and concern on your part.

Another form of support is to publicly bestow credit—but not blame. Even though prime accountability has been delegated, pointing out mistakes or faults in front of others embarrasses workers, creates defensiveness, fosters the impression that you are trying to pass the buck and get rid of final accountability, and guarantees that workers will be less willing to initiate action on their own in the future. Correcting mistakes, critiquing work, and providing negative feedback on task performance should be done in private, one-on-one, where the opportunity for problem-solving and training can be enhanced.

7. *Focus accountability on results.* Once you have engaged others in work, you generally should avoid closely monitoring the way in which individuals accomplish the work. Excessive supervision of methods destroys the five dimensions of empowerment. After all, the primary goal is successful accomplishment of a task, not use of your preferred procedures. This assumes, of course, that agreement on acceptable levels of performance has occurred, so you must clearly specify what level of quality or achievement is expected.

8. *Be consistent.* The time for you to engage others is before you have to. If you only involve others when you are overloaded or highly stressed, two problems result. First, a primary reason for engaging others is forgotten—namely, helping other people flourish. They feel that they are merely "pressure valves" for relieving your stress rather than valued team members. Second, there is no time for training, providing needed information, or engaging in two-way discussions. Instead of enhancing engagement, you create resistance or negative feelings in others.

Another key is to share both pleasant and unpleasant tasks. Sometimes you are tempted to keep for yourself the tasks you like to perform and pass less-desirable work along to others. It is easy to see the detrimental consequences this has on morale, motivation, and performance. When individuals feel that they are being used only to perform the "dirty work," engagement suffers.

9. *Avoid upward delegation.* Although it is important to engage others in work for their own development, you must be careful to avoid what is called "upward delegation." This means that other people try to have you solve their problems

or accept responsibility for their work. For example, suppose someone you have engaged in a task comes to you and says, "I have a problem. This assignment just isn't turning out very well. What do you suggest I do?" If you reply, "Gee, I'm not sure. Let me think about it, and I'll get back to you," you have just become the owner of the task and have promised to report back to the other person. You have accepted upward delegation, and this inhibits the other person from experiencing engagement.

One way to avoid upward delegation is to insist that the individuals develop their own solutions. A more appropriate response might have been, "What do you recommend?" "What alternatives do you think I should consider?" "What have you done so far?" "What do you think would be a good first step?" Rather than sharing problems and asking for advice, other people will be more engaged if they share proposed solutions or recommendations.

10. *Clarify consequences.* Be clear about the consequences of successful task accomplishment. What are the rewards for success, what opportunities might open up, what is the impact on the organization's mission, what learning and development can occur, what benefits will be provided to others, and so on. When people become aware that they can make a difference, that they can contribute something meaningful, and that there may be some payoffs for themselves and others, engagement is significantly more likely. Most importantly, the more you can highlight the meaningfulness of the work and the value that is being produced, the more engaged people will be in the work.

REVIEW OF ENGAGEMENT PRINCIPLES

We have provided you with 10 principles summarizing *how* to engage others, five criteria for determining *when* to engage others, and four questions for identifying *whom* to engage in work. Research results clearly show that when you foster empowered engagement, the following consequences occur:

❑ Other people readily accept the opportunity to be involved.

❑ The work has a high probability of being successfully completed.

❑ Morale and motivation remain high.

❑ Other peoples' problem-solving abilities are increased.

❑ More discretionary time becomes available.

❑ Interpersonal relationships are strengthened.

❑ People have a greater tendency to help one another and to display prosocial behavior.

Figure 8.3 summarizes the relationships among these principles.

International Caveats

Empowerment and engagement are sometimes misinterpreted as a soft approach to management, an abrogation of responsibility by leaders, an invitation for the inmates to run the asylum, or a prescription for chaos. Strong leadership, visionary managers, and take-charge bosses are usually the ones we read about in the newspapers and business magazines. A great deal of attention is given to people who "take command of the situation" and "stay out front of the troops."

With such a definition, empowerment is not a popular alternative in many cultures where, for example, *universalism, individualism, specificity,* and *ascription* are dominant. (Recall from Chapter 1 that the Trompenaars [1998; 2011] model differentiates cultures on the basis of seven dimensions: *universalism* versus *particularism; individualism* versus *communitarianism; neutrality* versus *affectivity; specificity* versus *diffuseness; achievement* versus *ascription; internal* versus *external* control; and *past, present,* or *future* time orientation.) Empowerment is sometimes viewed as contrary to some of these values in that maintaining consistency with rules and procedures (universalism) rather than encouraging experimentation and team innovation may seem to make empowerment less desirable. Focusing on individual performance (individualism) rather than team or collective effort may be viewed as contrary to empowerment. Involving only a limited amount of the self in the work setting or task assignment (specificity) rather than engaging multiple roles and in-depth relationships with colleagues also may be interpreted as inconsistent with empowerment and empowered engagement. A focus on ascribed status, title, and traditional position (ascription) rather than a blurring of hierarchical lines and focusing on merit or contribution also appears to contradict the aims of empowerment. Hence, empowerment may seem to be a concept that is more acceptable in cultures with a strong orientation toward particularism, collectivity, diffuseness, and achievement.

On the other hand, abundant research has found the principles of empowerment and engagement discussed in

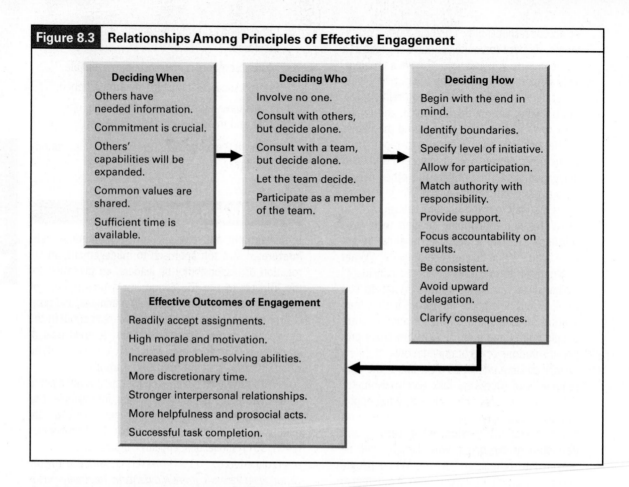

Figure 8.3 | Relationships Among Principles of Effective Engagement

Deciding When

Others have needed information.

Commitment is crucial.

Others' capabilities will be expanded.

Common values are shared.

Sufficient time is available.

Deciding Who

Involve no one.

Consult with others, but decide alone.

Consult with a team, but decide alone.

Let the team decide.

Participate as a member of the team.

Deciding How

Begin with the end in mind.

Identify boundaries.

Specify level of initiative.

Allow for participation.

Match authority with responsibility.

Provide support.

Focus accountability on results.

Be consistent.

Avoid upward delegation.

Clarify consequences.

Effective Outcomes of Engagement

Readily accept assignments.

High morale and motivation.

Increased problem-solving abilities.

More discretionary time.

Stronger interpersonal relationships.

More helpfulness and prosocial acts.

Successful task completion.

this chapter to be applicable across almost all cultures. It is a misconception to believe that these principles do not work effectively in Eastern cultures as well as Western cultures, Western Europe as well as South America, Africa as well as the Polynesian Islands. Principles of empowerment are relevant to old and young, male and female, Northern Hemisphere or Southern Hemisphere.

This is because the five principles of empowerment are connected to fundamental human needs that transcend national or ethnic cultures. Virtually everyone has a need for, and performs better when they are exposed to, an environment in which they: (1) feel capable, confident, and competent; (2) experience freedom, discretion, and choice; (3) believe they can make a difference, have an impact, and achieve a desired result; (4) sense meaning, value, and a higher purpose in their activities; and (5) trust that they will not be harmed or abused but honored and respected. In other words, the keys to effective empowerment are also keys to effective human performance at a fundamental level. Strong leaders are not lone rangers so much as they are savvy individuals who know how to mobilize those they lead and manage. Therefore,

whereas individual differences must certainly be taken into account and the pace at which empowerment and engagement can be fully implemented may vary with the circumstances, these principles of empowerment are essential to effective managerial performance.

Summary

Empowerment means helping to develop in others a sense of self-efficacy, self-determination, personal control, meaning, and trust. The current business environment is not particularly compatible with the principles of managerial empowerment. Because of the turbulent, complex, competitive circumstances that many organizations face, managers frequently experience a tendency to be less, rather than more, empowering. When managers feel threatened, they become rigid and seek more control over other people, not less control. However, without empowered employees, organizations cannot succeed in the long run. Learning how to be a competent empowering manager is a critical skill for individuals who will likely face overwhelming pressure not to practice empowerment.

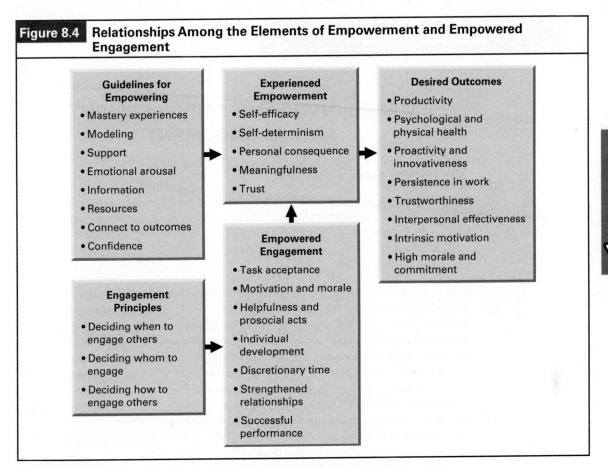

Nine prescriptions that managers can use to empower others were discussed. We also offered a series of principles and criteria for ensuring empowered engagement, which result in a variety of beneficial outcomes—both in terms of task accomplishment and in helping other people who are engaged in the work flourish. Figure 8.4 illustrates the relationships among the various elements of empowerment and engagement.

Behavioral Guidelines

As you practice empowering and engaging others, you will want to use the following guidelines as cues. *To foster empowerment in others, follow these guidelines:*

A. Foster self-efficacy or a sense of competence by providing personal mastery experiences and pointing out successful role models.

B. Foster self-determination or a sense of personal choice by providing alternatives and information to people.

C. Foster personal consequence or a sense of personal impact by highlighting the effects of the work on end users or on those affected by the results.

D. Foster meaningfulness or a sense of value by clarifying vision and values and connecting the outcomes to something of inherent value.

E. Foster trust or a sense of security by providing support and creating confidence, primarily by being consistent, honest, open, and fair.

F. Engage others in work by applying the guidelines provided in the chapter to determine *when* to engage others, *whom* to engage, and *how* to most effectively engage others.

CASES INVOLVING EMPOWERMENT AND ENGAGEMENT

Minding the Store

On January 1, Ruth Cummings was formally named branch manager for the Saks Fifth Avenue store in a suburb of Denver. Her boss, Shanaya Batra, gave her this assignment on her first day: "Ruth, I'm putting you in charge of this store. Your job will be to run it so that it becomes one of the best stores in the system. I have a lot of confidence in you, so don't let me down."

One of the first things Ruth did was to hire an administrative assistant to handle inventories. Because this was such an important part of the job, she agreed to pay her assistant slightly more than the top retail clerks were making. She felt that having an administrative assistant would free her to handle marketing, sales, and personnel matters—areas she felt were crucial if the store was to be a success.

Within the week, however, she received a call from Shanaya: "Say, Ruth, I heard that you hired an administrative assistant to handle inventories. Don't you think that is a bit risky? Besides, I think paying an assistant more than your top sales clerk is damaging to morale in the store. I wish you had cleared this with me before you made the move. It sets a bad precedent for the other stores, and it makes me look like I don't know what is going on in the branches."

Three weeks later, Ruth appeared on a local daytime talk show to discuss new trends in fashion. She had worked hard to make contact with the hosts of the show, and she felt that public exposure like this would increase the visibility of her store. Although the TV spot lasted only 10 minutes, she was pleased with her performance and with the chance to get public exposure.

Later that night at home, she received another phone call from Shanaya: "Don't you know the policy of Saks? Any TV appearances made on behalf of the store are to be cleared through the main office. Normally, we like to have representatives from the main store appear on these kinds of shows because they can do a better job of plugging our merchandise. It's too bad that you didn't notify someone of your intentions. This could be very embarrassing for me."

Just before Easter, Ruth was approached in the store by one of the sales clerks. A customer had asked to charge approximately $3,000 worth of china as a gift for his wife. He had been a customer of the store for several years and Ruth had seen him on several occasions, but store rules indicated that no charge could be made for more than $1,000 for any reason. She told the customer that she was not authorized to okay a charge of that amount, but that if he would visit the main store in Denver, maybe arrangements could be made.

Later in the day, an irate Shanaya called again: "What in the world are you thinking about, Ruth? Today we had a customer come into the main store and say that you wouldn't make a sale to him because the charge was too much. Do you know how long he has been a customer of ours? Do you know how much he spends in the store every year? I certainly hope we have not lost him as a customer because of your blunder. This makes me very upset. You've just got to learn to use your head."

Ruth thought about the conversation for several days and finally decided that she needed to see Shanaya. She called her administrative assistant to schedule an appointment for the following day.

Discussion Questions

8.1. What guidelines related to empowerment were violated by Shanaya? By Ruth?
8.2. What guidelines related to engagement were violated by Shanaya? By Ruth?
8.3. What should Ruth and Shanaya discuss in their meeting? Identify specific agenda items that should be raised.
8.4. What are the questions that Ruth should ask Shanaya to help her acquire the necessary elements of empowerment? What questions should Shanaya ask Ruth to be better able to ensure her success?
8.5. If you were an outside consultant attending the meeting, what advice would you give Shanaya? What advice would you give Ruth?

Changing the Portfolio

You are head of a staff unit reporting to the vice president of finance. He has asked you to provide a report on the firm's current portfolio, including recommendations for changes in the current selection criteria. Doubts have been raised about the efficiency of the existing system given the current market conditions, and there is considerable dissatisfaction with prevailing rates of return.

You plan to write the report, but at the moment you are perplexed about what type of approach to take. Your own specialty is the bond market, and it is clear to you that detailed knowledge of the equity market, which you lack, would greatly enhance the value of the report. Fortunately, four members of your staff are specialists in different segments of the equity market. Together, they possess a vast amount of knowledge about the intricacies of investment. However, they seldom agree on the best way to achieve anything when it comes to investment philosophy and strategy.

You have six weeks before the report is due. You have already begun to familiarize yourself with the firm's current portfolio and have been provided by management with a specific set of constraints that any portfolio must satisfy. Your immediate problem is to come up with some alternatives to the firm's present practices and to select the most promising for detailed analysis in your report.

Discussion Questions

8.6. Should this decision be made by you alone? Why or why not?
8.7. If your answer to the above question was to involve others, which alternative in Figure 8.2 should be used in making a decision? Justify your choice.
8.8. What are the most important considerations in deciding whom to involve in this task?
8.9. If others are to become involved, how much empowerment should they have? What would you do specifically to achieve the appropriate level of empowerment?

EXERCISES FOR EMPOWERMENT

Executive Development Associates

Assume you are Mary Ann O'Connell, general manager at Executive Development Associates. Your firm provides outplacement, training and development, career planning, and headhunting services for a large number of Fortune 500 companies. You have been at the corporate board meeting for the last three days in the Rocky Mountains, and you relied on your administrative assistant to screen out all but the most important or urgent messages. You slipped into the office on the way home from the airport Monday evening, just to check your electronic messages and your mail. Aside from a host of phone calls to return, here is the collection of messages retrieved from your email file and mail box.

Assignment

1. For each message, outline specifically the plan you will implement to empower others effectively to solve these problems. Determine who should be involved, what level of initiative should be taken, what actions you can take to ensure empowerment, how accountability should be maintained, and so on.

2. Write out the actions you'd take in response to each item. A worksheet has been provided on the next page to remind you of what you should consider as you record your responses.

3. After you have completed your own responses to each item, form a team of fellow students and share your plans. Provide feedback to one another on what is especially good, what could be improved, and what could be added to each person's action plan. In particular, which principles of empowerment are included, which are omitted, and which are contradicted?

Solving Problems Through Empowerment Worksheet

For each message, write out your plan of action. This plan should include answers to the questions listed below. Not every question is relevant to each message, but most are, and they can guide your action plan. After you have created your own responses, form a team of fellow students and share these plans in turn. Provide feedback to one another on what is especially good, what could be improved, and what could be added to each action plan.

1. Who should be involved in resolving this issue? Will you form a team?

2. What kinds of personal mastery experiences can be provided for whomever you involve? Can you model successful behavior?

3. What kinds of support, information, and resources can be provided?

4. How will you create emotional arousal and create confidence in others?

5. What are the main considerations in deciding if you should engage others in each task?

6. If you opt for engaging others, what will you do to:

Begin with the end in mind?
Identify boundaries?
Specify level of initiative?
Allow for participation?
Match authority with responsibility?
Provide support?
Maintain accountability?
Ensure consistency?
Avoid upward delegation?
Clarify consequences?

INTEROFFICE MEMORANDUM

DATA PROCESSING CENTER

DATE: June 15
TO: Mary Ann O'Connell, General Manager
FROM: Roosevelt Monroe, for the Data Processing Staff

After looking over last quarter's audit, it is clear that the number of complaints our group is receiving from individuals throughout the company is escalating. The problem is an obvious one to us. It is, simply, that several incompatible software systems have evolved over the last several years in various departments, and it is becoming increasingly difficult to coordinate across units. As you know, some data have to be retyped two or three times into different systems because of these incompatibilities.

The trouble is, our own employees, not to mention our customers, are becoming increasingly impatient with our slow turnaround time. They focus squarely on our group as the bottleneck. We think the rising complaint numbers in the quarterly audit are misleading, however, and they divert us from the real cause of the problem.

We're writing this memo to you to collectively urge you to address this issue as soon as possible. At a minimum, it should be discussed at our upcoming staff meeting on Tuesday. So far, the data processing staff is taking the blame for not getting data processed fast enough, yet it is really the fault of the system, not our unit.

We'll look forward to hearing from you on Tuesday.

INTEROFFICE MEMORANDUM

HUMAN RESOURCES DEPARTMENT

DATE: June 15
TO: Mary Ann
FROM: Lucy

I was excited by your speech at the senior management meeting last week in which you established a new challenge for all senior executives. With the new competitive environment that we face, the vision that you articulated for our future is both exciting and challenging and, I think, an important step forward. It really makes clear the key success factors that should drive our business.

In particular, I think your directive for all senior executives to disseminate the vision throughout the organization to their own subordinates is a good way to get the message delivered. However, you made a statement in your speech that has me troubled. You said, "We used to pay you on the basis of new accounts generated, quarterly earnings, customer satisfaction ratings, and new product designs. Our new barometer is going to be how you're doing in disseminating the vision throughout your own units."

Frankly, I'm perplexed as to how we'll ever measure this directive. As the one who has to administer the appraisal and compensation systems, I'm not sure what criteria we'll look for or what indicators we'll use to determine success. I'm afraid that we'll create dissatisfaction if we don't have something specific outlined. Our people, especially those who may not perform, will think it is purely arbitrary. Do you really mean to have us change the appraisal and compensation systems to include this new criterion? How do you propose we measure effective performance? What would you like me to do to support your statement? Did you mean to make the statement that you did?

This is rather urgent because I have a staff meeting Tuesday afternoon, and I promised to have a response by then. I've already stalled until I had a chance to talk to you.

COPY OF A LETTER

MIDWEST STATE UNIVERSITY

May 24

Dear Ms. O'Connell:

I am happy to be joining Executive Development Associates after several years at Midwest State University. As you know, leaving Midwest State has been quite traumatic for me, and that is what motivated me to make a request of you. I'm convinced that the reason I didn't receive tenure at Midwest State is because the expectations were never clear about what my responsibilities were and what the criteria were for success.

I know your company is very professional and employees are pretty much on their own, but I'm feeling a need to get some specific performance requirements outlined for me. I'm sure that I can be a good addition to your company, but I want to be clear about what your expectations are.

I have set a meeting with you on Tuesday through your administrative assistant. Would you please outline a specific set of responsibilities and expectations for my job as instructor in the training and development department? If possible, I'd like it in writing to avoid any misunderstanding. Regardless, I'll look forward to talking to you Tuesday.

Thank you for your consideration.

Sincerely,

Kwame Kilpack

INTEROFFICE MEMORANDUM

TRAINING AND DEVELOPMENT

DATE: Monday a.m.
TO: Mary Ann
FROM: Pam
RE: Chen Yu's Jury Duty

I know you're just getting back, but we've got an emergency on our hands.

I was just notified this morning by Chen that he has been selected for jury duty and that (can you believe it) he is being sequestered! Unfortunately, Mary Ann, this couldn't come at a worse time. As our expert on activity-based costing, Chen is the only guy we have who can teach the topic. So what's the trouble, you say? The trouble is that we have over 100 corporate trainers showing up here for a seminar on Friday, and the seminar isn't prepared yet. Chen said that he has some notes and a few PowerPoint slides prepared, but he had planned to spend this entire week designing and preparing it. Not only don't any of us know the topic very well, but we're not even sure what information we need, what data still needs to be gathered, who's got what, and how we go about filling in. Help! We're counting on this seminar to make budget this quarter, and we're feeling a little ticked off at Chen for waiting until the last minute. What do we do next?

By the way, how were the Rocky Mountains???

INTEROFFICE MEMORANDUM

OUTPLACEMENT DEPARTMENT

DATE: Monday a.m.
TO: Mary Ann O'Connell
FROM: Aneil Mishra
RE: Pending Plant Closure

You may have missed the news over the weekend. It was announced in the paper that Detroit Manufacturing has filed for Chapter 11 protection and that they're closing their Toledo plant. That means about 4,000 people will be out of work.

If we want the business, we've got to get moving right away. They will be looking at proposals from outplacement firms next week. We've got to get our proposal together, identify staff, determine a budget, and prepare a presentation in the next day or two.

Sounds like a great opportunity. I'll stop by tomorrow when you get back.

Empowering Ourselves

In this exercise, your task is to identify ways in which the empowerment of members of the graduating students this year in your own institution can be enhanced. You should use the principles of empowerment in the chapter to identify specific ways in which the empowerment of this group of people can be increased. What can be done, practically speaking, to effect empowerment?

Make certain that you don't merely identify what others could do, what the administration could implement, or what hypothetically could occur. Rather, identify practical and realistic factors that could empower this graduating class. What could they do as a group? What could you do? What personal responsibility could they take for their own empowerment?

Do not treat this exercise as hypothetical or fantasy. Identify actual behaviors that you can implement that will enhance empowerment. Use the suggestions in the text as well as others that you add to those lists.

	Things That Can Be Done to Enhance the Empowerment of the Graduating Class
Self-Efficacy (personal competence)	
Self-Determination (personal choice)	
Personal Consequence (personal impact)	
Meaningfulness (personal value)	
Trust (personal security)	

Now form a team with three or four colleagues. Share your ideas with the group. For each dimension of empowerment, identify the most powerful ideas you hear from the team members. Add at least one new idea to your list. Also, identify when and how you'll actually implement your list. Use your team to help specify actual behaviors that you can implement.

Deciding to Engage Others

Engaging others in work is one of the most deceiving management skills because it seems so easy to accomplish. Just tell someone what to do, or ask them to become involved, and they'll do it, right? Unfortunately, this is seldom the case, and this exercise is designed to help you determine when and how to engage others more effectively. To accomplish this exercise, you'll need to use the framework in Figure 8.2.

For each of the two scenarios that follow, ask the following questions:

- *Should I involve others or make the decision by myself?*
- *If I involve others, should I direct them to form a team, or should I consult them individually and make the decision by myself?*
- *If I form a team, should I grant decision-making authority to the team, or should I consult with the team but make the decision by myself?*
- *If I involve the team, should I participate in the team, or should I let the team decide?*

After you have made a decision about how to handle each of these two scenarios, form a group of colleagues. Share your decision and your rationale with the team. Reach a consensus regarding the most appropriate strategy to use in each of these two cases. For comparison purposes, experts have prepared an analysis of the two cases, which is found at the end of the chapter. It is provided only to enhance your team discussion.

An Emergency Request

You are a general plant supervisor, and seven product lines involving four of your eight foremen must be disrupted to satisfy an emergency request from an important client. You naturally wish to minimize the disruption. No additional personnel are available, and time limits to complete the new project are restrictive. The plant is new and is the only industrial plant in an economically depressed area dominated by farming. You can count on everyone pulling his or her own weight. The wages in the plant are substantially above farm wages, and the workers' jobs depend on the profitability of this plant—the first new industrial development in the area in 15 years. Your subordinates are relatively inexperienced, and you have been supervising them more closely than you might if the plant had been in a well-established industrial area and your subordinates were more experienced. The changes involve only standard procedures and are routine for someone of your experience. Effective supervision poses no problems. Your problem is how to reschedule the work to meet this emergency within the time limit with minimum disruption to the existing product lines. Your experience in such matters should enable you to figure out a way of meeting the request that will minimize the disruption of existing product lines.

Biological Warfare

You are the executive vice president of a small pharmaceutical manufacturer. You have the opportunity to bid on a contract for the Defense Department pertaining to biological warfare. The contract is outside the mainstream of your business; however, it could make economic sense, since you do have unused capacity in one of your plants, and the manufacturing processes are not dissimilar. You have written the document to accompany the bid and now have the problem of determining the dollar value of the quotation you think will win the job for your company. If the bid is too high, you will undoubtedly lose to one of your competitors. If it is too low, you could lose money on the program. There are many factors to consider in making this decision, including the cost of the new raw materials and the additional administrative burden of relationships with a new client, not to mention factors that are likely to influence the bids of your competitors, such as how much they need this particular contract. You have been busy assembling the necessary data to make this decision, but there remain several unknowns, one of which involves the manager of the plant in which the new products will be manufactured. Of all your subordinates, only he can estimate the costs of adapting the present equipment to its new purpose, and his cooperation and support will be necessary if the specifications of the contract are to be met. However, in an initial discussion with him when you first learned of the possibility of the contract, he seemed adamantly opposed to the idea. His experience has not particularly equipped him to evaluate projects like this one, so you were not overly influenced by his opinions. From the nature of his arguments, you inferred that his opposition was ideological rather than economic. You recall that he was once involved in a local peace organization and was one of the most vocal opponents in the company to the Iraq and Afghanistan troop deployments.

SKILL **APPLICATION**

ACTIVITIES FOR EMPOWERMENT
AND ENGAGEMENT

Suggested Assignments

8.10. Teach someone else (your spouse, a colleague, your boss) how to empower others and engage others effectively. Include the principles in Table 8.3 in your discussion. Use your own examples and illustrations.

8.11. Interview a manager about his or her empowerment practices. Try to determine what is especially effective, what doesn't work, what comes off as condescending, and what motivates people to perform. Identify the extent to which the manager knows and uses the principles discussed in the Skill Learning section of this chapter.

8.12. Think of a situation you now face with which you would like some help. It may be a task you want to accomplish, a tough decision you need to make, or a team you want to form. Make sure you think of something that requires the involvement of other people. Write down specific things you can do to engage other people to help you. How can you help them do what they want to do while simultaneously having them do what you want them to do?

8.13. Schedule a meeting with a manager who is not very good at empowerment. (Finding such a person shouldn't be difficult, because most leaders tend to be more authoritarian and bureaucratic than empowering.) As a student who has learned about and practiced empowerment and engagement, share what you have learned and offer suggestions that could help this manager improve.

Application Plan and Evaluation

The intent of this exercise is to help you apply this cluster of skills in a real-life, out-of-class setting. Now that you have become familiar with the behavioral guidelines that form the basis of effective skill performance, you will improve most by trying out those guidelines in an everyday context. Unlike a classroom activity, in which feedback is immediate and others can assist you with their evaluations, this skill application activity is one you must accomplish and evaluate on your own. There are two parts to this activity. Part 1 helps prepare you to apply the skill, and Part 2 helps you evaluate and improve on your experience. Be sure to write down answers to each item. Don't short-circuit the process by skipping steps.

Part 1: Planning

8.14. Write down the two or three aspects of this skill that are most important to you. These may be areas of weakness, areas you most want to improve, or areas that are most salient to a problem you face right now. Identify the specific aspects of this skill that you want to apply.

8.15. Now identify the setting or the situation in which you will apply this skill. Establish a plan for performance by actually writing down a description of the situation. Who else will be involved? When will you do it? Where will it be done?

Circumstances:
Who else?
When?
Where?

8.16. Identify the specific behaviors in which you will engage to apply this skill. Operationalize your skill performance.

8.17. What are the indicators of successful performance? How will you know you have been effective? What will indicate you have performed competently?

APPLICATION

Part 2: Evaluation

8.18. After you have completed your implementation, record the results. What happened? How successful were you? What was the effect on others?

8.19. How can you improve? What modifications can you make next time? What will you do differently in a similar situation in the future?

8.20. Looking back on your whole skill practice and application experience, what have you learned? What has been surprising? In what ways might this experience help you in the long term?

SCORING KEYS AND COMPARISON DATA

Go to www.pearson.com/mylab/management for scoring keys and comparison data for the following instruments:

Effective Empowerment and Engagement
Personal Empowerment Assessment

SKILL **ASSESSMENT**

- Team Development Behaviors
- Diagnosing the Need for Team Building

SKILL **LEARNING**

- The Advantages of Teams
- Team Development
- Leading Teams
- Team Membership
- Summary
- Behavioral Guidelines

SKILL **ANALYSIS**

- Losing to a Weaker Foe
- The Cash Register Incident

SKILL **PRACTICE**

- Leadership Roles in Teams
- Team Diagnosis and Team Development Exercise
- Winning the War for Talent
- Team Performance Exercise

SKILL **APPLICATION**

- Suggested Assignments
- Application Plan and Evaluation

SCORING KEYS AND *COMPARISON DATA*

9

Building Effective Teams and Teamwork

LEARNING OBJECTIVES

1. Diagnose and facilitate team development

2. Build high-performing teams

3. Facilitate team leadership

4. Foster effective team membership

MyLab Management

Go to www.pearson.com/mylab/management to complete the exercises marked with this icon ✪.

DIAGNOSTIC SURVEYS FOR BUILDING EFFECTIVE TEAMS

MyLab Management Personal Inventory Assessments

PERSONAL
INVENTORY
ASSESSMENT

TEAM DEVELOPMENT BEHAVIORS

The assessment instruments in this chapter are briefly described below. The assessments appear either in your text or in MyLab. The assessments marked with ✪ are available only in MyLab. If assigned, go to www.pearson.com/mylab/management to complete these assessments. The assessments without the ✪ appear only in the text.

All assessments should be completed before reading the chapter material.

After completing the first assessment, save your response to your hard drive. When you have finished reading the chapter, re-take the assessment and compare your responses to see what you have learned.

✪ ❑ The *Team Development Behaviors Assessment* measures the extent to which you demonstrate effective leadership behaviors when you are the leader of a team as well as the extent to which you are an effective team member.

✪ ❑ The *Diagnosing the Need for Team Building Assessment* helps you identify the extent to which a team you know well or a team of which you are a member is in need of development and improvement.

BUILDING EFFECTIVE TEAMS AND TEAMWORK

Assessment Section

DIAGNOSING THE NEED FOR TEAM BUILDING

Teamwork has been found to dramatically affect organizational performance. Some managers have credited teams with helping them to achieve incredible results. On the other hand, teams don't work all the time in all organizations. Therefore, managers must decide when teams should be organized. To determine the extent to which teams should be formed in order to accomplish tasks, respond to the items below.

Think of an organization in which you participate (or will participate) that needs to accomplish a task, provide a service, or produce a result. Answer these questions with that organization in mind.

Rating Scale

Using a scale of 1 to 5 (1 = little evidence; 5 = a lot of evidence), assign a number to each statement.

_____ 1. Output has declined or is lower than desired.

_____ 2. Complaints, grievances, or low morale are present or are increasing.

_____ 3. Conflicts or hostility between members is present or is increasing.

_____ 4. Some people are confused about assignments, or their relationships with other people are unclear.

_____ 5. Lack of clear goals and lack of commitment to goals exist.

_____ 6. Apathy or lack of interest and involvement by members is in evidence.

_____ 7. Insufficient innovation, risk-taking, imagination, or initiative exists.

_____ 8. Ineffective and inefficient meetings are common.

_____ 9. Working relationships across levels and units are unsatisfactory.

_____ 10. Lack of coordination among functions is apparent.

_____ 11. Poor communication exists; people are afraid to speak up; listening isn't occurring; and information isn't being shared.

_____ 12. Lack of trust exists among members and between members and senior leaders.

_____ 13. Decisions are made that some members don't understand, or with which they don't agree.

_____ 14. People feel that good work is not rewarded or that rewards are unfairly administered.

_____ 15. People are not encouraged to work together for the good of the organization.

_____ 16. Customers and suppliers are not part of organizational decision-making.

_____ 17. People work too slowly and there is too much redundancy in the work being done.

_____ 18. Issues and challenges that require the input of more than one person are being faced.

_____ 19. People must coordinate their activities in order for the work to be accomplished.

_____ 20. Difficult challenges that no single person can resolve or diagnose are being faced.

_____ **Total**

SOURCE: *Adapted from* Diagnosing the Need for Team Building, William G. Dyer. (1987). Team Building: Issues and Alternatives. *Reading, MA: Addison Wesley. Reprinted with permission of Addison Wesley.*

SKILL *LEARNING*

We have all heard statements describing the importance of teams. From athletics to architecture from corporations to communities, the value of teamwork and team building has been emphasized. For example:

"Teamwork is the fuel that allows common people to attain uncommon results." (Andrew Carnegie)

"We must all hang together, or most assuredly we shall all hang separately." (Benjamin Franklin)

"In the long history of humankind (and animal kind, too) those who learned to collaborate and improvise most effectively have prevailed." (Charles Darwin)

"Coming together is a beginning. Keeping together is progress. Working together is success." (Henry Ford)

"Great things in business are never done by one person. They are done by a team of people." (Steve Jobs)

"Talent wins games, but teamwork and intelligence win championships." (Michael Jordan)

"The main ingredient of stardom is the rest of the team." (John Wooden)

"The team, the team, the team." (Bo Schembechler, former University of Michigan football coach)

The Advantages of Teams

One important reason for an emphasis on teams is that participation in teams is fun for most people. There is something inherently attractive about engaging in teamwork. Consider, for example, the two advertisements that appeared next to one another in a metropolitan newspaper, both seeking to fill the same type of position. They are reproduced in Figure 9.1. While neither advertisement is negative or inappropriate, they are noticeably different. Which job would you rather take? Which firm would you rather work for? For most of us, the team-focused job seems much more desirable. This chapter focuses on helping you to flourish in these kinds of team settings.

Figure 9.1 A Team-Oriented and a Traditional Advertisement for a Position

Our Team Needs One Good Multiskilled Maintenance Associate

Our Team is down one good player. Join our group of multiskilled Maintenance Associates who work together to support our assembly teams at American Automotive Manufacturing.

We are looking for a versatile person with skills in one or more of the following: ability to set up and operate various welding machinery, knowledge in electric arc and M.I.G. welding, willingness to work on detailed projects for extended time periods, and general overall knowledge of the automobile manufacturing process. Willingness to learn all maintenance skills a must. You must be a real team player, have excellent interpersonal skills, and be motivated to work in a highly participative environment.

Send qualifications to:

AMM

American Automotive Manufacturing
P.O. Box 616
Ft. Wayne, Indiana 48606
Include phone number. We respond to all applicants.

Maintenance Technician/Welder

Leading automotive manufacturer looking for Maintenance Technician/Welder. Position requires the ability to set up and operate various welding machinery and a general knowledge of the automobile production process. Vocational school graduates or 3–5 years of on-the-job experience required. Competitive salary, full benefits, and tuition reimbursement offered.

Interviews Monday, May 6, at the Holiday Inn South, 3000 Semple Road, 9:00 A.M. to 7:00 P.M. Please bring pay stub as proof of last employment.

NMC

National Motors Corporation
5169 Blane Hill Center
Springfield, Illinois 62707

Whether you are a student, a manager, a subordinate, or a homemaker, it is almost impossible to avoid being a member of a team. Some form of teamwork permeates most people's daily lives. Most of us are members of discussion groups, friendship groups, neighborhood groups, sports teams, or even families in which tasks are accomplished and interpersonal interaction occurs. Teams, in other words, are simply groups of people who are interdependent in the tasks they perform, who affect one another's behavior through interaction, and who see themselves as a unique entity. What we discuss in this chapter is applicable to team activity in most kinds of settings, although we focus mainly on teams and teamwork in employing organizations rather than in homes, classrooms, or sports. The principles we review related to effective team performance, team leadership, and team participation, however, are virtually the same across all these kinds of teams.

For example, empowered teams, autonomous work groups, semiautonomous teams, self-managing teams, self-determining teams, crews, platoons, cross-functional teams, top management teams, **quality circles**, project teams, task forces, virtual teams, emergency response teams, and committees are all examples of the various manifestations of teams and teamwork that appear in the scholarly literature, and research has been conducted on each of them. Our focus is on helping you develop skills that are relevant in most or all of these kinds of situations, whether as a team leader or a team member.

Developing team skills is important because of the tremendous explosion in the use of teams in work organizations over the last couple of decades. For example, 79 percent of Fortune 1000 companies reported that they use self-managing work teams, and 91 percent reported that employee work groups are utilized (Lawler, 1998; Lawler, Mohrman, & Ledford, 1995; Solansky, 2008). More than two-thirds of college students participate in an organized team, and almost no one can graduate from a business school anymore without participating in several team projects or group activities. Teams are ubiquitous in both work life and at school. Possessing the ability to lead and manage teams and teamwork, in other words, has become a commonplace requirement in most organizations. In several studies, the most desired skill in new employees was found to be the ability to work in a team (Duart, et al., 2012; McChrystal, 2015).

One reason for the escalation in the desirability of teamwork is that increasing amounts of data show improvements in productivity, quality, and morale when teams are utilized. Many companies have attributed improvements in performance directly to the institution of teams in the workplace (Blaise, Bergeil, & Balsmeir, 2008; Cohen & Bailey, 1997; Guzzo & Dickson, 1996; Hamilton, Nickerson, & Owan, 2003). For example, by using teams in their organizations:

❑ Shenandoah Life Insurance Company in Roanoke, Virginia, saved $200,000 annually because of reduced staffing needs, while increasing its volume 33 percent.
❑ Westinghouse Furniture Systems increased productivity 74 percent in three years.
❑ AAL increased productivity by 20 percent, cut personnel by 10 percent, and handled 10 percent more transactions.
❑ Federal Express cut service errors by 13 percent.
❑ Carrier reduced unit turnaround time from two weeks to two days.
❑ Volvo's Kalamar facility reduced defects by 90 percent.
❑ General Electric's Salisbury, North Carolina, plant increased productivity by 250 percent compared to other GE plants producing the same product.
❑ Corning cellular ceramics plant decreased defect rates from 1,800 parts per million to 9 parts per million.
❑ AT&T's Richmond operator service increased service quality by 12 percent.
❑ Dana Corporation's Minneapolis valve plant trimmed customer lead time from six months to six weeks.
❑ General Mills plants became 40 percent more productive than plants operating without teams.
❑ A garment-making plant increased its productivity 14 percent by adopting a team-based production system.

Table 9.1 reports the positive relationships between employee involvement in teams and several dimensions of organizational and worker effectiveness. Lawler, Mohrman, and Ledford (1995) found that among firms that were actively using teams, both organizational and individual effectiveness were above average and improving in virtually all categories of performance. In firms without teams or in which teams were infrequently used, effectiveness was average or low in all categories.

Of course, a variety of factors can affect the performance and usefulness of teams. Teams are not inherently effective just because they exist. The Golden State Warriors NBA team in 2007, for example, set a record for the most consecutive seasons without a playoff appearance despite high draft picks and high-achieving players. By 2012, the team had made only one playoff appearance in more than 20 years, evidence that just because a group of talented people get together does not make for an effective team. (This same franchise, however, became a dynasty during the decade after 2010, winning multiple NBA championships.)

A variety of factors have been identified as inhibitors to effective team performance, including rewarding and recognizing individuals instead of the team, not maintaining stability of membership over time, not providing team members with autonomy, not fostering interdependence among team members, and failing to orient all team members (Edmondson & Harvey, 2017; Gibson, Zellmer-Bruhn, & Schwab, 2003; King, 2002). Verespei (1990) observed:

> All too often corporate chieftains read the success stories and ordain their companies to adopt work teams—NOW. Work teams don't always work and may even be the wrong solution to the situation in question.

The instrument titled "Diagnosing the Need for Team Building" in the Skill Assessment section of this chapter helps identify the extent to which the teams in which you are involved are performing effectively and the extent to which they need team building training. Often, teams can take too long to make decisions; they can drive out effective action by becoming too insular; and they can create confusion, conflict, and frustration for their members. All of us have been irritated by being members of an inefficient team, a team dominated by a single person, a team with slothful members, or a team in which standards are compromised in order to get agreement from everyone. The common adage that describes a camel as a racehorse designed by a team illustrates one of the many potential liabilities of a team.

On the other hand, a great deal of research has been conducted to identify the factors associated with high performance in teams. Factors such as *team composition* (e.g., heterogeneity of members, size of the team, familiarity among team members), *team motivation* (e.g., team potency, team goals, team rewards, team feedback), *team type* (e.g., virtual teams, cockpit

Table 9.1	Impact of Involvement in Teams on Organizations and Workers	
Performance Criteria		**Percent Indicating Improvement**
Changed management style to more participatory		78
Improved organizational processes and procedures		75
Improved management decision-making		69
Increased employee trust in management		66
Improved implementation of technology		60
Elimination of layers of management supervision		50
Improved safety and health		48
Improved union-management relations		47
Performance Criteria		**Percent Indicating Positive Impact**
Quality of products and services		70
Customer service		67
Worker satisfaction		66
Employee quality of work life		63
Productivity		61
Competitiveness		50
Profitability		45
Absenteeism		23
Turnover		22

(N = 439 of the Fortune 1000 firms)

SOURCES: *Lawler, E. E., Mohman, S. A., & Ledford, G. E. 1995; Mohrman, 1997.*

crews, quality circles), and *team structure* (e.g., team member autonomy, team norms, team decision-making processes) have been studied to determine how best to form and lead teams (see comprehensive reviews by Cohen & Bailey, 1997; Edmondson & Harvey, 2017; Guzzo & Dickson, 1996; Hackman, 2003; Shuffler, et al., 2012).

Several thousand studies of groups and teams have appeared in just the last decade, and we will not spend time in this chapter reviewing the extensive literature associated with teams, nor the multitude of factors that have been associated with team performance. Instead, we focus on a few key skills that will help you lead and participate effectively in most kinds of teams. We particularly focus on teams that are faced with a task to accomplish. This may be a work team at your job, a project team composed of fellow students, an ad hoc team discussing an issue, or a self-managing team in a service organization. Regardless of the kind of team in which you participate, you can improve your skills in helping the team become a high-performing unit.

Team success is a major factor in most people's individual success.

We concentrate first on helping you understand the development of teams and how to diagnose the key issues present in each of four stages of team development. Because the challenges teams encounter differ in various stages of team development, knowing about the developmental phases of teams and the predictable issues that arise will give you an advantage in being a more effective leader and team member. We focus on helping you improve your capability to lead teams in and through these various stages.

MyLab Management Watch it!
If your instructor has assigned this activity, go to www.pearson.com/mylab/management to complete the video exercise.

AN EXAMPLE OF AN EFFECTIVE TEAM

To illustrate some of the principles we discuss in this chapter, we briefly describe one of the most effective team efforts we know about. It is the team formed to plan and conduct the logistical support for the United States' engagement in the Persian Gulf War (Desert Storm)—the original conflict motivated by Iraq's threatened invasion of Kuwait. General Gus Pagonis was the designated leader of this team, which was organized as a result of an announcement by President George H. W. Bush that the U.S. would send troops to Saudi Arabia in order to confront the Iraqi aggression into Kuwait.

The tasks Pagonis faced were daunting. He was charged with building a team that could transport more than half a million people and their personal belongings to the other side of the world on short notice. But transporting the people was only part of the challenge. Supporting them once they arrived, moving them into position, supporting their battle plans, and then getting them and their equipment back home in record time were even greater challenges.

More than 122 million meals had to be planned, moved, and served—approximately the number eaten by all the residents of Wyoming and Vermont in three months. Fuel (1.3 billion gallons) had to be pumped—about the same amount used in Montana, North Dakota, and Idaho in a year—in order to support soldiers driving 52 million miles. Tanks, planes, ammunition, carpenters, cashiers, morticians, social workers, doctors, and a host of support personnel had to be transported, coordinated, fed, and housed. More than 500 new traffic signs had to be constructed and installed in order to help individuals speaking several different languages to navigate the relatively featureless terrain. Five hundred tons of mail had to be sorted and processed each day. More than 70,000 contracts with suppliers had to be negotiated and executed. All green-colored equipment—more than 12,000 tracked vehicles and 117,000 wheeled vehicles—had to be repainted desert brown and then repainted green when shipped home. Soldiers had to be trained to fit in with an unfamiliar culture that was intolerant of typical soldier-relaxation activity. Supplies had to be distributed at a moment's notice to several different locations, some of them behind enemy lines, in the heat of battle. Traffic control was monumental, as evidenced by one key checkpoint near the front where 18 vehicles per minute passed, seven days a week, 24 hours a day, for six weeks. More than 60,000 enemy prisoners of war had to be transported, cared for, and detained.

Because the war ended far sooner than predicted, an even more daunting challenge presented itself—getting all those supplies and personnel back home. Most of the equipment, ammunition, and food had to be brought back home because it had been unpacked but was mostly unused. That required thorough scrubbing to remove microorganisms or pests and rewrapping a huge amount of supplies. Since large, bulk containers had been broken up into smaller units during the war, it took twice as long to gather and ship materials out of Saudi Arabia as it did to ship them in. Yet personnel were eager to return home at the end of the campaign, so the pressure for speed was at least as great as at the outset of the conflict. In short, Pagonis's team faced a set of tasks that had never before been accomplished on that scale, and they were to do it in a time frame that would have been laughable if it weren't factual.

The team building and teamwork skills used to accomplish these tasks were detailed in Pagonis's book, *Moving Mountains*. Pagonis was awarded a third star during Desert Storm as a result of his outstanding leadership in the field of battle. He helped plan and execute the famous "end run" that took the Iraqi army completely by surprise. Most observers now agree that it was the success of the logistics team that really won the Persian Gulf War for the United States and saved tens of thousands, if not hundreds of thousands, of lives. Although now several decades old, this example highlights principles of effective team building and team leadership that are as current today as they were 30 years ago. The principles upon which effective teams are based have not changed in a thousand years.

Team Development

Regardless of whether you play the role of team leader or team member, in order to function effectively in a team it is important that you understand that all teams progress through stages of development. These stages cause the dynamics within the team to change, the relationships among team members to shift, and effective leader behaviors to be modified. In this section, we outline the four major stages that teams pass through, from early stages of development—when a team is still struggling to become a coherent entity—to a more mature stage of development when the team has become a highly effective, smoothly functioning unit. The skill we want you to develop is to be able to diagnose the stage of your team's development so that you will know what kinds of behaviors will most effectively enhance your team's performance. Each stage of development requires different management and leadership behaviors.

Evidence of predictable patterns of team development has been available since the early part of the twentieth century (Dewey, 1933; Freud, 1921). In fact, despite the variety in composition, purpose, and longevity of the teams investigated in a large array of studies, the stages of group and team development have been strikingly similar (Cameron & Whetten, 1984; Gordon, 2018; Quinn & Cameron, 1983; Rickards & Moger, 2000). The research shows that teams tend to develop through four separate, sequential stages. These stages were first labeled by Tuckman (1965, 2001) as **forming, norming, storming,** and **performing.** These easy-to-remember labels are still widely used today, although Tuckman's second and third stages are reversed in this chapter based on the research of Greiner (1972), Cameron and Whetten (1981), Richards and Moger (2000), and Bonebright (2010).

Table 9.2 summarizes the four main stages of team development. In order for teams to be effective and for team members to benefit most from team membership, teams must progress through the first three stages of development to achieve Stage 4. In each separate stage, unique challenges and issues predominate, and it is by successfully diagnosing and managing these issues and challenges that a team matures and becomes more effective. For each of the four stages, we first identify major team member issues and questions, and then we identify the management responses that help the team effectively transcend that stage of development.

THE FORMING STAGE

When team members first come together, they are much like an audience at the outset of a concert. They are not a team but an aggregation of individuals sharing a common setting. Something must happen for them to feel that they are a cohesive unit. When you meet with a group of people for the first time, for example, chances are that you do not feel integrated or cohesive with the group right away. Several questions are probably on your mind, such as:

❑ Who are these other people?

❑ What is expected of me?

❑ Who is going to lead?

❑ What is supposed to happen?

The questions foremost in the minds of participants in a new team have to do with establishing a sense of security and direction, getting oriented, and becoming comfortable with the new situation. Sometimes new team members can articulate these questions, while at other times they are little more than general feelings of discomfort or disconnectedness. Uncertainty and ambiguity tend to predominate as individuals seek some type of understanding and structure. Because there is no shared history with the team, there is no unity among members. Thus, the typical interpersonal relationships that predominate in this stage are:

❑ Silence

❑ Self-consciousness

❑ Dependence

❑ Superficiality

❑ Mild discomfort

Even though some individuals may enter a team situation with great enthusiasm and anticipation, they are usually hesitant to demonstrate their emotions

Table 9.2	Four Stages of Team Development
Stage	**Explanation**
Forming	Team members are faced with the need to become acquainted with each other, with the team's purpose, and with its structure. Relationships must be formed and trust established. Clarity of direction is needed from team leaders.
Norming	The team is faced with creating cohesion and unity, differentiating roles, identifying expectations for members, and enhancing collaboration. Providing supportive feedback and fostering commitment to a vision are needed from team leaders.
Storming	The team is faced with disagreements, counterdependence, differing points of view, and the need to manage conflict. Challenges include violations of team norms and expectations and overcoming groupthink. Focusing on process improvement, recognizing team achievement, and fostering win-win relationships are needed from team leaders.
Performing	The team is faced with the need for continuous improvement, innovation, speed, and capitalizing on core competencies. Sponsoring team members' new ideas, orchestrating their implementation, and fostering extraordinary performance are needed from team leaders.

to others until they begin to feel at ease. Moreover, without knowing the rules and boundaries, it feels risky to speak out or to even ask questions. Seldom are new members willing to actively query a leader when a team first meets together, even though uncertainty prevails. When a leader asks questions of team members, rarely does someone jump at the chance to give an answer. Silence predominates. When answers are given, they are likely to be brief. Little interaction occurs among team members themselves; most communication is targeted at the team leader or person in charge. Each individual is generally thinking more of himself or herself than of the team. Interactions tend to be formal and guarded. Self-protection and clarity create limited interaction.

Individuals cannot begin to feel like a team until they become familiar with the rules and boundaries of their setting. They don't know whom to trust, who will take initiative, what constitutes normal behavior, or what kinds of interactions are appropriate. They are not yet a real team but only a collection of individuals. Therefore, the task of the team in this stage is less focused on producing an output than on developing the team itself. Helping team members become comfortable with one another takes precedence over task accomplishment. To help a team effectively manage this first stage of development, effective managers should:

❑ Orient members and answer questions.

❑ Establish trust.

❑ Establish relationships between members and with the leader(s).

❑ Establish clarity of purpose, norms, procedures, and expectations.

This stage may be brief, but it is not a time to rely on free and open discussion and consensus decision-making to accomplish an outcome. Direction, clarity, and structure are needed instead. The first tasks are to ensure that all team members know one another and that their questions are answered. Because relatively little participation may occur during this stage, the temptation may be to rush ahead or to short-circuit introductions and instructions. However, teams tend to flounder later if the challenges of this stage are not adequately managed.

In the case of the Persian Gulf logistics team, the first critical task was to make certain that objectives, rules and regulations, time frames, and resources were clearly laid out. Each member of the team had to become comfortable with his or her team membership:

The team got down to work with a redoubled sense of urgency. They were soon fully familiar

with the plan that had been roughed out. We quickly got to a joint understanding of what I took to be our role in the theater. Our session... was very successful, mainly because from the outset we had a well-defined structure for invention. We worked toward several clearly expressed goals, and there was an imposed time limit to keep us on track. And finally, our various experiences were complementary. We needed each other and we knew it. (Pagonis, 1993, pp. 82–83)

THE NORMING STAGE

Once team members have become oriented, achieved clarity about the team's goals, and accepted their place in the team, the main challenge of the team is to create a cohesive unit with a sense of teamwork. Norms, rules, and expectations are clarified in the first stage, but an underlying team culture and informal relationships among members must also be developed. The need to move the team from a group of individuals sharing a common goal to a highly cohesive unit is the motivation that leads the team to a new stage of development—the norming stage. The more team members interact with one another, the more they develop common behaviors and perspectives. They experience a certain amount of pressure to conform to the expectations of other team members, so the team begins to develop a character and culture of its own. A new cohesive team culture affects the amount of work done by the team, its style of communicating, its approaches to problem-solving, and even team member dress.

The major focus of team members, in other words, shifts from overcoming uncertainty in the forming stage to developing the norms of a unified group. Typical questions in team members' minds during this stage include:

❑ What are the norms and values of the team?

❑ How can I best get along with everyone else?

❑ How can I show my support to others?

❑ How can I fit in?

During the norming stage, team members become contented with team membership and begin to value the team's goals as much as their own personal goals. Individual needs are met through the team's accomplishments. The team, rather than the leader or a single person, takes responsibility for solving problems, confronting and correcting mistakes, and ensuring success.

Agreement and a willingness to get along characterize the climate of the team. Individuals experience feelings of loyalty to one another, and the interpersonal relationships that most characterize team members include:

❑ Cooperativeness

❑ Conformity to standards and expectations

❑ Heightened interpersonal attraction

❑ Ignoring disagreements

This norming stage is a time when effective team leaders encourage members to build relationships. Participation by all team members is encouraged. To effectively manage this second stage of development, effective managers should:

❑ Maintain unity and cohesion.

❑ Facilitate participation and empowerment.

❑ Show support to team members.

❑ Provide feedback on team and team member performance.

A major problem may arise in this stage of development, however, and this is an increasing inability to engender diversity and varied perspectives in the team. Although team members may feel extremely satisfied with their tightly bonded unit, the team risks a danger of developing *groupthink* (Baron, 2005; Esser, 1998; Janis, 1972; Shafer & Crichlow, 2010). Groupthink occurs when the cohesiveness and inertia developed in a team drives out good decision-making and problem-solving. The preservation of the team takes precedence over accurate decisions or high-quality task accomplishment. Not enough differentiation and challenge to the team's mind-set occurs.

Groupthink

Irv Janis (1972) conducted research in which he chronicled several high-performing teams that in one instance performed in a stellar fashion but performed disastrously in another instance. His classic example was the cabinet of President John F. Kennedy. This team worked through what is often considered one of the best sets of decisions ever made in handling the Cuban Missile Crisis, in which the former Soviet Union was prevented from placing warhead missiles in Cuba by means of a high-stakes confrontation by Kennedy and his cabinet. This was the same team, however, that previously had made disastrous decisions in the Bay of Pigs fiasco, in which a planned overthrow of Fidel Castro's government in Cuba became a logistical nightmare, a confluence of indecision, and an embarrassing defeat.

What was the difference? Why did the same team do so well in one circumstance and so poorly in another? Janis's answer is groupthink. Groupthink typically occurs when the following attributes develop in teams that are stuck in the norming stage.

❑ *Illusion of invulnerability.* Members feel assured that the team's past success will continue. ("Our track record shows that we cannot fail.")

❑ *Shared stereotypes.* Members dismiss disconfirming information by discrediting its source. ("Those people just don't understand these things.")

❑ *Rationalization.* Members rationalize away threats to an emerging consensus. ("We know the wrongheaded reasons they don't agree with us.")

❑ *Illusion of morality.* Members believe that they, as moral individuals, are not likely to make wrong decisions. ("This team would never knowingly make a bad decision or do anything immoral or unethical.")

❑ *Self-censorship.* Members keep silent about misgivings and try to minimize doubts. ("I must be wrong if others don't think the way I do.")

❑ *Direct pressure.* Sanctions are imposed on members who explore deviant viewpoints. ("If you don't agree, why don't you just leave the team?")

❑ *Mind guarding.* Members protect the team from being exposed to disturbing ideas. ("Don't listen to them. We need to keep the rabble-rousers at bay.")

❑ *Illusion of unanimity.* Members conclude that the team must have reached a consensus since the most vocal members are in agreement. ("If a few vocal people express agreement, there must be a consensus.")

The problem with groupthink is that it leads teams to commit more errors than normal. For example, consider the following commonly observed scenario.

Not wanting to make a serious judgment error, a leader convenes a meeting of his or her team. In the process of discussing an issue, the leader expresses a preference for one option. Other team members, wanting to appear supportive, present arguments justifying his or her decision. One or two members tentatively suggest alternatives, but they are strongly overruled by the majority. The decision is carried out with even greater conviction than normal because everyone is in agreement, but the consequences are disastrous. How did this happen?

Although the leader brought the team together to avoid making a bad decision, the presence of groupthink actually made a bad decision more likely. Without the social support provided by the team, the leader may have been more cautious in implementing a personally preferred but uncertain decision.

To manage this tendency to develop groupthink, effective teams must move through the norming stage into the storming stage. The team must develop attributes that will foster diversity, heterogeneity, and even productive conflict in the team's processes (Ben-Hur, Kinley, & Jonsen, 2012; Roberto, 2005). In particular, Janis makes the following suggestions for addressing groupthink:

❑ *Critical evaluators.* At least one team member should be assigned to perform the role of critic or evaluator of the team's decisions.

❑ *Open discussion.* The team leader should not express an opinion at the outset of the team meeting but should encourage open discussion of differing perspectives by team members.

❑ *Subgroups.* Multiple subgroups in the team may be formed to develop independent proposals.

❑ *Outside experts.* Invite outside experts to listen to the rationale for the team's decision and critique it.

❑ *Devil's advocate.* Assign at least one team member to play devil's advocate during the discussion if it seems that too much homogeneity exists in the team's discussion.

❑ *Second-chance meetings.* Sleep on the team's decision and revisit it afresh the next day. The expression of team members' second thoughts should be encouraged.

In other words, teams in the norming stage become cohesive and highly integrated entities, and while this is critical to producing solidity, teamwork, and commitment, it may also create a tendency to preserve high involvement and good feeling at the expense of all else. Having a unified family feeling is necessary to pull the separate members together and to create a singular identity, but it can prove disastrous if important information is filtered out, contrary points of view are squelched, or nonconformity in any form is punished. Effective teams must also move on to the next stage, the storming stage of development.

THE STORMING STAGE

Whereas the comfortable climate that team members develop in the norming stage can lead to an excessive amount of agreement and homogeneity, it also can lead to the opposite phenomenon. That is, once team members begin to feel comfortable with the team, they often feel comfortable enough to explore different roles. Some may tend toward task facilitation—focusing on getting work done—while others may tend toward relationship building, focusing on interpersonal dynamics. This differentiation of team members' roles invariably leads the team into a stage of potential conflict and counterdependence—a storming stage.

Playing different roles causes team members to develop different perspectives and to develop opinions that challenge the leadership and direction of the team. Almost every effective team goes through a stage in which team members question the legitimacy of the team's direction, the leader, the roles of other team members, the opinions or decisions of others, and the task objectives. Up to now, the team was largely characterized by harmony and consensus. Individual differences were suppressed in order to create a sense of team. However, such a condition will not last forever without team members becoming uncomfortable about losing their individual identity, subjugating their feelings, or stifling differing perspectives. The team's long-term success, therefore, will depend on how well it manages the storming stage of development. Typical questions that arise in team members' minds during this stage are:

❑ How will we handle differences of opinion and dissension?

❑ How can we make decisions amid disagreement?

❑ How will we communicate negative feedback?

❑ Do I want to maintain my membership in the team?

❑ How far can I step out of bounds?

A Middle Eastern proverb states: "All sunshine makes a desert." Similarly, team development implies that some struggles must occur, some discomfort must be experienced, and some obstacles must be overcome for the team to prosper. The team must learn to deal with adversity—especially that produced by its own members. Tendencies toward groupthink must be addressed head-on. If team members are more interested in keeping peace than in solving problems and accomplishing tasks, the team will never become effective. No one wants to remain in a team that will not allow for individuality and uniqueness and that wants to maintain harmony more than it wants to accomplish its goals. Consequently, harmony is sometimes sacrificed as the team attacks problems and accomplishes objectives.

LEARNING

Team members do not cease to care about one another, and they remain committed to the team and its success. But they do begin to take sides on issues, to find that they are more compatible with some team members than others, and to align themselves with certain points of view. This leads to:

❑ Coalitions or cliques

❑ Competition among team members

❑ Disagreement with the leader

❑ Challenging others' points of view

During the troop deployment to Iraq, for example, a relatively rigid military command hierarchy—along with the urgency of the mission to be performed—inhibited large deviations from established norms and rules, but small deviations began to emerge as Pagonis's team developed. Logistics team members painted personal logos on some tanks and trucks, insider code names were given to people and locations as a bit of sarcasm, and challenges to top-brass mandates became more common in briefing rooms. This testing of norms and boundaries is sometimes merely an expression of a need for individuality, while in other instances it is a product of strong feelings that the team can be improved. The main task issues to be addressed by the team's leader in this stage include:

❑ Managing conflict

❑ Legitimizing productive expressions of individuality

❑ Turning counterdependence into interdependence

❑ Fostering consensus-building among heterogeneous perspectives

❑ Encouraging helpful expressions of disagreement

Conflict, coalition formation, and counterdependence create conditions that may lead to the norms and values of the team being questioned. Rather than stifling or resisting these differences, however, effective team leaders encourage members to turn those challenges into constructive suggestions for improvement. It is important for team members to feel that they can legitimately express their personal uniqueness and idiosyncrasies, so long as they are not destructive to the overall team.

It is clear from research that when teams face difficult or complex problems, they are more effective if membership is heterogeneous than if all team members act, believe, and see things the same way (Edmondson & Harvey, 2017; Shin, et al., 2012; Snow, 2018). Diversity is productive in fostering creativity, individuality, and solutions to difficult problems. It has been said that teams make complex problems simple. The trouble is, teams also make simple problems complex, so diversity and heterogeneity are not universally appropriate. The first two stages of team development, in fact, are purposeful in minimizing diversity and heterogeneity. In the third stage, however, maintaining flexibility in the team implies that tolerance for individuality is acceptable and that changes and improvements are promoted.

General Pagonis's philosophy about the way to manage differences was to encourage their expression:

The key is to be open to different experiences and perspectives. If you can't tolerate different kinds of people, you're not likely to learn from different kinds of perspectives. Effective leaders encourage contrary opinions, an important source of vitality. This is especially true in the military where good ideas come in an incredible variety of packages. (Pagonis, 1993, p. 24)

In the storming stage of development, the tensions and differentiation of roles may actually foster team cohesion and productivity rather than conflict if, as a leader in the team, you:

❑ Identify an external enemy (rather than one another) as a target for competition.

❑ Reinforce team commitment to and recognition of team-level performance.

❑ Maintain visibility of the overall vision and superordinate goals.

❑ Turn members into leaders by having team members teach the group's values and vision to others.

Pagonis's logistics team illustrates the value of the first three suggestions above—identifying an external enemy, team-level recognition, and vision.

In the presence of the enemy, our strength was flexibility, both as individuals and as a group. Organizations must be flexible enough to adjust and conform when their environments change. But the flexibility can degenerate into chaos in the absence of well-established goals.... Once everyone in the organization understands the goals of the organization, then each person sets out several objectives by which to attain those goals within his or her own sphere of activity.... When it works, cooperation and collegiality are enhanced, and in-fighting and suboptimization are minimized. (Pagonis, 1993, p. 83)

Figure 9.2 **The Xerox Dissemination Process**

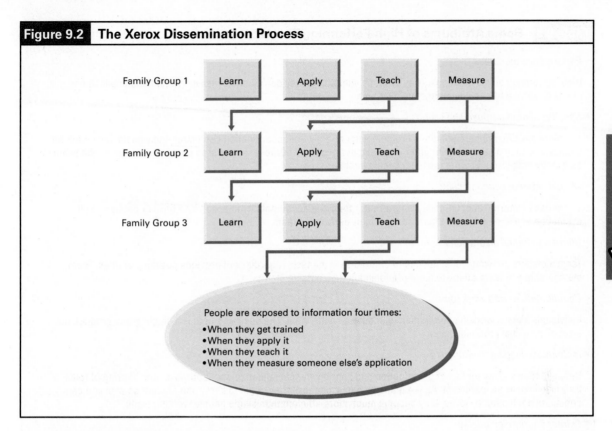

The fourth suggestion above is illustrated well by a process used effectively by Xerox Corporation to address stiff competition from external competitors. Figure 9.2 illustrates a process implemented by the firm in which members were turned into leaders in order to ensure that a common vision and common processes were realized throughout the company. To ensure that all units and all managers were working in harmony, the company divided itself into hierarchical family teams. A four-step process was then employed:

1. *Learn.* Core principles, vision, and values are taught and discussed.

2. *Apply.* Action plans are formed and an improvement agenda is implemented.

3. *Teach.* The principles and successful experiences are taught to the family team at the next lower level.

4. *Inspect.* The performance and action plans of this lower-level family team are measured and monitored.

Teams are exposed to the desired information four times: when they learn it, when they apply it, when they teach it, and when they inspect it. More importantly, because team members are engaged in teaching others, their commitment to the team, even in light of differentiated roles, is enhanced.

THE PERFORMING STAGE

The performing stage of development represents highly effective and efficient team functioning. Because the team has worked through the issues embedded in each of the previous stages of development, it is able to work at a high level of performance. The team has overcome issues of skepticism, uncertainty, nonparticipation, counterdependence, and self-centeredness typical of the first, or forming, stage of development. It has developed a clear mission, personal commitment to the team, and a high degree of loyalty and morale, and it has overcome tendencies toward groupthink that can occur in the norming stage. It has fostered differentiation and variety while also overcoming tendencies toward counterdependence, conflict, polarization, and disharmony typical of the storming stage. It now has the potential to develop the attributes of a high-performing team.

A listing of attributes of high-performance teams is provided in Table 9.3, based on research summarized in Blaise, Bergiel, and Balsmeier, (2008);

Table 9.3 — Some Attributes of High-Performing Teams

- *Performance outcomes*

  High-performing teams do things. They produce something; they don't just discuss it. Without accomplishment, teams dissolve and become ineffective over time.

- *Specific, shared purpose and vision*

  The more specific the purpose, the more commitment, trust, and coordination can occur. Individuals don't work for themselves; they work for one another in pursuit of the shared purpose. The shared purpose can also be the same as a motivating vision of what the team should achieve.

- *Mutual, internal accountability*

  The sense of internal accountability is far greater than any accountability imposed by a boss or outsider. Self-evaluation and accountability characterize a high-performing team.

- *Blurring of formal distinctions*

  Team members do whatever is needed to contribute to the task, regardless of previous positions or titles. Team membership and team roles are more predominant than outside status.

- *Coordinated, shared work roles*

  Individuals always work in coordination with others on the team. The desired output is a single group product, not a set of individual products.

- *Inefficiency leading to efficiency*

  Because teams allow for lots of participation and sharing, mutual influence about purpose, and blurring of roles, they may initially be inefficient. As the team develops, because they come to know one another so well and can anticipate each other's moves, they become much more efficient than single people working alone.

- *Extraordinarily high quality*

  Teams produce outcomes above and beyond current standards of performance. They surprise and delight their various constituencies with quality levels not expected and seldom, if ever, obtained before. An intolerance of mediocrity exists, so standards of performance are very high.

- *Creative continuous improvement*

  Large-scale innovations as well as never-ending small improvements characterize the team's processes and activities. Dissatisfaction with the status quo leads to a constant flow of new ideas, experimentation, and a quest for progress.

- *High credibility and trust*

  Team members trust one another implicitly, defend members who are not present, and form interdependent relationships with one another. Personal integrity and honesty characterize team activities and team member interactions.

- *Clarity of core competence*

  The unique talents and strategic advantages of the team and its members are clear. The ways in which these competencies can be utilized to further the team's objectives are well understood. Extraneous activities and deflections from the team's core mission are given low priority.

Edmondson and Harvey (2017); Gordon (2018); and Lawler (1998, 2003). This summarizes the characteristics that must be present in all high-performing teams, and it provides a good guideline for what you want to strive for when you are leading or participating in a team.

The team in the performing stage is not, however, free of challenges. The common issues that tend to dominate members of high-performing teams are:

- ❏ How can we help one another thrive?
- ❏ How can we foster continuous improvement and creativity?

- How can we build on our core competence?
- How can we maintain a high level of energy in the team?

Team members' questions in this stage change from being static to being dynamic. They shift in focus from merely accomplishing objectives to fostering change and improvement and achieving extraordinarily positive performance. Continuous improvement replaces accomplishment as an objective. Up to this point, the team has been trying to manage and resolve issues that lead to three key outcomes: (1) accomplishing tasks or objectives, (2) coordinating and integrating team members' roles, and (3) ensuring the personal well-being of all team members. It can now turn its attention to achieving a level of performance above the ordinary. The interpersonal relationships of team members are characterized by:

- High mutual trust
- Unconditional commitment to the team
- Mutual training and development
- Entrepreneurship

Team members in this stage exhibit a sense of shared responsibility and concern for one another as they carry out their work. Their relationships are not limited merely to accomplishing a task together, but also extend to ensuring that each team member is learning, developing, and flourishing. Coaching and assisting one another are common. In General Pagonis's high-performing team, for example, team members were continuously teaching one another and helping the team and its individual members become more competent.

I arranged to take a day or two away from headquarters with a group of key people from the command [team]. We used this brief respite from our everyday activities to take a long look at what our organization is doing. These sessions...gave us a chance to work as a group, in a focused way....From Day One, I held large, open classes where we discussed scenarios and potential solutions. I would pose a question to the group: "O.K., you have a ship that docked at Ad Dammam this morning. It's ready to be unloaded, and the onboard crane breaks. What's our response?" Collectively, the group would work toward one of several solutions.... These group sessions served several useful purposes at once. Obviously, they brought potential challenges into the open so

we could better prepare for them....Equally important, they promoted collaborative discussion across ranks and disciplines. (Pagonis, 1993, pp. 101, 177)

In addition to multifaceted relationships and unconditional commitment to one another, high-performing team members also take responsibility individually for continuously improving the team and its processes. Experimentation, trial-and-error learning, freewheeling discussions of new possibilities, and personal responsibility by everyone for upgrading performance is typical. The team adopts a set of behaviors that help to foster and perpetuate this stage of development, including:

- Capitalizing on their individual and collective core competencies
- Fostering innovation and continuous improvement
- Enhancing flourishing relationships
- Encouraging positive deviance

After having moved through the first three stages of development in the Persian Gulf War, for example, General Pagonis's logistics team moved into a stage characterized by activities that exceeded expected levels of performance. On one occasion, for example, Pagonis directed two team members to generate a solution to the problem of how to provide combat troops with decent meals on the front lines.

Imagine that you've been at some remote and desolate desert site for weeks, or even months, consuming dehydrated or vacuum-packed military rations. One day, unannounced, an odd-looking vehicle with the word "Wolfmobile" painted on it comes driving into your camp. The side panels open up, and a smiling crew inside offers to cook you a hamburger to order. "Side of fries? How about a Coke?" Morale shot up everywhere the Wolfmobiles pulled in—a little bit of home in the desert. (Pagonis, 1993, p. 129)

This example illustrates the major opportunity associated in the fourth stage of development—to help team members expand their focus from merely accomplishing their work and maintaining good interpersonal relationships to upgrading and elevating the team's performance. This level of performance unlocks positive energy and makes it impossible to ever return to a lower level of performance again.

Another example of the power of high-performing teams and their effects on members is a story told by our friend Bob Quinn (2005) in which an upper-level executive in a major manufacturing organization was expressing frustration with his company. "The trouble with my firm," lamented the executive, "is that they cannot stand excellence." He illustrated his frustration by recounting the following incident.

One day in his plant, a major problem occurred on the assembly line, and the line had to be shut down and repaired. The issue was serious and required personnel from multiple shifts to come to the plant to work on the problem. As a gesture of goodwill on his part, this executive purchased lunch—pizza, hot dogs, and soft drinks—for these employees who were going the extra mile for the company. They completed the task at the highest levels of quality and in record time. Sometime later, a representative from the finance department entered the office of this executive, slapped a piece of paper down on the desk, and exclaimed, "We can't pay this bill for the food. You know that it is against corporate policy to purchase food for employees from your budget. This bill will not be reimbursed."

Of course, no one could fault the finance department representative—he was simply doing his job and reinforcing the rules. Flabbergasted, however, the executive responded: "Look, I cannot do the same things we have always done and expect different results. I have to break rules once in a while in the service of achieving excellence or extraordinary performance. Buying lunch made all the difference to these employees. It's what accounted for our success."

"This incident just proves," stated the executive, "that my firm cannot stand excellence. They cannot tolerate being extraordinary." Our friend Bob offered this executive some advice. He simply proposed that the executive give up and conform to the rules and expectations. Stop trying to achieve extraordinary levels of success. The executive's reply was telling, however, and illustrates the power of high-performing teams in this fourth stage of development. His reply was: "I can't quit trying. Once I have experienced excellence, normal performance is just not good enough anymore. I can't stand still and not strive for extraordinary results."

Teams in this fourth stage of development are not all outstanding, of course, and unfortunately, **positive deviance** is rare. But, once team members experience this kind of excellence, team performance stuck in the first three stages of development will never be satisfactory again. Some of the prescriptions for achieving these levels of extraordinary success are highlighted in the sections below as we discuss skills involved in leading teams and in being an effective member of teams.

Leading Teams

One important factor in creating effective teams, of course, is the role of the leader. It is not the personal *style* of the leader that makes a difference. Multiple leadership styles can be effective, and no one style has particular advantages over others. Rather, it is the skills and capabilities of the leader and the tools and techniques put into practice that account for effective versus ineffective team performance. We highlight two especially critical aspects of team leadership here. Not only are these two aspects of team leadership observable in General Pagonis's leadership style, but they have emerged in the scholarly literature as critical factors in leading almost any kind of team (Cameron, 2012; Edmonson, 1999; Edmondson & Harvey, 2017; Gordon, 2018). The first is developing credibility and influence among team members. The second is establishing a motivating vision and goals for the team.

DEVELOPING CREDIBILITY

To be an effective team leader, you must have the respect and commitment of team members. That is, you must develop credibility (Kouzes & Posner, 1987, 2011). Establishing credibility and the capacity to influence team members is the first key challenge you will face as a leader of teams. Giving directions, articulating goals, or trying to motivate team members are all wasted efforts if you have not established credibility and respect (Helliwell & Huang, 2011). General Pagonis described this leadership challenge in the following way:

> I have found, time and time again in commands around the world, that my troops are more invested in their work and better motivated when they understand and buy into the ultimate goals of the operation. Reason counts for far more than rank when it comes to motivation. And motivation is the root of all organizational progress. Over the years I have developed a very distinctive leadership style. Gus Pagonis' command style, like everyone else's, is unique. This meant that I had choices to make. Would I rather have the world's best port operation officer, if he was someone who didn't already know my style? Or would I rather have the world's second best port operation officer who knew my style intimately

and was comfortable with it? The answer was obvious; we couldn't waste time fighting our own systems. Equally important, we couldn't afford the time that would be wasted as a new person tried to impress me, or get on my good side. We needed an instant body of leaders, strengthened by a united front. We needed to know that we could depend on one another unconditionally. We needed the confidence that the mission, and not personal advancement, would always be paramount in the mind of each participant. (Pagonis, 1993, p. 78, 84)

In earlier chapters, we identified ways to enhance a manager's influence (Chapter 5) and trust (Chapter 8), which are components of credibility. In this chapter, we highlight additional behaviors you can use to help establish leadership credibility in a team.

Team members, of course, will not follow a person they don't trust, who is hypocritical or dishonest, or whose motives appear to be personal aggrandizement instead of the welfare of the team. In fact, Kouzes and Posner (2011) identified credibility as the single most important requirement for leadership effectiveness. Once credibility has been established, then goals for the team can be articulated and the team can move toward high performance.

The seven behaviors summarized in Table 9.4 are keys to building and maintaining credibility and influence among team members. They are simple and straightforward, and there is much scholarly evidence that supports their efficacy (see Cialdini, 2008, 2018; Druskat & Wheeler, 2000; Hackman, 2003; Turner, 2000).

1. *Demonstrate integrity.* Chief among the behaviors that create leadership credibility is the demonstration of integrity. Integrity means that you do what you say, you behave congruently with your values, and you are believable in what you espouse. Individuals who appear to say one thing and do another, who are not honest in their feedback, or who do not follow through on their promises are perceived to lack integrity and are ineffective as leaders of teams.

2. *Be clear and consistent.* Expressing certainty about what you want and where you are going, without being dogmatic or stubborn, increases others' confidence in you. Being wishy-washy or inconsistent in your viewpoints impedes credibility. The electorate in most countries throughout the world rates their politicians very low in credibility because most candidates appear to be inconsistent in their statements, changing perspectives depending on the audience (Cialdini, 2008). Credible people, on the other hand, can be trusted to be consistent and transparent.

3. *Create positive energy.* Stay optimistic and complimentary. Most teams do not perform effectively when there is a climate of criticism, cynicism, or negativity. Criticizing team members, past leaders, others outside the team, or even being critical of the circumstances in which the team finds itself are usually not effective ways to help a team perform well. Individuals and teams perform better when positive energy exists—optimism, compliments, celebrations of success, and recognition of progress (Owens, et al., 2016). This does not mean being

---

Table 9.4	Ways to Build Team Leader Credibility

Team leaders build credibility with their team members by:

- Demonstrating integrity, representing authenticity, and displaying congruence (Walk the talk)

- Being clear and consistent about what they want to achieve (Be trustworthy and transparent)

- Creating positive energy by being optimistic and complimentary (Help others flourish)

- Using commonality and reciprocity (Build a foundation)

- Managing agreement and disagreement among team members by using one-sided and two-sided arguments appropriately—one-sided in situations when all team members agree, two-sided when consensus is not preexisting (Use effective influence techniques)

- Encouraging and coaching team members to help them improve (Mentor and tutor)

- Sharing information about the team, providing perspective from external sources, and encouraging participation (Inform and involve)

unrealistic or a "Pollyanna." Instead, it means that when you are seen as a source of positive energy and enthusiasm, you have more credibility and influence among team members.

4. *Use commonality and reciprocity.* If you express views that are held in common with team members, they are more likely to agree with your later statements. If you want to foster team change, or move the team toward an outcome that appears to be risky or uncomfortable, begin by expressing views with which other team members agree. It can be as simple as "I know you all have very busy schedules." Or, "We have a lot of diversity of opinion in our team on this issue." These kinds of statements work because of the principle of reciprocity. Team members have a tendency to agree with you more if they have received something from you in advance, even if it is merely your agreement with their point of view (Cialdini, 2018). After you have expressed agreement with them, you can then lead them toward goals or targets that may stretch them or may make them uncomfortable or uncertain.

5. *Manage agreement and disagreement.* When team members initially agree with you, it is more effective if you use a one-sided argument. That is, present only one point of view and support it with evidence. When team members tend to disagree with you at the outset, use two-sided arguments. That is, first present both sides of the case and then show how your own point of view is superior to the contrary perspective. Keep in mind that when team members agree with you, the first statements you make tend to hold more weight and are remembered the longest. When they disagree with you, the last statements made tend to carry the most weight (O'Keefe, 2016).

6. *Encourage and coach.* Encouragement means helping others develop courage—to tackle uncertainty, to achieve beyond their current performance, to disrupt the status quo. Encouraging team members not only involves compliments and supportive statements, it also involves assistance and resources. Coaching, as pointed out in Chapter 4, means helping to show the way, providing information or advice, and assisting team members with task requirements. Effective encouragement and coaching involve giving positively reinforcing comments as well as helpful advice or direction.

7. *Share information.* Building credibility means coming to understand the perspectives of team members as well as a sense of their talents and resources. Coming to know your team members well is crucial for successful leadership. One way to do this is to use the principle of "frequent checking." This merely involves asking questions and checking with team members regularly to determine levels of agreement, obstacles, dissatisfactions, needs, and interpersonal or team issues. Importantly, credibility grows as knowledge is shared. Being the source from which others can acquire needed information builds credibility and influence, so sharing is crucial (Mesmer-Magnus & DeChurch, 2009; Srivastava, Bartol, & Locke, 2006).

As stated by General Pagonis:

> *Keeping [team members] abreast of your actions, as well as the rationale behind those actions, puts everybody on an equal information footing. I believe that information is power, but only if it is shared.... Very early on I had gotten in the habit of sneaking my deputy, John Carr, into these briefing sessions with CINC [General Schwarzkopf and others]. That way, he stayed as smart and as current about the CINC's plans as I did.* (Pagonis, 1993, p. 88, 131)

ESTABLISH SMART GOALS AND EVEREST GOALS

Once team members have confidence in you as a leader, you can then identify goals and levels of performance to which team members can aspire.

There are two kinds of goals that characterize high-performing teams, and leaders must identify and espouse both kinds. The first are called **SMART goals**, and the second are called **Everest goals**. The purpose for establishing clear goals is so that every person on the team can give a similar answer to the questions: What are we trying to achieve? What is the result we are trying to create? Leaders who clearly articulate the desired outcomes are more likely to experience high performance from the team. Goal-directed performance, in fact, always exceeds performance disassociated with goals (Locke & Latham, 2012). Figure 9.3 illustrates this point.

It shows that when people are given *no goals* ("Here is your task. Go do it."), their performance tends to be low, even though most people will perform at a minimum level even when they are not certain of the standard that they should achieve. However, being provided with an *easy goal* ("The average is 10 tasks per day, but you can shoot for 6.") leads to even lower

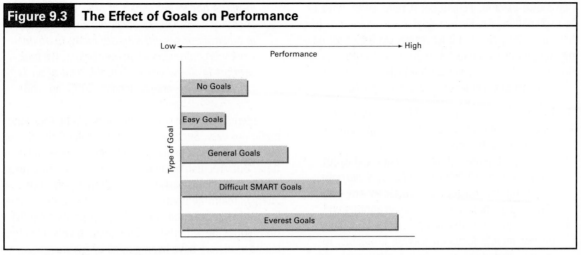

Figure 9.3   The Effect of Goals on Performance

SOURCE: *"Practicing Positive Leadership,"* Cameron, K. (2013).

performance. People tend to work toward the standard that has been established, and when it is easy, they slack off. Establishing *general goals* ("Do your best.") results in improved performance over easy goals, but identifying *difficult goals* ("The average is 10 tasks per day, but you should shoot for 12.") produces far higher levels of performance. The kinds of goals that produce the highest levels of performance, however, are difficult goals that possess five characteristics. The acronym SMART identifies these attributes. SMART goals are:

❑ **S**pecific—The goal is clear, and precise targets and standards are identified.

❑ **M**easurable—The goal can be assessed and quantified. The extent to which the goal has been achieved is obvious.

❑ **A**ligned—The goal is supportive of and consistent with the purposes and objectives of the broader organization. People are not pursuing their own objectives independent of their team.

❑ **R**ealistic—While being difficult and causing performance to stretch, the goal is not foolhardy or a fantasy.

❑ **T**ime-bound—An end point is identified or a completion date established so that goal achievement is not open-ended.

Consider the difference between a goal statement such as "We will be the best in our industry" and a goal statement that is SMART: "We will achieve a 5 percent improvement in the on-time delivery of our products by the end of the quarter." The latter provides a more motivating goal in that it is specific, measurable, aligned with

key outcomes, realistic, and time-bound. It gives people something they can easily understand and shoot for.

It is important to keep in mind, however, that articulating motivating goals and identifying the methods to achieve them are different. Goals specify the target. Methods specify the means for achieving the target. Goals are crucial to successful team leadership. Dictating methods is often lethal. Pagonis's leadership illustrates this well:

> *I never tell a subordinate how to carry out a specific goal. Dictating terms to a subordinate undermines innovation, decreases the subordinate's willingness to take responsibility for his or her actions, increases the potential for suboptimization of resources, and increases the chances that the command will be dysfunctional if circumstances change dramatically. Our first month in the theater only underscored my sense that our [team] would have to be incredibly elastic.* (Pagonis, 1993, p. 119)

The second type of goal that effective team leaders articulate is called an *Everest goal* (Cameron, 2013). An Everest goal goes beyond normal goal setting. It represents an ultimate achievement, an extraordinary accomplishment, or a beyond-the-norm outcome. Achieving it requires everything one can give. Like setting your sights on getting to the summit of Mount Everest, an Everest goal is clear and compelling, serves as a unifying focal point, builds team spirit, engages people, and creates positive energy and excitement. An Everest goal is stimulating because it connects to a profound passion. People get it right away, with little explanation. An Everest goal is visionary, not just tactical or strategic, and it leaves people better for having engaged in its pursuit. It requires extraordinary effort to achieve, and maybe a little luck.

Five attributes characterize Everest goals:

1. Everest goals represent *positive deviance.* They extend beyond expectations and represent extraordinary achievement.
2. Everest goals represent inherent value and worth. They possess *profound meaning and purpose.* Achieving the outcomes themselves are sufficient and are not a means to obtain another end.
3. Everest goals possess an *affirmative bias.* They do not merely focus on solving problems, reducing obstacles, overcoming challenges, or removing difficulties. Rather, they focus on opportunities, possibilities, and potential.
4. Everest goals represent a *contribution.* They focus on providing benefit to others or making a contribution rather than merely receiving a reward or recognition. Everest goals emphasize what individuals can give compared to what they can get.
5. Everest goals are *inherently energizing.* People do not need another source of motivation or reward in order to pursue them. People are not exhausted by pursuing Everest goals, but instead they are uplifted, elevated, and energized. Everest goals are not the same as mere stretch goals or difficult goals. They extend beyond the mere difficult.

An excerpt from a climber who finally made it to the top of Mount Everest after three failed attempts illustrates the difference between Everest goals and more traditional stretch or difficult goals:

> I realized something on that night in the dark on Everest. What I realized was that real winning had nothing to do with beating someone else, or crossing the finish line first, or standing on top. Winning wasn't anything external at all. It was an internal satisfaction, a deep inner sense of pride and joy. Success can only be measured within ourselves, by ourselves. It has nothing to do with other people's perception of our achievements. It has everything to do with our own perceptions of our efforts....Success isn't standing on the podium, or hearing the cheers of others, or standing on the summit at all. It's giving it your all....I think that in anything in life, if you give it everything you possibly can, you really do succeed....Our business

> in life is not to get ahead of others but to get ahead of ourselves, to break our own records, to outstrip our yesterday by our today, to do our work with more force than ever before. We took comfort in the words of Gandhi: 'Full effort is full victory'...(Clarke & Hobson, 2005, pp. 168)

Identifying such a goal, of course, is neither automatic nor easy. Such goals don't just roll off the tips of our tongues. Most people identify few of these in a lifetime. But articulating such a goal as a leader of a team creates automatic passion, commitment, and positive energy. Team members catch fire. They become more innovative, more cohesive, and higher performing than they could be otherwise. The most highly effective teams in history have been guided by Everest goals.

Examples of high-performing companies that established Everest goals include Ford Motor Company's goal to democratize the automobile (in the early 1900s); Boeing's goal to bring the world into the jet age (in the 1950s); Sony's goal to change the image of poor quality in Japan (in the 1960s); Apple's goal of one person, one computer (in the 1980s); the University of Michigan professor C. K. Prahalad's goal to help 500,000 Indians become employable in 10 years (in the 2000s); and the more recent General Motors goal of zero crashes, zero congestion, and zero pollution by 2025.

In summary, being an effective leader of a team requires at least two key skills that often do not receive adequate attention: (1) developing credibility among team members, and (2) articulating SMART and Everest goals for the team. Whereas these are obviously not the only skills that effective team leaders possess, without these two core capabilities, it is unlikely that the teams you lead will achieve high levels of Stage 4 performance.

INTERNATIONAL CAVEATS

We have pointed out throughout the book that individuals in different cultures exhibit differences in values and orientations (Trompenaars, 1996; Trompenaars & Hampden-Turner, 2011). Diagnosing, understanding, and capitalizing on individual differences, we repeat, is a crucial skill of competent managers. The seven value orientations identified by Trompenaars provide a useful tool for identifying those individual differences. That is, you can understand differences among people by assessing them on the extent to which they emphasize one value orientation over its opposite: *universalism* versus *particularism*; *individualism* versus *communitarianism*; *neutrality* versus *affectivity*; *specificity* versus *diffuseness*; *achievement* versus ascription; internal versus external control; and past, present, or future time orientation. The first chapter in this book provides a more detailed explanation of these value dimensions.

Individual differences may require that some modification be made in these team leadership behaviors. For example, if you are leading a team with members from cultures that tend to have a *collectivist* orientation (e.g., France, Japan, Mexico, Philippines) as opposed to an *individualist* orientation, team members will expect to be involved in the creation and articulation of the goals. They will be less comfortable with the goals coming from a single leader, regardless of his or her credibility and influence. Consequently, the Everest goal and its accompanying SMART goals should be designed with active participation of team members.

Similarly, team members from countries where a *neutral* culture (e.g., China, Japan, Korea, New Zealand) as opposed to an *affective* culture predominates may be less energized by language filled with superlatives and passion. Their orientation toward task accomplishment and factual data may mute their responses to emotional language. Consequently, being sensitive to the wording of your Everest goal statement will help make it more motivating.

On the other hand, the differences in cultural values among different nationalities are not so great as to negate the overall effectiveness of the two key skills mentioned above—building credibility and articulating goals. The data from thousands of managers worldwide support the effectiveness of these two key skills for team leaders, regardless of national differences (see Trompenaars & Hampden-Turner, 2011). You may need to be sensitive to the potential need to modify your behaviors based on the composition of your team, but team composition will not have as strong an influence on team effectiveness as the leadership skills you display (Edmondson & Harvey, 2017; Snow, 2018; Guzzo & Dickson, 1996.)

Team Membership

Most of the time, most of us will not serve as the leader of the teams in which we participate. It's wise to prepare for the leadership roles you will play in the future, but the vast majority of the time you will be an active member of a team, working for the common good of the group, rather than the person in charge. You will be valuable to your team because of the contributions you make in nonleadership roles. These contributions can have significant impact on your team's performance.

One of the most amazing statements made by General Pagonis as he reviewed the outcomes of the Iraq deployment related to the performance of his team, even when he was not the active leader:

> *I meet with skepticism, even disbelief, when I tell people that I didn't issue a single order during the ground war. This is only slightly a stretch of the truth. Yes, people sought and got guidance. But the people in my command knew exactly what they were supposed to do in almost every conceivable circumstance. They had been trained and encouraged to think on their feet. I felt they could even deal with the inconceivable.* (Pagonis, 1993, p. 148)

Team members were not only guided by an overarching goal and a clear understanding of what they were to accomplish, but they had become an extraordinarily high-performing team because of the roles played by team members. Pagonis described it this way: "Truth be told, we spent less of our time as logisticians, and more of our time as managers, fixers, firefighters, father confessors, and cheerleaders. There was simply nobody else around to play those roles" (p. 87).

In this section, we point out two main skills associated with team membership—playing advantageous roles, and providing helpful feedback to others. Once again, these skills are not complicated, but they have been found to be highly effective in helping team members influence team success (see Belbin, 2010).

ADVANTAGEOUS ROLES

Most teams face two main challenges: (1) accomplishing the task that has been assigned and (2) building unity and collaboration among the team members. You can enhance or inhibit those two challenges as a member of a team almost as much as you can as the team leader. All of us have experienced teams that just seem to click, that are able to get results quickly and effectively, and that are fun to be in. Those dynamics don't happen by chance but depend on certain key roles played by team members.

A great deal of research has been done on the power of group pressure and the influence of team members on one another. The classic Solomon Asch experiments (1951) were among the first to highlight the influence of team members on one another. The Asch experiments showed, for example, that when other team members verbally agreed with a statement that was obviously false—say, "The federal government controls the stock market"—the person being observed also tended to verbalize agreement with the obviously false statement—even if he or she disagreed with it. Team members' statements and behavior dramatically influence the behaviors of one another.

Most teams don't operate on the basis of blatant pressure tactics, of course, but team performance can be markedly enhanced by having team members play certain roles that facilitate task accomplishment and group cohesion.

Two main types of roles exist that enhance team performance: **task-facilitating roles** and **relationship-building roles**. It is difficult for team members to emphasize both types of roles equally, and most people tend to contribute in one area more than the other. That is, some team members tend to be more task-focused whereas others tend to be more relationship-focused. Task-facilitating roles are those that help the team accomplish its outcomes or objectives. Table 9.5 identifies the most common task-facilitating roles.

❑ *Direction giving.* Identifying ways to proceed or alternatives to pursue and clarifying goals and objectives.
❑ *Information seeking.* Asking questions; analyzing knowledge gaps; requesting opinions, beliefs, and perspectives.
❑ *Information giving.* Providing data, offering facts and judgments, and highlighting conclusions.
❑ *Elaborating.* Building on the ideas expressed by others; providing examples and illustrations.
❑ *Urging.* Imploring team members to stay on task and to achieve team goals.
❑ *Monitoring.* Checking on progress, developing measures of success, and helping to maintain accountability for results.
❑ *Process analyzing.* Analyzing processes and procedures used by the team in order to improve efficiency and timeliness.
❑ *Reality testing.* Exploring whether ideas presented are practical or workable; grounding comments in reality.

Table 9.5	Task-Facilitating Roles
Role	**Examples**
Direction giving	"This is the way we were instructed to approach our task."
	"Everyone write down your ideas, and then share them."
Information seeking	"What did you mean by that?"
	"Does anyone else have more information about this?"
Information giving	"Here are some relevant data."
	"I want to share some information that may be helpful."
Elaborating	"Building on your idea, here is an additional alternative."
	"An example of what you just said is…"
Urging	"We have only 10 minutes left, so we need to move more quickly."
	"We can't quit now. We're close to finalizing our proposal."
Monitoring	"You maintain accountability for the first recommendation, and I'll handle the second."
	"Here are some criteria we can use to judge our success."
Process analyzing	"It seems as if the energy level in the team is beginning to decline."
	"I've noticed that the women are participating less than the men in our team."
Reality testing	"Let's see if this is really practical."
	"Do you think this is workable given our resources?"
Enforcing	"We're beginning to wander in our comments; let's stay on task."
	"Since we agreed not to interrupt one another, I suggest we stick to our pact."
Summarizing	"It seems to me that these are the conclusions we have reached."
	"In summary, you have made three points…"

- *Enforcing.* Helping to reinforce team rules, reinforcing standards, and maintaining agreed-upon procedures.
- *Summarizing.* Combining ideas and summing up points made in the team; helping members understand the conclusions that have been reached.

When you perform task-facilitating roles, you help the team work more efficiently and effectively in achieving its objectives. Without having at least one team member displaying task-facilitating behaviors, teams tend to take longer to achieve their objectives and have difficulty staying focused. Sometimes keeping the team "on task" is the most important thing you can do. These roles are especially important when:

- Progress toward goal accomplishment is slow.
- The team is being deflected from its task.
- Time pressures exist.
- The assignment is complex or ambiguous and it is not clear how to proceed.
- No one else is helping the team move toward task accomplishment.

You don't have to be a taskmaster to be an effective facilitator of outcomes. In fact, just recognizing that the team is in need of task facilitation is a big part of being an effective team member. In most effective teams, you will find several members performing these task-facilitation roles.

An overwhelming amount of evidence exists suggesting that in addition to accomplishing tasks, high-performing teams pay attention to interpersonal issues. These teams are cohesive, interdependent, and have a positive affect among team members (Aguilar, 2016; Dutton, 2003; Kolb, 2014). Relationship-building roles are those that emphasize the interpersonal aspects of the team. These roles help team members feel good about one another, enjoy the team's work, and maintain a tension-free climate. Table 9.6 identifies the most common relationship-building roles:

- *Supporting.* Praising the ideas of others, showing friendliness, and pointing out others' contributions.
- *Harmonizing.* Mediating differences between others and finding a common ground in disputes and conflicting points of view.
- *Relieving tension.* Using jokes and humor to reduce tension and put others at ease.
- *Confronting.* Challenging unproductive or disruptive behaviors; helping to ensure proper behavior in the team.

Table 9.6	Relationship-Building Roles
Role	**Examples**
Supporting	"Your ideas are terrific!"
	"I really appreciate your honesty and openness. It's refreshing."
Harmonizing	"I hear the two of you saying essentially the same thing."
	"The disagreements being expressed don't seem to be all that crucial."
Relieving tension	"Hey folks, let's lighten up!"
	"This reminds me of the new conference table we bought. It sleeps 12."
Confronting	"How does your comment address the topic we are discussing?"
	"Your negative comments are really diminishing the positive energy in the group."
Energizing	"Your insights are really helpful!"
	"This team is the most enjoyable group I've been in for a long time."
Developing	"How can I help you?"
	"May I give you some assistance with that?"
Consensus building	"It seems like we're all saying pretty much the same thing."
	"Can we all at least agree on point number 1, even if we disagree on the rest?"
Empathizing	"I know how you feel."
	"This must be a very sensitive topic for you given your personal experience."

- *Energizing.* Motivating others toward greater effort; exuding enthusiasm.
- *Developing.* Helping others learn, grow, and achieve; orienting and coaching members of the team.
- *Consensus building.* Helping build solidarity among team members, encouraging agreement, and helping interactions to be smooth.
- *Empathizing.* Reflecting group feelings and expressing empathy and support for team members.

All of us have been on a team or in a class when a fellow participant is funny, actively engaging with others, or especially supportive of others. The chemistry of the group just seems to improve under such conditions. Work becomes easier and more enjoyable for team members. A certain amount of positive energy exists. People tend to take more responsibility, collaborate more readily, and try harder to find consensus. Relationship-building roles, in other words, help team members work more effectively together.

Teams that don't have both task facilitators and relationship builders struggle to perform effectively. Some members must ensure that the team accomplishes its tasks, and some must ensure that members remain bonded together interpersonally. These are usually not the same individuals, and at certain points in time, different roles may become more dominant than others. The key is to have a balance between task-oriented roles and relationship-building roles displayed in the team. The downfall of many teams is that they become unidimensional—for example, they emphasize task accomplishment exclusively, or they put too much emphasis on relationships.

UNPRODUCTIVE ROLES

Of course, each role can also have a downside if performed ineffectively or in inappropriate circumstances. For example, the *elaborating* role may be disruptive if the team is trying to reach a quick decision; the *tension relieving* role may be annoying if the team is trying to address a serious problem; the *enforcing* role may create resistance when the team is already experiencing high levels of pressure; the *consensus-building* role may mask real differences of opinion and tension among team members.

However, it is even more likely that team members will display other unproductive roles rather than inappropriately play task or relationship roles. Unproductive roles inhibit the team or its members from

achieving what they could have achieved, and they destroy morale and cohesion. They are called **blocking roles**. We point out a few of them here because, as you analyze the teams to which you belong, you may recognize these roles being performed and be able to confront them. Among the common blocking roles are:

- *Dominating.* Excessive talking, interrupting, or cutting others off.
- *Overanalyzing.* Splitting hairs and examining every detail excessively.
- *Stalling.* Not allowing the group to reach a decision or finalize a task by sidetracking the discussion, being unwilling to agree, repeating old arguments, and wasting time.
- *Remaining passive.* Not being willing to engage in the team's task. Staying on the fringe or refusing to interact with other team members; expecting others to do the team's work.
- *Overgeneralizing.* Blowing something out of proportion and drawing unfounded conclusions.
- *Faultfinding.* Being unwilling to see the merits of others' ideas or criticizing others excessively.
- *Premature decision-making.* Making decisions before goals are stated, information is shared, alternatives are discussed, or problems are defined.
- *Presenting opinions as facts.* Failing to examine the legitimacy of proposals and labeling personal opinions as truth.
- *Rejecting.* Rejecting ideas based on the person who stated them rather than on the ideas' merits.
- *Pulling rank.* Using status, expertise, or title to get ideas accepted rather than discussing and examining their value.
- *Resisting.* Blocking all attempts to change, improve, or make progress; being disagreeable and negative about suggestions from other team members.
- *Deflecting.* Not staying focused on the topic of the team's discussion; changing the subject of discussion or making comments that deflect attention away from the main points.

Each of these blocking roles has the potential to inhibit a team from efficiently and effectively accomplishing its task by crushing morale, destroying consensus, creating conflict, hampering progress, exhausting or frustrating members, and leading to ill-informed decisions. When you recognize that blocking roles are displayed, you will want to confront this unproductive behavior honestly and openly, and use supportive communication to suggest more helpful roles (see Chapter 4). When you are familiar with productive task facilitating and relationship-building roles, you will be able to assist others in making the team more effective.

PROVIDING FEEDBACK

When you provide feedback to others—whether corrective feedback in response to unproductive roles or mere suggestions for team improvement—you will want to keep in mind several well-proven rules of thumb. When giving feedback to anyone—team members, family members, colleagues, or even strangers—you should use the following principles of effective feedback summarized in Table 9.7 (Cameron, 2013; Wiggins, 2013).

- ❑ *Focus feedback on behavior rather than personal attributes.* Individuals can control and change their behavior. They cannot change their personalities or physical characteristics. For example, "Your comments do not address the topic" is more effective than "You are completely naïve."
- ❑ *Focus feedback on observations rather than inferences and on descriptions rather than judgments.* Facts and objective evidence are more trustworthy and acceptable than opinions and conjectures. For example, "The data don't support your point" is more effective than "You just don't get it, do you?"
- ❑ *Focus feedback on behavior related to a specific situation, preferably to the "here and now," rather than on abstract or past behavior.* It will merely frustrate people if they cannot pinpoint a specific incident or behavior to which you are referring. Similarly, people cannot change something that has already happened. For example, "You have yet to agree with any of the proposals" is more effective than "You have always been a problem in this team."

- ❑ *Focus feedback on sharing ideas and information rather than giving advice.* Unless requested, avoid giving direct instructions and demands. Instead, help recipients identify changes and improvements themselves. For example, "How do you suggest we break this logjam and move forward?" is more effective than "This is what we must do now."
- ❑ *Focus feedback on the amount of information that the recipient can use, rather than on the amount you might like to give.* Information overload causes people to stop listening. Not enough information leads to frustration and misunderstanding. For example, "You seem to have reached a conclusion before all the facts have been presented" is more effective than "Here is some evidence you should consider, and here is more evidence, and here is more evidence, and here is even more evidence."
- ❑ *Focus feedback on the value it may provide to the receiver, not on the emotional release it provides for you.* Feedback should be for the good of the recipient, not merely for you to let off steam. For example, "I must say that your excessive talking is very troublesome to me and not very helpful to our discussion" is more effective than "You are being a jerk, and you are making me mad."
- ❑ *Focus feedback on time and place so that personal data can be shared at appropriate times.* The more specific the feedback is, or the more it can be anchored in a specific context, the more helpful it can be. For example, "During a break, I would like to chat with you about something" is more effective than "You think your title gives you the right to force the rest of us to agree with you, but it's just making us resistant."

Table 9.7	Rules for Effective Team Feedback	
Effective Feedback	**Ineffective Feedback**
Focus on behaviors	Focus on the person
Focus on observations	Focus on inferences or opinions
Focus on descriptions	Focus on evaluations
Focus on a specific situation or incident	Focus on abstract or general situations
Focus on the present	Focus on the past
Focus on sharing ideas and information	Focus on giving advice
Give feedback that is valuable to the receiver	Give feedback that provides an emotional release
Give feedback at an appropriate time and place	Give feedback when it is convenient for you

INTERNATIONAL CAVEATS

These team member skills may require some modification in different international settings or with teams composed of international members (Trompenaars & Hampden-Turner, 2011). Whereas the team member skills discussed above have been found to be effective in a global context, it is naïve to expect that everyone will react the same way to team member roles.

For example, in cultures that emphasize *affectivity* (e.g., France, Iran, Italy, Mexico, and Spain), personal confrontations and emotional displays are more acceptable than in cultures that are more *neutral* (e.g., China, Japan, Korea, and Singapore), where personal references are more offensive. Humor and displaying enthusiastic behavior is also more acceptable in affective cultures than neutral cultures. Similarly, status differences are likely to play a more dominant role in *ascription*-oriented cultures (e.g., Czech Republic, Egypt, Korea, and Spain) than in *achievement*-oriented cultures (e.g., Australia, Canada, Norway, United Kingdom, and United States), in which knowledge and skills tend to be more important. Appealing to data and facts in Australia, Canada, Norway, the United Kingdom and the United States will carry more weight than in the Czech Republic, Egypt, Korea, and Spain.

Some misunderstanding may also arise in cultures emphasizing different *time frames*. Whereas some cultures emphasize just-in-time, short-term time frames (e.g., United States), others emphasize long-term future time frames (e.g., Japan). The story is told of the Japanese proposal to purchase Yosemite National Park in California. The first thing the Japanese submitted was a 250-year business plan. The reaction of the California authorities was, "Wow, that's 1,000 quarterly reports." The urgency to move a team forward toward task accomplishment, in other words, may be seen differently by different cultural groups. Some cultures (e.g., Japan) are more comfortable spending substantial amounts of time on relationship-building activities before moving toward task accomplishment.

Summary

All of us are members of multiple teams—at work, at home, at school, and in the community. Teams are increasingly prevalent in the workplace and in the classroom because they have been shown to be powerful tools to improve the performance of individuals and organizations. Effective teams almost always outperform even the most knowledgeable and skillful individuals. Consequently, it is important to become proficient in leading and participating in teams.

In this chapter, we reviewed three types of team skills: diagnosing and facilitating team development, leading a team, and being an effective team member. Figure 9.4 illustrates the relationship of these three key skills to high-performing team performance. These three skills are ones that you have no doubt engaged in before, but to be a skillful manager, you will need to hone your ability to perform each of these skill activities competently.

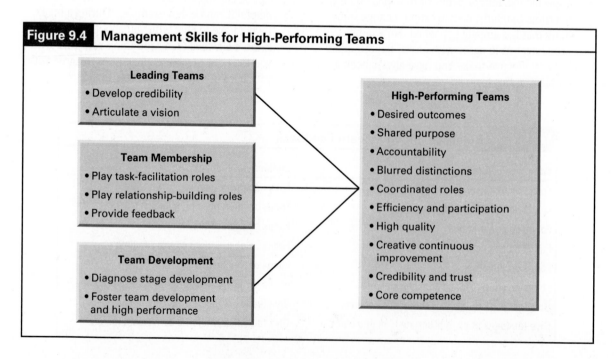

Figure 9.4 | **Management Skills for High-Performing Teams**

Leading Teams
- Develop credibility
- Articulate a vision

Team Membership
- Play task-facilitation roles
- Play relationship-building roles
- Provide feedback

Team Development
- Diagnose stage development
- Foster team development and high performance

High-Performing Teams
- Desired outcomes
- Shared purpose
- Accountability
- Blurred distinctions
- Coordinated roles
- Efficiency and participation
- High quality
- Creative continuous improvement
- Credibility and trust
- Core competence

Behavioral Guidelines

A. Learn to diagnose the stage in which your team is operating in order to facilitate team development and to perform your role appropriately. Know the key characteristics of the forming, norming, storming, and performing stages of development.

B. Provide structure and clarity in the forming stage, support and encouragement in the norming stage, and independence and exploration in the storming stage, and foster innovation and positive deviance in the performing stage.

C. When leading a team, first develop credibility as a prerequisite to having team members follow you.

D. Based on your established credibility, establish two types of goals for and with your team: SMART goals and Everest goals.

E. As a team member, facilitate task performance in your team by encouraging the performance of different roles listed in Table 9.5.

F. As a team member, facilitate the development of good relationships in your team by encouraging the performance of different roles listed in Table 9.6.

G. When encountering team members who block the team's performance with disruptive behaviors, confront the behavior directly and/or isolate the disruptive member.

H. Provide effective feedback to unhelpful team members that have characteristics listed in Table 9.7.

SKILL **ANALYSIS**

ANALYSIS

CASES INVOLVING BUILDING EFFECTIVE TEAMS

Losing to a Weaker Foe

What began as a heavily conventional military campaign to unseat the regime of Saddam Hussein had become a bitter, unconventional struggle against frustrated Sunnis who increasingly coalesced around a charismatic Jordanian who had taken the name Abu Musab al Zarqawi....The Joint Special Operations Task Force, although lavishly resourced and exquisitely trained, found ourselves losing to an enemy that, by traditional calculus, we should have dominated. Over time we began to realize that more than our foe, we were actually struggling to cope with an environment that was fundamentally different from anything we'd planned or trained for. The speed and interdependence of events had produced new dynamics that threatened to overwhelm the time-honored processes and culture we'd built. (p. 2)

Since its inception, the Task Force has conducted a regular cycle of training exercises...to refine the force's ability to execute missions. Relentlessly, quarter after quarter, year after year, intricate solutions to seemingly impossible situations have been developed, planned, rehearsed, and practiced around the world. (p. 117)

We could not claim we were mismatched against a world-class team. Honestly assessed, Al Qaeda was not a collection of supermen forged into a devilishly ingeniously organization by brilliant masterminds. They were tough, flexible, and resilient, but more often than not they were poorly trained and under-resourced....If we were the best of the best, why were we unable to defeat an under-resourced insurgency? Why were we losing? (p. 4, 19)

These factors are not unique to Iraq, or to warfare. They are affecting almost all of us in our lives and organizations every day. (p. 19)

When I joined the Ranger Regiment as a young captain, the standard operating procedures (SOPs) I followed were almost laughably detailed. My rucksack had to be packed with exactly the same equipment as every other Ranger's, and that equipment had to be in exactly the same pocket of the ruck. A folded entrenching tool was clipped to the left side and further held with parachute cord tied with prescribed knots. Failure to follow the SOPs brought immediate correction, and sometimes the punishment of a Saturday twelve-mile foot march—carrying the now correctly configured equipment. Such overweening rigor may seem ridiculous...but most of these regulations developed for a reason. Under fire and often in the dark, Rangers must be able to locate water, gauze, and ammunition in seconds. A correctly packed bag can mean the difference between life and death. (p. 35)

Basic SEAL training has earned a reputation as one of the toughest trials in the military. Of the 160-some students in each entering class, around 90 will drop out before the course ends, most in the first few weeks.... The formation of SEAL teams is less about preparing people to follow precise orders than it is to about developing trust and the ability to adapt within a small group. The purpose is not to produce supersoldiers. It is to build superteams. The first step of this is constructing a strong lattice of trusting relationships. (p. 95, 97)

When we first established our Task Force headquarters at Balad, we hung maps on almost every wall....But maps in Balad could not depict a battlefield in which the enemy could be uploading a video to an audience of millions from any house in any neighborhood, or driving a bomb around in any car on any street. In place of maps, whiteboards began to appear in our headquarters. Soon they were everywhere. Standing around them, markers in hand, we thought out loud, diagramming what we knew, what we suspected, and what we did not know. (p. 24, 25)

Every time we thought we had landed a debilitating blow to the organization as a whole, removing a ranking leader whose loss should have derailed them, they bounced back....From our vantage point, Al Qaeda should have devolved into an internal anarchy. But it didn't. It continued to function as persistently and implacably as ever, demonstrating a coherence of purpose and strategy. (p. 26)

To beat Al Qaeda, we would have to change into a type of force that the United States had never fielded. There was no manual for this transformation, and we had to conduct it in the middle of a war....Just as Al Qaeda had watched and learned from us at the start of the war, we would have to swallow our pride and learn from them. The messy diagrams on our whiteboards were not glitches—they were glimpses into the future organization of adaptable teams. (p. 84)

Our entire network—our teams across Iraq, intelligence agencies back in the United States and in the United Kingdom, headquarters of partner units across the region, and more than seventy liaison teams that the Task Force had positioned in headquarters, offices, and other critical locations—joined the effort. Across the network, teams coordinated the questions asked, shared the answers received, proffered suggestions, and exchanged insights. (p. 238)

The Task Force still had ranks and each member was still assigned a particular team and sub-sub-command, but we all understood that we were now part of a network....The structure that had, years earlier, taunted us from our whiteboards as we failed to prevent the murder of men, women, and children in attacks...had been repurposed. (p. 251)

A few years earlier, detainees would smugly dismiss our limited understanding of their organization. Now, they marveled at our intel, asking interrogators, "How are you doing this? How could you know that?" The answer was not some secret treasure trove of Al Qaeda data we stumbled across or a technological breakthrough in surveillance; it was the very edge that Al Qaeda had once held over us: a revolution in the mundane art of management. (p. 242)

SOURCE: Excerpts from General Stanley McChrystal's Team of Teams.
New York, NY: Penguin, 2015.

Discussion Questions

9.1. What stages of team development do you see unfold under the leadership of General McChrystal? What are the attributes you detect of each stage?

9.2. What was lacking at the outset of McChrystal's arrival in Iraq in the Joint Special Operations Task Force? Why wasn't it a high-performing team?

9.3. What role do purpose, vision, trust, and Everest goals play in developing a high-performing team?

9.4. What were the keys to the dramatic success of the Joint Special Operations Task Force?

9.5. If you were hired as a consultant to business teams based on what you learned from McChrystal, what two or three key pieces of advice would you give?

The Cash Register Incident

Read the following scenario by yourself. Then complete a three-step exercise: the first two steps by yourself, and the third step with a team. A time limit is associated with each step.

A store owner had just turned off the lights in the store when a man appeared and demanded money. The owner opened a cash register. The contents of the cash register were scooped up, and the man sped away. A member of the police force was notified promptly.

Step 1: After reading these instructions, close your book. Without looking at the scenario, rewrite it as accurately as you can. Describe the incident as best you can using your own words.

Step 2: Assume you observed the incident described in the paragraph above. Later, a reporter asks you questions about what you observed in order to write an article for the local newspaper. Answer the questions from the reporter by yourself. Do not talk with anyone else about your answers. Put a Y, N, or DK in the response column. Since reporters are always pressed for time, take no more than two minutes to complete step 2.

	Answer
Y	Yes, or true
N	No, or false
DK	Don't know, or there is no way to tell

Step 3: The reporter wants to interview your entire team together. As a team, discuss the answers to each question and reach a consensus decision—that is, one with which everyone on the team agrees. Do not vote or compromise just to finish the task. The reporter wants to know what you all agree on. Complete your team discussion in 10 minutes.

Statements About the Incident

"As a reporter, I am interested in what happened in this incident. Can you tell me what occurred? I'd like you to address the following questions."

Statement

Alone	Team	
_____	_____	1. Did a man appear after the owner turned off his store lights?
_____	_____	2. Was the robber a man?
_____	_____	3. Is it true that the man did not demand money?
_____	_____	4. The man who opened the cash register was the owner, right?
_____	_____	5. Did the store owner scoop up the contents of the cash register?
_____	_____	6. OK, so someone opened the cash register, right?
_____	_____	7. Let me get this straight...after the man who demanded the money scooped up the contents of the cash register, he ran away?
_____	_____	8. The contents of the cash register contained money, but you don't know how much?
_____	_____	9. Did the robber demand money of the owner?
_____	_____	10. OK, by way of summary, the incident concerns a series of events in which only three persons are involved: the owner of the store, a man who demanded money, and a member of the police force?
_____	_____	11. Let me be sure I understand. Is it true that the following events occurred: Someone demanded money, the cash register was opened, its contents were scooped up, and a man dashed out of the store?

When you have finished your team decision-making and mock interview with the reporter, the instructor will provide correct answers. Calculate how many answers you got right as an individual, and then calculate how many right answers your team achieved. Also go back and compare your own description of the incident with the actual wording of the scenario. How did you do? How accurate were you in your description?

Discussion Questions

9.5. How many individuals did better than the team as a whole? (In general, more than 80 percent of people do worse than the team.)

9.6. What changes would be needed in order for your team score to be even better?

9.7. How do you explain the superior performance of most teams over even the best individuals?

9.8. Under what conditions would individuals do better than teams in making decisions?

EXERCISES IN BUILDING EFFECTIVE TEAMS

Leadership Roles in Teams

Assume you have been appointed as the leader of a team of colleagues. In each of the scenarios below, identify the major issues you need to address and the key actions you should take to ensure the success of the team. *What is your role as a leader?*

9.9. The team has just come together for the first time, and this is its first meeting.

9.10. You join a team that has been together for several meetings and has, unfortunately, had a history of being unproductive, goofing off, and partying with one another a bit too much.

9.11. Your team is experiencing a lot of conflict among members. Strongly held points of view exist that seem not to be compatible. Factions have begun to arise in the team.

9.12. Your team is well oiled and highly functioning, and you want to make sure that this high level of performance not only continues but improves.

Team Diagnosis and Team Development Exercise

In order to help you develop the ability to diagnose team stage development, consider a team in which you are now a member. If you belong to a team as part of this class, select that one. You may also select a team at your place of employment, in your church or community, or a team in another class in school. Complete the following three-step exercise:

Step 1: Use the following questions to help you determine the stage of development in which your team is operating. Create a score for your team for each stage of development. Identify the stage in which the team seems to operate the most.

Step 2: Identify the actions or interventions that would lead your team to the next stage of development. Specify what dynamics need to change, what team members need to do, and/or how the team leader could foster more-advanced team development.

Step 3: Share your scores and your suggestions with others in class in a small-group setting, and add at least one good idea from someone else's diagnosis to your own design.

Use the following scale in your rating of your team right now.

Rating Scale

1. Not typical at all of my team
2. Not very typical of my team
3. Somewhat typical of my team
4. Very typical of my team

Stage 1

_____ 1. Not everyone is clear about the objectives and goals of the team.

_____ 2. Not everyone is personally acquainted with everyone else in the team.

_____ 3. Only a few team members actively participate.

_____ 4. Interactions among team members are very safe or somewhat superficial.

_____ 5. Trust among all team members has not yet been established.

_____ 6. Many team members seem to need direction from the leader in order to participate.

Stage 2

_____ 7. All team members know and agree with the objectives and goals of the team.

_____ 8. Team members all know one another.

_____ 9. Team members are very cooperative and actively participate in the activities of the team.

_____ 10. Interactions among team members are friendly, personal, and nonsuperficial.

_____ 11. A comfortable level of trust has been established among team members.

_____ 12. A strong unity exists in the team, and team members feel very much a part of a special group.

Stage 3

_____ 13. Disagreements and differing points of view are openly expressed by team members.

_____ 14. Competition exists among some team members.

_____ 15. Some team members do not follow the rules or the team norms.

_____ 16. Subgroups or coalitions exist within the team.

_____ 17. Some issues create major disagreements when discussed by the team, with some members on one side and some on the other side.

_____ 18. The authority or competence of the team leader is being questioned or challenged.

Stage 4

_____ 19. Team members are committed to the team and actively cooperate to improve the team's performance.

_____ 20. Team members feel free to try out new ideas, experiment, share something crazy, or do novel things.

_____ 21. A high level of energy is displayed by team members, and expectations for performance are very high.

_____ 22. Team members do not always agree, but a high level of trust exists and each person is given respect, so disagreements are resolved productively.

_____ 23. Team members are committed to helping one another succeed and improve, so self-aggrandizement is at a minimum.

_____ 24. The team can make fast decisions without sacrificing quality.

Scoring

Add up the scores for the items in each stage of team development. Generally, one stage clearly stands out as having the highest scores. Team stages develop sequentially, so the stage in which scores are highest is usually the dominant stage of development. Based on these scores, identify ways to move the team to the next level.

Total of Stage 1 items _____

Total of Stage 2 items _____

Total of Stage 3 items _____

Total of Stage 4 items _____

Winning the War for Talent

In this exercise, you will form teams of six members. Your team will have an overall objective to achieve, and each team member will have individual objectives. The exercise is accomplished in seven steps. Steps 1 through 6 should take a total of 50 minutes to complete.

Step 1: In your team, read the scenario on the next page about the problem of attracting and retaining talented employees in twenty-first-century organizations. Your team objective is to generate two innovative but workable ideas for how to retain good teachers in the public school system. You will have 15 minutes to develop the ideas.

Step 2: When each team has completed the assignment, each is given two minutes to present the two ideas. These ideas will be evaluated by the class, and a winning team will be selected based on the following criteria:

- ❏ The ideas are workable and affordable.
- ❏ The ideas are interesting, innovative, and unusual.
- ❏ The ideas have a good chance of making a difference if they are implemented.

Step 3: In addition to the team assignment, each team member is assigned to play three team member roles during the discussion. A role assignment schedule is listed on the next page. Team members may select the roles they wish to play, or an instructor can assign the roles. One purpose of this individual assignment is to give team members practice in playing either task-facilitation roles or relationship-building roles in a team setting, so you should take these assignments seriously. Remember, however, that you have only 15 minutes. When your team has completed its task, each team member will rate the effectiveness of every other team member in how well they played their roles and how much they helped the team accomplish its task. You will have five minutes to complete the ratings.

TEAM MEMBER NAME	ROLES	PERFORMANCE RATING: 1 (LOW)–10 (HIGH) PERFORMANCE FEEDBACK
1	Direction giving Urging Enforcing	
2	Information seeking Information giving Elaborating	
3	Monitoring Reality testing Summarizing	
4	Process analyzing Supporting Confronting	
5	Harmonizing Tension relieving Energizing	
6	Developing Consensus building Empathizing	

Step 4: Each team member uses the form above to rate the performance of, and provide feedback to, every other member of the team. In completing the form, make sure you focus on how well each person performed his or her assigned roles. Identify at least one thing you noticed about the performance of each team member so that you can provide personal feedback to each one. Remember that the overall purpose of this exercise is to give you practice in playing effective roles in teams and providing feedback to team members. You are given five minutes for this rating task.

Step 5: When each team has completed its task, one representative from each team is selected to form a judging team. This judging team evaluates the quality of the ideas produced by each team and announces a winning team. (Other class members should observe and rate the performance of this judging team and its members as they make their selection.) The judging team will be given 10 minutes to select the winning team.

Step 6: Teams meet again so that personal feedback can be given. Each team member takes a total of three minutes to give feedback to the other members of his or her team based on the evaluation form above. A total of 20 minutes will be required to provide this feedback.

Step 7: Hold a class discussion about what you observed regarding team members' roles. Especially, reflect on your own experience trying to play those roles and what seemed to be most effective in facilitating task accomplishment and in building team cohesion.

The Problem Scenario

Almost to a person, the chief concern expressed by senior executives in most "old economy" firms is how to attract and retain managerial talent. With the economy expected to grow at almost three times the growth of the job market, finding competent employees will be a continuing challenge for the next several years. The allure of dot.com firms, high-growth companies, and high-risk–high-return ventures has created an incredibly difficult environment for organizations whose chief competitive advantage is intellectual capital and human talent. Headhunters, venture capitalists, and even firms' customers are aggressively trying to lure away management talent any way they can. A recent survey of Wall Street investment bankers revealed that more than half had been approached by an Internet company. Armed with venture capital dollars and business plans promising swift public offerings, it is easy to see why many are succeeding in attracting managerial talent away from traditional companies. Compensation packages in the seven figures are not unusual.

In this highly competitive environment in which intellectual capital is at a premium, consider the difficulty faced by nonprofit organizations, local or state governments, arts organizations, or educational institutions whose budgets are constrained far below the high-priced world of the "new economy." How will they compete for talent when they cannot come close to the salaries of firms whose market capitalization exceeds the GDP of many African countries?

In particular, the U.S. public education system has suffered tremendously in this environment. The United States spends more per child on education than any country other than Norway, Sweden, and Austria, and the costs of education are increasing far faster than the consumer price index. However, it is well known that almost a fifth of public school students drop out before high school graduation, and of those who remain, the percent passing proficiency exams is woefully low—in some school districts, less than 10 percent. The average tenure of public school teachers is less than seven years, and that number is decreasing as these knowledge workers can find positions elsewhere at double and triple their school salaries. Add to that the difficulties escalating in the classroom resulting from students in single-parent homes, marginal economic circumstances, threats of violence, and behavioral disruptions, and it is clear why teaching is a difficult profession, even if monetary compensation were higher.

Numerous alternatives have been proposed, but few have addressed the problem of teacher attraction and retention. Your task as a team is to identify two answers to the question: How can we attract and retain teachers in the public schools of the United States? You may want to consider what is being done in the school systems in other countries or in highly effective school systems in America.

Team Performance Exercise

The purpose of this exercise is to help you practice the dynamics of team formation, development, and effective performance. The most important part of the exercise is practicing effective team leadership and team membership and accurately diagnosing the stages of team development so you can behave appropriately.

Your instructor will form you into teams of five members each. Your task as a team is to create a five-pointed star in the form that you drew when you were a child (see Figure 9.5). You will do this with a piece of rope or string that has been tied at the ends to form a circle. Here is how this exercise will occur:

1. You will find a 50-foot piece of rope or string on the floor. As a team, you will surround the rope or string and each member will take hold of it with both hands. Once you have taken hold of the rope or string, you cannot let go until the exercise has been completed.

Figure 9.5 | A Five-Pointed Star

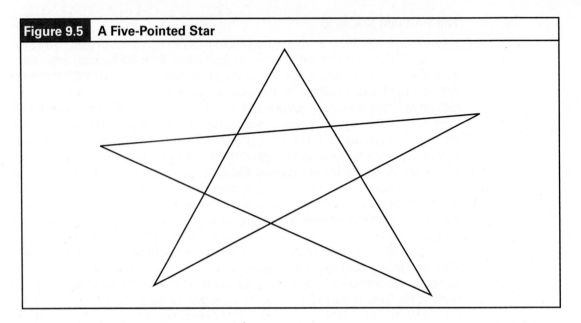

2. You will be given five minutes to plan how you are going to create the star, with all the appropriate crisscrosses. You may not move at all during this five-minute planning period. You must stay exactly where you are. Practicing is not permitted.

3. Once you have finished the five-minute planning session, you may not talk out loud again. The task must be completed in complete silence. You may not communicate verbally with any other member of your team. Only nonverbal communication is permitted. Remember, once you have taken hold of the rope or string, you cannot let go with either hand.

4. When the instructor gives the signal, you will start moving in order to create your five-pointed star. When you have finished, you will place the rope or string down on the floor in exactly the position in which you are standing. You may not rearrange or move the rope or string on the floor. It should accurately represent your team members' positions.

5. The quality of your results will be evaluated by the instructor and the winning team announced.

When you have finished the task, discuss the following questions:

9.13. As a team, what was especially effective and what was especially ineffective in planning for task accomplishment in advance?

9.14. What hints about initial stages of team development were utilized?

9.15. What happened to your team dynamics over the duration of the activity? Did they change from one stage to another? Did you end up as a high-performing team?

9.16. What team leadership and membership roles did each of your team members play? Which were the most effective?

9.17. What were the differences between teams that accomplished the task the quickest and with the highest quality compared to the others?

9.18. How did you make up for the inability to communicate as a team during the task?

9.19. What do you wish you could do differently to be more efficient and more effective if you were to do another task together?

ACTIVITIES FOR BUILDING EFFECTIVE TEAMS

Suggested Assignments

9.20. Teach someone else how to determine which stage of development a team is in and what behaviors are most effective in each separate stage.

9.21. Analyze the characteristics of a team in which you are a member. Determine in what ways its functioning could be improved. Based on the attributes of high-performance teams, identify what could be done to improve its performance.

9.22. Conduct a role analysis of a real team meeting in which members are trying to make a decision, solve a problem, or examine an issue. Who performed what roles? Which team members were most helpful? Which team members were least helpful? Provide feedback to the team on what roles you saw being played, what roles were missing, and what improvements could have made the team more effective.

9.23. Write out a formal vision statement for a team you are leading. Make certain that the vision possesses the attributes of effective, energizing vision statements discussed in the chapter. Identify specifically what you can do to get team members to commit to that vision.

9.24. Do an in-depth analysis of an effective team leader you know. Focus specifically on the ways in which he or she has developed credibility and continues to influence team members. Identify what followers say about credibility, not just the leader.

9.25. Teach someone, or coach someone, on how to become an effective leader of a team and how to become an effective team member. Demonstrate or exemplify the skills you teach that person.

Application Plan and Evaluation

The intent of this exercise is to help you apply this cluster of skills in a real-life, out-of-class setting. Now that you have become familiar with the behavioral guidelines that form the basis of effective skill performance, you will improve most by trying out those guidelines in an everyday context. Unlike a classroom activity, in which feedback is immediate and others can assist you with their evaluations, this skill application activity is one you must accomplish and evaluate on your own. There are two parts to this activity. Part 1 helps prepare you to apply the skill, and Part 2 helps you evaluate and improve on your experience. Be sure to write down answers to each item. Don't short-circuit the process by skipping steps.

Part 1: Planning

9.26. Write down the two or three aspects of this skill that are most important to you. These may be areas of weakness, areas you most want to improve, or areas that are most salient to a problem you face right now. Identify the specific aspects of this skill that you want to apply.

9.27. Now identify the setting or the situation in which you will apply this skill. Establish a plan for performance by actually writing down a description of the situation. Who else will be involved? When will you do it? Where will it be done?

     Circumstances:
     Who else?
     When?
     Where?

9.28. Identify the specific behaviors in which you will engage to apply this skill. Operationalize your skill performance.

9.29. What are the indicators of successful performance? How will you know you have been effective? What will indicate you have performed competently?

Part 2: Evaluation

9.30. After you have completed your implementation, record the results. What happened? How successful were you? What was the effect on others?

9.31. How can you improve? What modifications can you make next time? What will you do differently in a similar situation in the future?

9.32. Looking back on your whole skill practice and application experience, what have you learned? What has been surprising? In what ways might this experience help you in the long term?

SCORING KEYS AND COMPARISON DATA

✪ Go to www.pearson.com/mylab/management for scoring keys and comparison data for the following instruments:

    Team Development Behaviors

Diagnosing the Need for Team Building

Comparison Data (N = 10,000 students)

TOTAL SCORE	MEAN	BOTTOM QUARTILE	SECOND QUARTILE	THIRD QUARTILE	TOP QUARTILE
	54.22	38 or below	39–52	53–69	70 or above

Leadership Roles In Teams
(Examples of Correct Answers)

SCENARIO 1:

1. Explain the goals and objectives of the team.
2. Ensure that people get to know one another.
3. Give members a chance to ask questions. Address uncertainties.
4. Establish a relationship between yourself and each team member.
5. Build trust.

SCENARIO 2:

1. Facilitate participation of all team members.
2. Foster team cohesion so that peer pressure toward conformity is strong.
3. Provide honest feedback in a supportive way.
4. Guard against groupthink by establishing subgroups, devil's advocates, or critical evaluators.
5. Create a sense of team identify and ownership.

SCENARIO 3:

1. Make it legitimate for team members to disagree with one another in helpful ways.
2. Ensure respectful, supportive questioning and listening.
3. Work toward interdependence rather than independence so people work collaboratively.
4. Find areas of common agreement.
5. Reinforce the team's goal and purpose.

SCENARIO 4:

1. Encourage entrepreneurship and innovative ideas.
2. Push for positive deviance and extraordinary levels of high performance.
3. Capitalize on the most positive energizing team members.
4. Work to maintain high levels of openness and trust among team members.
5. Articulate and reinforce an Everest goal.

Instructor Guidelines for Discussion Questions: Losing to a Weaker Foe *(for I.M.)*

1. All four stages are illustrated in this abbreviated case study of building a winning team in the Middle East. Very basic instructions and training occurred at the outset (Stage 1). Cohesion and teamwork were drilled into the training of personnel (Stage 2). Lots of different perspectives and points of view were encouraged, and learning from the enemy had to occur (Stage 3). And the Task Force became such a high-performing team that even the detainees could not believe how efficient and effective they had become (Stage 4).
2. At the outset of McChrystal's arrival, the Task Force was operating primarily in stages 1 and 2—relying on standard operating procedures and rules that didn't apply to the current circumstances, and assuming that their rigorous training that created cohesive teams would lead them to victory.

SCORING KEYS AND COMPARISON DATA

BUILDING EFFECTIVE TEAMS AND TEAMWORK CHAPTER 9   **443**

3. Al Qaeda was successful primarily because they were attached to what they deemed as a core purpose, a vision, and an Everest goal. They used vicious and inhumane tactics in pursuit of those goals, but that passion led to their survival. Similarly, McChrystal indicated in his book that "the professionals with whom I served [had] an almost mystical devotion to mission accomplishment." (p. 3) Without this dedication and passion, teams will not survive the setbacks that invariably occur.

4. Success was based on a variety of factors, all of which cannot be enumerated here. Among the important factors were extraordinary training and advanced preparation, coordinated teams, a willingness to be flexible and adaptable, highly effective leaders, and an effective and coordinated use of technology.

5. Students should be encouraged to apply the information presented regarding stages of development, the different leadership challenges in each stage, and goal setting.

SKILL ASSESSMENT

- Leading Positive Change
- Reflected Best-Self Feedback Exercise
- Positive Practices Survey

SKILL LEARNING

- Leading Positive Change
- Ubiquitous and Escalating Change
- The Need for Frameworks
- Tendencies Toward Stability
- A Framework for Leading Positive Change
- Summary
- Behavioral Guidelines

SKILL ANALYSIS

- Corporate Vision Statements
- Jim Mallozzi: Implementing Positive Change in Prudential Real Estate and Relocation

SKILL PRACTICE

- Reflected Best-Self Portrait
- Positive Organizational Diagnosis Exercise
- A Positive Change Agenda

SKILL APPLICATION

- Suggested Assignments
- Application Plan and Evaluation

SCORING KEYS AND COMPARISON DATA

10

Leading Positive Change

LEARNING OBJECTIVES

1. Learn how to create positive deviance in organizations
2. Develop the capability to lead positive change
3. Acquire the ability to mobilize the capabilities of others in achieving positive change

DIAGNOSTIC SURVEYS FOR LEADING POSITIVE CHANGE

MyLab Management Personal Inventory Assessments

PERSONAL
INVENTORY
ASSESSMENT

The assessment instruments in this chapter are briefly described below. The assessments appear either in your text or in MyLab. The assessments marked with ✪ are available only in MyLab. If assigned, go to www.pearson.com/mylab/management to complete these assessments. The assessments without the ✪ appear only in the text.

All assessments should be completed before reading the chapter material.

After completing the first assessment, save your response to your hard drive. When you have finished reading the chapter, re-take the assessment and compare your responses to see what you have learned.

✪ ❑ The *Leading Positive Change Assessment* measures the extent to which you effectively lead the process of change and, especially, the degree to which you have developed skills in leading positive change.

❑ The *Reflected Best-Self Feedback Exercise* provides you with information on your greatest strengths, your behavior when you are at your very best, and the ways in which you make unique contributions.

✪ ❑ The *Positive Practices Survey* identifies the extent to which the organization you are rating possesses the characteristics of the very highest-performing organizations. It shows the degree to which your organization is flourishing and is likely to exceed performance expectations.

LEADING POSITIVE CHANGE

Assessment Section

REFLECTED BEST-SELF FEEDBACK

All of us can recall our own extraordinary moments, those moments when we felt that our best self was brought to light, affirmed by others, and put into practice. These memories are seared into our minds as moments in which we have felt alive, true to our deepest selves, and pursuing our full potential as human beings. Over time, we collect these experiences into a portrait of who we are when we are at our personal best. To help compose a best-self portrait, it is important to draw on the perceptions of significant others who have unique and valuable insights into our strengths and enduring talents. The Reflected Best-Self Feedback Exercise creates an opportunity for us to receive feedback regarding who we are when we are at our best. A detailed explanation of this exercise, including the research that supports its effectiveness in helping people become better leaders, can be found at https://positiveorgs.bus.umich.edu. Look under *DO*, then choose *Tools*.

In this exercise, you will gather information about yourself from other people who know you well. In the Skill Practice section of the chapter, you will be asked to develop a best-self portrait based on this feedback. The first step is to gather the information. Here is how to go about it.

Identify 20 people who know you well. These may be colleagues (former or current), friends (old or new), family members, neighbors, class members, or anyone who has had extended contact with you. Select individuals who will give you an honest opinion. The more diverse the group, the better. Also, realize that due to time constraints, everyone may not be able to respond. You need at least 10 responses to complete this part of the assignment, so ask enough people to ensure at least 10 responses, but try for 20.

Compose your feedback request using the sample email included below and send it to the 20 people you select. Although this request may seem awkward or difficult for you, people have found this assessment to be a profound learning activity, and other people are typically quite willing to participate in this exercise. You may find that this actually strengthens your relationships in many cases.

SOURCE: *Roberts, L. M., Spreitzer, G., Dutton, J., Quinn, R., Heaphy, E., Barker, B. (2005). How to play to your strengths, Harvard Business Review, 83: 75–80*

Sample Email Request for Feedback

I am taking a course that requires me to construct a profile of my unique strengths. I have been asked to contact 20 people who know me well. I would like to invite you to help me with this exercise. I have been assigned to request that each person provide me with three stories of when I added unique value, made a valuable contribution, or displayed my best strengths. What strengths did you see me display when I made a unique contribution?

This will require that you think about your interactions with me and identify times when you saw me add unique value and perform at my best. Please provide examples so I can understand the situation and the characteristics you are describing. I have attached some examples of what these stories could look like. Please use these only as a guide.

Feedback Examples

1. **One of your greatest strengths is:** *The ability to get people to work together and give all they have to a task.*

   For example, I think of the time that: *We were doing the Alpha project. We were getting behind and the stress was building. We started to close down and get very focused on just meeting our deadline. You noticed that we were not doing our best work and stopped the group to rethink our approach. You asked whether we wanted to just satisfy the requirements or whether we wanted to really do good and important work. You reminded us of what we were capable of doing and how each of us could contribute to a better outcome. No one else in that room would have thought to do that. As a result, we did meet the deadline and created a result we all feel proud of.*

2. **One of your greatest strengths is:** *Being happy all the time.*

   For example, I think of the time that: *We had just lost the league championship game, and we were all really down in the dumps. All of us knew we could have played better, and we were really in a funk. You were the one who pumped us up and made us feel better—not in a superficial or silly way, but by expressing genuine pleasure at having a chance to play and being together as friends. I really admire you for being able to see the good in a situation and being such a positive person.*

3. *One of your greatest strengths is:* The capacity to persist in the face of adversity.

For example, I think of the time that: We were past our deadline on a major report. Frank quit and we were left short-handed. Instead of getting discouraged, you became more focused than I have ever seen anyone get. I think you went 48 hours without sleep. I was amazed that you could produce such a quality product under those conditions.

Your feedback to me: Please provide me with three examples of the strengths you observed by completing the following statements.

1. *One of your greatest strengths is:*
   For example, I think of the time that:

2. *One of your greatest strengths is:*
   For example, I think of the time that:

3. *One of your greatest strengths is:*
   For example, I think of the time that:

Please email your responses to me by [insert a date]. Thank you very much for your cooperation. I will be sure to share with you what I learn.

When you have obtained this feedback, you will be guided in developing a Best-Self Portrait in the Skill Practice section of this chapter.

SOURCE: *Adapted from "Reflected best-self exercise: Assignment and instructions for participants." Center for Positive Organizations, Ross School of Business, University of Michigan, Product #01B, 2003.*

SKILL *LEARNING*

The word *leadership* is often used as a catchall term to describe almost any desirable behavior by a manager. "Good leadership" is frequently the explanation given for the success of almost any positive organizational performance—from stock price increases to upward national economic trends to happy employees. Magazine covers trumpet the remarkable achievements of leaders, and the person at the top is almost always credited with being the cause of the success or failure. Coaches are fired when players don't perform, CEOs lose their jobs when customers choose a competitor, and presidents are voted out of office when the economy goes south.

On the other hand, leaders are often given hero status when their organizations succeed (e.g., Jeff Bezos, Warren Buffett, Bill Gates, Steve Jobs). The leader as scapegoat, and hero, is an image that is alive and well in modern society. Rationally speaking, however, most of us recognize that there is much more to organizational success than the leader's behavior, but we also recognize that leadership is one of the most important influences in helping organizations perform well (Cameron, 2012; Cameron & Lavine, 2006; Pfeffer, 2015).

Some writers have differentiated between the concepts of leadership and management (Kotter, 1999; Maxwell & Covey, 2007). *Leadership* has often been described as what individuals do under conditions of change. When organizations are dynamic and undergoing transformation, people exhibit leadership. *Management*, on the other hand, has traditionally been associated with the status quo. Maintaining stability is the job of the manager. Leaders have been said to focus on setting direction, initiating change, and creating something new. Managers have been said to focus on maintaining steadiness, controlling variation, and refining current performance. Leadership has been equated with dynamism, vibrancy, and charisma; management with predictability, equilibrium, and control. Hence, leadership is often defined as "doing the right things," whereas management is often defined as "doing things right."

Recent research is clear, however, that such distinctions between leadership and management, which may have been appropriate in previous decades, are no longer useful (Cameron & Lavine, 2006; Cameron,

2012; Quinn & Quinn, 2015). Managers cannot be successful without being good leaders, and leaders cannot be successful without being good managers. No longer do organizations and individuals have the luxury of holding on to the status quo; worrying about doing things right without also doing the right things; keeping the system stable without also leading change and improvement; maintaining current performance without also creating something new; concentrating on equilibrium and control without also concentrating on vibrancy and charisma. Effective management and leadership are largely inseparable. The skills required to do one are also required for the other (Cameron, et al., 2014).

No organization in a postindustrial, hyperturbulent, twenty-first-century environment will survive without individuals capable of providing both management and leadership. Leading change and managing stability, establishing vision and accomplishing objectives, breaking the rules and monitoring conformance, although paradoxical, are all management skills that are required in order to be successful. Individuals who are effective managers are also effective leaders much of the time. The skills required to be effective as a leader and as a manager are essentially identical.

On the other hand, Quinn (2004) has reminded us that no person is a leader all of the time. Leadership is a *temporary* condition in which certain skills and competencies are displayed.

> *Understanding that leadership is a temporary, dynamic state brings us to a radical redefinition of how we think about, enact, and develop leadership. We come to discover that most of the time, most people, including CEOs, presidents, and prime ministers, are not leaders. We discover that anyone can be a leader. Most of the time, none of us are leaders.*

In this chapter, we focus on the most common activity that demonstrates leadership—leading change. It is while engaging in this task that the temporary state of leadership is most likely to be revealed. That is, despite the heroic image of leaders, every person can develop the skills needed to lead change. Everyone can, and most everyone does, demonstrate leadership at some point. On the other hand, effectively leading change involves a complex and difficult-to-master set of skills, so assistance is required in order to do it successfully. This is because of the difficulties associated with change.

Ubiquitous and Escalating Change

It is not news that we live in a dynamic, turbulent, and even chaotic world. Almost no one would try to predict with any degree of certainty what the world will be like in 10 years. Things change too fast. We know that the technology currently exists, for example, to put the equivalent of a full-size computer in a wristwatch, or inject the equivalent of a laptop computer into the bloodstream. New computers are beginning to be etched on molecules instead of silicon wafers. The half-life of any technology you can name—from complex computers to nuclear devices to software—is less than six months. Anything can be reproduced in less than half a year.

The mapping of the human genome is probably the greatest source for change, for not only can we now change a banana into an agent to inoculate people against malaria, but new organ development and physiological regulation promise to dramatically alter population lifestyles. As of this writing, more than 100 whole animals have been patented. Who can predict the changes that will result? Hence, not only is change ubiquitous and constant, but almost everyone predicts that it will escalate exponentially.

The Need for Frameworks

Frameworks or theories help provide stability and order in the midst of constant change. To illustrate the importance of frameworks, consider a simple experiment conducted by Nobel laureate Herbert A. Simon. Experimental subjects were shown a chessboard as it appeared midgame. Some of these individuals were experienced chess players, some were novices. They were allowed to observe the chessboard for 10 seconds, and then the board was wiped clean. The subjects were asked to replace the pieces on the board exactly as they had appeared before the board was cleared. This experiment was conducted on a computer, so wiping the chessboard clean was simple, and multiple trials could be generated for each person. Each trial showed a different configuration of a chess game midway through.

The question being investigated was: Which group was best at replacing the chess pieces, the novices or the experienced players? After looking at the board for 10 seconds, which individuals would be most accurate in placing each piece in its previous location? An argument could be made for either group.

On the one hand, the minds of novices would not be cluttered by preconceptions. They would look at the board with a fresh view. It is similar to the answer to the question: When is the best time to teach a person a new language, age 3 or age 30? The fact that 3-year-olds can learn a new language more quickly than 30-year-olds suggests that novices might also be better at this task because of their lack of preconceptions. On the other hand, the opposing argument is that experience ought to count for something, and the familiarity of experienced players with the chessboard should allow them to be more successful.

The results of the experiment were dramatic. Novices accurately replaced the pieces less than 5 percent of the time. Experienced players were accurate more than 80 percent of the time. When experienced chess players looked at the board, they saw familiar patterns, or what might be called frameworks. They said things such as, "This looks like the Leningrad defense, except this bishop is out of place and these two pawns are arranged differently." Experienced players identified the patterns quickly, and then they paid attention to the few exceptions on the board. Novices, on the other hand, needed to pay attention to every single piece as if it were an exception, since no pattern (or framework) was available to guide their decisions.

Frameworks serve the same function for managers. They clarify complex or ambiguous situations. Individuals familiar with frameworks are able to manage complex situations effectively because they can respond to fewer exceptions. Individuals without frameworks are left to react to every piece of information as a unique event or an exception. The best managers possess the most, and the most useful, frameworks. When they encounter a new situation, they do not become overwhelmed or stressed because they have frameworks that can help simplify and clarify the unfamiliar.

In this chapter, we provide you with a very useful framework for managing change. However, we are interested in having you not only manage change and learn to cope with the chaotic environment that currently exists, but also to become skillful at leading *positive change*. Leading positive change and managing change are not the same things.

To illustrate the difference between commonplace change and positive change, consider the continuum in Figure 10.1 (Cameron, 2003b). It shows a line depicting normal, healthy performance in the middle, with unhealthy, negative performance on the left and unusually positive performance on the right. Most

Figure 10.1   A Continuum of Negative and Positive Deviance

Individual:	Negative Deviance	Normal	Positive Deviance
Physiological (Medical research)	Illness	Health	Vitality
Psychological (Psychological research)	Illness	Health	Flow

Organizational and Managerial: (Management and organizational research)

	Negative Deviance	Normal	Positive Deviance
Revenues	Unprofitable	Profitable	Generous
Effectiveness	Ineffective	Effective	Excellent
Efficiency	Inefficient	Efficient	Extraordinary
Quality	Error-prone	Reliable	Flawless
Ethics	Unethical	Ethical	Virtuous
Relationships	Conflictual	Compatible	Caring
Adaptation	Threat-rigidity	Coping	Flourishing

Deficit gaps   *Abundance gaps*

Source: Cameron, 2003b.

organizations and most managers strive to maintain performance in the middle of the continuum—healthy, effective, efficient, reliable, compatible, and ethical. It is in the middle of the continuum where things are most comfortable.

We usually refer to the left end of the continuum as **negative deviance**. This refers to mistakes, errors, and problems. Most managers spend much of their time trying to get their employees and their units away from the negative deviance end of the continuum and near the more acceptable middle point. A lot of pressure is brought to bear on people who are negatively deviant.

However, the same pressure usually exists for individuals on the right side of the continuum. Think, for example, of people you have encountered who are positively deviant at work—flawless performers, flourishing in everything they do, and constantly extraordinary. They are too perfect. They make people feel uncomfortable. They make others feel guilty. They are rate-busters. We accuse them of showing up other people. A lot of pressure exists to get them back in line or within a normal range of performance. Most of the time, we insist that others stay in the middle range. Moving to either the left side or the right side of the continuum is usually interpreted as against the rules. Resistance occurs to both regular change—from negative deviance to normal performance—and to positive change—from normal performance to positive deviance.

For the most part, leaders and managers are charged with the responsibility of ensuring that their organizations are operating in the middle range of Figure 10.1. They are consumed with the problems and challenges that threaten their organizations from the left side of the continuum (e.g., unethical behavior, dissatisfied employees or customers, financial losses, market share deterioration.) Most leaders and managers are content if they can get their organizations to that middle state—profitable, effective, and reliable. In fact, almost all research on organizational change has focused on how to ensure that organizations can perform in the normal range (Cameron, 2014).

The right end of the continuum in Figure 10.1 represents organizations that are positively deviant—they strive to be extraordinarily positive. Instead of just being effective, efficient, and reliable, they might strive to be benevolent, flourishing, and flawless.

The right side of the continuum represents an **abundance approach** to performance. The left side of the continuum represents a **deficit approach** to performance (Cameron, 2012; Cameron & Lavine, 2006). Much more attention has been paid to solving problems, surmounting obstacles, battling competitors, eliminating errors, making a profit, and closing deficit gaps than to identifying the flourishing and life-giving aspects of organizations. Closing deficit gaps gets a lot more attention than closing abundance gaps (Cameron, 2008). Our colleague Jim Walsh (1999) found, for example, that words such as *win*, *beat*, and *competition* have dominated the business press over the past two decades, whereas words such as *virtue*, *caring*, and *compassion* have seldom appeared at all. Less is known, therefore, about managing the right side of the continuum in Figure 10.1, since most research on leadership, management, and organizations focuses on the left and center points of the continuum. Leading change usually means closing deficit gaps. In this chapter, however, we focus on leading change that closes abundance gaps.

A Framework for Leading Positive Change

Leading positive change is a management skill that focuses on unlocking positive human potential. Positive change enables individuals to experience appreciation, positive energy, vitality, and meaningfulness in their work. It focuses on creating abundance and human well-being. It fosters positive deviance. It acknowledges that positive change engages the heart as well as the mind.

A Case Example An example of this kind of change occurred in a New England hospital that faced a crisis of leadership when the popular vice president of operations was forced to resign (Cameron, 2012; Cameron & Caza, 2002). Most employees viewed him as the most innovative and effective administrator in the hospital and as the chief exemplar of positive energy and change. Upon his resignation, the organization was thrown into turmoil. Conflict, backbiting, criticism, and adversarial feelings permeated the system. Eventually, a group of employees appealed to the board of directors to replace the current president and CEO with this ousted vice president. Little confidence was expressed in the current leadership, and the hospital's performance was deteriorating. Their lobbying efforts were eventually successful, and the president and CEO resigned under pressure and the popular vice president was hired back as president and CEO.

Within six months of his return, however, the decimated financial circumstances at the hospital led to an announced downsizing aimed at reducing the workforce by 10 percent. The hospital faced millions of dollars in losses. This newly hired CEO had to eliminate the jobs of some of the very same people who had supported his return.

The most likely results of this action were an escalation in the negative effects of downsizing, including loss of loyalty and morale, perceptions of injustice and duplicity, and blaming and accusations. Based on research on the effects of downsizing, a continuation of the tumultuous, antagonistic climate was almost guaranteed (Cameron, Whetten, & Kim, 1987; Cooper, Pandley, & Quick, 2012; Datta, et al., 2010).

Instead, the opposite results occurred. Upon his return, the new CEO made a concerted effort to lead positive change in the organization, not merely manage the required change. He focused on closing abundance gaps, not merely deficit gaps. He consciously focused on positive change rather than following normal change formulas. He institutionalized forgiveness, optimism, trust, and integrity. Throughout the organization, stories of compassionate acts of kindness and virtue were almost daily fare.

One indication of a positive approach to change was the language used throughout the organization, which commonly included words such as *love, hope, compassion, forgiveness*, and *humility*, especially in reference to the leadership that announced the downsizing actions.

We are in a very competitive health care market, so we have differentiated ourselves through our compassionate and caring culture....I know it sounds trite, but we really do love our patients....People love working here, and their family members love us too....Even when we downsized, [our leader] maintained the highest levels of

integrity. He told the truth, and he shared everything. He got the support of everyone by his genuineness and personal concern....It wasn't hard to forgive. (Representative responses from a focus group interview of employees, 2012)

Even the redesigned physical architecture of the hospital reflected its positive approach to change, being designed to foster a more humane climate for patients and to communicate the virtuousness of the organization. For example, the maternity ward installed queen-sized beds so husbands could sleep with their wives rather than sitting in a chair at night; numerous communal rooms were created for family and friend gatherings; hallways and floors were all carpeted; service pets were brought in to comfort and cheer up patients; original paintings on walls displayed optimistic and inspiring themes; nurses' stations were all within eyesight of patients' beds; Jacuzzis were installed in the maternity ward; special meals were prepared to fit patients' dietary preferences; and so on. Employees indicated that the leadership of positive change—not merely the management of change—was the key to the hospital's recovery and subsequent ability to thrive. Figure 10.2 illustrates the financial turnaround associated with the hospital's concentrated focus on virtuousness.

Five Skills for Leading Positive Change

This chapter reviews the five key management skills and activities required to effectively lead positive change. They include (1) establishing a climate of positivity, (2) creating readiness for change, (3) articulating a vision of abundance, (4) generating commitment to the vision, and (5) creating sustainability of the positive change (Avey, Wernsing, & Luthans, 2008; Cameron, 2012; Cameron & Ulrich, 1986). Figure 10.3 summarizes these steps, and we discuss them below.

MyLab Management Watch it!
If your instructor has assigned this activity, go to www.pearson.com/mylab/management to complete the video exercise.

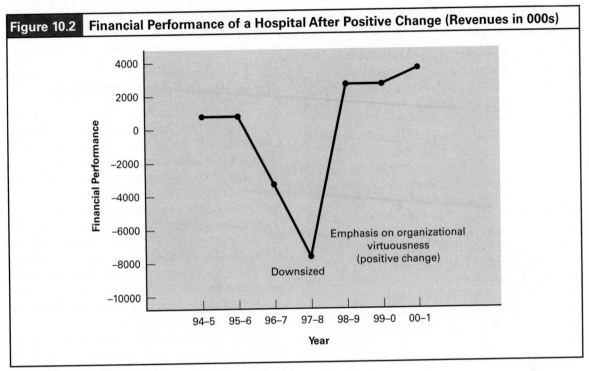

Figure 10.2 | **Financial Performance of a Hospital After Positive Change (Revenues in 000s)**

SOURCE: *Cameron, Bright, & Caza, 2003.*

Leaders of positive change are not all CEOs, of course, nor are they all in titled or powerful positions. On the contrary, the most important leadership demonstrated in organizations usually occurs in departments, divisions, and teams and by individuals who take it upon themselves to enter a temporary state of leadership (Meyerson, 2001; Quinn, 2004). These principles apply as much to the first-time manager, in other words, as to the experienced executive.

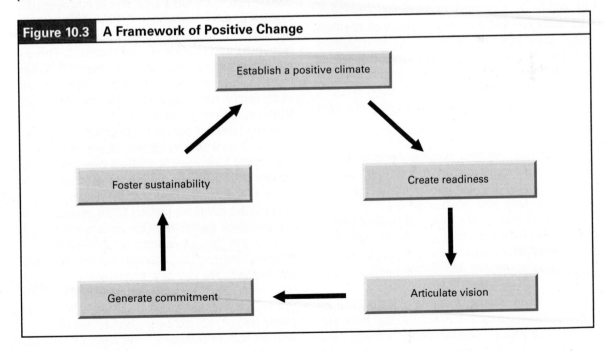

Figure 10.3 | **A Framework of Positive Change**

ESTABLISHING A CLIMATE OF POSITIVITY

The first step in leading positive change is to set the stage by establishing a climate that emphasizes and reinforces positivity. Because constant change is typical of all organizations, most of us, most of the time, focus on the problematic and negative aspects of change. Difficulties and obstacles capture more of our attention than pleasant and enjoyable events.

To illustrate, Baumeister and colleagues (2001) pointed out that negative occurrences, bad events, and disapproving feedback are more influential and longer lasting in people than positive, encouraging, and upbeat occurrences. For example, if someone breaks into your home and steals $1,000, it will create a larger reaction that will be more long-lasting in its effects than if someone sends you a $1,000 gift. If three people compliment you on your appearance and one person is critical of the way you look, the one criticism will carry more weight than the three compliments. In other words, according to Baumeister's review of the literature, "bad is stronger than good."

People tend to pay more attention to negative than positive phenomena, and for good reason. Ignoring a negative event or a threat could be costly or dangerous. Ignoring a positive, pleasant experience, on the other hand, just means that you missed out on something enjoyable. No major consequence is likely to occur. Therefore, managers and organizations—which are constantly confronted by problems, challenges, and obstacles—have a tendency to focus on negatives much more than on positives. Negative tendencies take precedence. To lead positive change, therefore, is to go against the grain. It is not necessarily a natural thing to do. On the other hand, Mahatma Gandhi's statement illustrates the necessity of positivity, even though it is difficult:

> *Keep your thoughts positive, because your thoughts become your words. Keep your words positive, because your words become your behavior. Keep your behavior positive, because your behavior becomes your habits. Keep your habits positive, because your habits become your values. Keep your values positive, because your values become your destiny.* (Gold, 2002)

In order to establish a climate of positivity in an organization, you must help establish at least three necessary conditions: (1) positive energy networks; (2) a climate of compassion, forgiveness, and gratitude; and (3) attention to strengths and the best self (see Cameron, 2013; Fredrickson & Branigan, 2005; Roberts, et al., 2005; Zhang & Bartol, 2010).

Create Positive Energy Networks

Have you ever been around a person who just makes you feel good? You leave every interaction happier, more energized, and uplifted? In contrast, do you know people who are constantly critical, negative, and discouraging? They seem to deplete your own reserve of positive energy? Recent research has discovered that people can be identified as "positive energizers" or "negative energizers" in their relationships with others (Baker, Cross, & Wooten, 2003; Cameron, 2013). **Positive energizers** are those who strengthen and create vitality and liveliness in others. **Negative energizers** are people who deplete the good feelings and enthusiasm in other people and make them feel diminished, devalued, or drained.

Recent research shows that positive energizers are higher performers, enable others to perform better, and help their own organizations succeed more than negative energizers (Baker, et al., 2003; Cameron, 2013; Powley, 2009; Ramlall, 2008). People who drain energy from others tend to be critical, express negative views, and fail to engage others, and they are more self-centered than positive energizers. Being a positive energizer is associated with being sensitive in interpersonal relationships, trustworthy, supportive of others, actively engaged in social interactions, flexible and tolerant in thinking, and unselfish. Positive energizers are not necessarily charismatic, giddy, or just Pollyannaish. They are not just enthusiastic and smiling all the time. Rather, positive energy creators are optimistic contributors, and others flourish when they are around them. Most importantly, positive energy can be developed. It is crucial for creating a climate of positivity in preparation for change.

To create a positive climate, identify positive energizers and place them in positions where others can interact with them and be influenced by them. The research findings are clear that people who interact with positive energizers perform better, as do the positive energizers themselves. One prescription, then, is to make sure that you and others rub shoulders with positive energizers. The performance of the entire team will improve. You can help foster positive energy in other people by (1) exemplifying or role modeling positive energy yourself—that is, focus on helping other people flourish; (2) recognizing and rewarding people who are positive energizers—they seldom receive any recognition or thanks; and (3) providing opportunities for individuals to form friendships at work—which usually are positive energy creators.

Ensure a Climate of Compassion, Forgiveness, and Gratitude

A second aspect of a climate of positivity is the appropriate display of compassion, forgiveness, and gratitude in organizations. These terms may sound a bit saccharine and soft—even out of place in a serious discussion of developing management skills for the competitive world of business. Yet, recent research has found them to be important predictors of organizational success. Companies with high scores on these attributes performed significantly better than others (Cameron, 2003b, 2012, 2013). That is, when managers fostered compassionate behavior among employees, forgiveness for missteps and mistakes, and gratitude resulting from positive occurrences, their firms excelled in profitability, productivity, quality, innovation, and customer retention. Managers who reinforced these virtues were more successful in producing bottom-line results (Cameron, et al., 2011; Rego, Ribeiro, & Cunha, 2010).

Paying attention to these concepts simply acknowledges that employees at work have human concerns—they feel pain, experience difficulty, and encounter injustice in their work and personal lives. More than 50 percent of the people you know are currently experiencing a severe family illness or a failed relationship, coping with hostile and unpleasant coworkers or associates, facing overload and burnout, or are struggling with a different personal concern (Cameron, 2017; Worline & Dutton, 2017). Most people you know are feeling some sort of personal pain right now. However, many organizations don't allow personal problems to get in the way of getting the job done. Human concerns take a backseat to work-related concerns. Regardless of what is happening personally, responsibilities and performance expectations remain the same.

To lead positive change, you will need to build a climate in which human concerns are acknowledged and where healing and restoration can occur. Because change always creates pain, discomfort, and disruption, you will want to be sensitive to the human concerns that can sabotage many change efforts. Without a reserve of goodwill and positive feelings, almost all change fails. Therefore, unlocking people's inherent tendency to feel compassion, to forgive mistakes, and to express gratitude helps build the human capital and reserve needed to successfully lead positive

change (Cameron, 2017; Hazen, 2008). How might that occur?

Compassion Worline and Dutton (2017) found that **compassion** is enhanced in organizations when you foster three things: **collective noticing, collective feeling,** and **collective responding** (also see Boyatzis, Smith, & Blaize, 2006; Kanov et al., 2003). When people are suffering or experiencing difficulty, the first step is to notice or be attentive to what is occurring. An ironclad rule exists at Cisco Systems, for example, stating that CEO John Chambers must be notified within 48 hours of the death or serious illness of any Cisco employee or family member. People are on the lookout for colleagues who need help.

The second step is to enable the expression of collective emotion. Gatherings or events where people can share feelings (grief, support, or love) help build a climate of compassion. For example, a memorial service for a recently deceased executive at which the CEO shed tears was a powerful signal to organization members that responding compassionately to human suffering was important to the organization (Frost, 2003).

The third step is collective responding, meaning that you ensure that an appropriate response is made when healing or restoration is needed. In the aftermath of 9/11, many examples of compassion—and noncompassion—were witnessed in organizations around the country. While some leaders modeled caring and compassion in the responses they fostered, others stifled the healing process (see Cameron, 2017; Dutton, et al., 2002; Worline & Dutton, 2017).

Forgiveness Most managers assume that **forgiveness** has a precarious place in the work setting. Because of high-quality standards, the need to eliminate mistakes, and a requirement to "do it right the first time," managers assume they cannot afford to let errors go unpunished. Forgiving mistakes will just encourage people to be careless and unthinking, they assume. However, forgiveness and high standards are not incompatible. This is because forgiveness is not the same as pardoning, condoning, excusing, forgetting, denying, minimizing, or trusting (Enright & Coyle, 1998).

To forgive does not mean relieving the offender of a penalty (i.e., pardoning), or concluding that the offense is acceptable, not really serious, or should be forgotten (i.e., condoned, excused, denied, minimized). The memory of the offense need not be erased for forgiveness to occur. Instead, forgiveness in an organization involves the capacity to abandon justified resentment, bitterness, and blame, and instead to adopt positive, forward-looking approaches in response to harm or damage and to learn from the misstep (Bright & Exline, 2012; Caldwell & Dixon, 2010; Cameron & Caza, 2002).

For example, because minor offenses and disagreements occur in almost all human interactions, especially in close relationships, most people are practiced forgivers. Without forgiveness, relationships could not endure and organizations would disintegrate into squabbles, conflicts, and hostilities. One explanation for the successful formation of the European Economic Union, for example, is forgiveness (Glynn, 1994). Collectively speaking, the French, Dutch, and British forgave the Germans for the atrocities of World War II, as did other damaged nations. Likewise, the reciprocal forgiveness demonstrated by the United States and Vietnam after the Vietnam War helps explain the flourishing economic and social interchange that developed in subsequent decades. On the other hand, the lack of peace in certain war-torn areas of the world can be at least partly explained by the refusal of organizations and nations to forgive one another for past trespasses (Helmick & Petersen, 2001).

The importance of forgiveness in organizations, and societies is illustrated by Nobel laureate Desmond Tutu in his description of post-apartheid South Africa:

> *Ultimately, you discover that without forgiveness, there is no future. We recognize that the past cannot be remade through punishment.... There is no point in exacting vengeance now, knowing that it will be the cause for future vengeance by the offspring of those we punish. Vengeance leads only to revenge. Vengeance destroys those it claims and those who become intoxicated with it... therefore, forgiveness is an absolute necessity for continued human existence.* (Tutu, 1998, p. xiii; 1999, p. 155)

Forgiveness is enhanced in organizations when you:

1. Acknowledge the trauma, harm, and injustice that organization members have experienced, but they define the occurrence of hurtful events as an opportunity to learn and to move forward toward a new goal.

2. Associate the outcomes of the organization (e.g., its products and services) with a higher purpose that provides personal meaning for organization members. This higher purpose replaces a focus on self (e.g., retribution, self-pity) with a focus on a higher objective.

3. Maintain high standards and communicate the fact that forgiveness is not synonymous with tolerance for error or lowered expectations. Use forgiveness to facilitate excellence by refusing to focus on the negative and, instead, focus on achieving excellence.

4. Provide support by communicating that human development and human welfare are as important in the organization's priorities as the financial bottom line. This kind of support helps employees catch sight of a way to move past the injury.

5. Pay attention to language, so that terms such as *forgiveness, compassion, humility, courage,* and *love* are acceptable; this language provides a humanistic foundation upon which most forgiveness occurs.

Gratitude Observing acts of compassion and forgiveness—not to mention being the recipient of them—creates a sense of **gratitude** in people (Emmons, 2007). Expressions of gratitude by one person tend to motivate others to express gratitude, so a self-perpetuating, virtuous cycle occurs. Gratitude is crucial in organizations because it leads people to return a favor, do good in return for receiving good, and behave compassionately and equitably.

Feelings of gratitude have been found to have dramatic effects on individual and organizational performance. For example, Emmons (2003) induced feelings of gratitude in students by assigning them to keep journals as part of a semester-long assignment. Some of the students were required to keep "gratitude journals" on a daily or weekly basis. They wrote down events or incidents that happened during the day (or week) for which they were grateful. Other students were assigned to write down events or incidents that were frustrating. Still other students were assigned to write down events or incidents that were merely neutral. Students keeping gratitude journals, compared to students who journaled about frustrating or neutral incidents, experienced fewer physical symptoms such as headaches, nausea, and colds; felt better about their lives as a whole; were more optimistic about the coming week; had higher states of alertness, attentiveness, determination, and energy; reported fewer hassles in their lives; engaged in more helping behavior toward other people; experienced better sleep quality; and had a sense of being more connected to others. In addition, they were absent and tardy less often and had higher grade point averages. Feelings of gratitude had significant impact on students' classroom performance as well as people's personal lives.

McCraty and Childre (2004) explained one reason positive effects of gratitude occur in people's lives. They studied heart rhythms of people experiencing frustrating or stressful work conditions, and compared those heart rhythms to changes that occurred when people were induced into a gratitude condition. Over a period of just 100 seconds, individuals' heart rhythms changed from erratic and inconsistent to steady and smooth within seconds of the shift from a stressful condition to a condition of gratitude. Physiologically, gratitude produces a substantial beneficial effect.

Emmons also found that gratitude elicits positive behaviors on the part of other people (e.g., they are more likely to loan money, provide compassionate support, and behave reciprocally). For example, a handwritten "thank you" on a restaurant bill by the server elicits about 11 percent higher tips, and visits by case workers and social workers are 80 percent higher if they are thanked for coming (McCullough, Emmons, & Tsang, 2002). People respond positively to expressions of gratitude. Thus, gratitude not only helps people *feel* good—it helps them *do* good as well.

You can engender gratitude in an organization simply by expressing "thank you" frequently and conspicuously, even for small acts and small successes. Do you ever thank the custodians, food service workers, or maintenance personnel in your building, for example? Expressing gratitude will have a powerful effect on performance

Pay Attention to Strengths and the Best Self

Identifying people's strengths (or what they do right) and then building on them creates more benefit than identifying weaknesses (or what people do wrong) and trying to correct them (*Gallup Business Journal*, 2018; Rath, 2009). For example, managers who spend more time with their strongest performers (rather than their weakest performers) achieved double the productivity. In organizations where workers have a chance to do what they do best every day, productivity is one-and-a-half times greater than in other organizations. People who are given feedback on their strengths are significantly more likely to feel highly engaged and to be more productive than people who are given feedback on their weaknesses. Students who are given feedback on their talents have fewer days of absenteeism, are tardy less often, and have higher GPAs than students who get no feedback on their talents. The strongest readers make more improvement in a speed-reading class designed to improve reading than the poor readers (Biswas-Diener, Kashdan, & Minhas, 2011; Clifton & Harter, 2003).

Reflected Best-Self Feedback One technique you can use to foster a positive climate and build on strengths is called the **"reflected best-self feedback"** process (Quinn, Dutton, & Spreitzer, 2003). It is a technique developed at the Ross School of Business at the University of Michigan and has been adopted at a large number of universities and corporations. It is designed to provide people with feedback on their strengths and unique capabilities. This kind of information is not frequently given to people, if ever, but receiving it allows individuals to build on their unique strengths in a positive way. Figure 10.4 illustrates the kind of feedback resulting from this exercise.

Begin at the bottom of the figure. Most of us have a lot of flaws and faults—areas that are underdeveloped, areas in which we are uninformed, areas in which we have little skill. Most feedback systems provide information on what those areas are and how we compare to other people's capabilities in the same areas. Those are labeled **weaknesses** in Figure 10.4. We also all have areas in which we perform competently. We do fine—not stellar, but good enough. Those are areas of **competence**. A third category is areas of well-developed skill. We're outstanding performers in some areas. We have special capabilities or talents, and we do better than most people. These are areas of **strength**. Finally, we all have areas that are unique to us. If we don't contribute what we have or know, or if we don't share our capacities and gifts, no one else has the ability to do so. Our talent or skill is special. We refer to this

Figure 10.4   Personal Weaknesses, Competencies, Strengths, and Uniquenesses

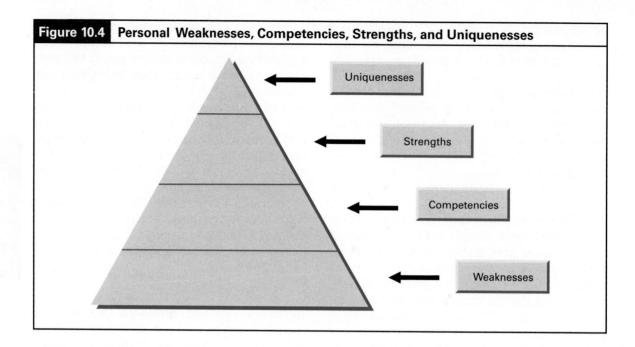

area as **uniquenesses**. Research indicates that capitalizing on our strengths and uniquenesses produces more success than trying to work on and overcome weaknesses—even though weaknesses may be more numerous and more obvious (Clifton & Harter, 2003; Rath, 2001).

If you engaged in the reflected best-self feedback process as part of the Skill Pre-Assessment section of this chapter, you received feedback that identifies your key strengths and unique talents—information that is both rare and extremely valuable. These themes represent your best-self strengths and uniquenesses.

The power of this feedback is that it comes in the form of incidents and stories, not numbers or trend lines, so it is connected directly to your behaviors and skills. These are the strengths and uniquenesses that you can build upon and display more often. This kind of feedback does not even mention faults or shortcomings, so it does not motivate you to overcome areas of deficiency. Rather, it helps you develop strategies to capitalize on your best self.

Of course, completely ignoring weaknesses and inadequacies is not healthy either. Focusing exclusively on the positive and disregarding critical weaknesses is not apt to be productive in the long run. It's just that most individuals, and most organizations, concentrate on the negative and are likely to ignore, or at least

short-change, the positive. The reflective best-self feedback technique is a way to counterbalance that tendency.

Summary   Few people live or work in a positive organizational climate in which people flourish and experience positive energy. The role of the leader of positive change, therefore, is to facilitate and engender these characteristics by creative a climate of positivity. Table 10.1 summarizes some specific behaviors that you can implement. Creating positive energy networks; fostering compassion, forgiveness, and gratitude; building on others' strengths; and using positive communication all are initial steps to effectively lead positive change.

CREATING READINESS FOR CHANGE

In addition to establishing a climate of positivity, you must help others understand the importance and urgency of the change. A positive climate is a crucial foundation, but leading positive change requires engaging individuals in the actual process of change. The second step in leading positive change, therefore, is to create readiness among those to be involved in the change. Many techniques are available to do this, and we mention just four here.

Table 10.1	Establishing a Climate of Positivity

1. Create positive energy networks.

   - Place positive energizers in places where others can interact with them and be influenced by them.
   - Model positive energy yourself.
   - Recognize and reward positive energizers.
   - Provide opportunities for people to form close friendships at work.

2. Ensure a climate of compassion, forgiveness, and gratitude.

   - Be on the lookout to notice human concerns.
   - Find ways to foster the collective expression of emotions.
   - Enable a collective response to difficulty, pain, or distress.
   - Publicly and personally acknowledge trauma and harm.
   - Identify higher-purpose outcomes that people will value.
   - Maintain high standards and look toward the future after mistakes.
   - Provide personal support to people who have been harmed.
   - Pay attention to language so that virtuous words are acceptable.
   - Express gratitude frequently and conspicuously, even for small acts.
   - Keep track of things that go right (not just that go wrong).

3. Identify and give people feedback on their strengths and unique competencies.

   - Implement a reflected best-self feedback process.
   - Spend time with your strongest performers.
   - Work to capitalize on strengths rather than focusing on overcoming weaknesses.
   - Use five positive comments for every negative comment in your interactions with others.

Benchmark Best Practice and Compare Current Performance to the Highest Standards

One way to create readiness for change is to compare current levels of performance to the highest standards you can find. Identifying who else performs at spectacular levels helps you set a standard toward which people can aspire. It identifies a target of opportunity. This is referred to as **benchmarking**, and it involves finding best practice, studying it in detail, and then planning to exceed that performance. "Shooting ahead of the duck" is the principle. This doesn't mean copying others. It means learning from and even exceeding what others do. Planned performance goes beyond the best practice; otherwise, benchmarking is merely mimicking.

When you compare your performance to others, you can use several different kinds of standards:

❑ **Comparative standards,** or comparing current performance to similar individuals or organizations (e.g., "Here is how we are doing relative to our best competitors.")

❑ **Goal standards**, or comparing current performance to your publicly stated goals (e.g., "Here is how we are doing compared to the goals we have established.")

❑ **Improvement standards**, or comparing current performance with your past improvements (e.g., "Here is how we are doing compared to our improvement trends of the past year.")

❑ **Ideal standards**, or comparing current performance with an idea or perfect standard (e.g., "Here is how we are doing relative to a zero defect standard.")

❑ **Stakeholder expectations**, or comparing current performance with the expectations of customers, employees, or other stakeholders (e.g., "Here is how we are doing in meeting customer demands.")

Which standard of comparison you choose will depend on which standard is the most important to your organization members and which standard is perceived to be reachable. The purpose of these comparisons is to highlight the opportunities available by finding a higher level of performance and showing the possibility of achieving it.

Identifying benchmark standards also helps ensure that new information, new ideas, and new perspectives will be imported, and that standards not considered possible before may become realistic. Studying others who may be doing the same job better than you may be accomplished by sponsoring visitors, holding learning events (symposia and colloquia) or conferences, creating study teams, and scheduling visits to other sites. The objective is to unfreeze people from reliance on past practice by learning that there may be a better way.

Institute Symbolic Events

To be successful in leading positive change you must signal the end of the old way of doing things and the beginning of a new way of doing things. One effective way to accomplish this is to use an event to signify a positive change or a new future.

For example, during the 1980s Chrysler was experiencing very dark days. The company was bankrupt, and no one knew for sure if it would survive. Lee Iacocca was hired to be the new CEO. Tens of thousands of cars sat idle in the "sales bank" (Chrysler's term for cars parked in vacant lots) waiting to be sold. In his first closed-door speech to senior executives, Iacocca announced that the sales bank would be abolished. All cars in the sales bank would be sold at "distressed prices." "But," he said, "I want to keep one. You know what people do when they pay off the mortgage; they burn it on the front lawn. I want to burn that last car on the front lawn of headquarters, so the whole world knows it's over!" (Cameron, 1985). A symbolic event was held, in fact, in which the last car in the sales bank was burned at headquarters, symbolizing a new future under Iacocca.

The symbolic imagery was far more powerful than a mere inspirational speech. Symbolic events capture hearts as well as heads of people, and this is required for positive change to occur.

Create a New Language

Another way to create readiness for change is to help organization members begin to use different words to describe old realities. When new language is used, perspectives change. For example, a key goal for the theme park division at Disney Corporation is to provide the best service in the world. The trouble is, most of Disney's theme park employees in the summer months are college students working at temporary jobs and are not particularly invested in being a park sweeper or concession stand cashier. Disney addresses this challenge by making sure that all new employees at Disney are taught that they have been hired by central casting, not the personnel department. They are cast members, not employees. They wear costumes, not uniforms. They serve guests and audience members, not tourists. They work in attractions, not rides or arcades. They have roles in the show and play characters (even as groundskeepers), not merely work a job. During working hours they are onstage, and they must go offstage to relax, eat, or socialize.

The intent of this alternative language is to change the way these employees think about their work, to place them in a mind-set that they wouldn't have considered otherwise. At Disney, summer employees are in show business—on stage, playing a role, performing for an audience. Changing language helps unfreeze old interpretations and create new ones.

Overcome Resistance

Change always creates resistance among some people. Because change is always uncomfortable and produces uncertainty about what the future will bring, many people are inclined to resist in some way. The three techniques for creating readiness mentioned above will be helpful, but in addition, you will want to consider these ideas for those who try to block change. The intent of these techniques is to get people who normally would resist the change to become supporters and advocates.

- ❏ Identify who the resisters are, who will let the change happen, who will help the change to happen, and who will be champions of the change. Nurture champions and first followers. Give them recognition, and encourage them to energize others.
- ❏ Encourage participation by others in the planning and execution of the change. Participation almost always reduces resistance and fosters support.
- ❏ Identify benefits, advantages, and future possibilities associated with the change. Specify WIIFM—"what's in it for me" for other people. Show what negative things will happen if the change is not successful. Identify examples of past success.
- ❏ Preserve the self-esteem of the resisters. Do not force them to comply. Do not denigrate their points of view. Find ways to legitimize their

opinions, fears, and rationale, but help them see a way through their obstacles.

- Find common areas of agreement. The cardinal rule in successful negotiation is to find something upon which both parties can agree and build from there. In overcoming resistance, the same rule applies. Identify something that you all agree on and capitalize on this common core for moving forward.

Summary

Creating readiness is a step designed to mobilize individuals in the organization to actively engage in the positive change process. It involves more than merely unfreezing people. Making people uncomfortable is a frequent prescription for getting people ready for change, and it often works; however, making people uncomfortable will usually escalate resistance. Leading positive change, therefore, focuses on creating readiness in ways that unlock positive motivations rather than resistance. It provides optimistic alternatives rather than fear.

Establishing a climate of positivity and creating readiness for change does little good if there is not a clear idea of where the positive change is heading. That is why the third step in the framework refers to articulating a clear, motivating vision of abundance.

ARTICULATING A VISION OF ABUNDANCE

Positive change seldom occurs without a leader articulating a **vision of abundance** (see Figure 10.1). By abundance we mean a vision that focuses on something that makes a profound difference, something that outlasts one's own life, something that has enduring impact. Visions of abundance are different from visions of goal achievement or effectiveness—such as earning a certain percent profit, becoming number one in the

Table 10.2	Creating Readiness in Others to Pursue Positive Change

1. Benchmark best practice, and compare current performance to the highest standards.

   - Use comparable others as standards.
   - Use stated goals as standards.
   - Use past improvement as a standard.
   - Use an ideal as a standard.
   - Use others' expectations as a standard.

2. Institute symbolic events to signal the positive change.

   - Interpret events or activities as indicators of the beginning of a new era.
   - Manage people's interpretations and mental images of incidents so that they reinforce the intended change.
   - Pay as much attention to the meaning of change as to the substance of the change.

3. Create a new language that illustrates the positive change.

   - Use words associated with the change that capture people's imagination.
   - Use passionate and inspiring language.
   - Use words that communicate and reinforce a new direction.

4. Overcome resistance.

   - Identify resisters, helpers, and champions. Reinforce champions and first followers.
   - Encourage participation.
   - Identify benefits, advantages, and future possibilities.
   - Preserve the self-esteem of resisters.
   - Find common areas of agreement.

marketplace, accomplishing a task, or receiving personal recognition. Visions of abundance speak to the heart as well as the head.

For example, the vision of abundance for Richard Bogomolny, the CEO of Finast Supermarkets in Cleveland, Ohio, was to improve the quality of life for residents of blighted areas of Cleveland who would otherwise never have access to a reasonably priced grocery store with competitive prices. He invested in new, state-of-the-art supermarkets in poor urban neighborhoods, stocking shelves with ethnic foods that were not popular in suburban stores and providing an environment of safety and cleanliness along with prices competitive with suburban shopping centers. Finast stores became social gathering places for entire neighborhoods, provided training and employment for the chronically unemployed, and, at the same time, became a highly profitable investment for the company (Bollier, 1996). Without the leader's clear statement of a vision of abundance, the overwhelming tendencies toward merely solving problems, addressing obstacles, and making money drive out positive change.

Most organizations have mission statements or goal statements, but an abundance **vision statement** is something different. Referring to Figure 10.1, it represents a positive deviant condition—not just problem-solving—and achieving something that represents the best of the human condition, not just monetary or reputational benefits.

Include Left-Brain and Right-Brain Features

Many years ago, neurosurgeons discovered that the brain consists of two hemispheres that can actually work independently when surgically separated. The left hemisphere controls rational cognitive activities, such as sequential thinking, logic, deduction, and numeric thought. Activities such as reading, solving math problems, and rational analysis are dominated by *left-brain thinking.*

The right hemisphere, on the other hand, controls nonrational cognitive activities, such as intuition, creativity, fantasy, emotions, pictorial images, and imagination. Composing music, storytelling, and artistic creation are most likely tied to *right-brain thinking.*

Of course, neither hemisphere operates autonomously from the other, and both kinds of mental activity are required in complex tasks. But that is precisely the point. Vision statements of leaders must contain rational targets, goals, and action plans (left-brain components), as well as metaphors, colorful language, and imagination (right-brain components). Unfortunately, most managers and most organizations emphasize the left-brain side in their mission and vision statements—for example, increased market share, becoming number one in the industry, or raising quality standards—but give little attention to exciting language, pictures and images of the future, or the emotions of members.

In the Skill Analysis section of this chapter, several corporate vision statements are provided for you to analyze. Note the differences among them in the relative emphasis on right-brain versus left-brain thinking.

Articulating the *left-brain* side of the vision is facilitated by answering the following questions:

❑ What are our most important strengths as an organization? Where do we have a strategic advantage?

❑ What major problems and obstacles do we face that need to be addressed? What stands in the way of significant improvement?

❑ What are the primary resources that we need? What information is required?

❑ Who are our key customers? What must be done to respond to their expectations?

❑ What measurable outcomes will we accomplish? What are the criteria to be monitored?

Articulating the *right-brain* side of the vision is aided by answering the following questions:

❑ What is the best we can achieve? What represents peak performance?

❑ What stories or events can we tell that characterize what we stand for?

❑ What metaphors or analogies can we use that will identify what the future of our organization will look like?

❑ What symbols are appropriate for helping capture people's imaginations?

❑ What colorful and inspirational language can exemplify what we believe in?

The most motivating vision statements—for example, Winston Churchill's "Never Give In" speech, John F. Kennedy's "Ask Not What Your Country Can Do for You" speech, Nelson Mandela's "A Dream for Which I Am Prepared to Die" speech, Martin Luther King Jr.'s "I Have a Dream" speech—all contain both left-brain and right-brain elements. Leaders of positive change pay attention to both in articulating their vision statements.

Make Vision Statements Interesting

Murray Davis (1971) published a now-classic article on what causes some kinds of information to be judged interesting or uninteresting. The truth or veracity of the information has little to do with that judgment, according to Davis. Rather, what's interesting depends on the extent to which the information contradicts weakly held assumptions and challenges the status quo. If new information is consistent with what is already known, people tend to dismiss it as common sense. If new information is obviously contradictory to strongly held assumptions, or if it blatantly challenges the core values of the organization's members, it is labeled ridiculous, silly, or blasphemous. Information that helps create new ways to view the future, that challenges the current state of things (but not core values), is viewed as interesting. New insights are created and people are drawn to the information because it makes them think, or it uncovers a new way to think (see Bartunek, Rynes, & Ireland, 2006).

Inspiring vision statements are interesting. They contain challenges and prods that confront and alter the ways people think about the past and the future. They are not outlandish or cavalier in their message, just provocative. For example, Ralph Peterson, former CEO of CH2M HILL (a large environmental and engineering firm), indicated that "corporate immortality" was the ultimate objective of the company, meaning that the firm was in business to create outcomes that would last well beyond the lifetime of the firm. Jeffrey Schwartz, CEO of Timberland, the shoe and clothing company, espoused a vision related to doing good in order to do well—that is, organizational virtuousness is equally important to organizational profitability. Tom Gloucer, former CEO of Reuters, espoused the vision that Reuters would become the fastest company in the world. Steve Jobs, former CEO of Apple, espoused a vision of "one person—one computer" throughout the entire world.

These examples are not intended to illustrate the best vision statements, of course, nor even vision statements that energize you personally. But, in each case, they carried a strong and motivating message for those in their organizations. They helped paint a mental picture of something that people cared about but that challenged the normal perception of things. The fact that they are interesting statements is what captured attention and the positive energy of others.

Include Passion and Principles

Visions of abundance are grounded in core values that organization members believe in, that have personal relevance, and about which they feel passionate. Such vision statements increase people's desire to affiliate with the leader and with the organization. A vision focused on "increasing productivity" is less energizing and inspiring than a vision based on "changing people's lives." "Achieving profitability" is less magnetic than "helping vulnerable people flourish."

In addition, elements of the vision are best phrased using adjectives and superlatives. Notice the difference in how you feel about the following comparisons: "phenomenal performance" versus "successful." Or, "passionately engaged" versus "committed." Or, "explosive growth" versus "good progress." Or, "awesome products" versus "useful items." Visions based on the former phrases engender more enthusiasm and passion than those based on the latter phrases.

Consider as an example of such language the vision statement of John Sculley, former CEO of Apple Computer Company:

> We are all part of a journey to create an extraordinary corporation. The things we intend to do in the years ahead have never been done before....One person, one computer is still our dream....We have a passion for changing the world. Apple people are paradigm shifters....We want to be the catalyst for discovering new ways for people to do things....Apple's way starts with a passion to create awesome products with a lot of distinctive value built in....We have chosen directions for Apple that will lead us to wonderful ideas we haven't as yet dreamed. (Sculley, 1987)

Finally, the vision statement must be straightforward and simple. A common error of leaders is to be too complicated, too lengthy, or too multifaceted in their vision statement. Most great leaders acknowledge that they have very few major objectives in mind. Their visions help people focus.

Attach the Vision to a Symbol

Effective vision statements are associated with a symbol. This is more than a symbolic event that helps create readiness for change. Rather, people must associate the vision with something tangible they see or hear. This reminds people of the vision on a regular basis.

Table 10.3	Articulating a Vision of Abundance

1. Focus on creating positive deviance rather than correcting problems.

   - Focus on possibilities more than probabilities.

   - Focus on extraordinary, spectacular achievement rather than just winning or being seen as successful.

2. Include left-brain images by asking questions such as:

   - What are our most important strengths?

   - What major problems and obstacles do we face?

   - What are the primary resources that we need?

   - What must be done to respond to customers' expectations?

   - What measurable outcomes will we accomplish?

   - What are the criteria to be monitored?

3. Include right-brain images by asking questions such as:

   - What represents peak performance?

   - What symbols, metaphors, or stories can help capture people's imaginations?

   - What colorful and inspirational language can exemplify what we believe in?

4. Make the vision interesting by challenging weakly held assumptions.

   - Associate the vision with core values that have personal meaning.

   - Ensure a straightforward and simple message.

   - Use exciting and energizing language.

5. Attach the vision to a symbol to constantly remind people of the vision.

   - Create visual images such as logos, flags, or signs.

   - Make certain that the visual symbol is closely associated with the vision so it remains a constant reminder.

That symbol may be a logo, a phrase from a speech, a flag, a physical structure, or other reminders of where the vision is taking the organization.

The turnaround at Ford Motor Company after William Clay Ford took over was symbolized by the resurrection of the blue Ford oval on the headquarters building. Chrysler returned to the classic Chrysler logo instead of the five-pointed star. Malden Mills reconstructed a plant that had been devastated by fire on the same property to symbolize human commitment and corporate compassion. The replacement structures for the World Trade Center towers were targeted specifically to symbolize a positive and uplifting future. Logos such as the Golden Arches, the Nike Swoosh, and Mickey Mouse are carefully publicized, even protected, because of the symbolic messages that they communicate about the companies they represent.

Table 10.3 summarizes some specific behaviors you can use in articulating a high-impact vision of abundance.

GENERATING COMMITMENT TO THE VISION

Once this vision of abundance has been articulated, it is necessary for leaders to help organization members commit to that vision, to sign up, to adopt the vision as their own, and to work toward its accomplishment. The whole intent of a vision is to mobilize the energy of individuals who are to implement and be affected by it. Among the ways to generate commitment to a vision are three discussed below. Others are discussed in depth in the chapters on motivation, empowerment, and teamwork.

Apply Principles of Recreation

An interesting truism was identified by Chuck Coonradt (2007): "*People will pay for the privilege of working harder than they will work when they are paid.*" Think about that for a minute. People are willing to spend more money in order to work harder than they will work when they are receiving remuneration. Under certain circumstances, individuals are more committed to doing work that actually costs them money than they are to doing work for which they receive remuneration wage. How can that be? In what circumstances might that be the case?

Consider the following hypothetical example. Suppose you live in Utah in the winter and, as you arrive at work, you find that the furnace is out of order. As the temperature falls to 65 degrees Fahrenheit you put on a coat. At 60 degrees you complain that it is too cold to work. At 55 degrees you leave, confident that no one could expect you to perform in such adverse conditions. Then you put on your $500 ski outfit, grab your $750 skis and boots, race off to the slopes in order to pay $115 for a lift ticket, $75 for gas, and $30 for a junk-food lunch. You will spend all day long in 10-degree weather working much harder skiing than you would have worked at the firm where you could have been paid.

If this sounds unusual, consider the skyrocketing absenteeism rates in companies and schools when the first big snow falls in ski areas, when the surf is up in cities close to the beach, or on the first day of hunting or fishing season. People regularly choose to pay to work harder than they work when they are paid.

Well, you say, that's because it's fun. It's recreation. And you're right. But there is no reason why the work performed in a regular job cannot be typified by the same principles that characterize recreation. In other words, what causes people to *want* to engage in recreational work can also be what causes them to be equally committed to their occupational work. At least five characteristics are typical of **recreational work** (Coonradt, 2007).

1. Goals are clearly defined.
2. Scorekeeping is objective, self-administered, peer-audited, and compared to past performance.
3. Feedback is frequent.
4. Personal choice is present; rules are consistent and don't change until the season is over.
5. A competitive environment is present.

Consider the game of (American) football. Each year the University of Michigan averages about 112,000 fans per game, every one of whom knows exactly what the goal is—to score more points than the opponent. There is no need for a periodic performance appraisal system, because the score changes only when a team crosses the goal line or kicks a field goal. There is no guessing about how to get ahead. Feedback is not only frequent, it is continuous. If the clock goes down,

they stop the game. No one would consider playing if the time and the score were not kept continuously.

Within the rules of the game, every participant and fan has personal choice. Players can go full speed or not; fans can cheer or not; the offense can run the ball or pass it. No one forces people to perform a role that they don't want to perform. Coordination and control occur because everyone knows the rules, and the rules don't change. Offside is offside, a first down is a first down, and a touchdown is a touchdown. When a receiver is wide open and makes an easy catch in the end zone, no one could imagine an NCAA committee deliberating about how many points the score is worth. No one would say, "Easy catch; wide open; worth only 4.5 points." No one would stand for that, and 112,000 people would go crazy. The rules don't change in recreation.

Plus, the environment is one of competition—both against an opponent and against personal past performance. The stimulation of competing against something is fun. Playing against someone who is markedly less skilled—beating them 100 to 0—is not much fun.

Despite the inherent motivation and commitment associated with recreational work, many leaders contradict them. Their vision is not stated clearly and precisely. There is no objective, self-administrated evaluation system. The scorekeeping system is controlled hierarchically, by managers one step above, instead of being peer-audited and continuous, as in recreation. Criteria of evaluation are vague, unreliable, and inconsistently administered. Organization feedback often comes only when quarterly earnings statements are tabulated, and then it is often focused on what went wrong. Personal freedom is too often constrained, as evidenced by the elaborate bureaucratic rules and policies that typify most large organizations. It is not unusual to have the criteria of success change in the middle of the game, especially if a new manager takes over. And, most employees never see how what they do makes any difference at all in obtaining the ultimate goal, or winning against a competitor.

The point is, one way for leaders to generate commitment to the vision is to implement principles of recreational work into the vision statement, and people will be inclined to pursue it eagerly.

Ensure Public Commitments

Another well-documented way to enhance commitment to a vision is to have people state their commitments aloud, in public. Individuals are motivated to behave consistently with their public declarations (Munson, et al., 2015; Salancik, 1977). The internal need for congruence ensures that public statements will be followed by consistent actions. After making public pronouncements, individuals are more committed and more consistent in their behavior to that which they have espoused (Baker, 2001; Cialdini, 2008).

For example, during World War II, good cuts of meat were in short supply in the United States. Lewin (1951) found that a significant difference existed between the commitment level of shoppers who promised out loud to buy more plentiful but less desirable cuts of meat (e.g., liver, kidneys, brains) compared to those who made the same promise in private.

In another study, students were divided in a college class into two groups. All students set goals for how much they would read and what kinds of scores they would get on exams. Only half the students were allowed to state these goals publicly to the rest of the class. By midsemester, the students who stated their goals publicly averaged 86 percent improvement. The nonpublic goal-setting students averaged 14 percent improvement.

When the Tennessee Valley Authority (TVA) was attempting to build a dam in the late 1940s, it found that local farmers vehemently resisted the efforts because of the land that would be flooded. To overcome this resistance and elicit farmers' commitment to the project, the TVA made local farmers members of the board that would supervise the construction efforts. These local farmers began to make public statements on behalf of the TVA project and, over time, became strongly committed to it (Selznick, 1949).

This point is, you will be more effective in leading positive change if you look for opportunities to have others make public statements in favor of your vision, or to restate the vision themselves. Assigning individuals to explain the vision to outside groups or to other employees, or forming discussion groups so that others can help refine or clarify the vision, are examples of how opportunities for public statements can be fostered in order to enhance commitment.

Institute a Small-Wins Strategy

People become committed to change when they see progress being made or success being achieved. We are all more committed to winners than to losers. Fans attend more games when the team has a good record than when it has a poor record. The number of people claiming to have voted for a winning candidate always exceeds by a large margin the actual number of votes received. In other words, when we see success, or progress being made, we are more committed to respond positively, to continue that path, and to offer our support.

Leaders of positive change create this kind of support by identifying small wins—a strategy that was discussed in Chapter 2, as well as mentioned in discussions of problem-solving and empowerment. This small-wins strategy is applicable in a variety of skill-building activities, so we repeat part of the discussion here. The key message is that surfacing and publicizing small wins creates commitment and builds momentum for desired change (Weick, 1981). For example, we have observed leaders, when beginning a major change initiative, starting with small changes such as a new coat of paint, abolishing reserved parking spaces, adding a display case for awards, flying a flag, holding regular social events, instituting a suggestion system, and so on. Each of these small changes is designed to create commitment to the visualized change.

A small-wins strategy is designed to create a sense of momentum by creating minor, quick changes. The basic rule of thumb for small wins is: *Find something that is easy to change. Change it. Publicize it, or recognize it publicly. Then, find a second thing that's easy to change, and repeat the process.*

Small wins create commitment because: (1) they reduce the importance of any one change ("It is no big deal to make this change."); (2) they reduce demands on any group or individual ("There isn't a lot to do."); (3) they improve the confidence of participants ("At least I can do that."); (4) they help avoid resistance or retaliation ("Even if they disagree, it's only a small loss."); (5) they attract allies and create a bandwagon effect ("I want to be associated with this success."); (6) they create the image of progress ("Things seem to be moving forward."); (7) if they don't work, they only create a small flop ("No major harm is done, and no long-lasting effects occur."); (8) they provide initiatives in multiple arenas ("Resistance cannot be coordinated or organized in a single area.") (Weick, 1993).

Creating commitment to your vision will be enhanced, in other words, by applying principles of recreational work, providing opportunities for public statements of commitment, and instituting small wins. As summarized in Table 10.4, you can create commitment to that which you *say*, that which you *do*, and that which you *reward*, but, without consistency and frequency, not necessarily to that which you *want*.

FOSTERING SUSTAINABILITY

The final step in leading positive change is to ensure that the change is sustained. General officers in the United States Army refer to this step as **"creating irreversible**

Table 10.4	Generating Commitment to the Vision

1. Apply principles of recreation to the work associated with the vision.

   - Clearly define goals.

   - Ensure that scorekeeping is objective, self-administered, peer-audited, and compared to past performance.

   - Ensure frequent (or continuous) feedback.

   - Provide opportunity for personal choice.

   - Ensure that rules are consistent and don't change.

   - Provide a competitive environment.

2. Provide opportunities for people to publicly commit to the vision.

   - Hold events where people can verbalize their commitment.

   - Ask people to teach others about, or recruit others to sign up for, the vision.

3. Institute a strategy of small wins.

   - Find something easy to change.

   - Change it.

   - Publicize it.

   - Repeat the process multiple times.

momentum"; that is, ensuring that the positive change gains such momentum that it cannot be thwarted (U.S. Army, 2003). The objective is to ensure that even if the leader leaves or circumstances change, the positive change will continue because of the sustainable impetus put in place and the irreversible momentum created.

Fostering sustainability doesn't happen quickly, of course, and the four previous steps in positive change—establishing a climate of positivity, creating readiness, articulating a vision, and generating commitment—all must be successfully accomplished first. But without sustainability the other steps are largely irrelevant because the change will not last. It will be a temporary false start. So, how do you foster sustainability for a positive change? We provide three suggestions.

Turn Students into Teachers

Most of the time we assume that it is the leader's responsibility to articulate the vision of abundance, and everyone else listens to it and accepts it. Teachers teach what students need to know and students learn it for the exam. The person in charge gives directions and the rest of us follow.

The most effective leaders, however, provide an opportunity for everyone in the organization to articulate the vision, or to teach others about the desired positive change. This process requires that every person develop "a teachable point of view" (Tichy, 1997). Developing your own teachable point of view means that you come to believe in something, and you can clearly explain what it is and why. In other words, you get to the point where you can articulate the vision in your own words. You are given opportunities to teach others what you understand the positive change to be. You are transformed from a student into a teacher.

Researchers at the National Training Laboratories in Bethel, Maine, developed a **"learning stair"** (see Figure 10.5). Their studies found that people remember 5 percent of what they hear in a lecture, 10 percent of what they read, 20 percent of what they view in a video, 30 percent of what they observe being demonstrated, 50 percent of what they discuss in a group, 75 percent of what they apply, and 90 percent of what they teach to others. By teaching someone else about the vision or the intended positive change, you remember it, become committed to it, and make it a part of your own personal agenda.

One manifestation of this principle was at Xerox Corporation under former chairman Rex Kern. Kern's focus was on rapidly institutionalizing a positive change process by turning students into teachers. He spent time sharing his vision of positive change with

Figure 10.5 | The Learning Stairs (from the NTL Institute)

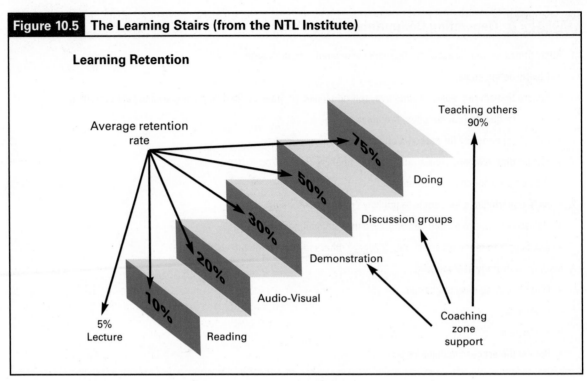

Learning Retention

SOURCE: *The Learning Stairs; NTL Institute for Applied Behavioral Science, 1091 South Bell Street, #300, Arlington, VA 22202.*

his top leadership team. Then these leaders were required to apply what they heard; that is, to implement personal action agendas and make personal changes.

Then, they were required to teach the positive change vision to someone else. Who would they teach? They taught the next level of leaders below them in the firm. They were also required to assess or monitor the positive change. This was in order to identify measurable indicators, milestones, and hard numbers to ensure that the positive change was really taking place. It was a way to guard against lip service with no real substance. What did they assess? It was the action agendas and managerial experiments implemented by the leaders they taught. The process continued down through all the organizational levels.

Each person, in other words, was exposed to the vision of abundance four times: when they learned it from their leader; when they applied it; when they taught it; and when they assessed it. Within a year of implementing Kern's process, Xerox achieved stunning results. It is widely acknowledged that this process was key in turning Xerox around as a company and in labeling Rex Kern as one of the great corporate leaders of the twentieth century.

Build Human Capital

Human capital refers to the resources inherent in the human beings who are employed by the organization. Like financial capital, human capital can be deployed, wasted, or developed. For positive change to have staying power, for it to last beyond the lifetime of the leader, people throughout the organization must have developed the capability to lead the vision themselves, to institute positive change, and to carry on under their own initiative. In other words, well-developed human capital is always the chief predictor of growth in financial capital.

Sustaining positive change occurs as individuals throughout the organization develop the capacity to lead positive change themselves. This can happen in many ways, of course, but a good example of the core principle is illustrated by a large Asian company in which we conducted research.

This particular company requires that each time a senior manager is promoted, he or she must take a three-month leave of absence. The person must actually leave work for three full months. For one of the months the manager is required to intensively study religion or ethics, and then document it, usually with a written report. For another month the individual is required to study history or a major historical figure, and then document it. The third month must be spent studying business, broadly defined. So, at the end of three months, three documents have been prepared. If, after the three months, the business has run smoothly with no major hitches, then the promotion occurs. That is, the person is promoted at the end of the three-month leave, not before.

Why would a large company implement such a strange promotion system at substantial risk and expense? Why not just send the manager to a weeklong executive education program at a university? Why remove a senior leader for three full months?

This is part of the process for creating sustainability. The three-month leave of absence provides a chance for self-development, personal enrichment, and broadening of perspective. Senior managers are required to study religion or ethics because all business decisions are based on some set of values or standards. The firm wants to make certain that these people spend time intelligently thinking through their own value system. To avoid the trap of becoming short-term in orientation, studying history helps broaden viewpoints and helps ensure that the mistakes of the past aren't repeated. Studying business principles helps expand the knowledge base and competence of the managers.

Most importantly, however, the leave of absence is essentially a test. The key value in this company is that human capital must be developed if success is to be achieved, so the leave of absence serves as a test of whether the manager has really developed his or her employees. If the organization performs less well when subordinates are in charge, then the manager is not prepared to be promoted. All managers have the responsibility to help develop others to be as competent as they are in leading positive change, and managers are held accountable for that development.

The point is, a key to ensuring that positive change is sustained is to have capable people in place. Providing organization members with developmental opportunities—that is, chances to increase their own skill set—is an investment in the long-term future of the organization and in the continuing success of positive change.

Metrics, Measurement, Milestones

A third aspect of sustainability is the establishment of **metrics** (or specific indicators of success), **measures** (or methods for assessing levels of success), and **milestones** (or benchmarks to determine when detectable progress will have occurred). These three factors help ensure accountability for change, make it clear whether or not progress is being made, and provide visible indicators that the change is successful. The adage "you get what you measure" is an illustration of this principle.

Change becomes institutionalized when it becomes a part of what people are held accountable to achieve. When it is clear what the measures are, people tend to respond to those measures. If you are measured on your test scores in a class but not on the extra reading you do, you will likely spend more effort and time studying for the exams than reading extra materials. It is only when you are measured on different criteria that you shift your focus. Consequently, institutionalizing positive change means that clear metrics are identified, a measurement system is put into place, and a milestone is identified for when the change must be accomplished.

The keys to establishing effective metrics, measures, and milestones for positive change are:

1. Identify two or three metrics or indicators that specify the result that is to be achieved. (A common mistake is to measure too many things. The key is to focus on a few core items.) These should not be metrics associated with effort or methods, but they should focus on results or outcomes. Specifically, they should address the outcomes desired from the vision of abundance. At Delta Airlines, for example, one metric for baggage handlers includes the elapsed time between the plane pulling up to the gate and the first bag being delivered on the carousel.

2. At Delta, daily logs are kept of baggage handler performance. These measures do not focus on hours worked or how many bags are handled. They focus on the key outcomes desired: namely, speed and accuracy of delivery.

3. Milestones are specified. At a certain point in time, a measurable amount of progress will have been achieved. For example, by the end of the month baggage handler timeliness will have improved 1 percent. By the end of the year, it will have improved 15 percent. Milestones simply create a time frame for keeping track of real progress.

Table 10.5	Institutionalizing the Vision and Creating Irreversible Momentum

1. Turn students into teachers.

   • Provide opportunities for people to develop a teachable point of view.

   • Make certain that others are required to articulate the vision themselves.

2. Build human capital.

   • Ensure training and development opportunities for others so they can be leaders of positive change.

   • Encourage the formation of networks and friendships that provide support.

3. Identify metrics, measures, and milestones.

   • Identify when measurable progress will be achieved.

   • Identify what the specific criteria will be for evaluating success.

   • Determine how successful achievement of the vision will be ascertained.

   • Maintain accountability for the success of the positive change.

Fostering sustainability for a vision of abundance and positive change, in sum, depends on making it a part of daily life and the habitual behavior displayed by individuals throughout the organization. No positive change can survive if it depends solely on the leader. Specific behaviors associated with these strategies are summarized in Table 10.5.

Summary

Most approaches to change focus on overcoming challenges, addressing obstacles, and solving problems. This chapter identifies an alternative approach to change in which the goal is to create abundance, or extraordinarily positive change. This kind of change unlocks something called the *heliotropic effect* (Cameron, 2013), or the tendency in all human beings toward positive energy and away from negative energy or toward that which gives life rather than detracts from life (Cameron, 2013).

When you are able to foster positive change in organizations, you unleash the heliotropic effect in your people. They tend to exude positive energy and to work toward positive outcomes, not just problem-solving or getting rid of obstacles. They achieve outcomes that would be improbable otherwise. Fostering virtuousness, positive energy, strengths, aspirational targets, and inspiring language are among the ways to unlock the heliotropic effect. This effect has been demonstrated in a variety of ways within organizations and individuals—physiologically, psychologically, emotionally, visually, and socially (see Cameron, 2003b, 2012, 2013; Cameron & Lavine, 2006; Bright, Cameron, & Caza, 2006).

In this chapter we provided a simple and easily remembered framework for accomplishing positive change and unleashing the power of the heliotropic effect. Five sets of skills and activities were explained: (1) establishing a climate of positivity, (2) creating readiness for change, (3) articulating a vision of abundance, (4) generating commitment to the vision, and (5) fostering sustainability of the positive change.

Behavioral Guidelines

Figure 10.6 summarizes the specific behaviors involved in leading positive change. Because change is so pervasive in organizations, every leader must manage change much of the time. However, positive change cuts across the grain and goes against the tendencies of most leaders. Negative, problem-focused concerns consume most leaders

Figure 10.6 **A Framework for Leading Positive Change**

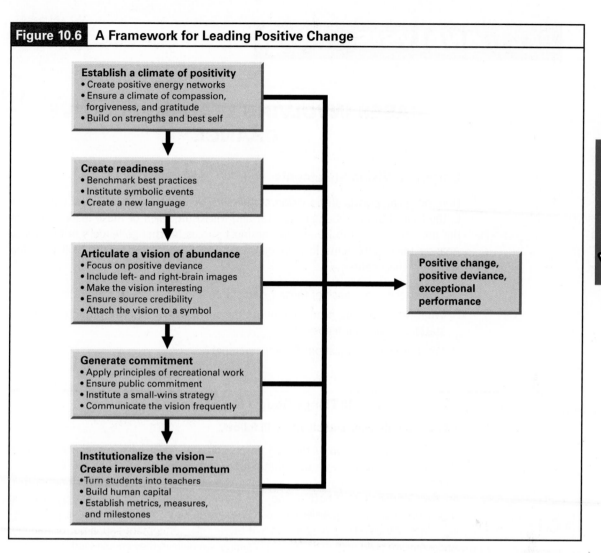

and managers. Leading positive change requires a different skill set. The following are the behavioral guidelines for achieving positive change:

A. Establish a climate of positivity by creating positive energy networks; ensure a climate of compassion, forgiveness, and gratitude; and identify and give feedback to people on their strengths and unique competencies.

B. Create readiness in others to pursue positive change by benchmarking best practice and comparing current performance to the highest standards; institute symbolic events to signal positive change; and create a new language that illustrates the positive change.

C. Articulate a vision of abundance by focusing on creating positive deviance rather than correcting negative deviance; include right-brain as well as left-brain images; and make the vision interesting by challenging weakly held assumptions.

D. Generate commitment to the vision by applying principles of recreational work associated with the vision; provide opportunities for people to publicly commit to the vision; and institute a strategy of small wins.

E. Foster sustainability of the vision, or create irreversible momentum, by turning students into teachers; help people develop teachable points of view and articulate the vision themselves; build human capital among others; and identify metrics, measures, and milestones for success.

CASES INVOLVING LEADING POSITIVE CHANGE

Corporate Vision Statements

Here are examples of three vision statements by well-known leaders of companies in the United States—Google, Toyota, and Microsoft. Each of these leaders was, at the time, considered to be among the most successful change leaders in the world. Analyze their statements in light of the principles discussed in the Skill Learning section of this chapter.

- ❑ How effective are each of these vision statements?
- ❑ What would be your prediction about the success of these firms based on the statements of their leaders?
- ❑ What are your suggestions for improvement?

10 Things Google Has Found to Be True

1. Focus on the user and all else will follow.

Since the beginning, we've focused on providing the best user experience possible. Whether we're designing a new Internet browser or a new tweak to the look of the homepage, we take great care to ensure that they will ultimately serve **you** rather than our own internal goal or bottom line. Our homepage interface is clear and simple, and pages load instantly. Placement in search results is never sold to anyone, and advertising is not only clearly marked as such, it offers relevant content and is not distracting. And when we build new tools and applications, we believe they should work so well you don't have to consider how they might have been designed differently.

2. It's best to do one thing really, really well.

We do search. With one of the world's largest research groups focused exclusively on solving search problems, we know what we do well, and how we could do it better. Through continued iteration on difficult problems, we've been able to solve complex issues and provide continuous improvements to a service that already makes finding information a fast and seamless experience for millions of people. Our dedication to improving search helps us apply what we've learned to new products, like Gmail and Google Maps. Our hope is to bring the power of search to previously unexplored areas, and to help people access and use even more of the ever-expanding information in their lives.

3. Fast is better than slow.

We know your time is valuable, so when you're seeking an answer on the web you want it right away—and we aim to please. We may be the only people in the world who can say our goal is to have people leave our homepage as quickly as possible. By shaving excess bits and bytes from our pages and increasing the efficiency of our serving environment, we've broken our own speed records many times over, so that the average response time on a search result is a fraction of a second. We keep speed in mind with each new product we release, whether it's a mobile application or Google Chrome, a browser designed to be fast enough for the modern web. And we continue to work on making it all go even faster.

4. Democracy on the web works.

Google search works because it relies on the billions of individuals posting links on websites to help determine which other sites offer content of value. We assess the importance of every web page using more than 200 signals and a variety of techniques, including our patented PageRank™ algorithm, which analyzes which sites have been "voted" to be the best sources of information by other pages across the web. As the web gets bigger, this approach actually improves, as each new site is another point of information and another vote to be counted. In the same vein, we are active in open source software development, where innovation takes place through the collective effort of many programmers.

5. You don't need to be at your desk to need an answer.

The world is increasingly mobile: People want access to information wherever they are, whenever they need it. We're pioneering new technologies and offering new solutions for mobile services that help people all over the globe to do any number of tasks on their phone, from checking email and calendar events to watching videos, not to mention the several different ways to access Google search on a phone. In addition, we're fueling greater innovation for mobile users everywhere with a free, open source mobile platform. Android brings the openness that shaped the Internet to the mobile world. Not only does Android benefit consumers, who have more choice and innovative new mobile experiences, but it opens up revenue opportunities for carriers, manufacturers and developers.

6. You can make money without doing evil.

Google is a business. The revenue we generate is derived from offering search technology to companies and from the sale of advertising displayed on our site and on other sites across the web. Hundreds of thousands of advertisers worldwide use AdWords to promote their products, and hundreds of thousands of publishers take advantage of our AdSense program to deliver ads relevant to their site content. To ensure that we're ultimately serving all our users (whether they are advertisers or not), we have a set of guiding principles for our advertising programs and practices:

❑ We don't allow ads to be displayed on our results pages unless they are relevant where they are shown. And we firmly believe that ads can provide useful information if, and only if, they are relevant to what you wish to find—so it's possible that certain searches won't lead to any ads at all.

❑ We believe that advertising can be effective without being flashy. We don't accept pop-up advertising, which interferes with your ability to see the content you've requested. We've found that text ads that are relevant to the person reading them draw much higher clickthrough rates than ads appearing randomly. Any advertiser, whether small or large, can take advantage of this highly targeted medium.

❑ Advertising on Google is always clearly identified as a "Sponsored Link," so it does not compromise the integrity of our search results. We never manipulate rankings to put our partners higher in our search results and no one can buy better page rank. Our users trust our objectivity and no short-term gain could ever justify breaching that trust.

7. There's always more information out there.

Once we'd indexed more of the HTML pages on the Internet than any other search service, our engineers turned their attention to information that was not as readily accessible.

Sometimes it was just a matter of integrating new databases into search, such as adding a phone number and address lookup and a business directory. Other efforts required a bit more creativity, like adding the ability to search news archives, patents, academic journals, billions of images and millions of books. And our researchers continue looking into ways to bring all the world's information to people seeking answers.

8. The need for information crosses all borders.

Our company was founded in California, but our mission is to facilitate access to information for the entire world, and in every language. To that end, we have offices in dozens of countries, maintain more than 180 Internet domains, and serve more than half of our results to people living outside the United States. We offer Google's search interface in more than 130 languages, offer people the ability to restrict results to content written in their own language, and aim to provide the rest of our applications and products in as many languages as possible. Using our translation tools, people can discover content written on the other side of the world in languages they don't speak. With these tools and the help of volunteer translators, we have been able to greatly improve both the variety and quality of services we can offer in even the most far-flung corners of the globe.

9. You can be serious without a suit.

Our founders built Google around the idea that work should be challenging, and the challenge should be fun. We believe that great, creative things are more likely to happen with the right company culture—and that doesn't just mean lava lamps and rubber balls. There is an emphasis on team achievements and pride in individual accomplishments that contribute to our overall success. We put great stock in our employees—energetic, passionate people from diverse backgrounds with creative approaches to work, play, and life. Our atmosphere may be casual, but as new ideas emerge in a café line, at a team meeting or at the gym, they are traded, tested, and put into practice with dizzying speed—and they may be the launch pad for a new project destined for worldwide use.

10. Great just isn't good enough.

We see being great at something as a starting point, not an endpoint. We set ourselves goals we know we can't reach yet, because we know that by stretching to meet them we can get further than we expected. Through innovation and iteration, we aim to take things that work well and improve upon them in unexpected ways. For example, when one of our engineers saw that search worked well for properly spelled words, he wondered about how it handled typos. That led him to create an intuitive and more helpful spell checker.

Even if you don't know exactly what you're looking for, finding an answer on the web is our problem, not yours. We try to anticipate needs not yet articulated by our global audience, and meet them with products and services that set new standards. When we launched Gmail, it had more storage space than any email service available. In retrospect offering that seems obvious—but that's because now we have new standards for email storage. Those are the kinds of changes we seek to make, and we're always looking for new places where we can make a difference. Ultimately, our constant dissatisfaction with the way things are becomes the driving force behind everything we do.

Update: We first wrote these "10 things" several years ago. From time to time we revisit this list to see if it still holds true. We hope it does—and you can hold us to that.

SOURCE: *Used by permission. google.com/corporate/tenthings.html*

Toyota's Mission and Guiding Principles

(Translation from original Japanese.)

1. Honor the language and spirit of the law of every nation and undertake open and fair corporate activities to be a good corporate citizen of the world.

2. Respect the culture and customs of every nation and contribute to economic and social development through corporate activities in the communities.

3. Dedicate ourselves to providing clean and safe products and to enhancing the quality of life everywhere through all our activities.

4. Create and develop advanced technologies and provide outstanding products and services that fulfill the needs of customers worldwide.

5. Foster a corporate culture that enhances individual creativity and teamwork value, while honoring mutual trust and respect between labor and management.

6. Pursue growth in harmony with the global community through innovative management.

7. Work with business partners in research and creation to achieve stable, long-term growth and mutual benefits, while keeping ourselves open to new partnerships.

Five Main Principles of Toyota

❑ Always be faithful to your duties, thereby contributing to the company and to the overall good.

❑ Always be studious and creative, striving to stay ahead of the times.

❑ Always be practical and avoid frivolousness.

❑ Always strive to build a homelike atmosphere at work that is warm and friendly.

❑ Always have respect for God, and remember to be grateful at all times.

SOURCE: *Based on English translation of Japanese mission statement from www.toyota.com.*

Microsoft

Bill Gates

Microsoft was built on innovation, and our future depends on it. We are in an extraordinary position to deliver even greater value to customers through a broad set of technologies, designed to complement each other and many third-party products and services. This is what we mean by *integrated innovation*, which is key to our business strategy.

To drive innovation, Microsoft has a long-term commitment to research and development. Our investment to date has brought about many of the successful products we offer today, and has built an increasingly valuable store of intellectual property. We are one of the largest patent filers in the world. Our innovations are available for broad use in others' products through our patent licensing programs.

A key focus of our innovation is security. We are developing advanced technologies that will help isolate computers from Internet attacks and make them more resilient when they are attacked. We are making it easier for customers to keep their systems updated with our latest, most secure software.

In addition, we are collaborating with other industry leaders to develop more effective community responses to security threats, and working closely with governments around the world to bring cybercriminals to justice. Through this broad, multipronged approach, our goal is to help bring significant improvements in security, and help preserve the benefits of technology for everyone.

As we innovate in technology, we are equally focused on crisp execution. In particular, we are working to deliver an unparalleled customer and partner experience. Across the company, we have created new listening, feedback, and response systems to help us get closer to customers and respond quickly and appropriately. Using automated error-reporting technologies, we have fixed a large majority of the computer crashes and hangs reported by customers, and our strengthened field response system has favorably resolved most nontechnical issues reported by customers.

Microsoft competes vigorously, and we always will. At the same time, we are committed to maintaining positive relationships within our industry, including with competitors, and to forging strong relationships with governments. We are also committed to helping make technology safer and easier to use. We work to help protect the safety of children online, for example, through our partnership with the International Centre for Missing and Exploited Children. We are deeply engaged in industry efforts to protect peoples' privacy online, counter the problem of identity theft, and curb the spam epidemic.

Discussion Questions

First answer the following questions by yourself, and then form a team of colleagues and share your answers. Reach consensus regarding a rank ordering.

Step 1: Rank these three firms in order based on these famous leaders' statements about their companies (1 = the best, and 3 = the worst).

	Google	Toyota	Microsoft
1. Which of the vision statements do you think represents the most effective positive leadership?	_____	_____	_____
2. Based on these statements, what is your prediction about future success in each firm in the next 10 years, from most to least successful? Ignore the health of the industry itself—e.g., computers, autos, software—and predict how each firm will do in its own industry based on these statements.	_____	_____	_____
3. Which statement has the clearest and most inspiring vision for the future?	_____	_____	_____
4. Which statement do you believe has been institutionalized the most thoroughly, and the least thoroughly?	_____	_____	_____

Step 2: Based on what you now know about leading positive change, what advice would you give each of these leaders if you were to make suggestions about how to more effectively establish a climate of positivity, create readiness for change, articulate a vision of abundance, generate commitment, and foster sustainability?

Jim Mallozzi: Implementing Positive Change in Prudential Real Estate and Relocation

In an extensive interview with Jim Mallozzi, CEO of Prudential Real Estate and Relocation Company, Jim describes the variety of ways in which he has implemented principles related to the positive change framework described in this chapter. Among the positive practices Jim implemented are utilizing positive energy networks to create a "change team"; developing a reciprocity network among company employees; articulating Everest goals; fostering positive leadership in the senior team; celebrating strengths, successes, and achievements; implementing reflected best-self feedback; and demonstrating caring and compassion with customers and potential customers. As a consequence of these initiatives, Jim achieved dramatic improvements in financial performance, improved customer satisfaction scores, and markedly enhanced employee engagement. This interview provides examples of how a leader can make a major impact in his organization's performance by creatively applying positive organizational change.

You were then appointed as the CEO of Prudential Real Estate and Relocation. What were the challenges and obstacles you found?

In the summer of 2009, as the financial markets were coming out of one of the worst recessions since the great depression, I was asked to take over Prudential's Real Estate and Relocation business (PRERS). The real estate side sells residential and commercial real estate franchises across North America. The relocation side helps families move throughout the world. It serves both U.S. government employees and large corporations. When I took over in the fall of 2009, we were facing a 70 million dollar loss per year. The company had lost 140 million dollars the year before. I could see that the organization just didn't have confidence in itself. Morale in our company and among our customers was not high. I called my good friend Kim Cameron and asked him to help me with the change effort. We started by bringing in Kim to work with our senior management team—what we call the "Gang of 30." Some of them were very reticent; others were curious. Fortunately, they were all patient.

What specifically did you do with your senior team? How did you start the process to turn around the company?

We started with a variety of exercises to show them that when you start with the positive, when you ask people to genuinely help you achieve what you're trying to do, fabulous things can happen. One very simple exercise we began with in our senior team was this: Select three people, one at a time, and tell those people three things you value about them. In corporate America, and in most places in life, people usually tell you, "Here are the three things that you need to change." Rarely do they tell you, "Here are the three things that you're fabulous at." When you do that, the energy just goes up. We started with that very simple but powerful exercise, and it got people's attention.

Did this activity translate into the rest of the organization?

About four months later we held our big annual convention. We invited 2,500 real estate agents from all over the country. This was my first presentation to this group as the new CEO. In the middle of my keynote address, I asked for the houselights to come up. I asked everybody to take out their Blackberries and their iPhones and turn them *on* as opposed to turn them *off*. I asked them all to text or email one great idea—how to get a new client, how to close a sale, how to keep a customer for life. I said, "Take your very best idea, your absolutely best one, and share it. Let's do it right now." I had somebody bring my Blackberry on stage, and I participated as well. We did that for about four or five minutes, and then I invited them to continue to do it for the next 36 hours—until the end of the convention. Do you know how many ideas we came up with? Over two thousand two hundred. We've been using those ideas for the last fifteen months. We've taken that very simple idea of reciprocity—just ask for help and you never know where help comes from—and we are building it into the culture of our company, and we're now using technology and social networking to keep it alive 24/7. We made remarkable progress in measurable targets such as growing revenues, keeping expenses flat, increasing customer service, and ultimately getting us back on a profitable basis. For us to accomplish any of this, we needed to draw on lots of sources of inspiration.

How is positive change different from the usual approach to change you have seen?
Like most companies, we do client surveys where 5 is outstanding and 1 is negative. We have always obsessed over the scores of 1, 2 and 3 and tried to get rid of those. To implement positive change we tried something different. We decided to look at the scores of 4 and 5 and figure out why were we outstanding. We want to know how to be a 5 company—how to define it, how to measure it, and how to replicate it. I happened to be in France three or four weeks ago. I was talking about positive principles with our French employees, and they were struggling a little bit. I asked, "So how do we get to be 5s?" They kind of looked at me very quizzically. I wondered if it was a language translation problem. Should I have said it in French? They responded: "No, we don't even measure anything north of 3." So I asked: "How do you know when you're outstanding?" It was a completely new idea to them. They said: "We don't." Then I asked them to try something. "Tell me when you have been outstanding. Tell me when you've seen our organization at its best." One person stood up and said, "Well I've seen our employees at our best, and I've seen us be a 5, just today. We have had people at the Charles De Gaulle Airport 24/7 for the last week greeting relocated employees who are coming back after being forced to evacuate Japan after the earthquake and tsunami." We are a relocation company, so we helped these people move there. She said, "They had to leave all their goods behind them. They have no place to live. They are being forced back into this country. We were there greeting them at the airport, helping them find a place to live, giving them bottled water as they get off the plane, helping them get back into France as quickly as we can. No other company is doing that. We are the only ones out there doing it on behalf of our clients." And I said, "That's it. You're a 5. You're helping people when they're the most vulnerable in their lives. That's to be celebrated. It's positively deviant and so different than everybody else." My job not only in France but throughout the whole firm is just to make sure people have the vision and the tools, and then I get the heck out of the way because they'll do it. It is important to try to create a culture that not only allows but encourages positive deviance.

You dramatically changed your customer satisfaction scores. Can you explain how that happened?
We set a goal to positively "wow" our best clients. For example, about 18 months ago, I was visiting our London operations meeting with a variety of clients. British Petroleum (BP) is one of our clients in Europe. I talked about positive change and how we were trying to change the culture of our company. I said that we wanted to engage them and learn from them. Then, about three or four weeks later, the Deep Water Horizon oil spill occurred with the unfortunate loss of a dozen or so lives and one of the largest environmental spills in history. You could read and see on TV that the folks at BP were being blasted in the U.S. and throughout the global press regarding their reaction times, what they were doing, what they were not doing, and so forth. The folks at BP were feeling pretty bad about all this. So I called up the senior HR person whom I knew, and I said, "Listen, I can see what's going on in the States. I'm sorry that this is happening for you. I understand you're trying to move a lot of people into the Gulf area to deal with this crisis. I would like to offer the services of our company to you, free of charge, for the duration of the crisis." He said, "Why would you make such an offer?" "The very simple answer is that we all have a responsibility for what's

going on in the Gulf. We all need to try to help in ways large and small. This is the best way that I can think of to help you. If you'd like to take us up on it, great, if you don't, that's fine. I certainly understand." About two days later I got a call back from the folks at BP. They said, "Well, first off, thank you so much for calling. There have been a number of vendors that we currently do business with throughout the world. Most have asked us to write them a check. You were the only one that offered to help us free of charge. We probably won't take you up on the offer, but we very much appreciate the gesture." I said, "That's fine. If you change your mind, we're happy to do whatever we can to help." Well, sure enough, about six months later they decided to go out for RFP (a request for a proposal) for a new vendor for relocation. We were invited to be one of the participants. Of course, the end of the story is not yet written. We don't know how it will turn out. But, we use this example with our associates to encourage them to be positively outrageous. It's okay to help others and not expect anything in return. When we do that, fabulous things can happen.

How did you roll out positive change to the rest of the organization?
As we started to introduce positive change into our organization, we began with the "Gang of 30." But we knew we needed to get the message out to our 1300 employees in seven countries representing 30 plus cultures. We knew we needed some help. So, we identified a set of positively energizing and positively deviant people. They were not the most senior or experienced people, but they were people who provided a real uplift to the organization. We selected 26 of them from across the world and brought them into headquarters. For some of these folks it was their first trip to the United States. I talked about how we wanted to change the company, and I told them that I needed their help. They were very excited by the challenge. I charged them to introduce positive change principles to 90 percent of our associates worldwide in 60 days, so that at least 1100 people had a working knowledge of what we mean by positive change in 60 days. That meant members of the change team had to understand what positive change is and have the ability to teach it to others. Then I said, "Tell me what you need to accomplish the challenge. I'm going to leave the room, and I'll come back in a couple of hours. Work with Kim. Tell me what you need to accomplish this." I came back a couple of hours later, and they said, "Okay, Jim, we're willing to take on the challenge, but here are four things we need from you. You know what? Within 60 days they had accomplished not only 90 percent, but it was 93 percent. Our employee opinion scores went up in 9 out of 10 categories. They have now created their own self-sustaining effort in continuing to bring the principles of positive change into our organization. It's been fabulous to see.

Did everyone get on-board? Did you get 100 percent agreement to adopt a positive perspective?
My own experience is about 50 to 60 percent of the people, if you're lucky, will get it pretty much out of the box. About 20 to 30 percent of the folks kind of sit on the sideline and say, "Is this just Jim's management thing du jour?" About ten percent of the people will positively reject everything that I talk about. They will just say, "It doesn't make any sense. Sorry, it's not working for me." And that's okay. I don't argue with them. They will be out of alignment with where we're trying to drive the organization, and they should go to a place where they will be in alignment. I quickly encourage them to go there. I've done a lot of recruiting of both senior and middle level executives into our company in the last 18 months, and people want to join a positively oriented company, even if you're asking them to accept the same or less pay. The younger the person is, the truer it is.

SOURCE: *Adapted from Cameron, K. S., and Plews, E. (2012) "Positive Leadership in Action."* Organizational Dynamics, *41: 99–105.*

ANALYSIS

Discussion Questions

10.1. What elements of positive change do you see implemented by Jim Mallozzi?

10.2. In what ways did Jim try to foster positively deviant performance?

10.3. What aspects of positive change did he leave out? What would you advise him to do going forward to foster sustainability?

10.4. What was Jim's vision of abundance?

EXERCISES IN LEADING POSITIVE CHANGE

Reflected Best-Self Portrait

The Skill Assessment section of this chapter suggested that you engage in a powerful assessment process that reveals your best self, or the unique strengths and contributions you display. If you obtained that feedback, you will want to analyze that data to create a best-self portrait. Read all of your feedback and take notes on the key insights. Look for commonalities across the individuals who provided you with feedback. Create themes where you find commonalities, and link the examples to them. You may find it useful to use a table such as the following.

COMMONALITY/THEME	EXAMPLES GIVEN	MY INTERPRETATION
1. Creative	1. Innovative builder of new projects at work. 2. Found new solutions for old problems. 3. Guided the team in transforming itself.	My ideas tend to be interesting and creative. I tend to bring new ideas to people with whom I work. I am innovative in my approach to problem-solving.
2.	1. 2. 3.	
3.	1. 2. 3.	

Step 1: Now, create a written portrait of your best self that captures the basic themes in your data. Identify when you are at your very best and what attributes and capabilities you display. Write at least one paragraph describing yourself using your best-self feedback as the data. Here are some reflective questions that you may want to consider as you craft your self-portrait.

- What have you learned about your own key strengths and uniquenesses?
- What was surprising to you about your feedback?
- What circumstances bring out your best?
- How do you intend to follow up or capitalize on this feedback?
- What career or life implications does this feedback hold?
- What has improved, or could improve, as a result of obtaining this feedback?

Write up your conclusions and your commitments as a result of reading through the feedback. Writing will have a clarifying and focusing effect, and you are not likely to get this kind of data very often in your life. Don't miss the opportunity to craft something meaningful for yourself.

Step 2: Share your best-self portrait with a team of colleagues. Get verbal feedback from them about what you have written. That is, your colleagues will help you clarify and become specific about your best-self attributes.

SOURCE: *http://positiveorgs.bus.umich.edu, search term "Reflected Best Self Exercise"*

Positive Organizational Diagnosis Exercise

Step 1: Select an organization that you can diagnose. If you are not currently working in one, volunteering in one, or leading one, select your own school or university. Your objective is to identify the strengths, peak experiences, and examples of positive deviance in the organization (rather than the problems and challenges). These kinds of data are seldom gathered in organizations, and people are not often asked to provide these kinds of data. However, in every organization, something works well. When asked, people can always identify things that are spectacular about their organization.

The questions we ask and the language we use helps determine our vision of abundance. When people have experienced success in the past, they are more willing to pursue a vision of the future, knowing that they have achieved extraordinary success in the past. They are confident that they can do it again.

Here are some examples of questions you should ask in diagnosing the positive aspects of an organization, a group, or even your own family.

- *Best-in-Class*: Put yourself in clients' or customers' shoes. What would they say makes this organization the best there is?
- *Careers*: What do you love about this organization that makes you want to come to work each day?
- *Leadership*: Who are the leaders in your organization you admire the most, and why? What do they do that is extraordinary?
- *Communication*: When did you have an extremely satisfying and productive interchange with someone you care deeply about? What happened?
- *Teamwork*: When have you experienced delight at extraordinary cooperation and teamwork that emerged in this organization? What happened?
- *Culture*: What is especially fun, energizing, revitalizing about your culture? What turns you on and gives you energy?
- *Aspiration*: What are your highest aspirations for this organization? What do you really hope for?
- *Work*: What is the best you have ever seen accomplished in the work here? What was achieved that exceeded everyone's expectations?

When you ask these kinds of questions, you will detect more enthusiasm being displayed by the person responding, and you will note an unleashing of positive energy. This is in contrast to more typical questions used in organizational diagnosis:

- ❑ What are your major problems and challenges?
- ❑ Where are your deficits?
- ❑ What is troublesome to people in this organization?
- ❑ What needs fixing?
- ❑ In what areas are you missing your targets?
- ❑ Who is doing better than you are, and why?

Craft your own interview format for conducting a positive diagnosis of an organization, a group, or a family. Use the positive questions above as a guide. Interview a representative sample of people in that organization (or all the members of your family).

Step 2: Now, write up the equivalent of a best-self portrait for the organization. Address these questions regarding the organization.

- ❑ What are the strengths and unique qualities of this organization?
- ❑ In what ways can it capitalize on its competencies?
- ❑ What is the vision that drives the organization?
- ❑ What recommendations do you have for positive change?

A Positive Change Agenda

Write out a detailed plan for leading positive change in an organization in which you are participating. You need not be the formal leader of that organization, since most real change is initiated from places within the organization other than the leader's office. Most great leaders simply capitalize on the ideas and agendas of their people.

In crafting your plan, address the following questions with specific and actionable ideas. Do not simply say something like: "I'll treat people better." That is not specific enough and does not identify an action. Instead, say, "I will compliment someone every day." That's more doable and measurable.

1. In what ways will you work to create a positive climate? What will you actually do?
2. In what specific ways will you create readiness in others to pursue positive change?
3. What is your specific vision of abundance? How will you communicate it so that it is accepted and energizing to people?
4. How will you generate commitment to that vision among others? Identify specific actions.
5. What will you do to institutionalize and create irreversible momentum for your positive change?

Now, identify the specific things you will need to do personally to exemplify and model your positive change. How will you enhance your own credibility?

ACTIVITIES FOR LEADING POSITIVE CHANGE

Suggested Assignments

10.6. Find someone you know well who is working in an organization. Teach him or her the principles of leading positive change. Use the concepts, principles, techniques, and exercises provided in this chapter. Describe what you taught and record the results in your journal.

10.7. Do a systematic analysis of the things that occur in your life for which you are grateful. What is going right, and what makes life worth living? Consider your job, family, school, and social life. Keep a "gratitude journal" for at least a semester (a three-month period). Make an entry in it at least once a week. Note what else changes in your life compared to before you began the journal.

10.8. Identify at least one person in your circle of acquaintances who is positively energizing to you. When you are around this person, you simply feel better. Make certain that you interact with that person on a frequent and consistent basis. Let the person know how you feel about him or her.

10.9. Identify an example of best practice. That is, find someone or some organization that is unique in being the best there is at something. Try to identify what it is that accounts for that extraordinary performance. What factors could be generalized to others or to other settings?

10.10. Identify a symbol that can serve as a constant reminder of your own—or your organization's—vision of abundance. Select something that is positively energizing and that can remind you every time you see it that you are pursuing a meaningful, uplifting vision.

10.11. Establish a close mentoring relationship with someone with whom you work or go to school. Your mentor may be a professor, a senior manager, or someone who has been around longer than you have. That relationship should build your self-esteem and be energizing to you. Make certain, however, that the relationship is reciprocal, not one-way.

Application Plan and Evaluation

The intent of this exercise is to help you apply this cluster of skills in a real-life, out-of-class setting. Now that you have become familiar with the behavioral guidelines that form the basis of effective skill performance, you will improve most by trying out those guidelines in an everyday context. Unlike a classroom activity, in which feedback is immediate and others can assist you with their evaluations, this skill application activity is one you must accomplish and evaluate on your own. There are two parts to this activity. Part 1 helps prepare you to apply the skill, and Part 2 helps you evaluate and improve on your experience. Be sure to write down answers to each item. Don't short-circuit the process by skipping steps.

Part 1: Planning

10.12. Write down the two or three aspects of this skill that are most important to you. These may be areas of weakness, areas of strength, or areas that are most salient to a situation you face right now. Identify the specific aspects of this skill that you want to apply.

10.13. Now identify the setting or the situation in which you will apply this skill. Establish a plan for performance by actually writing down a description of the situation. Who else will be involved? When will you do it? Where will it be done?

    Circumstances:
    Who else?
    When?
    Where?

10.14. Identify the specific behaviors in which you will engage to apply this skill. Operationalize your skill performance.

10.15. What are the indicators of successful performance? How will you know you have been effective? What will indicate you have performed competently?

Part 2: Evaluation

10.16. After you have completed your implementation, record the results. What happened? How successful were you? What was the effect on others?

10.17. How can you improve? What modifications can you make next time? What will you do differently in a similar situation in the future?

10.18. Looking back on your whole skill practice and application experience, what have you learned? What has been surprising? In what ways might this experience help you in the long term?

SCORING KEYS AND COMPARISON DATA

✪ Go to www.pearson.com/mylab/management for scoring keys and comparison data for the following instruments:

Leading Positive Change
Positive Practices Survey

Reflected Best-Self Feedback™ Exercise

This exercise does not have a solution or comparison data. Answers will vary among students.

A

ability: the product of aptitude multiplied by training and opportunity. p. 267

abundance approach: the right side of the performance continuum, characterized by concepts such as striving for excellence and being ethically virtuous, which are especially relevant to the skill of leading positive change. p. 451

accommodating approach: a response to conflict that tries to preserve a friendly interpersonal relationship by satisfying the other party's concerns while ignoring one's own. It generally ends with both parties losing. p. 318

achievement orientation: an emphasis on personal accomplishment and merit as the basis for getting ahead, used in contrast to an ascription orientation. One of the key dimensions that identifies international culture differences. p. 52

advising response: a response that provides direction, evaluation, personal opinion, or instructions. p. 205

affective orientation: an emphasis on open displays of emotion and feeling as being acceptable, used in contrast to a neutral orientation. One of the key dimensions that identifies international culture differences. p. 52

agreement communication: a form of validating communication marked by an approach that find agreement between the communicators. p. 200

ambidextrous thinking: the use of both the left and right sides of the brain, indicative of the most creative problem solvers. p. 153

analytical problem solving: a method of solving problems that involves four steps: (1) defining the problem; (2) generating alternative solutions; (3) evaluating and selecting an alternative; and (4) implementing and following up on the solution. p. 137, 148

anticipatory stressor: the anxious expectation of unfamiliar, uncertain, or disagreeable events. p. 93

ascription orientation: an emphasis on attributes such as age, gender, or family background as the basis for getting ahead, used in contrast to achievement orientation. One of the key dimensions that identifies international culture differences. p. 52

attraction: also referred to as personal attraction, "likability" stemming from agreeable behavior and attractive physical appearance; a combination of behaviors normally associated with friendships that has been shown to contribute to managerial success. p. 231

autonomy: the freedom to choose how and when to do a particular task; one of the characteristics of an intrinsically satisfying job. p. 101, 275

avoiding response: an unassertive, uncooperative reaction to conflict that neglects the interests of both parties by side-stepping the issue. The resulting frustration may engender power struggles as others rush to fill the leadership vacuum. p. 318

B

benchmarking: comparing current levels of performance to the highest standards available, by finding best practice, studying it in detail, and planning to exceed it. p. 459

bias against thinking: the inclination to avoid mental work, one indication of the conceptual block, complacency. p. 153

blocking roles: behaviors that stand in the way of or inhibit the effective performance of a team, or that subvert team member effectiveness. p. 428

brainstorming: a technique designed to help people solve problems by generating alternative solutions without prematurely evaluating and rejecting them. p. 159

C

centrality: the attribute of a position in which the occupant is a key member of informal networks of task-related and interpersonal relationships. The resulting access to information, resources, and the personal commitment of others is an important source of power. p. 235

challenging goals: one of the factors affecting the motivating potential of stated goals—hard goals tend to be more motivating than easy goals. p. 266

clarification probe: question(s) designed to clarify information given by the interviewee. p. 206

coaching: interpersonal communication used by managers to pass along advice and information or to set standards for subordinates. p. 194

cognitive style: the manner in which an individual gathers and evaluates information he/she receives. p. 47

collaborating approach: the cooperative, assertive, problem-solving mode of responding to conflict. It focuses on finding solutions to the basic problems and issues that are acceptable to both parties rather than on finding fault and assigning blame. Of the conflict management approaches, this is the only win-win strategy. p. 318

collective feeling: a feature of compassionate organizations, in which managers plan events where people can share feelings such as grief, support, or love. p. 455

collective noticing: a feature of compassionate organizations, in which managers notice or simply become aware when employees suffer or experience difficulty. p. 455

collective responding: a feature of compassionate organizations, in which managers ensure an appropriate response is made when healing or restoration is needed. p. 455

collectivism orientation: an emphasis on the predominance of groups, families, or collectives over individuals, used in contrast to individualism orientation. One of the key dimensions that identifies international culture differences. Also referred to as communitarianism. p. 51

commitment: the conceptual block that results when an individual endorses a particular point of view, definition, or solution. p. 149

comparative standards: standards that compare current performance to similar individuals or organizations, one of several different kinds of best practice standards. p. 459

compassion: in an organization, the capacity to foster collective noticing, feeling, and responding. p. 455

competence: areas in which a person performs fine—not stellar, but good enough. p. 275, 457

complacency: the conceptual block that occurs not because of poor thinking habits or inappropriate assumptions but because of fear, ignorance, self-satisfaction, or mental laziness. p. 152

compression: the conceptual block that results from an individual's looking at a problem too narrowly, screening out too much relevant data, or making assumptions that inhibit solving the problem. p. 150

compromising response: a reaction to conflict that attempts to find satisfaction for both parties by "splitting the difference." If overused, it sends the message that settling disputes is more important than solving problems. p. 318

conceptual blocks: mental obstacles that restrict the way a problem is defined and limit the number of alternative solutions that might otherwise be considered. p. 144

conformity level: the second level of values maturity, at which moral reasoning is based on agreement with and support of society's conventions and expectations. p. 53

congruence: exactly matching the communication, verbally and nonverbally, to what an individual is thinking and feeling. p. 195

conjunctive communication: connection of responses to previous messages in such a way that conversation flows smoothly. p. 202

consistent goals: one of the factors affecting the motivating potential of stated goals—it is difficult to pursue goals that are inconsistent or incompatible. p. 266

constancy: the conceptual block that results from using only one way to look at a problem—to approach, define, describe, or solve it. p. 146

continuous improvement: small, incremental changes team members initiate. p. 418

continuous reinforcement: administration of a reward every time a behavior occurs. p. 275

core competence: an aggregation of individual team member skills, including knowledge, styles, communication patterns, and ways of behaving. p. 418

core self-evaluation: a concept that captures the essential aspects of personality; it accounts for the five personality dimensions (neuroticism, extroversion, conscientiousness, agreeableness, and openness). p. 47

counseling: interpersonal communication used to help subordinates recognize their own problems rather than offering advice, direction, or a right answer. p. 194

creating irreversible momentum: ensuring positive change gains such momentum that it becomes institutionalized and cannot be thwarted. p. 466–467

creative problem solving: a method of solving problems that involves four stages: preparation, incubation, illumination, and verification. p. 137, 154

D

deep breathing: relaxation technique of taking several successive, slow deep breaths, then exhaling completely. p. 109

defensiveness: focusing on self-defense rather than listening; occurs when an individual feels threatened or punished by the communication. p. 194

deficit approach: the left side of the performance continuum, characterized by concepts such as solving problems and making a profit, which has garnered much more attention than the abundance approach but is less relevant to the skill of leading positive change. p. 451

deflecting response: a response that switches the focus from the communicator's subject to one selected by the listener; or simply the change of subject by the listener. p. 205

delegation: assignment of responsibility for tasks to subordinates. p. 390

descriptive communication: objective description of the event or behavior that needs modification; description of the reaction to the behavior or its consequences; and suggestion of a more acceptable alternative. p. 196

diffusion orientation: an emphasis on integrating work, family, and personal roles in a society, used in contrast to specificity orientation. One of the key dimensions that identifies international culture differences. p. 52

dignity (and liberty): the ethical decision principle that a decision is right and proper if it preserves the basic humanity of individuals and provides the opportunity for them to have greater freedom. p. 56

direct analogies: a Synectic problem-solving technique in which individuals apply facts, technology, and previous experience to solving a problem. p. 156

disciplining: a motivational strategy by which a manager reacts negatively to an employee's undesirable behavior in order to discourage further occurrences. Disciplining may be useful up to a point but does not encourage exceptional performance. p. 273

disconfirmation: a "put-down"; or the feeling resulting from communication that demeans or belittles the recipient and threatens his or her sense of self-worth. p. 194

disjunctive communication: responses that are disconnected from what was stated before. It can result from (1) a lack of equal opportunity to speak; (2) long pauses in a speech or before a response; or (3) when one person decides the topic of conversation. p. 202

disowned communication: attribution to an unknown person, group, or some external source; allows the communicator to avoid responsibility for the message and therefore avoid investing in the interaction. p. 202

distributive negotiaion: a negotiation tactic that requires both parties to sacrifice something to resolve the conflict—to divide up a "fixed pie." (Contrast with the integrative negotiation.) p. 309

E

effort: an important source of power suggesting personal commitment. p. 232

elaboration probe: question(s) designed to pursue a topic further when an interviewee has responded with superficial or inadequate information. p. 206

emotional intelligence: the ability to manage oneself emotionally and to manage relationships with others. p. 47

empowerment: the use of acquired power to give others power in order to accomplish objectives; it strikes a balance between lack of power and abuse of power. p. 372

enactive strategy: a method of managing stress that creates a new environment by eliminating the stressors. p. 90

encounter stressor: a type of stressor that results from interpersonal conflict. p. 92

environmentally induced stress: conflict-fostering tension induced by such organizational factors as budget tightening or uncertainty caused by rapid, repeated change. p. 316

equity: workers' perceptions of the fairness of rewards based on the comparison of what they are getting out of the work relationship (outcomes) to what they are putting into it (input). p. 282

ethical decision making: a well-developed set of moral principles used when making decisions. p. 55

evaluative communication: a statement that makes a judgment about or places a label on other individuals or on their behavior. p. 196

Everest goals: goals that represent an ultimate achievement, an extraordinary accomplishment, or a beyond-the-norm outcome. p. 422

expertise: cognitive ability resulting from formal training and education or from on-the-job experience; an important source of power in a technological society. p. 230

external attributions: to interpret someone's behavior as being caused by situational conditions. p. 284

external locus of control: the viewpoint of an individual who attributes the success or failure of particular behavior to outside forces. p. 60

extrinsic motivation: behavior motivated by rewards that are controlled by someone other than the employee—usually the supervisor—such as appreciation, job security, or good working conditions. (Compare with internal motivators.) p. 270

F

fantasy analogies: a synetic problem-solving technique in which individuals ask, "In my wildest dreams, how would I wish the problem to be resolved?" p. 156

feedback: information regularly received by individuals from superiors about their performance on a job. Knowledge of results permits workers to understand how their efforts have contributed to organizational goals. p. 101, 267

flexibility: the freedom to exercise one's judgment—an important prerequisite for gaining power in a position—particularly in tasks that are high in variety and novelty. p. 237

flexibility of thought: the diversity of ideas or concepts generated. p. 159

flexibility in communication: the result of the willingness of the coach or counselor to accept the existence of additional data or other alternatives and to acknowledge that other individuals may be able to make significant contributions both to the problem solution and to the relationship. p. 200

fluency of thought: the number of ideas or concepts produced in a given length of time. p. 159

forcing response: an assertive, uncooperative response to conflict that uses the exercise of authority to satisfy one's own needs at the expense of another's. p. 317

forgiveness: in an organization, the capacity to abandon justified resentment, bitterness, and blame, and instead, to adopt positive, forward-looking approaches in response to harm or damage. p. 455

forming stage: first stage of team development in which the team is oriented to each other and establishes clarity of purpose. p. 412

frameworks: familiar patterns that managers can use to clarify complex or ambiguous situations. p. 449

fundamental attribution error: the human tendency to explain another person's behavior on internal, dispositional factors and underestimate the effects of external or situational concerns. p. 284

G

goal characteristics: effective goals are specific, consistent, and appropriately challenging. p. 266

goal setting: the foundation of an effective motivational program, which consists of (1) including employees in the goal-setting process; (2) setting specific, consistent, and challenging goals; and (3) providing feedback. p. 102

goal-setting process: the critical consideration is that goals must be understood and accepted if they are to be effective. p. 266

goal standards: standards that compare current performance to publicly stated goals, one of several different kinds of best practice standards. p. 459

gratitude: in an organization, the frequent expression of thankfulness that leads to reciprocal behavior, equity, and justice. p. 456

groupthink: one of the pitfalls in group decision making that occurs when the pressure to reach consensus interferes with critical thinking. When the leader or the majority appear to prefer a particular solution, holders of dissenting views are reluctant to speak out. p. 165

H

hardiness: a combination of the three characteristics of a highly stress-resistant personality—control, commitment, and challenge. p. 106

hierarchical needs model: a general theory of motivation, positing that behavior is oriented toward need fulfillment, and that human needs tend to be arranged hierarchically (i.e., lower-level needs must be fulfilled before higher-order needs become salient). p. 279

human capital: a person's abilities and competencies ("I know the answer to the question"). Compare with social capital. p. 468

I

idea champion: person who comes up with the innovative solutions to problems. p. 166

ideal standards: standards that compare current performance to an ideal or perfect standard, one of several different kinds of best practice standards. p. 459

ignoring: a manager's neglect of both the performance and the satisfaction of employees. Such a lack of effective leadership can paralyze a work unit. p. 272

ignoring commonalities: a manifestation of the commitment block—the failure to identify similarities among seemingly disparate situations or data. p. 149

illumination stage: in creative thought, the third stage, which occurs when an insight is recognized and a creative solution is articulated. p. 154

imagery and fantasy: a relaxation technique using visualization to change the focus of one's thoughts. p. 110

imagination creativity: the pursuit of new ideas, breakthroughs, and radical approaches to problem solving. p. 142

imperviousness in communication: the failure of the communicator to acknowledge the feelings or opinions of the listener. p. 200

improvement creativity: the pursuit of incremental improvements on existing ideas. p. 143

improvement standards: standards that compare current performance to improvements made in the past, one of several different kinds of best practice standards. p. 459

incongruence: a mismatch between what one is experiencing and what one is aware of, or a mismatch between what one feels and what one communicates. p. 195

incubation creativity: the pursuit of creativity through teamwork, involvement, and coordination among individuals. p. 143

incubation stage: an early stage in creative thought in which mostly unconscious mental activity combines unrelated thoughts in pursuit of a solution to a problem. p. 154

indifference in communication: a type of communication in which the other person's existence or importance is not acknowledged. p. 199

individualism orientation: an emphasis on the self, uniqueness, and individuality, used in contrast to collectivism orientation. One of the key dimensions that identifies international cultural differences. p. 51

informational deficiencies: breakdowns in organizational communication. Conflicts based on the resulting misunderstandings tend to be common but easy to resolve. p. 316

initiator role: the part played in a conflict management model by the individual who first registers a complaint with another person who is the "responder." p. 322

innovation: large, visible, discontinuous changes; breakthroughs. p. 137

instrumental values: those values that prescribe desirable standards of conduct or methods to reach a goal. p. 53

integrative negotiation: a negotiation tactic in which the focus is on collaborative ways of "expanding the pie" by avoiding fixed, incompatible positions. (Contrast with distributive negotiation.) p. 309

internal attributions: to interpret someone's behavior as being caused by internal, or inherent, qualities. p. 284

internal locus of control: the viewpoint of an individual who attributes the success or failure of particular behavior to his/her own actions. p. 60

interpersonal competence: the ability to manage conflict, to build and manage high-performance teams, to conduct efficient meetings, to coach and counsel employees, to provide negative feedback in constructive ways, to influence others' opinions, and to motivate and energize employees. p. 46

intrinsic motivation: performance in which an employee is motivated by job characteristics inherent in the job itself, over which the manager has no control, and that determine whether or not a particular employee will find that job interesting and satisfying. (Compare with external motivators.) p. 286

invalidating communication: that which denies the other person the possibility of contributing to the communication. p. 199

investment creativity: the pursuit of rapid goal achievement and competitiveness. p. 143

issue-focused conflict: interpersonal conflicts that are substantive, or content, oriented. See people-focused conflict. p. 314

issue selling: influence strategy characterized by being the champion or representative of an issue. p. 244

J

Janusian thinking: thinking contradictory thoughts at the same time; conceiving two opposing ideas to be true concurrently. p. 158

job crafting: a variation of job design, allows workers to redesign their own jobs to promote job satisfaction and enhanced engagement. p. 276

job design: the process of matching job characteristics to workers' skills, interests, and needs. p. 276

L

leadership: a temporary, dynamic condition that can be developed and demonstrated by any person willing to choose to adopt a certain mind-set and implement certain key skills and competencies. p. 448

leading positive change: a management skill that focuses on unlocking positive human potential, creating abundance and human well-being, and acknowledging that positive change engages the heart as well as the mind. p. 450

learning stair: a model, developed by researchers at the National Training Laboratories in Bethel, Maine, that grades learning retention; at the lowest level, people remember only 5 percent of what they hear in a lecture, while at the highest level, people remember 90 percent of what they teach to others. p. 467

learning style: the way in which individuals perceive, interpret, and respond to information. Four main learning styles exist. p. 48

left-hemisphere thinking: brain activity concerned with logical, analytic, linear, or sequential tasks. p. 153

legitimacy: conformity with an organization's value system and practices, which increases one's acceptance and thus one's influence in that organization. p. 233

life balance: the development of resiliency in all areas of one's life in order to handle stress that cannot be eliminated. p. 104

locus of control: the second dimension of orientation toward change; the viewpoint from which an individual judges the extent to which he/she controls his/her own destiny. p. 60

M

manifest needs model: a general theory of motivation, positing that individuals can be classified according to the strengths of their various needs, which are often divergent and conflicting. p. 279

measures: methods for assessing levels of success. p. 469

meditative practices: technique of relaxation by meditation such as guided visualization or mantras. p. 110

mediator role: the conflict management role played by the third party who intervenes in a dispute between an "initiator" and a "responder." p. 327

metrics: specific indicators of success. p. 469

milestones: benchmarks to determine when detectable progress will have occurred. p. 469

morphological synthesis: a four-step process intended to expand the number of creative alternatives available for solving a problem. It involves combining the different attributes of a problem together in unique ways. p. 161

motivation: a combination of desire and commitment demonstrated by effort. p. 263

muscle relaxation: technique of relaxation by easing the tension in successive muscle groups. p. 109

N

need for achievement: an expressed desire for accomplishment and recognition. p. 280

need for affiliation: an expressed desire for social relations. p. 280

need for control: the desire to maintain for oneself a satisfactory balance of power and influence in relationships. p. 385

need for power: an expressed desire for control, or influence, over others. p. 280

negative deviance: change toward illness, error, conflict, and the like, usually depicted as a shift to the left along the continuum that shows normal, healthy performance in the middle. p. 451

negative energizers: people who deplete the good feelings and enthusiasm in others and make them feel diminished, devalued, or criticized. p. 454

negative reinforcement: involves removing something that is unpleasant from a task, with the aim of increasing the frequency of the behavior. p. 272

negotiation strategies: two broad approaches or perspectives used for resolving differences or allocating scarce resources—integrative and distributive. p. 309

neutral orientation: an emphasis on rational and stoic approaches to problem solving, used in contrast to an affective orientation. One of the key dimensions that identifies international cultural differences. p. 52

noninquisitiveness: the failure to ask questions, obtain information or search for data; an example of the complacency block. p. 152

norming stage: the second stage of a team's development in which expectations become clear, a group identity is formed, and the norms become clear and accepted. p. 412

O

orchestrator: person who brings together cross-functional groups and necessary political support to facilitate implementation of a creative idea. p. 166

organizational culture: the values and basic assumptions that typify an organization. It refers to the most basic elements of an organization, or "just the way things are around here." p. 53

orientation toward change: an individual's adaptability to ever-increasing levels of ambiguity and turbulence. p. 47

owned communication: statements for which a person takes responsibility, acknowledging that he or she is the source of the message; an indication of supportive communication. p. 202

P

partial, or intermittent, reinforcement: administration of a reward on an intermittent basis, when a behavior occurs. p. 275

particularism orientation: an emphasis on relationships and close personal connections to govern behavior, used in contrast to universalism orientation. One of the key dimensions that identifies international cultural differences. p. 51

"path goal" theory of leadership: The theory focuses on managers clearing a path toward their employees' goals. It proposes that a manager's involvement should vary according to what subordinates need, how much they expect, and how much support is available to them from other organizational sources, p. 268

people-focused conflict: interpersonal conflict that is personal (e.g., a clash between different personalities or interpersonal styles). See issue-focused conflict. p. 314

perceived equity: refers to a person's perception that valued outcomes are distributed fairly. p. 279

perceptual stereotyping: defining a problem by using preconceptions based on past experience, thus preventing the problem from being viewed in novel ways. p. 149

performance: the product of ability multiplied by motivation. p. 263

performance expectations: established goals that set the standard for performance. p. 263

performance goals: a level of performance above what is expected that, if attained, holds the promise of rewards. p. 265

performing stage: stage of a team when it is able to function as a highly effective and efficient unit. p. 412

personal analogies: recommended as part of Synectics, whereby individuals try to identify themselves as the problem, asking the question, "If I were the problem, what would I like? What would satisfy me?" p. 156

personal differences: variations among individuals' values and needs that have been shaped by different socialization processes. Interpersonal conflicts stemming from such incompatibilities are the most difficult for a manager to resolve. p. 315

personal management interview program (PMI): a regularly scheduled, one-on-one meeting between a manager and his or her subordinates. p. 208

personal values: an individual's standards that define what is good/bad, worthwhile/worthless, desirable/undesirable, true/false, moral/immoral. p. 48

positive deviance: change toward excellence, perfection, psychological "flow," and the like, usually depicted as a shift to the light along the continuum that shows normal, healthy performance in the middle. p. 420

positive energizers: people who strengthen and create vitality and liveliness in others. p. 454

positive energy networks: interconnected groups of vitality and liveliness creators, being a member of which has been shown to be more predictive of success than being at the center of an information network or influence network. p. 454

positive interpersonal relationships: relationships that create positive energy and physiological, emotional, intellectual, and social consequences. p. 188

positive reinforcement: involves adding something pleasant to a task to increase the frequency of behavior. p. 272

preparation stage: a stage in creative thought that includes gathering data, defining the problem, generating alternatives, and consciously examining all available information. p. 154

principled level: the third and highest level of values maturity in which an individual judges right from wrong by following internalized principles developed from personal experience. p. 53

proactive personality: a dispositional tendency to effect change in one's environment. p. 237

proactive strategy: a method of managing stress that initiates action in order to resist the negative effects of stress. p. 90

probing response: a response that asks a question about what the communicator just said or about a topic selected by the listener. p. 206

problem-solving process: an approach to conflict resolution that focuses on identifying underlying problems, or issues, and brainstorming solutions. p. 321

process: a sequential set of activities designed to lead to a specific outcome. p. 46

process improvement: stage in process management where process itself is changed so as to foster advancement. p. 412

punishment: involves adding something unpleasant when undesired behaviors occur, as a discouragement. p. 272

purpose: the reason a meeting is held, including information sharing, commitment building, information disseminating, and problem solving and decision making. p. 275

Q

quality circles: A problem-solving process originating in Japan in which teams who meet to discuss issues and make recommendations to upper management. p. 408

R

reactive strategy: a method for managing stress that copes with the stressors immediately, temporarily reducing their effects. p. 90

reason: the influence strategy that relies on persuasion and appeals to rational consideration of the inherent merits of the request in order to gain compliance. It is explicit and direct, not manipulative. p. 241

reciprocity: an influence strategy through which a manager uses bargaining as a tool for exacting a subordinate's compliance. This approach operates on the principle of self-interest and respect for the value of the interpersonal relationship. p. 241

recreational work: work that people willingly engage in due to characteristics such as clearly defined goals, objective evaluations, frequent feedback, the presence of personal choice, consistent rules, and a competitive environment. p. 465

reflected best-self feedback: a technique that managers can use to enhance positivity and focus on strengths, by providing people with feedback on their strengths and unique capabilities rather than their weaknesses. p. 457

reflecting response: a response that serves two purposes: (1) to confirm a message that was heard and (2) to communicate understanding and acceptance of the other person. p. 206

reflection probe: nondirective question(s) used for either elaboration or clarification of information; it generally mirrors or repeats some aspect of the interviewee's last answer. p. 206

reframing: stress-reduction technique of redefining a situation in a more positive light. p. 110

rehearsal: relaxation technique of trying out stressful scenarios and alternative reactions. p. 110

reinforcement: when rewards are linked to desired behaviors they are said to reinforce those behaviors (i.e., increase their frequency). p. 272

relatedness: pertains to our desire to connect with others in meaningful ways. p. 275

relational algorithm: a blockbusting technique for combining unrelated attributes in problem solving by connecting words to force a relationship between two elements in a problem. p. 161

relationship-building roles: those that emphasize the interpersonal aspects of the team. p. 426

relevance: the characteristic of a position whose tasks relate most closely to the dominant competitive goals of an organization and therefore enhance the power of the occupant. p. 238

repetition probe: a repeated or paraphrased question used if the interviewee has not directly answered a question the first time. p. 206

reprimand: a behavior-shaping approach used to transform unacceptable behaviors into acceptable ones; the discipline should be prompt and it should focus on the specific behavior. p. 273

resiliency: one's capacity to cope with stress. p. 104

respectful, egalitarian communication: treating subordinates as worth-while, competent, and insightful by emphasizing joint problem solving rather than projecting a superior position. p. 200

responder role: the part played in a conflict management model by the person who is supposedly the source of the "initiator's" problem. p. 325

retribution: an influence strategy that involves a threat—the denial of expected rewards or the imposition of punishment. It usually triggers an aversive response in the subordinate and the breakdown of the interpersonal relationship. p. 239

reverse the definition: a tool for improving and expanding problem definition by reversing the way you think of the problem. p. 157

rewarding: the motivational strategy that links desired behaviors with employee-valued outcomes. Such positive reinforcement gives an employee more incentive for exceptional accomplishment than does disciplining. p. 273

reward salience: refers to the extent to which an outcome is personally valued because it satisfies an important need. p. 279

right-hemisphere thinking: mental activity concerned with intuition, synthesis, playfulness, and qualitative judgment. p. 153

rigidity in communication: a type of message that portrays the communication as absolute, unequivocal, or unquestionable. p. 199

role incompatibility: the conflict-producing difference between workers whose tasks are interdependent but whose priorities differ because their responsibilities within the organization differ. The mediation of a common superior is usually the best solution. p. 316

rule breaker: the person who goes beyond organizational boundaries and barriers to ensure success of the creative solution. p. 166

S

self-awareness: a knowledge of one's own personality and individuality. p. 44

self-centered level: the first level of values maturity. It contains two stages of values development, moral reasoning and instrumental values, which are based on personal needs or wants and the consequences of an act. p. 53

self-determination: feelings of having a choice. p. 375

self-disclosure: revealing to others ambiguous or inconsistent aspects of oneself, a process necessary for growth. p. 46

self-efficacy: empowered feeling of possessing the capability and competence to perform a task successfully. p. 374

sensitive line: an invisible boundary around one's self-image, which, if threatened, will evoke a strong defensive reaction. p. 45

separating figure from ground: the ability to filter out inaccurate, misleading, or irrelevant information so the problem can be defined accurately and alternative solutions can be generated. p. 151

situational stressor: a type of stressor that arises from an individual's environment or circumstances, such as unfavorable working conditions. p. 92

skill variety: an attribute of a job that uses an individual's talents and abilities to the maximum and thus makes the job seem worthwhile and important. p. 101

small wins strategy: a strategy for individuals to use for coping with stress; it involves celebrating each small successful step, especially changes that are easy to implement and that build momentum, in the attack on a large project. p. 379

SMART goals: goals that are specific, measurable, aligned, realistic, and time-bound. p. 422

social capital: a person's social connections ("I know someone who knows the answer to the question"). Compare with human capital. p. 235, 552

source credibility: a judgment about the extent to which information can be believed, three attributes of which are trustworthiness, expertise, and dynamism. p. 471

specific goals: goals that are measurable, unambiguous, and behavioral. p. 266

specificity orientation: an emphasis on separating work, family, and personal roles in a society, used in contrast to diffusion orientation. One of the key dimensions that identifies international cultural differences. p. 52

sponsor: person who helps provide the resources, environment, and encouragement that the idea champion needs in order to work. p. 166

stakeholder expectations: a best-practice standard in which current performance is compared with the expectations of customers, employers, or other stakeholders. p. 459

storming stage: team development stage in which members question the team's direction, the leader, roles of other members, and task objectives. p. 412

strength: areas in which a person is an outstanding performer, has special capabilities or talents, and does better than most people. p. 457

stressors: stimuli that cause physiological and psychological reactions in individuals. p. 90

structural holes: a gap in your personal network such that two people to whom you are connected are not connected to each other. p. 236

subdivision: the breaking apart a problem into smaller parts. p. 160

superiority-oriented communication: a message that gives the impression that the communicator is informed while others are ignorant, adequate while others are inadequate, competent while others are incompetent, or powerful while others are impotent. p. 199

supportive communication: communication that helps managers share information accurately and honestly without jeopardizing interpersonal relationships. p. 195

symbolic analogies: symbols or images that are imposed on the problem; recommended as part of Synectics. p. 156

synectics: a technique for improving creative problem solving by putting something you don't know in terms of something you do know. p. 155

T

task-facilitating roles: those that help the team accomplish its outcome objectives. p. 426

task identity: an attribute of a job that enables an individual to perform a complete job from beginning to end. pp. 101, 382

task significance: the degree to which the performance of a task affects the work or lives of other people. The greater its significance, the more meaningful the job is to the worker. p. 101

terminal values: those values that designate desirable ends or goals for an individual. p. 53

thinking languages: the various ways in which a problem can be considered, from verbal to nonverbal or symbolic languages as well as through sensory and visual imagery. Using only one thinking language is one indication of the constancy block. p. 148

threat-rigidity response: the tendency of almost all individuals, groups, and organizations to become rigid, meaning conservative and self-protective, when faced with a threat. p. 45

time stressor: a type of stressor generally caused by having too much to do in too little time. p. 92

tolerance of ambiguity: an individual's ability to cope with ambiguous, fast-changing, or unpredictable situations in which information is incomplete, unclear, or complex. p. 59

two-way communication: the result of respectfulness and flexibility. p. 200

U

uniquenesses: areas in which a person has special capacities, gifts, talents, or skills. p. 458

universalism orientation: the ethical decision principle that a decision is right and proper if everyone would be expected to behave in the same way under the same circumstances. Used in contrast to particularism orientation. p. 51

V

validating communication: a message that helps people feel recognized, understood, accepted, and valued. It is respectful, flexible, two-way, and based on agreement. p. 199

values maturity: the level of moral development displayed by individuals. p. 53

verification stage: the final stage in creative thought in which the creative solution is evaluated relative to some standard of acceptability. p. 154

vertical thinking: defining a problem in a single way and then pursuing that definition without deviation until a solution is reached. p. 147

visibility: the power-enhancing attribute of a position that can usually be measured by the number of influential people one interacts with in the organization. p. 237

vision of abundance: an image of a positive future, a flourishing condition, and a legacy about which people care passionately, which a leader articulates in order to promote positive change. p. 461

vision statement: a leadership document that outlines an organization's guiding values and principles, provides a sense of direction and possibilities, and inspires optimism and hope for a better future. p. 462

W

weaknesses: areas in which a person is underdeveloped, uninformed, or has little skill. p. 457

work design: the process of matching job characteristics and workers' skills and interests. p. 278

INTRODUCTION REFERENCES

Abramson, N. R. & Moran, R. T. (2017). Managing Cultural Differences: Global Leadership for the 21st Century. Routledge.

American Management Association. (2000). Managerial skills and competence. National survey by AMA, March–April 2000. (N = 921)

Andersen Consulting Company. (2000). *Skills needed for the e-business environment.* Chicago: Author.

Bandura, A. (1977). *A social learning theory.* Englewood Cliffs, NJ: Prentice Hall.

Bass, B. (1990). *Handbook of leadership: Theory, research, and managerial applications*, 3rd ed. New York: Macmillan.

Blimes, L., K. Wetzker, & P. Xhonneux. (1997 February 10). Value in human resources. *Financial Times.*

Boyatzis, R. E. (1996). Consequences and rejuvenation of competency-based human resource and organization development. In Richard Woodman & William A. Pasmore (Eds.), *Research in organizational change and development*, Vol. 9. Greenwich, CT: JAI Press.

Boyatzis, R. E. (2000). Developing emotional intelligence. In C. Cherniss & D. Goleman (Eds.), *Development in emotional intelligence.* New York: Bantam.

Boyatzis, R. E. (2005). Self-directed change and learning as a necessary meta-competency for success and effectiveness in the 21st century. In R. Sims & J. G. Veres (Eds.), *Keys to employee success in the coming decades.* Westport, CT: Greenwood Publishing.

Boyatzis, R. E., S. S. Cowen, & D. A. Kolb. (1995). *Innovation in professional education: Steps on a journey from teaching to learning.* San Francisco: Jossey-Bass.

Boyatzis, R. E., D. Leonard, K. Rhee, & J. V. Wheeler. (1996). Competencies can be developed, but not in the way we thought. *Capability, 2:* 25–41.

Brodbeck, F., et al. (2000). Cultural variation of leadership prototypes across 22 countries. *Journal of Occupational and Organizational Psychology, 73:* 1–50.

Burnaska, R. F. (1976). The effects of behavioral modeling training upon managers' behavior and employees' perceptions. *Personnel Psychology, 29:* 329–335.

Cameron, K. S. (2017). "Cross-cultural research and positive organizational scholarship." *Cross-Cultural and Strategic Management Journal*, 24: 13–32.

Cameron, Kim S., & Robert E. Quinn. (2006). *Diagnosing and changing organizational culture.* San Francisco: Jossey-Bass.

Cameron, K. S., R. E. Quinn, J. DeGraff, & A. V. Thakor. (2006). *Competing values leadership: Creating value in organizations.* New York: Edward Elgar.

Cameron, K., & M. Tschirhart. (1988). Managerial competencies and organizational effectiveness. Working paper, School of Business Administration, University of Michigan.

Cameron, K. S., & D. O. Ulrich. (1986). Transformational leadership in colleges and universities. In J. Smart (Ed.), *Higher education: Handbook of theory and research* Vol. 2 (pp. 1–42). New York: Agathon.

Cameron, K. S., & D. A. Whetten. (1984). A model for teaching management skills. *Organizational Behavior Teaching Journal, 8:* 21–27.

Cohen, P. A. (1984). College grades and adult achievement: A research synthesis. *Research in Higher Education, 20:* 281–291.

Cox, T. H. (1994). *Cultural diversity in organizations: Theory, research, and practice.* San Francisco: Barrett-Koehler.

Cox, T. H., & R. L. Beal. (1997). *Developing competency to manage diversity.* San Francisco: Barrett-Koehler.

Curtis, D. B., J. L. Winsor, & D. Stephens. (1989). National preferences in business and communication education. *Communication Education, 38:* 6–15.

Davis, T. W., & F. Luthans. (1980). A social learning approach to organizational behavior. *Academy of Management Review, 5:* 281–290.

Executive Coaching Survey (2013). What areas are CEOs getting coaching in? *Harvard Business Review.*

Goleman, D. (1998). *Working with emotional intelligence.* New York: Bantam.

Greenberg, E. (1999). Broadcast Transcript, National Public Radio Morning Edition, October 26.

Hanson, G. (1986). *Determinants of firm performance: An integration of economic and organizational factors.* Unpublished doctoral dissertation, University of Michigan Business School.

Holt, J. (1964). *How children fail*. New York: Pitman.

Huselid, M. A. (1995). The impact of human resource management practices on turnover, productivity, and corporate financial performance. *Academy of Management Journal, 38:* 647.

Huselid, M. A., & B. E. Becker. (1997). The impact of high-performance work systems, implementing effectiveness, and alignment with strategy on shareholder wealth. *Academy of Management Best Papers Proceedings:* 144–148.

Katzenbach, J. R. (1995). *Real change leaders: How you can create growth and high performance in your company*. New York: New York Times Business, Random House.

Kolb, D. A. (1984). *Experiential learning: Experience as the source of learning and development*. Englewood Cliffs, NJ: Prentice Hall.

Latham, G. P., & L. P. Saari, (1979). Application of social learning theory to training supervisors through behavioral modeling. *Journal of Applied Psychology, 64:* 239–246.

Leonard, D. (1996). *The impact of learning goals on self-directed change in management development and education*. Unpublished doctoral dissertation, Weatherhead School of Management, Case Western Reserve University.

Luthans, F., S. A. Rosenkrantz, & H. W. Hennessey. (1985). What do successful managers really do? An observation study of managerial activities. *Journal of Applied Behavioral Science, 21:* 255–270.

Mintzberg, H. (1975). The manager's job: Folklore and fact. *Harvard Business Review, 53:* 49–71.

Moorehead, B. (n.d.). http://www.snopes.com/politics/soapbox/paradox.asp.

Moses, J. L., & R. J. Ritchie. (1976). Supervisory relationships training: A behavioral evaluation of a behavioral modeling program. *Personnel Psychology, 29:* 337–343.

Nair, K. (1994). *A higher standard of leadership*. San Francisco: Barrett-Koehler.

Pfeffer, J. (1998). *The human equation: Building profits by putting people first*. Boston Harvard Business School Press.

Pfeffer, J., & J. F. Veiga. (1999). Putting people first for organizational success. *Academy of Management Executive, 13:* 37–48.

Porras, J. I., & B. Anderson. (1991). Improving managerial effectiveness through modeling-based training. *Organizational Dynamics, 9:* 60–77.

Quinn, R. E. (2000). *Change the world*. San Francisco: Jossey-Bass.

Quinn, R. E., & J. Rohrbaugh. (1983). A special model of effectiveness criteria: Towards a competing values approach to organizational analysis. *Management Science, 29:* 363–377.

Rhee, K. (1997). *Journey of Discovery: A longitudinal study of learning during a graduate professional program*. Unpublished doctoral dissertation, Weatherhead School of Management, Case Western Reserve University.

Rigby, D. (1998). *Management tools and techniques*. Boston: Bain and Company.

Smith, P. E. (1976). Management modeling training to improve morale and customer satisfaction. *Personnel Psychology, 29:* 351–359.

Staw, B. M., L. Sandelands, & J. Dutton. (1981). Threat-rigidity effects in organizational behavior: A multi-level analysis. *Administrative Science Quarterly, 26:* 501–524.

Tichy, N. M. (1993). *Control your destiny or someone else will*. New York: Doubleday.

Tichy, N. M. (1999). *The leadership engine*. New York: Harper Business.

Trompenaars, F., & C. Hampden-Turner. (2012). *Riding the waves of culture*. Understanding diversity in global business. New York: McGraw-Hill.

U.S. Office of the Comptroller of the Currency. (1990). http://www.occ.treas.gov.

Vance, C. M. (1993). *Mastering management education*. Newbury Park, CA: Sage.

Van Velsor, E., & L. Jean Britain. (1995). Why executives derail: Perspectives across time and culture. *Academy of Management Executive, 9:* 62–72.

Weick, K. E. (1995). *Sensemaking in organizations*. Thousand Oaks, CA: Sage.

Welbourne, T., & A. Andrews. (1996). Predicting performance of initial public offering firms: Should HRM be in the equation? *Academy of Management Journal, 39:* 891–919.

Wheeler, J. V. (1999). *Organizational and environmental supports and opportunities for self-directed learning following graduate education*. Unpublished doctoral dissertation, Weatherhead School of Management, Case Western Reserve University.

Whetten, D. A., & K. S. Cameron. (1983). Management skill training: A needed addition to the management curriculum. *Organizational Behavior Teaching Journal, 8:* 10–15.

CHAPTER 1 REFERENCES

Agor, W. H. (1985). Intuition as a brain skill in management. *Public Personnel Management, 14:* 15–25.

Alberts, H. J., Martijn, C., & De Vries, N. K. (2011). Fighting self-control failure: Overcoming ego depletion by increasing self-awareness. *Journal of Experimental Social Psychology, 47*(1), 58–62.

Alexander, K. L. (2000, February 22). No Mr. Nice Guy for Disney. *USA Today:* B1–B2.

Allan, H., & J. Waclawski. (1999). Influence behaviors and managerial effectiveness in lateral relations. *Human Resource Development Quarterly, 10:* 3–34.

Allport, G., P. Vernon, & G. Lindzey. (1960). *Study of values*. Boston: Houghton Mifflin.

Allport, G., R. Gordon, & P. Vernon. (1931, 1960). *The study of values manual*. Boston: Houghton Mifflin.

Anderson, C., & C. E. Schneider. (1978). Locus of control, leader behavior, and leader performance among management students. *Academy of Management Journal, 21:* 690–698.

Andrews, K. (1989, September–October). Ethics in practice. *Harvard Business Review:* 99–104.

April, K. A., Dharani, B., & Peters, K. (2012). Impact of locus of control expectancy on level of well-being. *Review of European Studies, 4*(2), 124.

Armstrong, S. J. (2000). The influence of cognitive style on performance in management education. *Educational Psychology, 20:* 323–339.

Armstrong-Stassen, M. (1998). Downsizing the federal government: A longitudinal study of managers' reactions. *Revue Canadienne des Sciences de l'Administration, 15:* 310–321.

Ashley, G. C., & Reiter-Palmon, R. (2012). Self-awareness and the evolution of leaders: The need for a better measure of self-awareness. *Journal of Behavioral and Applied Management, 14*(1), 2.

Barbuto Jr, J. E., Weltmer, D. F., & Pennisi, L. A. (2010). Locus of Control, Sources of Motivation, and Mental Boundaries as Antecedents of Leader–Member Exchange Quality. *Psychological reports, 106*(1), 175–188.

Bar-On, R. (1997). *Bar-On emotional quotient inventory: Users manual.* Toronto: Multi-Health Systems.

Bazerman, M. H. & Tenbrunsel, A. E. (2011). Why do good people let bad things happen? Harvard Business review, April.

Bernardi, R. (1997). The relationships among locus of control, perceptions of stress, and performance. *Journal of Applied Business Research, 13:* 108.

Berscheid, E., & E. H. Walster. (1978). *Interpersonal attraction.* Reading, MA: Addison-Wesley.

Bigoness, W., & G. Blakely. (1996). A cross-national study of managerial values. *Journal of International Business Studies, 27:* 739–752.

Bilsky, W., & S. H. Schwartz. (1994). Values and personality. *European Journal of Personality, 8:* 163–181.

Bonnett, C., & A. Furnham. (1991). Who wants to be an entrepreneur? *Journal of Economic Psychology, 66:* 125–138.

Bono, J. E., & T. A. Judge. (2003). Core self-evaluations: A review of the trait and its role in job satisfaction and job performance. *European Journal of Personality, 17:* 5–18.

Boone, C., & B. de Brabander. (1997). Self-reports and CEO locus of control research: A note. *Organizational Studies, 18:* 949–971.

Bowling, N. A., Eschleman, K. J., & Wang, Q. (2010). A meta-analytic examination of the relationship between job satisfaction and subjective well-being. Journal of Organizational and Occupational Psychology, 83 (4) 915–934.

Boyatzis, R. E. (1982). *The competent manager: A model for effective performance.* New York: Wiley.

Boyatzis, R. E. (1998). Self-directed change and learning as a necessary meta-competency for success and effectiveness in the 21st century. In R. Sims and J. G. Veres (Eds.), *Keys to employee success in the coming decade.* Westport, CT: Greenwood.

Boyatzis, R. E., D. Goleman, & K. Rhee. (2000). Clustering competence in emotional intelligence: Insights from the Emotional Intelligence Inventory. In R. Bar-On and J. D. A. Parker (Eds.), *Handbook of emotional intelligence* (pp. 343–352). San Francisco: Jossey-Bass.

Brown, N. W. (1997). Description of personality similarities and differences of a sample of black and white female engineering students. *Psychological Reports, 81:* 603–610.

Budner, S. (1962). Intolerance of ambiguity as a personality variable. *Journal of Personality, 30:* 29–50.

Cable, D., & T. A. Judge. (1996). Person-organization fit, job choice decisions, and organizational entry. *Organizational Behavior and Human Decision Processes, 67:* 294–311.

Cameron, K. S., & R. E. Quinn. (2006). *Diagnosing and changing organizational culture.* San Francisco: Jossey-Bass.

Cassidy, S. (2004). Learning styles: An overview of theories, models, and measures. *Educational Psychology, 24:* 419–444.

Cavanaugh, G. F. (1980). *American business values in transition.* Englewood Cliffs, NJ: Prentice-Hall.

Cervone, D. (1997). Social-cognitive mechanisms and personality coherence: Self-knowledge, situational beliefs, and cross-situational coherence in perceived self-efficacy. *Psychological Science, 8:* 156–165.

Chan, D. (1966). Cognitive misfit of problem-solving style at work: A facet of person-organization fit. *Organizational Behavior and Human Decision Processes, 68:* 194–207.

Chang, C. H., Ferris, D. L., Johnson, R. E., Rosen, C. C., & Tan, J. A. (2012). Core self-evaluations: A review and evaluation of the literature. *Journal of Management, 38*(1), 81–128.

Chenhall, R., & D. Morris. (1991). The effect of cognitive style and sponsorship bias on the treatment of opportunity costs in resource allocation decisions. *Accounting, Organizations, and Society, 16:* 27–46.

Clare, D. A., & D. G. Sanford. (1979). Mapping personal value space: A study of managers in four organizations. *Human Relations, 32:* 659–666.

Clarke, N. (2010). Emotional intelligence and its relationship to transformational leadership and key project manager competences. *Project Management Journal, 41*(2), 5–20. doi:http://dx.doi.org/10.1002/pmj.20162

Coleman, D., G. Irving, & C. Cooper. (1999). Another look at the locus of control-organizational commitment relationship: It depends on the form of commitment. *Journal of Organizational Behavior, 20:* 995–1001.

Cools, E., & H. Van den Broeck. (2007). Development and validation of the Cognitive Style Indicator. *Journal of Psychology, 14:* 359–387.

Côté, S., Lopes, P. N., Salovey, P., & Miners, C. T. (2010). Emotional intelligence and leadership emergence in small groups. *The Leadership Quarterly, 21*(3), 496–508.

Covey, S. R. (1989). *The seven habits of highly effective people.* New York: Simon & Schuster.

Cox, T. H. (1994). *Cultural diversity in organizations.* San Francisco: Barrett-Koehler.

Cromie, S., I. Callaghan, & M. Jansen. (1992). The entrepreneurial tendencies of managers. *British Journal of Management, 3:* 1–5.

Darrow, B. (1998, November 16). Michael Dell. *Computer Reseller News:* 124–125.

Dollinger, S. J., F. T. L. Leong, & S. K. Ulicni. (1996). On traits and values: With special reference to openness to experience. *Journal of Research in Personality, 30:* 23–41.

Eckstrom, R. B., J. W. French, & H. H. Harmon. (1979). Cognitive factors: Their identification and replication. *Multivariate Behavioral Research Monographs, 72:* 3–84.

Elliott, A. L., & R. J. Schroth. (2002). *How companies lie: Why Enron is just the tip of the iceberg.* New York: Crown Business.

Elsayed-Elkhouly, S. M., & R. Buda. (1997). A cross–cultural comparison of value systems of Egyptians, Americans, Africans, and Arab executives. *International Journal of Commerce and Management, 7:* 102–119.

Erez, A., & T. A. Judge. (2001). Relationship of core self–evaluations to goal setting, motivation, and performance. *Journal of Applied Psychology, 86:* 1270–1279.

Feist, G. J., & F. Barron. (1996). Emotional intelligence and academic intelligence in career and life success. Presented at the American Psychological Association Meeting, San Francisco.

Fisher, S. G., W. D. K. Macrosson, & C. A. Walker. (1995). FIRO-B: The power of love and the love of power. *Psychological Reports, 76:* 195–206.

Fisher, S. G., W. D. K. Macrosson, & M. R. Yusuff. (1996). Team performance and human values. *Psychological Reports, 79:* 1019–1024.

Freud, S. (1956). *Collected papers* (Vols. 3 and 4). London: Hogarth.

Furnham, A., & Marks, J. (2013). Tolerance of ambiguity: A review of the recent literature. *Psychology, 4*(09), 717.

Gallup News (2017) December 4-11, page 1.

Gardner, D. G., & Pierce, J. L. (2010). The core self-evaluation scale: Further construct validation evidence. *Educational and Psychological Measurement, 70*(2), 291–304.

Gilligan, C. (1979). Women's place in man's lifecycle. *Harvard Educational Review, 49:* 431–446.

Gilligan, C. (1980). Moral development in late adolescence: A critique and reconstruction of Kohlberg's theory. *Human Development, 23:* 77–104.

Gilligan, C. (1982). In a different voice: Women's conceptions of self and morality. *Harvard Educational Review, 47:* 481–517.

Gilligan, C. (1988). Two moral orientations: Gender differences and similarities. *Merrill-Palmer Quarterly, 34:* 223–237.

Goleman, D. (1995). *Emotional intelligence.* New York: Bantam.

Goleman, D. (1998). What makes a leader? *Harvard Business Review, 76:* 92–102.

Goleman, D. (1998). *Working with emotional intelligence.* New York: Bantam.

Goleman, D., Boyatzis, R. E., & McKee, A. (2013). *Primal leadership: Unleashing the power of emotional intelligence.* Harvard Business Press.

Haase, R. F., D. Yul Lee, & D. L. Banks. (1979). Cognitive correlates of polychronicity. *Perceptual and Motor Skills, 49:* 271–282.

Hammer, T. H., & Y. Vardi. (1981). Locus of control and career self-management among nonsupervisory employees in industrial settings. *Journal of Vocational Behavior, 18:* 13–29.

Harris, S. (1981, October 6). Know yourself? It's a paradox. *Associated Press.*

Harter, S. (1990). Causes, correlates, and the functional role of global self-worth. In R. J. Sternberg & J. Kolligan (Eds.), *Competence reconsidered.* (pp. 67–97). New Haven: Yale University Press.

Hayes, J., & C. W. Allinson. (1994). Cognitive style and its relevance for management practice. *British Journal of Management, 5:* 53–71.

Henderson, J. C., & Paul C. Nutt. (1980). The influence of decision style on decision making behavior. *Management Science, 26:* 371–386.

Hendricks, J. A. (1985, May–June). Locus of control: Implications for managers and accountants. *Cost and Management:* 25–29.

Hewett, T. T., G. E. O'Brien, & J. Hornik. (1974). The effects of work organization, leadership style, and member compatibility upon the productivity of small groups working on a manipulative task. *Organizational Behavior and Human Performance, 11:* 283–301.

Higgs, M., & Rowland, D. (2010). Emperors with clothes on: The role of self-awareness in developing effective change leadership. *Journal of Change Management, 10*(4), 369–385.

Hoffman, B. J., Bynum, B. H., Piccolo, R. F., & Sutton, A. W. (2011). Person-organization value congruence: How transformational leaders influence work group effectiveness. *Academy of Management Journal, 54*(4), 779–796.

Hone, L. C., Jarden, A., Duncan, S., & Schofield, G. M. (2015). Flourishing in New Zealand workers: Associations with lifestyle behaviors, physical health, psychosocial, and work-related indicators. Journal of Occupational and Environmental Medicine, 57(9),973–983.

Jacobson, C. M. (1993). Cognitive styles of creativity: Relations of scores on the Kirton Adaptation-Innovation Inventory and the Myers-Briggs Type Indicator among managers in the USA. *Psychological Reports, 72:* 1131–1138.

Johnston, C. S. (1995). The Rokeach Value Survey: Underlying structure and multidimensional scaling. *Journal of Psychology, 129:* 583–597.

Judge, T. A., & Kammeyer-Mueller, J. D. (2011). Implications of core self-evaluations for a changing organizational context. *Human Resource Management Review, 21*(4), 331–341.

Judge, T. A., A. Erez, J. E. Bono, & C. J. Thoreson. (2002). Are measures of self-esteem, neuroticism, locus of control, and generalized self-efficacy indicators of a common core construct? *Journal of Personality and Social Psychology, 83:* 693–710.

Judge, T. A., A. Erez, J. E. Bono, & C. J. Thoreson. (2003). The core self-evaluation scale: Development of a measure. *Personnel Psychology, 56:* 303–331.

Judge, T. A., & J. E. Bono. (2001). Relationship of core self-evaluations traits—self-esteem, generalized self-efficacy, locus of control, and emotional stability—with job satisfaction and job performance: A meta-analysis. *Journal of Applied Psychology, 86:* 80–92.

Karimi, R., & Alipour, F. (2011). Reduce job stress in organizations: Role of locus of control. *International Journal of Business and Social Science, 2*(18).

Kirton, M. J. (2003). *Adaptation–innovation in the context of diversity and change.* London: Routledge.

Kohlberg, L. (1969). The cognitive-developmental approach to socialization. In D. A. Goslin (Ed.), *Handbook of socialization theory and research.* Chicago: Rand McNally.

Kohlberg, L. (1976). Moral stages and moralization, the cognitive-developmental approach. In T. Lickona (Ed.), *Moral development and behavior.* New York: Holt, Rinehart & Winston.

Kohlberg, L. (1981). *Essays in moral development,* Vol. 1. New York: Harper & Row, pp. 409–412.

Kohlberg, L., & R. A. Ryncarz. (1990). Beyond justice reasoning: Moral development and consideration of a seventh stage. In C. Alexander & E. J. Langer (Eds.), *Higher stages of human development.* New York: Oxford University Press.

Kolb, D. A., R. E. Boyatzis, & C. Mainemelis. (2000). Experiential learning theory: Previous research and new directions.

In R. J. Sternberg & L. F. Zhang (Eds.), *Perspectives on cognitive, learning, and thinking styles.* Mahwah, NJ: Lawrence Erlbaum.

Kren, L. (1992). The moderating effects of locus of control on performance incentives and participation. *Human Relations, 45:* 991–1012.

Lavy, S., & Littman-Ovadia, H. (2016). My better self: Using strengths at work and work productivity, organizational citizenship behavior and satisfaction. *Journal of Career Development*, 1–15. DOI: 10.1177/0894845316634056

Lickona, T. (1976). Critical issues in the study of moral development and behavior. In T. Lickona (Ed.), *Moral development and behavior: Theory, research, and social issues.* New York: Holt, Rinehart & Winston.

Liddel, W. W., & John W. Slocum Jr. (1976). The effects of individual-role compatibility upon group performance: An extension of Schutz's FIRO theory. *Academy of Management Journal, 19:* 413–426.

Littman-Ovadia, H., Lavy, S., & Boiman-Meshita, M. (2016a). When theory and research collide: Examining correlates of signature strengths use at work. *Journal of Happiness Studies.*

Locke, E. A., K. McClear, & D. Knight. (1996). Self-esteem at work. *International Review of Industrial/Organizational Psychology, 11:* 1–32.

Maslow, A. H. (1962). *Toward a psychology of being.* Princeton, NJ: D. Von Nostrand.

Meyer, J. P., Hecht, T. D., Gill, H., & Toplonytsky, L. (2010). Person–organization (culture) fit and employee commitment under conditions of organizational change: A longitudinal study. *Journal of Vocational Behavior, 76*(3), 458–473.

Milgram, S. (1963). Behavioral study of obedience. *Journal of Abnormal and Social Psychology, 67:* 371–378.

Miller, D., M. F. R. Kets de Vries, & J. M. Toulouse. (1982). Top executive locus of control and its relationship to strategy-making, structure, and environment. *Academy of Management Journal, 25:* 237–253.

Mitchell, L. E. (2002). *Corporate irresponsibility: America's newest export.* New Haven: Yale University Press.

Moore, T. (1987, March 30). Personality tests are back. *Fortune:* 74–82.

Newton, T., & A. Keenan. (1990). The moderating effect of Type A behavior pattern and locus of control upon the relationship between change in job demands and change in psychological strain. *Human Relations, 43:* 1229–1255.

Ng, T. W., & Feldman, D. C. (2011). Locus of control and organizational embeddedness. *Journal of Occupational and Organizational Psychology, 84*(1), 173–190.

Nwachukwu, S. L. S., & S. J. Vitell. (1997). The influence of corporate culture on managerial ethical judgments. *Journal of Business Ethics, 16:* 757–776.

O'Reilly, B. (1999). The mechanic who fixed Continental. *Fortune, 140:* 176–186.

Parker, V., & K. Kram. (1993). Women mentoring women. *Business Horizons, 36:* 101–102.

Phillips, J., & S. Gully. (1997). Role of goal orientation, ability, need for achievement, and locus of control in self-efficacy and goal-setting processes. *Journal of Applied Psychology, 82:* 792–802.

Posner, B. Z. (2010). Another look at the impact of personal and organizational values congruency. *Journal of Business Ethics, 97*(4), 535–541.

Posner, B., & J. Kouzes. (1993). Values congruence and differences between the interplay of personal and organizational values. *Journal of Business Ethics, 12:* 341–347.

Rest, J. R. (1979). *Revised manual for the Defining Issues Test: An objective test of moral judgment development.* Minneapolis: Minnesota Moral Research Projects.

Rice, Michelle. (1999). Rugged mountains and lifelong connections: Adrian Manger. *Australian CPA, 69:* 36–37.

Roddenberry, A., & Renk, K. (2010). Locus of control and self-efficacy: potential mediators of stress, illness, and utilization of health services in college students. *Child Psychiatry & Human Development, 41*(4), 353–370.

Rogers, C. R. (1961). *On becoming a person.* Boston: Houghton Mifflin.

Rokeach, M. (1973). *The nature of human values.* New York: Free Press.

Rosenthal, R. (1977). The PONS Test: Measuring sensitivity to nonverbal cues. In P. McReynolds (Ed.), *Advancement on psychological assessment.* San Francisco: Jossey-Bass.

Rotter, J. B. (1966). Generalized expectancies for internal versus external control of reinforcement. *Psychological Monographs, 80:* 1–28.

Ryan, L. R. (1970). *Clinical interpretation of the FIRO-B.* Palo Alto, CA: Consulting Psychologists Press.

Salovey, P., & J. Mayer. (1990). Emotional intelligence. *Imagination, Cognition, and Personality, 9:* 185–211.

Schein, E. H. (1960). Interpersonal communication, group solidarity, and social influence. *Sociometry, 23:* 148–161.

Seeman, M. (1982). On the personal consequences of alienation in work. *American Sociological Review, 32:* 273–285.

Showry, M., & Manasa, K. V. L. (2014). Self-awareness-key to effective leadership. *IUP Journal of Soft Skills, 8*(1), 15.

Simsek, Z., Heavey, C., & Veiga, J. J. F. (2010). The impact of CEO core self-evaluation on the firm's entrepreneurial orientation. *Strategic Management Journal, 31*(1), 110–119.

Snarey, J. R., & G. E. Vaillant. (1985). How lower- and working-class youth become middle-class adults: The association between ego defense mechanisms and upward social mobility. *Child Development, 56:* 899–910.

Sosik, J., & L. E. Megerian. (1999). Understanding leader emotional intelligence and performance: The role of self–other agreement on transformational leadership perceptions. *Group and Organization Management, 24:* 367–390.

Spector, P. E. (1982). Behavior in organizations as a function of employee's locus of control. *Psychological Bulletin, 47:* 487–489.

Spencer, L. M., & S. M. Spencer. (1993). *Competence at work: Models for superior performance.* New York: Wiley.

Sprecher, S., Treger, S., Wondra, J. D., Hilaire, N., & Wallpe, K. (2013). Taking turns: Reciprocal self-disclosure promotes liking in initial interactions. *Journal of Experimental Social Psychology, 49*(5), 860–866.

Sternberg, R. J. (1996). *Successful intelligence*. New York: Simon & Schuster.

Sternberg, R. J., & L. F. Zhang (Eds.). (2000). *Perspectives on cognitive, learning, and thinking styles*. Mahwah, NJ: Lawrence Erlbaum.

Sweeney, P., D. McFarlin, & J. Cotton. (1991). Locus of control as a moderator of the relationship between perceived influence and procedural justice. *Human Relations, 44:* 333–342.

Teoh, H. Y., & S. L. Foo. (1997). Moderating effects of tolerance for ambiguity and risk–taking propensity on the role conflict–perceived performance relationship: Evidence from Singaporean entrepreneurs. *Journal of Business Venturing, 12:* 67–81.

Tillman, C. J., Smith, F. A., & Tillman, W. R. (2010). Work locus of control and the multi-dimensionality of job satisfaction. *Journal of Organizational Culture, Communications and Conflict, 14*(2), 107.

Timothy, A., C. Thoresen, V. Pucik, & T. Welbourne. (1999). Managerial coping with organizational change: A dispositional perspective. *Journal of Applied Psychology, 84:* 107–122.

Trompenaars, F. (1996). Resolving international conflict: Culture and business strategy. *Business Strategy Review, 7:* 51–68.

Trompenaars, F., & C. Hampton-Turner. (2012). *Riding the waves of culture*. New York: McGraw-Hill.

Tubbs, W. (1994). The roots of stress-death and juvenile delinquency in Japan: Disciplinary ambivalence and perceived locus of control. *Journal of Business Ethics, 13:* 507–522.

Vance, C. M., K. S. Groves, Y. Paik, & H. Kindler. (2007). Understanding and measuring linear–nonlinear thinking style for enhanced management education and professional practice. *Academy of Management Learning and Education Journal, 6:* 167–185.

Watson, D. (2000). *Mood and temperament*. New York: Guilford.

Weick, K. E. (1993). The collapse of sensemaking in organizations. *Administrative Science Quarterly, 38:* 628–652.

Weick, K. E., & K. Sutcliffe. (2000). High reliability: The power of mindfulness. *Leader to Leader, 17:* 33–38.

Wheeler, R. W., & J. M. Davis. (1979). Decision making as a function of locus of control and cognitive dissonance. *Psychological Reports, 44:* 499–502.

Zeidner, M., Matthews, G., & Roberts, R. D. (2012). *What we know about emotional intelligence: How it affects learning, work, relationships, and our mental health*. MIT press.

Zhu, J. (2018). Why self-awareness matters and how you can be more self-aware. https://positivepsychologyprogram.com/self-awareness-matters-how-you-can-be-more-self-aware.

CHAPTER 2 REFERENCES

Adler, C. M., & J. J. Hillhouse (1996). Stress, health, and immunity: A review of the literature. In Thomas W. Miller (Ed.), *Theory and assessment of stressful life events*. Madison, CT: International University Press.

Adler, J. (2005). *My prescription for anti-depressive living*. New York: Regan.

Adler, J. (1999, June 14). Stress, *Newsweek*; 56–61.

Adler, V. (1989). Little control equals lots of stress. *Psychology Today, 23:* 18–19.

American Institute of Stress. (2000). www.stress.org/problem.htm.

Anderson, C. R. (1977). Locus of control, coping behaviors and performance in a stress setting: A longitudinal study. *Journal of Applied Psychology, 62:* 446–451.

Auerbach, S. M. (1998). *Stress management: Psychological foundations*. Upper Saddle River, NJ: Prentice Hall.

Balzer, W. K., M. E. Doherty, & R. O'Connor. (1989). Effects of cognitive feedback on performance. *Psychological Bulletin, 106:* 410–433.

Bandura, A. (1997). *Self-efficacy: The exercise of control*. New York: W. H. Freeman.

Beary, J. F., & H. Benson. (1977). A simple psychophysiologic technique which elicits the hypometabolic changes in the relaxation response. *Psychosomatic Medicine, 36:* 115–120.

Bell, C. R. (1998). *Managers as mentors*. San Francisco: Barrett-Koehler.

Benson, H. (1975). *The relaxation response*. New York: William Morrow.

Bramwell, S. T., M. Masuda, N. N. Wagner, & T. H. Holmes. (1975). Psychosocial factors in athletic injuries. *Journal of Human Stress, 1:* 6.

Brockner, J., & B. M. Weisenfeld. (1993). Living on the edge: The effects of layoffs on those who remain. In J. Keith Murnighan (Ed.), *Social psychology in organizations: Advances in theory and research*. Englewood Cliffs, NJ: Prentice Hall.

Cameron, K. S. (1998). Strategic organizational downsizing: An extreme case. *Research in Organizational Behavior, 20:* 185–229.

Cameron, K. S. (1994). Strategies for successful organizational downsizing. *Human Resource Management Journal, 33:* 189–212.

Cameron, K. S., S. J. Freeman, & A. K. Mishra. (1991). Best practices in white-collar downsizing: Managing contradictions. *Academy of Management Executive, 5:* 57–73.

Cameron, K. S., M. U. Kim, & D. A. Whetten. (1987). Organizational effects of decline and turbulence. *Administrative Science Quarterly, 32:* 222–240.

Cameron, K. S., D. A. Whetten, & M. U. Kim. (1987). Organizational dysfunctions of decline. *Academy of Management Journal, 30:* 126–138.

Cantor, N., & J. F. Kihlstrom. (1987). *Personality and social intelligence*. Englewood Cliffs, NJ: Prentice Hall.

Coddington, R. D., & J. R. Troxell. (1980). The effect of emotional factors on football injury rates: A pilot study. *Journal of Human Stress, 6:* 3–5.

Cooper, C. L., & M. J. Davidson. (1982). The high cost of stress on women managers. *Organizational Dynamics, 11:* 44–53.

Cooper, C. L. (1998). *Theories of organizational stress*. New York: Oxford University Press.

Cooper, M. J., & M. M. Aygen. (1979). A relaxation technique in the management of hypocholesterolemia. *Journal of Human Stress, 5:* 24–27.

Cordes, C. L., & T. W. Dougherty. (1993). Review and an integration of research on job burnout. *Academy of Management Review, 18:* 621–656.

Covey, S. (1989). *Seven habits of highly effective people*. New York: Wiley.

Cowley, C. (2000, June 14). Stress-busters: What works. *Newsweek*: 60.

Curtis, J. D., & R. A. Detert. (1981). *How to relax: A holistic approach to stress management.* Palo Alto: Mayfield Publishing Co.

Davidson, J. (1995). *Managing your time.* Indianapolis: Alpha Books.

Davis, M., E. Eshelman, & M. McKay. (1980). *The relaxation and stress reduction workbook.* Richmond, CA: New Harbinger Publications.

Deepak, M. D. (1995). *Creating health: How to wake up the body's intelligence.* New York: Houghton Mifflin.

Dellbeck, M., & S. Shatkin. (1991). *Scientific research on the transcendental meditation process.* Fairfield, IA: Maharishi International University of Management Press.

Dyer, W. G. (1987). *Teambuilding.* Reading, MA: Addison-Wesley.

Eliot, R. S., & D. L. Breo. (1984). *Is it worth dying for?* New York: Bantam Books.

Farnham, A. (1991, October 7). Who beats stress and how? *Fortune:* 71–86.

Fisher, C., & R. Gitelson. (1983). A meta-analysis of the correlates of role conflict and role ambiguity. *Journal of Applied Psychology, 68:* 320–333.

French, J. R. R., & R. D. Caplan. (1972). Organizational stress and individual strain. In A. J. Marrow (Ed.), *The failure of success.* New York: AMACOM.

Friedman, M., & R. H. Rosenman. (1974). *Type A behavior and your heart.* New York: Knopf.

Friedman, M., & D. Ulmer. (1984). *Treating type A behavior and your heart.* New York: Alfred A. Knopf, 84–85.

Friedman, M. (1996). *Type A behavior: Its diagnosis and treatment.* New York: Kluwer Academic Publishers.

Gardner, H. (1993). *Multiple intelligences: The theory in practice.* New York: Basic Books.

Gittell, J., K. Cameron, & S. Lim. (2006). Relationships, layoffs, and organizational resilience. *Journal of Applied Behavioral Science.*

Goldberg, H. (1976). *The hazards of being male.* New York: Nash.

Goleman, D. (1998). *Working with emotional intelligence.* New York: Bantam Books.

Gordon, A. (1959). *A day at the beach.* Copyright © 1959 by Arthur Gordon. All rights reserved. Reprinted by permission of the author. First published in the *Reader's Digest.*

Greenberg, J. (1987). *Comprehensive stress management,* 2nd ed. Dubuque, IA: William C. Brown Publishers.

Greenberger, D. B., & S. Stasser. (1991). The role of situational and dispositional factors in the enhancement of personal control in organizations. *Research in Organizational Behavior, 13:* 111–145.

Griest, J. H., et al. (1979). Running as treatment for depression. *Comparative Psychology, 20:* 41–56.

Hackman, J. R., G. R. Oldham, R. Janson, & K. Purdy. (1975). A new strategy for job enrichment. *California Management Review, 17:* 57–71.

Hackman, R. J., & G. R. Oldham. (1980). *Work redesign.* Reading, MA: Addison-Wesley.

Hall, D. T. (1976). *Careers in organizations.* Santa Monica, CA: Goodyear.

Hendricks, W. (1996). *Coaching, mentoring, and managing.* Franklin Lakes, NJ: Career Press.

Hepburn, G. C., C. A. McLoughlin, & J. Barling. (1997). Coping with chronic work stress. In B. H. Gottlieb (Ed.), *Coping with chronic stress.* (pp. 343–366). New York: Plenum.

Hobson, C. J., J. Kamen, J. Szostek, C. M. Nethercutt, J. W. Tiedmann, & S. Wojnarowicz. (1998). Stressful life events: A revision and update of the Social Readjustment Rating Scale. *International Journal of Stress Management, 5:* 1–23.

Holmes, T. H., & R. H. Rahe. (1967). The social readjustment rating scale. *Journal of Psychosomatic Research, 11:* 213–218.

Holmes, T. H., & R. H. Rahe. (1970). The social readjustment rating scale. *Journal of Psychosomatic Research, 14:* 121–132.

Hubbard, J. R., & E. A. Workman. (1998). *Handbook of stress medicine: An organ system approach.* Boca Raton, FL: CRC Press.

Ivancevich, J., & D. Ganster. (1987). *Job stress: From theory to suggestions.* New York: Haworth.

Ivancevich, J. M., & M. T. Matteson. (1980). *Stress & work: A managerial perspective.* Glenview, IL: Scott Foresman.

Jourard, S. M. (1964). *The transparent self.* Princeton, NJ: Von Nostrand.

Judge, T. A., & J. E. Bono. (2001). Relationship of core self-evaluations traits—self-esteem, generalized self-efficacy, locus of control, and emotional stability—with job satisfaction and job performance: A meta-analysis. *Journal of Applied Psychology, 86:* 80–92.

Kahn, R. L., et al. (1964). *Organizational stress: Studies in role conflict and ambiguity.* New York: Wiley.

Kahn, R. L., & P. Byosiere. (1992). Stress in organizations. In Marvin Dunnette & L. M. Hough (Eds.), *Handbook of industrial and organizational psychology* (pp. 571–650). Palo Alto: Consulting Psychologists.

Karasek, R. A., T. Theorell, J. E. Schwartz, P. L. Schnall, C. F. Pieper, & J. L. Michela. (1988). Job characteristics in relation to the prevalence of myocardial infarction in the U.S. Health Examination Survey and the Health and Nutrition Examination Survey. *American Journal of Public Health, 78:* 910–918.

Katzenbach, J. R., & D. K. Smith. (1993). *The wisdom of teams.* Boston: Harvard Business School Press.

Kobasa, S. C. (1979). Stressful life events, personality, and health: An inquiry into hardiness. *Journal of Personality and Social Psychology, 37:* 1–12.

Kobasa, S. (1982). Commitment and coping in stress resistance among lawyers. *Journal of Personality and Social Psychology, 42:* 707–717.

Kram, K. (1985). *Mentoring at work.* Glenview, IL: Scott Foresman.

Kuhn, A., & R. D. Beam. (1982). *The logic of organizations.* San Francisco: Jossey-Bass.

Lakein, D. (1989). *How to get control of your time and your life.* New York: McKay.

Latack, J., A. J. Kinicki, & G. Prussia. (1995). An integrative process model of coping with job loss. *Academy of Management Review, 20:* 311–342.

Lawler, E. E., S. A. Mohrman, & G. E. Ledford. (1992). *Employee involvement and total quality management.* San Francisco: Jossey-Bass.

Lehrer, P. M. (1996). *The Hatherleigh guide to issues in modern therapy.* New York: Hatherleigh Press.

Levinson, J. D. (1978). *Seasons of a man's life.* New York: Knopf.

Lewin, K. (1951). *Field theory in social science.* New York: Harper & Row.

Likert, R. (1967). *The human organization.* New York: McGraw-Hill.

Locke, E., & G. Latham. (1990). *A theory of goal setting and task performance.* Englewood Cliffs, NJ: Prentice Hall.

Lusch, R. F., & R. R. Serpkenci. (1990). Personal differences, job tension, job outcomes, and store performance: A study of retail managers. *Journal of Marketing, 54:* 85–101.

Maddi, S., & S. C. Kobasa. (1984). *The hardy executive: Health under stress.* Homewood, IL: Dow Jones-Irwin.

Masten, A. S., & M. J. Reed. (2002). Resilience in development. In C. R. Snyder, & S. J. Lopez (Eds.), *Handbook of positive psychology* (pp. 74–88). New York: Oxford University Press.

McNichols, T. J. (1973). *The case of the missing time.* Evanston, IL: Northwestern University Kellogg School of Business.

Mednick, M. T. (1982). Woman and the psychology of achievement: Implications for personal and social change. In H. J. Bernardin (Ed.), *Women in the workforce.* New York: Praeger.

Milgram, S. (1963). Behavioral study of obedience. *Journal of Abnormal and Social Psychology, 63:* 371–378.

Mintzberg, H. (1973). *The nature of managerial work.* New York: Harper & Row.

Mishra, A. K. (1992). *Organizational responses to crisis.* Unpublished doctoral dissertation, University of Michigan School of Business Administration.

Murphy, L. R. (1996). Stress management in work settings: A critical review of health effects. *American Journal of Health Promotion, 11:* 112–135.

Northwestern National Life Insurance Company (NNL). (1992). *Employee burnout: Causes and cures.* Minneapolis, MN: Author.

Orme-Johnson, D. W. (1973). Autonomic stability and transcendental meditation. *Psychosomatic Medicine, 35:* 341–349.

Peters, T. (1988). *Thriving on chaos.* New York: Knopf.

Pfeffer, J. (1998). *The human equation: Building profits by putting people first.* Boston: Harvard Business School Press.

Pilling, B. K., & S. Eroglu. (1994). An empirical examination of the impact of salesperson empathy and professionalism and merchandise salability on retail buyer's evaluations. *Journal of Personal Selling and Sales Management, 14:* 55–58.

Rahe, R. H., D. H. Ryman, & H. W. Ward. (1980). Simplified scaling for life change events. *Journal of Human Stress, 6:* 22–27.

Rosenthal, R. (1977). The PONS Test: Measuring sensitivity to nonverbal cues. In P. McReynolds (Ed.), *Advances in psychological measurement.* San Francisco: Jossey-Bass.

Rostad, F. G., & B. C. Long. (1996). Exercise as a coping strategy for stress: A review. *International Journal of Sport Psychology, 27:* 197–222.

Saarni, C. (1997). Emotional competence and self-regulation in childhood. In P. Savoey & D. J. Sluyter (Eds.), *Emotional development and emotional intelligence.* New York: Basic Books.

Schein, E. H. (1960). Interpersonal communication, group solidarity, and social influence. *Sociometry, 23:* 148–161.

Selye, H. (1976). *The stress of life*, 2nd ed. New York: McGraw-Hill.

Shoda, Y., W. Mischel, & P. K. Peake. (1990). Predicting adolescent cognitive and self-regulatory competencies from preschool delay of gratification: Identifying diagnostic conditions. *Developmental Psychology, 26:* 978–986.

Siegman, A. W., & T. W. Smith (Eds.). (1994). *Anger, hostility, and the heart.* Mahwah, NJ: Lawrence Erlbaum and Associates.

Singh, J. (1993). Boundary role ambiguity: Facts, determinants, and impacts. *Journal of Marketing, 57:* 11–30.

Singh, J. (1998). Striking balance in boundary-spanning positions: An investigation of some unconventional influences of role stressors and job characteristics on job outcomes or salespeople. *Journal of Marketing, 62:* 69–86.

Sorenson, M. J. (1998). *Breaking the chain of low self-esteem.* Stone Mountain, GA: Wolf Publications.

Spencer, L. M., & S. M. Spencer. (1993). *Competence at work: Models for superior performance.* New York: Wiley.

Stalk, G., & T. M. Hout. (1990). *Competing against time.* New York: Free Press.

Staw, B. M., L. Sandelands, & J. Dutton. (1981). Threat-rigidity effects in organizational behavior. *Administrative Science Quarterly, 26:* 501–524.

Sternberg, R. (1997). *Successful intelligence.* New York: Simon & Schuster.

Stone, R. A., & J. Deleo. (1976). Psychotherapeutic control of hypertension. *New England Journal of Medicine, 294:* 80–84.

Sutcliffe, K., & T. Vogus. (2003). Organizing for resilience. In K. S. Cameron, J. E. Dutton, & R. E. Quinn (Eds.), Positive organizational scholarship. San Francisco: Barrett-Koehler.

Thoits, P. A. (1995). Stress, coping, and social support processes: Where are we? What next? *Journal of Health and Social Behavior, 36:* 53–79.

Trompenaars, F. (1996). Resolving international conflict: Culture and business strategy. *Business Strategy Review, 7:* 51–68.

Trompenaars, F., & C. Hampden-Turner. (2012). *Riding the waves of culture.* New York: McGraw-Hill.

Turkington, C. (1998). *Stress management for busy people.* New York: McGraw-Hill.

Vinton, D. E. (1992). A new look at time, speed, and the manager. *Academy of Management Executive, 6:* 1–16.

Weick, K. (1984). Small wins. *American Psychologist, 39:* 40–49.

Weick, K. E. (1993a). The collapse of sensemaking in organizations. *Administrative Science Quarterly, 38:* 628–652.

Weick, K. E. (1993b). The KOR experiment. Working paper, University of Michigan School of Business Administration.

Weick, K. E. (1995). *Sensemaking in organizations.* Beverly Hills, CA: Sage.

William, R., & V. Williams. (1998). *Anger kills: 17 strategies to control the hostility that can harm your health.* New York: Harper Collins.

Wolff, H. G., S. G. Wolf, & C. C. Hare (Eds.). (1950). *Life stress and bodily disease.* Baltimore: Williams and Wilkins.

Yogi, M. (1994). *Science of being and art of living: Transcendental meditation.* New Haven, CT: Meridian Books.

CHAPTER 3 REFERENCES

Adams, J. L. (2001). *Conceptual blockbusting: A guide to better ideas*. Cambridge, MA: Perseus Publishing.

Albert, R. S., & M. A. Runco. (1999). A history of research on creativity. In R. J. Sternberg (Ed.), *Handbook of creativity*. Cambridge: Cambridge University Press.

Amabile, T. M. (1988). A model of creativity and innovation in organizations. In L. L. Cummings & B. M. Staw (Eds.), *Research in Organizational Behavior, 10:* 123–167.

Basadur, M. S. (1979). *Training in creative problem solving: Effects of deferred judgment and problem finding and solving in an industrial research organization*. Unpublished doctoral dissertation, University of Cincinnati.

Ben-Amos, P. (1986). Artistic creativity in Benin Kingdom. *African Arts, 19:* 60–63.

Black, J. S., & H. B. Gregersen. (1997). Participative decision making: An integration of multiple dimensions. *Human Relations, 50:* 859–878.

Blasko, V. J., & M. P. Mokwa. (1986). Creativity in advertising: A Janusian perspective. *Journal of Advertising, 15:* 43–50.

Bodycombe, D. J. (1977). *The mammoth puzzle carnival*. New York: Carroll & Graf.

Cameron, K. S., R. E. Quinn, J. DeGraff, & A. V. Thakor. (2006). *Competing values leadership: Creating values in organizations*. New York: Edward Elgar.

Chu, Y-K. (1970). Oriented views of creativity. In A. Angloff & B. Shapiro (Eds.), *Psi factors in creativity* (pp. 35–50). New York: Parapsychology Foundation.

Cialdini, R. B. (2008). *Influence: Science and practice*. Needham Heights, MA: Allyn and Bacon.

Collins, M. A., & T. M. Amabile. (1999). Motivation and creativity. In R. J. Sternberg (Ed.), *Handbook of creativity*. Cambridge, UK: Cambridge University Press.

Covey, S. R. (1998) "Creative orientation." *Executive Excellence, 1:* 13–14.

Crovitz, H. F. (1970). *Galton's walk*. New York: Harper & Row.

Csikszentmihalyi, M. (1996). *Creativity: Flow and the psychology of discovery and invention*. New York: Harper Collins.

de Bono, E. (1968). *New think*. New York: Basic Books.

de Bono, E. (2015a). *Lateral thinking*. New York: Harper Collins.

de Bono, E. (2015b). *Serious creativity*. New York: Random House.

de Bono, E. (2000). *New thinking for the new millennium*. New York: New Millennium Press.

DeDreu, C.K.W. (2010). Human creativity: Reflections on the role of culture. *Management and Organization Review, 6:* 437–446.

DeGraff, J. & DeGraff, S. (2017). *The innovation code*. San Francisco: Berrett Koehler.

DeGraff, J., & K. A. Lawrence. (2002). *Creativity at work: Developing the right practices to make innovation happen*. San Francisco: Jossey-Bass.

Dutton, J. E., & S. J. Ashford. (1993). Selling issues to top management. *Academy of Management Review, 18:* 397–421.

Einstein, A. (1919). Fundamental ideas and methods of relativity theory, presented in their development. (© 1919, G. Holton). Unpublished manuscript.

Eisenfuhr, F., Weber, M. & Langer, T. (2010). *Rational decision making*. New York: Springer.

Ettlie, J. E., & R. D. O'Keefe. (1982). Innovative attitudes, values, and intentions in organizations. *Journal of Management Studies, 19:* 163–182.

Feldman, D. H. (1999). The development of creativity. In R. J. Sternberg (Ed.), *Handbook of creativity*. Cambridge, UK: Cambridge University Press.

Festinger, L. (1957). *A theory of cognitive dissonance*. Stanford: Stanford University Press.

Finke, R. A., T. B. Ward, & S. M. Smith. (1992). *Creative cognition: Theory, research, and applications*. Cambridge, MA: MIT Press.

Getzels, J. W., & M. Csikszentmihalyi. (1976). *The creative vision: A longitudinal study of problem finding*. New York: Wiley.

Gladwell, M. (2005). *Blink*. Boston: Little, Brown.

Goll, I., & A. M. A. Rasheed. (1997). Rational decision making and firm performance: The moderating role of environment. *Strategic Management Journal, 18:* 583–591.

Gordon, W. J. J. (1961). *Synectics: The development of creative capacity*. New York: Collier.

Guagagno, R.E. & Cialdini, R.B. (2010). Preference for consistency and Social influence: A review of current research findings. *Social Influence, 5:* 152–163.

Hastie, R. & Dawes, R.M. (2009). *Rational choice in an uncertain world: The psychology of judgment and decision making*. New York: Sage.

Hawn, C. (2004, January). If he's so smart... *Fast Company:* 68–74.

Heider, F. (1946). Attitudes and cognitive organization. *Journal of Psychology, 21:* 107–112.

Hermann, N. (1991). The creative brain. *The Journal of Creative Behavior, 25:* 11–16.

Hudspith, S. (1985). *The neurological correlates of creative thought*. Unpublished PhD Dissertation, University of Southern California.

Hyatt, J. (1989, February). The odyssey of an excellent man. *Inc.:* 63–68. Copyright © 1989 by Goldhirsch Group, Inc. Reprinted with permission of the publishers, 38 Commercial Wharf, Boston, MA 02110.

Interaction Associates. (1971). *Tools for change*. San Francisco: Author.

Iyengar, B. K. S., Evans, J. J., & Abrams, D. (2006). Light on life: The yoga journey to wholeness, inner peace, and ultimate freedom. New York: Rodale.

Janis, I. L. (1971). *Groupthink*. New York: Free Press.

Janis, I. L., & L. Mann. (1977). *Decision making: A psychological analysis of conflict, choice, and commitment*. New York: Free Press. Copyright © 1977 by the Free Press. Reprinted with the permission of the Free Press, an imprint of Simon & Schuster.

Juran, J. (1988). *Juran on planning management*. New York: Free Press.

Kahneman, D. (2013). *Thinking fast and slow*. New York: Farrar, Straus and Giroux.

Kaufman, J. C. (2016) *Creativity 101*. New York: Springer.

Kaufman, J. C. & Sternberg, R. J. (2010). *The Cambridge handbook of creativity*. Cambridge: Cambridge University Press.

Koberg, D., & J. Bagnall. (2003). *The universal traveler: A soft system guidebook to creativity, problem solving, and the process of design.* Los Altos, CA: William Kaufmann.

Koestler, A. (1964). *The act of creation.* New York: Dell.

Koopman, P. L., J. W. Broekhuijsen, & A. F. M. Wierdsma. (1998). Complex decision making in organizations. In P. J. D. Drenth & H. Thierry (Eds.), *Handbook of work and organizational psychology,* Vol. 4 (pp. 357–386). Hove, England: Psychology Press/Erlbaum.

Kuo, Y-Y. (1996). Toaistic psychology of creativity. *Journal of Creative Behavior, 30:* 197–212.

Maduro, R. (1976). *Artistic creativity in a Brahmin painter community* (Monograph 14). Berkeley: University of California Center for South and Southeast Asia Cultures.

March, J. G. (1994). *A primer on decision making: How decisions happen.* New York: Free Press.

March, J. G. (Ed.). (1999). *The pursuit of organizational intelligence.* New York: Blackwell.

March, J. G., & H. A. Simon. (1958). *Organizations.* New York: Wiley.

Markoff, J. (1988, November 2). For scientists using supercomputers, visual imagery speeds discoveries. New York Times News Service, *Ann Arbor News,* D3.

Martindale, C. (1999). Biological bases of creativity. In R. J. Sternberg (Ed.), *Handbook of creativity.* Cambridge, UK: Cambridge University Press.

McKim, R. H. (1997). *Thinking visually: A strategy manual for problem solving.* Parsippany, NJ: Dale Seymour Publications.

McMillan, I. (1985). Progress in research on corporate venturing. Working paper, Center for Entrepreneurial Studies, New York University.

Medawar, P. B. (1967). *The art of the soluble.* London: Methuen.

Miller, S. J., D. J. Hickson, & D. C. Wilson. (1996). Decision making in organizations. In S. R. Clegg & C. Hardy (Eds.), *Handbook of organizational studies* (pp. 293–312). London: Sage.

Mitroff, I. I. (1998). *Smart thinking for crazy times: The art of solving the right problems.* San Francisco: Barrett-Koehler.

Molina, G. G., Bruekers, F., Presura, C., Damstra, M., van der Veen, M. (29015). Morphological synthesis of ECG signals for person authentication. Poznan, Poland: *IEEE Xplore.*

Morris, M.W. & Leung, K. (2010) Creativity East and West: Perspectives and parallels. *Management and Organization Review,* 6: 313–327.

Mumford, M. D., W. A. Baughman, M. A. Maher, D. P. Costanza, & E. P. Supinski. (1997). Process-based measures of creative problem solving skills. *Creativity Research Journal, 10:* 59–71.

Nayak, P. R., & J. M. Ketteringham. (1986). *Breakthroughs!* New York: Rawson Associates.

Nemeth, C. J. (1986). Differential contributions of majority and minority influence. *Psychological Review, 93:* 23–32.

Newcomb, T. (1954). An approach to the study of communicative acts. *Psychological Review, 60:* 393–404.

Nickerson, R. S. (1999). Enhancing creativity. In R. J. Sternberg (Ed.), *Handbook of creativity.* Cambridge: Cambridge University Press.

Nolan, V. & Williams, C. (2010). *Imagine That!* Publishers Graphics, LLC, 2010.

Osborn, A. (1953). *Applied imagination.* New York: Scribner.

Paulus, P. B. & Nijstad, B. A. (2003). *Group creativity.* London: Oxford University Press.

Poincare, H. (1921). *The foundation of science.* New York: Science Press.

Raudsepp, E. (1981). *How creative are you?* New York: Perigee Books/G.P. Putnam's Sons. Copyright © 1981 by Eugene Raudsepp. Reprinted with the permission of the author, c/o Dominick Abel Literary Agency, Inc.

Raudsepp, E., & G. P. Hough. (1977). *Creative growth games.* New York: Putnam.

Reiter-Palmon, R. (2014). The rokle of problem construction in creative production. *The Journal of Creative Behavior,* 51: 323–326.

Ribot, T. A. (1906). *Essay on the creative imagination.* Chicago: Open Court.

Riley, S. (1998). *Critical thinking and problem solving.* Upper Saddle River, NJ: Simon & Schuster.

Rothenberg, A. (1979). *The emerging goddess.* Chicago: University of Chicago Press.

Rothenberg, A. (1991). Creativity, health, and alcoholism. *Creativity Research Journal, 3:* 179–202.

Rothenberg, A. (2014). *Flight from wonder: An investigation of scientific creativity.* Oxford University Press.

Rothenberg, A., & C. Hausman. (2000). Metaphor and creativity. In M. A. Runco (Ed.), *Creativity research handbook,* Vol. 2. Cresskill, NJ: Hampton.

Roukes, N. (1988). *Design synectics: Stimulating creativity in design.* Berkeley, CA: Davis Publications.

Scope, E. E. (1999). *A meta-analysis of research on creativity: The effects of instructional variables.* Ann Arbor, MI: Dissertation Abstracts International, Section A: Humanities and Social Sciences.

Scott, O. J. (1974). *The creative ordeal: The story of Raytheon.* New York: Atheneum.

Siau, K. L. (1995). Group creativity and technology. *Journal of Creative Behavior, 29:* 201–216.

Smith, G. F. (1998). Idea-generation techniques: A formulary of active ingredients. *Journal of Creative Behavior, 32:* 107–133.

Starko, A. J. (2001). *Creativity in the classroom: Schools of curious delight.* Mahwah, NJ: Lawrence Erlbaum.

Sternberg, R. J. (Ed.). (1999). *Handbook of creativity.* Cambridge: Cambridge University Press.

Sunstein, C. R. & Hastie, R. (2015). *Wiser: Getting beyond groupthink to make groups smarter.* Boston: Harvard Business Review Press.

Tichy, N. (1983). *Strategic human resource management.* New York: Wiley.

Trompenaars, F., & C. Hampden-Turner. (2012). *Riding the waves of culture: Understanding cultural diversity in business.* Yarmouth, ME: Nicholas Brealey Publishing.

Trompenaars, F., & C. Hampden-Turner. (2004). *Managing people across cultures.* Mankato, MN: Capstone Publishing.

Tushman, M. L., & P. Anderson. (1997). *Managing strategic innovation and change*. New York: Oxford University Press.

Van de Ven, A. (1997). Technological innovation, learning, and leadership. In R. Garud, P. Rattan Nayyar, & Z. Baruch Shapira (Eds.), *Technological innovation: Oversights and foresights*. Cambridge: Cambridge University Press.

von Oech, R. (1986). *A kick in the seat of the pants*. New York: Harper & Row.

Vroom, V. H., & P. W. Yetton. (1973). *Leadership and decision making*. Pittsburgh: University of Pittsburgh Press.

Vygotsky, L. (1962). *Thought and language*. Cambridge, MA: MIT Press.

Wallas, G. (1926). *The art of thought*. London: C. A. Watts.

Ward, T. B., S. M. Smith, & R. A. Finke. (1999). Creative cognition. In R. J. Sternberg (Ed.), *Handbook of creativity*. Cambridge: Cambridge University Press.

Weick, K. E. (1979). *The social psychology of organizing*. Reading, MA: Addison-Wesley.

Weick, K. E. (1984). Small wins. *American Psychologist, 39:* 40–49.

Weick, K. E. (1995). *Sensemaking in organizations*. Beverly Hills, CA: Sage.

Williams, W. M., & L. T. Yang. (1999). Organizational creativity. In R. J. Sternberg (Ed.), *Handbook of creativity*. Cambridge, UK: Cambridge University Press.

Wonder, J., & J. Blake. (1992). Creativity East and West: Intuition versus logic. *Journal of Creative Behavior, 26:* 172–185.

Zeitz, P. (1999). *The art and craft of problem solving*. New York: Wiley.

Zhou, J., & C. E. Shalley. (2003). Research on employee creativity: A critical review and directions or future research. *Research in Personnel and Human Resources Management, 22:* 165–217.

CHAPTER 4 REFERENCES

Argyris, C. (1991). Teaching smart people how to learn. *Harvard Business Review, 63:* 99–109.

Baker, W. (2000). *Achieving success through social capital*. San Francisco: Jossey-Bass.

Barnlund, D. C. (1968). *Interpersonal communication: Survey and studies*. Boston: Houghton Mifflin.

Beebe, S. A., S. J. Beebe, & M. V. Redmond. (1996). *Interpersonal communication*. Boston: Allyn & Bacon.

Boss, W. L. (1983). Team building and the problem of regression: The personal management interview as an intervention. *Journal of Applied Behavioral Science, 19:* 67–83.

Bostrom, R. N. (1997). The process of listening. In O. D. W. Hargie (Ed.), *The handbook of communication skills*. London: Routledge.

Bowman, G. W. (1964). What helps or harms promotability? *Harvard Business Review, 42:* 14.

Brownell, J. (1986). *Building active listening skills*. Englewood Cliffs, NJ: Prentice Hall.

Brownell, J. (1990). Perceptions of effective listeners. *Journal of Business Communication, 27:* 401–415.

Cameron, K. S. (1994). Strategies for successful organizational downsizing. *Human Resource Management Journal, 33:* 89–122.

Cameron, K.S. (2012). *Positive leadership*. San Francisco: Berrett Koehler.

Carrell, L. J., & S. C. Willmington. (1996). A comparison of self-report and performance data in assessing speaking and listening competence. *Communication Reports, 9:* 185–191.

Council of Communication Management. (1996). Electronic communication is important, but face-to-face communication is still rated high. *Communication World, 13:* 12–13.

Covey, S. R. (1989). *The seven habits of highly effective people*. New York: Simon & Schuster.

Cupach, W. R., & B. H. Spitzberg. (1994). *The dark side of interpersonal communication*. Hillsdale, NJ: Lawrence Erlbaum.

DeVito, J.A. (2015). *The interpersonal communication book* (14th edition). Boston: Pearson.

Dutton, J. E. (2003). *Energize your workplace: How to create and sustain high quality relationships at work*. San Francisco: Jossey-Bass.

Dutton, J.E. (2014). Build high quality connections. In J. Dutton & G. Spreitzer *How to be a Positive Leader: Small Actions, Big Impact*, San Francisco: Berrett–Koehler Publishers,

Dyer, W. G. (1972). Congruence. In *The sensitive manipulator*. Provo, UT: Brigham Young University Press.

Fredrickson, B. L. (2001). The role of positive emotions in positive psychology: The broaden-and-build theory of positive emotions. *American Psychologist, 56:* 218–226.

Gackenbach, J. (1998). *Psychology and the Internet: Intrapersonal, interpersonal, and transpersonal implications*. New York: Academic Press.

Geddie, T. (1999). Moving communication across cultures. *Communication World, 16:* 37–40.

Gibb, J. R. (1961). Defensive communication. *Journal of Communication, 11:* 141–148.

Gittell, J. H. (2003). A theory of relational coordination. In K. S. Cameron, J. E. Dutton, & R. E. Quinn (Eds.), *Positive organizational scholarship*. San Francisco: Barrett-Koehler.

Gittell, J. H., K. S. Cameron, & S. Lim. (2006). Relationships, layoffs, and organizational resilience: Airline industry responses to September 11th. *Journal of Applied Behavioral* Science, *42:* 300–329.

Glasser, W. (1965). *Reality therapy: A new approach to psychiatry*. New York: Harper & Row.

Glasser, W. (2000). *Reality therapy in action*. New York: Harper Collins.

Golen, S. (1990). A factor analysis of barriers to effective listening. *Journal of Business Communication, 27:* 25–35.

Gordon, R. D. (1988). The difference between feeling defensive and feeling understood. *Journal of Business Communication, 25:* 53–64.

Gudykunst, W. B., & S. Ting-Toomey. (1988). *Culture and interpersonal communication*. Newbury Park, CA: Sage.

Gudykunst, W. B., S. Ting-Toomey, & T. Nishida. (1996). *Communication in personal relationships across cultures*. Thousand Oaks, CA: Sage.

Haas, J. W., & C. L. Arnold. (1995). An examination of the role of listening in judgments of communication competence in coworkers. *Journal of Business Communication, 32:* 123–139.

Haney, W. V. (1992). *Communication and interpersonal relations*. Homewood, IL: Irwin.

Hanson, G. (1986). *Determinants of firm performance: An integration of economic and organizational factors*. Unpublished doctoral dissertation, University of Michigan Business School.

Hargie, O. D. W. (1997). Communication as skilled performance. In O. D. W. Hargie (Ed.), *The handbook of communication skills*. London: Routledge.

Heaphy, E. D., & J. E. Dutton. (2006). Embodying social interactions: Integrating physiology into the study of positive connections and relationships at work. *Academy of Management Review* (in press).

Hyman, R. (1989). The psychology of deception. *Annual Review of Psychology, 40:* 133–154.

James, W., cited in D. R. Laing (1965). Mystification, confusion, and conflict. In I. Boszormenya-Nagy & J. L. Franco (Eds.), *Intensive family therapy*. New York: Harper & Row.

Knapp, M. L., & A. L. Vangelisti. (1996). *Interpersonal communication and human relationships*. Boston: Allyn & Bacon.

Kramer, D. A. (2000). Wisdom as a classical source of human strength: Conceptualization and empirical inquiry. *Journal of Social and Clinical Psychology, 19:* 83–101.

Kramer, R. (1997). *Leading by listening: An empirical test of Carl Rogers' theory of human relationship using interpersonal assessments of leaders by followers*. Ann Arbor, MI: Dissertation Abstracts International Section A: Humanities and Social Sciences, Volume 58.

Loomis, F. (1939). *The consultation room*. New York: Knopf.

Losada, M., & E. Heaphy. (2004). The role of positivity and connectivity in the performance of business teams. *American Behavioral Scientist, 47:* 740–765.

McGregor, D. (1960). *The human side of enterprise*. New York: McGraw-Hill.

Ouchi, W. (1981). *Theory Z*. Reading, MA: Addison-Wesley.

Peters, T. (1988). *Thriving on chaos*. New York: Knopf.

Pfeffer, J. (1998). *The human equation: Building profits by putting people first*. Boston: Harvard Business School Press.

Reis, H., & S. L. Gable. (2003). Toward a positive psychology of relationships. In C. L. M. Keyes & J. Haidt. *Flourishing: Positive psychology and the life well-lived* (pp. 129–160). Washington, DC: American Psychological Association.

Rogers, C. W. (1961). *On becoming a person*. Boston: Houghton Mifflin.

Rogers, C., & R. Farson. (1976). *Active listening*. Chicago: Industrial Relations Center.

Rosen, S. (1998). A lump of clay. *Communication World, 15:* 58–59.

Sieburg, E. (1978). *Confirming and disconfirming organizational communication*. Working paper, University of Denver.

Spitzberg, B. H. (1994). The dark side of (in)competence. In William R. Cupach & Brian H. Spitzberg (Eds.), *The dark side of interpersonal communication*. Hillsdale, NJ: Lawrence Erlbaum.

Sternberg, R. J. (1990). *Wisdom: Its nature, origins, and development*. Cambridge: Cambridge University Press.

Synopsis Communication Consulting of London. (1998). *The human factor: New rules for the digital workplace*. London: Author.

Szligyi, A. D., & M. J. Wallace. (1983). *Organizational behavior and human performance*. Glenview, IL: Scott Foresman.

Time. (2000, June 19). Embarrassing miscue: 31.

Triandis, H. C. (1994). *Culture and social behavior*. New York: McGraw-Hill.

Trompenaars, F. (1996). Resolving international conflict: Culture and business strategy. *Business Strategy Review, 7:* 51–68.

Trompenaars, F., & C. Hampden-Turner. (2011). *Riding the waves of culture*. New York: McGraw-Hill.

Wiemann, J. M. (1977). Explanation and test of a model of communication competence. *Human Communication Research, 3:* 145–213.

Wolvin, A., & C. Coakley. (1988). *Listening*. Dubuque, IA: W. C. Brown.

CHAPTER 5 REFERENCES

Adler, P. S., & S. Kwon. (2002). Social capital: Prospects for a new concept. *Academy of Management Review, 27:* 17–40.

Allen, R. W., D. L. Madison, L. W. Porter, P. A. Renwick, & B. T. Mayer. (1979). Organizational politics: Tactics and characteristics of actors. *California Management Review, 22:* 77–83.

Allinson, C. W., S. J. Armstrong, & J. Hayes. (2001). The effects of cognitive style on leader-member exchange: A study of manager-subordinate dyads. *Journal of Occupational and Organizational Psychology, 74:* 201–220.

Anderson, C., O. P. John, D. Keltner, & A. M. Kring. (2001). Who attains social status? Effects of personality and physical attractiveness in social groups. *Journal of Personality and Social Psychology, 81:* 116–132.

Agle, B. R., N. J. Nagarajan, J. A. Sonnenfeld, & D. Srinivasan. (2006). Does CEO charisma matter? An empirical analysis of the relationships among organizational performance, environmental uncertainty, and top management team perceptions of CEO charisma. *Academy of Management Journal, 49:* 161–174.

Bacharach, S. B. (2005, May). Making things happen by mastering the game of day-to-day politics. *Fast Company:* 93.

Baum, L., & J. A. Byre. (1986, April). Executive secretary: A new rung on the corporate ladder; but hitching her star to the boss can work both ways. *BusinessWeek:* 74.

Bennis, W., & B. Nanus. (2003). *Leaders: Strategies for taking charge*, 2nd ed. New York: Harper Collins.

Bies, R. J., & T. M. Tripp. (1998). Two faces of the powerless: Coping with tyranny in organizations. In R. M. Kramer, & M. A. Neale (Eds.), *Power and influence in organizations*. Thousand Oaks, CA: Sage.

Bolman, L. G., & T. E. Deal. (1997). *Reframing organizations: Artistry, choice, and leadership*. San Francisco: Jossey-Bass.

Breen, B. (2001, November). Trickle-up leadership. *Fast Company:* 70.

Buell, B., & A. L. Cowan. (1985, August). Learning how to play the corporate power game. *BusinessWeek:* 54–55.

Bunderson, J. S. (2002). Team member functional background and involvement in management teams. *Academy of Management Proceedings, OB:* 11–16.

Bunderson, J. S. (2003). Team member functional background and involvement in management teams: Direct effects and the moderating role of power centralization. *Academy of Management Journal, 46:* 458–474.

Bunker, K. A., K. E. Kram, & S. Ting. (2002). The young and the clueless. *Harvard Business Review, 80:* 80–87.

Burt, R. S. (1997). The contingent value of social capital. *Administrative Science Quarterly, 42:* 339–365.

Canfield, F. E., & J. J. LaGaipa. (1970). Friendship expectations at different stages in the development of friendship. Paper read at the annual meeting of the Southeastern Psychological Association, Louisville.

Chiu, L. H. (1972). A cross-cultural comparison of cognitive styles in Chinese and American children. *International Journal of Psychology, 8:* 235–242.

Chiu, L. (2001). Locus of control differences between American and Chinese adolescents. *Journal of Social Psychology, 128:* 411–413.

Choi, I., R. E. Nisbett, & A. Norenzayan. (1999). Causal attribution across cultures: Variation and universality. *Psychological Bulletin, 125:* 47–63.

Cialdini, R. B. (2001). *Influence: Science and practice*, 4th ed. Boston: Allyn & Bacon.

Cohen, A. R., & D. L. Bradford. (2003). Influence without authority: The use of alliances, reciprocity, and exchange to accomplish work. In B. M. Staw (Ed.), *Psychological dimensions of organizational behavior*, 3rd ed. (pp. 359–367). Englewood Cliffs, NJ: Prentice Hall.

Conger, J. A., & R. N. Kanungo. (1998). *Charismatic leadership in organizations*. Thousand Oaks, CA: Sage.

Conner, J., & D. Ulrich. (1996). Human resource roles: Creating value, not rhetoric. *Human Resource Planning, 19:* 38–49.

Cuming, P. (1984). *The power handbook*. Boston: CBI Publishing Co.

Daly, J. P. (1995). Explaining changes to employees: The influence of justifications and change outcomes on employees' fairness judgments. *Journal of Applied Behavioral Science, 31:* 415–428.

Deal, T. E., & A. A. Kennedy. (1982). *Corporate cultures: The rites and rituals of corporate life*. Reading, MA: Addison-Wesley.

DeGeorge, R. T. (1999). *Business ethics*. Upper Saddle River, NJ: Prentice Hall.

Dirks, K. T., & D. L. Ferrin. (2001). The role of trust in organizational settings. *Organization Science, 12:* 450–467.

Dutton, J. E., & S. J. Ashford. (1993). Selling issues to top management. *Academy of Management Review, 18(3):* 397–428.

Dutton, J. E., & R. B. Duncan. (1987). The creation of momentum for change through the process of strategic issue diagnosis. *Strategic Management Journal, 83(3):* 279–295.

Dyer, W. G. (1972). Congruence. In *The sensitive manipulator*. Provo, UT: Brigham Young University Press.

Emerson, R. M. (1962). Power-dependence relations. *American Sociological Review, 27:* 31–40.

Erez, A., V. F. Misangyi, D. E. Johnson, M. A. LePine, & K. C. Halverson. (2008). Stirring the hearts of followers: Charismatic leadership as the transferal of affect. *Journal of Applied Psychology, 93:* 602–616.

Fisher, A. (2005, March 7). Starting a new job? Don't blow it. *Fortune*: 48.

Furman, W. (2001). Working models of friendship. *Journal of Social and Personal Relationships, 18:* 583–602.

Gabarro, J. J., & J. P. Kotter. (1980). Managing your boss. *Harvard Business Review, 58:* 92–100.

Gabarro, J. J., & J. P. Kotter. (2007). Managing your boss. In K. P. Coyne, E. J. Coyne, L. Bossidy, J. J. Gabarro, & J. P. Kotter (Eds.). *Managing UP*, 2nd ed. (HBR Article Collection). Boston: *Harvard Business Review*.

Gardner, J. (1990). *On leadership*. New York: Free Press.

Gelman, E. (1985, September). Playing office politics. *Newsweek:* 56.

Giamatti, A. B. (1981). *The university and public interest*. New York: Atheneum.

Grove, A. (1983). *High output management*. London: Souvenir Press.

Gruber, J., & M. Smith. (1995). Women's responses to sexual harassment: A multivariate analysis. *Basic and Applied Social Psychology, 17:* 543–562.

Hinings, C. R., D. J. Hickson, J. M. Pennings, & R. E. Schneck. (1974). Structural conditions of intraorganizational power. *Administrative Science Quarterly, 21:* 22–44.

Hoerr, J. (1985, December). Human resource managers aren't corporate nobodies anymore. *BusinessWeek:* 58.

Hogg, M. A. (2001). A social identity theory of leadership. *Personality and Social Psychology Review, 5:* 184–200.

Hosmer, L. T. (1995). Trust: The connecting link between organizational theory and philosophical ethics. *Academy of Management Review, 20:* 379–403.

Hosoda, M., E. F. Stone-Romero, & G. Coats. (2003). The effects of physical attractiveness on job-related outcomes: A meta-analysis of experimental studies. *Personnel Psychology, 56:* 431–462.

Kanter, R. (1979). Power failures in management circuits. *Harvard Business Review, 57:* 65–75. Copyright © 1979 by The President and Fellows of Harvard College. Reprinted with the permission of *Harvard Business Review*. All rights reserved.

Kaplan, R. E., & M. Mazique. (1983). *Trade routes: The manager's network of relationships* (Technical Report #22). Greensboro, NC: Center for Creative Leadership.

Kipnis, D. (1987). Psychology and behavioral technology. *American Psychologist, 42:* 30–36.

Kipnis, D., & S. M. Schmidt. (1988). Upward-influence styles: Relationship with performance evaluations, salary, and stress. *Administrative Science Quarterly, 33:* 528–542.

Kipnis, D., S. M. Schmidt, & I. Wilkinson. (1980). Intraorganizational influence tactics: Explorations in getting one's way. *Journal of Applied Psychology, 65:* 440–452.

Korda, M. (1991). *Power: How to get it, how to use it*. New York: Warner Books.

Kotter, J. P. (1977). Power, dependence and effective management. *Harvard Business Review, 55:* 125–136.

Labich, K. (1995, February 20). Kissing off corporate America. *Fortune, 131:* 44–52.

Langlois, J. H., L. Kalakanis, A. J. Rubenstein, A. Larson, M. Hallam, & M. Smoot. (2000). Maxims of myths of beauty? A meta-analytic and theoretical review. *Psychological Bulletin 126:* 390–423.

Lawrence, R. R., & J. W. Lorsch. (1986). *Organization and environment: Managing differentiation and integration.* Boston: Harvard University Press.

Leger, D. M. (2000, May). Help! I'm the new boss. *Fortune:* 281–284.

Marwell, G., & D. R. Schmitt, (1967). Dimensions of compliance-gaining strategies: A dimensional analysis. *Sociometry, 30:* 350–364.

May, R. (1998). *Power and innocence: A search for the sources of violence.* New York: Norton.

McCall, M. M., Jr., & M. M. Lombardo. (1983). What makes a top executive? *Psychology Today, 26:* 28–31. Copyright © 1983 by Sussex Publishers Inc. Reprinted with the permission of *Psychology Today.*

McClelland, D. C., & D. H. Burnham. (2003). Power is the great motivator. *Motivating People, 81:* 117–126.

Mechanic, D. (1962). Sources of power of lower participants in complex organizations. *Administrative Science Quarterly, 7:* 349–364.

Miller, R. (1985). Three who made a difference. *Management Review, 74:* 16–19.

Morris, M. W., J. M. Podolny, & S. Ariel. (2000). Missing relations: Incorporating relational constructs into models of culture. In P. C. Earley & H. Singh (Eds.), *Innovation in international and cross-cultural management* (pp. 52–90). Thousand Oaks, CA: Sage.

Mulder, M., L. Koppelaar, R. V. de Jong, & J. Verhage. (1986). Organizational field study. *Journal of Applied Psychology, 7:* 566–570.

Mulgan, G. (1998). *Connexity: How to live in a connected world.* Boston: Harvard Business School Press.

Pascale, R. (1985). The paradox of "corporate culture": Reconciling ourselves to socialization. *California Management Review, 27:* 26–41.

Perrow, C. (1970). Departmental power and perspectives in industrial firms. In M. N. Zold, (Ed.), *Power in organizations.* Nashville, TN: Vanderbilt University Press.

Peters, T. (1978). Symbols, patterns, and settings: An optimistic case for getting things done. *Organizational Dynamics, 7:* 3–22.

Pfeffer, J. (1977). Power and resource allocation in organizations. In B. Staw & G. Salancik (Eds.), *New direction in organizational behavior.* Chicago: St. Clair Press.

Pfeffer, J. (1981). *Power in organizations.* Marshfield, MA: Pitman.

Pfeffer, J. (1994). *Power and influence in organizations.* Boston: Harvard Business School Press.

Pfeffer, J., & A. Konrad. (1991). The effects of individual power on earnings. *Work and Occupations, 18:* 385–414.

Schein, E. H. (1999). *The corporate culture survival guide: Sense and nonsense about culture change.* San Francisco: Jossey-Bass.

Schmidt, S., & D. Kipnis. (1987). The perils of persistence. *Psychology Today, 21:* 32–33.

Shipper, F., & J. E. Dillard. (2000). A study of impending derailment and recovery of middle managers across career stages. *Human Resource Management, 39:* 331–345.

Sparrowe, R. T., R. C. Liden, & M. L. Kraimer. (2001). Social networks and the performance of individuals and groups. *Academy of Management Journal, 44:* 316–325.

Stewart, T. A. (1992, May 18). The search for the organization of tomorrow. *Fortune:* 92–98.

Tedeschi, J. T. (1974). Attributions, liking and power. In T. L. Huston (Ed.), *Foundations of interpersonal attraction.* New York: Academic Press.

Thompson, L. (2001). *The mind and heart of the negotiator.* Upper Saddle River, NJ: Prentice Hall.

Triandis, H. (1994). *Culture and social behavior.* New York: McGraw-Hill.

Trompenaars, F. (1996). Resolving international conflict: Culture and business strategy. *Business Strategy Review, 7:* 51–68.

Tully, S. (1993, February 8). The modular corporation. *Fortune:* 106–114.

Vijayasiri, G. (2008). Reporting sexual sarassment: The importance of organizational culture and trust. *Gender Issues, 25:* 43–61.

Yukl, G. (2002). *Leadership in organizations,* 5th ed. Upper Saddle River, NJ: Prentice Hall.

CHAPTER 6 REFERENCES

Abbott, R. K. (1997). Flexible compensation: Past, present, and future. *Compensation & Benefits Management, 13:* 18–24.

Adria, M. (2000). Making the most of e-mail. *Academy of Management Executive, 14:* 153–154.

Alderfer, C. P. (1977). A critique of Salancik and Pfeffer's examination of need-satisfaction theories. *Administrative Science Quarterly, 22:* 658–672.

Atkinson, J. W. (1992). Motivational determinants of thematic apperception? In C. P. Smith (Ed.), *Motivation and personality: Handbook of thematic content analysis.* New York: Cambridge University Press.

Bennis, W. (1984). The four competencies of leadership. *Training and Development Journal, 38:* 15–19.

Bennis, W. (2003). *On becoming a leader.* Cambridge, MA: Perseus Books Group.

Berg, J. M., J. E. Dutton, & A. Wrzesniewski. (2013). Job crafting and meaningful work. In B. J. Dik, Z. S. Byrne, & M. F. Steger (Eds.), *Purpose and meaning in the workplace* (pp. 81–104). Washington, DC: American Psychological Association.

Birch, D., & J. Veroff. (1966). *Motivation: A study of action.* Monterey, CA: Brooks-Cole.

Bitter, M. E., & W. L. Gardner. (1995). A mid-range theory of the leader/member attribution process in professional service organizations: The role of the organizational environment and impression management. In M. J. Martinko (Ed.), *Attribution theory: An organizational perspective.* Delray Beach, FL: St. Lucie Press.

Boehle, S., K. Dobbs, & D. Stamps. (2000). Two views of distance learning. *Training, 37:* 34.

Butler, T., & J. Waldroop. (1999, September–October). Job sculpting: The art of retaining your best people. *Harvard Business Review:* 144–152.

Choi, I., R. E. Nisbett, & A. Norenzayan. (1999). Causal attribution across cultures: Variation and universality. *Psychological Bulletin, 125:* 47–63.

Cook, A. (2005, May). Money's a sure-fire motivator—Isn't it? *Promotions and Incentives:* 56–59.

Cropanzano, R., & R. Folger. (1996). Procedural justice and worker motivation. In R. M. Steers, L. W. Porter, & G. A. Bigley (Eds.), *Motivation and leadership at work.* New York: McGraw-Hill.

Daniels, K., C. Gedikli, D. Watson, A. Semkina, & O. Vaughn. (2017). Job design, employment practices and well-being: a systematic review of intervention studies. *Ergonomics, 60:* 1177–1196.

Davidson, O. B., & D. Eden. (2000). Remedial self-fulfilling prophecy: Two field experiments to prevent golem effects among disadvantaged women. *Journal of Applied Psychology 85:* 386–398.

Deci, E. L., & R. M. Ryan. (1985). *Intrinsic motivation and self-determination in human behavior.* Basel Switzerland: Springer Nature.

Fisher, A. (2005, March 7). Starting a new job? Don't blow it. *Fortune:* 5.

Fisher, A. (2005, March 7). Starting a new job? Don't blow it. *Fortune:* 5.

Ganzach, Y. (1998). Intelligence and job satisfaction. *Academy of Management Journal, 41:* 526–536.

Gerhart, B. A. (2003). *Compensation: Theory, evidence, and strategic implications.* Thousand Oaks, CA: Sage.

Graham, M. E., & C. O. Trevor. (2000). Managing new pay program introductions to enhance the competitiveness of multinational corporations (MNCS). *Competitiveness Review, 10:* 136–154.

Hackman, J. R., & G. R. Oldham. (1980). *Work redesign.* Reading, MA: Addison-Wesley.

Harter, J. K., F. L. Schmidt, & T. L. Hayes. (2002). Business-unit-level relationship between employee satisfaction, employee engagement, and business outcomes: A meta-analysis. *Journal of Applied Psychology, 87:* 268–279.

Heider, F. (1958). *The psychology of interpersonal relations.* New York: Wiley. https://www.psychologytoday.com/us/blog/positively-media/201111/social-networks-what-maslow-misses-0)

House, R. J., & T. R. Mitchell. (1974). Path-goal theory of leadership. *Journal of Contemporary Business, 3:* 81–97.

Jackson, P. (2000). Interview with Phil Jackson by Bob Costas. MSNBC.

Janssen, O. (2001). Fairness perceptions as a moderator in the curvilinear relationships between job demands, and job performance and job satisfaction. *Academy of Management Journal, 44:* 1039–1050.

Jay, A. (1967). *Management and Machiavelli, an inquiry into the politics of corporate life.* New York: Holt, Rinehart & Winston.

Kerr, S. (1995). On the folly of rewarding A, while hoping for B. *Academy of Management Executive, 9(1):* 7–14.

Kerr, S. (1996, July 22). Risky business: The new pay game. *Fortune:* 94–97.

Kinley, N., & S. Ben-Hur. (2015). *Changing employee behavior: A practical guide for managers.* London: Palgrave MacMillan.

Kleiman, C. (2005, June 14). Awards for workers get better as they get personal. *Chicago Tribune:* 2.

Knight, D., C. C. Durham, & E. A. Locke. (2001). The relationship of term goals, incentives, and efficacy to strategic risk, tactical implementation, and performance. *Academy of Management Journal, 44:* 326–338.

Komaki, J., T. Coombs, & S. Schepman. (1996). Motivational implications of reinforcement theory. In R. M. Steers, L. W. Porter, & G. A. Bigley (Eds.), *Motivation and leadership at work.* New York: McGraw-Hill.

Kopelman, R. E. (1985, Summer). Job redesign and productivity: A review of evidence. *National Productivity Review:* 237–255.

Kotter, J. (1996, August 5). Kill complacency. *Fortune:* 168–170.

Latham, G. P. (2004). The motivational benefits of goal-setting. *Academy of Management Executive, 8:* 4–128.

Latham, G. P., & E. A. Locke. (2006) Enhancing the benefits and overcoming the pitfalls of goal setting. *Organizational Dynamics, 5:* 332–340.

Latham, G., M. Erez, & E. Locke. (1988). Resolving scientific disputes by the joint design of crucial experiments by the antagonists: Application to the Erez-Latham disputes regarding participation in goal setting. *Journal of Applied Psychology, 73:* 753–772.

Lawler, E. E. (1987). The design of effective reward systems. In J. Lorsch (Ed.), *Handbook of organizational behavior.* Englewood Cliffs, NJ: Prentice Hall.

Lawler, E. E. (1968). Equity theory as a predictor of productivity and work quality. *Psychological Bulletin, 70:* 596–610.

Lawler, E. E. (1988). Gainsharing theory and research: Findings and future directions. In W. A. Pasmore & E. R. Woodman (Eds.), *Research in organizational change and development* (Vol. 2). Greenwich, CT: JAI Press.

Lawler, E. E. (2000a). *Strategic pay.* San Francisco: Jossey-Bass.

Lawler, E. E., III. (2000b). *Pay strategies for the new economy.* San Francisco: Jossey-Bass.

LeDue, A. I., Jr. (1980). Motivation of programmers. *Data Base, 3:* 5.

Levering, R., & M. Moskowitz. (2003, January 20). 100 best companies to work for. *Fortune, 147:* 127.

Lilienfeld, S. O., S. J. Lynn, L. L. Namy, & N. J. Woolf. (2010). *Psychology: A framework for everyday thinking.* New York: Pearson Education.

Locke, E. A., & G. P. Latham. (2002, September). Building a practically useful theory of goal setting and task motivation. *American Psychologist, 57:* 705–717.

Luthans, F., & A. D. Stajkovic. (1999). Reinforce for performance: The need to go beyond pay and even rewards. *Academy of Management Executive, 13(2):* 49–57.

Malle, B. F. (2004). *How the mind explains behavior: Folk explanations, meaning, and social interaction.* Boston: MIT Press.

Maslow, A. H. (1954). *Motivation and personality.* New York: Harper.

Maslow, A. H. (1970). *Motivation and personality*, 2nd ed. New York: Harper & Row.

McCauley, L. (1999). Next stop—the 21st century. *Fast Company, 27:* 108–112.

McClelland, D. *Human motivation*, 1988. Cambridge University Press.

McClelland, D. C., J. W. Arkinson, R. A. Clark, & E. L. Lowell. (1953). *The achievement motive.* New York: Appleton-Century-Crofts.

McClelland, D. C., & D. H. Burnham. (2003). Power is the great motivator. *Harvard Business Review, 81:* 117–126.

McGregor, D. (1960). *The human side of enterprise.* New York: McGraw-Hill.

Michener, H. A., J. A. Fleishman, & J. J. Vaske. (1976). A test of the bargaining theory of coalition formulation in four-person groups. *Journal of Personality and Social Psychology, 34:* 1114–1126.

Moe, M. T., & H. Blodget. (2000, May 23). *The knowledge web. Part 4: corporate e-learning—feeding hungry minds.* Merrill Lynch & Co.

Murlis, H., & A. Wright. (1985). Rewarding the performance of the eager beaver. *Personnel Management, 17:* 28–31.

Murray, B., & B. Gerhart. (1998). An empirical analysis of a skill-based pay program and plant performance outcomes. *Academy of Management Journal, 41:* 68–78.

Nelson, B. (2000). Are performance appraisals obsolete? *Compensation and Benefits Review, 32:* 39–42.

Nelson, N. (2005). *The power of appreciation in business: How an obsession with value increases performance, productivity, and profits.* Malibu, CA: MindLab Publishing.

Nelton, S. (1988, March). Motivating for success. *Nation's Business:* 25.

News-Gazette. (1987, January): 6.

Oldham, G. R., & Y. Fried. (2016). Job design research and theory: Past, present and future. *Organizational Behavior and Human Decision Processes, 136:* 20–35.

O'leary-kelly, A. M., j. j. Marocchio, & D. D. Fink. (1994). A review of the influence of group goals on group performance. *Academy of Management Journal, 37:* 1285–1301.

Parker, G. (2001). Establishing remuneration practices across culturally diverse environments. *Compensation & Benefits Management, 17:* 23–27.

Perry, M. (2000, January). Working in the dark. *Training Media Review:* 13–14.

Peters, T., & R. H. Waterman. (1982). *In search of excellence.* New York: Warner Books.

Pfeffer, J. (1995). Producing sustainable competitive advantage through the effective management of people. *Academy of Management Executive, 9:* 55–71.

Pink, D. H. (2009). Drive: The surprising truth about what motivates us. Newmarket, Ontario Canada: Riverwood Publisher.

Quick, T. L. (1977). *Person to person managing.* New York: St. Martin's Press.

Quick, T. L. (1991). Motivation: Help your star performers shine even brighter. *Sales and Marketing Management, 143:* 96.

Reese, S. (1999, July). Getting your money's worth from training. *Business and Health:* 26–29.

Ross, L. (1977). The intuitive psychologist and his shortcomings: Distortions in the attribution process. In L. Berkowitz, *Advances in experimental social psychology.* **10**. New York: Academic Press. pp. 173–220

Rutledge, P. (2011). Social networks: What maslow misses. *Psychology Today, Blog entry, posted: November 8, 2011.*

Ryan, R. M., & E. L. Deci. (2000). Self-determination theory and the facilitation of intrinsic motivation, social development, and well-being. *American Psychologist, 55:* 68–78.

Sanderson, C. (2010). *Social psychology.* Hoboken, NJ: John Wiley & Sons.

Schriesheim, C. A., & L. L. Neider. (1996). Path-goal leadership theory: The long and winding road. *Leadership Quarterly, 7:* 317–321.

Shamir, B., R. J. House, & M. B. Arthur. (1993). The motivational effects of charismatic leadership: A self-concept based theory. *Organization Science, 4(4):* 577–594.

Stajkovic, A. D., & F. Luthans. (2001). Differential effects of incentive motivators on work performance. *Academy of Management Journal, 4:* 580–500.

Steers, R. M., L. W. Porter, & G. A. Bigley. (1996). *Motivation and leadership at work.* New York: McGraw-Hill.

Sue-Chan, C., & M. Ong. (2002). Goal assignment and performance: Assessing the mediating roles of goal commitment and self-efficacy and the moderating role of power distance. *Organizational Behavior and Human Decision Processes, 89:* 1140–1161.

Taylor, W. C. (1995). At Verifone it's a dog's life (and they love it?). *Fast Company, 1:* 115.

Thompson, D. W. (1978). *Managing people: Influencing behavior.* St. Louis, MO: C. V. Mosby Co.

Tichy, N. (1997, April). Bob Knowling's change manual. *Fast Company:* 76.

Tomlinson, A. (2002, March 25). T&D spending up in U.S. as Canada lags behind. *Canadian HR Reporter, 15:* 1–18.

Triandis, H. C. (1994). *Culture and social behavior.* New York: McGraw-Hill.

Vroom, V. (1964). *Work and motivation.* New York: Wiley.

Walster, E., G. W. Walster, & E. Bershcheid. (1978). *Equity: theory and research.* Boston: Allyn and Bacon, Inc.

Weiner, B. (2000). Intrapersonal and interpersonal theories of motivation from an attributional perspective. *Educational Psychology Review, 12:* 1–14.

Wood, R., & A. Bandura. (1989). Social cognitive theory of organizational management. *Academy of Management Review, 14 (3):* 361–383.

Wrzesniewski, A. & J. Dutton. (2001). Job crafting: Revisioning employees as active crafters of their work. *Academy of Management Review, 26:* 179–201.

Zingheim, P. K., & J. R. Schuster. (1995). Introduction: How are the new pay tools being deployed? *Compensation and Benefits Review* (July–August): 10–11.

CHAPTER 7 REFERENCES

Adler, N. J. (2002). *International dimensions of organizational behavior*, 4th ed. Cincinnati, OH: South-Western.

Adler, R. B. (1977). Satisfying personal needs: Managing conflicts, making requests, and saying no. In *Confidence in communication:*

A guide to assertive and social skills. New York: Holt, Rinehart & Winston.

Adler, R. B., L. B. Rosenfeld, & R. F. Proctor. (2001). *Interplay: The process of interpersonal communication.* Fort Worth, TX: Harcourt, Inc.

Adler, R. B., & G. Rodman. (2003). *Understanding human communication*, 8th ed. New York: Oxford University Press.

Agndal, H., L. Åge, & J. Eklinder-Frick. (2017). Two decades of business negotiation research: an overview and suggestions for future studies. *Journal of Business & Industrial Marketing, 32:* 487–504.

Argenti, J. (1976). *Corporate collapse: The causes and symptoms.* New York: Wiley.

The boss as referee. [Accountemps survey]. (1996, September). *CMA Management Accounting Magazine, 70(7):* 32.

Brown, L. D. (1983). *Managing conflict at organizational interfaces.* Reading, MA: Addison-Wesley.

Cameron, K. S., M. U. Kim, & D. A. Whetten. (1987). Organizational effects of decline and turbulence. *Administrative Science Quarterly, 32:* 222–240.

Caputo, A. (2013). A literature review of cognitive biases in negotiation processes. *International Journal of Conflict Management, 24:* 374–398.

Catch a falling star. (1988, April 23). *The Economist,* 88–90.

Caudron, S. (1992). Subculture strife hinders productivity. *Personnel Journal, 71(2):* 60–64.

Cox, T. H. (1994). *Cultural diversity in organizations: Theory, research, and practice.* San Francisco: Barrett-Koehler.

Cox, T. H., & Blake, S. (1991). Managing cultural diversity: Implications for organizational competitiveness. *Academy of Management Executive, 5(3):* 45–56.

Cummings, L. L., D. L. Harnett, & O. J. Stevens. (1971). Risk, fate, conciliation, and trust: An international study of attitudinal differences among executives. *Academy of Management Journal, 14:* 285–304.

Dana, D. (1984). The costs of organizational conflict. *Organizational Development Journal, 2:* 5–7.

Dana, D. (2014) The Dana Measure of Financial Cost of Conflict. https://mediationworks.com/wp-content/uploads/2016/11/cost-of-conflict-whitepaper-.pdf

de Dreu, C. K. W., S. L. Koole, & W. Steinel. (2000). Unfixing the fixed pie: A motivated information-processing approach to integrative negotiation. *Journal of Personality and Social Psychology, 79:* 975–987.

de Dreu, C. K. W., & L. R. Weingart. (2002). Task versus relationship conflict: A meta-analysis. *Academy of Management Proceedings, CM:* B1–B6.

Eisenhardt, K. M., J. L. Kahwajy, & L. J. Bourgeois III. (1997, July–August). How management teams can have a good fight. *Harvard Business Review:* 77–85.

Fisher, R., & S. Brown. (1988). *Getting together: Building a relationship that gets to yes.* Boston: Houghton Mifflin.

Gage, D. (1999, December). Is having partners a bad idea? *IndustryWeek,* Growing Companies Edition: 46–47.

Gendron, G., & B. O. Burlingham. (1989, April). The entrepreneur of the decade: An interview with Steve Jobs. *Inc.:* 123.

The GM system is like a blanket of fog. (1988, February 15). *Fortune:* 48–49.

Gordon, T. (2000). *Parent effectiveness training.* New York: Three Rivers Press.

Grove, A. (1984, July). How to make confrontation work for you. *Fortune:* 74.

Hines, J. S. (1980). *Conflict and conflict management.* Athens: University of Georgia Press.

Hofstede, G. (1980, Summer). Motivation, leadership, and organization: Do American theories apply abroad? *Organizational Dynamics:* 42–63.

Jehn, K. A. (1997). A qualitative analysis of conflict types and dimensions of organizational groups. *Administrative Science Quarterly, 41:* 530–557.

Jehn, K., & E. A. Mannix. (2001). The dynamic nature of conflict: A longitudinal study of intragroup conflict and group performance. *Academy of Management Journal, 44:* 238–251.

Keashly, L. (1994). Gender and conflict: What does psychological research tell us? In A. Taylor & J. B. Miller (Eds.), *Conflict and gender.* Cresskill, NJ: Hampton Press.

Kelly, J. (1970, July–August). Make conflict work for you. *Harvard Business Review, 48:* 103–113.

Kilmann, R. H., & K. W. Thomas. (1977). Developing a forced-choice measure of conflict-handling behavior: The MODE instrument. *Educational and Psychological Measurement, 37:* 309–325.

Kim, S. H., & R. H. Smith. (1993). Revenge and conflict escalation. *Negotiation Journal. 9:* 37–44.

Korabik, D., G. L. Baril, & C. Watson. (1993). Managers' conflict management style and leadership effectiveness: The moderating effects of gender. *Sex Roles, 29(5/6):* 405–420.

Latham, G., & K. Wexley. (1994). *Increasing productivity through performance appraisal.* Reading, MA: Addison-Wesley.

Lombardo, M. M., & R. W. Eichinger. (1996). *The Career ARCHITECT Development Planner.* Minneapolis: Lominger Ltd.

Loscheldera, D. D., M. Frieseb, & R. Trötschelc. (2017). How and why precise anchors distinctly affect anchor recipients and senders. *Journal of Experimental Social Psychology, 70:* 164–176.

Malhotra, D., & M. Bazerman. (2008). *Negotiation genius: How to overcome obstacles and achieve brilliant results at the bargaining table and beyond.* Boston: Harvard Business School.

Maslow, A. (1965). *Eupsychian management.* Homewood, IL: Irwin.

Memeth, C. J., B. Personnaz, M. Personnaz, & J. A. Goucalo. (2004). The liberating role of conflict in group creativity: A study in two countries. *European Journal of Social Psychology, 34:* 365–374.

Morris, W., & M. Sashkin. (1976). *Organizational behavior in action.* St. Paul, MN: West Publishing.

Morrison, A. M. (1996). *The new leaders: Leadership diversity in America.* San Francisco: Jossey-Bass.

Patterson, K., J. Grenny, R. McMillan & A. Switzler. (2012). *Crucial conversations: Tools for talking when stakes are high.* New York: McGraw Hill.

Pelled, L. H., K. M. Eisenhardt, & K. R. Xin. (1999). Exploring the black box: An analysis of work group diversity, conflict, and performance. *Administrative Science Quarterly, 44:* 1–28.

Perot, H. R. (1988, February). How I would turn around GM. *Fortune:* 48–49.

Phillips, K. W., K. A. Liljenquist, & M. A. Neale. (2009). Is the pain worth the gain? The advantages and liabilities of agreeing with socially distinct newcomers. *Personality and Social Psychology Bulletin, 35:* 336–350.

Porter, E. H. (1973). *Manual of administration and interpretation for strength deployment inventory.* La Jolla, CA: Personal Strengths Assessment Service.

Rahim, M. A., & A. A. Blum. (1994). *Global perspectives on organizational conflict.* Westport, CT: Praeger.

Ruble, T., & J. A. Schneer. (1994). Gender differences in conflict-handling styles: Less than meets the eye? In A. Wrzesniewski, & J. B. Miller, (Eds.), *Conflict and gender.* Cresskill, NJ: Hampton Press.

Ruble, T., & K. Thomas. (1976). Support for a two-dimensional model of conflict behavior. *Organizational Behavior and Human Performance, 16:* 145.

Runde, C. & T. Flanagan. (2012). *Becoming a conflict competent leader* (2nd ed.). San Francisco: Jossey-Bass.

Schmidt, W. H., & R. Tannenbaum. (1965, November–December). Management of differences. *Harvard Business Review, 38:* 107–115.

Sillars, A., & J. Weisberg. (1987). Conflict as a social skill. In M. E. Roloff & G. R. Miller (Eds.), *Interpersonal processes: New directions in communication research.* Beverly Hills, CA: Sage.

Smith, W. P. (1987). Conflict and negotiation: Trends and emerging issues. *Journal of Applied Social Psychology, 17:* 631–677.

Thomas, K. (1976). Conflict and conflict management. In M. D. Dunnette (Ed.), *Handbook of industrial and organizational psychology.* London: Routledge and Kegan Paul.

Thompson, L. (2001). *The mind and heart of the negotiator,* 2nd ed. Upper Saddle River, NJ: Prentice Hall.

Ting-Toomey, S., G. Gao, P. Trubisky, Z. Yang, H. S. Kim, S. L. Lin, & T. Nishida. (1991). Culture, face maintenance, and styles of handling interpersonal conflict: A study in five cultures. *International Journal of Conflict Management, 2:* 275–296.

Trompenaars, F. (1994). *Riding the waves of culture: Understanding diversity in global business.* New York: Irwin.

Trompenaars, F. (1996). Resolving international conflict: Culture and business strategy. *Business Strategy Review, 7:* 51–68.

Volkema, R. J., & T. J. Bergmann. (2001). Conflict styles as indicators of behavioral patterns in interpersonal conflicts. *Journal of Social Psychology, 135:* 5–15.

Weldon, E., & K. A. Jehn. (1995). Examining crosscultural differences in conflict management behavior: Strategy for future research. *International Journal of Conflict Management, 6:* 387–403.

Wilmot, W. W., & J. L. Hocker. (2001). *Interpersonal conflict.* New York: McGraw-Hill.

Xie, J., X. M. Song, & A. Stringfellow. (1998). Interfunctional conflict, conflict resolution styles, and new product success: A four-culture comparison. *Management Science, 44:* S192–S206.

CHAPTER 8 REFERENCES

Abrahamson, E. (1996). Management fashion. *Academy of Management Review, 21:* 254–285.

Adler, A. (1927). *Understanding human nature.* Garden City, NY: Garden City Publishing.

Alinsky, S. D. (1971). *Rules for radicals: A pragmatic primer for realistic radicals.* New York: Vintage Books.

Alloy, L. B., C. Peterson, L. Y. Abrahamson, & M. E. P. Seligman. (1984). Attributional style and the generality of learned helplessness. *Journal of Personality and Social Psychology, 46:* 681–687.

Anderson, C., D. Hellriegel, & J. Slocum. (1977). Managerial response to environmentally induced stress. *Academy of Management Journal, 20:* 260–272.

Ashby, R. (1956). *Design for the brain.* London: Science Paperbacks.

Averill, J. R. (1973). Personal control over aversive stimuli and its relationships to stress. *Psychological Bulletin, 80:* 286–303.

Baker, W., R. Cross, & M. Wooten. (2003). Positive organizational network analysis and energizing relationships. In K. S. Cameron, J. E. Dutton, & R. E. Quinn (Eds.), *Positive Organizational Scholarship* (pp. 328–342). San Francisco: Barrett-Koehler.

Bandura, A. (1977). Self-efficacy: Toward a unifying theory of behavioral change. *Psychological Review, 84:* 191–215.

Bandura, A. (1986). *Social foundations of thought and action: A social cognitive theory.* Englewood Cliffs, NJ: Prentice Hall.

Bandura, A. (1989). Human agency in social cognition theory. *American Psychologist, 44:* 1175–1184.

Bandura, A. (1997). Self-efficacy: The exercise of control. New York: W.H. Freeman.

Barber, B. (1983). *The logic and limits of trust.* New Brunswick, NJ: Rutgers University Press.

Bennis, W., & B. Nanus. (1985). *Leaders: The strategies for taking charge.* New York: Harper & Row.

Bernard, C. I. (1938). *The functions of the executive.* Cambridge, MA: Harvard University Press.

Block, P. (1987). *The empowered manager: Positive political skills at work.* San Francisco: Jossey-Bass.

Bookman, A., & S. Morgan. (1988). *Women and the politics of empowerment.* Philadelphia: Temple University Press.

Bowles, F.A. & Pearlman, C.J. (2017). Self-efficacy in action: Tales from the classroom for teaching, learning, and professional development. Lanham, MD: Rowman & Littlefield Publishers.

Bramucci, R. (1977). A factorial examination of the self-empowerment construct. Unpublished doctoral dissertation, University of Oregon.

Brehm, J. W. (1966). *Response to loss of freedom: A theory of psychological reactance.* New York: Academic Press.

Brief, A., & W. Nord. (1990). *Meanings of occupational work.* Lexington, MA: Lexington Books.

Byham, W. C. (1988). *Zapp! The lightening of empowerment.* New York: Harmony Books.

Cameron, K. S. (1998). Strategic organizational downsizing: An extreme case. *Research in Organizational Behavior, 20:* 185–229.

Cameron, K. S., J. E. Dutton, & R. E. Quinn. (2003). *Positive organizational scholarship.* San Francisco: Barrett-Koehler.

Cameron, K. S., S. J. Freeman, & A. K. Mishra. (1991). Best practices in white-collar downsizing: Managing contradictions. *Academy of Management Executive, 5:* 57–73.

Cameron, K. S., S. J. Freeman, & A. K. Mishra. (1993). Organization downsizing and redesign. In G. P. Huber, & W. Glick (Eds.), *Organizational change and design*. New York: Oxford University Press.

Cameron, K. S., M. U. Kim, & D. A. Whetten. (1987). Organizational effects of decline and turbulence. *Administrative Science Quarterly, 32:* 222–240.

Cameron, K. S., D. A. Whetten, & M. U. Kim. (1987). Organizational dysfunctions of decline. *Academy of Management Journal, 30:* 126–138.

Cameron, K. S., & R. E. Quinn. (2006). *Diagnosing and changing organizational culture*. San Francisco: Jossey-Bass.

Coch, L., & J. R. P. French. (1948). Overcoming resistance to change. *Human Relations, 11:* 512–532.

Conger, J. A. (1989). Leadership: The art of empowering others. *Academy of Management Executive, 3:* 17–24.

Conger, J. A., & R. N. Kanungo. (1988). The empowerment process. *Academy of Management Review, 13:* 471–482.

Coonradt, C. A. (1985). *The game of work*. Salt Lake City: Shadow Mountain Press.

DeCharms, R. (1979). Personal causation and perceived control. In L. C. Perlmuter & R. A. Monty (Eds.), *Choice and perceived control*. Hillsdale, NJ: Erlbaum.

Deci, E. L., & R. M. Ryan. (1987). The support of autonomy and control of behavior. *Journal of Personality and Social Psychology, 53:* 1024–1037.

Deci, E. L., J. P. Connell, & R. M. Ryan. (1989). Self-determination in a work organization. *Journal of Applied Psychology, 74:* 580–590.

DeGraff, J., & K. A. Lawrence. (2002). *Creativity at work: Developing the right practices to make innovation happen*. San Francisco: Jossey-Bass.

Deutsch, M. (1973). *The resolution of conflict: Constructive and destructive processes*. New Haven, CT: Yale University Press.

DiClemente, C. C. (1985). Perceived efficacy in smoking cessation. Paper presented at the Annual meeting of the American Association for the Advancement of Science, Los Angeles.

Drucker, P. (1988, January–February). The coming of the new organization. *Harvard Business Review:* 45–53.

Durkheim, E. (1964). *The division of labor in society*. New York: Free Press.

Eisenhart, K. M., & D. Charlie Galunic. (1993). Renewing the strategy-structure-performance paradigm. *Research in organizational behavior*. Greenwich, CT: JAI Press.

French, J. P. R., Jr., & B. Raven. (1960). The bases of social power. In D. Cartwright & A. Zander (Eds.), *Group dynamics* (pp. 607–623). New York: Harper & Row.

Freire, P., & A. Faundez. (1989). *Learning to question: A pedagogy of liberation*. New York: Continuum Publishing.

Gambetta, D. (1988). *Trust: Making and breaking cooperative relations*. Cambridge, MA: Basil Blackwell.

Gecas, V. (1989). The social psychology of self-efficacy. *Annual Review of Sociology, 15:* 291–316.

Gecas, V., M. A. Seff, & M. P. Ray. (1988). Injury and depression: The mediating effects of self concept. Paper presented at the Pacific Sociological Association Meetings, Las Vegas.

Gemmill, G. R., & W. J. Heisler. (1972). Fatalism as a factor in managerial job satisfaction. *Personnel Psychology, 25:* 241–250.

Gibb, J. R., & L. M. Gibb. (1969). Role freedom in a TORI group. In A. Burton (Ed.), *Encounter theory and practice of encounter groups*. San Francisco: Jossey-Bass.

Goddard, R. D., W. K. Hoy, & A. W. Hoy. (2003). Collective efficacy beliefs: Theoretical developments, empirical evidence, and future directions. *Educational Researcher, 33:* 3–13.

Golembiewski, R. T., & M. McConkie. (1975). The centrality of trust in group processes. In C. Cooper (Ed.), *Theories of group processes*. New York: Wiley.

Greenberger, D. B., & S. Stasser. (1991). The role of situational and dispositional factors in the enhancement of personal control in organizations. *Research in Organizational Behavior*, Vol. 13, (pp. 111–145). Greenwich, CT: JAI Press.

Greenberger, D. B., S. Stasser, L. L. Cummings, & R. B. Dunham. (1989). The impact of personal control on performance and satisfaction. *Organizational Behavior and Human Decision Processes, 43:* 29–51.

Hackman, J. R., & G. R. Oldham. (1980). *Work design*. Reading, MA: Addison-Wesley.

Hackman, J. R., G. R. Oldham, R. Janson, & K. Purdy. (1975). A new strategy for job enrichment. *California Management Review, 17:* 57–71.

Hammer, T. H., & Y. Vardi. (1981). Locus of control and career self-management among nonsupervisory employees in industrial settings. *Journal of Vocational Behavior, 18:* 13–29.

Harris, L. (2002). *Harris Poll #31*. New York: Harris Interactive.

Harter, S. (1978). Effectance motivation reconsidered: Toward a developmental model. *Human Development, 21:* 34–64.

Huber, G. P. (1980). *Managerial decision making*. Glenview, IL: Scott Foresman.

Kahn, W. A. (1990). Psychological conditions of personal engagement and disengagement at work. *Academy of Management Journal, 33:* 692–724.

Kanter, R. (1983). *The change masters*. New York: Simon & Schuster.

Langer, E. J. (1983). *The psychology of control*. Beverly Hills, CA: Sage.

Langer, E. J., & J. Rodin. (1976). The effects of choice and enhanced personal responsibility. *Journal of Personality and Social Psychology, 34:* 191–198.

Lawler, E. E. (1992) *The ultimate advantage: Creating the high involvement organization*. San Francisco: Jossey-Bass.

Lawrence, P., & J. Lorsch. (1967). *Organizations and environments*. Homewood, IL: Irwin.

Leana, C. R. (1987). Power relinquishment versus power sharing: Theoretical clarification and empirical comparison on delegation and participation. *Journal of Applied Psychology, 72:* 228–233.

Locke, E. A., & D. M. Schweiger. (1979). Participation in decision making: One more look. In B. M. Staw & L. L. Cummings (Eds.), *Research in organizational behavior*, Vol. 1 (pp. 265–340). Greenwich, CT: JAI Press.

Luhmann, N. (1979). *Trust and power.* New York: Wiley.

Maddux, J. E. (2002). Self-efficacy. In C. R. Snyder & S. J. Lopez, *Handbook of positive psychology* (pp. 277–287). New York: Oxford.

Manz, C. C., & H. Sims. (1989). *Super-leadership: Teaching others to lead themselves.* Englewood Cliffs, NJ: Prentice Hall.

Martin, J., M. Feldman, M. J. Hatch, & S. Sitkin. (1983). The uniqueness paradox of organizational stories. *Administrative Science Quarterly, 28:* 438–452.

Marx, K. (1844). *Early writings.* Edited and translated by T. B. Bottomore. New York: McGraw-Hill.

McClellend, D. (1975). *Power: The inner experience.* New York: Irvington.

Mishra, A. K. (1992). Organizational response to crisis: The role of mutual trust and top management teams. Unpublished doctoral dissertation, University of Michigan.

Neufeld, R. W. J., & P. Thomas. (1977) Effects of perceived efficacy of a prophylactic controlling mechanism on self-control under painful stimulation. *Canadian Journal of Behavioral Science, 9:* 224–232.

Newman, W. H., & K. Warren. (1977). *The process of management.* Englewood Cliffs, NJ: Prentice Hall.

Organ, D., & C. N. Greene. (1974). Role ambiguity, locus of control, and work satisfaction. *Journal of Applied Psychology, 59:* 101–112.

Ozer, E. M., & A. Bandura. (1990). Mechanisms governing empowerment effects: A self-efficacy analysis. *Journal of Personality and Social Psychology, 58:* 472–486.

Pratt, M. G., & B. E. Ashforth. (2003). Fostering meaningfulness in working and at work. In K. S. Cameron, J. E. Dutton, & R. E. Quinn (Eds.), *Positive organizational scholarship* (pp. 309–327). San Francisco: Barrett-Koehler.

Preston, P., & T. W. Zimmerer. (1978). *Management for supervisors.* Englewood Cliffs, NJ: Prentice Hall.

Quinn, R. E. (2005). *Building the bridge as you walk on it.* San Francisco: Jossey-Bass.

Quinn, R. E., & G. Spreitzer. (1997). The road to empowerment: Seven questions every leader should consider. *Organizational Dynamics, 25:* 37–49.

Rappoport, J., C. Swift, & R. Hess. (1984). *Studies in empowerment: Steps toward understanding and action.* New York: Haworth Press.

Rose, S. M., & B. L. Black. (1985). *Advocacy and empowerment: Mental health care in the community.* Boston: Routledge and Kegan Paul.

Rothbaum, F., J. R. Weisz, & S. S. Snyder. (1982). Changing the world and changing the self: A two-process model of perceived control. *Journal of Personality and Social Psychology, 42:* 5–37.

Runyon, K. E. (1973). Some interaction between personality variables and management style. *Journal of Applied Psychology, 57:* 288–294.

Sashkin, M. (1982). *A manager's guide to participative management.* New York: American Management Association.

Sashkin, M. (1984). Participative management is an ethical imperative. *Organizational Dynamics, 12:* 4–22.

Schneider, J. A., & W. W. Agras. (1985). A cognitive behavioral treatment of bulimia. *British Journal of Psychiatry, 146:* 66–69.

Schwalbe, M. L., & V. Gecas. (1988). Social psychological consequences of job-related disabilities. In J. T. Mortimer & K. M. Borman (Eds.), *Work experience and psychological development through life span.* Boulder, CO: Westview.

Seeman, M., & C. S. Anderson. (1983). Alienation and alcohol. *American Sociological Review, 48:* 60–77.

Seligman, M. E. P. (1975). *Helplessness: On depression, development, and death.* San Francisco: Freeman.

Sewell, Carl. (1990). *Customers for life.* New York: Pocket Books.

Solomon, B. B. (1976). *Black empowerment: Social work in oppressed communities.* New York: Columbia University Press.

Spreitzer, G. M. (1992). *When organizations dare: The dynamics of individual empowerment in the workplace.* Unpublished doctoral dissertation, University of Michigan.

Staples, L. H. (1990). Powerful ideas about empowerment. *Administration in Social Work, 14:* 29–42.

Staw, B., L. Sandelands, & J. Dutton. (1981). Threat-rigidity effects in organizational behavior: A multilevel analysis. *Administrative Science Quarterly, 26:* 501–524.

Thomas, K. W., & B. A. Velthouse. (1990). Cognitive elements of empowerment: An interpretive model of intrinsic task motivation. *Academy of Management Review, 15:* 666–681.

Trompenaars, F. (1996). Resolving international conflict: Culture and business strategy. *Business Strategy Review,* 7: 51–68.

Trompenaars, F., & C. Hampden-Turner. (1998). *Riding the waves of culture.* New York: McGraw-Hill.

Urwick, L. (1944). *Elements of administration.* New York: Harper and Brothers.

Vogt, J. F., & K. L. Murrell. (1990). *Empowerment in organizations.* San Diego: University Associates.

Vroom, V. H., & A. G. Jago. (1974). Decision making as social process: Normative and descriptive models of leader behavior. *Decision Sciences, 5:* 743–769.

Vroom, V. H., & P. W. Yetton. (1973). *Leadership and decision making.* Pittsburgh: University of Pittsburgh Press.

Weick, K. E. (1979). *The social psychology of organizing.* Reading, MA: Addison-Wesley.

Weick, K. E. (1984). Small wins. *American Psychologist, 39:* 40–49.

Weick, K. E. (1993). Collapse of sense-making in organizations. *Administrative Science Quarterly, 38:* 628–652.

White, R. W. (1959). Motivation reconsidered: The concept of competence. *Psychological Review, 66:* 297–333.

Wrzesniewski, A. (2003). Finding positive meaning in work. In K. S. Cameron, J. E. Dutton, & R. E. Quinn (Eds.), *Positive organizational scholarship* (pp. 296–308). San Francisco: Barrett-Koehler.

Zand, D. E. (1972). Trust and managerial problem solving. *Administrative Science Quarterly, 17:* 229–239.

Zimmerman, M. A., & J. Rappaport. (1988). Citizen participation, perceived control, and psychological empowerment. *American Journal of Community Psychology, 16:* 725–750.

Zimmerman, M. A. (1990). Taking aim on empowerment research: On the distinction between individual and psychological conceptions. *American Journal of Community Psychology, 18:* 169–177.

CHAPTER 9 REFERENCES

Ancona, D. G., & D. Caldwell. (1992). Bridging the boundary: External activity and performance in organizational teams. *Administrative Science Quarterly, 27:* 459–489.

Asch, S. E. (1951). Effects of group pressure upon the modification and distortion of judgments. In H. Guetzkow (Ed.), *Groups, leadership, and men.* Pittsburgh: Carnegie Press.

Cameron, K. S., & D. A. Whetten. (1981). Perceptions of organizational effectiveness in organizational life cycles. *Administrative Science Quarterly, 27:* 524–544.

Cameron, K. S., & D. A. Whetten. (1984). Organizational life cycle approaches: Overview and applications to higher education. *Review of Higher Education, 6:* 60–102.

Campion, M. A., G. J. Medsker, & A. C. Higgs. (1993). Relations between work group characteristics and effectiveness: Implications for designing effective work groups. *Personnel Psychology, 46:* 823–850.

Cialdini, R. B. (1995). *Influence: Science and practice*, 3rd ed. Glenview, IL: Scott Foresman.

Clarke, J., & A. Hobson. (2005). *Above all else: The Everest dream.* Toronto: Stewart Publishing.

Cohen, S. G., & D. E. Bailey. (1997). What makes teams work: Group effectiveness research from the shop floor to the executive suite. *Journal of Management, 23:* 239–290.

Cox, T. H. (1994). *Cultural diversity in organizations: Theory, research, and practice.* San Francisco: Barrett-Koehler.

Dew, J. R. (1998). *Managing in a team environment.* Westport, CT: Quorum.

Dewey, J. (1933). *How we think.* Boston: Heath.

Druskat, V., & J. Wheeler. (2000). Effective leadership of self-managing teams: Behaviors that make a difference. Working paper, Weatherhead School of Management, Case Western Reserve University.

Druskat, V., & S. Wolff. (1999). The link between emotions and team effectiveness: How teams engage members and build effective task processes. *Academy of Management Best Paper Proceedings*, Organizational Behavior Division.

Dyer, W. G. (1987). *Team building: Issues and alternatives.* Reading, MA: Addison-Wesley.

Edmonson, A. (1999). Psychological safety and learning behavior in work teams. *Administrative Science Quarterly, 44:* 350–383.

Freud, S. (1921). *Group psychology and the analysis of the ego.* London: Hogarth Press.

Gladstein, D. (1984). Group in context: A model of task group effectiveness. *Administrative Science Quarterly, 29:* 497–517.

Greiner, L. (1972, July–August). Evolution and revolution as organizations grow. *Harvard Business Review:* 37–46.

Gully, S. M., D. S. Divine, & D. J. Whitney. (1995). A meta-analysis of cohesion and performance: Effects of level of analysis and task interdependence. *Small Group Research, 26:* 497–520.

Guzzo, R. A., & M. W. Dickson. (1996). Teams in organizations: Recent research on performance and effectiveness. *Annual Review of Psychology, 47:* 307–338.

Hackman, J. R. (1987). The design of work teams. In J. W. Lorsch (Ed.), *Handbook of organizational behavior.* Englewood Cliffs, NJ: Prentice Hall.

Hackman, J. R. (1990). *Groups that work (and those that don't).* San Francisco: Jossey-Bass.

Hackman, J. R. (1993). Teams and group failure. Presentation at the Interdisciplinary College on Organization Studies, University of Michigan, October.

Hackman, J. R. (2003). *Leading teams.* Cambridge, MA: Harvard Business School Press.

Hamilton, B. H., J. A. Nickerson, & H. Owan. (2003). Team incentives and worker heterogeneity: An empirical analysis of the impact of teams on productivity and participation. *Journal of Political Economy, 111:* 465–497.

Hayes, N. (1997). *Successful team management.* Boston: International Thompson Business Press.

Janis, I. (1972). *Victims of groupthink.* Boston: Houghton Mifflin.

Katzenbach, J. R., & D. K. Smith. (1993). *The wisdom of teams.* Boston: Harvard Business School Press.

Kouzes, J., & B. Posner. (1987). *The leadership challenge.* San Francisco: Jossey-Bass.

Kramer, R. M. (1999). Trust and distrust in organizations: Emerging perspectives, enduring questions. *Annual Review of Psychology, 50:* 569–598.

Lawler, E. E. (1998). *Strategies for high performance organizations.* San Francisco: Jossey-Bass.

Lawler, E. E. (2003). *Treat people right.* San Francisco: Jossey-Bass.

Lawler, E. E., S. A. Mohrman, & G. E. Ledford. (1995). *Creating high performance organizations: Practices and results of employee involvement and total quality management in* Fortune 1000 *companies.* San Francisco: Jossey-Bass.

Lidz, F. (2000). Up and down in Beverly Hills. *Sports Illustrated, 92(16):* 60–68.

Locke, E. (1990). *A theory of goal setting and task performance.* Upper Saddle River, NJ: Prentice Hall.

Manz, C., & H. Sims. (1987). Leading workers to lead themselves: The external leadership of self-managing work teams. *Administrative Science Quarterly, 32:* 106–128.

Mullen, B., & C. Copper. (1994). The relation between group cohesiveness and performance: An integration. *Psychological Bulletin, 115:* 210–227.

Pagonis, W. G. (1993). *Moving mountains.* Cambridge, MA: Harvard Business School Press.

Parker, G. M. (1996). *Team players and teamwork: The new competitive business strategy.* San Francisco: Jossey-Bass.

Peters, T. (1987). *Thriving on chaos.* New York: Knopf.

Quinn, R. E. (2005). *Building the bridge as you walk on it.* San Francisco: Jossey-Bass.

Quinn, R. E., & K. S. Cameron. (1983). Organizational life cycles and shifting criteria of effectiveness: Some preliminary evidence. *Management Science, 29:* 33–51.

Schein, E. H. (1976). What to observe in a group. In C. R. Mill & L. C. Porter (Eds.), *Reading book for human relations training.* Bethel, ME: NTL Institute.

Senge, P. (1991). *The fifth discipline.* New York: Doubleday.

Trompenaars, F. (1996). Resolving international conflict: Culture and business strategy. *Business Strategy Review, 7:* 51–68.

Trompenaars, F., & C. Hampden-Turner. (1998). *Riding the waves of culture.* New York: McGraw-Hill.

Tuckman, B. W. (1965). Developmental sequence in small groups. *Psychological Bulletin, 63:* 384–399.

Turner, M. E. (Ed.). (2000). *Groups at work: Advances in theory and research.* New York: Lawrence Erlbaum.

Verespei, M. A. (1990, June 18). Yea, teams? Not always. *Industry Week:* 103–105.

Wellins, R. S., W. C. Byham, & J. M. Wilson. (1991). *Empowered teams.* San Francisco: Jossey-Bass.

Yeatts, D. E., & C. Hyten (1998). *High performing self-managing work teams: A comparison of theory to practice.* Thousand Oaks, CA: Sage.

CHAPTER 10 REFERENCES

Avey, J. B., Wernsing, T. S., & Luthans, F. (2008). Can positive employees help positive organizational change? Impact of psychological capital and emotions on relevant attitudes and behaviors. *The Journal of Applied Behavioral Science, 44*(1), 48–70.

Baker, W. (2001). *Achieving success through social capital.* San Francisco: Jossey-Bass.

Baker, W., R. Cross, & M. Wooten. (2003). Positive organizational network analysis and energizing relationships. In K. S. Cameron, J. E. Dutton, & R. E. Quinn (Eds.), *Positive organizational scholarship: Foundations of a new discipline* (pp. 328–342). San Francisco: Barrett-Koehler.

Bartunek, J. M., Rynes, S. L., & Ireland, R. D. (2006). What makes management research interesting, and why does it matter? *Academy of Management Journal, 49*(1), 9–15.

Baumeister, R. F., E. Bratslavsky, C. Finkenauer, & K. D. Vohs. (2001). Bad is stronger than good. *Review of General Psychology, 5:* 323–370.

Bennis, W., & B. Nanus. (1985). *Leaders: The strategies for taking charge.* New York: Harper & Row.

Biswas-Diener, R., Kashdan, T. B., & Minhas, G. (2011). A dynamic approach to psychological strength development and intervention. *The Journal of Positive Psychology, 6*(2), 106–118.

Bollier, D. (1996). *Aiming higher: Twenty-five stories of how companies prosper by combining sound management and social vision.* New York: Amacom.

Boyatzis, R. E., Smith, M. L., & Blaize, N. (2006). Developing sustainable leaders through coaching and compassion. *Academy of Management Learning & Education, 5*(1), 8–24.

Bright, D. S., & Exline, J. J. (2012). Forgiveness at four levels: Intrapersonal, relational, organizational, and collective group. In Cameron, K. S., & Spreitzer, G. M., (Eds.), Oxford *Handbook of Positive Organizational Scholarship.* New York: Oxford University Press.

Bright, D. S., K. S. Cameron, & A. Caza. (2006). The ethos of virtuousness in downsized organizations. *Journal of Business Ethics, 64:* 249–269.

Caldwell, C., & Dixon, R. D. (2010). Love, forgiveness, and trust: Critical values of the modern leader. *Journal of Business Ethics, 93*(1), 91–101.

Cameron, K. S. (1985). Iacocca's transformation of Chrysler; Excerpts from Lee Iacocca's speeches to his top management team, 1979–1984. (In possession of the author.)

Cameron, K. S. (2003a). Ethics, virtuousness, and constant change. In N. M. Tichy & A. R. McGill (Eds.), *The ethical challenge* (pp. 185–193). San Francisco: Jossey-Bass.

Cameron, K. S. (2003b). Organizational virtuousness and performance. In K. S. Cameron, J. E. Dutton, & R. E. Quinn (Eds.), *Positive organizational scholarship: Foundations of a new discipline* (pp. 48–65). San Francisco: Barrett-Koehler.

Cameron, K. S. (2008). Paradox in positive organizational change. *The Journal of Applied Behavioral Science, 44*(1), 7–24.

Cameron, K. S. (2012). *Positive leadership.* San Francisco: Berrett Koehler.

Cameron, K. S. (2013). *Practicing positive leadership.* San Francisco: Berrett Koehler.

Cameron, K. S. (2014). Advances in positive organizational scholarship. *Advances in Positive Organizational Psychology, 1,* 23–44.

Cameron, K. S. (2017). Organizational compassion: Manifestations through organizations. *Oxford Handbook of Compassion.* London: Oxford University Press.

Cameron, K. S., & A. Caza. (2002). Organizational and leadership virtues and the role of forgiveness. *Journal of Leadership and Organizational Studies, 9:* 33–48.

Cameron, K. S., & M. Lavine. (2006). *Making the impossible possible: Leading extraordinary performance—The Rocky Flats story.* San Francisco: Barrett-Koehler.

Cameron, K. S., & R. E. Quinn. (1999). *Diagnosing and changing organizational culture.* Reading, MA: Addison-Wesley.

Cameron, K. S., & D. O. Ulrich. (1986). Transformational leadership in colleges and universities. *Higher Education: Handbook of Theory and Research, 2:* 1–42.

Cameron, K. S., D. A. Whetten, & M. U. Kim. (1987). Organizational effects of decline and turbulence. *Administration Science Quarterly, 32:* 222–240.

Cameron, K. S., Mora, C., Leutscher, T., & Calarco, M. (2011). Effects of positive practices on organizational effectiveness. *Journal of Applied Behavioral Science, 47,* 266–308.

Cameron, K. S., Quinn, R. E., DeGraff, J., & Thakor, A. (2014). *Competing values leadership: creating value in organizations.* Revised Edition. Northampton, MA: Edward Elgar.

Carlzon, J. (1987). *Moments of truth.* Cambridge, MA: Ballinger.

Christie, R., & S. Lehman. (1970). The structure of Machiavellian orientations. In R. Christie & F. Geis (Eds.), *Studies in Machiavellianism* (pp. 359–387). New York: Academic Press.

Cialdini, R. B. (2000). *Influence: The science of persuasion.* New York: Allyn & Bacon.

Clifton, D. O., & J. K. Harter. (2003). Investing in strengths. In K. S. Cameron, J. E. Dutton, & R. E. Quinn (Eds.), *Positive organizational scholarship: Foundations of a new discipline* (pp. 111–121). San Francisco: Barrett-Koehler.

Coonradt, C. (2007). *The game of work.* Layton, UT: Gibbs Smith Press.

Cooper, C. L., Pandley, A., & Quick, J. C. (2012). *Downsizing: Is less still more?* Cambridge: Cambridge University Press.

Cooperrider, D. L. (1990). *Appreciative management and leadership: The power of positive thought and action in organizations.* San Francisco: Jossey-Bass.

Csikszentmihalyi, M. (1990). *Flow: The psychology of optimal experience.* New York: Harper Perennial.

Datta, D. K., Guthrie, J. P., Basuil, D., & Pandey, A. (2010). Causes and effects of employee downsizing: A review and synthesis. *Journal of Management, 36*(1), 281–348.

Davis, M. (1971). That's interesting! *Philosophy of the Social Sciences, 1:* 309–344.

Dutton, J. E., P. J. Frost, M. C. Worline, J. M. Lilius, & J. M. Kanov. (2002, *January*). Leading in times of trauma. *Harvard Business Review: 54–61.*

Emmons, R. A. (2003). Acts of gratitude in organizations. In K. S. Cameron, J. E. Dutton, & R. E. Quinn (Eds.), *Positive organizational scholarship: Foundations of a new discipline* (pp. 81–93). San Francisco: Barrett-Koehler.

Emmons, R. A. (2007). *Thanks!* New York: Houghton Mifflin.

Enright, R. D., & C. Coyle. (1998). Researching the process model of forgiveness within psychological interventions. In E. L. Worthington (Ed.), *Dimensions of forgiveness* (pp. 139–161). Philadelphia: Templeton Foundation Press.

Enrique, J. (2000). *As the future catches you.* New York: Crown Business.

Fredrickson, B. L. (2003). Positive emotions and upward spirals in organizations. In K. S. Cameron, J. E. Dutton, & R. E. Quinn (Eds.), *Positive organizational scholarship: Foundations of a new discipline* (pp. 163–175). San Francisco: Barrett-Koehler.

Fredrickson, B. L., & Branigan, C. (2005). Positive emotions broaden the scope of attention and thought-action repertoires. *Cognition & Emotion, 19*(3), 313–332.

Frost, P. J. (2003). *Toxic emotions at work: How compassionate managers handle pain and conflict.* Cambridge, MA: Harvard Business School Press.

Gallup Business Journal (2018). State of the American workplace. https://news.gallup.com/topic/employee_engagement.aspx.

Glynn, P. (1994). Toward a politics of forgiveness. *American Enterprise, 5:* 48–53.

Gold, T. (2002). *Open your mind, open your life.* Springfield, IL: Andrews McNeel Publishing.

Gottman, J. (1994). *Why marriages succeed and fail.* New York: Simon & Schuster.

Hazen, M. A. (2008). Grief and the workplace. *Academy of Management Perspectives, 22,* 78–86.

Helmick, R. G., & R. L. Petersen. (2001). *Forgiveness and reconciliation: Religion, public policy, and conflict.* Philadelphia: Templeton Foundation Press.

Kanov, J. M., S. Maitlis, M. C. Worline, J. E. Dutton, & P. J. Frost. (2003). Compassion in organizational life. *American Behavioral Scientist:* 1–54.

Kirschenbaum, D. (1984). Self-regulation and sport psychology: Nurturing and emerging symbiosis. *Journal of Sport Psychology, 8:* 26–34.

Kotter, J. (1999). *John Kotter on what leaders really do.* Cambridge, MA: Harvard Business School Press.

Lewin, K. (1951). *Field theory in social science.* New York: Harper & Row.

Losada, M., & E. Heaphy. (2003). The role of positivity and connectivity in the performance of business teams: A nonlinear dynamics model. *American Behavioral Scientist, 47:* 740–765.

Maxwell, J. C. (2007). *The 21 Irrefutable Laws of Leadership: Follow Them and People Will Follow You.* Nashville: Thomas Nelson.

McCraty, R., & Childre, D. (2004). The grateful heart. In R. A. Emmons & M. E. McCullough (Eds.), *The psychology of gratitude* (pp. 230–255). New York: Oxford University Press.

McCullough, M. E., R. A. Emmons, & J. Tsang. (2002). The grateful disposition: A conceptual and empirical topography. *Journal of Personality and Social Psychology, 82:* 112–127.

Meyerson, D. (2001). *Tempered radicals.* Cambridge, MA: Harvard Business School Press.

Munson, S. A., Krupka, E., Richardson, C., & Resnick, P. (2015). Effects of public commitments and accountability in a technology-supported physical activity intervention. *Proceedings of the 33rd Annual ACM Conference on Human Factors in Computing Systems.* 2015: 1135–1144.

Nahrgang, J. D., DeRue, D. S., Hollenbeck, J. R., Spitzmuller, M., Jundt, D. K., & Ilgen, D. R. (2013). Goal setting in teams: The impact of learning and performance goals on process and performance. *Organizational Behavior and Human Decision Processes, 122*(1), 12–21.

Perot, H. R. (1988). A vision for General Motors. Internal company document. General Motors Corporation, Detroit, MI.

Pfeffer, J. (1998). *The human equation: Building profits by putting people first.* Boston: Harvard Business School Press.

Pfeffer, J. (2015). *Leadership BS: Fixing Workplaces and Careers One Truth at a Time.* Boston: HarperCollins.

Powley, E. H. (2009). Reclaiming resilience and safety: Resilience activation in the critical period of crisis. *Human Relations, 62*(9), 1289–1326.

Quinn, R. E. (2000). *Change the world.* San Francisco: Jossey-Bass.

Quinn, R. E. (2004). *Building the bridge as you walk on it.* San Francisco: Jossey-Bass.

Quinn, R. E., J. E. Dutton, & G. M. Spreitzer. (2003). Reflected best-self exercise: Assignment and instructions for participants. Center for Positive Organizational Scholarship, Ross School of Business, University of Michigan. Product #001B.

Quinn, R. W., & Quinn, R. E. (2015). *Lift: The Fundamental State of Leadership.* San Francisco: Berrett Koehler.

Ramlall, S. J. (2008). Enhancing employee performance through positive organizational behavior. *Journal of Applied Social Psychology, 38*(6), 1580–1600.

Rath, T. (2001). *Now Discover Your Strengths.* New York: Gallup Press.

Rego, A., Ribeiro, N., & Cunha, M. P. (2010). Perceptions of organizational virtuousness and happiness as predictors of organizational citizenship behaviors. *Journal of Business Ethics, 93*(2), 215–235.

Roberts, L. M., Dutton, J. E., Spreitzer, G. M., Heaphy, E. D., & Quinn, R. E. (2005). Composing the reflected best self portrait: Building pathways for becoming extraordinary in work organizations. *Academy of Management Review, 30*(4), 712–736.

Roberts, L. M., G. Spreitzer, J. Dutton, R. Quinn, E. Heaphy, & B. Barker. (2005). How to play to your strengths. *Harvard Business Review, 83:* 75–80.

Salancik, G. R. (1977). Commitment of control of organizational behavior and belief. In B. M. Staw & G. R. Salancik (Eds.), *News directions in organizational behavior.* Chicago: St. Clair Press.

Sculley, J. (1987). Apple's identity and goals. Internal company document. Apple Computer, Inc., Cupertino, CA.

Seligman, M. E. P. (2002). *Authentic happiness.* New York: Free Press.

Selznick, P. (1949). *TVA and the grass roots.* Berkeley: University of California Press.

Simmel, G. (1950). *The sociology of Georg Simmel.* Glencoe, IL: Free Press.

Tichy, N. M. (1993). *Control your destiny or someone else will.* New York: Doubleday.

Tichy, N. M. (1997). *The leadership engine.* New York: Harper Collins.

Tutu, D. (1998). Without forgiveness there is no future. In R. D. Enright & J. North (Eds.), *Exploring forgiveness.* Madison: University of Wisconsin Press.

Tutu, D. (1999). *No future without forgiveness.* New York: Doubleday.

U. S. Army Strategic Leadership Program. (2003). Personal communication. Boston, MA.

Walsh, J. P. (1999). Business must talk about its social role. In T. Dickson (Ed.), *Mastering strategy* (pp. 289–294). London: Financial Times/Prentice Hall.

Weick, K. E. (1981). Small wins: Redefining the scale of social problems. *American Psychologist, 39:* 40–49.

Weick, K. E. (1993, Winter). Small wins in organizational life. *Dividend:* 20–24.

Worline, M., & Dutton, J. E. (2017). *Awakening Compassion at Work: The Quiet Power that Elevates People and Organizations.* San Francisco: Berrett Koehler.

Zhang, X., & Bartol, K. M. (2010). Linking empowering leadership and employee creativity: The influence of psychological empowerment, intrinsic motivation, and creative process engagement. *Academy of Management Journal, 53*(1), 107–128.

INDEX

Page numbers followed by an f or t represent figures and tables respectively.